A Practical Guide

to Food and Drug Law and Regulation

Third Edition

Edited by Kenneth R. Piña
and Wayne L. Pines

Published by the Food and Drug Law Institute
FDLI

ISBN 978-1-935065-02-9

FDLI

1155 15th Street NW, Ste. 800
Washington, D.C. 20005
Tel: (202) 371-1420; Fax: (202) 371-0649
www.fdli.org

Table of Contents

Introduction

The goal of this third edition of *A Practical Guide to Food and Drug Law and Regulation* is to explain the law and regulations that govern the development, marketing, and sale of food, medical products, and cosmetics in simple, nontechnical terms.

The idea for this book originated more than a decade ago, when Ken was invited to teach the food and drug law course for the Temple University School of Pharmacy's Graduate Studies Program for Quality Assurance and Regulatory Affairs. He noted that existing books on food and drug law were written in the "case law" format commonly used to teach law students, or were written for audiences with pre-existing knowledge of Food and Drug Administration (FDA) laws. What was needed was a practical legal/regulatory primer that was substantive but that also could be readily understood by a wide range of persons with an interest in FDA-related laws and regulations.

The Food and Drug Law Institute (FDLI) welcomed the idea for such a volume. When Wayne, with vast experience as a nonlawyer in the FDA regulatory world, learned of the idea of a text that would explain simply the requirements of the law and regulations, he embraced the project and joined Ken as co-editor, becoming *the* key force behind its timely publication.

In the decade since the first edition was published, this book has become a basic resource both academically and within regulated industries. It has become a standard textbook in several food and drug law courses in law schools and has been cited as a reference in judicial opinions (including a U.S. Supreme Court opinion). For many entering the FDA regulatory world, it is their first primer.

The intended readers of this book include students in law schools and in other professional schools, plus professionals who work for regulated companies and in related fields. Their commonality is that they want and need to understand how the law and regulations that guide FDA's activities work and are interpreted in practical, real-world terms.

In this third edition, we have attempted to remain true to our original goals. The format is intended to represent a natural progression from subject to subject, so that it is useful not only as a resource but also as a teaching tool. Each chapter has been updated, consistent with the new laws enacted by Congress, as well as recent developments. Chapters have been added on pharmacovigilance, combination products, and the regulation of research.

Our unending gratitude goes to each of the chapter authors. They have dedicated substantial time and energy not just to their original authorship, but now to updating it twice. They continue to provide not just their practical knowledge but also their insights. Thanks to Rita Fullem of FDLI, who assisted in making sure this third edition became a reality; and to our families, who supported this effort with patience and love.

We hope that this volume serves as a valuable introduction to the Federal Food, Drug and Cosmetic Act—what the law says and how it and its implementing regulations really work.

Kenneth R. Piña
kpina@coreriskstd.com

Wayne L. Pines
wpines@apcoworldwide.com

About the Editors

Kenneth R. Piña, J.D., R.Ph., is a founding Principal of Core Risks Ltd. LLC (CRL), a global provider of compliance and risk solution services to the life science industry. Mr. Piña's practice focuses upon the development and maintenance of corporate compliance and ethics training programs, critical Enterprise Risk Management assessments, the development of corporate crisis management plans and infrastructure, and neutral fact-finding capabilities for sensitive internal investigations involving compliance-related claims.

Prior to joining CRL, Mr. Piña was the Senior Vice President, Chief Legal Officer, and Secretary of Henkel Corporation, a consumer product and specialty chemical company. Before joining Henkel, Mr. Piña served as Vice President, General Counsel, and Secretary of Rhone-Poulenc Rorer Pharmaceuticals Inc., directing legal matters for the company within North, Central, and South America, as well as the Pacific Rim area.

Mr. Piña received his Juris Doctorate from the Dickinson School of Law, The Pennsylvania State University, where he was named a Food and Drug Law Institute Scholar and also received the American Jurisprudence Award in Food and Drug Law. He is also a graduate of the Rutgers University College of Pharmacy. Mr. Piña is active in numerous professional and charitable organizations.

Wayne L. Pines is President of Health Care and Regulatory Services at APCO Worldwide in Washington, D.C. He is an international consultant on FDA-related issues, specializing in crisis management, drug/device approvals, advertising and promotion issues, advisory committee preparation, and media outreach.

A graduate of Rutgers University, Mr. Pines served as Director of Consumer Education, Chief of Press Relations, and Associate Commissioner for Public Affairs at FDA. He has written or edited a dozen books, including *How to Work with the FDA, FDA: A Century of Consumer Protection*, two books on risk management, three books on crisis management, and the *FDA Advertising and Promotion Manual*. He has chaired since their inception in the late 1980s the annual advertising education conferences for both the Food and Drug Law Institute and the Drug Information Association, and is a frequent speaker at other conferences.

Mr. Pines serves as President of the Alliance for a Stronger FDA and as Chairman of the MedStar Research Institute. He also serves on the boards of several companies and other organizations. His awards include the FDA Award of Merit twice, the Public Health Service Superior Service Award, and the FDA Alumnus of the Year award.

Chapter 1

Overview of the U.S. Legal System

Edward P. Richards, III, J.D., M.P.H., Paul M. Hebert Law Center, Louisiana State University, Baton Rouge, LA

Key Points

- **The Constitution is the fundamental source of U.S. law.**
- **The Constitution divides legal powers between the states and the federal government.**
- **The federal government is divided into three parts to create checks and balances on its power.**
- **The Supreme Court ensures that other branches of the government do not violate the Constitution.**
- **Agencies are created by Congress and overseen by the President.**
- **Federal agencies such as FDA are in the executive branch of the federal government.**
- **FDA may only regulate products that affect interstate commerce.**
- **The courts defer to agency decisions.**
- **Agencies may take emergency actions to protect the public health and safety.**
- **Formal agency regulations are subject to public notice and comment.**

Introduction

The food, drug, and medical devices industries are unique in their breadth and complexity, and their intimate impact on individual lives. They are heavily regulated by state and federal government agencies to ensure that the public is protected from unsafe goods and from intentional contamination. This chapter introduces the basic structure and process of the legal system as it affects food, drug, and medical device regulation.

Federalism

The American legal system is a federal system, with powers divided between the states and the central government. This system was shaped by the Revolutionary War. Each of the thirteen original colonies had an independent government that was overseen by England. Communications were slow, and England's concerns generally were limited to taxes and keeping the exports and imports flowing. The colonies had great freedom to govern themselves in most matters. With the Declaration of Independence, they became separate nations with complete control over their legal affairs. When they joined together under the Articles of Confederation to fight the war, none was willing to give up control of its government to a central authority. The result was a weak federation that almost lost the war because it could not raise troops and supplies.

When the Constitution was drafted, the colonies realized that they could not stand against the European powers without a strong central government. The federal government was given the power to deal with foreign governments and disputes between the states. The states retained many other powers, including the right to run their state governments with only limited interference from the federal government.

This division between state and federal governments, and the distribution of power between them, is pivotal to the American legal system. Every national business must deal with fifty state governments and the federal government. In some areas the federal government has imposed a uniform standard that all the states must follow. For example, a new drug must be approved only by the Food and Drug Administration (FDA) to be sold in the fifty states. In other areas, such as compensation for persons injured by prescription drugs, a state may have a liability standard that varies greatly from, and sometimes conflicts with, the standards of other states.

State Versus Federal Powers

The Constitution gives the federal government sole authority over the regulation of interstate commerce, foreign affairs, and the power to declare and wage war. These powers were constrained by the Bill of Rights, a series of ten amendments to the Constitution that protect individual liberty from federal government action. Amendments adopted after the Civil War banned slavery and gave the federal government additional powers to protect individual rights. These amendments also extended the Bill of Rights protections to actions by state governments. The powers that were not restricted to the federal government were retained by the states and some were shared between the state and federal governments. For food, drug, and medical device law and regulation, the important federal powers are the right to regulate interstate and international commerce; the important state power is the police power to protect the public health and safety.

For food, drug, and medical device law and regulation, the important federal powers are the right to regulate interstate and international commerce; the important state power is the police power to protect the public health and safety.

Regulation of Commerce

The federal government controls international commerce as well as commerce between the states. The import and export of foods, drugs, and medical devices is regulated through treaties with other countries and statutes passed by Congress. While the states ceded the power to regulate interstate commerce to the federal government, they retained, via their police powers, the right to regulate any activity that poses a threat to the public health or safety of their citizens. Thus, state laws that banned milk from out-of-state dairies were held unconstitutional because they interfered with interstate commerce in their attempts to protect local businesses. State consumer protection laws, such as those requiring the inspection of imported milk and banning the import of contaminated milk, are constitutional, provided they also apply to milk produced within the state.

U.S. Constitution
Commerce Clause
Section 8. The Congress shall have the Power . . . To regulate Commerce with foreign Nations, and among the several States, and with the Indian Tribes.
U.S. CONST. art I, § 8, cl. 3.

The breadth of federal power to regulate interstate commerce is defined by Congress, subject to limits imposed by the U.S. Supreme Court. Generally speaking, anything that moves between the states, any business that uses raw materials that come from out of state, or any business that affects interstate commerce is subject to regulation under the Commerce Clause. The Civil Rights Act uses this broad definition of interstate commerce, and a court found that a barbecue restaurant whose only customers were local in-state residents was involved in interstate commerce because it bought food and condiments that originated outside the state.

Food, drug, and medical device laws use a more limited definition that requires that the product (or at least one of its ingredients) travel in interstate commerce. Thus, a pharmaceutical firm that wants to market a new drug throughout the country must have FDA approval before it can be advertised or shipped in interstate commerce. While most states require FDA approval for drugs sold within the state, there have been occasions when states have permitted the prescription of non-FDA-approved drugs. As long as these state-approved drugs and their ingredients were made wholly within the state and used only by physicians in the same state, FDA has no authority to ban the use of the drug. This is a congressional, rather than a constitutional, limit. Congress could allow FDA to use the broad definition of interstate commerce and regulate all drug sales and also the practice of medicine.

The Police Power

Police power is the right to protect the country and its population from threats to the public health and safety. The police power is fundamental to government, and predates organized police forces. In the colonial period, police power was used to control nuisances, such as tanneries that fouled the air and water in towns; to prevent the sale of bad food; and to quarantine persons who were infected with communicable diseases.

Under the Constitution, the states and the federal government share police power, with the federal equivalent of the police power being exercised through the Interstate Commerce Clause. Food, drug, and medical device regulation is a federal health and safety function, as are environmental protection laws and workplace safety laws. The states have companion laws in most of these areas, plus local public health enforcement such as restaurant inspections, communicable disease control, and drinking water sanitation. The courts usually find that true public health and safety concerns take priority over individual rights. For example, persons with dangerous communicable diseases, such as tuberculosis, can be confined or quarantined until they are no longer infectious and thus pose no threat to the community. As long as the confinement is to protect the public against future harm and not to punish the individual for past acts, it may be done as a civil law matter without giving the individual criminal law protections.

U.S. Constitution Supremacy Clause
This Constitution and the Laws of the United States which shall be made in Pursuance thereof . . . shall be the supreme Law of the Land; . . . any Thing in the Constitution or Laws of any State to the Contrary notwithstanding.
U.S. Const. art VI, cl. 2.

Federal Preemption

Food, drug, and medical device regulation involves both state and federal laws governing the same activity. As long as the laws do not conflict, they both can be enforced by the appropriate government. If they do conflict, the Constitution provides that federal law preempts the conflicting state regulation. This conflict can arise because the federal law *explicitly* states that it is taking away the states' power to regulate. For example, federal law specifies the necessary labeling for hearing aids and limits what additional requirements a state may impose without FDA permission. When Massachusetts passed a law requiring more information on hearing aid labels, a federal court barred enforcement of the law.

Federal law can *implicitly* preempt a state's right to regulate if the federal government so completely controls the area that there is no room for state regulation. The federal government regulates electronic communications, such as television and radio, which are intrinsically interstate activities because of the potential for their signals to cross state lines. These regulations cover all aspects of electronic communication, leaving no room for state regulation.

In some cases, federal law also preempts private lawsuits brought under state law. The Cigarette Labeling Act provided that states cannot require more or different health warnings on a cigarette package than those required by federal law. The Supreme Court found that this preempted state court lawsuits by smokers who claimed that the cigarettes were defective because the packages did not carry adequate warnings. Federal law also preempts certain lawsuits alleging vaccine-related injuries, and substitutes an administrative compensation fund for possible state tort recoveries. FDA regulation of drugs does not provide any preemption of state tort law claims, but the Medical Device Amendments of 1976 (MDA) do preempt some claims against medical device manufacturers.

Limits to Federal Power

Federal power is limited. If there is no interstate commerce involved and the matter does not involve individual rights under the Constitution, the states have the right to control their affairs. The federal government has limited authority to commandeer state personnel to enforce federal law (after the terrorist attacks on September 11, 2001, and the Hurricane Katrina disaster, however, Congress gave the President broad emergency authority over state government). If the federal government wants to regulate an area that is reserved to the states, or does not have the funds to take a specific action with a federal agency, it can provide the states with a financial incentive to encourage them to follow federal guidelines. When Congress wanted the states to pass laws requiring people in cars to wear seatbelts, it told the states to pass seatbelt laws or lose some of their federal highway construction money. The Medicaid program is a state-federal partnership in which the federal government controls actions of state personnel through restrictions on the federal matching money. This use of the spending power to provide financial incentives to states has become more important as the U.S. Supreme Court has limited the federal government's authority to regulate state government.

If there is no interstate commerce involved and the matter does not involve individual rights under the Constitution, the states have the right to control their affairs.

Separation of Powers

The Constitution divides the federal government into three branches: the legislative (Congress), the executive (President), and the judicial (Supreme Court). These divisions are intended to act as checks and balances to prevent any branch from dominating the government. The states have basically the same organizational structure, although some states make one branch of the government much stronger than the others. For the purpose of the discussion, this chapter focuses on the federal system.

The Legislative Branch

Congress has two houses: the Senate and the House of Representatives. These houses have different procedural rules and their members serve terms of different lengths. Both Senators and Representatives are popularly elected. Congress is the only branch of government that can authorize the spending of government funds and the imposition of taxes.

Each proposed law (bill) must be passed by both houses of Congress and signed by the President. The President can veto legislation, and Congress can override a presidential veto only by a two-thirds majority vote. The President can propose legislation, and does so each year when he or she presents the proposed budget. Ultimately, however, it is Congress that passes laws. To keep Congress from becoming too powerful, the Constitution gave the power to enforce the laws to the President.

The Executive Branch

The President is head of the executive branch and is charged with enforcing the laws passed by Congress. The President has two areas of power: domestic and international. In domestic affairs, most of the President's power comes from laws passed by Congress, such as the Federal Food, Drug, and Cosmetic Act. These laws constrain domestic action to areas specifically approved by Congress, although the President does have some flexibility to respond to emergencies. The Constitution grants the President broad powers over international affairs, including international trade, foreign policy, and national security. These powers are subject to only limited review by Congress and the courts.

Enforcement is carried out through various agencies, including FDA. Congress creates agencies and gives them power through laws called "enabling legislation," which specifies what the agency is to do, how the agency is structured, and its budget. Once an agency is established, Congress can modify or expand its duties with subsequent legislation; for example, FDA was given authority to regulate medical devices by amendments that were made in 1976 to its enabling legislation. Congress also controls agency action through setting the agency's budget, which can include specific limits on money for each agency activity. Congress may not interfere directly with agency management.

Congress creates agencies and gives them power through laws called "enabling legislation," which specifies what the agency is to do, how the agency is structured, and its budget.

The heads of most agencies and their top administrators, such as FDA's Commissioner of Food and Drugs, are political appointees and the President may change them at will. This allows the President to set agency policy within the constraints of the legislation governing the agency. There are also independent agencies, such as the Securities and Exchange Commission and the Federal Trade Commission, which are governed by appointed boards whose members have staggered terms. The

President can replace board members only when their terms expire, which gives the agency greater political independence than agencies that report directly to the President. Independent agencies typically are charged with politically sensitive enforcement.

The Department of Justice (DOJ) is the only agency that can prosecute criminal charges. If FDA wants to bring a criminal charge against an individual or business, it must bring its case to DOJ for prosecution. Agencies like FDA possess civil power and can enforce their own rules through actions such as injunctions and seizures. An injunction is a court order that requires that an entity or person desist from some action, such as selling tainted food or manufacturing a drug or device that does not conform to FDA regulations. Because FDA can use an injunction to close a business, it is a powerful enforcement tool. There are variations on injunctions, called embargoes or seizure orders, that allow products to be kept off the market. When a product is seized because it presents a threat to the public health or safety, the government does not have to pay compensation because dangerous property that is not fit for its intended use is treated as having no value.

The Department of Justice is the only agency that can prosecute criminal charges.

The Judicial Branch

The judicial branch consists of the Supreme Court, the courts of appeal (circuit courts), and the district (local) federal courts. The district courts hold trials for federal criminal cases, decide disputes arising under federal law or the Constitution, and hear cases involving citizens of different states under "diversity jurisdiction." The courts of appeal do not conduct trials but review the trial records from the district courts. Because many agency actions generate a record like a trial, Congress often provides that these agency actions be reviewed directly by the court of appeals. When a case is heard on appeal, the court does not collect new evidence or hear the testimony of the witnesses; it only considers the record generated at the district court or administrative level.

Cases before the Supreme Court are one of four types: 1) cases involving one state suing another; 2) cases that arise from courts of appeal rulings; 3) cases reviewing state court decisions involving questions of federal law or rights under the Constitution; and 4) cases where Congress has given "original jurisdiction" to the Supreme Court. The Supreme Court ensures that federal laws are given the same meaning by all courts of appeal, it resolves conflicts between state and federal laws, and it determines if state or federal laws impermissibly infringe on rights guaranteed by the Constitution. If the Supreme Court determines that a state law, federal law, or administrative regulation such as an FDA rule conflicts with the Constitution, it will strike the law down so that it may no longer be enforced.

How the Courts Work

When most people think of law, they think of the courtroom. While most law and lawyering does not happen in the courtroom, it is important to understand how the courts work because the courtroom is where disputes, both private and governmental, end up if they cannot be resolved in any other way.

Characteristics of the U.S. litigation system:
- *a common law system*
- *an adversarial system*
- *divided into civil and criminal law*

The U.S. litigation system has three key characteristics: 1) it is a common law system, meaning that judges rely on the opinions of other judges; 2) it is an adversarial system (i.e., it is driven by the litigants rather than the judges); and 3) it is divided into civil and criminal law, with the greatest legal protections reserved for persons accused of a crime and at risk of imprisonment or execution.

Understanding the Common Law

England is a common law country. As a consequence, so were the original British colonies in America. The Constitution accepted most of the English common law that was in force when it was written. Common law means that the law evolves through judges applying the law to specific cases and writing opinions about how the law applies in those cases. The laws they apply may be from earlier court decisions enforcing even earlier traditions, or they may apply statutes passed by legislatures. Cases still arise that involve rules laid down in cases decided more than 200 years ago. Each case decided by a common law court becomes a precedent, or guideline, for subsequent decisions involving similar disputes.

The evolution of the law on the preemption of state tort claims against medical device manufacturers is a good example of how the common law system functions. The MDA of 1976 gave FDA the authority to regulate sale of medical devices. Congress wanted to assure uniform standards for medical devices so the MDA contains language that the states cannot impose additional standards on medical devices. In an early case under the MDA, the court ruled that state regulation of hearing aids was preempted by the MDA because it conflicted with federal regulations. This was a simple application of the law to a direct regulatory conflict.

In 1992, the U.S. Supreme Court ruled that the Cigarette Labeling Act preempted state tort claims against tobacco companies, holding that tort claims were a form of state regulation. Because the language in the Cigarette Labeling Act was similar to the MDA, defendants in tort cases involving medical devices began to argue that the MDA preempted these tort claims. Some federal courts accepted this argument, and some rejected it. In 1996, the U.S. Supreme Court reviewed the law to resolve these conflicting opinions. The court found that there could be preemption, but only if FDA really regulated the device, rather than just letting it be sold because it was like a device already on the market. This led to a second wave of cases with conflicting decisions over how much oversight FDA had to have over the device before preemption was triggered. The U.S. Supreme Court further clarified the law by finding preemption in a case decided in 2008.

The value of a common law system is that the law can be adapted to situations that were not contemplated by the legislature.

The value of a common law system is that the law can be adapted to situations that were not contemplated by the legislature. There are two disadvantages. First, the law will often be unclear for years; cases with similar facts can have differing outcomes depending on which court reviews them. Second, the court will resolve only the issues before it, so even the 2008 case on the MDA, decided more than thirty years after the passage of the MDA, still leaves some preemption issues unresolved.

The Adversarial System

The U.S. judicial system uses an adversarial model in which the judge acts as an impartial referee to ensure that the case is presented properly to jurors but does not assist the parties in developing their cases (although, in some instances, cases can be decided by the judge without a jury). In private litigation, the plaintiff—the person who brings the litigation—hires a lawyer to file a complaint against the defendant. The defendant then hires a lawyer to oppose the plaintiff's charges and to bring any possible counterclaims against the plaintiff. In criminal cases and in agency enforcement actions, it is the government that brings the proceedings against the defendant. There are some federal statutes, such as the False Claims Act, that allow a private person to bring a civil action on behalf of the government and share in any recovery as an incentive to vindicate the government's interest. A few states allow private citizens to bring criminal actions in very limited circumstances.

The courts protect against bias by excluding judges or jurors who have a relationship with the plaintiff or the defendant or who are familiar with the factual issues in the case. Each side presents its case to the court or the jury, and the opposing side tries to discredit it. Lawyers must be truthful to the court, but do not have a duty to volunteer all the information they possess about their client's case, even if not doing so misleads the judge or jury. If the case involves scientific or medical matters, each side will have persons testify as experts to tell the jury what that side claims happened. Because neither the jurors nor the judge are knowledgeable about the specific facts being litigated, they have to decide which expert to trust based on credentials and demeanor. The great strength of the jury system is that it allows citizens to control the power of the government in criminal cases and to resolve difficult policy problems when these involve only the parties to the case. The great weakness of the jury system is that it cannot deal with complex scientific issues, and it cannot balance the rights of persons not involved in the case. For example, in product liability cases involving persons claiming to have been injured by pharmaceuticals, the jury has no way to balance the interests of the injured person against those who may be denied access to the drug if the litigation is successful.

Criminal Law

The key distinction between civil and criminal law is that only criminal laws can punish a person with imprisonment or execution. A law that imposes a five-year prison sentence for selling heroin would be a criminal law. A civil law can force the defendant to part with money or property, or to refrain from taking an illegal action. (There are also criminal laws that punish with a fine.) Mental health commitment laws and communicable disease quarantine laws are not criminal laws, even if they require the person to be kept in prison, because the purpose of the law is public protection, not punishment. Most food, drug, and medical device litigation involves civil law, but there are circumstances where criminal prosecution is an issue.

Criminal laws are intended to protect society at large and are enforced by the government in its own name. An example is *United States v. Leichter*, in which Leichter was prosecuted for defrauding FDA. Another example is a murder case; the government rather than the person who was injured brings the criminal lawsuit. The victim appears only as a witness, and has little say in whether the government prosecutes the case.

Because the federal and state governments are so powerful, the Constitution provides special protections for criminal defendants. Criminal defendants have a right to: 1) free legal counsel if they are indigent, 2) a jury trial, 3) not be forced to testify against themselves, 4) refuse to talk to the police, 5) be free from unreasonable searches and seizures, and 6) force the government to prove its case beyond a reasonable doubt. The Constitution also bars laws that criminalize actions that happened before the law was passed (ex post facto law). If the jury finds the defendant not guilty, the government cannot try the defendant again for the same crime (no double jeopardy). This does not, however, bar another government from prosecuting the defendant. Thus, it is not unusual to see the federal government retry a defendant who has been acquitted by a jury in state court.

Criminal defendants ... *have a right to 1) free legal counsel if they are indigent, 2) a jury trial, 3) not be forced to testify against themselves, 4) refuse to talk to the police, 5) be free from unreasonable searches and seizures, and 6) force the government to prove its case beyond a reasonable doubt.*

Criminal prosecutions can be devastating to a legitimate business, even if the business is ultimately found not guilty. The publicity can hurt the value of the stock, the company records may be seized as evidence, and individual employees may have to hire lawyers because their interests are different from the company's. Criminal defense is very expensive, and is not covered by most insurance policies. A regulated industry may be forced to give up its operating license if indicted. The government will sometimes threaten criminal prosecution to persuade a company to pay a large civil fine.

Civil Law

Civil lawsuits . . .
can also be brought to make the defendant stop doing something, such as selling unpasteurized milk (injunctions). In the usual civil case, there is no right to counsel and the defendant can be forced to testify.

Civil lawsuits generally involve claims for losses or injuries suffered by a person or their property. Civil lawsuits called injunctions ask the court to order the defendant to stop doing something illegal, such as selling unpasteurized milk. If the defendant disobeys the injunction, the court may hold the defendant in contempt of court and impose a fine or imprisonment. In the usual civil case, there is no right to counsel and the defendant can be forced to testify. The case need only be proved by a preponderance (>50%) of the evidence, which is much lower than the "beyond a reasonable doubt" standard used in criminal cases. The more the case resembles a criminal law case, however, the more protections to which the defendant is entitled. Thus, while a case to institutionalize a person who is dangerous because of mental illness is a civil case, the defendant may be entitled to a lawyer and a higher standard of proof than in a proceeding to collect money.

Civil lawsuits can be brought by the government or by private citizens. Government agencies often use civil litigation to enforce regulatory rulings. They can seek an injunction or institute a seizure or embargo action to take possession or forbid the sale of property. These are very powerful measures in the food and drug industry, where seized or embargoed inventory can become outdated faster than the defendant can get a trial to contest the court's order. The agency has great leverage to negotiate a settlement if the defendant has 1,000 tons of fresh fruit that cannot be moved off a ship.

Private civil litigation includes business disputes over private law matters, such as compliance with contracts and ownership of property. These often are settled under the rules of the Uniform Commercial Code, a set of uniform laws adopted by all the states that facilitate the quick resolution of simple business disputes. Private plaintiffs can sue FDA to enjoin it from enforcing questionable statutes or regulations. FDA can be sued for negligence causing personal injury under the Federal Tort Claims Act (FTCA). The FTCA allows ordinary negligence actions, such as suing FDA for failing to test and detect a dangerous batch of polio vaccine. Unlike private tort actions, however, if the plaintiff is injured because of an intentional policy choice, the agency is not liable. For example, the government tested atomic weapons in the western desert, knowing that this would put local residents at risk. When these residents sued, the case was eventually dismissed because the injuries were the result of a policy decision, rather than negligence.

Personal injury lawsuits . . . *generally are based on negligence, which means proving that the defendant did not act as a reasonable person and thus exposed the plaintiff to unnecessary risk.*

Lawsuits for compensation for personal injuries, called tort lawsuits, are very important to the food and drug industry. Simple tort lawsuits generally are based on negligence, which means proving that the defendant did not act as a reasonable person and thus exposed the plaintiff to unnecessary risk. An example would be a diagnostic laboratory that improperly read a laboratory test and thus delayed a patient's diagnosis of cancer. To win a negligence case, the plaintiff must show what a reasonable laboratory would have done, how the defendant laboratory failed to meet this standard, and that this failure caused plaintiff's harm. This generally requires a lot of information from the defendant, which is obtained by court orders in a process called "discovery."

The most expensive tort lawsuits are brought against product manufacturers under the theory of strict liability. All states have adopted some form of strict liability, which requires that, to recover, an injured person show that the product was defective and unreasonably dangerous and that it was the cause of his or her injury. Unlike a negligence lawsuit, the plaintiff does not need to prove that the defendant acted "unreasonably." Thus, even if the defendant was more careful than other manufacturers and the plaintiff cannot show that the defendant could have prevented the injury, the plaintiff still can recover. For example, assume that after a drug has been on the market for three years, some patients begin to show serious liver damage. The evidence shows that this could not have been detected during clinical testing because it was either too rare or required a cofactor that could not have been anticipated during the clinical trial. Under the theory of strict (products) liability, the manufacturer could be held liable to the patients for their injuries.

Discovery

Discovery is the process for obtaining information in legal proceedings. Discovery is used in civil and criminal litigation, and in administrative proceedings. There are three types of discovery: 1) depositions, where the witness answers questions in person and the answers are recorded by a court reporter or by video tape; 2) interrogatories, which are written questions that are served on a party to a lawsuit and filled out with the help of the party's lawyer; and 3) subpoenas, which are legal orders to produce documents or other physical evidence, such as a batch of allegedly contaminated drugs. As companies have moved to electronic communications and document storage, courts have extended discovery rules to electronic records and e-mail. Discovery of electronic records ("e-discovery") poses new legal and practical issues. It is easier for parties to convince the court to grant broad discovery orders when it will result only in a few DVDs of data, rather than truckloads of paper records.

Discovery is the most time-consuming and expensive part of litigation. For example, in a product liability lawsuit over the side effects of a new drug, a plaintiff will want copies of all the documents that contain any information about the drug, including the thousands of pages contained within the new drug application submitted to FDA. These will be reviewed carefully for comments by researchers or others that might indicate that the company knew of the problem or structured the research in ways that would minimize discovery of side effects. The plaintiff also would want to depose the senior executives of the company.

Privileged Information

U.S. law recognizes several circumstances where information is privileged from discovery, particularly in criminal trials. These include the information that a priest gets in confession, that one spouse learns from the other, that comes under attorney-client privilege, and certain privileges that have been created by statute. There is no common law physician-patient privilege, although some states have created one. There is greater access to information in civil lawsuits than in criminal prosecutions, but the attorney-client privilege is still in force.

U.S. law recognizes several circumstances where information is privileged from discovery.

The attorney-client privilege protects information a client tells his or her attorney. It does not protect documents or other materials that the client gives the attorney, unless these were protected already under a different privilege. If the client tells the same information to a nonattorney, such as a coworker, then the information can be obtained by deposing the coworker. If the attorney is the corporation's employee, the attorney-client privilege runs to the corporation. If there is a conflict between the corporation's interests and employee's interests, the attorney must choose to protect the corporation. Thus, in criminal cases, employees who are being investigated need to retain their own attorneys.

There is also protection for the work that the attorney does for the client (the attorney work product doctrine). It applies to work done for the client in anticipation of litigation, meaning that it is not available if the attorney is acting as a business advisor rather than as legal counsel. This doctrine protects information, such as accident investigation reports, if they are done under the supervision of the attorney. It also protects the legal research done by the attorney. The protection is not absolute, however. A court can order the production (turning over to the other side) of attorney work product if necessary to ensure fairness in the case. For example, assume that the attorney has an engineer test a medical device that was involved in an accident. The test destroys the device, making the engineer's report the only evidence of performance of the device. Even though the report was prepared at the instruction and under the supervision of an attorney, the court could order that the report be produced.

The Administrative Law System

Most food, drug, and medical device law is administrative law enforced by executive branch agencies, primarily FDA. In the United States, administrative law dates back to sanitary commissions and other citizens' boards in the colonial period. The growth of federal agencies reflects the growth of federal government after World War II. Administrative law is civil law, although agencies can refer cases to DOJ or state prosecutors if they find criminal activity. The agencies that conduct administrative practice are diverse, ranging in size and power from the Department of Health and Human Services (DHHS), which has a budget exceeding many small states, to specialized state agencies that have small budgets and no full-time staff.

Deference to Agency Expertise

Agencies occupy a privileged legal position because courts generally defer to agency decisions, as long as the agency is acting within the legal authority it was given by Congress in its enabling legislation. The courts recognize that there are many regulatory matters that can be resolved only through expert decision making because they turn on highly technical issues, they demand quick action, or some combination of both. In the classic Frozen Chicken case from 1908, the owners of a freezer plant attacked the right of a public health agency to seize and destroy thousands of pounds of chicken that had thawed when the refrigeration failed. The court ruled that the agency was justified in seizing and destroying the chicken because of the potential threat to the public.

Deference to Agency Expertise
Agencies occupy a privileged legal position because courts generally defer to agency decisions, as long as the agency is acting within the legal authority it was given by Congress in its enabling legislation.

This deference to agency decision making gives agencies flexibility in responding to problems. If a foodborne illness like listeriosis breaks out because of problems with cheese made from unpasteurized milk, health agencies can institute control measures much faster than Congress or the state legislatures could pass specific laws on the subject. The agency also has the freedom to modify its regulations as it learns more about a problem.

Administrative Procedure

While agencies may act quickly and with little oversight during emergencies, they are more limited in their actions that deal with routine matters. Federal agencies are governed by the Administrative Procedure Act (APA), and each state has a comparable set of rules for its agencies. Among other things, the APA establishes how federal agencies make regulations (rules) and how they conduct hearings.

Rulemaking
FDA must follow a defined process before it can release a new rule. In addition, it must first publish the proposed regulation in the Federal Register.

Rulemaking

A federal agency can do only what Congress gives it the power to do in its enabling legislation. In many cases, however, that enabling legislation is broad and general. This gives the agencies flexibility, but can make it difficult to understand what is required to comply with agency regulations. Agencies write regulations to provide industries and individuals with more detailed and specific information than the enabling legislation does. The APA and an agency's enabling legislation provide a formal process for the promulgation of regulations so as to ensure that there is public notice of proposed regulations and a chance for public comment before the regulation is finalized (notice-and-comment rulemaking). Properly promulgated regulations have the same force as a law passed by Congress. For example, its enabling legislation may direct FDA to prevent the sale of food packed under unsanitary conditions. The agency must define "unsanitary" in such a way as to carry out the wishes of Congress, while recognizing the realities of food production and handling.

One such rule could define how many insect parts are allowed in a pound of butter. The FDA must first publish its proposed regulation in the *Federal Register*, which is a compilation of the federal notices, including proposed and final rules, by agencies. This notice could exceed 100 pages. All interested persons, which might include butter and cookie makers, are given a period to comment on the rule. If the proposed rule allows three insect parts per pound, the butter industry might complain that reducing insect parts to less than twenty per pound would increase the cost of butter. A public interest group might comment that there should be no insect parts in butter and, if there are, notice of them should appear on the label so consumers know what they are buying.

FDA must review the responses to the proposed regulation, and in some cases must hold public hearings to get more input. It then decides whether it wants to change the standard. In this case, assume it decides to raise the level to five insect parts per pound. It then publishes in the *Federal Register* a final rule with this standard. The final rule will include a summary of the comments FDA received and explanations of why it did or did not follow them. In this case, the agency would say that it was persuaded that three insect parts per pound would be too expensive, but that twenty would be too many and indicate filthy conditions. It also would say that it is too expensive to ban insect parts, and because they do not carry disease, including notice of insect parts on the label would give consumers the wrong impression that the butter was unsafe.

When the final rule goes into effect, it is published as part of a series of books called the *Code of Federal Regulations* (C.F.R.). A food manufacturer who wants to start producing butter could look in Title 21 of the C.F.R., where FDA regulations are codified. Agencies also can publish informal guides for the industries they regulate. While these do not have the same legal standing as regulations that were subject to notice-and-comment in the *Federal Register*, they are useful guides to agency practice. FDA publishes both formal regulations and more informal guidelines to help industry comply with its requirements.

The Right to Inspect
FDA inspectors may visit regulated facilities to check for violations without a search warrant.

Administrative Searches

When a party to a lawsuit wants discovery, it must file its request with the court. The opposing party can contest the request and the court will have a hearing to determine if the request must be complied with or if it will be quashed (denied). When the government wants to enter the premises of a business to collect evidence for a criminal case, it must obtain a search warrant from a judge.

Administrative agencies have greater freedom to collect information from the industries they regulate. In many regulated industries, a company must agree to provide the agency with whatever information it requests and allow inspections without a search warrant as conditions of obtaining a license. Thus, a drug company has to allow an FDA inspector onto its manufacturing site to check for current Good Manufacturing Practices (cGMPs) because the permit to produce drugs includes the right to inspect. If the company refuses and demands that the agency get a search warrant, the agency can revoke the company's permit to make drugs at the facility while it seeks the warrant.

Information collected during administrative searches can be used for regulatory actions, but there are limits on how it can be used in criminal prosecutions. If FDA believes that a criminal prosecution is possible, it should refer the case to DOJ so the prosecutors can obtain a search warrant that complies with criminal due process requirements.

Administrative Hearings

In some situations, agencies must conduct hearings to allow regulated industries to have a say in proceedings against them. These hearings are presided over by an administrative law judge. Unlike a judge in an adversary civil or criminal case, the administrative law judge can act as both prosecutor and judge; this is called an inquisitorial system. The role of the administrative law judge is different from that of a judge in an adversary proceeding. Adversary judges are not generally permitted to talk with one party in the absence of the other party and are prohibited from assisting either party in the presentation of its case. The adversary judge considers only the procedural aspects of the case and is not expected to be an expert in the subject matter. The jurors are chosen to ensure that they do not know about the matters being litigated. Thus, the judge and jury in an adversarial case must depend on the litigants to develop and present their cases and must rule based only on what is presented.

In contrast, agency proceedings are generally much more informal. Agencies typically allow regulated parties to talk directly to the staff, who usually are encouraged to help the regulated party prepare their case or comply with the regulation. Usually adversary proceedings take a lot more time and cost a lot more money than administrative proceedings.

Agency hearings do not have juries. While live witness testimony is permitted, agencies generally prefer written reports from experts because they are easier to evaluate than live testimony. The judge is frequently an expert and will question the parties to ensure that the lawyers are presenting all the relevant evidence. Most importantly, in agency practice the lawyers and their clients will deal with the same agency personnel on many different matters. The agency will know whether they are credible and will act accordingly. Parties that have a reputation for cutting corners will be regulated more closely.

Judicial Review of Agency Actions

In situations where an agency believes a public health and safety risk is imminent, it can act without first going to court. In the aforementioned Frozen Chicken case, the health agency seized the chicken without first getting a court order. The agency was sued for an unconstitutional taking—illegal seizure—of the property. The court ruled that seizing the chicken without first going to court was proper, given the imminent threat to the public health. The defendant's due process rights were satisfied by a postseizure hearing. If the agency was found to have acted without proper authority or justification, it could be ordered to pay for damages.

In situations where an agency believes a public health and safety risk is imminent, it can act without first going to court.

The U.S. Supreme Court has ruled that in reviewing the order of a public health agency, the courts should not second-guess the underlying scientific basis of the agency's decision: "It is not for the courts to determine which scientific view is correct in ruling upon whether the police power has been properly exercised. The judicial function is exhausted with the discovery that the relation between means and end is not wholly vain and fanciful, an illusory pretense." To successfully attack an agency's expert decision making, it must be shown that the agency acted "arbitrarily or capriciously," which means that the agency acted without a rational basis for its decision. To defeat such a challenge, the agency must present a proper record explaining the factual and legal basis for its actions.

The courts do not defer to agencies' interpretation of laws because that is the area of the courts' expertise. It is not unusual for a court to prohibit an agency from regulating a given activity because the court determines that Congress did not give the agency authority for the contested regulations. For example, when FDA tried to restrict a physician's right to give patients his homemade drugs, the court found that the agency's enabling legislation did not give it the power to regulate medical practice. In litigation over regulation of nicotine by FDA, it was clear that nicotine was a drug under the definition of the statute, but the question before the court was whether Congress had intended to withhold the authority to regulate nicotine from FDA. While the court considered FDA's interpretation of the statutes, it relied on its own review and interpretation to support its ruling that Congress had not intended for FDA to regulate nicotine.

In rare cases, courts will review an agency's failure to act.

In rare cases, the courts will also review an agency's failure to act. In one case, the Secretary of DHHS refused to promulgate a rule banning the interstate shipment of unpasteurized milk. A public interest group sued the agency, arguing that such a rule was necessary to protect the public's health. The agency record showed that FDA scientists had built an overwhelming record that unpasteurized milk posed a threat to the public health. The court found that the Secretary was acting arbitrarily and capriciously in refusing to promulgate the rule, and ordered her to do so.

Summary

Food, drug, and medical device regulation can be understood only in the larger context of the U.S. legal system. All actions of FDA must be authorized by Congress and overseen by the President. All food and drug regulation by FDA is civil law, although FDA can refer cases to DOJ for criminal prosecution. Any industry regulated by FDA must be familiar with the statutes and the specific regulations promulgated by FDA governing their industry. Failure to follow these regulations can result in seizures, closing of facilities, and civil and criminal penalties.

Chapter 2

U.S. Food and Drug Law and FDA—A Historical Background

*Paul Hyman, Hyman, Phelps & McNamara, PC, Washington, D.C.**

Key Points

- Food and drug law dates back to the beginning of commerce, arising with laws to protect consumers of food from false weights and measures.
- U.S. food and drug law derives primarily from British food laws adopted by the colonies and the states after the Revolutionary War.
- Until the mid-19th century, almost all food and drug regulation occurred at the local level, reflecting the prevailing pattern of commerce.
- With regional and national expansion of food distribution, the states became more involved; the few federal laws focused primarily on imports, taxes, and duties rather than consumer protection.
- The Vaccine Act of 1902 marked the federal government's venture into domestic drug regulation, and included premarket approval.
- The Food and Drugs Act of 1906, the first comprehensive federal law regulating foods and drugs, was strictly an enforcement statute, designed to punish violations.
- A tragedy involving a new dosage form of a sulfa drug, Elixir Sulfanilamide, which contained an unlabeled solvent and killed almost 100 people, helped induce Congress to enact the Federal Food, Drug, and Cosmetic Act of 1938 (FDCA), the basic law today.
- In addition to strengthening enforcement and federal jurisdiction, the 1938 act included government premarket clearance of drugs for safety.
- The FDCA has been amended numerous times, strengthening the regulation of drugs, food and color additives, and medical devices, and, more recently, promoting the availability of generic drugs, new therapeutic agents, nutrition information for foods, and dietary supplements.
- FDA, which enforces the FDCA, is the oldest federal regulatory agency, beginning in 1848 as the Agricultural Division of the Patent Office, subsequently becoming part of the U.S. Department of Agriculture; the Federal Security Agency; the Department of Health, Education and Welfare; and now the Department of Health and Human Services, but lacking a statutory existence until 1988.

---

* The author gratefully acknowledges the invaluable assistance of Kurt R. Karst and Cassandra A. Soltis in the update of this chapter.

The basic statute under which the federal government regulates food, drugs, medical devices, and cosmetics is the Federal Food, Drug, and Cosmetic Act of 1938 (FDCA). The history of food and drug regulation, however, goes back virtually to the beginning of recorded history, or at least since such products were offered for sale to consumers. Moreover, that history did not stop with the 1938 act. There have been numerous amendments to the statute, both expanding and contracting its reach, as well as court decisions that have changed the interpretation of the statutory language in ways that frequently have surprised the law's congressional proponents, government regulators, regulated industry, and consumers.

Roots of Food and Drug Law and Regulation

The development of food and drug law can be said to have paralleled the development of civilization.

The development of food and drug law can be said to have paralleled the development of civilization. Laws to protect consumers from adulterated food products and from false weights and measures date back at least to biblical times and can be found in all civilizations. Until relatively recent times, and the development of analytical chemistry and the beginnings of modern medicine, the regulation of food encompassed drugs as well. With the development of "consumer" products, early civilizations had to take steps to protect consumers who, like today's consumers, could not readily protect themselves from fraudulent practices. Early regulations can be found in the Code of Hammurabi in the 18th century B.C., and in early Chinese and Indian laws.

The Greeks and Romans enacted increasingly complicated food laws, addressing adulteration of staples such as wine, wheat, flour, and bread. In Rome, the sale of watered, flavored, and colored wines; the use of false weights and measures; and other fraudulent practices could give rise to a private right of action or to a civil crime punishable by condemnation to the mines or temporary exile. Thus, the Romans did not rely entirely on the doctrine of *caveat emptor* ("buyer beware") to regulate foods.

In the Middle Ages, following the Crusades, certain regulatory functions, particularly with respect to short weights and measures, were the responsibility of mercantile guilds. For instance, the Pepperers Guild was appointed custodian of official weight standards in the 13th century by King Henry III of England and its members became the first public food inspectors in England.

Concern over inadequate policing by these private, commercial interests eventually led to the enactment of local ordinances or state laws to regulate sales of particular commodities. Laws in England and the Continent regulated the quality of bread, wine, beer, ale, meat, fish, honey, spices, butter, milk, and water. Punishment for violations of these laws could range from public humiliation to fines to corporal or even capital punishment.

During the 16th and 17th centuries, colonial expansion brought more exotic goods—such as chocolate, tea, coffee, and sugar—to Europe. The substitution of cheaper ingredients and other fraudulent practices became more sophisticated and more widespread. The ability of regulatory officials to detect these adulterated foods was limited, although many ordinances and laws were enacted to try to prevent these practices. It was only with the development of the science of chemistry, however, that modern food and drug regulation could begin to develop. By the middle of the 19th century, the advance of analytical chemistry and the use of the microscope to analyze foods led at last to broad food and drug laws in Europe and the United States.

The American colonies followed English legal precedents for food regulation, but the early laws and ordinances primarily were intended to protect trade in the colonies. Independence did not change this legal tradition. Most states, like Virginia, formally adopted all of the English common law. Massachusetts enacted its own food adulteration law as early as 1785, again modeled on British regulations. Throughout the 19th century and into the 20th century, the United States was influenced most strongly by British law and regulation.

In the 1800s, Great Britain and other European countries began to update their laws to protect the public from unsafe and fraudulently presented foods and drugs. Their laws shifted from protection of revenue to protection of consumers as more fraud and adulteration were recognized and the public demanded better protection.

1820
Frederick Accum, a German chemist working in London, publishes A Treatise on Adulteration of Food and Culinary Poisons.

In 1820, a German chemist working in London, Frederick Accum, published *A Treatise on Adulteration of Food and Culinary Poisons*, which described the fraudulent adulteration of bread, beer, wine, liquor, tea, coffee, cream, confectionery, vinegar, mustard, pepper, cheese, olive oil, and pickles. Accum bravely identified merchants who were selling adulterated foods and drugs. His book also discussed various methods available to detect these frauds.

As exposed by Accum and others, adulteration of food and drugs was widespread. Candy was colored with highly toxic mineral pigments such as compounds of lead, arsenic, copper, mercury, and chromium. "Rock-and-rye" candy, popular among children, was made of glucose, flour, and fusel oil. Coffee was regularly adulterated with chicory, as well as roasted ox or horse liver. Tea was adulterated with copper arsenite, lead chromate, and indigo.

Dr. A.H. Hassall, an English physician, performed microscopic analyses on common food adulterations that were published in the medical journal *The Lancet*, and then republished in a book in 1855. Like Accum, Dr. Hassall's articles identified merchants responsible for the adulterations, and they received much public attention. In analyses of many samples of foods such as coffee, bread, flour, milk, and tea, Dr. Hassall found most to be adulterated with cheaper food ingredients and such extraneous materials as metals, colors, shells, husks, sand, and grit.

In response to public pressure, in 1860 the English Parliament enacted the first general food law in England, the Adulteration of Food and Drink Act. This legislation was extended to medicines in 1868 and 1872. In 1875, these acts were replaced by the Sale of Food and Drugs Act.

In the United States, until the middle of the 19th century, most food and drug regulation was carried out on a local level, reflecting the type of commerce prevalent at that time. As with other commerce, however, food distribution expanded regionally and nationally, and the states became more involved. By 1900, almost every state had some type of food and drug law in place.

Federal legislation through the 19th century focused on foreign commerce. Thus, in 1848, Congress passed the Drug Importation Act that ordered U.S. Customs to prevent entry of foreign adulterated drugs. The law's primary purpose was to levy taxes and duties on imported articles, and to protect U.S. industry. Protecting consumers was of secondary importance. Other laws enacted during the latter half of the 19th century included the Tea Acts of 1883 and 1897, the Oleomargarine Act of 1886, and the Filled Cheese Act of 1896. All were enforced by the Treasury Department and had similar commercial purposes.

Accum's treatise had raised public concern in the United States, as well as in Europe, about food adulteration. Several similar investigations in the United States added to this concern. Among these was a report by Lemuel Shattuck in 1850 that showed that average life expectancy had decreased in Boston from 27.85 years to 21.43 years and in New York from 26.15 years to 19.69 years between the years 1810 to 1820, and 1840 to 1845. He attributed this in part to adulterated food and drugs and recommended establishing boards of health to counter the problems.

1850
Lemuel Shattuck attributes a decrease in average life expectancy to adulterated food and drugs, and he recommends establishing boards of health to counter the problems.

Findings of this type helped put pressure on Congress to pass federal legislation. Many scientists, journalists, and social reformers joined the effort. Dr. Harvey W. Wiley, who became the Chief Chemist of the U.S. Department of Agriculture (USDA) (the forerunner of Commissioner of Food and Drugs) in 1883, took an aggressive public role in exposing food adulteration and demanding a federal response. Some industry leaders also spoke out on the need for federal regulation, based both on their concerns over lax enforcement and on the difficulties of complying with the patchwork of state and local laws. More than 100 food and drug bills were introduced in Congress, unsuccessfully save one, from the 1880s to 1906.

The one federal law enacted in that period was the Virus Act of 1902 (subsequently known as the Biologics Control Act), which was intended to ensure purity and safety of therapeutic serums, vaccines, toxins, antitoxins, and similar products used to prevent, treat, or cure diseases in humans. Vaccines had long been widely accepted in the United States, but regulation of their safety and purity was left to the states. The direct impetus for the 1902 federal law arose from two tragedies that occurred in 1901: one involving contaminated smallpox vaccine that caused an outbreak of tetanus in Camden, New Jersey; the other involving diphtheria antitoxin contaminated with tetanus in St. Louis, Missouri. These incidents convinced Congress that federal action was necessary to protect the public from contaminated products. Ironically, vaccines originally were regulated by the Vaccines Act of 1813, apparently the first federal regulatory law, but that law was repealed in 1822 after similar incidents of contaminated batches occurred.

The 1902 act for the first time required government premarket approval of a product. Biologics manufacturers were required to obtain both product and establishment licenses. The act also, for the first time, authorized federal agents (from the Treasury Department) to inspect biologics establishments. Enforcement of the human biologics law subsequently was transferred to the National Institutes of Health and became the Food and Drug Administration's (FDA's) responsibility in 1972. Animal biologics are still regulated by USDA.

The Food and Drugs Act of 1906

The pressure on Congress to enact federal legislation from Dr. Wiley and others was heightened around the turn of the century by public opinion whipped up by "muckrakers," "investigative reporters" who exposed food and drug adulteration, consumer fraud, and other social issues. Probably the most influential was Upton Sinclair, whose 1906 novel *The Jungle* dramatically portrayed food adulteration in the meat industry as part of his description of the exploitation of workers and the poor in Chicago. In response, President Theodore Roosevelt sent his own representatives to Chicago who confirmed the abominable conditions. President Roosevelt then added his support for federal legislation.

1906
The original Food and Drugs Act is passed by Congress and signed by President Theodore Roosevelt. It prohibits interstate commerce in misbranded and adulterated foods, drinks, and drugs.

On June 30, 1906, both the Food and Drugs Act (often called the "Pure Food and Drugs Act") and the Meat Inspection Act were signed into law. The former was enforced by the predecessor to today's FDA. The latter was, and remains, the jurisdiction of the USDA, continuing the historic split in regulatory authority between the two agencies and the corresponding segments of the food industry.

The 1906 act commanded the federal government to ferret out adulterated and misbranded foods and drugs in interstate commerce but it did not authorize the government to establish industrywide standards or broad rules to protect the public health.

The 1906 act was the first comprehensive U.S. legislation relating to foods and drugs. It was designed as an "enforcement" statute intended to punish violations by criminal prosecution or by seizure of the offending goods. In concise and simple terms, the 1906 act commanded the federal government to ferret out adulterated and misbranded foods and drugs in interstate commerce. The government was not authorized to establish industrywide standards or broad rules to protect the public health or to approve any products before they could be marketed.

Section 2 of the 1906 act prohibited the interstate shipment, including import from and export to a foreign country, of any adulterated or misbranded food or drug. The person who delivered a violative product *and* the person who subsequently delivered such an article "in original unbroken packages" were guilty of a misdemeanor and subject to a fine of up to $200. A subsequent offense was punishable by either or both a $300 fine and one year in prison. A dealer who could show a "guaranty" from a U.S. supplier to the effect that the article was not adulterated or misbranded would be exempt from prosecution (section 9 of the 1906 act).

Section 6 of the 1906 act defined "drug" to include "all medicines and preparations recognized in the United States Pharmacopoeia (USP) or National Formulary (NF) for internal or external use, and any substance or mixture of substances intended to be used for the cure, mitigation, or prevention of disease of either man or animals." The act provided that a drug was "adulterated" if: 1) the drug failed to meet the standards of "strength, quality, or purity" as prescribed by the USP or the NF, unless the drug's container "plainly stated" a different standard of purity; or 2) the drug failed to meet its own labeled strength or purity (section 7 of the 1906 act).

Section 6 of the 1906 act also defined "food" to include "all articles used for food, drink, confectionary, or condiment by man or other animals, whether simple, mixed, or compound." A food was adulterated:

> **First.** If any substance has been mixed and packed with it so as to reduce or lower or injuriously affect its quality or strength.
>
> **Second.** If any substance has been substituted wholly or in part for the article.
>
> **Third.** If any valuable constituent of the article has been wholly or in part abstracted.

> **Fourth.** If it be mixed, colored, powdered, coated, or stained in a manner whereby damage or inferiority is concealed.
>
> **Fifth.** If it contain any added poisonous or other added deleterious ingredient which may render such article injurious to health. . . .
>
> **Sixth.** If it consists in whole or in part of a filthy, decomposed, or putrid animal or vegetable substance, or any portion of an animal unfit for food, whether manufactured or not, or if it is the product of a diseased animal, or one that has died otherwise than by slaughter.

The statute further declared confectionary to be adulterated if it contained certain minerals, poisonous color or flavor, other ingredients harmful to health, "spirituous liquor," or narcotic drugs (section 7 of the 1906 act).

The 1906 act also listed several acts that would constitute "misbranding" as to both food and drugs. In particular, any drug, food, or food ingredient "the package or label of which shall bear any statement, design, or device regarding such article [or its components] which shall be false or misleading in any particular" would be misbranded (section 8 of the 1906 act). A drug could also be misbranded if: 1) it was an imitation of or was offered for sale under the name of another drug; 2) the original contents were replaced by other materials; or 3) the package label failed to state "the quantity or proportion of any alcohol, morphine, opium, cocaine, heroine, alpha or beta eucaine, chloroform, cannabis indica, chloral hydrate, or acetanilide" or any derivatives of those substances. A food could be misbranded for the same conditions and also if the package contained: 1) an inaccurate quantity of contents statement or 2) a false statement about the food's ingredients.

"Misbranded" as defined in the 1906 act:
In particular, any drug, food, or food ingredient "the package or label of which shall bear any statement, design, or device regarding such article [or its components] which shall be false or misleading in any particular" would be misbranded.

An adulterated or misbranded article in interstate commerce, or still "unloaded, unsold, or in original unbroken packages," could be seized and condemned by a U.S. district court (section 10 of the 1906 act). The procedures were to conform to admiralty proceedings except that either the claimant of the article or the government could demand a jury trial.

The act was administered jointly under "uniform rules and regulations" established by the Secretaries of Agriculture, Commerce, and Treasury, including "collection and examination of specimens of foods and drugs" (section 3 of the 1906 act). The Secretaries established a committee to draw up rules and regulations for enforcement of the law. The committee included Dr. Wiley, Chief of the USDA Bureau of Chemistry, which was primarily responsible for the enforcement of the act. The bureau, in particular, examined samples and, if they appeared to be violative, notified and provided the party from whom the samples were obtained an opportunity to be heard. "[I]f it appears that any of the provisions of [the 1906] Act have been violated," the Secretary of Agriculture certified the matter to the appropriate U.S. District Attorney for formal action in the federal district court (sections 4 and 5 of the 1906 act).

A controversy soon arose over whether a drug label was "false or misleading in any particular" if it contained unproved therapeutic claims. The Supreme Court, in *United States v. Johnson*, 211 U.S. 488 (1911), held that "Cancerine tablets," offered as part of "Dr. Johnson's Mild Combination Treatment for Cancer, Tumor and Other Chronic Diseases," were not misbranded because the statute prohibited only misleading statements about the ingredients of a drug, not about the drug's effectiveness.

Congress reacted in 1912 with the Sherley Amendment, which expanded the definition of misbranding for drugs to include "any statement, design, or device regarding the curative or therapeutic effect of such article or [its components], which is false and fraudulent." Significantly, the government still had the burden of proving fraudulent intent.

Five Amendments to the 1906 act:

- *The "Net Weight" Amendment*
- *The "Kenyon" Amendment*
- *"Butter" Amendment*
- *"McNary-Napes" Amendment*
- *"Shrimp Inspection" Amendment*

There were only five other amendments to the 1906 act before it was replaced by the FDCA in 1938:

- The Net Weight Amendment of 1913 required the quantity of a packaged food's contents to be plainly and conspicuously marked on the outer package in terms of weight, measure, or numerical count.
- The Kenyon Amendment of 1919 overturned an adverse administrative decision by defining the word "package," as used in the act, to include "wrapped meats inclosed [sic] in papers."
- In 1923 Congress responded to requests from the dairy industry to provide the first standard definition of a food product in "An Act to Define Butter and to Provide a Standard Therefore."
- At the urging of the canned foods industry, Congress passed the McNary-Napes Amendment in 1930, authorizing the Secretary of Agriculture to establish standards of quality, condition, and fill of container for each class of canned foods.
- In 1934 Congress implemented the Shrimp Inspection Amendment, which authorized the Secretary of Agriculture to create a voluntary seafood inspection program that would allow a participant to market its shrimp as "USDA Approved."

The Bureau of Chemistry and others quickly recognized deficiencies in the 1906 act. Among other things, the bureau was concerned that the law did not reach dangerous cosmetics and medical devices. The bureau also was concerned that the 1906 act did not extend to fraudulent statements made in food and drug advertising, as opposed to package labels. Although the bureau and other critics initially believed amendments to the existing statute would remedy the 1906 act's failings, they came to the conclusion over time that a completely new statute would be necessary.

The Federal Food, Drug, and Cosmetic Act

In the 1920s and early 1930s, consumers were exposed to increasing numbers of processed and manufactured foods, drugs, cosmetics, and medical devices. Occasionally, these new products had tragic consequences. For example, a depilatory known as "Koremlu Cream," advertised as a cosmetic, contained thallium acetate that caused severe injury to unsuspecting users. Various "slenderizing" compounds, containing powerful pharmacologic agents, could not be regulated as drugs under the 1906 act because obesity was not recognized as a disease. These products were outside the scope of the 1906 act and the government had no means to remove them from the market.

1938
The FDCA was passed by Congress, containing new provisions:
- *Extending control to cosmetics and therapeutic devices.*
- *Requiring new drugs to be shown safe before marketing—starting a new system of drug regulation.*
- *Eliminating the Sherley Amendment requirement to prove intent to defraud in drug misbranding cases.*
- *Providing that safe tolerances be set for unavoidable poisonous substances.*
- *Authorizing standards of identity, quality, and fill-of-container for foods.*
- *Authorizing factory inspections.*
- *Adding the remedy of court injunctions to the previous penalties of seizures and prosecutions.*

In another notorious example, "Radiothor" was labeled accurately as "radium-containing water." Because that statement was true and the label made no fraudulent therapeutic claims, the government could not take action against the manufacturer. The agency could only warn consumers not to use "Radiothor," even as people were dying from radiation poisoning.

Further, the 1906 act prohibited fraudulent advertising only if attached to, or packaged with, the product. Thus, both consumers and honest manufacturers were susceptible to the deceptive advertising practices of the unscrupulous producer (and the 1906 act provided for only the mildest criminal penalties).

By 1933, critics of the 1906 act included consumer advocates, politicians, reporters, and other commentators, as well as officials of FDA (the bureau became FDA in 1930).

Rexford G. Tugwell, who became Assistant Secretary of Agriculture in 1933 under President Franklin D. Roosevelt, assembled a committee of FDA officials, USDA attorneys, and several administrative law professors. Their objective was the complete overhaul of the 1906 act. These efforts resulted in a bill introduced by Senator Copeland of New York in 1933 as S. 1944.

Consistent with New Deal political theory, the bill would have increased greatly FDA's regulation of the food and drug industries. Most contentious was a provision that authorized the Secretary of Agriculture to issue any regulations deemed necessary to enforce the law. (It was generally understood that the Secretary would delegate all authority to FDA to enforce the law unless the law specifically barred such delegation.) The regulations would have the force and effect of law. The Secretary also would have the authority to set the procedures for issuing regulations.

Jurisdiction over medical devices would be established by including them in the definition of "drug." Cosmetics, previously subject to little regulation, would be brought within the jurisdiction of FDA. Factories that manufactured or processed foods, drugs, or cosmetics, and warehouses that stored such goods would be subject to inspection. FDA also by regulation could require permits for manufacturing, processing, and packaging facilities. False advertising of regulated products would also be prohibited.

S. 1944 would have expanded greatly the criteria for "adulterated" or "misbranded" foods, drugs, cosmetics, or devices. For example, in response to various "quack" remedies then on the market, a drug would be adulterated if dangerous when used according to its labeling and misbranded if it claimed to have an effect that general medical opinion did not support. Food would be misbranded if it failed to meet standards of quality, standards of identity, and standards of package fill that the Secretary was to promulgate by regulation. Adulterated or misbranded goods in interstate commerce were subject to seizure, and any person (including corporate officers) responsible for introducing or receiving such goods could be subject to criminal liability. Significantly, the bill established a strict liability standard; a "knowing" violation of these provisions was not necessary (although more severe penalties applied if a person acted with scienter). In addition, the Secretary was authorized to use "publicity" when necessary to protect the public health or prevent consumer fraud.

S. 1944, introduced in 1933 by Senator Copeland, sparked a five-year legislative battle that reflected the ongoing debate over the rise in administrative autonomy under the New Deal.

S. 1944 sparked a five-year legislative battle that reflected, in large part, the ongoing debate over the rise in administrative autonomy under the New Deal. Critics focused on the broad discretionary authority vested in the Secretary of Agriculture and the lack of procedural safeguards to prevent misuse of power. Although the Secretary was authorized to issue many regulations only after "notice and hearing," the Secretary also was given the authority to define "notice" and "hearing" by regulation. Moreover, any findings of fact after such a hearing were deemed to be conclusively established for purposes of judicial review. The false advertising provisions were another major target of criticism. Both advertisers and publishers believed that the definition of false advertising was too vague and the penalties for publishing such advertising were too severe.

As a result, S. 1944 was revised over successive years in attempts to agree with the objectives of the affected industries. The first revision (S.

2000), submitted to the Senate in 1934, attempted to enhance procedural safeguards by establishing two five-member advisory panels, the Committee on Public Health and the Committee on Food. A majority vote of the appropriate committee was required before FDA could propose a regulation. After a hearing, another majority vote was required before FDA could issue the regulation. The bill also gave jurisdiction to the U.S. district courts to enjoin the enforcement of any regulation that would cause substantial harm to the petitioner "if it is shown that the regulation is unreasonable, arbitrary, or capricious, or not in accordance with the law." "False advertising" was required to be "false or misleading in any particular relevant to the purposes" of the act. The bill died in committee, but was amended and resurfaced in the same session as S. 2800.

In a concession to the publishing industry, S. 2800 modified some provisions relating to advertising and specifically exempted publishers from liability for false advertisements. To deflect criticism that the government was attempting to regulate the practice of medicine, the bill contained an explicit statement to the contrary. A drug was still considered misbranded, however, if the labeling contained the name of a disease for which the drug was not a cure, as supported by "substantial medical opinion" or "demonstrable scientific facts." The Senate Committee on Commerce held hearings on S. 2800 and, after further modification, reported it favorably to the Senate but Congress adjourned without action on the bill.

Senator Copeland persisted, and in 1935 he introduced a new bill, S. 5. This bill retained the Committee on Food and the Committee on Public Health and granted them broader authority to formulate and issue regulations. The bill authorized the Secretary to appoint additional advisory committees to include representatives of the food, drug, cosmetic, and advertising industries and consumers in the regulatory process. S. 5 eliminated the provision granting the Secretary conclusive power with respect to questions of fact and transferred this to the judicial system. Judicial authority to review regulations was made explicit. FDA was given jurisdiction over false advertising. The bill passed in the Senate.

Senator Copeland persisted, and in 1935 he introduced a new bill, S. 5.

In the House of Representatives, a subcommittee of the Committee on Interstate and Foreign Commerce held hearings on S. 5 and competing legislation sponsored in the House. In May 1936, this subcommittee agreed to a bill. Among other things, this bill granted sole authority for enforcing the false advertising prohibitions to the Federal Trade Commission (FTC). The House bill eliminated the Committees on Public Health and Food and the advisory committees. Rulemaking authority was transferred back to the Secretary, with some restrictions.

The bill passed the House and went to conference. However, neither side would yield on the issue of which agency should control advertising, and the bill failed again.

In January 1937, Senator Copeland reintroduced S. 5 in another attempt to achieve a food and drug bill. To address one of the advertising issues, the bill would use injunctions, rather than criminal sanctions, to enforce the prohibition of advertising that was "false or misleading in any particular." Further, the "particulars" that a court could enjoin were enumerated, including statements regarding the identity, strength, quality, purity, safety, dietary, curative, therapeutic, or beneficial effects of a food, drug, device, or cosmetic. Jurisdiction over advertising was placed in FDA on the theory that advertising was an extension of labeling. The FTC would retain jurisdiction over advertising that was an unfair method of competition. With several other amendments (including a separate definition for "device"), the Senate passed S. 5 and the bill was referred to the House Committee on Interstate and Foreign Commerce.

The Elixir Sulfanilamide tragedy led to passage of the 1938 law.

While the bill was in the House committee, a drug manufacturer released a product labeled "Elixir Sulfanilamide," a new dosage form of a sulfa drug. Before the elixir was marketed, the manufacturer tested the product for flavor, but not for safety. One ingredient in the elixir, which was not listed on the label, was diethylene glycol, a solvent used to prepare the elixir. Almost 100 people died from ingesting the drug. FDA immediately initiated a recall, but could base its actions only on a technical violation of the 1906 act: "elixir" could be used only to describe a solution that contained alcohol; as Elixir Sulfanilamide did not contain alcohol, it was misbranded. The manufacturer's failure to test the drug for safety or to list a lethal ingredient on the label did not violate the 1906 act.

This tragedy reinvigorated the efforts to enact a food and drug bill. In addition, the jurisdictional controversy over advertising was resolved early in 1938 by the Wheeler-Lea Amendments to the Federal Trade Commission Act, which gave the FTC jurisdiction over false advertising of food, drugs, devices, and cosmetics as an unfair or deceptive trade practice. The House committee amended S. 5 to specify that foods, drugs, devices, or cosmetics were misbranded if the labeling was false or misleading in any particular. The committee added a list of factors that would be considered to decide whether labeling was misleading, including representations or suggestions of fact and the omission of any material facts. This provision was intended to prevent manufacturers of drugs and devices from making false effectiveness claims. The bill, however, deleted the provision that deemed a drug misbranded if scientific opinion did not support a labeling claim of efficacy.

As a response to the Elixir Sulfanilamide tragedy, the committee added a provision to S. 5 that defined "new drugs" and required manufacturers to apply to FDA before a new drug could be marketed. As part of the application, the manufacturer had to test the new drug for safety and submit full reports of the investigations conducted to establish safety to FDA for review. If FDA did not act within sixty days, the manufacturer could market the drug. If FDA questioned an application's assertion of safety, the agency could initiate a hearing. Whether by oversight or intention, devices were not subject to premarket safety review.

To facilitate judicial oversight of administrative action, an administrative hearing was required before FDA could issue many regulations. The Secretary could issue, modify, or repeal a proposed regulation only on evidence of record at the hearing. The bill required that the Secretary publicize detailed findings of fact before taking action. Within ninety days after a regulation issued, individuals or businesses could challenge the regulation in any district court. If challenged, the Secretary was required to furnish a certified copy of the administrative record. The court could then review the agency's findings of fact and, in appropriate circumstances, could supplement the record with additional evidence.

The Senate disagreed with some of these amendments and another conference committee was convened. The committee decided that judicial review would be more consistent and less burdensome to the agency if it were conducted in the circuit courts of appeal. Further, to the extent that evidence outside the administrative record was to be taken, it would be done in a proceeding before the Secretary. Other amendments clarified certain labeling provisions. Both houses then approved the bill, and President Roosevelt signed the FDCA on June 25, 1938.

Structure of the Federal Food, Drug, and Cosmetic Act of 1938

As enacted, the FDCA is divided into nine chapters. While each chapter will be explained in greater detail later in this text, the following brief summary of each chapter's subject matter should prove beneficial at this juncture.

The Federal Food, Drug, and Cosmetic Act of 1938
The FDCA remains the basic law governing food and drug regulation.

Chapter one is the short title of the act. Chapter two provides definitions of important terms.

Chapter three sets forth the prohibited acts and penalties. In particular, section 301 states that "the following acts *and causing thereof* are hereby prohibited" (emphasis added), thus including aiding and abetting. Among other things, the act prohibits the "adulteration" or "misbranding" of food, drugs, devices, and cosmetics in interstate commerce, or the introduction or delivery for introduction of adulterated or misbranded goods into interstate commerce.

The FDCA also established, for the first time, jurisdiction in the district courts to restrain violations of the act by injunction. A violation of any of the prohibited acts in section 301 can be prosecuted as a misdemeanor under a strict liability standard, applicable to both companies and individuals. The Supreme Court upheld this standard in *United States v. Dotterweich*, 320 U.S. 277 (1943), and in *United States v. Park*, 421 U.S. 658 (1975). As in the 1906 act, a person could avoid criminal penalties by showing a supplier's guaranty. The act also provides the accused an opportunity to present oral or written views to FDA before the agency reports the case to the U.S. Attorney for prosecution. The Supreme Court in *Dotterweich*, however, held that failure to provide that opportunity does not preclude prosecution. In addition, the Secretary is authorized to enforce "minor" violations of the act by means of "written notice or warning." All formal enforcement proceedings are brought by the government, meaning that FDA must act through the Department of Justice (DOJ).

As in the 1906 act, violative articles are subject to seizure and condemnation in the district courts. Multiple seizures are authorized for adulterated products, unapproved new drugs, or products previously adjudicated as misbranded.

Chapter four addresses regulation of foods. The Secretary is authorized to promulgate regulations establishing standards of identity, quality, and fill of containers for foods. In a concession to the agricultural and dairy industries, most fresh or dried fruits and vegetables, as well as butter, are exempt from these regulations. An adulterated food is defined as a food that contains any "poisonous or deleterious substance," or any "filthy, putrid, or decomposed substance," or that was prepared, packaged, or stored "under unsanitary conditions." Food is also adulterated if missing a "valuable constituent," or if any substance has been added to increase its bulk or make it appear to be of greater value (known as "economic adulteration").

Food is deemed misbranded if its labeling is "false or misleading in any particular," if it is an imitation of another food (unless clearly labeled as an imitation), or if it does not meet FDA regulations setting standards of identity, quality, or container fill.

Food is deemed misbranded, among other things, if its labeling is "false or misleading in any particular," if it is an imitation of another food (unless clearly labeled as an imitation), or if it does not meet FDA regulations setting standards of identity, quality, or container fill. Foods for special dietary use must comply with FDA regulations.

The act also provides for FDA to impose emergency permit controls by regulation, requiring a permit to manufacture certain foods where microbial contamination cannot be readily controlled after the fact. FDA is also authorized to set tolerances for poisonous or deleterious substances that cannot be avoided by good manufacturing practices.

Drugs and devices are the subject of chapter five. A drug or device is deemed adulterated if it is unsafe or unsanitary. Drugs that fall below the standards of strength and purity established in specified official references (unless clearly labeled as such) or that do not meet the standards of strength or purity represented on the label also are adulterated.

A drug or device is misbranded, among other reasons, if its labeling is "false or misleading in any particular"; fails to identify the manufacturer, packer, or distributor; lacks a statement of net contents; does not list the common name of the drug and every active ingredient; does not contain "adequate directions for use" and "adequate warnings"; or is dangerous to health when used according to the labeling.

"Misbranded" as defined in the 1938 act
A drug or device is misbranded, among other reasons, if its labeling is "false or misleading in any particular"; fails to identify the manufacturer, packer, or distributor; lacks a statement of net contents; does not list the common name of the drug and every active ingredient; does not contain "adequate directions for use" and "adequate warnings"; or is dangerous to health when used according to the labeling.

"New drugs" cannot be introduced into interstate commerce unless an application has been filed with the Secretary that includes reports showing that the new drug is safe for use. The application becomes effective in sixty days unless FDA notifies the applicant to the contrary. An opportunity for hearing is provided, and the applicant can appeal an adverse decision to a federal district court. Drugs for investigational purposes are exempted from these requirements.

Chapter six describes the adulteration and misbranding provisions for cosmetics and is the shortest chapter. A cosmetic is adulterated if it:

- contains any "poisonous or deleterious substance which may render it injurious to users" when used as directed (except that a coal tar hair dye is exempt if it bears a label warning);
- is or contains any "filthy, putrid, or decomposed substance";
- was "prepared, packaged or held under unsanitary conditions" and became contaminated or rendered injurious to health;
- has a poisonous or deleterious container; or except for a hair dye, contains an unapproved color or one from an uncertified batch.

FDA is authorized to list and batch certify harmless colors.

A cosmetic is misbranded if its labeling is "false or misleading in any particular," fails to list the manufacturer and quantity of contents on any package label, lacks prominence and conspicuousness for required label statements, or is in a misleading container. FDA is authorized to exempt cosmetics shipped in bulk to be labeled or repacked elsewhere.

Administrative provisions are the subject of chapter seven. Section 701(a) authorizes FDA "to promulgate regulations for the efficient enforcement of this Act." No procedures are specified. More formal rulemaking procedures are set out for regulations to implement such rules as food standards; standards of strength, purity, and quality for noncompendial drugs; and listing of habit-forming drugs. FDA must offer an opportunity for hearing and the agency's decision must be based on "substantial evidence of record at the hearing." Within ninety days, any adversely affected party can appeal the order to an appropriate circuit court of appeals.

FDA's principal enforcement tool is the establishment inspection.

Chapter seven also spells out the authority and limits of FDA's principal enforcement tool, the establishment inspection. It authorizes the agency to:

- Use its own or state agents to conduct examinations and investigations.
- Take samples of foods, drugs, or cosmetics. (This is stated in a backhanded way in section 702(b), which requires FDA to give a portion of the sample to the owner "where a sample . . . is collected for analysis.")
- Review and copy records of interstate shipment in the possession of a carrier or the recipient of a food, drug, device, or cosmetic. Refusal of a written request is unlawful, but FDA may not use evidence so obtained in a criminal action against the person who provided the evidence.
- Enter and inspect, "at reasonable times," any factory, warehouse, establishment, or vehicle where food, drugs, devices, or cosmetics are produced, packed, or held for introduction into interstate commerce, or after such introduction. FDA inspectors must first obtain permission, but refusal is a prohibited act. The inspection may extend to the facilities, vehicle, equipment, finished and unfinished materials, container, and labeling, but not to records.
- Publish reports of formal actions under the act and disseminate information where FDA believes there is an imminent danger to health or "gross" consumer deception.

Chapter eight governs imports and exports of products. The Secretary of the Treasury is ordered to deliver samples of food, drugs, devices, or cosmetics offered for import as requested by the Secretary of Agriculture. Section 801 states: "If it appears from the examination of such samples or otherwise that" the products violate the FDCA, such products may be refused admission. The refused article must be exported or destroyed. Significantly, no direct right to judicial review is provided.

Articles intended for export are exempt from the adulteration or misbranding provisions of the act only if they comply with the foreign purchaser's specifications, do not violate foreign law, are labeled on the shipping package for export only, and have not been offered in domestic commerce. Unapproved new drugs can not be exported.

Finally, chapter nine repealed the Federal Food and Drugs Act of 1906. It also exempts meat and meat food products, biologics, and certain other products from the provisions of the act because they are governed by other statutes.

AMENDMENTS TO THE FDCA

Since 1938, there have been numerous amendments of the FDCA; however, there has been no general overhaul of the entire regulatory scheme comparable to the 1938 act's relationship to the 1906 act. Early amendments primarily were aimed at overcoming omissions and shortcomings in the law, often following court decisions. These statutes generally broadened FDA's regulatory authority and left implementation largely to FDA. More recent amendments have required FDA to focus on commercial and economic issues, frequently specifying precisely how and when FDA must implement the FDCA. In 1997 and 2007, Congress enacted laws that represented the most comprehensive efforts to "reform" the agency and improve regulation of all products since 1938.

There have been numerous amendments of the FDCA since 1938, but there has been no overhaul of the entire regulatory scheme comparable to the 1938 act's relationship to the 1906 act.

Significant Amendments from 1938 to 1962

Scientific developments, as well as the demands of World War II, led to a number of new laws directed at specific drugs. In December 1941, Congress amended the FDCA to require batch certification of the strength, quality, and purity of insulin in order "to adequately ensure safety and efficacy of use." (FDCA § 506.) Congress was persuaded of the need to ensure uniformity among batches because of the difficulties in making this drug. Significantly, this law gave FDA, for the first time, specific authority to regulate the efficacy of a particular drug.

Batch certification subsequently was required for penicillin (1945); streptomycin (1947); aureomycin, chloramphenicol, and bacitracin (1949); and all antibiotics (1962). By 1982, however, FDA was convinced that the quality of these drugs was now adequate to permit them to be regulated the same as other new drugs, and the agency ceased requiring batch certification in most instances.

In 1948, after an appellate court held that the FDCA did not reach products after shipment in interstate commerce, Congress amended the FDCA to hold expressly that a product may be in violation of the act while "held for sale (whether or not the first sale) after shipment in interstate

1951
The Durham-Humphrey Amendment
The Durham-Humphrey Amendment defines the kinds of drugs that cannot be safely used without medical supervision and restricts their sale to prescription by a licensed practitioner.

commerce." This brought local warehouses and retailers within FDA's jurisdiction.

♦ The Durham-Humphrey Amendment

In 1951, in the Durham-Humphrey Amendment, Congress for the first time defined prescription drugs for purposes of FDA regulation. Prescription and over-the-counter (OTC) status previously were determined by state law or by industry, although FDA had used the misbranding provision requiring "adequate directions for use" to impose prescription limits on some drugs. As amended, the FDCA defines a prescription drug to include habit-forming drugs; drugs that are dangerous for use except under the supervision of a (state) licensed practitioner because of their "toxicity or other potentiality for harmful effect,. . . method of use, or the collateral measures necessary to [their] use"; and those that are limited to prescription dispensing by approved new drug applications (NDAs). OTC drugs are not defined but comprise all those drugs that do not meet the prescription drug criteria.

For several years, FDA used this definition (as well as the misbranding and new drug provisions) to prohibit sales of stimulant, depressant, and hallucinogenic drugs, which, unlike narcotics, were not subject to specific laws outlawing their abuse. During the 1950s and 1960s, FDA criminally prosecuted manufacturers, distributors, importers, physicians, truck stop operators, and others engaged in the illicit diversion of these drugs. In the late 1960s, FDA prosecuted a few students for distribution of LSD and other hallucinogens. Congress subsequently passed several controlled substances laws that ultimately were transferred to DOJ and are now enforced by the Drug Enforcement Administration (DEA).

In 1953, after a court restricted FDA's inspectional authority, Congress amended section 704 of the act to make clear that FDA had the right to inspect without the permission of the owner or operator of the establishment.

In 1954, and again in 1958, Congress attended to problems relating to chemical contamination of foods. In 1954, Congress set tolerances for pesticide chemicals in or on raw agricultural commodities, including a complex premarket approval system based on a demonstration of safety for use of pesticides in foods intended for human use (FDCA §§ 201(q), (r), 402(a)(2), 408). Authority for establishing the tolerances subsequently was transferred to the Environmental Protection Agency, with FDA retaining the authority to proceed against foods that contain unapproved or unsafe levels of pesticides.

♦ The Food Additives Amendment of 1958

Congress subsequently enacted the Food Additives Amendment of 1958, which gave FDA authority to require premarket approval for safety of components added to foods (FDCA §§ 201(s), (t), 402(a)(2), 409). This followed several years of hearings on the appropriate regulatory mechanism to ensure the safety of food ingredients.

Under this law, a food additive is defined as any substance intended or reasonably expected to become a food component or to affect a food's characteristics that is "not generally recognized [by] qualified experts" as safe (GRAS) for its intended use based on "scientific procedures" or, for substances marketed prior to 1958, based on experience from common use in food (FDCA § 201(s)). A food additive is deemed unsafe unless FDA has reviewed data proving its safety and issued a regulation allowing its use. Human safety data is not required. The law established formal rulemaking procedures for the process.

1958
Food Additives Amendment
The Food Additives Amendment required manufacturers of new food additives to establish safety. The Delaney Provision prohibits the approval of any food additive shown to induce cancer in humans or animals.

In addition, the law contains an anticancer provision, known as the Delaney Clause after its leading sponsor, Representative James Delaney (D-NY), which prohibits approval of any food additive that has been "found to induce cancer when ingested by man or animal" or found to induce cancer in appropriate tests. As analytic testing has advanced, this "one molecule" approach has affected several widely used food components, such as the artificial sweeteners cyclamate and saccharin and the preservative nitrite. On two occasions, Congress has taken steps to exempt specific substances from the Delaney Clause. In 1962, the FDCA was amended to exempt ingredients of animal feeds (primarily diethylstilbestrol) if no residue is found in edible portions of the animal. In the Saccharin Study and Labeling Act of 1977, Congress put a moratorium on FDA action to ban saccharin, but required labeling of products containing the sweetener. That act was repealed in December 2000. The Delaney Clause was modified in 1996 with respect to pesticides but otherwise remains in place.

♦ The Color Additive Amendments of 1960

Congress enacted the Color Additive Amendments of 1960 to regulate colors added to foods, drugs, or cosmetics separately from the Food Additives Amendment. A color additive is defined in the amendment as a dye, pigment, or other coloring agent that "is capable (alone or through reaction with other substance) of imparting color" when added to a food, drug, cosmetic, or the human body. Unlike food additives, the definition of color additives does not contain any grandfather protection for a GRAS color. FDA can approve a color for one use and not others. For example, some colors are approved for external use; some are approved for use everywhere but around the eye.

1960
Color Additive Amendments
The Color Additive Amendments required manufacturers to establish the safety of color additives in foods, drugs, and cosmetics.

Like food additives, color additives are unsafe unless used in compliance with a regulation issued by FDA. The color also must be "listed" in the FDA regulation for specific uses, and must be batch certified or exempted by FDA regulation. FDA previously had established a provisional listing of "harmless" coal tar colors based on the 1938 act. FDA was authorized to continue this "provisional listing of commercially established colors" for thirty months. The provisional listing, however, lasted until 1981, and several colors still are provisionally regarded as safe by FDA pending receipt of further data.

The amendment also contains a Delaney Clause that prohibits FDA from approving any color additive found to induce cancer when ingested by man or animal, or found to induce cancer "after tests which are appropriate for the evaluation of the safety of additives for use in food." The prohibition thus is slightly narrower than the similar provision for food additives.

1962 Drug Amendments
Thalidomide tragedy leads to passage of major amendment to the law. Since 1962, drugs must be proven effective as well as safe.

♦ The 1962 Drug Amendments

In the late 1950s, Senator Estes Kefauver began a series of investigations of the drug industry for antitrust and price-fixing violations. In the midst of these investigations, there was, as in 1938, a public health tragedy that convinced Congress to enact legislation to protect the public. The incident involved thalidomide, a tranquilizer that was available in the United States only as an investigational drug, but was commercially marketed in other countries. The drug was found to cause birth defects in children whose mothers took the drug during their pregnancy. As a result of the thalidomide tragedy, Congress reexamined the new drug approval process. This led to enactment of the Drug Amendments of 1962, the most comprehensive revision of the drug regulatory law since 1938.

Ironically, although thalidomide raised drug safety concerns, the most significant change brought about by the 1962 Drug Amendments was the added requirement to prove *effectiveness* to obtain premarket approval of a new drug. The definition of "new drug" also was amended to include a drug that was not generally recognized by qualified experts as "safe and effective" for its labeled use (FDCA § 201(p)(1)).

In addition, the drug approval provisions were changed substantially:

- FDA now must affirmatively approve a product before it can be marketed;
- FDA can deny approval for false or misleading labeling;
- there must be "substantial evidence" of efficacy, "consisting of adequate and well-controlled investigations, including clinical investigations, by experts qualified by scientific training and experience to evaluate the effectiveness of the drug involved";
- new record and reporting requirements were added;
- the investigational new drug exemption authority was broadened to authorize FDA to issue regulations to require reports of preclinical

tests, investigator agreements, informed consent, and other records and reports; and

- the Secretary of the Department of Health and Human Services (DHHS), but not FDA, can suspend the NDA immediately if there is an imminent hazard to health.

The 1962 Drug Amendments also broadened FDA's regulatory authority over all drugs in several respects, authorizing:

- good manufacturing practice regulations for all drugs,
- increased authority over antibiotics,
- mandatory use of the generic name in drug labeling,
- inspection authority over prescription drug records,
- mandatory inspection of drug establishments every two years,
- annual drug establishment registration,
- regulation of prescription drug advertising, and
- a requirement to prove the efficacy of all new drugs approved from 1938 to 1962.

Legislation From 1962 to 1976

Considerable emphasis was placed on regulation in the decade and a half following the Drug Amendments of 1962, but the types of legislation affecting FDA were unusually varied.

In the decade and a half following the Drug Amendments of 1962, there was considerable emphasis on regulation, but the types of legislation affecting FDA were unusually varied. For example, Congress passed the Drug Abuse Control Amendments of 1965, authorizing FDA to act against depressant, stimulant, and hallucinogenic drugs, which previously had been regulated only as adulterated, misbranded, or unapproved new drugs under the FDCA. The statute added felony penalties for selling such drugs, including counterfeit drugs, and authorized FDA personnel enforcing the law to carry firearms, execute and serve search and arrest warrants, seize products under court order, and arrest an individual who violated the law in the investigator's presence or where there was probable cause to believe that the individual had committed or was committing a felony.

FDA established the Bureau of Drug Abuse Control (BDAC), recruiting those FDA inspectors who enjoyed such activity, as well as law enforcement personnel from other federal and state agencies. BDAC was transferred to DOJ in 1968 as part of the Bureau of Narcotics and Dangerous Drugs and, more recently, to DEA.

♦ The Child Protection Act

In 1966, the Federal Hazardous Substances Labeling Act was modified by the Child Protection Act to ban hazardous toys and other articles, broadening FDA's jurisdiction over products not covered by the FDCA. In 1972, jurisdiction was transferred to the newly created Consumer Product Safety Commission (CPSC).

1966
Fair Packaging and Labeling Act
The Fair Packaging and Labeling Act requires all consumer products in interstate commerce to be honestly and informatively labeled, with FDA enforcing provisions on foods, drugs, cosmetics, and medical devices.

♦ The Fair Packaging and Labeling Act

The Fair Packaging and Labeling Act (FPLA) also was passed that year, requiring truthful and informative labeling for all consumer products in interstate commerce. FDA shared jurisdiction with the FTC, focusing on foods, drugs, cosmetics, and medical devices. FDA used the FPLA to require cosmetics to bear ingredient labeling. Both the FDCA and the FPLA were amended by the Poison Prevention Packaging Act of 1970, which required child-resistant packaging for household substances that could be hazardous to children. CPSC now enforces that Act.

♦ The Animal Drug Amendments of 1968

In the Animal Drug Amendments of 1968, Congress established procedures for approving new animal drugs and animal feed containing new animal drugs. This included the certification of antibiotics intended for use in animals.

♦ The Radiation Control for Health and Safety Act

That same year, Congress passed the Radiation Control for Health and Safety Act, which was intended to protect the public from unnecessary exposure to radiation from electronic products. The law authorizes FDA to set standards for emissions for such products as microwave ovens, X-ray machines, color televisions, and cathode ray tubes for computers. Civil penalties may be imposed for noncompliance and, since 1990, the criminal penalties applicable to devices under the FDCA apply as well to radiologic products. The act originally was enforced by the Bureau of Radiological Health, a division of the Public Health Service. In 1971, that bureau was transferred to FDA where it ultimately was merged with the Bureau of Devices to become today's Center for Devices and Radiological Health. The law itself was added to the FDCA.

♦ The Drug Listing Act

In 1972, Congress enacted the Drug Listing Act requiring that all marketed drugs be listed with FDA when a company first registers, and that the lists be updated each June and December. The listing must include all labeling and representative advertisements for prescription drugs, and labels, package inserts, and representative labeling for OTC drugs. Like establishment registration, listing does not involve FDA approval, although FDA occasionally does respond to a listing by questioning whether a product is a new drug.

The Medical Device Amendments of 1976

Under the 1938 Act, FDA's authority to regulate medical devices was limited to action against adulterated or misbranded devices. FDA could not review or approve medical devices to confirm that they were safe and effective before they could be distributed commercially. FDA reacted by trying to regulate devices as drugs whenever possible in order to obtain the premarket approval authority that existed for new drugs. Thus, FDA regulated absorbable sutures and injectable liquid silicone as drugs, although they were chemically inert.

1976
Medical Device Amendments
The Medical Device Amendments were passed to ensure the safety and effectiveness of medical devices, including diagnostic products. The amendments require manufacturers to register with FDA and follow quality control procedures. Some products must have premarket approval by FDA; others must meet performance standards before marketing.

After the 1962 Drug Amendments, greater attention was given to regulation of devices. This came from industry, health professionals, some patient groups, and even Congress. Concerns arose over the dangers of some devices, such as the Dalkon Shield, an intra-uterine device that was associated with a number of injuries to women.

In response to these pressures, in 1969 the Secretary of Health, Education and Welfare appointed a departmental study group on medical devices, chaired by Dr. Theodore Cooper, director of the National Heart and Lung Institute. The Cooper Committee issued a report in 1970, which concluded that greater device regulation was needed, but should not follow the drug regulatory scheme. The report recommended, among other things, nongovernmental expert reviews and varying degrees of regulation based on risks of different types of devices. The Cooper Committee report was influential in shaping the Medical Device Amendments of 1976 (MDA), the first comprehensive federal regulatory framework for medical devices in the United States.

Among other things, the MDA revised the definition of "device" to distinguish it from "drug," thereby clarifying some of the confusion that existed in the 1938 act. Specifically, a "device" is intended for the same therapeutic use as a drug, but is

> . . . an instrument, apparatus, implement, machine, contrivance, implant, in vitro reagent, or other similar or related article. . . which does not achieve its primary intended purposes through chemical action within or on the body of man or other animals and which is not dependent upon being metabolized for the achievement of its primary intended purpose [FDCA § 201(h)].

Devices that previously had been regulated as drugs were to be returned to device status as "transitional devices."

The MDA established a comprehensive system for classifying and clearing medical devices, based on risk, for introduction in interstate commerce. The MDA distinguished between devices on the market before and after enactment of the 1976 law (i.e., "pre-amendment" or "predicate" devices, and "post-enactment" or "post-amendment" devices). Any device not marketed before the enactment date is automatically placed in the highest risk class of devices (Class III) unless it is "substantially equivalent" to a predicate device already on the market and classified at a lower risk to the public health. To enable FDA to determine if such substantial equivalence exists, the MDA added section 510(k), which requires a person who proposes to market such a device to notify FDA at least ninety days in advance of introduction of the device (commonly referred to as "the 510(k)"). A Class III device requires premarket approval, similar to new drug approval. Class I devices are regulated by general controls. Class II devices may require performance standards.

FDA also was given broad regulatory powers by the MDA, including the authority to:

- require registration of device establishments and listings of device products;
- prescribe good manufacturing practice regulations; to ban worthless or dangerous products;
- require notification, repair, replacement, and/or refund for defective devices; to require records and reports on devices;
- define by regulation "restricted devices," which go beyond prescription devices and for which FDA may inspect records;
- detain suspected violative devices for twenty days pending the filing of a formal action; and
- recall dangerous devices.

The MDA elevated the importance of device regulation within FDA, and reflected the increasing significance of devices in medical practice.

Several of these powers are unique to device regulation.

The MDA elevated the importance of device regulation within FDA, and reflected the increasing significance of devices in medical practice.

Legislation From 1977 to Present

♦ The Orphan Drug Act

In 1982, after much lobbying by patient groups and some manufacturers, Congress concluded that the pharmaceutical industry was not sufficiently committed to the development of drugs to treat rare diseases. Because of the limited market for such drugs, and because patents for them often had expired, manufacturers could not expect to recoup their research and development costs through sales. In 1983 Congress responded with a package of economic incentives embodied in the Orphan Drug Act.

The act applies to drugs "for a rare disease or condition," which initially was defined as one that "occurs so infrequently in the U.S. that there is no reasonable expectation" of recovering development costs. This definition proved unworkable and the act was amended in 1985 to include diseases that affect fewer than 200,000 people in the United States. Sponsors of orphan drugs qualify for tax credits to offset their research costs and may be eligible for FDA research grants. Most important, the sponsor is granted seven years of "market exclusivity," which prevents FDA from approving a competitor's version of the identical drug for the same disease. This is separate from any patent protection and has been a major economic benefit for some companies.

♦ The Drug Price Competition and Patent Term Restoration Act

1984
Drug Price Competition and Patent Term Restoration Act
This act expedites the availability of less costly generic drugs by permitting FDA to approve applications to market generic versions of brand-name drugs without repeating the research done to prove them safe and effective. At the same time, the brand-name companies can apply for up to five years longer patent protection for the medicines they developed to make up for time lost while their products were going through FDA's approval process.

Several factors during the 1970s and early 1980s led Congress to address more broadly competitive issues in the drug market. These included concerns over the cost of drugs to patients, the development of the generic drug industry, the increasing number of important drugs whose patents were due to expire, and the need to encourage pharmaceutical research. These factors led to the Drug Price Competition and Patent Term Restoration Act of 1984, commonly called Waxman-Hatch after its two principal sponsors, Representative Henry Waxman (D-CA) and Senator Orrin Hatch (R-UT). The act was designed as a compromise to promote competition by encouraging the development of low-cost generic drugs, and to encourage research by granting certain competitive benefits to innovators.

The act requires FDA to approve generic drugs that are shown to be "bioequivalent" to a previously approved drug that is "listed" in an FDA publication, without requiring new proof of safety or effectiveness. By filing this "abbreviated" new drug application (ANDA), the generic manufacturer is spared the cost of conducting clinical studies and can offer the product to consumers at a reduced price.

In return, the act grants brand-name manufacturers two important benefits to encourage drug research. The first is the opportunity to extend the patent term to make up for time lost while a drug is undergoing development and FDA review. The second benefit is a period of "market exclusivity" granted to a sponsor that develops a new chemical entity or a new use for a previously approved drug. For a new chemical entity, the act grants five years of exclusivity against approval of an ANDA or other application that lacks clinical data. For a new use for a previously approved drug, in a new full NDA or a supplement that contains clinical tests "essential" to approval, the act grants three years of exclusivity against an ANDA. FDA also must honor a patent and withhold approval of a generic drug until the patent expires or is held invalid by a court.

The Waxman-Hatch Act has resulted in an explosion of generic drug approvals. There also have been a number of lawsuits brought to interpret some of its provisions. The act was followed by FDA's worst scandal, involving bribes to FDA generic drug staff and submission of false information in several ANDAs.

♦ The Generic Animal Drug and Patent Term Restoration Act

In 1988, Congress passed the Generic Animal Drug and Patent Term Restoration Act, extending to veterinary products the same benefits given to human drugs under the Waxman-Hatch Act. Companies are authorized to produce and sell generic versions of animal drugs using abbreviated new animal drug applications for previously approved drugs based on evidence demonstrating their safety and efficacy.

1987
Prescription Drug Marketing Act
Addressed the unacceptable risks associated with counterfeit, adulterated, misbranded, subpotent or expired drugs.

♦ The Prescription Drug Marketing Act of 1987

In the mid-1980s, Congress became concerned about diverted or counterfeit drugs in the marketplace. The response was the Prescription Drug Marketing Act of 1987 (PDMA), which was intended to address "an unacceptable risk that counterfeit, adulterated, misbranded, subpotent, or expired drugs will be sold to American consumers." In addition to attempting to regulate diversion of legitimate prescription drugs and counterfeits in domestic commerce, the law prohibits the re-import of exported drugs as U.S. goods returned except to the original manufacturer or for emergency use.

The PDMA bans the sale or purchase of or trade in prescription drug samples and establishes comprehensive storage, handling, and recordkeeping requirements for such samples. The PDMA also prohibits, with certain exceptions, the resale of prescription drugs purchased by hospitals, healthcare entities, and charitable institutions, and regulates prescription drug wholesale distributors by requiring states to license them in accordance with federal guidelines. Manufacturers must report loss or theft of samples and the conviction of their sales representatives for illegal diversion. There is a substantial civil penalty for a manufacturer's failure to take appropriate steps to prevent diversion (up to $1,000,000 per violation after two convictions of the firm's representatives). There is also a bounty for whistle-blowers of one-half the criminal fine, up to $125,000.

♦ Safe Medical Devices Act of 1990

The Safe Medical Devices Act of 1990 (SMDA) was the first major revision of the medical device requirements of 1976. The SMDA increases FDA's regulatory authority over the medical device industry, particularly in the areas of postmarketing requirements and the premarket notification and approval process. The SMDA was particularly intended to expedite device premarket clearances and approvals by shifting some of FDA's emphasis from premarket reviews to postmarket regulation and surveillance.

The SMDA defines substantial equivalence, essentially codifying FDA's substantial equivalence decision-making structure. Under the SMDA, to determine that a device is substantially equivalent (and therefore, subject to 510(k) clearance), FDA must find that it has the same intended use as the predicate device. The SMDA gives FDA authority to order special controls for Class II devices beyond the performance standards allowed under the MDA, including postmarket surveillance, patient registry, development and dissemination of guidelines, and other appropriate actions deemed necessary by FDA. The SMDA also includes provisions enabling FDA to implement postmarket surveillance, civil penalties, temporary suspension of premarket approval (PMA) applications, required reports of removals and corrections, user and distributor reporting, and medical device tracking. Perhaps the most important postmarketing provision is the requirement of notification to FDA and the manufacturer of all incidents that contribute to serious injury, death, or illness that may have been associated with the use of a medical device. Under the SMDA, anyone who is aware of or has knowledge of an incident that reasonably suggests that a medical device has caused or contributed to the death, serious injury, or serious illness of a patient, visitor, or staff member of a healthcare facility must report the incident to FDA.

1992
Generic Drug Enforcement Act
The Generic Drug Enforcement Act imposes debarment and other penalties for illegal acts involving approval of abbreviated new drug applications.

♦ The Generic Drug Enforcement Act of 1992

In 1992, following a notorious scandal in which officials of FDA's Generic Drugs Division were convicted of taking bribes and a number of generic drug industry personnel were convicted of bribing FDA officials or submitting false data to the agency, Congress enacted the Generic Drug Enforcement Act (GDEA). The act authorizes FDA to "debar" firms and individuals convicted of felonies in connection with the drug approval process from participating in that process for periods ranging from one to ten years for firms and as long as lifetime for individuals. Despite its name, the law applies to both generic and brand-name drug companies. FDA also can bar a "high managerial agent" who had actual knowledge of a violation, and failed to take steps to report or prevent the violation. FDA can temporarily deny approval of an ANDA submitted by a person under criminal investigation for bribery or false statements.

The GDEA also imposes civil penalties for false statements, bribes, destruction of documents, failure to disclose a required material fact, obstruction of an investigation, use of a debarred person to help prepare a drug application, or work on an application by a debarred person. The fines are severe: up to $250,000 per violation for an individual and $1,000,000 for others. The penalty can be levied by FDA via an administrative proceeding or through a court proceeding brought by DOJ. In either case, there is a right of appeal. Informants are entitled to an award of the lesser of $250,000 or one-half the penalty collected.

♦ The Prescription Drug User Fee Act of 1992

As FDA became more engrossed in approving generic drugs, the research-based industry began to push Congress to give FDA more resources to review full NDAs. The political and economic climate, however, was not conducive to enlarging the budget of any government agency. Instead, there developed a philosophy of applying marketplace principles to government activity. In particular, the administration and Congress began to look to the beneficiaries of government services to pay for those services rather than putting a greater burden on taxpayers.

1992
Prescription Drug User Fee Act
PDUFA adds more resources to FDA's review process for drugs and biologics.

The Prescription Drug User Fee Act of 1992 (PDUFA) established requirements for drug and biologics manufacturers to pay fees for applications and supplements that require FDA to review clinical studies. These user fees are intended to enable FDA to hire more reviewers to assess the clinical studies in these applications. In return, FDA pledged (but was not statutorily committed) to speed up the review of NDAs. The act also included annual establishment fees and annual product fees for companies with approved NDAs. The PDUFA was scheduled to expire on September 30, 1997, but was extended by the FDAMA of 1997.

1990
Nutrition Labeling and Education Act
Health claims on foods are regulated under the Nutrition Labeling and Education Act of 1990.

♦ The Nutrition Labeling and Education Act of 1990

In the mid- to late-1980s, increased consumer interest and advances in studies of nutrition and health led some major food companies to begin to experiment with nutritional claims in advertising and labeling. In particular, one manufacturer launched a labeling and advertising program for cereal that claimed the product could be useful in a high-fiber diet to help prevent cancer. The claim had been reviewed and approved by the National Cancer Institute and the FTC. FDA was more critical but ultimately took no regulatory action.

Congress also became interested in this subject, enacting the Nutrition Labeling and Education Act of 1990 (NLEA), the first comprehensive revision of the food labeling requirements of the FDCA since 1938. Building on FDA's much earlier voluntary nutrition labeling requirements and more recent proposals to permit health claims for food products, the NLEA ordered FDA to encourage the food industry to "assist consumers in maintaining healthy dietary practices." Among other things, the NLEA provides for mandatory nutrition labeling in a uniform format, including serving size, number of servings per container, and the nutrition content of the food per serving based on a common household measure.

The NLEA authorized, for the first time, the use of a "health claim" in food labeling. This is a claim "that characterizes the relationship of [a] nutrient. . . to a disease or a health-related condition." Such health claims were permitted only in compliance with FDA regulations. Congress, however, ordered FDA to consider issuing regulations pertaining to the relationship of calcium and osteoporosis, fiber and cancer, lipids and cardiovascular disease, lipids and cancer, sodium and hypertension, fiber and cardiovascular disease, folic acid and neural tube defects, antioxidant vitamins and cancer, zinc and immune function in the elderly, and omega-3 fatty acids and heart disease. Regulations must be based on "significant agreement" of qualified experts that "the totality of publicly available scientific evidence" supports the claims.

The NLEA imposed federal preemption for any food labeling requirements mandated by the FDCA, preempting any state regulation not identical to the FDA requirements. This does not apply to actions against false or misleading labeling or to food advertising.

1994
Dietary Supplement Health and Education Act
Addresses the regulation of dietary supplements by exempting them from some regulatory requirements.

♦ The Dietary Supplement Health and Education Act of 1994

Manufacturers of dietary supplements and other "health foods" felt that the NLEA did not address adequately their interests. After considerable lobbying and a great deal of grass-roots support, Congress was persuaded to enact the Dietary Supplement Health and Education Act of 1994 (DSHEA). In doing so, Congress expressly recognized, defined, and allowed specific claims for dietary supplements, exempting them from some regulatory requirements applicable to other foods.

Among other things, the DSHEA provides a definition of dietary supplement that includes vitamins; minerals; herbs or other botanicals; amino acids; dietary substances used by man to supplement the diet by increasing the total dietary intake; and any concentrate, metabolite, constituent, extract, or combination of any of these ingredients. The law expressly states that such dietary supplements are foods. Dietary supplements are exempt from the "food additive" provisions of the law, thus placing the burden on FDA to demonstrate that dietary supplements are unsafe. New dietary ingredients, not marketed in the United States before October 15, 1994, must contain only ingredients that have been used in the food supply before that time, or have a history of use elsewhere or other evidence of safety.

The DSHEA also permits dissemination of published scientific information and labeling statements pertaining to nutritional claims for dietary supplements, subject to certain specified conditions. FDA was required to issue regulations for nutrition labeling for dietary supplements and for good manufacturing practices (GMPs) for these products, which are required to be modeled after FDA's food GMPs.

The DSHEA also established a Commission on Dietary Supplement Labels and an Office of Dietary Supplements within the National Institutes of Health to study label claims for dietary supplements and report to the President and Congress with recommendations for legislation and changes in regulations. The office was created to study the potential role of dietary supplements as part of the effort to improve U.S. health-care, and to promote scientific study of dietary supplements to maintain health, prevent chronic disease, and for other health-related conditions.

In November 1997, the commission issued its report, which included several recommendations to FDA for distinguishing unauthorized disease claims from permissible claims that describe the effect of a dietary supplement on the structure or function of the body ("structure-function" claims). The commission's report served as a basis for FDA's final rule in January 2000 regarding permissible label claims for dietary supplements.

♦ Export Reform and Enhancement Act of 1996

The Export Reform and Enhancement Act of 1996 (EREA) amended the FDCA to alter FDA's role in regulating the trade of drugs, biologics, and medical devices, and eased import and export restrictions on drugs and medical devices. Under the EREA, manufacturers may export both approved and unapproved medical products to certain foreign countries, and may import the components and raw materials necessary to manufacture products intended for export.

1997
Food and Drug Administration Modernization Act
FDAMA, enacted in 1997, broadened FDA's authority and reformed several areas of regulation.

♦ The Food and Drug Administration Modernization Act of 1997

Over the years, FDA's regulatory role has expanded considerably from that of removing unsafe or misbranded products from the marketplace, to determining whether drugs and medical devices are safe and effective for their intended use. Critics, including members of Congress, industry, patient groups, and others, became convinced that FDA's ability to accomplish the duties embodied in this expanded role had not kept pace with the agency's statutory responsibilities, resulting in an overly burdensome and inefficient regulatory system. The requirements for the clinical testing and premarket review of new products had become increasingly complex, time-consuming, and costly, with the result that patients had been denied timely access to safe and useful drugs and medical devices.

The Food and Drug Administration Modernization Act of 1997 (FDAMA) is the culmination of a comprehensive legislative reform effort designed to streamline regulatory procedures within FDA and to improve the regulation of drugs, medical devices, and foods. Passed with wide bipartisan support, the legislation is the broadest amendment of the basic law since 1938. The FDAMA is principally designed to ensure the timely availability of safe and effective drugs, biologics, and medical devices by expediting the premarket review process for new products, while maintaining FDA's "gold standard" for product approval.

Building on the re-authorization of the Prescription Drug User Fee Act of 1992 (PDUFA I) for five more years, the FDAMA improves FDA's public accountability, requires an FDA mission statement to define the scope of the agency's regulatory responsibilities, and requires FDA to publish a compliance plan, in consultation with appropriate scientific and academic experts, healthcare professionals, representatives of patient and consumer advocacy groups, and the regulated industry. This is intended to eliminate backlogs in the drug and medical device approval process and ensure the timely review of applications. As part of the agency's new mission statement, FDA must promptly and efficiently review clinical research and take appropriate action on the marketing of regulated products so that innovation and product availability are not impeded or discouraged.

The FDAMA included a unique provision, which amended the FDCA to encourage drug manufacturers to study their drugs in pediatric populations. This new provision grants the sponsor of a pending or approved NDA for a drug with current exclusivity under the Waxman-Hatch Act or the Orphan Drug Amendments an extra six months of market exclusivity for performing certain studies in pediatric populations. Pediatric exclusivity attaches to an active moiety and not to a specific drug product, allowing a manufacturer's entire product line containing the active moiety to receive six months of additional market protection. Although this authorization was subject to a sunset provision on January 1, 2002, Congress has re-authorized the provision in 2002 and 2007, and its current sunset date is October 1, 2012.

The FDAMA included a unique provision, which amended the FDCA to encourage drug manufacturers to study their drugs in pediatric populations.

The FDAMA also creates a statutory fast track approval process for drugs for serious or life-threatening diseases and conditions (based on existing FDA regulations), establishes a data bank of information on clinical trials for such conditions (with the help of the National Institutes of Health), authorizes the use of expert scientific panels to review clinical investigations of drugs, and expands the rights of drug and device manufacturers to disseminate treatment information.

The FDAMA also broadened FDA's authority over OTC drugs by extending the agency's inspection authority over OTC drug records to the same extent allowed for prescription drugs. Ingredient labeling requirements are also expanded to include inactive ingredients. The FDAMA preempts labeling for OTC drugs (and cosmetics) from state regulation where federal requirements are in place.

The FDAMA reforms the regulation of medical devices with regard to the review of applications, standards, and data requirements. For example, the law mandates priority review for breakthrough technologies in medical devices and grants FDA the authority to contract with outside scientific experts to review medical device applications.

The FDAMA provides streamlined procedures and greater flexibility in FDA regulations regarding nutrient content and health claims for foods. Such claims may be permitted on food labels, without the need for FDA to issue a regulation, if a scientific body of the U.S. government has published an authoritative statement endorsing the claim. The law also establishes a "notification" procedure for the marketing of indirect food additives.

♦ Fiscal Year 2001 Agricultural Appropriations—Drug Import Provisions

The Fiscal Year 2001 Agricultural Appropriations, Pub. L. 106-387 (Oct. 28, 2000), included two provisions, which amend the FDCA to allow the importation of prescription drugs into the United States from foreign countries. The Medicine Equity and Drug Safety Act of 2000 (MEDS Act) allows wholesalers and pharmacists to import prescription drugs from specified foreign countries, provided certain documentation and testing information, to be defined in FDA regulations, is included with the drugs. The Prescription Drug Import Fairness Act of 2000 prevents FDA from issuing warning notices to individuals, not in the business of importing drugs, who import drugs for personal use. The purpose was to try to lower the costs of prescription drugs in the United States. However, on December 26, 2000, the outgoing Secretary of DHHS declined to implement the MEDS Act, and this decision was reaffirmed by the new Secretary of DHHS on July 9, 2001.

♦ Best Pharmaceuticals for Children Act

The Best Pharmaceuticals for Children Act, Pub. L. No. 107-109 (Jan. 4, 2002), *inter alia,* renewed FDA's authority to grant six months of exclusivity for pediatric studies; eliminated the user fee waiver for pediatric use supplements; gave priority review status for pediatric supplements; and authorized government contracts for pediatric studies of drugs that lack patent protection or marketing exclusivity. The law also allowed ANDAs for generic drugs with added pediatric information. In addition, the law directed the Secretary of DHHS to establish an Office of Pediatric Therapeutics within the FDA Commissioner's office to coordinate all FDA pediatric activities.

BIOHAZARD

♦ The Bioterrorism Act

In June 2002, the Public Health Security and Bioterrorism Preparedness and Response Act of 2002 (Pub. L. No. 107-188) (Bioterrorism Act) amended the FDCA and the Public Health Service Act to increase the capacity of government at all levels to detect and respond effectively to public health emergencies related to bioterrorist attacks. Among other things, the Bioterrorism Act provided for accelerated approval, licensing, or clearance, as a "priority countermeasure," for a drug, biologic product, medical device, vaccine, vaccine adjuvant, antiviral, or diagnostic test, intended to treat, identify, or prevent infections or diagnose conditions caused by biological agents or toxins. The act required the creation of a national database of biological agents and toxins that could pose a severe threat to human, animal, or plant health; development of security safeguards and mandatory registration for the possession, use, or transfer of such agents and toxins; and inspections, with limited exceptions for clinical or diagnostic laboratories and certain investigational, approved, or licensed products. Prescription drug user fees were extended through the year 2007 with only minor changes.

Most importantly, the Bioterrorism Act granted FDA significant new authority with respect to foods, including dietary supplements and animal feeds. Domestic and foreign facilities that manufacture, process, pack, or hold food for U.S. consumption must register with FDA. Inspections are permitted upon "a reasonable belief that a food article is adulterated and presents a threat of serious adverse health consequences or death to humans or animals." The Bioterrorism Act also provides for maintenance of certain manufacturing and shipping records; administrative detention of adulterated foods; pre-importation notifications; prohibition against port shopping; and debarment for repeated violations.

The Bioterrorism Act also provides for:
- *maintenance of certain manufacturing and shipping records*
- *administrative detention of adulterated foods*
- *pre-importation notifications*
- *prohibition against port shopping*
- *debarment for repeated violations*

The existing "import for export" requirements were broadened to include submission of information and data upon importation of drug components, device components or accessories, food additives, color additives and dietary supplements (including those in bulk form) that are intended for further processing or incorporation into a regulated product and for subsequent export.

♦ Medical Device User Fee and Modernization Act of 2002

Following the trend to seek user fees from regulated industry, the Medical Device User Fee and Modernization Act of 2002, Pub. L. No. 107-250 (Oct. 26, 2002) (MDUFMA), was enacted to amend the FDCA to subject medical device manufacturers to medical device user fees for certain applications, reports, application supplements, and submissions sent to FDA for evaluation. The law also established certain performance goals for FDA to meet. In addition, the law included provisions for device establishment inspections by accredited third parties, established new regulatory requirements for reprocessed single-use devices, and provided for modular (i.e., discrete sections) review of PMAs.

♦ Rare Diseases Orphan Product Development Act of 2002

Stating its concerns over 25 million Americans suffering from more than 6,000 rare diseases, and recognizing the role of the National Organization for Rare Diseases, Congress passed the Rare Diseases Orphan Product Development Act of 2002, Pub. L. No. 107-281 (Nov. 6, 2002), to amend the Orphan Drug Act by re-authorizing the Orphan Products Research Grant program to authorize appropriations for Fiscal Years

2002-2006 for grants and contracts for the development of orphan drugs. Fiscal Year 2003-2006 appropriations were set at $25 million per year.

♦ Animal Drug User Fee Act of 2003

Congress added user fees for veterinary products in the Animal Drug User Fee Act of 2003, Pub. L. No. 107-130 (Nov. 18, 2003), directing FDA to assess and collect user fees for animal drug applications. The law is scheduled to sunset at the end of Fiscal Year 2008, unless it is re-authorized for an additional period of time or made permanent.

♦ Medicare Prescription Drug, Improvement, and Modernization Act of 2003

Title XI of the Medicare Prescription Drug, Improvement, and Modernization Act of 2003 is the culmination of several years of congressional attempts to reduce the cost of drug products to consumers.

Title XI of the Medicare Prescription Drug, Improvement, and Modernization Act of 2003, Pub. L. No. 108-173 (Dec. 8, 2003), titled "Access to Affordable Pharmaceuticals," is the culmination of several years of congressional attempts to reduce the cost of drug products to consumers. To accomplish this goal, the changes in Title XI target two issues: generic drug approvals (including government review of marketing agreements between companies) and the importation of prescription drugs from Canada into the United States. The generic drug revisions in the law primarily amend provisions of the FDCA that were added in 1984 by the Drug Price Competition and Patent Term Restoration Act.

The provisions on importation of prescription drugs from Canada recognized that Americans increasingly have sought to purchase drugs from Canada and other foreign countries. This law authorized importation from Canada, under specific conditions, if the Secretary of DHHS certifies to Congress that the imports will not pose any additional risk to the public health and will result in a significant savings to American consumers. To date, the Secretary has declined to provide such certification.

♦ Pediatric Research Equity Act of 2003

To encourage drug research for pediatric use, Congress enacted the Pediatric Research Equity Act of 2003, Pub. L. No. 107-155 (Dec. 3, 2003), amending the FDCA to require that applications for a new active ingredient, new indication, new dosage form, new dosing regimen, or new route of administration for drugs and biological products include a pediatric assessment (unless waived or deferred), and that sponsors of marketed drugs and biologics conduct such an assessment by a specified date (unless waived) under certain circumstances. This law essentially codified FDA's 1998 "Regulations Requiring Manufacturers to Assess the Safety and Effectiveness of New Drugs and Biological Products in Pediatric Patients" (commonly referred to as the "Pediatric Rule"), which had been invalidated by a federal district court for exceeding FDA's authority under the act.

♦ Minor Use and Minor Species Animal Health Act of 2004

Concerned over lack of animal drugs for marginal uses, Congress enacted the Minor Use and Minor Species Animal Health Act of 2004, Title I of Pub. L. No. 108-282 (Aug. 2, 2004), to encourage the development of new animal drugs intended for a minor use (i.e., an indication that occurs infrequently in a few animals, or in limited geographic areas, and in a small number of animals annually) or for a use in a minor species (i.e., other than cattle, horses, swine, chickens, turkeys, dogs, and cats). It provides a conditional approval mechanism under which existing safety requirements must be met but the effectiveness standard is "a reasonable expectation of effectiveness" rather than "substantial evidence of effectiveness." In addition, a sponsor of a new animal drug for a minor use or use in a minor species may petition FDA to declare its product a "designated new animal drug," similar to the status of human drugs under the Orphan Drug Act.

♦ Food Allergen Labeling and Consumer Protection Act of 2004

In Title II of Pub. L. No. 108-282, Congress enacted the Food Allergen Labeling and Consumer Protection Act of 2004, requiring food labels to declare any major food allergen present. The major food allergens are milk; eggs; fish; crustacean shellfish; tree nuts (e.g., almonds, pecans, or walnuts); wheat; peanuts; and soybeans, as well as any protein derived from those allergens, unless it is a "highly refined oil." Tree nuts, fish, and crustacean shellfish must be identified by specific type or species.

♦ Anabolic Steroid Control Act of 2004

Congress enacted the Anabolic Steroid Control Act of 2004, Pub. L. No. 108-358 (Oct. 22, 2004), to address the abuse of steroids by professional athletes and the widespread use of steroids and steroid precursors among students. The act amended the Controlled Substances Act in several ways, including revising the definition of "anabolic steroid" to eliminate the requirement that the substance promote muscle growth. The act also expanded the list of substances regulated as controlled substances to fifty-nine steroids, including active steroids and steroid precursors.

The Anabolic Steroid Control Act of 2004 addresses the abuse of steroids by professional athletes and the widespread use of steroids and steroid precursors among students.

♦ Project BioShield Act of 2004

Passed largely in response to the terrorist attacks in the fall of 2001, Project BioShield Act of 2004, Pub. L. No. 108-276 (July 21, 2004), provides industry with incentives to develop new chemical, biological, radiological, and nuclear medical countermeasures. The act also grants FDA the authority to allow the interim emergency use of investigational drugs, biological products, and devices to respond to domestic emergencies.

♦ Medical Device User Fee Stabilization Act of 2005

Congress revisited the medical device user fees established in the Medical Device User Fee Stabilization Act of 2005, Pub. L. No. 109-43 (Aug. 1, 2005). Among other things, the law set the PMA application fees for Fiscal Years 2006 and 2007, increased the annual gross receipts or sales threshold below which businesses are eligible for reduced user fees or a user fee waiver, and added a provision holding any reprocessed single-use device to be misbranded unless it identifies the manufacturer.

♦ Regulation of Contact Lenses as Medical Devices (2005)

Congress amended the FDCA to deem all contact lenses to be medical devices.

Because FDA had previously regulated some noncorrective, decorative contact lenses as cosmetics, Congress amended the FDCA to deem all contact lenses to be medical devices in this very succinct statute, Pub. L. No. 109-96 (Nov. 9, 2005).

♦ Stem Cell Therapeutic and Research Act of 2005

The Stem Cell Therapeutic and Research Act of 2005, Pub. L. No. 109-129 (Dec. 26, 2005), provides "for the collection and maintenance of human cord blood stem cells for the treatment of patients and research." It amended the Public Health Service Act to authorize the C.W. Bill Young Cell Transplantation Program, which is intended to increase "the number of transplants for recipients suitably matched to biologically unrelated donors of bone marrow and cord blood."

♦ Sanitary Food Transportation Act of 2005

Title VII, section 7201 of Pub. L. No. 109-59, the Sanitary Food Transportation Act of 2005, authorizes FDA to promulgate regulations establishing sanitary food transportation practices, including sanitation, packaging, recordkeeping, and isolation, among other things. In addition, FDA is to issue regulations specifying those nonfood products that may not be shipped with food products. To date, FDA has not issued such regulations.

♦ Pandemic and All-Hazards Preparedness Act of 2006

To address some of the shortcomings of the BioShield Act of 2004, Congress enacted the Pandemic and All-Hazards Preparedness Act of 2006, Pub. L. No. 109-417 (Dec. 19, 2006). Among other things, the act requires FDA to establish a team of manufacturing and regulatory experts to provide chemical, biological, radiological, and nuclear countermeasure manufacturers with technical assistance and it allows DHHS to convene meetings with industry under specified circumstances that would otherwise violate federal antitrust laws.

♦ Dietary Supplement and Nonprescription Drug Consumer Protection Act of 2006

The Dietary Supplement and Nonprescription Drug Consumer Protection Act of 2006, Pub. L. No. 109-462 (Dec. 22, 2006), requires manufacturers, packers, or distributors of dietary supplements and OTC drugs to submit to FDA all serious adverse event reports associated with the use of their products in the United States. The act also requires dietary supplements and OTC drugs to bear either a domestic telephone number or domestic street address where consumers can call or write to report serious adverse events.

♦ Food and Drug Administration Amendments Act of 2007

In what has been described as the broadest amendment of the FDCA in recent memory, the Food and Drug Administration Amendments Act of 2007, Pub. L. No. 110-85 (Sept. 27, 2007) (FDAAA), re-authorized and amended several drug and medical device statutory provisions that were scheduled to sunset, provides FDA with new funding and drug safety oversight responsibility, and addresses virtually all regulated product categories. The law includes eleven titles, the first five of which re-authorize drug and medical device user fee and pediatric-related programs through Fiscal Year 2012, including PDUFA, MDUFMA, the Best Pharmaceuticals for Children Act, and the Pediatric Research Equity Act. Title III also amends the FDCA to provide new incentives to medical device manufacturers to develop devices for pediatric patients and to give FDA new authority to review and regulate such devices. Titles VI-VIII establish a new private-public partnership intended to modernize medical product development and enhance product safety, amend the FDCA with respect to certain conflict of interest issues among FDA advisory committee members, and establish databases for clinical trial registries and results.

The Food and Drug Administration Amendments Act of 2007 reauthorized and amended several drug and medical device statutory provisions that were scheduled to sunset, provides FDA with new funding and drug safety oversight responsibility, and addresses virtually all regulated product categories.

Title IX, perhaps the farthest-reaching provision of the law, includes various programs intended to improve the postmarket safety of drugs, including giving FDA the authority to impose risk evaluation and mitigation strategies. Title IX modifies the citizen petition process with respect to petitions having the potential to delay approval of generic drug products. The section also prohibits the sale of any food that contains an approved drug, an approved biological product, or a "drug [or biological product] for which substantial clinical investigations have been instituted and for which the existence of such investigations has been made public," unless the food containing the drug or biologic had been marketed prior to such approval or testing. This provision, in particular, might have a significant impact on the development of functional food ingredients.

Title X concerns food safety, requiring the creation of a reportable food registry for foods "for which there is a reasonable probability that the use of, or exposure to, such article of food will cause serious adverse health consequences or death to humans or animals." Title X also includes a provision requiring FDA to establish ingredient and processing standards and definitions for pet food and update standards for the labeling of pet food. FDA must also establish early warning and surveillance and notification systems "to identify adulteration of the pet food supply and outbreaks of illness associated with pet food." Finally, Title XI includes several miscellaneous provisions intended, among other things, to improve antibiotic access and innovation.

The History of the Food and Drug Administration

FDA is the oldest federal regulatory agency, dating back to its initial establishment in 1848 as the Agricultural Division of the Patent Office.

FDA is the oldest federal regulatory agency, dating back to its initial establishment in 1848 as the Agricultural Division of the Patent Office. The agency has had several, essentially accumulating, roles. For its first six decades, it was a scientific and technical advisor to other agencies. It added a law enforcement function in 1906. In 1938, the agency was given responsibility for approving the marketing of new drugs, and that premarket licensing function has been broadened by subsequent legislation. Today the agency is regarded as a science-based law enforcement agency responsible for ensuring safe foods and cosmetics, and safe and effective drugs and medical devices in the U.S. marketplace.

More than half of FDA's existence was spent in the USDA, beginning with the transfer of the Agricultural Division to USDA upon the department's creation in 1862. The division's chemical laboratory became known as the USDA Chemical Division. The agency became the Division of Chemistry in 1890 and the Bureau of Chemistry in 1901. Until 1906, the agency had no statutory enforcement duties but primarily provided information and advice to other USDA offices and other agencies, such as the Treasury Department, responsible for enforcing the few relevant federal laws during that time.

Although there were six Commissioners of the agency from 1862 to 1883, it was the seventh Commissioner, Harvey W. Wiley, M.D., who is generally acknowledged as the "father of the FDA." Dr. Wiley strengthened and transformed the staff of the division into an advocacy organization and, ultimately, a law enforcement agency. He crusaded for the creation of a national food and drug law, and was credited with a major role in the passage of the 1906 act. Political and personal differences with his superiors, however, led to the establishment of a three-person Board of Food and Drug Inspection, including Dr. Wiley, to approve all legal actions recommended by the bureau. Dr. Wiley frequently was outvoted, and he ultimately resigned under pressure in 1912.

For the next fifty-three years, until 1965, FDA was directed by career employees, only a few of whom were physicians. Moreover, there were only seven Commissioners or top officials of FDA from 1883 to 1965. Since then, there have been thirteen Commissioners in slightly more than forty years, all but one (Dr. Herbert Ley, 1968-1969) of who had never previously worked for the agency.

When the 1906 act passed, the Bureau of Chemistry had six field laboratories (San Francisco, New York, Boston, Philadelphia, Chicago, and New Orleans). Seventeen more were opened from 1907 to 1911. The agency's budget in that period was less than $1,000,000, and the agency employed fewer than 100 people.

In 1914, the agency's second "modern" commissioner, Dr. Carl Alsberg, reorganized the agency. He established the Division of Food Control and delegated control of the field laboratories, which were reduced from twenty-three to sixteen to save money, to three food and drug inspection districts (Eastern, Central, and Western). This decentralized the agency's inspection activities and joined the enforcement functions more closely with the scientific functions, and remained the basic organization for the agency until 1948.

In 1927, the agricultural research and the enforcement functions of the Bureau of Chemistry were separated, with the latter becoming the Food, Drug, and Insecticide Administration (FDIA). The Drug Control Laboratory, which was responsible for surveillance of proprietary drugs, was included in the FDIA. In 1930, the FDIA became the Food and Drug Administration, although the agency did not officially exist by statute until the Food and Drug Administration Act of 1988.

FDA did not officially exist by statute until the Food and Drug Administration Act of 1988.

FDA remained a part of USDA until 1940 when it was transferred to the Federal Security Agency, which also included such agencies as the Public Health Service, the Office of Education, the Civilian Conservation Corps, and the Social Security Administration. The move was in part due to the differing missions and inherent conflict between FDA and its parent, USDA. At the same time, the head of FDA became known as the Commissioner of Food and Drugs, the present title of the post, although no commission existed. The Federal Security Agency became the Department of Health, Education and Welfare in 1953, and subsequently DHHS in 1979, when a separate Department of Education was established.

In 1948, due to concerns over lack of uniformity and efficiency among the three operating districts, the agency was reorganized to centralize authority in Washington, D.C. Commissioner Paul B. Dunbar, whose career with the agency dated to 1907, dismantled the three districts, moving many of the staff to Washington, D.C., to join the divisions of Field Operations, Regulatory Management, and Program Research. The sixteen field stations became district offices and reported directly to the

Commissioner. There were some morale and related problems, as the districts had developed different enforcement styles over the years.

In 1963, following several years of increasing statutory authority and wider jurisdiction, a tripling of the agency's enforcement budget, and two citizen advisory committee reports (in 1955 and 1962), then Commissioner George P. Larrick reorganized the agency to try to emphasize scientific research, education, and voluntary compliance. He added a Bureau of Education and Voluntary Compliance, and divided the previously existing scientific bureau into the Bureau of Scientific Research and the Bureau of Scientific Standards and Evaluation. These three bureaus joined the Bureau of Medicine and the Bureau of Regulatory Compliance.

Congressional criticism led, in 1966, to the appointment of the first outsider, and the first physician in more than forty years, as the Commissioner of Food and Drugs.

Despite this reorganization, congressional criticism led, in 1966, to the appointment of the first outsider, and the first physician in more than forty years, as the Commissioner of Food and Drugs, Dr. James L. Goddard. Dr. Goddard came from the Communicable Disease Center of the Public Health Service, and had a reputation as a reformer and aggressive regulator. He was given a mandate to reform FDA. In 1966, he extensively reorganized FDA, essentially reversing the 1963 changes. Among other things, the two separate science bureaus were recombined as the Bureau of Science and the district offices reported directly to the Commissioner rather than the Bureau of Regulatory Compliance. A new Bureau of Drug Abuse Control was added, following the Drug Abuse Control Amendments of 1965. (This was transferred to the Department of Justice in 1968.) In addition, the Bureau of Veterinary Medicine was created.

Dr. Goddard's brief stay (less than two and one-half years) marked the beginning of what has been called the period of "short-term" Commissioners. Since then, FDA has had twelve Commissioners: Herbert Ley Jr., M.D. (7/1/1968—12/12/1969), Charles Edwards, M.D. (12/13/1969—3/15/1973), Alexander M. Schmidt, M.D. (7/20/1973—11/30/1976), Donald Kennedy, Ph.D. (4/4/1977—6/30/1979), Jere E. Goyan, Ph.D. (10/21/1979—1/20/1981), Arthur Hull Hayes Jr., M.D. (4/13/1981—9/11/1983), Frank E. Young, M.D. (7/15/1984—12/17/1989), David A. Kessler, M.D. (11/8/1990—2/28/1997), Jane E. Henney, M.D. (1/17/1999—1/19/2001), Mark B. McClellan, M.D., Ph.D. (11/14/2002—3/26/2004), Lester M. Crawford, D.V.M., Ph.D. (7/18/2005—9/23/2005), and Andrew C. von Eschenbach, M.D. (12/13/2006—present). All of these twelve Commissioners were appointed from outside the agency, and most were physicians. At times, the post of Commissioner was vacant and temporarily filled by an acting Commissioner. (Full biographies of all FDA Commissioners since Harvey W. Wiley, M.D. are available on FDA's website at http://www.fda.gov/oc/commissioners/default.htm.)

In addition, more professionals began to join the agency in positions of authority, often as political appointees. There also has been increasing scrutiny and involvement in FDA's activities by Congress, its parent department, and the White House.

In 1968, FDA was placed by the Department of Health, Education and Welfare under the Public Health Service, then combined with other agencies in the new Consumer Protection and Environmental Health Service (CPEHS). This placed another official above the Commissioner, but CPEHS was abolished less than two years later and FDA again became part of the Public Health Service.

Reorganization
FDA's current structure stems from the 1970s reorganization along product lines. FDA regulates twenty-five cents of every consumer dollar.

FDA was reorganized in 1970, with the regulatory and voluntary compliance bureaus combined into the Bureau of Compliance and with the establishment of ten Regional Food and Drug Directors, paralleling the department regional structure. The agency also reorganized along product lines, establishing a Bureau of Drugs and a Bureau of Foods, Pesticides, and Product Safety. Almost thirty years later, FDA still follows that basic organization, although the bureaus have all become centers with the following names: the Center for Drug Evaluation and Research, the Center for Biologics Evaluation and Research, the Center for Devices and Radiological Health, the Center for Food Safety and Applied Nutrition, and the Center for Veterinary Medicine. Each center has undergone its own changes and reorganizations, but the general organization remains the same.

Over the years, FDA has had to contend with tight budgets and battles with Congress and other agencies over resources and authority. FDA has grown from a budget of some $12,000 in 1890 to a proposed budget of more than $2.1 billion for fiscal year 2009, and from a handful of employees to more than 9,000 employees. The products regulated by FDA account for some twenty-five cents of every dollar spent by U.S. consumers. The agency has an immense, if often unsung, effect on the economy and the public's health, safety, and well being.

Chapter 3

The Philosophy of Food and Drug Law

Richard M. Cooper, Williams & Connolly LLP, Washington, D.C.

Key Points

- **Food and drug law is primarily about physical things.**
- **The overriding purpose of the FDCA is to protect the consuming public.**
- **As new risks have been recognized, the FDCA has been amended to make it more protective.**
- **Expansion of FDA authority has coincided with expansion of administrative tools throughout the federal government.**
- **There has been a substantial transfer of power from the courts to FDA.**
- **FDA has been, and will continue to be, a scientific regulatory agency that protects the public from unsafe or ineffective medical products.**
- **The review process must be rigorous enough to ensure that new products meet the statutory standards.**
- **FDA technically does not regulate the practice of medicine; however, its regulations do bear directly on physicians conducting FDA-regulated clinical investigations.**
- **Consumers now have greater opportunity and necessity to make informed decisions about matters that affect their own health.**
- **FDA is accountable to the Public Health Service, Congress, and the courts, as well as practically to the scientific and medical communities.**
- **FDA takes an expansive view of its mission and authority.**
- **FDA is rethinking its role in the international economy.**

Introduction

Food and drug law is primarily about physical things—foods, drugs (including biological products such as blood and vaccines), medical devices, cosmetics, and radiation-emitting products. It is only secondarily about the companies and people who manufacture, distribute, sell, and prescribe those things.

This focus on things is reflected in many aspects of the law and practice under it. The main segments of the governing statute—the Federal Food, Drug, and Cosmetic Act (FDCA)—are organized by type of product: food (chapter four); drugs, devices, and electronic products (chapter five); and cosmetics (chapter six). The agency that administers the statute—the Food and Drug Administration (FDA)—is also organized by product type. Its main operating units include the Center for Food Safety and Applied Nutrition (which also regulates cosmetics), the Center for Drug Evaluation and Research, the Center for Biologics Evaluation and Research, the Center for Devices and Radiological Health, and the Center for Veterinary Medicine (which regulates foods and drugs for animals).

Principal types of FDCA violations:

- *"adulterated" products*
- *"misbranded" products*
- *products marketed without required FDA approval*

In general, the principal types of violation of the statute are defined so as to make a product "adulterated" or "misbranded" or marketed without a required FDA approval. In identifying a violation by a company or individual, it generally (although not universally) is necessary to identify a product that violates the statute in one of those three ways.

When the government goes to court under the FDCA, the remedy it often seeks is a seizure and condemnation of a product it claims is in violation of the statute or an injunction against shipment of one or more products in interstate commerce. Indeed, the official legal title of such a seizure action is of the form, "United States v. [an estimated number of units of a particular kind of product]." In such a case, the units of the product literally are the defendants. Anyone who claims to own them may enter the lawsuit to defend on their behalf; but, if no one does, the government wins by default, and the products generally are condemned and destroyed.

The reason for this primary focus on things is that the overriding purpose of the FDCA is to protect the consuming public from regulated products that are unsafe (food, drugs, devices, cosmetics, radiation-emitting products), ineffective (drugs and devices), or deceptively or otherwise inadequately labeled (food, drugs, devices, and cosmetics). Where a product is violative, FDA's first objective is to protect the public from the product, itself, by bringing about its removal from commerce. Accordingly, the most common informal remedy for a violative product is a recall, which is a more or less voluntary alternative to a seizure by the government.

In some cases, FDA, acting through the Department of Justice (DOJ), may pursue an additional objective. It may seek to prevent future violations through an injunction against those likely to cause a violation in the future. In addition or in the alternative, it may seek punishment of companies and individuals for past violations, through criminal prosecution in the courts or an administrative proceeding for civil penalties.

The FDCA's main judicial remedies—seizure, injunction, and criminal prosecution—are very forceful. Upon the filing of a complaint for seizure by

DOJ—before any defense is presented—the products proceeded against are legally seized by U.S. Marshals; and, in general, they are released from seizure only if a claimant appears, and the government fails to persuade the court that the products are violative of the FDCA. If the government obtains an injunction, it generally shuts down a manufacturing facility unless and until FDA is satisfied that the facility can manufacture products that comply with the statute. A company or an individual can be convicted of a misdemeanor (an offense punishable by fine and imprisonment for not more than one year) under the FDCA merely for causing or being responsible for the shipment of a product in violation of the act—even without an intent to violate the statute, and even without knowledge that a violation was occurring. Where there is intent to defraud, a violation may be treated, under the FDCA or the general criminal law, as a felony (which is punishable by a higher fine and longer term of imprisonment).

A company or an individual can be convicted of a misdemeanor under the FDCA merely for causing or being responsible for the shipment of a product in violation of the act—even without an intent to violate the statute, and even without knowledge that a violation was occurring.

The law's enforcement scheme is so severe because its purposes, as the Supreme Court put it in 1943, "touch phases of the lives and health of people which, in the circumstances of modern industrialism, are largely beyond self-protection." In explaining why the FDCA imposes strict misdemeanor liability on individuals involved in violations, the Supreme Court stated in 1975 that the FDCA "imposes not only a positive duty to seek out and remedy violations when they occur but also, and primarily, a duty to implement measures that will insure that violations will not occur. The requirements of foresight and vigilance imposed on responsible corporate agents are beyond question demanding, and perhaps onerous, but they are no more stringent than the public has a right to expect . . . ."

This overriding concern to protect the public is, of course, also fully reflected in the statutory standards applicable to regulated products. For example, a food additive may be approved only if its sponsor affirmatively shows that there is a reasonable certainty that it will not harm any consumers. In general, the sponsor of a new drug or medical device must affirmatively show that its product is effective for some appropriate medical use, and that the benefits provided by that effectiveness outweigh the risks to health presented by the product. Where there are reasonable scientific or medical doubts about whether these standards have been met, the product is not approved.

Food and drug law, however, was not always this protective. As new risks to the public health have been recognized, Congress has amended the law scores of times to make it more protective.

The first general federal food and drug statute, the Pure Food and Drugs Act of 1906, was much simpler than today's law. It applied only to foods and drugs, and did not require any governmental review of any such product before it was put onto the market. If a product was marketed in violation of the statute, the government had to find out about it and bring a court action against the product or against those who were marketing it. Over time, it became clear that the scope of the statute was too narrow, and that the statutory scheme did not adequately protect the public.

The FDCA was enacted in 1938. It extended food and drug law coverage to medical devices and cosmetics. It also established a mechanism for FDA to regulate research on drugs, and required FDA review of new drugs to ensure that they were safe before they could be marketed. This "premarket review" was limited to safety, and did not apply to devices, cosmetics, or foods (except that FDA was authorized to impose a permit requirement on certain classes of foods that can present a severe risk to health if not processed properly). The 1938 act also gave FDA authority to inspect establishments where regulated products are manufactured, processed, packed, or held.

Although the original FDCA was a marked improvement over the 1906 statute, it, too, proved deficient in protecting the public. Consequently, the statute has been strengthened by a series of amendments, among the most important of which were these: premarket review for safety was extended to food additives (1958) and color additives (1960); premarket review of drugs was extended to effectiveness as well as safety (1962); premarket review for safety and effectiveness and FDA regulation of research were extended to devices (1976). Numerous other aspects of FDA regulation have been strengthened in other amendments, culminating (thus far) in the Food and Drug Administration Amendments Act of 2007.

Expansion of FDA authority has coincided with expansion of administration tools throughout the federal government.

The philosophy of premarket review is simple: to the extent reasonably possible, the most significant benefits and risks of a product should be identified and assessed before the product is marketed. If the risks are not justified, the product should not be marketed. If the risks are justified only if the product is used in accordance with certain conditions, or if certain conditions can reduce even the justified risks, those conditions should be identified and disclosed.

The enactment of the premarket review requirements from 1958 to 1976 coincided with a vast expansion throughout the federal government of the use of administrative tools rather than court actions to impose regulatory requirements. Prior to this change in method of governing, FDA had established new interpretations of the statutory standards for regulated products principally through judicial opinions in court actions. Through the DOJ, FDA would file court actions against regulated products and marketers of such products; it would argue in court that the general words of the statute should be interpreted to impose particular detailed requirements, and that those requirements had been violated; and generally the courts would accept FDA's interpretations and embody them in judicial opinions, on which FDA could rely in later cases. Manufacturers and other marketers interested in learning what the applicable requirements were would consult the statute and the judicial decisions interpreting it. FDA supplemented these sources principally with so-called "trade correspondence" and announcements.

There has been a substantial transfer of power from the courts to FDA. The courts, however, still have the final say on the validity of regulatory requirements. In practice the courts defer to FDA's views most of the time.

Through its new premarket approval authority and the use of rulemaking (the issuance of regulations of general applicability) and administrative adjudication (the deciding of individual cases in administrative rather than judicial proceedings), FDA developed much more efficient ways (faster, less expensive, more systematic, more coherent, more within the agency's control) to establish binding regulatory requirements. Thus, today, the court cases FDA initiates serve principally not to create new regulatory requirements but rather to enforce regulatory requirements already established through administrative means. Consequently, during the last forty years there has been not only a large increase in regulatory requirements but also a substantial transfer of power over such requirements from the federal courts to FDA. The courts still have the final say on the validity of regulatory requirements, but in practice the courts defer to FDA's views most of the time. Today, someone seeking to learn the requirements applicable to a particular product would consult the statute, the regulations in title 21 of the *Code of Federal Regulations*, regulations not yet codified and other issuances in the *Federal Register*, FDA guidance documents, letters, speeches, congressional testimony, and judicial decisions.

Premarket review and the increased use of administrative techniques to establish regulatory requirements and policy have substantially changed the nature of food and drug law and FDA. In its early years, FDA was essentially a law enforcement agency. The operating units that are now called centers were then called bureaus. Science in the agency was a handmaiden to enforcement: its role was to identify problems in the marketplace, and help the agency react to the problems and win in court.

FDA is a scientific regulatory agency.

More recently, currently, and for the foreseeable future, FDA has been, is, and will continue to be essentially a scientific regulatory agency. It protects the public health principally by screening out unsafe or otherwise inadequate products in premarket review, and by establishing, on the basis of scientific knowledge, general regulatory requirements for the design, manufacture, testing, labeling, and, in limited circumstances, advertising, of marketed products. The vast bulk of public protection is achieved through these *preventive* activities. They are backed up, of course, by the agency's continued ability and willingness to react to violations by having DOJ file court actions against violative products and those who market them. Thus, today, court enforcement is a handmaiden to scientific regulation.

This change in the nature of FDA's role has created or sharpened a number of issues central to the philosophy of food and drug regulation, including these:

- the general relationship between FDA and the industries it regulates, the agency's roles with respect to health promotion and health protection, and the relative importance of enforcement and voluntary compliance;
- the relation between FDA's regulation of medical products (drugs and devices) and the practice of medicine and related professions;
- the relation between FDA's regulation of medical products and reimbursement for those products under federal healthcare programs (and private health insurance programs);
- the extent to which FDA should or, as a practical matter, must rely on consumers to protect their own health, and the role of FDA's regulation of product labeling in that connection;
- with its greatly increased regulatory authority, to whom and through what means FDA is ultimately accountable;
- in what ways, and to what extent, FDA should adapt its regulatory role to the international market; and
- to what extent FDA's activities should be paid for by special fees from the firms FDA regulates rather than by revenues from taxation of the general population.

The remainder of this chapter will address these issues.

The Tension Between Prevention of Harm and Promotion of Benefit

FDA's Mission:
"promote public health by promptly and efficiently reviewing clinical research and taking appropriate action on the marketing of regulated products in a timely manner."

Public health is improved when safe and effective drugs and devices are made available and when those that are unsafe or ineffective are kept off the market. Clearly, it is part of FDA's mission to protect the public from medical products that are unsafe or ineffective. Under legislation enacted in 1997, it is also part of the agency's mission to "promote public health by promptly and efficiently reviewing clinical research and taking appropriate action on the marketing of regulated products in a timely manner." How should FDA harmonize those objectives? To what extent and in what ways should FDA's premarket review of new drugs and devices be made more searching, more detailed, and more deliberate in order to detect inadequacies that would make a product unsafe or ineffective or to develop additional information that would make product use more safe or more effective; and to what extent and in what ways should FDA review be simplified, streamlined, and speeded up in order to ease entry to the market for products that may improve health? More generally, should FDA's relationship with the research-based corporations that develop new drugs and devices be at arm's length and hierarchical (regulator/regulated firm) or should there be a significant cooperative and collegial element?

Plainly, there are no simple answers. In our free enterprise system, although much basic research is sponsored by government, most new medical technologies and the products that embody them are developed by private firms operating for profit. Under the FDCA, the responsibility for testing new products also rests with private firms, not with FDA. FDA's role is to review proposed new products on the basis of information on safety and effectiveness developed and presented by private firms and to determine on the basis of that information (and general scientific and medical knowledge) whether the products meet statutory requirements for marketing.

The review process must be rigorous enough to ensure that new products meet the statutory standards, and that the information submitted is sufficient to make possible the writing of adequate directions for prescribing and use. The review process must not be so demanding, however, that the availability of good products is unduly delayed.

Similarly, FDA must not abdicate its regulatory role, its responsibility to ensure that no product is approved unless it satisfies the statutory standards, or its legal duty to review all products independently, objectively, and impartially. These objectives might be compromised if FDA reviewers became too deeply involved in product development or interacted too collegially with employees of private firms, so that they came to have an emotional stake in product approval. The development of beneficial products will be hindered, however, if FDA reviewers do not work collaboratively with knowledgeable counterpart physicians, scientists, engineers, and statisticians at private companies to develop appropriate test protocols and criteria for review, to identify appropriate medical uses for new products, and to draft maximally useful guidance for prescribing physicians.

FDA and AIDS: *AIDS caused FDA to establish a trade-off between current patients and future patients.*

A striking example of an adjustment in the review process in response to urgent need was FDA's reaction to acquired immunodeficiency syndrome (AIDS). Under political pressure for rapid development and approval of drugs to treat persons infected with human immunodeficiency virus (HIV), the agency adopted an actively cooperative role, adopted lenient interpretations of the statutory criteria, drastically reduced its normal demands for test data, and greatly streamlined its review process. The result was swift market entry of any drug that appeared beneficial in the treatment of AIDS. The cost of this success was, in most cases, a lack of the usual quantity and quality of data to support solid conclusions about the detailed benefits and risks presented by particular products and to provide the basis for adequate directions to physicians for use of the products. This overall approach involved a trade-off between the interests of current patients and those of future patients. Because, at the time, there was no effective treatment and the disease was considered fatal in all cases, this was a fully understandable but nevertheless difficult trade-off.

In the area of enforcement, FDA necessarily is a cop; but it cannot, itself, continuously patrol every factory where the products it regulates are made or test the actual quality of every unit of every product on the market. Thus, the agency has had to develop strategies that maximize the effectiveness of its limited resources in inducing compliance by regulated firms. The agency has had to blend elements of strict enforcement with technical assistance in the form of guidelines, development of consensus implementation standards, and random and for-cause inspections and sampling of products.

For example, FDA regulations require that foods, drugs, and devices be manufactured in accordance with "current good manufacturing practices." The regulations set forth only very general standards, such as that buildings and facilities shall be clean and sanitary, equipment shall be suitable for its purposes, and employees shall be adequately qualified and trained. Introduction into commerce of a product made in violation of these requirements is technically unlawful. Detailed elaborations of the general requirements in the regulations are set forth in guidance documents created by FDA, in consensus documents developed by experts from FDA and the regulated industries, and in a substantial literature developed by private experts. Additional elaboration is set forth in documents resulting from FDA compliance and enforcement activities—reports of violations observed during FDA inspections, FDA warning letters, and judicial decisions resulting from court cases initiated by FDA.

FDA regulations require that foods, drugs, and devices be manufactured in accordance with "current good manufacturing practices."

Of course, to some extent, an additional incentive for compliance is provided by the law of products liability administered by the states. Where a consumer claims to have been harmed by an FDA-regulated product, violation of an FDA requirement generally may be considered as evidence that the product was defective and that its manufacturer was negligent.

FDA's control over warnings and other information in drug and device labeling and other regulatory decisions the agency makes can have a significant effect on products liability litigation. Issues have been raised as to whether, and if so how, FDA should take account of this effect in carrying out its regulatory responsibilities; and as to whether FDA approval of certain aspects of a product and the product's compliance with the conditions for FDA approval should preempt the imposition of products liability on a theory that such approval and compliance were insufficient under state law.

In the past, the agency generally attempted to be neutral as between injured plaintiffs and defendant manufacturers, and regarded products liability as a useful adjunct to regulation, and therefore generally opposed arguments that its regulatory requirements preempt different or additional requirements under state law. In recent years, the agency has asserted that certain aspects of its regulation of medical products do preempt different or additional state law requirements. Moreover, concerns about liability have contributed to a recognized insufficiency of medical products in certain categories (e.g., drugs to treat illnesses in pregnant women, products for neonates, and contraceptives). There is ongoing public debate about what degree of preemption best serves the public health in the long term.

FDA and the Practice of Medicine

Although FDA's product-approval decisions and other regulatory actions have a large effect on healthcare, FDA technically does not regulate the practice of medicine, nursing, pharmacy, or the other healing professions, except when they conduct clinical trials within FDA's jurisdiction and when they become involved in the manufacture, distribution, or promotion of products within that jurisdiction. Outside those exceptions, the healthcare professions are regulated by the states.

FDA technically does not regulate the practice of medicine.

FDA's regulations bear directly on physicians and nurses when they conduct FDA-regulated clinical investigations to develop information for product approval. In general, when a physician's relationship with a patient is also that of a scientific investigator with a research subject, FDA's role is to protect the rights and welfare of the subject by ensuring that risks to the subjects have been reduced to the practical minimum and that the subjects' informed consent to participation in the investigation has been properly obtained, to ensure that the remaining risks entailed by use of an investigational drug or device are justified by the likelihood that the investigation will yield useful scientific data, and to ensure that the investigational product is not used outside the FDA-approved investigational protocol.

Use of an approved drug or device by a healthcare professional treating a patient is outside FDA's jurisdiction. When FDA approves a drug or device, it approves it for use only in specific medical circumstances (called "indications"). The manufacturer of an approved product may advertise and promote it only for the approved indications. Physicians and others authorized by state law to prescribe medical products, however, may prescribe the product for any indication they choose, subject only to the requirements of state law with respect to medical licensure and malpractice.

Many products develop medically accepted indications that are outside the FDA-approved indications; some unapproved indications may even become the standard of care.

Over time, many products develop medically accepted indications that are outside the FDA-approved indications; some unapproved indications may even become the standard of care. Unless a manufacturer submits to FDA data adequate to support approval of an additional indication, it will remain unapproved. Consequently, it commonly occurs that a drug or device has a medically significant use outside its approved indications, but the product's manufacturer is prohibited from recommending or promoting, or providing guidance for, that use to physicians and other healthcare providers (except in response to an unsolicited inquiry by a provider to the manufacturer). Organizations that are independent of the manufacturer are not subject to any such prohibition, and are free to meet any marketplace need for information about unapproved uses of FDA-regulated products.

Manufacturers have nevertheless objected to this restriction on their freedom to disseminate information about their products. Historically, FDA has responded that, if manufacturers were free to disseminate information about unapproved uses, they would have much less incentive to seek FDA approval of additional indications and to develop the scientific data required for such approval. Thus, on this issue, our society's general commitment to free competitive dissemination of truthful information collides with FDA's role as approver of new drugs and devices and reviewer of manufacturers' statements in the marketplace about their FDA-regulated products. A limited compromise of the competing views was included in FDA reform legislation enacted in 1997, but has now expired. Recently, in a draft guidance document, FDA has endorsed (with certain conditions) dissemination by manufacturers of reprints of medical journal articles and medical and scientific publications relating to unapproved uses of their approved or cleared medical products. The debate, however, persists.

The issue extends beyond purely medical information. As economic considerations have come explicitly to play a much larger role in decisions about healthcare, and as important elements of healthcare decision making have shifted from individual physicians to managed care organizations and third-party payers, the demand for economic information about the performance of drugs and medical devices also has increased. The managed care organizations and third-party payers want to know not only whether a drug or device is safe and effective and for which indications but also whether it is cost-effective as compared to alternative products and other treatments (such as surgery).

When manufacturers undertake to provide such information, should it have to be approved by FDA before the manufacturers can disseminate it? Even if the recipients are sophisticated organizations? Is such a role for FDA an appropriate or an inappropriate extension of its existing role as reviewer of information on product safety and effectiveness?

FDA's current position is that such information, when disseminated by regulated firms, is subject to its jurisdiction and to the FDCA's standards for scientific validity. The studies that are needed to satisfy those standards are expensive and time-consuming. Plainly, there is a trade-off between the availability of information from regulated firms and its quality: if only high-quality and costly information may be disseminated by such firms, they will provide less information. Where manufacturers do not provide information, decision makers who would benefit from such information will have to turn to whatever information may be available from other sources or do without. It is a fair question whether, in the circumstances, FDA has made the optimal trade-off between availability and quality of medical-economic information from regulated firms.

It is a fair question whether FDA has made the optimal trade-off between availability and quality of medical-economic information from regulated firms.

The Responsibilities of Consumers

As a result of vastly increased knowledge in the health-related sciences and changes in the healthcare delivery system, consumers now have greater opportunity and necessity than in recent decades to make informed decisions about matters that affect their own health. These changes are most clearly reflected by the labeling of foods and over-the-counter (OTC) drugs.

As to both types of products, FDA has implemented a philosophy of encouraging competition in product innovation by increasing manufacturers' communications about their products to consumers. The result has been a plethora of new products in food stores and drug stores, and new claims and information on product labels and in advertisements. Congress has particularly encouraged this development with respect to foods.

FDA encourages competition in product innovation.

Increased scientific understanding of human nutrition and of the role of diet in general health has led to fundamental revision of food labels, so as to provide increased information to consumers, and incentives to food processors to produce more healthful foods. Food labels now contain more easily usable information about the nutrient content of foods and, as permitted by FDA pursuant to statutory criteria, claims about the relationship between particular food products and specific diseases.

FDA's strategy in overseeing food labels is to enable consumers to make informed choices in the construction of a healthful overall diet. One might ask, however, how well such a strategy actually serves a population that includes many people who never see such information (in institutions where meals are served—schools, nursing homes, prisons, etc.), who cannot understand or use such information (because, e.g., their language is other than English, or they are functionally illiterate or innumerate), or simply do not have the time or energy to use it.

In recent years, many medically significant drugs have been switched by FDA from prescription to OTC status. Pharmaceutical manufacturers seek such switches when they see attractive marketing opportunities for OTC sales (e.g., after profits from prescription sales have been reduced by generic competition). Such switches make drugs more accessible to consumers and reduce the overall cost of using them by eliminating the requirement of contact with a physician. They also shift the cost of the drugs from the healthcare system to the drugs' users because most insurance and other third-party payer systems that cover prescription drugs do not also cover OTC drugs.

Even where consumers do consult a physician, they are more likely now than in the past to use an OTC rather than a prescription drug. Because managed care systems generally do not cover OTC drugs, the systems have a financial incentive to induce their physicians to direct patients to OTC, rather than prescription, drugs when suitable OTC drugs are available; and the widening range of OTC drugs available expands the opportunities for physicians to do so. Thus, FDA policy combines with the incentives facing pharmaceutical manufacturers and managed care systems to lead to greater usage of OTC drugs.

Increased societal reliance on OTC drugs means increased reliance on consumers to deal with their own medical needs: increased consumer autonomy, but also increased consumer responsibility. The economics of health care drives in this direction, as, perhaps, does the demand of sophisticated consumers. There are important issues of how far and how fast the shift from prescription to OTC should go, and as to what extent, and at what cost, society can or should protect those who cannot cope with the increased personal responsibility.

FDA Accountability

FDA is accountable to:

- *Public Health Service*
- *Congress*
- *the courts*
- *scientific and medical communities*

In making decisions critical to the health of the American people, to whom is FDA accountable? Within the government, FDA is triply accountable.

First, it is part of the Public Health Service in the Department of Health and Human Services (DHHS), and thus part of the executive branch. The agency and its head, the Commissioner of Food and Drugs, are answerable to the Secretary of DHHS, the Office of Management and Budget, and, ultimately, the President. The agency's major regulatory and personnel decisions, budget, congressional testimony, and legislative proposals all are reviewable by one or more of these officials or offices.

Second, the agency is overseen by Congress. The Senate Committee on Health, Education, Labor and Pensions and the House Committee on Energy and Commerce have jurisdiction over the FDCA and other statutes that FDA administers; authorize the agency's budget; and conduct frequent hearings (in the House, through the Subcommittee on Oversight and Investigations and the Subcommittee on Health) on the agency's performance. Because FDA originated as the Bureau of Chemistry in the Department of Agriculture (before it was transferred to what is now DHHS), FDA's appropriations are determined by agricultural subcommittees of the Appropriations Committees in the House and Senate. Thus, those committees, too, have a continuing interest in FDA, which is reflected in FDA's annual appropriations hearings. From time to time, other Senate and House committees also take an interest in FDA.

Third, FDA is overseen by the courts. The agency's enforcement program is conducted mostly in the courts, although in recent years Congress has given it increased authority to impose civil monetary penalties administratively. Regulated firms, public interest groups, and others dissatisfied with an FDA action (or inaction) can seek recourse in the courts. Because FDA can appear in court only through the DOJ, that department can also impose some check on the agency.

Regulated firms, public interest groups, and others dissatisfied with an FDA action (or inaction) can seek recourse in the courts.

As a practical matter, FDA is also accountable to the scientific and medical communities, and particularly to their academic components. Most of the principal decision makers at FDA are physicians or scientists, to whom the respect of their professional peers is of great importance. Particularly when FDA makes decisions about cutting-edge technologies or other matters at the scientific frontier (as it often does), the agency's decision makers want to make decisions that will be respected as sensible in the relevant scientific and medical disciplines. Routinely, the agency, when faced with such decisions, formally seeks the advice of its advisory committees, which are composed principally of leading academic physicians and scientists. FDA generally follows their advice.

Like all government agencies, FDA is also accountable to public opinion, as shaped by the press. The agency's relations with all the constituencies with which it deals—regulated firms, trade associations, federal and state governmental bodies, scientific and medical groups, organizations representing patients, and others—are all influenced significantly by the agency's standing with the public.

Nevertheless, in a large and critical part of its work—review of new products—FDA is largely insulated from effective outside oversight. Such reviews are based on trade secret data generally not otherwise disclosed elsewhere, except to similar regulatory bodies in other countries. The reviews are highly technical, require highly specialized competence in several disciplines, and are extremely labor-intensive. Probably no other governmental institution currently is equipped to oversee the quality of FDA's performance of this distinctive function on an ongoing basis.

FDA new-product decisions are critical to the fate of regulated firms.

Because, over time, FDA's new product decisions are critical to the fate of regulated firms, they are extremely reluctant to challenge any particular FDA product-review decision in another forum. Resort to the courts to challenge an FDA denial of approval of a new product is particularly unappealing for several reasons:

- the technical nature of the subject matter;
- prevailing doctrines of administrative law, which lead to deference to administrative agencies on scientific and technical matters;
- the institutional limits on the judiciary, which is not well equipped to make judgments about scientific and technical matters; and
- the unattractiveness of trying to market a product that FDA has initially refused to approve.

The result is a limited, but important, area in which the exercise of governmental power is, to a considerable extent, unaccountable.

FDA is held accountable, however, on infrequent occasions when a segment of the public takes a particularly strong interest in a pending review of a proposed new product or when a past approval of a product has turned out to be a serious mistake. In such circumstances, extraordinary public attention focuses on FDA's decision-making process, and the agency is called to public account for its decision.

For example, organized groups representing patients, such as those with the AIDS virus or Alzheimer's disease, have brought public pressure on FDA to approve proposed new drugs. News media sometimes have championed particular drugs or devices. When an approved product has turned out to be much more harmful than was anticipated when FDA approved it, FDA has been called before a congressional committee to explain its decision.

These two types of scenarios create conflicting pressures on FDA. The agency may be subjected to public pressure to hasten the approval of an apparently promising new product, but the agency knows it is likely to be criticized severely if its approval turns out to have been a mistake. Few products, however, attract public support before approval, and few FDA approvals turn out to have been mistaken. In the general run of decision making about approvals of new products—including decisions about what indications and claims for a product will be permitted and how other information will be presented in the product's official labeling—FDA is largely unaccountable as a practical matter.

FDA takes an expansive view of its mission and its authorities.

Ultimately, FDA's accountability is a function not only of how other governmental bodies and other constituencies view the agency, but also of other, competing demands on the attention and resources of those to whom FDA is accountable. The variability in effective oversight of the agency presents a persistent philosophical issue for FDA: what should be its basic stance toward the statute it administers? Should FDA officials view the statute as a set of detailed instructions from Congress to be carried out in a manner as faithful as possible to what congressional drafters presumably intended? Or should the statute be viewed as basically a set of authorities for FDA to use to advance its views of what promotes the public health, through whatever means FDA can use without being overridden by some governmental body or group to which the agency is formally accountable?

For example, if the agency views a particular statutory limitation on its authority as reflecting a congressional compromise inimical to the public health, should the agency respect the limitation faithfully or seek ways to evade it through other statutorily permitted means? To what extent should the agency seek to expand its powers in the face of inertia or distraction in other centers of power? To what extent should the agency be creative and aggressive in asserting its power to advance policies it considers beneficial to the public health? Alternatively, should the agency seek to discern and carry out the policy preferences of its political superiors in the executive branch and of Congress? In sum, what is the appropriate role of a subordinate agency entrusted with a mission to protect the public health?

Over the decades, different FDA decision makers have responded differently to this set of issues. In general, the agency has taken an expansive view of its mission and its authorities, and has used its statutory tools aggressively to advance its institutional views of what is good for the public health. The most striking example was FDA's assertion of jurisdiction over tobacco products without an express delegation of statutory authority—an assertion of authority the Supreme Court held to be invalid.

FDA in the International Community

Before the advent of what today is called "the global economy," FDA's concerns were focused almost entirely on protecting consumers in the United States. FDA viewed itself as having only limited responsibility toward consumers abroad, and only a limited role in facilitating the marketing of American products abroad. The agency also devoted relatively little effort to monitoring imports. Amendments to the FDCA and globalization have required FDA to rethink the proper role of the American national food and drug regulator in the international economy.

What is America's responsibility with respect to FDA-regulated products exported from this country to a foreign country?

What is America's responsibility with respect to FDA-regulated products exported from this country to a foreign country? Should the United States be an international nanny? Should its attitude toward foreign consumers be "let the buying country beware"? Should its role be something in between—and, if so, what? Does it matter whether the importing country does or does not have its own sophisticated regulatory system? Does it matter whether products exported from the United States may be re-exported from the original importing country to a third country? (If the products are re-exported back to the United States, that clearly is a matter of legitimate FDA concern.) If the United States does have some responsibility toward consumers in foreign countries, does it follow that the very same standards of safety, effectiveness, labeling, and product quality that apply to domestically distributed products should also apply to exported products, even when they are going to countries that are very different in population characteristics, healthcare systems, healthcare needs, and general economic level? If different standards should apply, what are they? What level of FDA effort and resources should be allocated to reviewing exported products, under any standard? To these difficult questions, there are no simple, obviously correct answers.

In general, FDA would prefer that American firms not export products within its jurisdiction whose safety and effectiveness for the ultimate consumers have not been demonstrated. FDA recognizes, however, that standards of safety and effectiveness appropriate for the affluent United States, with its sophisticated healthcare system, may not be appropriate for countries that are much poorer and have only rudimentary healthcare systems. Moreover, FDA owes respect to the authority and responsibility of foreign governments to decide what products may be marketed to their own people. In addition, the limitations on FDA's resources and the undesirability of driving export manufacturing facilities abroad constrain FDA's ability to act, and the willingness of Congress to have FDA act, as the protector of all the world's consumers.

The increasing dependence of the United States on imports of medical products and foods and, since 9/11, concerns about bioterrorism have raised serious issues about FDA's ability to protect American consumers from products that are fraudulent or adulterated, have been tampered with, or are otherwise defective. Plainly, in cooperation with Congress and through agreements with foreign governments, FDA will have to upgrade its programs for protection against unlawful imports. This effort will, of course, require the allocation of significantly increased resources, as well as the development and implementation of significantly improved monitoring and inspection systems.

To facilitate the international movement of foods, drugs, and devices, FDA has made a major effort to harmonize its regulatory requirements and standards with those of counterpart agencies in other countries. A host of issues relate to the extent to which FDA should compromise with foreign regulators in order to promote international uniformity in data development to support the approval of new products, product labeling, manufacturing systems and practices, factory inspection standards, and other matters. A further issue relates to the level of effort and resources that FDA should devote to assisting U.S. manufacturers to meet importation requirements of foreign governments.

How FDA Should Be Funded

An issue that arose in the 1990s and continues to be the subject of debate is whether, and if so to what extent, the activities of FDA should be funded by "user fees" from regulated firms.

Finally, an issue that arose in the 1990s and continues to be the subject of debate is whether, and if so to what extent, the activities of FDA should be funded by "user fees" from regulated firms rather than from the federal government's general revenues (collected principally from taxpayers). Plainly, from the perspective of the national budget and the interest of taxpayers, any shift of the burden of payment to regulated firms is desirable. Does such a shift, however, raise legitimate concerns?

Is product review properly viewed as a service provided by FDA to regulated firms, for which it is appropriate that those firms pay a fee? Was not the system of product review established for the benefit of the public rather than the regulated firms? Are there likely to be adverse practical consequences of reconceptualizing product review as a service to regulated firms?

If regulated firms are paying for a particular FDA activity (e.g., review of an application for approval of a new drug), is there a risk that the fact of payment by the firms will affect the performance of the function and the interaction between the agency personnel performing it and the personnel of the paying firms? Over time, might the firms become more assertive in their dealings with the agency; and might FDA personnel feel that they "owe" the paying firms more? If such consequences do occur, are they necessarily undesirable?

Is there a risk that FDA functions paid for by regulated firms will receive disproportionate financial support as compared to agency functions funded by the taxpayers, so that, over time, an imbalance will occur between product review (paid for by firms) and enforcement (paid for by the taxpayers)? Has such an imbalance already occurred, and with undesirable consequences? Can the political process, including congressional oversight and the appropriations process, be relied on to maintain a reasonable balance?

If FDA functions are paid for by private firms rather than from the public treasury, is there a risk that there will be a natural bureaucratic tendency for the firm-supported functions (and FDA jobs) to proliferate unnecessarily? Or can it reasonably be expected that firms and their trade associations will have sufficient political capital with Congress and the administration to maintain checks on such a development?

The political system has been unwilling to provide, from general revenues, an adequate level of resources for timely FDA reviews of new products.

These questions raise fundamental issues about the principles underlying the regulatory system FDA administers. The risks just described are real, but it is also undeniable that the political system has been unwilling to provide, from general revenues, an adequate level of resources for timely FDA reviews of new products, and that the additional resources from user fees have accelerated product reviews and approvals, to the general benefit of the public. Whether the advantages of this approach outweigh the disadvantages over the long term will depend principally on the quality of FDA management and the ability of outside constituencies (principally Congress and the news media) to find an effective way to monitor the quality of FDA's performance despite the relative imperviousness of FDA product reviews to public scrutiny. As funding of FDA by user fees extends beyond product reviews to other functions, these concerns and the need for effective management and oversight of FDA will increase.

Conclusion

Food and drug law is a fascinating microcosm of old and new issues in political and social philosophy, including many facets of social justice among different groups affected by regulatory decisions. These issues influence day-to-day administration of the law and the large controversies that erupt from time to time.

Chapter 4

The Food and Drug Administration—How It Is Organized and Works

Fred H. Degnan, King & Spalding, Washington, D.C.

Key Points

- **Although FDA is not an independent agency, it makes every effort to operate as if it were one. It is unique among its sister agencies within DHHS because of the variety of products and scientific issues it confronts and because of the extensive regulatory and enforcement authority it wields, not to mention the latitude it has been given to police the domestic and international commerce of the products it regulates.**
- **The agency's evolution from a small bureau in USDA in 1906 to a very visible and active component of DHHS reveals the development of a highly specialized agency that can adapt and adjust to increased regulatory burdens.**
- **The fundamental structure and organization of FDA for decades has remained unchanged: the Office of the Commissioner, substantive centers, and field offices form the nucleus of agency activity and initiatives.**
- **Because of the complexity, variety, and importance of the issues within its responsibilities, FDA has been forced to lead the way in developing and employing regulatory tools, such as rulemaking and advisory committees, and has forged generally strong collaborative working arrangements with sister agencies and state authorities. As a result, the agency has enhanced its ability to function efficiently and in a substantively and scientifically sound way.**

Introduction

Although perhaps the most visible and well-known of all public health organizations, the U.S. Food and Drug Administration (FDA) is not an independent agency. Rather, it is a component of the U.S. Department of Health and Human Services (DHHS). Moreover, and perhaps even more surprising, only very limited statutory authority (e.g., authority with respect to dispute resolution regarding the timeliness of agency review of drug, device, or biological combination product applications) is directly vested in the Commissioner of Food and Drugs. The governing core legislation, the Federal Food, Drug, and Cosmetic Act

(FDCA), is designed to be administered almost exclusively by the Secretary of Health and Human Services. In fact, until 1988, the Commissioner, for all practical purposes, served at the pleasure of the Secretary. The FDCA was modified in 1988 to require that the Commissioner be appointed by the President and confirmed by the Senate. Although now in a more favorable political position, the Commissioner, nevertheless, remains answerable to the Secretary of DHHS, as well as to others in the political system.

The routine administration of the FDCA is conducted by FDA.

Notwithstanding the language of the FDCA, the Secretary has delegated the majority of authority under the act to the Commissioner. In turn, the Commissioner has redelegated the bulk of the authority received from the Secretary to the Directors of FDA's "centers" and regional offices. Delegations and redelegations under the act can be found in Part 5 of FDA's regulations (21 C.F.R. §§ 5.10, 5.20). Thus, as a practical matter, the routine administration of the FDCA is conducted by FDA. The Secretary, however, has not delegated—and, in fact, has specifically reserved—the authority to approve FDA regulations that present significant public issues involving the quality, availability, marketing, or cost of foods, drugs, cosmetics, medical devices, biologics, or any other article subject to regulation by FDA. This hierarchy is important to understanding the role of various parts of the government in highly visible and important FDA activities.

FDA is unique among its sister agencies within DHHS because of the variety of products and scientific issues it confronts, because of the extensive regulatory and enforcement authority it wields, and due to the latitude it has been given to police the domestic and international commerce of the products it regulates. In large part because of the complexity, variety, and importance of the issues within its responsibility, FDA frequently has restructured itself in an effort to enhance its efficiency. And, to be successful in its public health mission, the agency has led the way in developing and employing regulatory tools such as rulemaking and advisory committees, and has forged generally strong, collaborative working arrangements with sister agencies and state authorities. In the process, the agency attempts to maintain a workable balance with Congress and its overseers in the executive branch, DHHS, and the Office of Management and Budget (OMB).

How FDA Is Organized

Headquarters and the Field

In 1906 the Bureau of Chemistry of the U.S. Department of Agriculture (USDA), FDA's first lineal ancestor, faced real challenges. At issue was how best to regulate the safety and labeling of foods and drugs in interstate commerce. Right from the start there was recognition that such regulation, to be effective, required not only policy guidance and decision making from a central organization (the Bureau of Chemistry), but also a strong presence throughout the diverse regions of the United States. As a result, "field" laboratories in New York, Boston, Philadelphia, Chicago, New Orleans, and San Francisco were established to provide critical reports and information needed to enforce what were viewed as the sweeping provisions of the Pure Food and Drugs Act of 1906.

With the passage of time, the complexity of the challenges confronting FDA has increased dramatically. The agency's regulatory authority extends far beyond the food and drug products subject to the 1906 act. Moreover, whereas the tasks and responsibilities that faced the Bureau of Chemistry in 1906 centered primarily around ensuring against the adulteration and misbranding of food and drugs, the tasks and responsibilities confronting the agency today include the development of scientific and regulatory policy; the expert and prompt scientific review of premarket applications; the comprehensive investigation of an array of diverse manufacturers; the even-handed enforcement of statutory prohibitions and standards; the security of regulated products from tampering and terrorist activity; and the coordination of international policies and regulation to foster trade, yet protect domestic consumers from harmful or bogus products.

The agency's structure must accommodate these diverse and broad-ranging initiatives and goals. Although restructuring, or at least tinkering with existing structures, has occurred frequently, the fundamental structure of the agency continues to embrace the concept of a national headquarters for policy and decision making and an extensive, professional field force throughout the country to provide informed, consistent public health decision making and regulatory enforcement.

Headquarters: The Office of the Commissioner

FDA is a highly centralized administrative agency. The Office of the Commissioner is structured with the goal of coordinating agency enforcement activity and public policy and ensuring consistency of approach between various agency components in their interpretation of scientific understanding, application of regulatory requirements, and exercise of discretion and judgment. See Figure 1. Simply put, the Office of the Commissioner is involved in every significant agency activity.

FDA is a highly centralized administrative agency.

It is not uncommon for the Commissioner's office to be reorganized to reflect a particular administration's or a particular Commissioner's perception of the agency and preferred way of conducting business. The office

Figure 1

Department of Health and Human Services
Food and Drug Administration

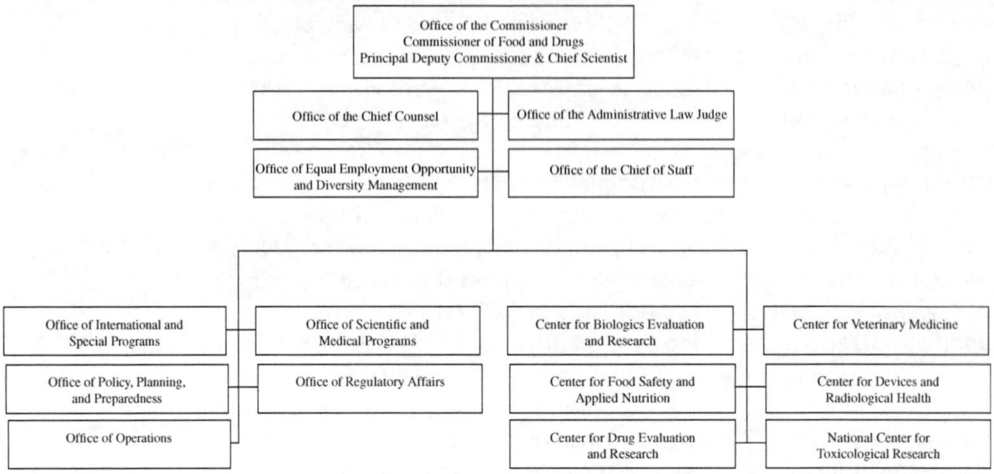

was most recently reorganized in 2007. The restructuring included the establishment of four deputy-level offices within the Office of the Commissioner. This marked a return to aspects of a four-deputy structure that was abandoned in 1999 in favor of a more streamlined design.

The four deputy-level offices are Scientific and Medical Programs; Policy, Planning and Preparedness; Operations; and International and Special Programs. The new deputy structure has resulted in a shift in the reporting lines of authority and reduced the number of offices in the Office of the Commissioner that report directly to the Commissioner. Now, for example, the Offices of Legislation, Crisis Management, Counterterrorism, and Science and Health Coordination no longer report to the Commissioner but rather to a designated deputy commissioner.

FDA's five centers:

- *Center for Biologics Evaluation and Research (CBER)*
- *Center for Devices and Radiological Health (CDRH)*
- *Center for Drug Evaluation and Research (CDER)*
- *Center for Food Safety and Applied Nutrition (CFSAN)*
- *Center for Veterinary Medicine*

The reorganization left untouched the direct access to the Commissioner on the part of the agency's substantive "centers" and its Office of Regulatory Affairs (ORA), the office that coordinates FDA's enforcement activities nationwide. FDA centers conduct the bulk of FDA's scientific and regulatory evaluations and interpret and apply FDA's statutory authority over food, drugs, cosmetics, devices, and radiological products. The centers are: the Center for Biologics Evaluation and Research (CBER), the Center for Devices and Radiological Health (CDRH), the Center for Veterinary Medicine (CVM), the Center for Drug Evaluation and Research (CDER), and the Center for Food Safety and Applied Nutrition (CFSAN). Enhancing the communication lines between the Office of the Commissioner and the centers helps ensure that scientific issues are fully aired and understood.

A Closer Look at the Operation of FDA's Five Substantive Centers

Each substantive center possesses the machinery of an administrative agency. Each center has a director and related hierarchy of managers. Moreover, each center has a focal point for policy guidance, programs, and enforcement actions, as well as the necessary scientific capabilities to support policy and compliance activities.

Each center has a focal point for policy guidance, programs, and enforcement actions, as well as the necessary scientific capabilities to support policy and compliance activities.

Consider, for example, CFSAN. Its offices include but are not limited to: the Office of Food Additive Safety, which provides a centralized coordinated focal point for food and color additive petition review; the Office of Food Defense, Communication and Emergency Response, which provides a single focus for all CFSAN programs affecting food security and protection; the Office of Management Systems, which focuses on administrative processes and the management of resources; the Office of Scientific Analysis and Support, which provides centralized support throughout the center in specialty areas such as mathematics and statistics, pathology, physical chemical analysis, consumer studies, economics, and epidemiology; and the Office of Constituent Operations, which provides educational and liaison functions with groups outside the center. The agency's other four centers are, generally, similarly structured.

Although a center can be active in responding to policies and programs suggested by the Office of Commissioner or the executive branch, the mainstay of most centers' initiatives involves reviewing premarket applications; developing scientific and regulatory policy in the form of guidance documents or regulations; proactively and reactively addressing issues of potential public health concern; preventing, intervening, and responding to food-related risks; and ensuring compliance with the food adulteration and misbranding provisions of the FDCA. Thus, as a practical matter, the first stop in dealing with FDA is usually with the center whose jurisdiction covers the substantive matter at issue. The Office of the Commissioner is unlikely to act in the absence of substantive input from a center and rarely disagrees with a center's science-based analysis of an issue.

"The Field"

Although the field offices report to the Office of the Commissioner, they have traditionally served—and continue to serve—rather specialized functions related to enforcement of the FDCA and its implementing regulations. The "field" is divided into five regions, each responsible for a distinct part of the country. There are more than twenty "district" offices and over 100 additional resident inspection posts within the regions. See Figure 2.

Figure 2

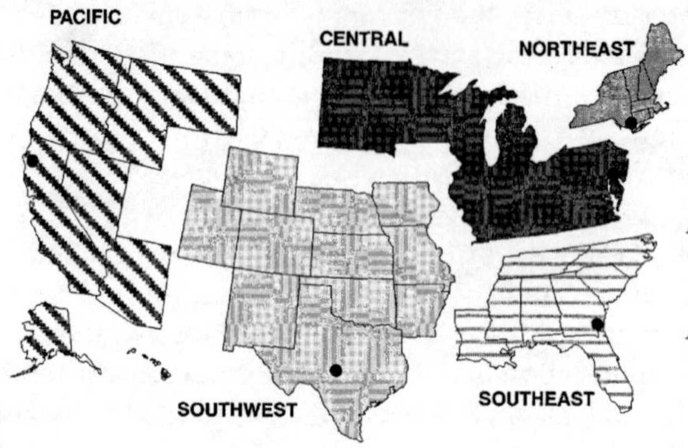

Five regions, each responsible for a distinct part of the country, comprise FDA's field operations. District offices and resident inspection posts are located throughout the United States.

A regional field office is responsible for agency activities within its boundary.

A regional field office is responsible for agency activities within its boundary. Its primary focus is to ensure that regulated industry within a given region complies with the laws and regulations enforced by the agency. Regional directors report to the Associate Commissioner of Regulatory Affairs who, in turn, reports to the Deputy Commissioner of Operations.

The district offices, as well as the much smaller resident inspection posts, perform the nuts-and-bolts, hands-on work. They inspect the facilities in which regulated products are prepared, packed, manufactured, processed, or held, and perform the initial task of evaluating compliance with agency criteria, standards, and regulations. These offices also work cooperatively with state, local, and other federal agencies; encourage local consumer protection programs in areas related to agency-enforced laws and regulations; and provide valuable consumer education.

Field offices are also an important source of information for headquarters. They are often the first to identify new or emerging problems and trends, future program needs, and priorities. Moreover, they refine and improve existing analytical methodologies and explore and develop new monitoring systems (e.g., techniques to detect a specific contaminant in a food or drug product). The field offices also play a major role in managing product recalls, conducting follow-up checks to determine the effectiveness of a recall, and preventing recurring violations of the FDCA. The field recommends legal action to headquarters and to the Office of the Chief Counsel or, as necessary, to the U.S. Attorney in its area. A key role for the field involves providing extensive factual and evidentiary support in civil or criminal proceedings.

The Office of the Chief Counsel

Although integral to the functioning of the agency, the Office of the Chief Counsel is not part of FDA. Rather the office is, technically, the Food and Drug Division of DHHS's Office of General Counsel. Nevertheless, for all practical purposes, the Office of the Chief Counsel generally has served as FDA's lawyer and the Chief Counsel as the Commissioner's lawyer.

Although integral to the functioning of the agency, the Office of the Chief Counsel is not part of FDA.

The Office of the Chief Counsel reviews and evaluates the propriety of proposed agency actions to enforce the FDCA, helps defend the agency in litigation, works closely with the centers in developing proposed and final regulations, and generally advises all components of the agency on the requirements of the law and the legal implications of an action or inaction.

Basically, the role the Office of the Chief Counsel serves in advising various components of the agency is to identify issues of law, policy, and fact that are likely to arise in the context of a given initiative and assess the lawfulness of—or perhaps, more precisely, the probability that the agency will prevail in—such issues. Simply put, the fundamental role of the Office of the Chief Counsel is to measure agency decision making by the prevailing legal standard.

So. . . How Does It All Work? A Hypothetical

The interplay among the various components of FDA perhaps can be made more concrete by resort to a hypothetical. Assume a producer of fresh-cut and packaged salad greens fails to follow good agricultural or manufacturing practices in the production of a large lot of product. Assume further that the failure causes an indeterminable number of packages of salad greens to be contaminated with a potentially harmful microorganism. Packages from the lot of salad greens at issue are shipped to retail stores in three states. In time, a few people who have consumed salad greens from packages from the lot in question begin to suffer adverse reactions.

Working independently, two healthcare providers send stool specimens to different clinical laboratories for analysis. In both cases, a strain of *Escherichia coli (E. coli)* is isolated. Both laboratories send the *E. coli* strain to separate public health laboratories which perform DNA fingerprinting and submit the pattern to pulse-field gel electrophoresis (PFGE). Additional people become ill and similar testing occurs.

Connecticut is the first state to identify a cluster of *E. coli* cases with matching PFGE patterns. Connecticut health authorities notify the Centers for Disease Control and Prevention (CDC). CDC looks for the strain in other reports of possible outbreaks and quickly confirms matching patterns in the two other states. CDC contacts FDA's Office of Crisis Management, which begins coordinating the agency's internal and external investigational, scientific, and communication activities.

CFSAN, ORA, the Office of Public Affairs, and the two district offices having jurisdiction in the respective states all become involved. CDC works with the states and FDA to create a standard questionnaire and to develop a process for identifying and reporting cases. Working in cooperation with CDC, FDA districts coordinate investigations to gather information related to the illnesses and identify the possible source of contamination. Meanwhile the Commissioner's office has been preparing for media, consumer, and legislative inquiries and has designated an official in the Office of the Commissioner as the primary contact for CFSAN with respect to any new developments concerning the outbreaks.

CFSAN experts, working with CDC experts, identify an apparent association between a number of the outbreaks and consumption of the producer's salad greens. The applicable district office sends investigators to visit the producer's facility and inspect its records, equipment, processing line, and overall harvesting, shipping, cooling, and related practices. While that inspection is going on, an FDA laboratory analyst identifies a strain of *E. coli* in one of the open packages of salad greens retrieved by an agency investigator from the home of one of the outbreak victims. The strain matches the infectious strain reported by the state public health laboratories.

Officials in CFSAN immediately contact the chief executive officer (CEO) of the producer, inform him or her of the confirmatory laboratory results, and request the CEO to cease production of product and to begin a recall of all salad green products currently marketed. The CEO requests a short time to consider the information. CFSAN officials consult with the Office of the Chief Counsel, which in turn advises that based on the facts at hand, the center is justified in immediately issuing a public alert on its own initiative and also, working through the FDA District Director in the district where the producer is located, to automatically detain the producer's salad greens in light of the credible evidence indicating that the food presents a threat of serious adverse health consequences. Notified of these developments, the CEO agrees to stop distribution and implement a recall immediately, accompanied by a press release. FDA investigators at the company's facility verify that the product was shipped to only three states and that, therefore, there is no need to alert public health counterparts in other states or in Canada and Mexico.

The immediate threat to health now avoided, officials in CFSAN and the Office of the Commissioner study the implications of the episode particularly in light of similar past episodes involving these products. The episode serves as a priority-setting event for the agency to intensify its cooperative efforts with industry and state regulatory officials to develop comprehensive agricultural and manufacturing practices for such products. The Commissioner's office and the center agree that the center should look into the key elements of and the scientific basis and justification for such practices. The center consults with the Office of the Chief Counsel as to the legal authority to impose such requirements and the scientific burdens the center must meet to invoke that authority via regulation. Working with state counterparts and CDC, center officials begin to assemble the required database and craft a proposed regulation. In the process, public hearings are scheduled and held to collect information and recommendations from industry and consumers alike.

Ultimately, the center prepares a proposed regulation. The Office of the Chief Counsel reviews the proposal for legal and evidentiary sufficiency. The center, in light of comments from the Chief Counsel, collects more information and expert opinion and scientific support to strengthen its case. The draft of the proposed rule is submitted for review and consideration to the Office of the Commissioner.

Meanwhile, the district, in a follow-up inspection of the facility, finds evidence that the producer had reason to suspect the contamination of its products but opted to distribute them. Working closely with the Office of the Chief Counsel and the Office of Criminal Investigations, the district helps develop a criminal action against the producer.

This hypothetical, although bereft of specifics, nevertheless reveals the coordinated approach that FDA routinely applies in handling such public health issues.

This hypothetical, although bereft of specifics, nevertheless reveals the coordinated approach that FDA routinely applies in handling such public health issues. Field, center, Commissioner's office, and the Office of the Chief Counsel work together, combining their respective expertise to address not only the immediate problem but also long-term solutions to avoid or deter comparable threats to public health.

FDA's Administrative and Regulatory Tools and How It Uses Them

Rulemaking

Like all agencies, FDA has finite resources that force it to ask hard questions about the best way to regulate. Before 1970 most regulatory agencies like FDA answered the question in a traditional manner, emphasizing enforcement litigation against products, companies, or individuals in violation of the FDCA. There is merit to this approach—particularly for FDA. Because FDA has broad litigation authority, the agency can rely on that authority to bring an array of regulatory actions. It can invoke, for example, the seizure provisions of the act to promptly and efficiently withdraw violative products from the marketplace. In addition, the agency has statutory authority to enjoin manufacturers from producing and marketing violative products. Moreover, FDA has broad authority to recommend that the Department of Justice (DOJ) criminally prosecute, either as a misdemeanor or felony, or both, individuals involved in the interstate commerce of violative products.

As a regulatory tool, however, there can be practical drawbacks to enforcement litigation. It is time-consuming and resource intensive. It is reactive to a situation or problem. It can encourage a "cop" mentality as opposed to an objective, fact-driven assessment of how best to accomplish statutory and regulatory goals.

FDA pioneered rulemaking as a regulatory tool.

By the 1970s the complex issues accompanying the variety of products and the distinctive manufacturing disciplines FDA was charged to police prodded the agency to consider, in addition to litigation, proactive means of encouraging and accomplishing compliance. The primary tool the agency chose for this purpose was "informal" rulemaking. In the process FDA "pioneered" rulemaking as a regulatory tool.

FDA's statutory authority to conduct rulemaking is found in sections 701(a) and 701(e) of the FDCA. Section 701(e) contains "formal" rulemaking authority—authority that involves issuing regulations on the basis of a rulemaking record that may be tested in a quasi-judicial administrative proceeding. Simply put, elaborate procedural safeguards are built into section 701(e) of the act—in fact, the provisions in section 701(e) may be the most elaborate rulemaking procedures under which any federal agency operates.

In stark contrast to section 701(e), section 701(a) is a model of brevity. It reads, in full, as follows: "The authority to promulgate regulations for the efficient enforcement of this Act, except as otherwise provided in this section, is hereby vested in the Secretary."

Under this authority, FDA recognized it could achieve compliance by publishing regulations prescribing how firms interested in being in compliance in the first place could so conform. For example, instead of relying exclusively on seizing misbranded products, the agency recognized that it could publish regulations prescribing how to label a product—e.g., how to name a product, how to craft a principal display panel, how to phrase declarations concerning net weight, sodium content, etc. Instead of relying exclusively on injunctions to force manufacturers to manufacture a food or drug in an appropriate manner, the agency could promulgate regulations containing basic procedures to follow in manufacturing such a product and which, if followed, would enhance the likelihood that a product would not be found to be adulterated or misbranded. Instead of case-by-case consideration of the procedures used by a new drug developer for evaluating data, the agency could issue regulations describing the attributes of a well-controlled investigation, identifying requirements for informed consent, oversight by institutional review boards, etc.

FDA's concept of rulemaking as a regulatory tool was premised on the fundamental notion that regulated industries would, if not welcome, at least follow guidance as to how to manufacture and market compliant, nonviolative products. The notion that an aggressive regulatory agency could enhance its ability to protect the public health by issuing guidance-based regulations was novel in the 1970s. What made the use of rulemaking truly "pioneering," however, was the weight that courts accorded to the agency's regulations.

An agency can issue interpretative or substantive rules.

This is an especially critical point. There are basically two kinds of regulations that an administrative agency can issue. One is "interpretative," the other "substantive." Interpretative rules or regulations are, for purposes of this discussion, synonymous; they contain the agency's view of what the statute means. Enforcement, therefore, is hinged on whether the agency can establish that a particular statutory requirement has been violated. Although an interpretative rule may add persuasive insight to a court's interpretation of the statute, it lacks the force of law and courts are free to disagree with it. A substantive rule or regulation is quite different. It expands an existing substantive provision of law and specifies what that provision requires. If held to be a valid extension of the statutory scheme, a substantive regulation has the force and effect of law—thereby rendering an administrative agency, to an extent, a legislative power.

A string of court cases has recognized the substantive force of a regulation issued under section 701(a). The most notable of these is *Weinberger v. Hynson, Westcott & Dunning*, 412 U.S. 609 (1973), in which the Supreme Court upheld as substantive FDA's regulations defining the fundamental elements of what constitutes "substantial evidence" of effectiveness. By permitting FDA to adopt substantive rules delineating the contours of what constituted an adequate and well-controlled investigation, the court converted controversial questions of scientific fact that normally would be the subject of extensive litigation into the very narrow objective issue of whether a manufacturer complied with the regulation.

The validity of any FDA regulation may be tested in court.

The validity of any FDA regulation may be tested in court. In determining whether a regulation is appropriate, courts focus on whether the statutory scheme and the specific provisions cited by the agency justify the promulgation of the regulation. Such an inquiry focuses on not only the statutory purpose but also such practicalities as the types of enforcement problems that may be encountered and the type of supervision required to accomplish the goals of the FDCA. Moreover, a hallmark of any rulemaking is the "administrative record" compiled by the agency in support of the regulation. The administrative record includes comments received from the public on the agency's initial notice of its proposed regulation. In finalizing a rule, the agency must respond with a reasonable explanation as to why the regulation is legitimate, lawful, and supported by the facts.

One of FDA's most creative exercises of its substantive rulemaking authority involved its efforts to regulate the nutrition labeling of food. The FDCA did not mention the word "nutrition" until the passage in 1990 of the Nutrition Labeling and Education Act (NLEA). Nevertheless, nearly twenty years earlier, FDA had embarked on rulemaking initiatives that specifically defined when nutrition food labeling would be necessary, the required format for such information, and the criteria by which the adequacy of certain claims (e.g., "low sodium") would be judged. The promulgation of FDA's nutrition labeling regulations in the 1970s effectively prescribed—with the force and effect of law—how an entire industry had to label its products and formulate product claims. This type of rulemaking, as should be readily apparent, is far more efficient industrywide as an enforcement tool than are individual lawsuits.

Today, FDA continues to rely on its substantive rulemaking authority. The internal process of issuing regulations is somewhat more cumbersome than it was in the 1970s. While the essential elements of informal notice and comment remain the same, the layers of review in the Office of the Commissioner, the Office of the Secretary of DHHS, and OMB in the White House are more numerous. Moreover, concerns such as environmental impacts, economic burdens, and paperwork reduction must now be taken into account in every major new regulatory proposal. Nevertheless, the point is as true today as it was decades ago: FDA's ability to issue substantive regulations has changed dramatically how it operates as an administrative agency.

Agency Guidance Documents

Although rulemaking in many ways remains the tool of choice to provide guidance to the regulated community and to gauge regulatory compliance, FDA more and more frequently today resorts to issuing less formal "guidance documents" to assist manufacturers in efficiently dealing with it on matters of mutual interest and concern. The purposes of such "guidance documents" are: 1) to provide assistance by clarifying requirements that have been imposed by Congress or issued by FDA in regulations, 2) to explain how compliance with those statutory and regulatory requirements may be achieved, and 3) to outline specific review and enforcement approaches so as to ensure that the agency acts in an effective, fair, and consistent manner.

Guidance documents are less formal and assist manufacturers by clarifying requirements, explaining compliance, and outlining specific review and enforcement approaches.

A guidance document, for example, may define what the agency considers to be the important characteristics of preclinical and clinical test procedures, manufacturing practices, and scientific protocols. Other guidance documents explain FDA's views on how to comply with relevant statutes and regulations, and how to avoid enforcement actions. CFSAN, for example, has issued guidance documents on issues such as how to submit a food additive petition, the types of changes that constitute a "major change" in an infant formula and thus require documented premarket notification, and—with the passage of the NLEA—how to avoid misbranding a product. One of the most successful guidance documents is the agency's "Questions and Answers" publication addressing some of the more common issues raised by the agency's implementation of the NLEA.

FDA distinguishes between "Level 1" and "Level 2" guidance documents. Level 1 guidance documents include documents that set forth initial interpretations of statutory or regulatory requirements, or set forth changes in interpretation or policy that are of more than a minor nature (including complex scientific issues or highly controversial issues). Level 2 guidance documents set forth existing practices or minor changes in the interpretation of a policy.

Before FDA prepares a draft of a Level 1 guidance document, the agency often seeks or accepts early input from individuals or groups outside the agency via public meetings and workshops. After FDA prepares a draft Level 1 guidance, the agency publishes a notice in the *Federal Register* announcing that the draft guidance is available and inviting comment on it. If it wishes, FDA may hold public meetings on the draft guidance or present it to an advisory committee for review. After receiving and reviewing comments, the agency will prepare the final version of the document and publish a notice in the *Federal Register* announcing that the guidance document is available.

No such procedures attend the issuance of a Level 2 guidance. FDA may post and immediately implement a Level 2 guidance document and may request and accept comment.

Guidance documents do not establish legally enforceable rights or responsibilities, and are not legally binding on the public or the agency. Rather, they explain how the agency believes relevant statutes and regulations apply to certain regulated activities. Because a guidance document represents the agency's current thinking on a given subject, FDA has formally committed to ensure that its staff does not deviate from it unless there is an appropriate justification and "appropriate supervisory concurrence." Agency guidances are available by request or over the Internet. When dealing with a center on a particular issue, it is critical to ask whether a relevant guidance document exists.

In between regulations and guidance documents are "guidelines." For years, FDA relied on guidelines to refine and explain the principles and details in an existing regulation. Guidelines also have been used by the agency to lay out clinical test procedures, manufacturing practices, product standards, scientific protocols, ingredient specifications, and other technical or policy criteria. Because, however, the agency's position has been that a guideline represents the formal position of FDA and obligates the agency to follow it, the agency in recent years has placed far more time and resources into the preparation of guidance documents that do not carry such obligatory force.

Meetings

FDA officials want the agency to be as "transparent" as practicable. This posture clearly has evolved over the years as the agency broadened from mere enforcement to helping ensure maximum voluntary compliance on the part of industry. This is not to say that FDA is not an aggressive enforcer when the situation merits; it is. But, in recent years the agency has made real efforts to communicate guiding criteria and standards to help industry steer clear of conduct that could give rise to enforcement-related concerns. In addition to regulations and guidance documents, meetings and correspondence are valuable ways the agency attempts to respond to industry questions, issues, and concerns. Meetings can be initiated either by industry or the agency. They may be private or public. Before a meeting takes place, FDA generally wants the company or group to provide an agenda and a list of attendees. Minutes of every private meeting are prepared and placed on public review in the administrative file of the proceeding. Rather comprehensive regulations govern the conduct of any meeting with the agency. See 21 C.F.R. § 10.65.

FDA officials want the agency to be as "transparent" as practicable.

Hearings

Another valuable regulatory tool is the administrative "hearing." FDA has extensive regulations governing the conduct of administrative hearings. Formal hearings involving the approval or withdrawal of a licensed product (e.g., under a drug, a food additive, etc.) are conducted generally like formal trials (formal evidentiary public hearings, 21 C.F.R. Part 12) or like scientific boards of inquiry (public hearings before a public board of inquiry, 21 C.F.R. Part 13). Traditionally, these hearings, like most any form of litigation, have been both time-consuming and resource intensive, and, as a result, have become increasingly rare as FDA and industry look to more efficient dispute resolution mechanisms.

Another valuable regulatory tool is the administrative "hearing."

Regulations also govern the procedures to be followed at hearings before the Commissioner or his or her delegate. Public hearings before the Commissioner have served, particularly in the last fifteen years, to permit the agency to hear directly from public and industry sectors alike in various locations nationwide, and to collect informed scientific opinion regarding possible agency initiatives or requirements. In implementing the NLEA, for example, FDA held a series of nationwide hearings regarding the purpose of the food label, and the nature and extent of the nutrition information that should be required to appear on it. The agency also has held hearings on the risks presented by microbial contamination in the manufacture of food and possible procedures designed to prevent such contamination. This type of hearing provides a valuable mechanism for industry and the public to have input in agency policies and practices well before they have been decided.

Agency Interaction With Outside Experts

Although FDA is a science-based organization possessing a great deal of expertise, outside expert advice has become increasingly critical to its decision making. In part, this is due to the fact that some of the laws administered by the agency (e.g., the Medical Device Amendments of 1976) require the use of outside expert advisory committees. But, in addition, the increasing complexity associated with advances in science and reduced internal resources for developing "in-house" expertise, creates the need to include advice from "outside" experts. This heightened role of outside experts seems likely to increase in the future.

Two key sets of regulations govern FDA's "advisory" committees. The General Services Administration has published regulations that apply to all government advisory committees. See 41 C.F.R. Parts 105-154. These

Two key sets of regulations govern FDA's "advisory" committees.

regulations set forth basic policies and procedures regarding the establishment, operation, termination, and control of advisory committees.

FDA's own regulations deal with basic administrative aspects that apply to the conduct of an advisory committee. See 21 C.F.R. Part 14. The regulations delineate meeting procedures: what portions of the committee proceedings can be "closed" to the public; the rules of general conduct for a hearing; the preparation of minutes and reports; the maintenance of transcripts; and the handling of public inquiries and requests for advisory committee recommendations. FDA's regulations require that members of an advisory committee must have diverse interests, education, training, and experience. They also describe the procedures for nominating voting and nonvoting members to "technical" and "nontechnical" committees. FDA treats all of its current advisory committees as technical committees, which is important because technical committees may have consumer or industry members. In any event, however, only technical experts can serve as voting members. On technical committees, nonvoting members are meant to serve as liaisons between the groups or constituencies they represent and the committee.

The responsibilities and powers of nonvoting members and voting members are similar. The primary difference between them is that a nonvoting member may vote only on procedural matters, such as the adoption of rules or the approval of minutes and future meeting dates. Moreover, a nonvoting member who represents industry, for example, may have access to data and information that constitute a trade secret, or confidential or commercial financial information, only if that member has been appointed as a special government employee.

FDA pays its advisory committee members a fixed daily rate when the committee meets, and also reimburses for travel, food, and lodging. While most members are physicians, committee memberships also generally include registered nurses, statisticians, epidemiologists, pharmacists, and pharmacologists. In addition to the expert members, one consumer representative and usually one industry representative serve on each committee.

Professional members are recruited through notices published at least once a year in the *Federal Register* and through other means, such as contacting professional organizations and medical schools. Nominations are reviewed by FDA staff and the Commissioner of Food and Drugs. A list of candidates is then submitted to the Secretary of DHHS for final selection. Committee chairpersons are appointed from among the nominees; they are not elected by their committees. Committee members are subject to federal laws that prohibit them from taking part in any official action in which they have a financial interest. Members must file financial disclosure forms and declare in advance of a meeting any conflict of interest that exists.

FDA'S STANDING ADVISORY COMMITTEES
Office of the Commissioner
Science Board
Risk Communication Advisory Committee
Pediatric Advisory Committee
Center for Biologics Evaluation and Research
Allergenic Products Advisory Committee
Cellular, Tissue, and Gene Therapies Advisory Committee
Blood Products Advisory Committee
Transmissible Spongiform Encephalopathies Advisory Committee
Vaccines and Related Biological Products Advisory Committee
Center for Drug Evaluation and Research
Anesthetic and Life Support Drugs Advisory Committee
Anti-Infective Drugs Advisory Committee
Antiviral Drugs Advisory Committee
Arthritis Drugs Advisory Committee
Cardiovascular and Renal Drugs Advisory Committee
Dermatologic and Ophthalmic Drugs Advisory Committee
Drug Safety and Risk Management Committee
Endocrinologic and Metabolic Drugs Advisory Committee
Gastrointestinal Drugs Advisory Committee
Nonprescription Drugs Advisory Committee
Oncologic Drugs Advisory Committee
Peripheral and Central Nervous System Drugs Advisory Committee
Pharmaceutical Science and Clinical Pharmacology Advisory Committee
Psychopharmacologic Drugs Advisory Committee
Pulmonary-Allergy Drugs Advisory Committee
Reproductive Health Drugs Advisory Committee
Center for Food Safety and Applied Nutrition
Food Advisory Committee
Center for Devices and Radiological Health
Devices Good Manufacturing Practice (GMP) Advisory Committee
National Mammography Quality Assurance Advisory Committee
Anesthesiology and Respiratory Therapy Devices Panel
Circulatory System Devices Panel
Clinical Chemistry and Clinical Toxicology Devices Panel
Dental Products Panel
Ear, Nose, and Throat Devices Panel

Gastroenterology and Urology Devices Panel
General and Plastic Surgery Devices Panel
General Hospital and Personal Use Devices Panel
Hematology and Pathology Devices Panel
Immunology Devices Panel
Medical Devices Dispute Resolution Panel
Microbiology Devices Panel
Molecular and Clinical Genetics Panel
Neurological Devices Panel
Obstetrics and Gynecology Devices Panel
Ophthalmic Devices Panel
Orthopaedic and Rehabilitation Devices Panel
Radiological Devices Panel
Technical Electronic Product Radiation Safety Standards Committee
Center for Veterinary Medicine
Veterinary Medicine Advisory Committee
National Center for Toxicological Research
Special Studies Relating to the Possible Long-Term Health Effects of Phenoxyl Herbicides Contaminants Committee (Ranch Hand Committee)
Science Advisory Board

The size of FDA committees ranges from nine to fifteen members. The committees vary in the extent to which they are used. The average number of meetings per year per advisory committee is less than two, but that is misleading as one committee could have six meetings and another none.

Committee agendas are created by FDA staff. Most commonly, committees are asked to recommend whether a product should be approved. They also may be asked for advice on policy. A *Federal Register* notice announcing the meeting is published in advance of the date, along with the products or issues to be considered.

Companies prepare extensively to present to advisory committees because the outcome of the committee vote is extremely important to the fate of the product at issue. In the case of a product review, usually both FDA and the manufacturer present their data or analysis. Any member of the public who has so requested also may make a presentation. The presentations, the committee's deliberations, and the final vote—in short, every aspect of the meeting—are on the record. A transcript of the record is made available.

Once a committee has voted and submitted its advice to FDA, the agency is free to follow, or not follow, the advice. In 2007, in an effort to maximize the integrity, consistency, and utility of advisory committee voting results, FDA issued a guidance recommending that advisory committees adhere to a process of simultaneous voting in which all members vote at once. According to the guidance, the results of the vote should be announced immediately and how each voted should become part of the public administrative record.

In recent years, the integrity of advisory committees has become increasingly a matter of public focus and attention. The reason is obvious: in the wake of public concern over issues involving the safety of FDA-approved products (e.g., Vioxx), it is considered essential that the input from the agency's expert advisory committees help ensure the credibility of agency decision making. As a result, the disclosure of financial interest information has received legislative as well as agency attention. Effective in October 2007, section 712(c)(2) of the FDCA prohibits advisory committee members from participating in a committee matter if they or any immediate family members have a financial interest that could be affected by the advice proffered. Disqualification may be avoided if FDA grants a waiver. Section 712 and 18 U.S.C. § 208 specify the circumstances under which FDA may grant participation. Section 712 of the FDCA also requires that FDA disclose on its website the type, nature, and magnitude of the financial interests of each advisory committee member who has received a waiver.

Advisory committee members are prohibited from participating in a committee matter if they or any immediate family members have a financial interest that could be affected by the advice proffered.

Based on section 712, FDA issued a guidance detailing procedures for determining whether a conflict of interest exists and, as a result, the eligibility of a candidate to participate in an advisory committee's consideration of a particular matter. The guidance sets out a rather stringent policy for considering eligibility for participation than is permitted under the current legal authorities. Under the approach recommended in the guidance, a member possessing a conflict of interest may participate only in the narrowest of circumstances: where the potential conflict is minimal and the member's expertise is needed for the committee's deliberations.

Specifically, if an individual has a disqualifying financial interest, the combined value of which exceeds $50,000, the member "generally" would not be permitted to participate in an advisory committee meeting on the particular matter in which the conflict arises regardless of the need for the member's expertise. If the disqualifying financial interests are $50,000 or less, the member would be eligible to participate only if he or she meets the applicable statutory standard for participation—the need for his or her services outweighs the potential conflict. Third, if the standard for participation is met, the individual's participation is to be limited to nonvoting. Moreover, in cases where there may be a perception of a conflict of interest, FDA reserves the right to limit participation even though full participation would be permitted under the applicable laws.

In addition to standing advisory committees, FDA has submitted with some regularity over the last two decades projects or problems to outside experts for their consideration and recommended resolution. The agency on occasion has used such highly regarded bodies as the National Academy of Sciences, the National Research Council, and the Life Sciences Research Office of the Federation of American Societies for Experimental Biology. Requests for such outside help, as well all the supporting, nonproprietary information reviewed by the outside group, and the final recommendations of such a group, are publicly available and open to public comment.

How FDA Deals and Interacts With Other Federal Agencies

Introduction

Although the laws that FDA administers provide generally comprehensive authority to regulate products, the agency's authority is not always exclusive. In some cases its jurisdiction may overlap with other federal agencies. In other cases, the agency's jurisdiction may simply be complementary. And, in still other cases, its statutory authority may conflict with that of other agencies.

Agencies That FDA Works Closely With:

- *U.S. Department of Agriculture*
- *Environmental Protection Agency*
- *Federal Trade Commission*
- *Consumer Product Safety Commission*
- *Drug Enforcement Agency*
- *National Institute on Drug Abuse*
- *Department of State*
- *U.S. Customs Service*
- *Department of Justice*

Although these circumstances easily could lead to chaos, they have not. For decades, FDA has relied on agreements and memoranda of understanding (MOUs) to clarify regulatory responsibilities, areas of primary jurisdiction, reciprocal regulatory and information-based roles, and funding responsibilities with other agencies involved in aspects of food and drug regulation.

U.S. Department of Agriculture

Historically, no agency is closer to FDA than USDA. As noted earlier, FDA's predecessor, the Bureau of Chemistry, originated in USDA and undertook its food and drug responsibilities upon enactment of the Pure Food and Drugs Act of 1906. Although the bureau eventually evolved into the Food and Drug Administration in 1930, it remained part of USDA until 1940. Thereupon, FDA became part of the Federal Security

Agency which, in turn, became the Department of Health, Education and Welfare and then, as it is now, DHHS.

USDA has broad authority over the food supply, including the inspection of meat and poultry and the labeling of food products containing meat or poultry.

USDA continues to have broad authority over the food supply, including the inspection of meat and poultry and the labeling of food products containing meat or poultry. USDA also inspects and grades fresh fruits, vegetables, and grains.

FDA and USDA have entered into scores of MOUs. For example, while FDA has broad authority over the safety and labeling of food, including fresh fruits and vegetables, USDA's Agricultural Marketing Service (AMS) carries out a number of functions designed to aid in the efficient marketing of agricultural products. AMS develops commercial grade standards and specifications for foods, and the rendering of inspection and grading services to producers, processors, shippers, buyers, or other interested parties.

MOUs between the two agencies commit AMS to advising FDA of all the food processing and packaging plants operating under AMS supervision, and to report to FDA, for possible enforcement, any processor or packer who has not corrected objectionable conditions found to exist by FDA and who otherwise, based upon AMS's first-hand information, may not have the capability to consistently produce and market quality food. In turn, FDA agrees to work closely with AMS inspectors and cooperate with them in their efforts to grade and inspect produce. Similar agreements exist between FDA and USDA's Animal and Plant Health Inspection Service, Food Safety Inspection Service (FSIS), and, concerning public education initiatives, the USDA itself.

FSIS and FDA also coordinate efforts in the meat and seafood industries to curtail the contamination of meat, poultry, and fish products from harmful microorganisms. The agencies have worked extensively to develop consistent, forward-looking Hazard Analysis and Critical Control Point (HACCP) procedures designed to ensure the safest possible food supply. In accomplishing these ends, there has been a significant exchange between the agencies of scientific data and information, as well as expertise.

USDA, FDA, and the Environmental Protection Agency (EPA) coordinate the agencies' respective regulatory authorities over products developed by plant biotechnology, and USDA and FDA coordinate their respective authorities with respect to products developed by animal biotechnology techniques. In 1986 the agencies established the Coordinated Framework for regulating genetically engineered organisms and products. This coordination has been essential in the overall efforts of the federal government to encourage new technologies while at the same time to ensure that every aspect of the use of such technology, from initial investigation to the ultimate production of a consumer product, is carefully and appropriately regulated.

In light of the numerous "overlapping" opportunities in the regulation of food, the notion of vesting one agency with all federal responsibility for food regulation has been considered frequently. Regardless of how this organizational issue is eventually resolved, the cooperative efforts between FDA and USDA have unquestionably formed a foundation for meeting future regulatory challenges involving the evaluation of scientific data, the accommodation of new innovations, and how the public health goals of the country's various food safety laws can be applied in a meaningful fashion.

EPA and Foods
Two EPA laws directly impact on the food supply: the Federal Insecticide, Fungicide, and Rodenticide Act (FIFRA) and the Safe Drinking Water Act (SDWA).

Environmental Protection Agency

EPA administers two laws that have direct impact on the food supply: the Federal Insecticide, Fungicide, and Rodenticide Act (FIFRA) and the Safe Drinking Water Act (SDWA). FIFRA governs the registration of pesticides. Without such registration, a pesticide cannot be sold lawfully for use in the United States. A major part of the registration process for food use pesticides involves tolerance setting, which is conducted under section 408 of the FDCA. EPA was vested with this tolerance-setting authority in 1970 pursuant to a reorganization plan. As a result, EPA determines the safety of pesticide residues in food, while FDA takes enforcement action under the FDCA for products violating the standards established by EPA.

Under the SDWA, EPA controls contaminants in drinking water that may have adverse effects on the public health. The SDWA gives exclusive control over the safety of public water to EPA. FDA, however, always has considered drinking water to be a food under section 201(f) of the FDCA. Through an MOU both parties agreed that the passage of the SDWA in 1974 implicitly repealed FDA's authority under the FDCA over water used for drinking purposes (although section 410 of the FDCA makes clear that FDA retains exclusive control over bottled drinking water). The MOU goes on to establish that EPA in essence controls all aspects related to the safety of water prior to the water coming out of a public tap, and that water used as an ingredient in food or in food processing remains subject to the FDCA.

FDA and EPA also share authority over chemical additives. The Toxic Substances Control Act (TSCA) gives EPA authority to regulate mixtures of chemical substances and articles containing such substances or mixtures. EPA can require testing of a chemical substance or a mixture based on possible unreasonable risk of injury to health or the environment. Under TSCA, for example, EPA regulates the addition of direct and indirect additives to drinking water. The agencies have agreed that the appropriate interpretation of TSCA excludes from the definition of "chemical substance" products regulated under the FDCA.

The commonality of safety concerns presented by the products regulated by each agency (the toxicity of pesticides, chemical substances, and additives to food or water) has resulted in significant efforts between FDA and EPA to coordinate their scientific approaches to assessing the safety of such substances. MOUs provide general guidance and encouragement to the agencies in accomplishing such harmonization. Nevertheless, differences in opinion as to how most accurately to assess risks do exist between the two agencies. For example, only recently, after years of debate, FDA decided to accept EPA's use of "scaling factors" in extrapolating the results of data from laboratory animals to assess their significance and relevance to the health of people.

FTC and FDA
FTC and FDA work together under a 1971 liaison agreement.

The Federal Trade Commission

FDA and the Federal Trade Commission (FTC) possess concurrent jurisdiction over the labeling and advertising of foods, over-the-counter drugs, veterinary drugs and related products, and cosmetics. The two agencies have agreed that the FTC should exercise primary responsibility concerning the advertising of such products, and that FDA will do likewise for matters relating to product labeling. Accordingly, under the Federal Trade Commission Act (FTC Act), the FTC investigates and prosecutes "unfair methods of competition" including "unfair or deceptive practices" and "methods of competition." The FTC's goal is to protect consumers from unfair and deceptive advertising and marketing practices, and to prohibit unfair trade practices that could impact on competitive markets and business relationships. FDA's jurisdiction over product labeling is more consumer oriented, and is designed to ensure that products and all the printed graphic or related material that may accompany their sale do not mislead consumers and are presented in a truthful, unambiguous manner.

By virtue of a "liaison agreement" entered into in 1971, the agencies coordinate their activities, and share information and expertise. The arrangement, however, is complicated by the fact that substantiation requirements for labeling under the FDCA are more stringent than those for advertising under the FTC Act. Thus, on occasion, the FTC is placed in the position of appearing more lax in its enforcement posture when compared to FDA. The FTC's unique enforcement powers, however, which include adjudication by the five FTC commissioners as well as the ability to issue cease and desist orders enforceable by injunctive, civil penalty, and criminal contempt proceedings, compensate for whatever lesser substantiation standard the agency may possess.

In many cases, the FTC's follow through in enforcing advertising is important, if not essential, to FDA initiatives over labeling. For example, FDA's comprehensive efforts to implement the NLEA and limit the type of health-related information that may be communicated about the relationship between a component of a diet and the prevention of a disease or health-related condition would be severely diluted if the FTC did not endorse a comparable regulatory philosophy with regard to the advertising of such food components. Working together on this issue the two agencies have developed a comprehensive approach to regulating and ensuring the comparability of health claims on food.

The FTC has also played an important role in helping FDA adapt to judicial precedent requiring FDA to consider the commercial speech implications of any regulatory effort with respect to product misbranding. The FTC's history of relying upon 1) consumer survey data to show that a given advertising claim has the potential to mislead and 2) disclaimers to cure any such potential has provided a helpful framework for FDA in considering enforcement and regulatory policy concerning the lawful contours of product promotion.

CPSC
FDA generally prevails in jurisdiction questions with CPSC.

Consumer Product Safety Commission

The Consumer Product Safety Act protects the public from unreasonable risks of injury associated with consumer products. The Consumer Product Safety Commission (CPSC) was formally established in 1973. A major component was FDA's Bureau of Product Safety, established in the early 1960s to administer provisions of the Federal Hazardous Substances Act relating to the labeling of products presenting consumer hazards.

In spite of, or perhaps because of, the etiology of CPSC, disputes arose quite early between the two agencies over jurisdictional points. Whereas FDA believed that a container having a food contact surface should be regulated by FDA as a "food additive" (i.e., because of the potential for migration of a component to the food), CPSC considered such an article within its jurisdiction as a consumer commodity. After much discussion, the agencies agreed to draw the jurisdictional line on the basis of whether an article could cause contamination or spoilage of food as a result of migrating to or otherwise becoming a component of food. Under this approach, home canning equipment that fails to provide a seal adequate to keep air from passing into stored food is regulated by CPSC, as are pressure cookers, slow cookers, refrigerators, or freezers that fail to perform at proper temperatures thereby rendering food unfit to eat. A food container that presents the possibility of components migrating into the food itself (e.g., lead leeching from the soldered lining of a tin can into the food or beverage) would be regulated by FDA as a food contaminant or additive.

This focus on the "mechanical" versus "component" nature of a hazardous substance has come to form the fundamental distinction between CPSC and FDA jurisdiction. Thus, FDA retains its basic jurisdiction over foods, medical devices, drugs, and cosmetics except in those cases where the container of such articles possesses a defect such as sharp edges or a propensity to explode or break. Such situations are regulated by CPSC.

Disputes between the two agencies continue on occasion, and are resolved either informally or through the somewhat time-consuming process of issuing an advisory opinion. In close-call situations, FDA generally prevails, perhaps because of its more efficient and successful track record in enforcement litigation.

The Drug Enforcement Administration, the National Institute on Drug Abuse, and the U.S. Department of State

Federal regulation of drugs of abuse is a shared enterprise among four distinct entities: FDA, the Drug Enforcement Administration (DEA), National Institute on Drug Abuse (NIDA), and the U.S. Department of State (DOS). One area of joint enterprise is establishing "schedules" for drugs of abuse. The "schedules" establish the level of control in the manufacture, importing, prescribing, or handling of drugs of abuse.

FDA, DEA, NIDA, and DOS share in the federal regulation of drugs of abuse.

Acting on behalf of the Secretary of DHHS, FDA has the authority to make domestic drug scheduling recommendations, which, in turn, determine the level of control that will accompany an addictive substance under the Controlled Substances Act. DEA, however, conducts the relevant scheduling proceedings and administers the scheduling, amendment, or repeal of any domestic classification. NIDA, by formal agreement with FDA, provides FDA with recommendations and views regarding the addictive potential of a drug substance. FDA, DEA, and DOS collaborate on issues relating to the administration of international treaties governing the scheduling and classification of narcotics and psychotropic drugs. FDA, NIDA, and DEA also collaborate in administering provisions of the Narcotic Addict Treatment Act that establishes a basis for control of narcotic addict treatment programs to prevent the diversion of narcotic drugs, and to ensure proper treatment of narcotic addicts. All of these relationships are spelled out in MOUs.

Responsibility among the agencies in these areas is generally well defined. FDA and NIDA limit their focus to scientific factors relating to the safety, pharmacology, and addiction potential. DEA implements the scientific findings of FDA and NIDA, and conducts comprehensive enforcement of the control, distribution, and diversion of scheduled substances. In the context of narcotic addict treatment programs, including methadone, FDA and DEA work closely together, with FDA obtaining DEA approval prior to authorizing any treatment program. Both FDA and DEA maintain the authority to deny or revoke approval of a treatment program independent of each other.

U.S. Customs Service

Perhaps in no other area of food and drug regulation does FDA have broader authority than it does over imported products.

Perhaps in no other area of food and drug regulation does FDA have broader authority than it does over imported products. FDA exercises that authority in conjunction and cooperation with the U.S. Customs Service. Section 801(a) of the FDCA permits FDA to refuse admission to an imported article if "it appears" that the article is in violation of the act. FDA has no burden to prove that a product for import actually violates the act. The fundamental test for refusal merely rests upon the "appearance" of a violation—a standard that, when considered literally, is impossible for the agency not to meet should it believe a product to be violative.

Customs' authority over imports arises under the Tariff Act of 1930 as well as under section 801. Section 801 vests the Secretary of the Treasury with the authority to deliver samples of imported products to FDA for analysis. In actual practice, FDA personnel at most ports collect the samples, issue the appropriate notice of sampling, and, where applicable, having determined that an article is in violation and may not be brought into compliance, issue a refusal notice. If FDA does not have the personnel to carry out these functions, Customs will do so in close cooperation with agency officials.

In 1979, Customs and FDA entered into an MOU formalizing this process, and delegating to FDA the authority to collect samples, issue notices of sampling, and issue notices of refusal of admission. The MOU permits designation of FDA employees as Customs officers. If an importer wishes to recondition a violative product or to contest a refusal of admission, a bond must be filed. Only Customs can issue the bond. Although FDA can admit a product to import, Customs still must release the product for entry into the market.

Policing the safety of imported food is perhaps FDA's most daunting job. Currently, more than $65 billion worth of food products is imported annually. The sheer volume precludes inspection of every imported product and, as a practical matter, demands the cooperation FDA and the Customs Service have forged. The problems presented by potentially violative products being introduced through import regularly invite congressional scrutiny of FDA actions and consideration of ways, usually through greater resources, to augment FDA's and the Customs Service's abilities to protect the public from risks presented by imported products.

Notably, in 2002 Congress passed legislation designed to help reduce the ability of international terrorists to contaminate foods imported into the

United States. The legislation requires food importers to provide FDA with advance notice of shipments of human and animal food imported or offered for import into the United States. This advance information permits FDA, in conjunction with U.S. Customs, to channel resources and target inspections—a necessity in light of the fact that every day FDA receives approximately 25,000 notifications with respect to incoming shipments of food. The legislation also authorizes FDA to ask Customs to institute a temporary hold for twenty-four hours on any food offered for import if FDA has credible evidence or information indicating that the food presents a threat of serious adverse harm and FDA is unable to immediately inspect or examine the food.

In sum, as a legal—and practical—matter, import issues demand daily cooperation between FDA and Customs. The case can be made that, in light of the volume of FDA-regulated products imported annually, coordination between the two agencies is more crucial to the public health than the coordination between FDA and any other agency.

Going to Court
FDA cannot go to court itself; it is always represented by the Department of Justice.

Department of Justice

FDA does not possess independent authority to represent itself in judicial proceedings. As is the case with most other federal agencies, FDA is represented in court by DOJ. DOJ's Office of Consumer Litigation is the primary overseer of agency-related litigation—litigation that may be either enforcement-based (i.e., brought by the government) or defensive in nature. Because of the frequent science-based expertise that comes into play in FDA-related litigation, DOJ has historically and continues to welcome participation by lawyers from FDA's Office of the Chief Counsel in the conduct of such litigation. Although occasionally characterized by differences in litigation strategy or assessments of legal empowerment, FDA and DOJ generally have worked well together in defending agency actions and in enforcing the provisions of the FDCA—as the agency's successful litigation track record bears out.

Centers for Disease Control and Prevention

Although FDA unquestionably has the lead responsibility within DHHS for ensuring the safety of food and the safety and effectiveness of drugs and devices, FDA's sister agency, CDC, has an important complementary and nonregulatory public health role. As the lead federal agency for conducting disease surveillance, CDC monitors the occurrence of illness and

FDA's sister agency, CDC, plays an important complementary and nonregulatory public health role.

outbreaks in the United States attributable to food and other FDA-regulated products. The disease surveillance systems coordinated by CDC constitute an essential information network for early warnings about dangers presented by regulated products.

With respect to food in particular, CDC's surveillance systems are helpful in measuring federal, state, and local initiatives to reduce food-borne illness. Moreover, CDC's surveillance systems are critical indicators of new and changing patterns of food-borne illness. CDC, time and again, has been able to promptly alert FDA of products implicated in food-borne disease and has provided both agencies with expert scientific opinion on the effectiveness of food-borne disease prevention strategies.

CDC's role in providing critical expertise with respect to disease control and prevention will only increase in the coming years. With that increased role, however, comes the potential for the two agencies to hold inconsistent or divergent positions. Ultimately, any FDA regulatory action based on a potential public health threat identified by CDC must be evaluated in light of the governing legal standards FDA is charged to enforce.

Because it is not a regulatory agency, however, CDC is unconstrained by statutory burdens of proof and is free to opine on the extent and severity of potential hazards it defines. Apparent, or real, conflicts between the two agencies can arise. Consider, for example, the use of the compound Bisphenol A (BPA) in plastic bottles. FDA has advised that the food contact uses of BPA have been found to be "safe" within the meaning of existing regulatory standards. CDC, on the other hand, has taken the more aggressive public position that more study and investigation are needed to assess whether BPA, which may have hormone-like effects on the reproductive system, is not, in fact, injuring consumers. The extent to which the two agencies work together to harmonize discordant views and, where such views remain at odds, to help educate consumers as to why each view is responsibly held, is a coordination goal worthy of attention.

Other Agencies

Other agencies play critical roles in FDA's ability to efficiently exercise its jurisdiction. FDA has developed MOUs or agreements with these agencies to ensure cooperation, including the exchange of scientific information and investigative evidence. These other agencies and their areas of overlapping interests include: the Nuclear Regulatory Commission (licensing and regulation of the nuclear industry, and knowledge and information regarding radiation); the Federal Bureau of Investigation (Federal Anti-tampering Act implementation); the National Marine Fisheries Service (voluntary seafood inspection program); and the Bureau of Alcohol,

Tobacco and Firearms (the regulation of alcoholic beverages and tobacco).

FDA and Congress

For any federal agency, Congress basically has three distinct functions: legislative (the development, modification, or repeal of legislation); oversight (overseeing how the agency is administering its legislative authority); and appropriations (funding agency programs).

Particularly within the last two decades, FDA has paid increasing attention to managing its relations with Congress. The Office of Legislative Affairs (OLA) in the Office of the Commissioner is the agency's primary liaison with Capitol Hill. OLA initiates, coordinates, and provides in-depth analyses of agency legislative needs and prepares supporting documents and position papers not only for the Commissioner and agency officials but also for Congress and OMB. A large part of OLA activities also involves responding to congressional and legislative inquiries—inquiries that from time to time may involve sensitive correspondence critical of agency action or inaction. In cooperation with the FDA centers, OLA coordinates hearings before Congress and coordinates briefings with congressional members and staff.

FDA decisions affect, sometimes dramatically, discrete constituencies. As a result, FDA issues are often lightning rods for congressional attention. The resulting congressional oversight hearings can be contentious affairs that can affect the course of agency regulation and decision making. Saccharin, infant formulas, AIDS treatments, dietary supplements, the pace of product approvals, tobacco, and numerous other issues have been the subject of high-publicity, high-profile, and intense congressional scrutiny. FDA takes these encounters seriously and treats them with enormous care. A large part of FDA's role at any congressional hearing involves education—concise, clear explanations of the roles scientific data, public policy, and legal requirements have in the melding of its positions, decisions, and practices.

FDA issues are often lightning rods for congressional attention.

Several House and Senate committees have a degree of jurisdiction over FDA activity. As a vestige of FDA's days as part of USDA, the Agricultural Subcommittees of the House and Senate Appropriations Committees continue to review and determine FDA's annual appropriation. The agency's authorizing committees, however, are the House Committee on Energy and Commerce and the Senate Committee on Labor and Human Resources. The House Subcommittee on Oversight and Investigations and the Subcommittee on Health and the Environment traditionally have been very active in surveying and directing agency activity. Other committees with FDA-related responsibilities include, in the Senate, the Committee on Agriculture, Nutrition, and Forestry and the Committee on Governmental Affairs and, in the House of Representatives, the Committee on Agriculture, the Committee on Government Operations, the Committee on Merchant Marine and Fisheries, the Committee on Science, Space and Technology, and the Committee on Small Business.

Another feature of FDA's congressional relations involves the Government Accountability Office (GAO), formerly known as the General Accounting Office. Since the early 1970s, GAO has been called upon by Congress to investigate and report back to Congress on an array of FDA-related matters. As a result, a significant part of FDA's congressional activity is spent in cooperation with GAO in its investigations. OLA coordinates agency responses and serves as the primary liaison with GAO.

FDA and Its Relations With the States

FDA's ability to efficiently regulate hinges to a certain extent on its relationship with state and local authorities. Although FDA possesses the lion's share of regulatory authority, states nevertheless play an important role in public health protection. Every state has a food and drug act, in most cases patterned quite closely upon the FDCA. Moreover, local authorities may have specific regulations or ordinances governing product labeling, weight, and related attributes.

Every state has a food and drug act, in most cases patterned quite closely upon the FDCA.

The Association of Food and Drug Officials of the United States and the Association of Official Analytical Chemists generally work closely with FDA to accomplish the public health protection goals of both the FDCA and its state counterparts. State food and drug officials often are trained by FDA and, in return, provide valuable service to FDA in enforcing provisions of the FDCA. In the food area, for example, an extensive array of model codes governing the sanitation of milk and other retail foods characterize the cooperation between FDA and state officials. In general, FDA prepares the model codes and ensures that they contain the latest and best scientifically based advice about food safety issues. The agency also helps implement the codes at the state level. These codes recognize that thousands of local and state agencies assume the frontline responsibility for inspecting and enforcing food safety laws.

In recent years FDA has intensified these initiatives with the development of a model Food Code designed to prevent food-borne illness.

Although neither federal law nor federal regulation, the Food Code provides the states with FDA's best advice for a uniform system of regulation to ensure that food is safe and properly protected at the retail and food service level.

FDA's substantive licensing decisions concerning food additives, drugs, and medical devices generally are deferred to by the states. From time to time a state (e.g., California, under its ballot referendum legislation Proposition 65) may wish to impose an additional requirement, such as a warning, on an FDA authorized product but this is rare.

Under the NLEA and the Safe Medical Device Amendments of 1990, FDA possesses express preemption authority over inconsistent state requirements. The agency also has extensive implied preemption authority under the Supremacy Clause and the Commerce Clause of the U.S. Constitution. The agency, however, rarely seeks to exercise its preemptive authority over state actions. The agency's policy regarding preemption reflects a general presumption against preemption, and favors working together with state authorities to make the state and federal schemes at issue consistent with one another. On occasion these efforts have not been successful and the agency has preempted with regular success, thereby rendering null and void inconsistent state requirements or activities (e.g., state efforts to regulate imitation food labeling in a manner inconsistent with FDA's nationwide efforts have been found, by two U.S. Courts of Appeals, to be preempted).

Under the NLEA and the Safe Medical Device Amendments of 1990, FDA possesses express preemption authority over inconsistent state requirements.

Part of FDA's deference to and willingness to work with states, and thereby avoid preemption, is grounded in the recognition that states provide FDA needed support in conducting regulated facility and manufacture inspections, in accomplishing significant product recalls, and in collecting valuable enforcement- and compliance-related information (the nature and extent of these various state activities are contained in scores of MOUs with the agency). These examples of state assistance provide very real deterrents to actions by FDA—like preemption—that could be viewed as being meaningfully at odds with long-term federal and state relations.

One key exception to the foregoing involves state common law claims for negligence and strict liability that conflict with, because they are different from or in addition to, requirements imposed by FDA during the premarket approval processes for medical devices. Although FDA is not likely to bring a preemption case in such an instance, it is likely to support such an action if requested by a court or interested party to weigh in. The agency may also, on its own initiative, file an *amicus* brief in such a proceeding. To this end, a 2008 Supreme Court case (*Riegel v. Medtronic, Inc.*, No. 06-179) confirmed the holdings of several federal circuit courts to the effect that FDA's premarket approval requirements for Class III medical devices preempt conflicting state common law claims.

Another key exception to FDA's traditional deference and forbearance in the context of preemption involves prescription drug labeling. In the preamble to FDA's 2006 final rule amending its regulations governing the content and format of prescription drug labeling, FDA offered the view that under existing preemption principles, FDA approval of prescription drug labeling under the FDCA preempts conflicting or contrary state law. The agency went on to advise that state common law-based product liability and failure-to-warn cases have the potential to directly threaten the agency's ability to regulate the dissemination of risk information in accordance with the FDCA and good science and, thus, can frustrate FDA's implementation of its statutory mandate. The precise scope and extent to which FDA may lawfully preempt in this area remains undefined and is being, and will likely continue to be, contested in the courts.

FDA's International Relations

For years FDA has inspected foreign new drug manufacturers who wish to market their products in the United States, processed and granted approvals for the export of investigational new drugs, negotiated MOUs on regulatory matters and agreements with foreign governments, and conducted international training programs and conferences. Although FDA continues these important activities, its most fundamental international function today involves efforts to "harmonize" international enforcement and trade-related matters. The impetus for this focus arises from the Uruguay Round Agreement on Tariffs and Trade (also referred to as GATT), the Agreement on the Application of Sanitary and Phytosanitary Measures, and the Agreement on Technical Barriers to Trade.

FDA's most fundamental international function today involves efforts to "harmonize" international enforcement and trade-related matters.

As might be expected, FDA's international affairs staff in the Office of the Commissioner works closely with the Office of the U.S. Trade Representative and various trade groups in dealing with issues arising from these agreements. FDA also participates with the Codex Alimentarius Commission to develop international standards regarding the safety and sanitation of food. Moreover, FDA works closely with foreign governments to harmonize international technical requirements for pharmaceuticals and biologics, international vaccines, and cosmetics and veterinary drugs.

Although FDA activities in this area are largely overseen by the Office of the Commissioner, experts in each of the agency's centers are actively involved. Moreover, FDA publishes for comment in the *Federal Register* the procedures it proposes to follow and the criteria it believes appropriate on which to base harmonization decisions.

FDA and the Executive Branch

FDA is a component of DHHS. Thus, it is part of the executive branch. Accordingly, the agency's activities are not only subject to oversight from or by the Secretary of DHHS but also from OMB. Thus, the agency's major regulatory initiatives and rulemaking proposals, legislative proposals, congressional appearances and testimony, and budgetary requests are subject to review, scrutiny, and approval by OMB. OMB's oversight of FDA budget requests is not new, but OMB's oversight and review of agency rulemaking and related initiatives begun under the Carter administration in the late 1970s was increased under the Reagan administration, and continues through today.

One additional source of FDA oversight resides in the Inspector General (IG) of DHHS. The IG has the authority to investigate fraud and "abuses" of FDA's substantive program authority. In the late 1980s and early 1990s the IG was involved in a number of issues concerning the agency, most notably a series of matters arising from the agency's administration of its generic drug approval program.

The OIG DHHS has the authority to investigate fraud and "abuses" of FDA's substantive program authority.

Conclusion

History reveals that FDA is frequently subjected to reorganization. The reorganizations often reflect economic reality as well as the political orientations of the incumbent administration. The fundamental structure of FDA, however, has remained unchanged: the Office of the Commissioner, the substantive centers, and the field offices form the nucleus of agency activity and initiatives. Relations with sister agencies are generally positive and based on years of collaboration and compromise, with only an occasional incident of controversy. The agency also has developed tools, such as rulemaking and advisory panels, to enhance its ability to function efficiently and in a substantively and scientifically sound way.

The agency's evolution from a small bureau in USDA to a very visible and active component of DHHS reveals the development of a highly specialized agency that can adapt and adjust to increased regulatory burdens. By and large, the processes and structures put into place by both Congress and FDA have provided regulation that is commensurate with the risks to be prevented and the goals to be achieved. Among the more intractable problems that confront the agency today is the issue of resources. The pressure placed upon an agency with as many public health responsibilities as FDA to address and resolve complex public health issues with ever diminishing resources is enormous. As a result, the agency's cooperative efforts with sister agencies, state authorities,

Among the more intractable problems that confront the agency today is the issue of resources.

and international governments appear likely to increase over time. Moreover, reliance on outside expertise and substantive transparent efforts by industry at voluntary compliance are likely to be key components of any agency effort to continue to function effectively.

Chapter 5

The Drugs/Biologics Approval Process

Geoffrey M. Levitt, Wyeth Pharmaceuticals, Philadelphia, PA

Key Points

- The new drug application (NDA) process follows a series of defined phases, including:
  1) preclinical investigation (laboratory and animal testing);
  2) clinical investigation (human testing);
  3) FDA review of the application;
  4) postmarketing.

  Each of these phases involves varying levels of FDA oversight.
- At the preclinical phase, there is little direct FDA oversight. If proper practices and guidelines are not observed, however, the applicant's ability to use preclinical data in support of its application may be jeopardized.
- Clinical investigation is carried out under much closer FDA supervision. During this phase, the applicant must file investigational new drug (IND) applications with FDA before beginning new clinical studies, and must operate under rules and procedures designed to protect the rights and safety of human subjects. In addition, the applicant normally consults closely with FDA on the design of human studies (particularly in the later stages) with the goal of ensuring that the studies will support approval of its NDA.
- The FDA review phase is initiated by submission of the NDA. This phase is typically characterized by an ongoing dialogue between the applicant and FDA, wherein the applicant tries to satisfy the agency on outstanding questions and concerns. If FDA concludes the drug is safe and effective for its intended use or uses, this phase culminates in approval; if not, the NDA may be denied (or more often, withdrawn for an overhaul).
- The ANDA is an important variant of the NDA. With an ANDA, the applicant must pass all the same hurdles as for a full NDA, with one critical exception: the ANDA applicant does not have to demonstrate the safety and efficacy of its drug. Instead, the ANDA relies on the proven safety and efficacy of an already approved drug to which it refers (the "reference drug"). Therefore, the ANDA applicant, instead of showing safety and efficacy, must show that its drug will work the same in the body (i.e., will be "bioequivalent") to that reference drug.
- There are various forms of exclusivity that are of concern to both NDA and ANDA applicants, including patent protection, statutory exclusivity for the first approval of a new chemical entity or of certain new variations on an existing drug, and potential generic exclusivity for the first ANDA applicant who challenges a patent covering a reference drug. A distinct form of exclusivity, orphan exclusivity, is available to biologics license application (BLA) as well as NDA applicants.

Key Points Continued

- **Various mechanisms are available for expedited availability of a drug, including treatment investigational new drug applications (under which an investigational product is distributed more widely than otherwise, and for more treatment-oriented purposes) and fast-track approval (under which a drug or biologic that shows potential to address unmet therapeutic needs for serious or life-threatening diseases is given priority treatment by FDA). These mechanisms are worth bearing in mind for the new drug or biologic applicant as a way of getting wider and/or faster access to the market.**

Introduction

Before a new drug or biologic may be lawfully marketed in the United States, it must be approved by the Food and Drug Administration.

Before a new drug or biologic may be lawfully marketed in the United States, it must be approved by the Food and Drug Administration (FDA). In reality, there is not one single FDA approval framework that covers all drugs and biologics, but rather a set of distinct frameworks, each of which applies to a specific category of product. These include new drug approvals, abbreviated new drug approvals, the over-the-counter (OTC) review process, new animal drug applications, abbreviated new animal drug applications, and biologics.

All these frameworks have some important elements in common, but also some key differences. The new drug approval process is, in many ways, the standard model and provides a basic framework for understanding the other processes.

FDA Drug Review: The New Drug Application

What Is a "Drug"? What Is a "New Drug"?

Under section 201(g)(1) of the Federal Food, Drug, and Cosmetic Act (FDCA), a "drug" includes: 1) articles recognized in the U.S. Pharmacopoeia, the U.S. Homeopathic Pharmacopoeia, or the National Formulary; 2) articles "intended for use in the diagnosis, cure, mitigation, treatment, or prevention of disease"; 3) articles (other than food) "intended to affect the structure or any function of the body"; and 4) articles intended for use as a component of any of the above. "New drug," as defined in section 201(p) of the FDCA, means virtually any drug that first came onto the market, or is offered for entry onto the market, after the enactment of the act in 1938 (which includes the overwhelming majority of drugs in existence today), unless the drug is "generally recognized as safe and effective"—a category whose main practical importance is in the context of OTC drugs. A "new drug" must have an approved new drug application (NDA), or one of the recognized variants of an NDA, such as an abbreviated new drug application (ANDA), to be marketed lawfully in the United States.

Although the specifics of product development and FDA review may differ for each new drug product, the process of bringing a new compound onto the market generally follows a series of defined phases: preclinical investigation, clinical trials, submission and review of the NDA, and post-marketing.

Preclinical Investigation

The first stage in a drug's regulatory life cycle is preclinical investigation.

The first stage in a drug's regulatory life cycle is preclinical investigation. The basic goals of preclinical investigation are: 1) to identify the potential effects in the body of the chemical substance being investigated, through laboratory experimentation and animal testing; and 2) to gather enough evidence on the potential new drug to determine if it is reasonably safe to begin preliminary trials in humans.

Unlike human clinical trials, prior notification to FDA is not required to begin a preclinical investigation, although the preclinical phase is subject to specific FDA regulations known as good laboratory practices (GLPs). Unapproved new drugs shipped interstate as part of a preclinical investigation are exempted from the FDCA's general prohibition on interstate shipments of unapproved drugs as long as the drugs are appropriately labeled and adequate records of shipment and receipt are maintained. FDA may, however, terminate a preclinical investigator's ability to ship unapproved drugs if it determines that continuing the investigation is unsafe or otherwise contrary to the public interest, or that the drugs are being used for purposes other than bona fide scientific investigation.

Direct FDA involvement in a preclinical investigation ordinarily comes at the conclusion of the investigation, when the agency reviews the investigational new drug (IND) application that the drug sponsor submits prior to beginning human clinical trials. FDA then evaluates the soundness of the data the sponsor has gathered through preclinical investigation, as well as the adequacy of the methods used to gather those data. The agency's evaluation focuses in particular on the preclinical data the sponsor relied on to reach the conclusion that it was reasonably safe to conduct the proposed human clinical investigations. This primarily involves data regarding what effects the drug actually has in the body (pharmacology) and how toxic it is at various possible dose levels (toxicology).

FDA's GLP regulations, which are codified in Part 58 of Title 21 of the *Code of Federal Regulations* (C.F.R.), govern the laboratory work and facilities associated with any nonclinical study intended to support a marketing application for an FDA-regulated product, including drugs and biologics. These regulations establish certain minimum requirements for different aspects of a testing laboratory's practices, subject the laboratory to FDA inspectional oversight, and provide penalties for noncompliance.

The GLP regulations specify minimum standards in such areas as personnel, facilities, equipment, and operations. The regulations typically set these standards through procedural and structural safeguards, rather than through specific substantive requirements.

For example, in the area of personnel, the GLP regulations require that individuals involved in preclinical studies be sufficiently trained to conduct the study appropriately, but do not specify what such training must encompass. The personnel controls also require the designation of a study director to oversee, monitor, and certify the study and require the establishment of a separate quality assurance unit charged with independently monitoring the progress and scientific soundness of any study. This quality assurance unit, among other tasks, must maintain copies of study schedules and written protocols; conduct periodic inspections to ensure compliance with all regulations and specifications; submit regular status reports to the management of the testing facility; and prepare and sign a written statement outlining quality assurance efforts, which is to be included in the final study report.

The GLP regulations also require facilities to be of suitable size and construction, including proper animal care facilities, as applicable. The regulations provide that any study to be submitted to FDA in support of an IND (or other official application) must be conducted with a detailed protocol specifying the study's objectives and methodologies, and that all relevant records and data from the study must be retained for specified periods. FDA may inspect any GLP-covered facility and its records to determine its compliance with applicable standards.

A testing facility's failure to conform to applicable GLP requirements can result in various sanctions.

A testing facility's failure to conform to applicable GLP requirements can result in various sanctions. If the violation adversely affected the validity of a preclinical study and FDA considers lesser regulatory actions inadequate, the violation can result in the facility's being disqualified from carrying out any preclinical testing. In addition, any studies undertaken at a disqualified testing facility that are submitted in support of a subsequent product application may be excluded from consideration. FDA also may disregard a preclinical laboratory study done at a nonconforming facility, even if the nonconformance would not warrant disqualification of the facility. Exclusion of a preclinical study under either of these circumstances may lead, in extreme cases, to the termination or withdrawal of approval of the application.

Although the direct burden of GLP compliance is on the testing facility, the GLP regulations create strong incentives for sponsors who plan to rely on preclinical studies for subsequent FDA applications to take an active role in overseeing those studies.

Clinical Investigation

The primary purpose of the preclinical investigation is to gather sufficient evidence about the proposed new drug to proceed to the next regulatory stage—testing the product in people. The primary goal of human clinical investigation, in turn, is to gather sufficient information about the safety and efficacy of the drug to support an NDA. In contrast to the preclinical stage, clinical trials involve much more active FDA oversight, designed both to protect the health and safety of the human test subjects and to ensure the integrity and usefulness of the clinical study data.

The Investigational New Drug Application

Unlike the preclinical stage, commencement of clinical trials requires formal notification to FDA. At least thirty days before the drug's sponsor wishes to begin such trials, the sponsor must submit an IND to the agency (basic IND requirements are set out at title 21 C.F.R. Part 312 and in section 505(i) of the FDCA). If FDA does not object to the IND within thirty days, it automatically becomes effective and clinical trials may begin. If FDA finds a problem with the application, however, it may impose a "clinical hold," barring commencement of the investigational studies proposed in the application until the problem is resolved to the agency's satisfaction.

The specific contents of an IND depend both on the nature of the drug and the scope of the proposed trials. All INDs, however, must include the following basic elements: 1) a detailed cover sheet; 2) a table of contents; 3) an introductory statement and general investigative plan; 4) an investigator's brochure, except in the case of sponsor-investigator applications (i.e., where the investigator herself or himself is the sponsor); 5) a set of comprehensive investigative protocols; 6) information on the proposed drug's chemistry, manufacturing, and controls; 7) pharmacology and toxicology information; 8) a summary of previous human experience with the drug; and 9) any additional information FDA deems necessary.

An IND includes:

- *information on the study drug itself*
- *information on the proposed clinical investigation*

Thus, the IND covers two basic categories of information: information on the study drug itself, and information on the proposed clinical investigation. As to the study drug, the sponsor must provide the pharmacological and toxicological data upon which the sponsor concluded it was reasonably safe to propose clinical trials involving humans. The IND also must include information describing the manufacturing and control of the study drug, as well as comprehensive information on the drug's chemical composition, structural formula, proposed dosage form, and proposed route of administration. Information on any prior human experience with the drug also is required, including any relevant foreign experience, as well as any history of the drug's being withdrawn from investigation or marketing.

As to the information on the proposed investigation, the application must include proposed study protocols, with varying levels of detail depending on the phase of the clinical trial being undertaken. Generally, protocols must identify the objectives and purpose of the study; names and qualifications of investigators; patient selection criteria; study design and methodologies, and the study's measurement criteria, including clinical or laboratory monitoring. The IND also must identify the person(s) with overall responsibility for monitoring the study, as well as outside contract research organizations.

In addition, the application must include a detailed "investigative plan" addressing, among other things, the rationale behind the planned clinical research, an outline of the proposed approach, the types of clinical trials to be conducted, an estimate as to the number of patients involved, and a discussion of any significant anticipated patient risks based on toxicological data. Further, the application must contain a commitment from the sponsor to conduct clinical trials under the supervision of an Institutional Review Board (IRB), and to follow all applicable rules and regulations, including those pertaining to informed consent.

Informed Consent and Institutional Review Boards

A fundamental goal of regulatory requirements for informed consent and review of clinical studies by IRBs is to ensure the protection of the rights and welfare of human subjects. FDA investigators regularly check for compliance with these regulations and an institution or sponsor's noncompliance can result in the temporary suspension or formal termination of a clinical study, as well as other administrative sanctions or legal proceedings.

Potential participants in clinical trials must be informed adequately about risks, possible benefits, and alternative courses of treatment before making the decision to participate in the experimental research.

The thrust of the informed consent regulations, which are codified at 21 C.F.R. Part 50, is to ensure that patient participation in clinical trials is entirely voluntary and knowing. Potential participants in clinical trials must be informed adequately about risks, possible benefits, and alternative courses of treatment *before* making the decision to participate in the experimental research. Such consent must be documented, and research subjects cannot be forced to waive any potential future claims for negligence against the study's investigator, sponsor, or institution. Furthermore, when prisoners are used as research subjects, additional restrictions and requirements exist to ensure truly voluntary participation in light of the inherently more coercive prison environment.

The regulations pertaining to IRBs, codified at 21 C.F.R. Part 56, require IRB oversight of a clinical study in order to ensure that the rights of the human test subjects are adequately protected, while, at the same time, rigorous scientific and medical standards are maintained. The IRB is essentially a committee designated by an institution (e.g., university medical center, contract research organization, or hospital) to review biomedical research involving human subjects. The IRB must approve a proposed clinical study before the study can begin and must continue to monitor the research as it progresses. IRB approval of a proposed clinical study can be given only if certain conditions are met, including that the proposed research appropriately minimizes patient risks and that such risks are reasonable in relation to anticipated benefits.

The regulations also set up relatively detailed requirements for an IRB's internal "housekeeping." Thus, the IRB must establish written procedures detailing, among other things, its review processes and criteria, and its procedures designed to ensure the prompt reporting of changes in ongoing clinical research or in informed consent documents. Moreover, IRB members must come from sufficiently diverse disciplines to enable the IRB to review the study not only in terms of specific research issues but also in terms of the study's acceptability under community and legal standards, as well as professional conduct and practice norms. The IRB also must keep detailed records of its activities; those records are subject to FDA inspection.

The Phases of a Clinical Investigation

Clinical investigations are typically divided into three phases, which often overlap in practice.

Clinical investigations are typically divided into three phases.

Phase 1 studies ordinarily involve the initial administration of the drug to a small number (typically twenty to eighty) of healthy test subjects or patients. Such studies are designed to determine the metabolism and pharmacologic actions of the drug in humans and the side effects associated with increasing doses, and, if possible, to gain early evidence on effectiveness. The drug's sponsor also must derive sufficient pharmacological data from Phase 1 trials to devise appropriate Phase 2 studies. In the case of more toxic drugs intended to treat serious or life-threatening conditions, such as many cancer drugs, Phase I trials may take place in patients with the target condition.

Phase 2 investigations involve an expanded patient group (up to several hundred patients) afflicted with the disease or condition being studied.

The thrust of Phase 2 trials is to obtain evidence of the drug's effectiveness against the targeted disease, to explore further risk and side effect issues, and to confirm preliminary data regarding optimal dosage ranges. At the end of Phase 2 trials, the sponsor typically meets with FDA to discuss specific regulatory or scientific concerns the sponsor must address in designing and conducting its Phase 3 studies. While such conferences are technically optional, they are almost always advisable as they can provide an invaluable opportunity to address agency concerns that might otherwise impede review of the application.

The sponsor may request a formal meeting with responsible FDA officials to reach a binding agreement on the size or design of clinical or bioequivalence trials. After testing begins, such agreements may be changed only with the written consent of the sponsor or if the director of the responsible FDA division issues a written decision identifying a substantial scientific issue "essential to determining the safety or effectiveness of the drug" that would not otherwise have been addressed.

Phase 3 clinical trials may commence, with appropriate notification to FDA, once the drug's sponsor has gathered preliminary evidence that suggests the drug may be effective. Such studies may involve up to several thousand patients. They frequently take place at multiple locations and involve more clinical investigators than in earlier phases. The primary goal of a Phase 3 clinical trial, or "pivotal" trial, is to collect the data necessary to meet the safety and efficacy standards required for FDA approval.

Obligations of Sponsors and Investigators:

- *ensuring patient safety*
- *ensuring appropriate scientific conduct*
- *keeping FDA informed*
- *selecting appropriate investigators*
- *adhering to proper protocols and practices*
- *recordkeeping*
- *shipping and handling of product*
- *reporting any adverse event*
- *obtaining valid informed consent*

Obligations of Clinical Sponsors and Investigators

Throughout all phases of a clinical investigation, both the sponsor of the study and the individual investigators have responsibilities and duties designed to ensure patient safety as well as the integrity and soundness of the data derived from the investigation. Noncompliance with these requirements may result in FDA regulatory actions including warning letters, exclusion of a disqualified investigator's study results, suspension of an IND or NDA predicated on discredited study data, or even civil or criminal proceedings.

The study sponsor is responsible for ensuring patient safety and appropriate scientific conduct, and has the primary responsibility to keep FDA informed of the progress of the study and of any significant safety-related events. The sponsor also bears responsibility for selecting appropriate investigators, ensuring adherence to proper protocols and practices, recordkeeping, and shipping and handling of investigational product. In addition, sponsors are responsible for compliance with regulations on informed consent and IRBs.

The sponsor also bears responsibility for reporting to FDA and to clinical investigators any adverse safety events that occur during clinical trials. If the adverse event suggests a significant life-threatening hazard or side effect that has not been sufficiently identified in the written investigative materials accompanying the study, the sponsor must report it to FDA and to investigators within fifteen calendar days of receiving the information. A telephone report to the agency within seven calendar days is required if an unexpectedly life-threatening or fatal event has occurred.

Under the Food and Drug Administration Amendments Act of 2007 (FDAAA), the sponsor is required to post on a public registry certain summary information about any clinical trial for a serious or life-threatening disease, other than a Phase I investigation, that was underway as of December 26, 2007 (the effective date of the requirement), no later than that date. For any such trial started after that date, the sponsor is required to post the summary information within twenty-one days after the first patient is enrolled in the trial. For clinical trials that are not for a serious or life-threatening disease and that were underway as of September 27, 2007 (the date of enactment of the FDAAA), the posting requirement goes into effect on September 27, 2008. Sponsors are required to certify to FDA that they have complied with these requirements at the time they submit any "application" under section 505 of the FDCA (for drugs) or section 351 of the Public Health Service Act (for biologics). As of this writing the precise scope of this certification requirement was still under debate, although it appears clear that the requirement will apply at least to the submission of NDAs, BLAs, and efficacy supplements. Finally, starting on September 27, 2008, the registry database will be expanded to include certain basic information about clinical trial results for approved drugs and biologics; this results portion of the database is to be further expanded over the subsequent two years through a rulemaking.

Clinical investigators are required, among other things, to obtain valid informed consent from any participating subjects, to follow study protocols, to ensure that other study personnel follow the required protocols, and to report significant adverse events. An investigator may be disqualified from conducting studies for repeated violations of the regulations, or may be subject to further administrative, civil, or criminal proceedings. If an investigator disqualification occurs, the study's sponsor will be required to establish that the study's overall viability is not threatened by the investigator's misconduct. Investigator misconduct also may result in an FDA determination that the IND can no longer remain in effect, or, in extreme cases, that an NDA predicated upon the investigator's data must be withdrawn.

The Food and Drug Administration Amendments Act of 2007 requires a sponsor to post on a public registry certain summary information about any clinical trial for a serious or life-threatening disease, other than a Phase 1 investigation.

FDA Oversight: Clinical Holds

Through the imposition of a "clinical hold," FDA may forestall a proposed clinical investigation or suspend an existing one. A clinical hold can be imposed for a number of reasons, including an unreasonable and significant risk to patients, the use of improperly qualified investigators, a deficient or disregarded investigative protocol, or any other serious deficiency in an IND or a particular clinical trial. FDA must communicate the imposition of a clinical hold by telephone or other form of rapid communication, and must provide the drug sponsor, within thirty days, with a written explanation of the basis for the clinical hold. As a general rule, until the agency's consent to lift a clinical hold is obtained, any clinical trial or trials subject to the hold cannot commence or resume. Under the Food and Drug Administration Modernization Act of 1997 (FDAMA), a sponsor faced with a clinical hold may submit a written request to FDA that the hold be removed. FDA must respond to such a request in writing within thirty days.

IND Withdrawal

As with the imposition of a clinical hold, FDA can halt further use or distribution of an investigational drug through withdrawal or suspension of an IND. Similar concerns, such as undue patient risk or serious deficiencies in the application or the clinical protocol, trigger both types of agency action, with withdrawal obviously reserved for the more serious cases.

Where the continuation of a clinical study poses, in FDA's judgment, an immediate and substantial danger to human subjects, the agency may order immediate termination of an IND, subject to possible reinstatement. Where no such immediate risk is present, however, if FDA proposes to withdraw an IND, the agency will notify the sponsor in writing and provide thirty days to submit any corrections or explanations. The sponsor's failure to respond within the specified time frame results in the termination of the IND. The sponsor, however, may request a formal hearing if FDA refuses to accept a submitted correction or explanation.

The New Drug Application: Standards and Procedures

Once Phase 3 clinical trials are completed, the applicant prepares to submit its NDA. This preparation process ordinarily includes a pre-NDA meeting with FDA staff, with the goal of helping to ensure that the application will contain all required data.

Data requirements in a NDA cover seven broad categories.

Contents of the New Drug Application

The regulatory requirements that govern the contents of an NDA, codified at 21 C.F.R. Part 314, are intended to give FDA enough information to make a meaningful evaluation of the drug. Specific NDA data requirements are lengthy and detailed, covering seven broad categories: 1) preclinical data, such as animal and laboratory studies, evaluating the drug's pharmacology and toxicology; 2) human pharmacokinetic and bioavailability data; 3) clinical data (i.e., data obtained from administering the drug to humans, which must include adequate tests to demonstrate that the drug is safe under the proposed conditions of use, as well as "substantial evidence" that the drug is effective under such proposed conditions); 4) a description of proposed methods by which the drug will be manufactured, processed, and packed; 5) a description of the drug product and drug substance; 6) a list of each patent claiming the drug, drug product, or method of use, or a statement that there are no relevant patents making such claims; and 7) the drug's proposed labeling. The applicant also must provide a summary of the application, concluding with a presentation of both the risks and benefits of the new drug. In addition, the NDA must contain various regulatory certifications covering such matters as financial ties between the sponsor and clinical investigators and compliance with clinical trial registry requirements.

Unless an application is publicly disclosed or acknowledged, FDA will keep the application's existence a secret until the agency sends an approval letter. Similarly, the contents of an application generally are kept secret until an approval letter is sent, even if the existence of the application is known. Following approval of the NDA, material in the application that contains trade secrets or confidential commercial information continues to be protected from disclosure, at least in theory. FDAAA added the requirement that FDA must publish on its website within forty-eight hours of approval of a new drug or biologic a summary review documenting conclusions about the drug from all reviewing disciplines, noting any critical issues or disagreements that arose during the review and how they were resolved. In addition, FDA must publish on its website, within thirty days of approval, the action package for approval of any new drug or biologic that is a new chemical entity; for any other new drug or biologic, the action package must be published within thirty days of receipt of the third Freedom of Information Act request for the package.

Risk Evaluation and Mitigation Strategy

FDA may require a sponsor to include a REMS in its NDA when the agency deems it "necessary to ensure that the benefits of the drug outweigh the risks of the drug."

An additional element that may be required as part of an NDA is the risk evaluation and mitigation strategy (REMS), as provided under the FDAAA. FDA may require a sponsor to include a REMS in its NDA when the agency deems it "necessary to ensure that the benefits of the drug outweigh the risks of the drug."

A REMS must contain, at a minimum, a timetable for submission to FDA by the sponsor of REMS assessments at set intervals (eighteen months, three years, and in the seventh year after approval), subject to possible variations in frequency and possible elimination of the assessment requirement altogether if, after the initial three-year period, FDA determines that the drug's serious risks have been adequately identified and are being adequately managed (FDCA § 505-1(d)). A sponsor may also submit an assessment of an existing REMS to FDA at any time, along with a proposed modification of the REMS. In addition, a sponsor must submit a REMS assessment (which may include a proposal for modification of the strategy):

- when submitting a supplemental application for a prescription drug for a new indication;
- when specifically required under the REMS;
- as specified by FDA if the agency determines that new safety or efficacy information indicates that any REMS element should be modified or added; or
- within fifteen days if the Secretary of the Department of Health and Human Services (DHHS) determines there may be cause to withdraw the drug's NDA under section 505(e) of the act.

In addition to the required periodic assessments, a REMS may also be required to provide for the distribution of a Medication Guide or a patient package insert to each patient when the drug is dispensed if FDA determines that such a requirement may help "mitigate a serious risk of the drug." A communication plan aimed at healthcare professionals may also be required if FDA determines that such a plan may support implementation of an element of the REMS.

A more stringent set of REMS elements may be required if FDA determines them necessary to "assure safe use of the drug, because of its inherent toxicity or potential harmfulness." These elements may require:

- that healthcare professionals who prescribe or dispense the drug have particular training or experience or are specially certified;
- that the drug be dispensed only in specified settings such as hospitals;
- that patient testing, monitoring, and/or enrollment in a registry be required in connection with dispensing the drug.

Whenever a REMS assessment is submitted, FDA must initiate discussion with the sponsor within sixty days, except for assessments required because the Secretary of DHHS has determined there may be cause to withdraw the NDA, in which case such discussions must begin within thirty days after submission. For proposed REMS modifications submitted as part of an NDA or supplement, FDA must describe the final REMS or any modification to the REMS, as applicable, in the action letter on the application. For proposed REMS modifications submitted as part of a REMS assessment, FDA must describe the final REMS, in most cases, within ninety days of the beginning of the required discussions with the sponsor. Detailed dispute resolution processes apply if FDA and the sponsor disagree on a REMS or REMS modification.

Generic drugs referencing a drug approved with a REMS are subject to all elements of the REMS except the requirement to submit assessments and proposed modifications. For those REMS elements involving restrictions on distribution and use, the generic drug applicant and the reference drug applicant are to use a single, shared system, unless FDA determines that the burdens of such a system outweigh the benefits, or that any aspect of the REMS elements in question is patent-protected or proprietary and the ANDA applicant is not able to obtain a license. In this connection, the law prohibits an NDA sponsor from using any REMS element required to assure safe use in order to "block or delay" approval of an ANDA.

FDA Will Refuse to File an NDA if:

- *it is incomplete*
- *it is in improper form*
- *it omits critical data*
- *it fails to make required certifications*

Submitting and Filing the New Drug Application

When an NDA arrives at FDA, the agency considers it to be "received," not "filed." The application is considered "filed" only when formally accepted for review by FDA. The agency must determine whether or not to file an application within sixty days of its receipt. If no grounds for refusing to file the application exist, FDA must file it; the filing date will be sixty days after the date of receipt.

FDA will accept an application for filing only if it is sufficiently complete to permit a substantive review. FDA has the authority to refuse to file an application on several grounds, for example: 1) if the application is incomplete or in improper form, or omits data critical to assessing safety, efficacy, or adequate directions for use; or 2) if the application fails to make required certifications regarding how the preclinical and clinical trials were conducted.

Although its refusal to file (RTF) authority sounds quite broad, FDA typically uses that authority only for obvious deficiencies in the application, not in cases that involve "matters of subtle judgment." The agency's RTF guidance document states: "It is important . . . that [RTF] be reserved for applications . . . plainly inadequate, non-reviewable without major repair, or that make review unreasonably difficult." Applications that contain deficiencies this severe will be subject to refusal, because FDA believes that accepting applications in need of extensive repair is unfair to new drug sponsors whose submissions were complete and properly formatted. (One notable exception to the normal requirement for a complete NDA submission is the category of "fast-track" drugs, discussed below. FDAMA explicitly permits FDA to review applications for fast-track drugs on a "rolling" basis.)

There are three circumstances where FDA is especially likely to use its RTF power: 1) omission of a required section of the NDA, or presentation of a section in so haphazard a manner as to render it incomplete on its face; 2) clear failure to include evidence of effectiveness that can meet the statutory and regulatory standards; and 3) omission of critical data, information, or analyses needed to evaluate safety and effectiveness, or to provide adequate directions for use. Because the agency's RTF power is discretionary, it can choose not to use this procedure for particularly critical drugs even if specific grounds for invoking it exist. In practice, potential RTF issues usually are addressed and resolved before the NDA is submitted. The pre-NDA meeting often provides a forum for this process. (Because the ANDA process does not typically involve pre-application meetings between the sponsor and FDA, RTFs are more common for ANDAs.)

If FDA chooses to use its RTF authority, it will notify the applicant, which can then request an informal conference. After the conference, the applicant can request that FDA file the application, with or without amendments to correct the deficiencies. The agency then will file the application "over protest." As a practical matter, however, an applicant has little or no incentive to ask the agency to do this. If FDA believes the application contains deficiencies egregious enough to warrant an RTF response, there is little chance of subsequent favorable FDA action on the application. Therefore, requests to file an application "over protest" are extremely rare.

Substantive Standards for Review

FDA reviewers must find that an application meets several substantive requirements before the agency will approve the NDA. The most basic requirement is that the drug be both "safe" and "effective." These words have specialized meanings in the new drug approval context.

"Safe" and "effective" have special meanings in the new drug approval context.

The FDCA, as enacted in 1938, did not require a sponsor to address efficacy as part of its application to market a new drug—only safety. The Drug Amendments of 1962 added the requirement that a new drug must be supported by "substantial evidence" that the drug will have the effect it purports to have under the indicated conditions of use. "Substantial evidence" is defined in the law as evidence from adequate and well-controlled clinical studies. Although FDA has traditionally required two independent pivotal studies to demonstrate efficacy, FDAMA provided that one "adequate and well-controlled" study accompanied by confirmatory evidence could constitute substantial evidence of effectiveness if FDA determines, "based on relevant science," that data from the study are sufficient to establish effectiveness.

In addition, a drug may not be approved unless there are "adequate tests by all methods reasonably applicable to show whether or not such drug is safe for use under the conditions prescribed, recommended, or suggested in the proposed labeling thereof." In applying this standard, FDA recognizes that there is no such thing as an absolutely safe drug; in addition to the benefits it provides, every drug will present some risks. Therefore, FDA's safety assessment requires consideration of a product's efficacy. As the agency said in its 1995 statement on the efficacy standard, "FDA weighs the product's demonstrated effectiveness against its risks to determine whether the benefits outweigh the risks." This risk/benefit analysis takes account of information such as the seriousness of the disease, the adequacy of any existing remedies, and adverse reaction and any other safety data.

In addition to evidence of safety and effectiveness, there also must be adequate manufacturing controls in place before FDA will approve a drug. In particular, the methods used in, and the controls and facilities used for, manufacturing, processing, packing, and holding the drug substance and finished product must comply with FDA's current good manufacturing practice (cGMP) requirements, and must be adequate to maintain the drug's purity, quality, strength, identity, and bioavailability. A pre-approval inspection of the applicant's facilities typically will be conducted to verify compliance with these requirements.

An additional prerequisite to approval is that the drug's labeling must meet applicable statutory and regulatory requirements. The labeling cannot be false or misleading, and must comply with general requirements concerning content and form, including such matters as presentation of clinical data, warnings, and dosage and administration information. The labeling review is usually the final step in the approval process.

Under the Pediatric Research Equity Act of 2003 (PREA) (as re-authorized by the FDAAA in 2007), an NDA or biologic license application (BLA) for a new drug or biologic must include an assessment of the safety and efficacy of the product in all relevant pediatric subpopulations (as defined by FDA in consultation with the sponsor), as well as data to support dosing and administration for each pediatric subpopulation for which the product is to be deemed safe and effective. These requirements may be deferred for various reasons, including an FDA finding that the product is ready for approval for use by adults before pediatric studies are complete. The requirement may also be waived partially or entirely on a variety of grounds, including that 1) the necessary studies are impossible or highly impractical; 2) there is evidence strongly suggesting that the product would be ineffective or unsafe in children; 3) the product does not represent a meaningful benefit over existing therapies for children and is not likely to be used in a substantial number of children; or 4) (for a partial waiver applicable to a specific age group) reasonable efforts to produce a pediatric formulation necessary for that age group have failed. FDA also has authority under PREA to require pediatric assessments for marketed products if FDA finds that 1) the product is used in a substantial number of children for the labeled indications and adequate pediatric labeling could confer a benefit on pediatric patients; 2) there is reason to believe the product would represent a meaningful therapeutic benefit over existing therapies for pediatric patients for one or more claimed indications; or 3) the absence of adequate pediatric labeling could pose a risk to pediatric patients.

Advisory Committees
Important issues raised by an NDA (or BLA) may be reviewed by FDA advisory committees made up of outside experts.

Advisory Committee Review

Although the primary review of an NDA is carried out by the appropriate division within the Center for Drug Evaluation and Research (CDER), FDA may also seek the advice of its expert advisory committees. These committees may review studies of the drug under consideration, as well as its proposed labeling, and provide recommendations on issues pertaining to approval of the drug. Each review division within CDER has access to one or more advisory committees. Advisory committees are composed primarily of prominent research and clinical specialists, but also must include a representative of consumer interests, a representative of the drug manufacturing industry not directly affected by the matter before the panel, and at least two specialists in the disease or condition for which the drug under review is to be indicated.

Advisory committees respond to specific questions posed by the agency regarding safety and efficacy, and evaluate whether additional studies are needed to support approval. FDA typically has been more likely to use advisory committee review if the new drug is particularly significant therapeutically, or if review of the drug involves evaluation of complex scientific data. The FDAAA now requires FDA to refer any BLA or any NDA for a new chemical entity to an advisory committee for review prior to approval or to summarize in the action letter why it did not do so. In addition to advisory committees, FDA also has discretion to consult outside expert reviewers from the scientific community. Advisory committee and outside review recommendations, however, are not binding on the agency. Under FDAMA, FDA must make a final decision on a matter reviewed by an advisory committee and notify the affected parties, or explain why no decision has been reached, within ninety days after the advisory committee's recommendation.

The New Drug Application: FDA Action and Time Frames

Note: In July 2008, FDA published a final rule that substantially modified the system for reviewing and acting upon NDAs, including the replacement of the former "approvable" and "nonapprovable" letters with a single "complete response" letter (Applications for Approval to Market a New Drug; Complete Response Letter; Amendments to Unapproved Applications, 73 Fed. Reg. 39,588 (July 10, 2008)). The following section reflects the modified system in place starting on August 11, 2008, the effective date of the new rule. Readers seeking information on the previous NDA review system should consult prior editions of this book.

The FDCA provides that within 180 days after the filing of an NDA "or such additional period as may be agreed" between FDA and the applicant, FDA must either approve the application or give the applicant notice of an opportunity for a hearing as to whether the application is approvable (essentially, a procedural step required before FDA may formally reject an NDA). Because FDA rarely is in a position to reach a final yes-or-no decision on an NDA within 180 days after it is filed, the agency has created a procedural framework that allows it to engage in multiple rounds of review of an NDA that may stretch on much longer than 180 days without running afoul of the statutory deadline.

First, as described above, FDA has by regulation established a sixty-day period following actual receipt of the NDA during which the agency decides if the application is sufficiently complete to allow it be "filed." Only after this determination is made does the statutory "filing clock" start to run.

While the filing step effectively extends the 180-day statutory deadline by sixty days, even this additional amount of time is usually insufficient for FDA to reach a final decision on an application. Accordingly, the primary mechanism by which FDA ensures itself the timing flexibility it needs to complete its review of an application without violating the statutory deadline is to rely on the "or such additional period as may be agreed" language of the statute to create a system in which the NDA applicant in effect agrees to allow the review of the application to continue until FDA is either ready to approve it or makes clear that the application is not approvable in its current form, in which case the applicant typically withdraws the application on its own. (Situations in which an applicant forces FDA to provide a formal hearing on approvability, as the statute contemplates, are quite rare.)

This mechanism in turn is premised on the concept of the review cycle, formerly referred to in FDA regulations as the "review clock." FDA regulations state that within 180 days of the receipt of an NDA, FDA will review it and send the applicant either an approval letter or a "complete response" letter describing the deficiencies that must be satisfactorily addressed before the application can be approved. This 180-day period is called the "initial review cycle." Significantly, however, the regulations also provide that the initial review cycle "may be adjusted by mutual agreement between FDA and an applicant or as . . . the result of a major amendment" (amendments to the NDA are discussed below).

A key vehicle for expressing applicants' agreement to extending the initial review cycle is FDA's performance goals under the Prescription Drug User Fee Act (PDUFA), which are negotiated between industry and FDA and formally presented to Congress. First enacted in 1992 with the intent of providing additional resources for FDA drug review and accelerating drug review times, PDUFA is re-authorized on a five-year cycle, with the most recent re-authorization taking place in 2007 as part of the FDAAA. PDUFA applies only to NDAs and BLAs, not to generic drug applications.

Under PDUFA, FDA collects a substantial user fee for each NDA (and BLA) it receives, with certain minor exceptions. In exchange, FDA commits to the PDUFA performance goals, which provide for specific review times for NDAs and BLAs. Though technically not legally binding, these performance goals represent FDA's side of a three-way bargain under which industry agrees to pay the user fees and Congress authorizes FDA to collect the fees and use them for drug reviews and related tasks. As such, the performance goals are taken very seriously by the agency.

In its PDUFA performance goals under the 2007 re-authorization, FDA committed to review and act on 90 percent of standard original NDA and BLA submissions (i.e., submissions for drugs similar to existing treatments) within ten months of receipt, and 90 percent of priority original NDA and BLA submissions (i.e., submissions for drugs that represent significant advances over existing treatments) within six months of receipt. Thus, by signing on to the PDUFA performance goals, industry has effectively agreed to an extension of the initial review cycle for standard NDA and BLA applications from six months to ten months.

As noted above, at the conclusion of the initial review cycle, FDA will send the applicant either an approval letter or a complete response letter. Because outright approval at the end of the initial review cycle is quite rare, in the vast majority of cases the applicant will receive a complete response letter outlining the additional steps that need to taken before the application can be approved. Upon receipt of a complete response letter, the applicant must either resubmit the application, addressing the deficiencies noted in the letter; withdraw the application;

or ask FDA to provide an opportunity for a hearing on the approvability of the application. Under FDA regulations, the applicant who receives a complete response letter automatically agrees to an extension of the statutory review deadline until it takes any of these actions. Failure to take any of the specified actions within one year after the issuance of a complete response letter will be considered a request by the applicant to withdraw the application, unless the applicant has requested an extension. If FDA considers the applicant's failure to take action within one year to be a request to withdraw the application, the agency will give the applicant written notice and a thirty-day period in which to explain why the application should not be withdrawn and to request an extension of time to resubmit it.

Resubmissions of an application following receipt of a complete response letter fall into two categories. A Class 1 resubmission is one that contains relatively minor information such as final printed labeling, draft labeling, certain safety or stability updates, postmarketing study commitments, assay validation data, final release testing on lots used to support approval, or minor re-analyses of previously submitted data. Under FDA's regulations a Class 1 resubmission constitutes an agreement by the applicant to start a new two-month review cycle beginning on the date FDA receives the resubmission. A Class 2 resubmission is one that includes any item not specified as part of a Class 1 resubmission, including any item that would require presentation to an advisory committee. A Class 2 resubmission constitutes an agreement by the applicant to start a new six-month review cycle beginning on the date FDA receives the resubmission.

Submission by the applicant of an amendment to a pending application can also affect the review timelines. If the applicant submits a "major amendment" within three months of the end of a review cycle, FDA's regulations state that this constitutes an agreement by the applicant to extend the review cycle by three months. Submission of a major amendment prior to that time will not extend the review cycle, although FDA may, at its discretion, defer review of such an amendment until the next review cycle. Submission of an amendment that is not major at any time during a review cycle will not extend the cycle, although FDA also may defer review of such an amendment to the next cycle. Although the prior version of FDA's regulations gave an example of a major amendment (an amendment that contains significant new data from a previously unreported study or detailed new analyses of previously submitted data), the agency explicitly refused to provide any definition, explanation, or example of a major amendment in its current regulations, leaving itself with almost unrestricted discretion to define an amendment as major or not, and therefore with a maximum of control over the timing of NDA review.

The Postmarketing Period

An applicant's responsibilities with respect to its NDA do not cease upon approval. The postapproval stage brings with it its own set of obligations for the NDA holder. Of particular note, FDAAA gave expanded FDA powers over such areas as safety-related labeling changes and the conduct of postmarketing studies.

Changes Affecting an Approved Application

Changes affecting an approved drug are grouped into three categories, each of which carries different procedural requirements. For some changes, the sponsor must submit a supplement to its NDA, and FDA must approve that supplement, before the sponsor can implement the desired changes. This is a "prior approval" supplement. A second group of changes also requires supplementing the NDA, but the sponsor can implement the changes before FDA approves the supplement. These supplements are commonly referred to as "change being effected" supplements. A third category of changes need only be listed in the annual report that the sponsor must file with FDA concerning the drug covered by the NDA.

Prior approval supplements are required for any change to the drug or its manufacturing processes, equipment, or facilities that has "a substantial potential to have an adverse effect" on the drug's identity, strength, quality, purity or potency as these factors may relate to its safety or effectiveness. On the manufacturing side, this may include changes in the drug's qualitative or quantitative formulation or approved specifications; changes that may affect the sterility assurance of the drug; and changes in the synthesis of the drug substance that may affect its impurity profile or its physical, chemical, or biological properties. All changes in labeling—including new indications, dosing regimens, populations, and the like—require a prior approval supplement, with limited exceptions that will be discussed below.

"Changes being effected" supplements are utilized for changes with only a moderate potential for an adverse effect on the performance of the drug. These supplements fall into two subcategories. The first subcategory requires the sponsor to wait thirty days after submitting the supplement before starting distribution of the drug product incorporating the change in question—the so-called "CBE-30." CBE-30s are to be used, for instance, for a change in the drug's container-closure system that does not affect its quality, or for relaxation of an acceptance criterion or deletion of a test to comply with an official compendium that is consistent with FDA statutory and regulatory requirements. When an applicant submits a CBE-30, it may not distribute the drug incorporating the change in question if within the thirty-day period following submission

FDA informs it that the change requires prior approval or that required information is missing from the supplement. For the second subcategory of CBE changes, the applicant may begin distribution of the affected drug product immediately upon receipt by FDA of the supplement. These CBEs are often referred to as CBE-0s. CBE-0s may be used for changes involving addition to a specification or changes in methods or controls to provide increased assurance that the drug will have the characteristics it purports to possess, or a change in labeling that adds or strengthens a contraindication, warning, precaution, or adverse reaction; adds or strengthens dosage and administration information to increase safe use of the product; or deletes false or misleading information.

Finally, changes in conditions with only a minimal potential for an adverse effect on the drug's performance need only be described in the annual report submitted by the applicant. Examples of such changes include editorial or minor changes in labeling, deletion or reduction of an ingredient that only affects the product's color, and changes in the drug's container size or shape without changes in the closure system (for nonsterile solid dosage forms).

Postmarketing Safety-Related Label Changes

A key FDAAA provision aimed at strengthening FDA's safety oversight powers provides FDA with new authority to compel a sponsor to make safety-related changes in drug labeling after approval of the drug. Under this new authority, if FDA becomes aware of "new safety information" about a serious drug risk that the agency believes should be included in the drug's labeling, the agency must promptly notify the sponsor. The sponsor then has thirty days to either submit a labeling supplement reflecting the new safety information or explain why it does not believe a labeling change is warranted. If the agency disagrees with the sponsor's conclusion, it must initiate discussions with the sponsor that may not take more than thirty days from the due date of the sponsor's response, unless extended by the agency. Within fifteen days of the conclusion of these discussions, FDA may issue an order requiring the sponsor to make those labeling changes the FDA deems appropriate to address the new safety information. Violations of any of these requirements by the sponsor will subject the sponsor to misbranding charges and potential civil money penalties.

Adverse Reaction Reporting

"Adverse drug experiences" are somewhat circularly defined under FDA's regulations as any adverse events associated with the use of a drug in humans. An applicant holding an approved NDA must promptly review reports of adverse drug experiences associated with its drug, regardless of the source from which such reports are obtained. If a reaction is both serious (e.g., fatal, life threatening, or permanently disabling) and unexpected (not listed in labeling, or differing from reactions listed in the labeling due to greater severity or specificity), it must be reported to FDA in an "alert report" within fifteen calendar days of the applicant's receipt of the information. All adverse reactions that are not serious and unexpected must be reported at quarterly intervals for three years after an application is approved, and annually thereafter.

Withdrawal
Although FDA rarely invokes its statutory authority to withdraw NDAs, there are several circumstances under which it can initiate such action.

Withdrawal

Although FDA rarely invokes its statutory authority to withdraw NDAs, there are several circumstances under which it can initiate such action. As might be expected, the conditions that can trigger NDA withdrawal generally relate to serious problems with the drug or the application. For instance, FDA can withdraw an NDA if the drug is unsafe for use under the conditions of use for which the application was approved. Similarly, FDA can use its withdrawal authority if new clinical evidence shows that the drug is not safe under approved conditions, or if the drug is not effective. Additionally, FDA can seek withdrawal of an application if the drug's labeling is false or misleading, or if there are inadequate assurances that the drug's quality, strength, and purity are as claimed. The agency also can withdraw an NDA if the sponsor fails to file required patent information in a timely manner, or if the NDA contains false statements of material fact.

If FDA seeks to withdraw an NDA, usually it must give the applicant notice and the opportunity for a hearing. If the drug in question presents an "imminent hazard," however, the Secretary of DHHS can summarily suspend approval of the application and give the applicant the opportunity for an expedited hearing. The Secretary cannot delegate the authority to summarily suspend NDAs in this fashion, but can and has delegated to FDA the authority to hold the expedited hearing. In practice, FDA rarely invokes its authority to withdraw or summarily suspend NDAs.

Phase IV
After a new drug is approved, FDA often requires additional studies to obtain more information.

Phase IV Studies

Although clinical studies are a prerequisite to approval, they also are performed after approval as "Phase IV" studies. Such studies can be designed to: 1) obtain additional safety data, 2) obtain additional efficacy data, 3) detect new uses for or abuses of a drug, or 4) determine effectiveness for labeled indications under conditions of widespread usage.

There are at least two reasons FDA may be interested in Phase IV studies. First, such studies allow FDA to grant approval of a new drug on the condition that the applicant complete studies that shed additional light on the drug's safety and efficacy subsequent to approval. Phase IV studies also can be used to facilitate FDA's postapproval monitoring of an approved drug.

The FDAAA added to FDA's postmarketing study toolkit new authority to outright require a sponsor to complete a previously agreed postmarketing study or to impose a new requirement to conduct and complete a postmarketing study on a marketed drug either to 1) assess a known serious risk related to use of the drug; 2) assess signals of serious risk related to use of the drug; or 3) identify an unexpected serious risk when available data indicate the potential for such risk. This new authority comes with several restrictions, including that FDA may require a postmarketing study only if adverse event reporting and active surveillance would not be sufficient to fulfill the purpose of the study, and that the required study may take the form of a clinical trial only if a less burdensome kind of study (e.g., a patient registry or an epidemiological study) would not be adequate. Failure to comply with a postmarketing study requirement imposed under this new authority carries with it a potential misbranding charge and substantial civil monetary penalties.

The three main statutory market protections are:
- *the patent extension provisions;*
- *statutory exclusivity for new chemical entities and approvals requiring new clinical studies; and*
- *exclusivity for orphan drugs.*

Marketing Protection

An issue virtually every drug sponsor faces at some point is what kind of market protection, if any, its product is eligible for, or, conversely, how its product can overcome a competitor's exclusivity in order to enter the market. There are three main statutory routes to securing market protection for qualifying new drug products outside of, or in addition to, standard patent protection: 1) the patent term extension provisions; 2) nonpatent statutory exclusivity provisions for new chemical entities and approvals requiring new clinical studies; and 3) nonpatent exclusivity for orphan drugs.

Patent Term Extension

The statutory patent term extension provision, codified at section 156 of Title 35 of the *United States Code* (U.S.C.), recognizes the reality that many pharmaceutical products receive patents long before they are approved for marketing. Because the premarketing regulatory review period may last for a large portion of the product's patent life, Congress amended the patent law as part of the 1984 amendments to the FDCA to allow extensions of a product's patent term in certain situations.

A drug is eligible for a patent term extension if its patent has not expired and has not been extended previously, and if the drug has been subject to a regulatory review period prior to commercial marketing or use. Only one patent per product is eligible for extension.

The length of the extension is based on the length of the regulatory review period. This includes a "testing period," which begins on the date the IND became effective and ends on the date the NDA was submitted, and an "approval period," which covers the time from the submission of the NDA to its approval. In determining the patent extension, each of these two periods will be reduced by: 1) any portion of the period that took place prior to the patent's issuance, and 2) any amount of time during which the applicant did not act with "due diligence" in pursuing regulatory review. After each component of the review period has been calculated and adjusted, the patent will be extended for one-half of the "testing" period and all of the "approval" period, up to a maximum of a five-year extension and a total of fourteen years of extended patent life postapproval.

A drug patent owner seeking an extension must submit an application to the Commissioner of Patents and Trademarks within sixty days of receiving NDA approval. FDA assists the Patent and Trademark Office (PTO) in reviewing the application, because only FDA has the information necessary to calculate the regulatory review period and make the due diligence determination. At the end of the review process, the PTO issues or denies the extension.

Statutory Exclusivity for New Chemical Entities and Approvals Based on New Studies

In addition to patent term extension, the FDCA contains provisions that authorize various periods of statutory exclusivity independent of a product's patent status. The goal of these exclusivity provisions is to give innovator drug companies a monetary incentive to invest in the research and testing needed to develop new products, while simultaneously affording consumers broader access to drug products by making available generic products that rely on studies conducted by an innovator company.

Under the FDCA's exclusivity provisions, if an NDA is approved for a drug containing an active ingredient never before approved under an NDA (or "new chemical entity"), then no application for a generic drug that references the drug may be submitted for five years from the date of approval of the drug. Thus, the law in this situation effectively delays generic competition for five years from NDA approval plus the time it takes FDA to review and approve the first generic application. An exception to this five-year rule allows a generic applicant to submit its application beginning four years from the date of NDA approval if that applicant is challenging a patent covering the reference drug (such patent challenges are discussed in more detail below). Another form of statutory market protection is the three years of exclusivity for an NDA or NDA supplement for a previously approved active ingredient if the application contains reports of new clinical studies essential to approval. A second applicant who wishes to market its drug sooner than these exclusivity provisions allow can always do its own clinical studies and submit a full NDA for its version of the product, instead of a generic application, although in practice few companies choose this route because of the cost involved.

Orphan Drugs
Orphan drugs are drugs for diseases that affect 200,000 people or less.

Orphan Drug Exclusivity

The goal of the Orphan Drug Act of 1983 was to motivate pharmaceutical manufacturers to develop and bring to market drugs for orphan diseases—that is, diseases thought to be too rare to attract the commercial interest of pharmaceutical manufacturers in the ordinary course of business. A "rare" disease is defined in the statute as any disease that affects fewer than 200,000 persons in the United States, or that affects more than 200,000 persons and for which there is no reasonable expectation that the manufacturer will recover from U.S. sales the cost of developing and making the drug available in the United States.

Although the Orphan Drug Act created a series of incentives for manufacturers to develop drugs for these rare diseases—including FDA assistance with clinical protocols, available grant assistance for clinical development, and a tax credit for a portion of research and development expenses—by far the most important incentive under this act is the seven-year market exclusivity awarded to the first applicant to obtain marketing approval of a designated orphan drug for a particular disease or condition. To obtain this exclusivity, the applicant must request orphan drug designation for the drug before the submission of the marketing application, and the drug must be so designated before approval of the application. Upon approval of the drug, and assuming that these conditions are met, FDA may not approve another sponsor's application for the same drug for the same disease or condition until seven years from the date of the first applicant's approval, unless: 1) the drug's orphan designation is revoked, 2) its marketing approval is withdrawn, 3) the orphan exclusivity holder consents to the approval of another applicant's product, or 4) the orphan exclusivity holder is unable to assure the availability of a sufficient quantity of the drug.

FDA's orphan drug regulations also provide that a sponsor's drug will not be blocked by a previous sponsor's orphan exclusivity, even if the two sponsors' drugs otherwise would be considered structurally the same, if the second sponsor's drug is "clinically superior" to the first sponsor's drug. Clinical superiority may be shown by greater efficacy, greater safety, or a major contribution to patient care.

Pediatric Exclusivity

Under the Best Pharmaceuticals for Children Act (BPCA), patent terms, statutory exclusivities, and orphan exclusivity are all eligible for a six-month extension (for an NDA-approved drug only) if the NDA sponsor completes a pediatric study for the drug in response to a written request from FDA. Under the 2007 re-authorization of the BPCA contained in the FDAAA, the FDA has 180 days to review studies submitted in response to a written request in order to determine whether the studies comply with the terms of the request, and that determination must be made no later than nine months prior to the expiration of any exclusivity the sponsor wishes to extend. Thus, in practice, a sponsor wishing to qualify for an extension of a particular exclusivity (patent, statutory, or orphan) now must submit its pediatric studies in response to a written request not less than fifteen months (180 days plus nine months) prior to the expiration of that exclusivity.

FDA Regulation of Drugs: Variations on the Standard Model

Non-NDA Routes to Market: Historical Development

Meeting the safety and efficacy standards required to obtain approval of an NDA entails substantial expense, effort, and expertise. These factors create significant barriers to market entry, a situation that, as in any area of economic activity, can lead to higher prices to consumers. This situation in turn sets up an inherent tension between maintaining the regulatory standards needed to protect the public health and safety, on the one hand, and mitigating the economic burdens imposed by drug prices, on the other. When the need to offer adequate financial incentives to induce companies to undertake the formidable task of new drug development is added to this mixture, the policy equation becomes complex indeed.

Since the passage of the FDCA in 1938, Congress and FDA have made periodic efforts to readjust the balance between each of these goals. Such efforts generally result in further moves to re-level the economic playing field.

"Not-New" Drugs

Before the enactment of the FDCA in 1938, there were no significant regulatory barriers to generic competition in the drug market. With the statutory establishment of the "new drug" category, however, a drug could not be marketed unless it was either "generally recognized as safe" or its NDA was allowed to become effective absent FDA disapproval, which was the standard approval process under the 1938 version of the act until the 1962 Drug Amendments added the requirement for affirmative FDA approval, as well as the substantive efficacy standard. This process was minimal by today's standards, but it was not cost-free, and as a result imposed certain barriers to entry.

Thus, to facilitate generic competition for post-1938 drugs, FDA established an informal practice whereby, on request, it would inform an interested party whether a particular drug was generally recognized as safe, and consequently not a "new drug" subject to a premarket application. The factual basis for such a "general recognition" decision was typically a history of safe marketing of the pioneer version of the drug in the United States. This policy continued under the 1962 amendments (modified to consider general recognition of both safety and efficacy), but at a slower pace, until the practice was discontinued in 1968 and all such "not new drug" letters were formally revoked by the agency.

The DESI Review examines all available data on drugs approved between 1938 and 1962 and makes recommendations as to their efficacy.

The Drug Efficacy Study Implementation Review

The 1962 Drug Amendments contained a provision for the retroactive evaluation of the efficacy of drugs approved as safe (or which had been subject to a "not new drug" letter) between 1938 and 1962. The Drug Efficacy Study Implementation (DESI) Review, established by FDA in 1968, designated the National Academy of Sciences/National Research Council to establish expert panels to review available data on all marketed post-1938 drugs, and to make recommendations as to their efficacy. FDA was then to act on those recommendations by withdrawing drugs found ineffective and by notifying potential generic manufacturers of what information would be required for approval of a generic version of a marketed drug (other than proof of safety and efficacy, which were deemed to have been established by the DESI Review panel).

In response, the agency created a new form of NDA, the ANDA, for which approval was based on sameness of active ingredients and on bioequivalence rather than on safety and efficacy data. This ANDA process for DESI drugs later was codified by statute in the 1984 drug amendments.

The "Paper NDA" Policy

As the patent terms on post-1962 drugs began to expire in the 1970s and the early 1980s, it became evident that under existing law there were no feasible means to get competing versions of approved drugs on the market without costly and repetitive testing for safety and efficacy. Because such repeat testing would unnecessarily put more human test subjects at risk, and would waste scarce clinical and agency resources, FDA sought a way to expand the concept of the DESI Review and ANDA policy to generic versions of certain post-1962 drugs. The result was the "paper NDA" policy which, although short-lived, provides a historical and conceptual bridge between the "old drug" and "general recognition" bases for generic drug marketing and the modern statutory ANDA approval process.

The paper NDA policy permitted competing versions of approved new drugs to be approved based on the submission of publicly available reports of well-controlled studies demonstrating the drug's safety and efficacy. The policy was challenged and ultimately upheld in court (*Burroughs Wellcome Co. v. Schweiker*, 649 F.2d 221 (4th Cir. 1981)). Because adequate published studies documenting safety and efficacy were available for only a few post-1962 drugs, however, and because FDA review of such paper NDAs was not significantly easier than for full NDAs, the policy made only a marginal contribution to fostering generic competition. It survives today in modified form as the "505(b)(2)" application.

Generic Drugs and the Abbreviated New Drug Application Process

Legislative Background

In the late 1970s and early 1980s Congress began to consider legislative options in response to the lack of a viable generic drug approval process for post-1962 drugs. During that time, other legislative efforts were underway to restore the part of drug patents' effective life lost due to increasingly lengthy FDA review times. In 1983, a patent term restoration bill was narrowly defeated in the House of Representatives, and it became apparent that neither an ANDA bill nor a patent term restoration bill could pass Congress independently. As a result, leaders of the generic and innovator sides of the pharmaceutical industry agreed to cooperate in crafting a bill incorporating both the ANDA mechanism sought by generic manufacturers, and patent restoration protections desired by research-based companies. The resulting legislation—the Drug Price Competition and Patent Term Restoration Act—was enacted in 1984.

The dual purposes of this legislation were to expedite the availability of safe and effective, but less expensive, generic versions of approved drugs, while simultaneously encouraging the costly research and development efforts that led to the discovery of therapeutically important new drugs. The amendments created an abbreviated process whereby a generic company could gain approval of its version of a drug without repeating the expensive and lengthy clinical trials already performed for the drug. As previously discussed, innovator companies received restoration of patent rights to compensate for the time expended in the FDA review process, as well as nonpatent exclusivity for qualifying drug products.

The 1984 amendments also provided protection for the generic drug industry in the form of a provision establishing that it is not an act of patent infringement for a nonpatent holder to make, use, or sell a patented drug during the term of the patent, as long as such activity is reasonably related to the contemplated submission of an application to FDA. This provision, which specifically overruled the early 1984 decision of the newly created Court of Appeals for the Federal Circuit in *Roche Prod., Inc. v. Bolar Pharmaceutical Co.* (733 F.2d 858 (Fed. Cir. 1984)), was necessary to allow generic applicants to have their ANDAs submitted and approved in time to begin marketing on the date of patent expiration. If the court's ruling had stood, development of ANDAs could not have begun until patent expiration. As a result, *de facto* market exclusivity would have extended well beyond the term of the patent. The protection provided by the statutory provision overruling the *Bolar* decision was counterbalanced by a provision allowing an innovator to sue an ANDA applicant upon submission of an ANDA challenging the innovator's patent.

The Statutory ANDA Requirements

The required contents of an ANDA are set forth in section 505(j) of the FDCA and in agency regulations (21 C.F.R. § 314.94). The statute requires that an ANDA contain:

- information showing that the proposed conditions of use for the drug have previously been approved for a drug that is listed by FDA as approved for safety and efficacy;
- proof that the active ingredient(s) are the same as in the listed drug;

- proof that the generic drug will use the same route of administration, dosage form, and strength as the listed drug;
- proof that the generic drug is bioequivalent to the listed reference drug;
- information showing that the proposed generic labeling is the same as the labeling approved for the listed drug, except for differences related to an approved "suitability petition";
- the basic technical information required of a full NDA, including a list of components, statement of the composition of the drug, and description of the methods and facilities used in the production of the drug;
- samples of the generic product and proposed labeling; and
- a patent certification informing FDA of the patent status of the listed reference drug relied upon by the ANDA.

Although the statutory requirements for an ANDA appear relatively straightforward on their face, many of these requirements have been the basis of contentious administrative and judicial battles.

The Prior Approval and Current Listing Requirements

Two threshold requirements for a drug to be ANDA-eligible are: 1) that the drug's active ingredient has been approved already by FDA for the conditions of use proposed in the ANDA, and 2) that nothing has changed to call into question the basis of approval of the original drug's NDA.

The 1984 amendments require FDA to publish a monthly list of all approved drugs. That publication, commonly known as the "*Orange Book*" (officially titled *Approved Drug Products And Therapeutic Equivalence Evaluations*), serves as the crucial point of reference for many aspects of the ANDA process. In particular, an ANDA may only be submitted if the drug it copies is currently listed in the *Orange Book* as a "reference" listed drug. Such a listing signifies that the drug has been approved, and that as of the date of the *Orange Book* edition consulted, the drug has not been withdrawn from the market over issues of safety or efficacy. Although it is rare for approved drugs later to be found unsafe, an approved drug is on occasion withdrawn from the market voluntarily by the manufacturer. In such cases, FDA must make a determination of whether the drug was withdrawn for safety or effectiveness reasons 1) before approving any ANDA that refers to the listed drug, 2) if any ANDAs that reference the drug have already been approved, or 3) if an interested person petitions FDA to make such a determination.

The other situation in which a current listing in the *Orange Book* is significant is when FDA withdraws approval of an NDA pursuant to FDCA section 505(e), as discussed above. This rare occurrence will prevent approval of any pending ANDA for the product and also will serve to withdraw approval of any existing approved ANDAs.

"Suitability Petitions" for Different Active Ingredient(s), Routes of Administration, Dosage Forms, and Strengths

Although a product approved under an ANDA presumptively must have the same active ingredient(s), route of administration, dosage form, and strength as the listed drug it seeks to copy, the FDCA also permits generic products to incorporate differences from those requirements where such differences ultimately will not affect the safety and efficacy of the generic product. (The potential for approval of a generic drug with a different active ingredient from the reference drug only applies to a combination drug for which the generic applicant proposes to substitute a different active ingredient for one of the active ingredients in the reference drug.)

To market a generic product with any of these differences, however, the generic applicant must first submit, and FDA must approve, an ANDA "suitability petition." FDA is required to approve any such petition unless it finds that investigations must be conducted in order to demonstrate the safety and efficacy of the generic drug in question.

Bioequivalence

A primary requirement for approval of an ANDA is that the proposed generic drug be shown to be "bioequivalent" to the innovator drug it purports to copy. For generic products that meet the bioequivalence requirement, the FDCA allows the presumption that the generic version of the drug will be as safe and as effective as the original version.

The core of the bioequivalence concept, as interpreted by FDA in regulations, is an "absence of a significant difference" in the extent to which, and the rate at which, two different drug products' active ingredients "become available at the site of drug action when administered at the same molar dose under similar conditions in an appropriately designed study." For the typical solid oral dosage form drug, this concept means that one version of the drug provides the same total and peak blood concentrations of the active ingredient as another version. FDA regulations and policy, however, provide a number of different methods for assessing bioequivalence.

FDA regulations require ANDAs to contain either 1) "evidence" of bioequivalence of the ANDA product to the listed reference drug, or 2) "information" showing bioequivalence that is sufficient to allow FDA to waive the "evidence" requirement. In practice, this means that an ANDA must contain either results of human studies showing bioequivalence, or other facts on which FDA can conclude that the ANDA product will be bioequivalent to its reference listed drug.

The regulations regarding "evidence" of bioequivalence specifically state that FDA may accept such evidence based on human (*in vivo*) testing, laboratory (*in vitro*) testing, or both. Those regulations also set out, in rank order of acceptability, types of *in vivo* and *in vitro* tests that may be used to establish bioequivalence. Those tests include *in vivo* blood concentration tests, *in vitro* tests that have been correlated to such *in vivo* blood tests, urinary excretion tests, measurement of observable pharmacological effects over time, comparative clinical trials of safety and efficacy, FDA-accepted *in vitro* dissolution tests, or the catchall "any other approach deemed adequate by FDA" to establish bioequivalence. Consistent with these options, the regulations permit FDA, "for good cause," to "waive a requirement for the submission of evidence of *in vivo* bioavailability if waiver is compatible with the public health."

Bioequivalence issues associated with generic versions of innovator drugs have created considerable debate and litigation between and among innovator and generic drug companies and FDA. This debate has been particularly focused on drugs that are not "systemically effective"—that is, whose active moiety is not delivered to the site of drug action by systemic blood flow (e.g., drugs that are inhaled, topically applied, or locally active in the gastrointestinal tract, such as antiparasitics).

Patent Certification

The final procedural requirement for an ANDA is a patent certification with respect to each patent that covers the reference listed drug the ANDA seeks to copy, or that claims a use for the listed drug. The statute sets out four types of certifications that can be made by a generic applicant in relation to a patent on the reference listed drug:

> (I) that information on the patent has not been filed with FDA by the patent owner;
> (II) that the patent already has expired;
> (III) a statement of the date on which the patent will expire; or
> (IV) that the patent is invalid or will not be infringed by the manufacture, use, or sale of the generic applicant's drug.

FDA by regulation has expanded the paragraph IV certification to include an allegation of unenforceability as well as invalidity or noninfringement and has added a fifth type of certification: a statement that there are no patents that claim the listed drug. It is also possible for a generic applicant to "carve out" a listed method of use patent by stating that it is not seeking approval for the particular indication covered by that patent (the so-called "section viii statement," after the statutory subparagraph that addresses it).

If a paragraph I or II certification, or a certification of no relevant patents, is filed, FDA may make approval of the ANDA effective immediately upon completion of its review. If a paragraph III certification is filed, the approval may be made effective on the patent expiration date specified in the ANDA, although a tentative approval may be issued before that time. If the ANDA contains a paragraph IV certification, however, a complex series of events will be triggered, the outcome of which will determine the effective date of approval of the ANDA.

This process begins when a generic company submits an ANDA containing a paragraph IV certification and, as required, notifies the patent owner and the NDA holder that it has submitted such a certification, which is done once FDA has formally accepted the ANDA for review (typically thirty to sixty days after the ANDA is initially submitted, unless the ANDA is refused for filing [see discussion above under "Submitting and Filing the New Drug Application"]). The notification must set forth in detail the factual and legal bases for the ANDA applicant's belief that the listed patent is invalid or will not be infringed by the ANDA applicant's drug.

After receiving this paragraph IV notification, the patent/NDA holder must evaluate the legal and factual arguments asserted by the ANDA applicant. If the patent/NDA holder so decides, it may file a lawsuit against the applicant for patent infringement. The lawsuit must be filed within forty-five days of receipt of the paragraph IV notification, or FDA may make approval of the ANDA effective immediately upon the conclusion of the review process. If a lawsuit is brought, an automatic statutory injunction prohibits FDA from making approval of the ANDA effective for thirty months, unless the court rules in favor of the generic company prior to that time or unless the thirty-month injunction is shortened or lengthened by the district court in response to undue delay by either party.

Filing a paragraph IV certification is an "artificial act" of patent infringement created by the 1984 amendments to allow the courts to decide whether the patent is valid, or if the proposed future manufacture and sale of the generic version would infringe the patent. Without making the paragraph IV certification itself an act of infringement, it was believed that the courts would be barred under the Constitution from issuing what would otherwise amount to an advisory opinion about potential future infringement by the generic competitor. Once a patent suit based on a paragraph IV certification is brought, the only issues to be decided are whether the proposed generic marketing of the drug will infringe the patent, or whether the patent is otherwise invalid or unenforceable.

Although a paragraph IV challenge is often costly and difficult, the 1984 amendments included an incentive for a generic company to bring such a challenge in the form of a 180-day delay in FDA approval of other companies' ANDAs to the benefit of a generic company that first challenges a listed drug patent. The original version of this incentive provision was ambiguous in several respects and gave rise to frequent litigation, creating uncertainty that seriously undermined its effectiveness. In December 2003 Congress amended the 180-day exclusivity provision, resolving a good deal of the previous uncertainty in favor of an approach aimed at balancing the exclusivity incentive with the interest of getting generic drugs onto the market more quickly and reliably. In particular, the December 2003 amendments established a mechanism whereby a first paragraph IV challenger could forfeit its right to the 180-day exclusivity under a variety of circumstances, including the failure to put its generic drug on the market within a specified period following approval.

The New "Paper NDA"—Section 505(b)(2) Applications

505(b)(2)

In addition to codifying procedures for ANDAs, the 1984 amendments also established a new category of NDA under section 505(b) of the FDCA—the "505(b)(2) application." This type of application, like the earlier paper NDA, provides for NDAs submitted by an applicant in reliance on safety and efficacy data supplied by another applicant, and to which the 505(b)(2) applicant has no right of reference. Unlike with the old paper NDA, however, the 505(b)(2) applicant is not restricted to reliance on published studies, but may also rely on previous FDA findings of safety and efficacy for another applicant's drug based on unpublished data in FDA's files that is no longer legally protected.

There are several scenarios where a 505(b)(2) application may come into play. One involves an applicant that seeks to market its version of an established drug for a new therapeutic indication or with some other modification requiring new clinical studies, and seeks to rely on relevant safety findings on the drug in a previously approved NDA. Another scenario is where an ANDA suitability petition for a significantly different version of an approved drug—such as a different dosage form or route of administration—is inappropriate because clinical studies are required, but prior studies on the original drug product are still relevant to showing the overall safety and efficacy of the new version of the drug.

The 505(b)(2) application also is similar to an ANDA in that the applicant is required to certify as to the patent status of the drug for which the referenced investigations were conducted, by stating either that the relevant patent information has not been filed by the original applicant (as evidenced by the lack of a listing in the *Orange Book*), that such patent has expired, the date on which the patent will expire, that there are no patents that cover the listed drug, or that the patent is invalid, unenforceable, or will not be infringed by the manufacture, use, or sale of the proposed 505(b)(2) drug. Also, as with ANDAs, the 505(b)(2) applicant who files a paragraph IV patent certification of invalidity or noninfringement must notify the patent holder, who then has forty-five days to decide whether to sue the applicant for patent infringement and trigger an automatic thirty-month statutory injunction while the courts decide the substantive patent issues involved. Unlike the ANDA situation, however, no 180-day exclusivity is available in connection with a 505(b)(2) application.

Over-the-Counter Drugs

The OTC Review

As noted above, in order to avoid regulation as a new drug, a drug ordinarily must be deemed generally recognized as safe and effective (GRAS/GRAE). The test for general recognition of safety and effectiveness, as it has been applied by FDA and the courts, is a stringent one. In brief, it requires 1) that the drug be "generally recognized, among experts qualified by scientific training and experience to evaluate the safety and effectiveness of drugs, as safe and effective for use under the conditions prescribed, recommended, or suggested in the labeling thereof"; 2) that such general recognition be based on adequate published data demonstrating the drug's safety and efficacy (*Weinberger v. Bentex Pharm., Inc.*, 412 U.S. 645, 652 (1973)); and 3) that the drug have been used "to a material extent" and "for a material time" under the labeled conditions. The courts have stipulated that general recognition of effectiveness for an individual drug product must be supported by the same level of evidence as required for an NDA, including adequate and well-controlled investigations demonstrating efficacy (*Weinberger v. Hynson, Westcott & Dunning, Inc.*, 412 U.S. 609, 629-32 (1973)).

The test for general recognition of safety and effectiveness requires:

1) *that the drug be "generally recognized, among experts qualified by scientific training and experience to evaluate the safety and effectiveness of drugs, as safe and effective for use under the conditions prescribed, recommended, or suggested in the labeling thereof;"*
2) *that such general recognition be based on adequate published data demonstrating the drug's safety and efficacy; and*
3) *that the drug have been used "to a material extent" and "for a material time" under the labeled conditions.*

Although it is exceedingly difficult for a drug product to qualify as GRAS/GRAE on an individual basis, the GRAS/GRAE concept has provided FDA with a key legal tool to regulate OTC drugs, namely the OTC review. Starting in 1972, FDA instituted a system to review the safety and efficacy of active ingredients (as opposed to individual drug products) in each category of OTC drugs. For each such category, FDA issues a call-for-data notice that is published in the *Federal Register*. These notices ask manufacturers to submit clinical/marketing data for the individual active ingredients contained in their products. The agency then convenes expert advisory panels that are responsible for reviewing the data submissions for the active ingredients in each category.

Once each panel is finished with its review of the active ingredients and the submitted data, it is responsible for providing a final report to FDA. This report reviews each ingredient and places it into one of three categories. Category I ingredients are deemed GRAS/GRAE; Category II ingredients are considered either unsafe, ineffective, or both; and Category III ingredients are viewed as having insufficient data to determine safety and/or efficacy. The report is published by FDA in the *Federal Register* as an advance notice of proposed rulemaking with an opportunity for public comment. FDA then reviews the report, takes into account any public comment, and publishes in the *Federal Register* its interpretation of the report, sometimes disagreeing with the panel's interpretations and making changes as necessary. This action, which is also open for public comment, is referred to as the Tentative Final Monograph, and is technically a notice of proposed rulemaking.

FDA then undertakes a final review of the ingredients, again taking into account any public comments, which could include new or additional data. On this basis, the agency publishes in the *Federal Register* a rule establishing a Final Monograph. Following the effective date of the Final Monograph (usually a year after publication), continued marketing is permitted only for drug products with active ingredients, labeling claims, dosage strengths, and other specified conditions included in the Final Monograph.

Occasionally, companies petition FDA to re-open or amend an OTC monograph, or FDA sees a need to re-open the review of a particular category of drugs. The agency will publish a notice in the *Federal Register* to that effect. This action is considered a proposed monograph amendment (technically a Notice of Proposed Rulemaking) and is open for public comment. The review process then proceeds as explained above.

While most OTC drug categories have been finalized by FDA, the OTC Drug Review process technically remains open, with certain categories of drugs still under review. Until a Final Monograph is published in the *Federal Register* and takes effect, all products containing active ingredients under review in a particular category and meeting certain other conditions regarding labeling claims and other product attributes may continue to be marketed although FDA may take regulatory action against an individual ingredient or product over safety or efficacy issues.

There are three ways to make an Rx-to-OTC switch:

- *the manufacturer supplements an existing NDA*
- *FDA creates or amends an OTC monograph*
- *the manufacturer can petition FDA for the switch*

Rx-to-OTC Switches

A rapidly increasing proportion of the OTC market is made up of products that originally were approved as prescription drugs and subsequently were switched to OTC status, a transition commonly referred to as an "Rx-to-OTC switch." There are three ways to accomplish such a switch. A drug manufacturer can supplement the drug's existing NDA; FDA may create or amend an OTC monograph; or the manufacturer may petition FDA to make the switch.

Currently, by far the most common way to accomplish the Rx-to-OTC switch is by supplementing the drug's NDA. This is in large part due to the opportunity this route affords the drug's sponsor to obtain marketing exclusivity for the switched product. In particular, if the Rx-to-OTC switch supplement involves a change to the drug that is supported by "new clinical investigations" that are "conducted or sponsored by [the applicant]" and are "essential to the [supplement's] approval," the applicant will gain three additional years of marketing exclusivity for the OTC product, as discussed above. There is no set formula for determining what kinds of changes will meet the exclusivity requirements; such changes can relate to such matters as active ingredient, dosage form, route of administration, conditions of use, or dosing regimen.

Procedurally, an applicant seeking to switch a product must file a supplemental application to the drug's NDA and must include a statement explaining why its studies meet the requirements for exclusivity, as described above. Next, FDA will decide whether to approve the switch, and subsequently will make the exclusivity determination. Generic manufacturers of the switched product, however, may file citizen petitions or take other administrative or legal actions to encourage FDA to deny exclusivity. Conversely, a manufacturer who is unhappy with an agency denial of exclusivity may challenge that denial in court.

Expedited Availability

The treatment IND mechanism, established by regulation in 1987 and codified by FDAMA, allows an investigational drug to be provided outside controlled clinical trials to treat patients with serious or immediately life-threatening diseases for which no comparable or satisfactory alternative therapy is available.

As discussed above, one major response to concerns about drug approval delays has been the establishment of the user fee system. Separate and apart from that system, however, a number of special pathways have been created both by FDA and Congress to expedite the availability of drugs for seriously ill patients. This section provides a brief review of those pathways.

Treatment INDs

The treatment IND mechanism, established by regulation in 1987 and codified by FDAMA, allows an investigational drug to be provided outside controlled clinical trials to treat patients with serious or immediately life-threatening diseases for which no comparable or satisfactory alternative therapy is available. The standard for FDA clearance of a treatment IND for a "life-threatening disease" is whether the available scientific evidence, taken as a whole, provides a reasonable basis for concluding that the drug "may be effective for its intended use" and would not expose patients to an "unreasonable and significant risk of illness or injury." For a "serious" disease, the standard is whether there is "sufficient evidence of safety and effectiveness" to support treatment use. Most IND procedural requirements apply to treatment INDs, including informed consent requirements and prohibitions on pre-approval promotion or other commercialization of experimental treatments (although companies may charge patients enough to cover costs). In addition, the drug sponsor is expected to continue conventional clinical trials and to pursue marketing approval of the drug with "due diligence."

Individual Patient Access to Investigational Drugs for Serious Diseases

Under the expanded access mechanism established by FDAMA in 1997, a patient acting through a physician may request an investigational drug, and a manufacturer may provide such a drug, if the patient's physician determines that the patient has no comparable or satisfactory alternative therapy, and that the risk to the patient from the investigational drug is no greater than the risk from the disease or condition. For a drug to qualify for this mechanism, FDA must determine that there is sufficient evidence of safety and effectiveness to support its use and that provision of the investigational drug will not interfere with clinical investigations in support of marketing approval. In addition, the sponsor or clinical investigator must submit to FDA a protocol describing the use of the drug in a single patient or small group of patients.

Emergency Access

FDAMA also codified current regulations permitting the shipment of investigational new drugs for the diagnosis, monitoring, or treatment of a serious condition or disease in emergency situations as determined by FDA.

Fast-track designation is available for drugs or biologics that demonstrate the potential to address unmet medical needs for serious or life-threatening conditions.

Fast-Track Approval

Under the fast-track authority established by FDAMA, fast-track designation is available for drugs or biologics that demonstrate the potential to address unmet medical needs for serious or life-threatening conditions.

The first step in the fast-track program is that the sponsor requests FDA to designate its drug as a fast-track product. If the drug is given fast-track status, the law permits approval based on evidence of the drug's effect on a "surrogate endpoint" that reasonably suggests clinical benefit, or on a clinical endpoint. Such approval may be conditioned on the completion of postmarketing, or Phase IV, clinical studies to verify and describe the drug's clinical benefit and to resolve remaining uncertainty about the surrogate endpoint or clinical endpoint on the basis of which the product was approved. Drugs and biologics approved under the fast-track procedure may also be subject to predissemination review requirements for promotional labeling and advertising, and to a streamlined procedure for withdrawal of approval if, among other reasons, a post-marketing clinical study fails to verify clinical benefit. The law also provides that FDA may review marketing applications for fast-track products on a rolling basis (i.e., may begin review based on partial submissions); user fee deadlines, however, do not apply to such an application until it is complete.

The Combination Drug Policy

FDA's combination drug policy provides that:

> (a) Two or more drugs may be combined in a single dosage form when each component makes a contribution to the claimed effects and the dosage of each component (amount, frequency, duration) is such that the combination is safe and effective for a significant patient population requiring such concurrent therapy as defined in the labeling for the drug. Special cases of this general rule are where a component is added:
>
> (1) To enhance the safety or effectiveness of the principal active component; and

> (2) To minimize the potential for abuse of the principal active component.
>
> 21 C.F.R. § 300.50.

Although this regulation on its face reads as a permissive policy, it was actually promulgated to require additional evidence of efficacy for many fixed combination drug products already on the market. For an NDA for a combination drug containing two (or more) active ingredients, the combination policy means that evidence of safety and efficacy would be required not only for the drug as a whole, but also for each of the components. In other words, each component must be shown to contribute individually to the claimed overall effects of the product. This contribution, however, need not relate to efficacy—a component also may be added if it is shown to increase the safety of the other component or components. Of key importance under the combination drug policy is the principle that prior efficacy (or safety) results on individual active components cannot be extrapolated to a proposed combination drug; rather, that combination drug must undergo its own clinical investigations to demonstrate safety, efficacy, and the contribution of the active components. Like many such principles in the drug approval setting, however, this one is not necessarily absolute, and FDA may exhibit more (or less) flexibility in individual cases.

Animal Drugs

Basic Elements

In broad outline, the approval process for animal drugs tracks that for human drugs. Indeed, the legal definition of a "drug" itself includes articles "intended for use in the diagnosis, cure, mitigation, treatment, or prevention of disease *in man or other animals*" or "intended to affect the structure or any function of the body *of man or other animals*," (FDCA § 201(g)(1)(B), (C) (emphasis added)). Although the law provides separate definitions of a "new drug" requiring affirmative FDA approval for human drugs and animal drugs, respectively, these definitions are virtually identical in substance. The "new animal drug" definition, however, explicitly includes drugs intended for use in animal feed (but excludes the feed itself) (FDCA § 201(v)).

Like new drugs intended for use in humans, a new animal drug must ordinarily be investigated in preclinical and then clinical studies in order to gather evidence about its safety and efficacy. Clinical studies typically take place under the animal counterpart of an IND, the "Notice of Claimed Investigational Exemption for a New Animal Drug" (commonly referred to as an INAD), covered in 21 C.F.R. Part 511. The procedures and standards for the submission and FDA review of a new animal drug application (NADA) (codified in section 512 of the FDCA and 21 C.F.R. Part 514) are, in turn, very much like those for an NDA. In particular, a new animal drug must be shown to be safe and effective in order to obtain FDA approval. (One procedural difference between human and animal drug approvals is that all new animal drug approvals are published as regulations in the C.F.R.) Once the new animal drug is approved, proposed changes in the conditions of approval trigger the requirements of the supplemental NADA process, which are roughly similar to those of the supplemental NDA process.

In addition, although animal drugs were not included in the 1984 amendments that established the current patent term extension and generic drug approval provisions for human drugs, they were the subject of counterpart legislation four years later, in the form of the 1988 Generic Animal Drug and Patent Term Restoration Act (GAD-PTR Act). As the 1984 amendments had done for human drugs, the GAD-PTR Act established a framework in the area of animal drugs for patent term restoration, approval of generic products, and exclusivity protection for innovator products.

Special Issues

Beneath the overall structural similarities between the approval processes for human and animal drugs, there are a few important differences in policy and approach, particularly with respect to drugs for use in food-producing animals. One such difference stems from the fact that such drugs are often administered in animal feed. In such cases FDA regulates not only the drug itself, but also the premixes and concentrates into which the drug is initially mixed (the so-called "Type A medicated articles" and "Type B medicated feeds") as well as the final medicated feed incorporating such concentrates to be fed to animals in the field (the so-called "Type C medicated feed") (21 C.F.R. Part 558). A drug intended for incorporation in animal feed may be lawfully shipped only to the holder of an approval for the medicated feed in question (FDCA § 512(a)). That feed, in turn, must be used in accordance with the conditions of its approval (FDCA § 512(m)).

In addition, as might be expected for drugs administered to food-producing animals, the safety of humans who may ultimately ingest products derived from such animals is an overriding concern. FDA accordingly oversees not only the safety and efficacy of such drugs in the animal "patients" themselves but also the possible health effects of potential residues of such drugs in meat, milk, or other products of those animals. Of particular importance here is the FDCA's prohibition on the use of any cancer-causing compound in food animals, unless it can be determined by methods satisfactory to FDA that no residue of such compound will be found in food produced from such animals under conditions reasonably certain to be followed in practice (the so-called "DES proviso") (FDCA § 512(d)(1(I); 21 C.F.R. Part 500, Subpart E).

Animal Biologics

As in the human arena, biological products—that is, products produced from living beings, such as sera, antitoxins, and the like—intended for therapeutic use in animals are subject to a separate legal and regulatory regime from that for drugs, under the 1913 Virus-Serum-Toxin Act (VST Act). Unlike human biologics, however, animal biologics are regulated not only under a separate legal regime but also by an altogether separate agency, the U.S. Department of Agriculture (USDA).

The VST Act made it illegal to ship from one state to another any virus, serum, toxin, or analogous product intended for use in the treatment of domestic animals unless the product in question was prepared in accordance with regulations issued by USDA at an establishment holding a current license from USDA (21 U.S.C. § 151). On the basis of this rather sparse legislative statement, USDA has erected a system of licensing animal biologics and the establishments that produce them whose main substantive features parallel those of FDA animal drug regulation (this system is codified in 9 C.F.R. subch. E). New animal biologics must be supported by adequate showings of safety and efficacy in order to obtain approval, and are subject to more or less the same level of postapproval regulatory oversight as new animal drugs. One peculiarity in the animal biologics area is that the original language of the VST Act was read to exempt the preparation and shipment of animal biologics entirely within one state from USDA regulation. Congress filled this gap in 1985 when it amended the act to cover shipments of animal biologics "in or from the United States" (Pub. L. 99-198, 99 Stat. 1654).

Biologics

In simple terms, biological products (sometimes referred to as "biologics" or "biologicals") are medical products derived from living organisms. Such products are regulated under section 351 of the Public Health Service Act (PHSA) (42 U.S.C. § 262), as well as under various provisions of the FDCA. Legally, biological products are defined under section 351 of the PHSA as including "a virus, therapeutic serum, toxin, antitoxin, vaccine, blood, blood component or derivative, allergenic product, or analogous product, or arsphenamine or derivatives of arsphenamine (or any other trivalent organic arsenic compound) applicable to the prevention, treatment, or cure of a disease or condition of human beings." To be lawfully marketed in interstate commerce, a biological product must be the subject of a biologics license, issued by FDA on the basis of a demonstration that the product is "safe, pure, and potent," and that the facility in which the product is manufactured meets standards to assure that it continues to be safe, pure, and potent.

Originally, the regulatory scheme for biologics was quite distinct from that for nonbiologic drugs.

Originally, the regulatory scheme for biologics was quite distinct from that for nonbiologic drugs. The most prominent difference was that whereas drugs must obtain NDAs in order to be lawfully marketed, biological products were the subject of a bifurcated approval system under which a product had to obtain a product license, by means of a product license application (PLA), *and* the establishment where the product was manufactured had to obtain an establishment license, through an establishment license application (ELA), before the product could be lawfully marketed.

In 1997, however, FDAMA amended section 351 of the PHSA to establish the single biologics license in place of the former product and establishment licenses for all biological products. FDAMA also stipulated that the FDCA applies to a biological product, with the sole exception that a product for which a license has been approved under PHSA § 351 is not required to have an approved NDA. Finally, Congress stated directly in FDAMA that FDA "shall take measures to minimize differences in the review and approval" of new drugs and biologics. For most practical purposes, therefore, the regulation of human therapeutic biologics in both the pre-approval and postapproval periods is closely similar to that of new drugs.

Thus, as in the new drug model previously discussed, to gain marketing approval for a therapeutic biologic, the sponsor of that biologic must demonstrate its safety and efficacy for its recommended uses. Along the road to that approval, the IND requirements applicable to new drugs also apply to the investigation of therapeutic biologics. Similarly, in the postapproval world, biologics manufacturers must report adverse events under a scheme similar to that for drugs (21 C.F.R. Part 600, Subpart D).

One major remaining difference between drugs and biologics, however, is that because almost all biologics continue to be licensed under the PHSA rather than approved under section 505 of the FDCA, they are not subject to the exclusivity and generic application provisions of section 505. Thus, at least for the time being, biologics are not eligible for the statutory exclusivity protections of section 505, nor is it possible, with rare exceptions, to obtain approval of "generic biologics" or "biosimilars," although as of this writing legislation to establish a pathway for such approval is under active consideration.

Biologics are not eligible for the statutory exclusivity protections of section 505, nor is it possible, with rare exceptions, to obtain approval of generic biologics.

Biologics are, however, eligible for orphan drug status, and many of the major disputes over orphan exclusivity have in fact involved biological products.

Case Studies

Case Study: Court Enforcement of FDA Approval Deadline

The futility of trying to enforce the statutory 180-day filing clock deadline in court seemed to have been confirmed by a 1991 case in which a disgruntled drug company, Barr Laboratories, Inc., sued FDA for not completing the review of its drug applications within the deadline. The court agreed that FDA's delay violated the statute, but refused to do anything about it on the ground that it was up to the agency, not the court, to set drug review priorities, and that to order FDA to meet the deadline on the plaintiff's applications would disadvantage other, equally worthy applicants. *In re Barr Lab., Inc.,* 930 F.2d 72 (D.C. Cir. 1991), *cert. denied,* 502 U.S. 906 (1991).

In 2005, however, a section 505(b)(2) NDA applicant challenged the conventional wisdom, with unexpected results. Sandoz, Inc. had submitted its NDA for the recombinant human growth hormone product Omnitrope in July 2003, relying in part on FDA's prior approval of Pfizer's recombinant human growth hormone product Genotropin. In April 2004, Pfizer objected to the Omnitrope application. In August 2004, FDA told Sandoz that although the agency had completed its review of Omnitrope, it was deferring a decision because of the application's "nature and complexity." *Sandoz v. Leavitt et al.*, Civ. No. 05-1810 (RMU), D.D.C. April 10, 2006, at 3.

In September 2005 Sandoz sued FDA, asserting that the agency had violated the statutory 180-day action deadline. FDA did not dispute that assertion, but argued that the statutory deadline was "aspirational" and had effectively been modified by the subsequent user fee action date structure agreed upon with Congress. The court brushed this defense aside and granted summary judgment for Sandoz, concluding that the statutory requirement was clear, unambiguous, and unchanged, and that to hold otherwise would be to "accept governmental mediocrity and vitiate the statute's mandatory language." The court distinguished the *Barr* case on the grounds that FDA had approved a number of other subsequently filed NDAs, including 505(b)(2) NDAs, for both naturally sourced and recombinant biologic drugs since Sandoz had submitted its application, so that it was evident that ordering FDA action on Sandoz's NDA would not "directly bottleneck other NDAs." Further, with additional resources now available to FDA under PDUFA, the court felt the agency should be held to a higher standard. Accordingly, the court ordered FDA to comply with the statutory requirement and either approve the application or provide Sandoz with the required notice and opportunity for a hearing on the approvability of the application. To the surprise of some, FDA chose in response to approve Sandoz's application.

As of this writing, however, the *Sandoz* case has led neither to a meaningful change of FDA's NDA review practices nor to a wholesale legal assault on those practices by drug sponsors. For one thing, the specific facts of the case are relatively unique, in particular FDA's written acknowledgement to the sponsor that it had completed its substantive review of the application but was nonetheless refusing to take final action, presumably at least in part because of Pfizer's objections, without any clear end in sight. This left FDA with a glaring legal vulnerability the agency would be unlikely to take on again. More broadly, under the user fee system, it remains the case that sponsors typically have much more to gain by working with FDA within the framework of their action dates to move the application forward than by taking the agency on in court. Nonetheless, the *Sandoz* case illustrates that there are limits to FDA's discretion under the user fee system and that the statutory filing clock deadline retains at least some life still.

Case Study: Early Access to Investigational Drugs

Evidently unsatisfied with the existing mechanisms for expedited availability of experimental drugs described above, the patient advocacy group Abigail Alliance sued FDA over the agency's refusal to allow dying patients unrestricted access to unapproved drugs. After an unexpected ruling by a panel of the D.C. Circuit Court of Appeals in 2006 that the Due Process Clause of the U.S. Constitution protects terminally ill patients' rights to have access to "potentially life-saving" investigational drugs that have passed successfully through Phase I studies, FDA sought reconsideration by the full court. In August 2007 the court rejected the panel's conclusion and ruled that "there is no fundamental right . . . of access to experimental drugs for the terminally ill." *Abigail Alliance v. von Eschenbach*, 495 F.3d 695, 697 (D.C. Cir. 2007).

Case Study: Bioequivalence for Nonsystemically Absorbed Drugs

A prominent example of conflict over bioequivalence involved the asthma drug albuterol administered by metered dose inhaler (MDI). The NDA holder for the drug, Schering-Plough, submitted a petition to FDA arguing that the statutory bioequivalence requirement, which specifies only measurements of "rate and extent of absorption," categorically precluded FDA from approving any ANDAs for nonsystemically absorbed drugs, including, of course, MDI albuterol. FDA denied the petition on the basis that the statute specifically contemplates determinations of bioequivalency based on evidence other than rate and extent of absorption. Schering-Plough then sued FDA in federal district court, but the court agreed with FDA's interpretation and dismissed the complaint. (*Schering Corp. v. Sullivan*, 782 F. Supp. 645, 647 (D.D.C. 1992), *vacated*, 995 F.2d 1103 (D.C. Cir. 1993).) On appeal, the substance of the district court's holding was affirmed. The appellate court stated that although the FDCA's definition of bioequivalence is "ambiguous," FDA's interpretation of that definition, on the basis of which the agency proposed to approve generic MDI albuterol products, was "reasonable." (*Schering Corp. v. FDA*, 51 F.3d 390, 400 (3d Cir. 1995), *cert. denied*, 116 S. Ct. 274 (1995).) Subsequent cases involving similar issues of bioequivalence for nonsystemic ANDA products have reached basically the same outcome.

Chapter 6

A Pharmacovigilance Primer

Edward John Allera, Buchanan Ingersoll & Rooney PC, Washington, D.C.

Key Points

- **Pharmacovigilance includes all activities directed toward detecting, assessing, understanding, and preventing adverse events or other product-related problems.**
- **The regulatory framework for pharmacovigilance has been in place for decades, imposing postapproval requirements on all categories of drugs.**
- **Any adverse experience that is not listed on a drug's current label is considered an "unexpected" drug experience.**
- **There are five basic types of postmarketing reports, whose requirements are dictated by the seriousness of the adverse experience.**
- **Congress, in the Food and Drug Administration Amendments of 2007, created a statutory mechanism in recognition of the importance of pharmacovigilance: risk evaluation and mitigation strategy.**
- **Pharmacovigilance reporting requirements are designed to safeguard public health and safety by creating a system for improving the labeling of drug products.**

Introduction

Pharmacovigilance encompasses all postapproval scientific and data-gathering activities relating to the detection, assessment, understanding, and prevention of adverse events or any other product-related problems. Interestingly, no statutory definition of the practice exists under the Federal Food, Drug, and Cosmetic Act (FDCA) or the Food and Drug Administration's (FDA's) regulations. FDA has created the regulatory framework for pharmacovigilance indirectly under its authority to regulate all drug labeling as well as its authority to require maintenance of records for new drugs.

Pharmacovigilance has played a role in the safe use of pharmaceuticals for decades. For example, the declaration of phenformin as an "imminent hazard to health" in the 1970s was based on pharmacovigilance information. The role of pharmacovigilance has dramatically increased in recent years as public policy considerations and public perceptions and acceptance of risk have shifted.

It has long been accepted that the risk analysis that occurs during the drug development process has to be thorough and rigorous. In recent years, there has been increased recognition of the need and importance of monitoring a drug's safety after approval, while in actual medical use. As a result, the discipline of pharmacovigilance has become increasingly central to the regulatory life cycle of drugs.

It is well recognized that not all safety concerns will be identified during the clinical trial process.

It is well recognized that not all safety concerns will be identified during the clinical trial process. Even drugs intended for chronic use are seldom tested in more than 3,000 to 5,000 patients prior to approval. In contrast, postapproval patient exposure to a new drug increases by orders of magnitude. Of particular concern are patients with co-morbid conditions and those who are taking other drugs.

Heavy publicity about postapproval adverse events allegedly associated with drugs such as Vioxx and Avandia have heightened both public and political awareness of the important role that pharmacovigilance plays in protecting public health. In the Food and Drug Administration Amendments Act of 2007 (FDAAA), Congress recognized the importance of pharmacovigilance and created a statutory mechanism—the risk evaluation and mitigation strategy—for increasing the scrutiny of safety for premarket approval and postmarket approval. This activity has also led to an increase in the amount of product liability litigation involving the safety of drugs. Further, the Centers for Medicare and Medicaid Services (CMS) has issued regulations to facilitate gathering data from the Medicare Part D drug program to aid, in part, pharmacovigilance. All these factors magnify the importance of pharmacovigilance.

Background

The regulatory framework for pharmacovigilance has been in place for decades. Specific FDA regulations impose postapproval pharmacovigilance requirements on all categories of drugs: grandfathered drugs (21 C.F.R. § 310.305); drugs approved under a new drug application (NDA) (21 C.F.R. § 314.80); drugs approved under an abbreviated new drug application (ANDA) (21 C.F.R. § 314.90); and biologics (21 C.F.R. § 600.80). Additional regulations exist for postapproval testing requirements (21 C.F.R. § 310.303), highlighting the need for congruency between the information gathered during the pre-approval phase with information that is collected postapproval. The symmetry of the pharmacovigilance process is further confirmed in 21 C.F.R. § 314.70(c)(6)(iii)(A) where supplemental applications are required to add or strengthen a contraindication, warning, precaution, or adverse reaction; the supplement is subject to thirty-day pre-implementation FDA review and approval of the proposed language.

Reporting Requirements

Overview

Even before the current focus on pharmacovigilance, two principles for adverse event reporting were set forth in FDA's regulations: timeliness and accuracy.

Even before the current focus on pharmacovigilance, two principles for adverse event reporting were set forth in FDA's regulations: timeliness and accuracy. Each has weaknesses given the partially voluntary nature of elements of the reporting system, the limitations on the data and clinical information available, and the need for data interpretation.

With regard to timing, the current environment of an ever-increasing number of reports to FDA, faster FDA review cycles for NDAs, more complex new drug submissions, and the greater use of drugs by an aging population has placed more pressure on FDA, and as a consequence, manufacturers, to develop sophisticated infrastructures that will help them to quickly and aggressively obtain and report adverse effects.

The accuracy of reporting, however, represents a unique challenge. The accurate interpretation of reported information can be difficult, especially considering the common usage of gross or crude terms from various lexicons, and differences in human perception (i.e., different clinicians and patients may define specific adverse effects vastly differently).

Because crises involving drug safety always permit cynical hindsight second-guessing of pharmacovigilance data, the timeliness of submitting adverse event reports to FDA is also critical. FDA has vast experience in adverse events, drug safety reports, and safety evaluation not only concerning the drug in question, but also identical, similar, and related drugs. This database affords FDA a perspective on risk that is unavailable to any single applicant because no single report or series of reports is dispositive; it is only a piece of the greater safety picture. For a manufacturer, not only is thorough and timely reporting of adverse events necessary but it is also important that it maintain an active dialogue with FDA about the reports, trends, and any other data that may affect the labeling or status of the drug. Significantly, U.S. courts have viewed such collaborative efforts by manufacturers with FDA to be a basis for limiting product liability.

Definitions

FDA has developed a glossary of terms to deal with pharmacovigilance (21 C.F.R. §§ 310.305, 312.32, 314.80, and 600.80). An "adverse drug experience" is defined as any adverse event associated with the use of a drug in humans, whether or not drug related, in the course of professional practice, including intentional or unintentional overdosage, drug abuse, drug withdrawal, or the failure of the drug to have its intended effect.

"Disability" is a substantial disruption in a person's ability to conduct normal life functions.

"Life-threatening" is an adverse drug experience that places the patient at the immediate risk of death, but does not include an adverse experience that, had it occurred in a more severe form, might have caused death.

A "serious adverse experience" is one occurring at any dose of a drug that results in death, a life-threatening experience, inpatient hospitalization or prolongation of an existing hospitalization, a persistent or significant disability or incapacity, or a congenital anomaly or birth defect. Other events that do not cause the foregoing are also deemed serious if they may jeopardize the patient and require medical or surgical intervention to prevent those events.

Any adverse experience that is not listed in the current labeling of the drug is regarded as an unexpected drug experience.

The role of labeling surfaces in the definition of unexpected drug experiences. Any adverse experience that is not listed in the current labeling of the drug is regarded as an unexpected drug experience. These include events that may be symptomatically and pathophysiologically related to an event listed in the labeling but differ due to greater severity or specificity. FDA interprets "unexpected" as relating to the actual observation rather than the theoretical pharmacological possibility.

For unapproved drugs, approved drugs, and approved biologics these terms are considered to be identical, and reporting should be handled consistently. Attempts to create different systems within a company only increase the likelihood of failing to comply with FDA's regulations and expectations.

Reports

Five basic types of postmarketing reports exist, and their reporting requirements are dictated by the seriousness of the adverse experiences: 15-day Alert Reports, 15-day Follow-Up Reports, Periodic Adverse Experience Reports, Field Alerts, and Annual Reports.

♦ 15-day "Alert Report"

An applicant is required to report each adverse drug experience that it becomes aware of that is both serious and unexpected, whether foreign or domestic, as soon as possible but not later than fifteen calendar days from initial receipt of the information.

An applicant is required to report each adverse drug experience that it becomes aware of that is both serious and unexpected, whether foreign or domestic, as soon as possible but not later than fifteen calendar days from initial receipt of the information. For an unapproved drug, any person whose name appears on the label, whether as its manufacturer, packer, or distributor, has the filing obligation. Thus, the obligation applies to any adverse reaction that does not appear on the label and is serious by virtue of either its increased severity or incidence. Information from scientific literature or from abroad is subject to the 15-day Alert reporting requirement if the information is found in scientific or medical journals as case reports or as the result of a clinical trial. A copy of the published article is to be filed with the report

These reports are designed to quickly provide FDA with relevant data from participants in the healthcare delivery system about a potentially adverse event related to a drug. The focus is on new or potentially new adverse experiences. While the adverse reports system in the United States has been termed voluntary in the general sense (healthcare providers and others in the healthcare distribution system), it is mandatory for drug applicants or persons whose names appear on the label.

♦ 15-day "Alert Report" Follow-Up

The obligation for follow-up falls directly on every person identified on the label of the drug product whether the holder of the approved application, the manufacturer, the packer, or the distributor, of either approved drugs or those drugs marketed without approvals. The reports must be prominently identified as to their content (i.e., "15-day Alert Report" or "15-day Alert Report Follow-Up"). The format for submission has historically been FDA Form 3500A, or a computer-generated version that provides an equivalent in all elements of data and is agreed to by FDA.

The holder of the application is obligated to conduct a comprehensive follow-up investigation. This point is critical. FDA's regulations impose an additional 15-calendar-day requirement on the report of new information or as requested by the agency. FDA's regulations require records to be maintained of the steps taken in the investigation even if no new information is detected. If new information is detected, it is subject to a new 15-day reporting requirement. Normally, however, FDA will be in contact with the company, and a thorough report will be prepared in accord with a time frame agreed to by the parties. Similar obligations apply to the manufacturer of the drug, whether approved or unapproved. To reduce duplicative reporting, companies listed on the labeling can fulfill their obligations by providing notice to the applicant or manufacturer within five calendar days of the receipt of the adverse experience. In the contemporary environment, there appears to be no restriction on persons listed on the label from fulfilling these obligations in lieu of the holder of the approval or the manufacturer.

Persons or companies included on the labeling who report the adverse experience to the manufacturer or holder of the approval must maintain records of their adverse experience reporting, including the following: the date the adverse event was reported to them; the date it was reported to its business cohort (e.g., the manufacturer); and the name and address of the applicant or manufacturer.

The reason for confusion regarding who is responsible for reporting arises because pharmaceutical industry operations have become more "virtual" in recent years.

The reason for confusion regarding who is responsible for reporting arises because pharmaceutical industry operations have become more "virtual" in recent years. The subcontracting by pharmaceutical companies of key operations, such as manufacturing, distribution, marketing, and recordkeeping, has become commonplace. While it is commonly recognized that such arrangements require the creation of defined contractual obligations, this does not always take place in practice, creating reporting vulnerabilities where there is the absence of precise delegation of responsibilities among the parties. Confusion can arise about fulfillment of the legal obligations under the FDCA, resulting not only in the failure to comply with obligations of the act but also the potential for substantive commercial liabilities among the parties. The specific issues associated with follow-up are discussed below because they are the basis for the Periodic Adverse Experience Reports.

♦ Periodic Adverse Experience Reports

For the first three years after approval of an application, the applicant must submit quarterly reports of all adverse events that do not fall within the 15-day Alert Reports (i.e., those reported adverse events that are already noted within the product labeling or are not deemed to be "serious and life threatening"). The reports must be filed within thirty days of the end of the quarter, and the annual report must be filed within sixty days of the date of the NDA or ANDA approval. The reports must contain a narrative summary and analysis of the available information, an analysis of the 15-day Alert Reports (which are to be fully referenced), and a description of any action taken by the manufacturer since its receipt of the most recent report of the adverse event.

Information from postmarketing studies, reports from the scientific literature, and foreign marketing experience are exempt from the periodic reporting system. Should an applicant conclude, however, that an adverse event is associated with a recently approved drug being studied under a new investigational NDA, FDA regulations provide that the applicant should include this event in its periodic report but should also clearly mark this incident as being distinct from those experiences that are being spontaneously reported.

All records submitted must protect the privacy of the patients involved, and therefore should not include the specific names and addresses of the individual patients. Unique identifiers that are assigned by the reporter of no more than eight characters should be created. The applicant should also include the name of the reporter. Under FDA's regulations the names of the patients, healthcare professionals, hospitals, and geographical identifiers are not publicly releasable.

The submission of a report does not necessarily reflect a conclusion by the filer or FDA that the report or information constitutes an admission that the drug has caused or contributed to an adverse event.

Further, the agency has a regulation that states that the submission of a report does not necessarily reflect a conclusion by the filer or FDA that the report or information constitutes an admission that the drug has caused or contributed to an adverse event. The regulation leaves open the ability of the applicant or other filer to not admit or deny that any report constitutes an admission.

Limitations exist with any reporting system—whether spontaneous, mandatory, or voluntary—and FDA recognizes them: passivity, under reporting, variable quality and incompleteness, duplicate reporting, and inability to determine accurately the incidence rate because the numerator is uncertain and the denominator must be projected. More than 90 percent of the adverse experience reports are manufacturer reports, and the majority of them are periodic reports, although the rate of fifteen-day reports is increasing. Fewer than 10 percent of the reports are direct reports from healthcare professionals.

Acknowledging these limitations, FDA has issued guidelines intended to improve both the accuracy and the consistency of adverse experience reporting, thus hoping to further improve the public health value of pharmacovigilance. Optimally, FDA desires that reports contain a description of the adverse event or disease experience, including the time to onset of signs and symptoms. Suspected and concomitant therapy details should be provided, including the regimen. A listing of over-the-counter, nutrient supplement, and discontinued medications that were being taken concomitantly should be included in the description. Patient characteristics, to the extent possible, should be provided. In essence, the agency is seeking important baseline patient information that is relevant to the detection and diagnosis of the adverse event, as well as the methods used in making the diagnosis and the clinical course of the event and outcome. Relevant therapeutic measures and laboratory data are also sought, both at baseline and during the event, if available. Any information about response to dechallenge or rechallenge should also be submitted.

FDA has developed principles to assess submitted reports. Some of the questions that it poses include: Did the event occur within an expected time frame? Was there an absence of symptoms prior to drug exposure? Was there a positive challenge or dechallenge? Is the event consistent with the pharmacological effect of the drug or the class of drugs administered? Was the event identified in clinical trials? Is there an absence of alternative explanations?

FDA does not presently recommend any specific categorization of causality, although commentators have used the categories of probable, possible, and unlikely.

Currently, there is no internationally agreed-upon standard or criteria for assessing causality. Moreover, confounded cases are common, and it is rarely possible to know with a high level of certainty that a specific event was specifically caused solely by a drug product. Of critical importance, FDA does not presently recommend any specific categorization of causality, although commentators have used the categories of probable, possible, and unlikely.

For both approved and unapproved drugs subject to the recordkeeping requirements, a ten-year requirement exists for maintaining raw material and records, although the periodic reporting requirement does not apply to unapproved drugs.

♦ Field Alerts

The notification may be provided by telephone or other method of rapid communication, and a prompt written follow-up is required that is plainly marked "NDA-Field Alert Report." These reports are filed directly with the local field office, and by regulation are applicable only to approved products. There is no specific requirement in FDA's regulations for manufacturers of unapproved drugs to make such filings.

Such reports have the shortest time requirement—three days. The clock is normally considered to start after the completion of the investigations into the potential manufacturing deficiencies. For marketed approved applications, whether NDAs or ANDAs, Field Alerts can be the most critical filings. These reports normally concern manufacturing problems and they often relate to more imminent public health risks. Accordingly, many consider such filings an integral part of current Good Manufacturing Practices (cGMPs) that are applicable to all drugs, whether approved or marketed without an approval. As previously noted, within three working days of the receipt of information about distributed drugs or drugs about to be distributed, the application holder is to notify the district office that is responsible for the manufacturing facility should it believe that or become aware that its drug product is mislabeled or adulterated; that the drug product's labeling is not correct; and/or that the drug product could be mistaken for and/or erroneously used in place of another product. Some specific types of circumstances that require notification within three days include bacterial contamination; significant chemical, physical or other change; deterioration in the distributed drug product; or any failure of one or more distributed batches to meet the specifications established for it in its applications.

♦ Annual Reports

Within sixty days of the anniversary date of the application's approval, the applicant is required to file its annual report with the FDA reviewing division that was responsible for its approval. Two copies are required, accompanied by a transmittal Form FDA 2252. The report is to contain a summary of all significant new information that might affect the safety, effectiveness, or labeling of the drug product subject to the application. The description is to include any actions taken or that the applicant intends to take as a result of any new information gathered during the year (e.g., labeling changes, new studies). A description of steps taken to evaluate pediatric use of the product should also be included.

The various pharmacovigilance reporting requirements are designed to safeguard public health and safety by creating a system for improving the labeling of drug products.

Drug advertisements and promotional labeling are subject to the annual report. Specimens of mailing pieces and other labeling or advertising devised for promotion of the drug product at the time of the initial submission of the labeling and at the time of the initial publication of the advertisement must be submitted.

Distribution data according to National Drug Code number, the number of units, and quantities distributed for domestic and foreign use are to be reported. Patient, professional, and package inserts are to be supplied, including all text, tables, etc. Electronic submissions are now available. A summary of any labeling changes is to be filed. Also to be filed are chemistry, manufacturing, and controls changes, but only for new information that may affect the agency's previous conclusions about the drug product's safety or effectiveness. Any change that does not require a supplemental filing should be included in the annual report.

Clinical data submissions are essential. Published clinical trials of the drug, or abstracts that include trials on the safety and effectiveness of the drug, must be submitted. Clinical trials on new uses, biopharmaceutics studies, pharmacokinetics, and clinical pharmacology studies must also be submitted. Reports of clinical experience pertinent to safety, such as epidemiologic studies or analyses of experience in monitored patients, must be filed whether they are conducted by the applicant or otherwise obtained by it. Summaries of completed unpublished clinical trials are to be filed. The status of postmarketing study commitments must be filed as well as a log of outstanding regulatory commitments.

The various pharmacovigilance reporting requirements are designed to safeguard public health and safety by creating a system for improving the labeling of drug products. The annual report is the most comprehensive and lucid document intended for this purpose. Each report is designed to highlight the occurrence of new, unexpected adverse events or an increase in the incidence of adverse events. In contemporary terms, FDA's various pronouncements in speeches and guidelines define the mission of pharmacovigilance as to facilitate the safe and effective use of drug products by promptly gathering and evaluating drug safety data

A "safety signal" is an apparent excess of adverse events that can be found in a single well-documented case report, preclinical findings, or experience with other similar products in the drug's pharmacological class.

and identifying "safety signals" that in turn allow for the most accurate labeling of drug products and their safe use.

A safety signal is, simply stated, a key component of an effective risk management program. FDA uses the term to refer to a concern that needs to be further assessed when an excess number of adverse events is detected and potentially associated with the use of a specific drug product as compared to what one would expect based on the drug's current labeling. The importance of strong pharmacovigilance activities was underscored by Congress, which specifically created a statutory "signal of a serious risk" in the FDAAA. The term pharmacovigilance and related term "signal of a serious risk" are analogous to terms such as cGMPs and current Good Clinical Practices. The terms are not static. They are evolving and have the potential for retroactive application by adversaries attempting to prove that the labeling of the drug product failed to contain all the relevant information.

According to both contemporary guidance and FDAAA, a "safety signal" is an apparent excess of adverse events that can be found in a single well-documented case report, preclinical findings, or experience with other similar products in the drug's pharmacological class. It can come also from literature or risk management programs. Such signals should be assessed in terms of magnitude, population at risk, changes in risk of time, biological plausibility, and interactions.

FDA expects companies to develop and maintain effective pharmacovigilance signal detection and reporting systems. Generally, such systems search available case reports, adverse experience databases, the literature, and FDA's adverse experience review system to look for product-related data. Data searches are often carried out using sophisticated database mining systems, with updated coding terminology like that of the Medical Dictionary for Regulatory Activities. The goal is to identify potential product-event linkages that may be considered signals and calculate the rate of risk (i.e., the reporting rates versus the actual incidence rate). Effective risk management systems will not only help detect these signals but also help manage them and reduce the risks.

When a signal is detected, investigation is considered appropriate through observational studies, either randomized or nonrandomized. Types of nonrandomized studies include pharmacoepidemiologic, surveys, and registries. Signals that may warrant further investigation include new unlabeled adverse events (especially if serious); an apparent increase in the severity of a labeled event; the occurrence of serious events presently thought to be rare; new interactions; identification of previously unrecognized at-risk populations; confusion about the product's name or use; or inadequacies that are detected relative to current risk minimization efforts.

FDA's policies relative to pharmacovigilance activities are constantly evolving to reflect changes in technology as well as the growing sophistication of drug products. In this regard, it is important to note that retrospective data reviews, as well as reviews of currently reported data, can both play an important role in drug product safety. Thus, manufacturers must constantly be evaluating available data, both old and new, to safeguard the public health. Such a landscape, especially where the guidelines are broad and constantly evolving, also represents a challenge to drug manufacturers, who can potentially face significant liability risks despite vigilant efforts to maintain effective pharmacovigilance programs.

Supplemental Applications—Closing the Loop

The pharmacovigilance process is continuous, as is the need to improve the labeling of a product during its entire life cycle.

The goal of pharmacovigilance is to ensure that labeling of drug products is comprehensive and contains the most contemporary description of the drugs' safe and effective data. In this way the risks associated with the drugs' use can be intelligently weighed, and physicians, healthcare providers, and, in today's information technology age, patients can make informed decisions about the drugs' usage. Based upon the information gathered by pharmacovigilance plans and submitted to FDA, informed decisions can be made about any changes necessary to the product's current labeling. The pharmacovigilance process is continuous, as is the need to improve the labeling of a product during its entire life cycle.

It is unquestioned that the holder of an approved NDA must satisfy the fundamental requirements of pharmacovigilance. Until generic competition arrives, the holder of the approved application is the focal point of all the relevant data. Today, generic drug products constitute more than 60 percent of the drug units sold in the U.S. market. Once an ANDA is approved for a drug, generic penetration can reach 90 percent in just ninety days. After a period of years, the generic version unquestionably will become the market leader, and the evidence on the drug's use gleaned from the market for reporting may be primarily about generic versions of the drug. FDA's regulations setting forth obligations of holders of approved NDAs are incorporated by reference into the agency's regulations imposing obligations on holders of approved ANDAs (see 21 C.F.R. §§ 314.70 (c), 314.97, and 314.98). As the role of generic drugs grows, the obligations of the holders of approved ANDAs in the area of pharmacovigilance may increase dramatically. Holders of these approvals must be aware of the current and evolving environment.

If the pharmacovigilance data lead one or more than one holder of an approval to conclude that a labeling change may be appropriate, the critical question becomes the proper approach for implementing the change. Theoretically, FDA's regulations permit the holder of an approved application, either NDA or ANDA, to file a supplemental application to implement the change at least within thirty days to strengthen a contraindication, warning, precaution, and adverse experience. That interpretation is often proffered in product liability litigation, and the failure of companies to implement the change is alleged to be negligence or a breach of the appropriate standard of care.

This interpretation of the agency's regulations is seductive but it is erroneous as a practical matter. FDA is meticulous in maintaining its preeminent role in ensuring that the labeling of drugs is truthful, accurately warns of risks and does not distort them, and assures consistency in the labeling of all applications for the same drug and for all drugs within the same class.

The most appropriate way for a company to protect itself is to maintain a dialogue with FDA on the issues associated with pharmacovigilance and to be as meticulous as possible in filing necessary reports.

The most appropriate way for a company to protect itself is to maintain a dialogue with FDA on the issues associated with pharmacovigilance and to be as meticulous as possible in filing necessary reports. We are entering a new era when pharmacovigilance will be the foundation for improved drug product labeling and potential litigation. FDA, CMS, and other agencies such as the Veterans Administration in its electronic records effort are committed to improving their skills in this area. In the current atmosphere the courts have been receptive to limiting liability when proper dialogue and diligent filing are followed. Following the principles that apply to pharmacovigilance is one step toward following the standards of care that are evolving in the industry.

Chapter 7

The Medical Device Approval Process

Edward C. Wilson, Jr.[1] *& Michael S. Heyl, Hogan & Hartson LLP, Washington, D.C.*

Key Points

- **Medical devices include thousands of healthcare products, from simple articles such as thermometers, tongue depressors, and heating pads, to more complex products such as heart pacemakers, kidney dialysis machines, and drug-eluting stents.**
- **Medical device manufacturers generally must obtain clearance of a 510(k) premarket notification or approval of a premarket approval application (PMA) for any device they intend to commercially distribute for the first time in the United States, unless the device is exempt from such requirements.**
- **Medical devices are classified into one of three classes according to their level of risk, with Class I devices posing the least amount of risk and Class III devices generally posing the greatest risk.**
- **The 510(k) premarket notification process refers to section 510(k) of the Federal Food, Drug, and Cosmetic Act (FDCA), and is used for devices that are substantially equivalent to a legally marketed Class I or Class II device, or to a Class III device for which FDA has not yet called for PMAs. The 510(k) premarket notification process is shorter than the PMA process because FDA usually requires significantly less data in 510(k) notifications in order to demonstrate that the device is substantially equivalent to a predicate device.**
- **High-risk devices and devices not found to be substantially equivalent to a legally marketed predicate device require approval of PMAs. The PMA process is lengthy because FDA generally requires clinical data demonstrating the safety and effectiveness of the device for its intended use.**
- **The FDCA permits device manufacturers to ship devices solely for investigational use without an approved PMA or cleared 510(k) notice if they meet the requirements of FDA's investigational device exemption (IDE) regulations.**

Introduction

The Food and Drug Administration's (FDA's) regulation of medical devices is extremely complex. As new technologies emerge, the challenges of determining how products will be regulated, and navigating the premarket clearance and approval process, is complicated and often daunting. Once products are cleared or approved to market, companies face rigorous regulatory requirements to keep them there. Until 1976, Congress had never enacted specific legislation governing the regulation of medical devices. Prior to that date, public protection from defective devices depended on FDA's enforcement of the limited provisions in the Federal Food, Drug, and Cosmetic Act of 1938 (FDCA) and on judicial interpretations that extended FDA's regulatory authority over drugs to devices. This combination of sources for the agency's authority proved cumbersome.

The Medical Device Amendments of 1976 expanded FDA's statutory authority over devices.

By the mid-1970s, it had become clear that, due to significant and rapid scientific advances, and because some unsafe, ineffective, and even fraudulent devices were occasionally marketed, an increase in federal regulation was needed. In 1976, Congress passed the Medical Device Amendments (amendments) (Pub. L. No. 94-295, 90 Stat. 539), which vastly expanded FDA's statutory authority over devices. Since that time, Congress has enacted several pieces of legislation in an attempt to create a workable system to ensure the safety and effectiveness of medical devices. Among other things, congressional amendments to the FDCA have further expanded FDA's authority to clear or approve medical devices prior to marketing. For example, FDA is authorized to collect user fees from applicants of medical device submissions. Congressional amendments, however, also have required FDA to increase the transparency of the medical device clearance and approval process. In sum, FDA's medical premarket clearance and approval processes have evolved over time to a somewhat complicated set of regulatory requirements and FDA policies. The purpose of this chapter is to provide a practical summary and perspective to those premarket clearance and approval requirements that are applicable to most medical devices.

What the Statute and Regulations Say

FDA defines the term "medical device" as:

> . . . an instrument, apparatus, implement, machine, contrivance, implant, in vitro reagent, or other similar or related article, including any component, part, or accessory, which is: (1) recognized in the official National Formulary, or the United States Pharmacopoeia, or any supplement to them, (2) intended for use in the diagnosis of disease or other conditions, or in the cure, mitigation, treatment, or prevention of disease, in man or other animals, or (3) intended to affect the structure or any function of the body of man or other animals, and which does not achieve its primary intended purposes

through chemical action within or on the body of man or other animals and which is not dependent upon being metabolized for the achievement of its primary intended purposes.

In contrast, products that accomplish their principal objectives by chemical action or by being metabolized by the body are considered drugs. Examples of devices range from simple devices such as thermometers, tongue depressors, and heating pads, to more complex products such as intrauterine contraceptive devices, heart pacemakers, kidney dialysis machines, and drug-eluting stents. It is not always easy to determine if a product would be considered by FDA to be a drug or a device and some products are considered "combination products"—meaning they are a combination of a device and a drug or a biologic.

Classification of Devices

Generally, medical devices available on the market on or before May 28, 1976 (called "pre-amendment devices"), and devices similar to them, are distinguished from devices introduced after that date. Unless they are significantly modified, pre-amendment devices are permitted to remain on the market, pending final classification or other action by FDA, without any FDA review.

Medical devices are assigned to one of three regulatory classes based on the level of control necessary to ensure their safety and effectiveness.

On the other hand, devices introduced after the enactment date are subject to a certain level of FDA review depending on the amount of control necessary to ensure their safety and effectiveness. Those medical devices are assigned to one of three regulatory classes based on the level of control necessary to ensure their safety and effectiveness. Thus, the most risk-laden medical devices require the highest level of government review and approval. For example, Class I devices are generally subject only to "general controls" because they are perceived as presenting the least potential harm to the user. Class II devices, on the other hand, are normally subject to general controls and "special controls," while Class III devices are the most regulated and generally require premarket approval in addition to these controls. Overall, FDA has established classifications for approximately 1,700 different types of devices and grouped them into nineteen medical specialties, such as Hematology, Ophthalmology, OB/GYN, and General Surgery.

Class I devices include elastic bandages, examination gloves, and certain hand-held surgical instruments, and, barring the exemptions discussed below, are subject only to general controls. These controls include requirements for facility registration and product listing with FDA; premarket notification (unless specifically exempt from those requirements); maintenance of records and filing reports with respect to device marketing experience; adherence to good manufacturing practices (GMPs), known as the Quality System Regulation (QSR) (unless exempt); and any distribution and use limitations FDA may impose. In addition, the general controls provide FDA with the authority to ban devices that present substantial deception or significant risks, as well as to detain devices that are alleged to violate the FDCA, pending legal action. Finally, FDA may require manufacturers to notify purchasers and users of devices that present unreasonable risks, and to impose corrective action in certain situations.

The Food and Drug Administration Modernization Act of 1997 (FDAMA) (Pub. L. No. 105-115, 111 Stat. 2296) exempted all Class I devices from FDA's premarket notification requirements except those that are intended for a use which is of substantial importance in preventing the impairment of human health or that present a potentially unreasonable risk of injury or illness (Class I reserved devices). Several dozen devices fall into the Class I reserved category, such as bloodbank supplies, keratomes, ventricular cannulas, and positron cameras. In addition, many Class I devices are exempt from the design control provisions of the QSR requirements. Still other Class I devices are exempt from most of the QSR requirements, with the exception of complaint handling and record-keeping.

Class II devices are those for which general controls alone are insufficient to ensure their safety and effectiveness. Class II devices are subject to both general and special controls (e.g., performance standards, postmarket surveillance, patient registries, and FDA guidelines). Examples of Class II devices are powered wheelchairs, infusion pumps, and surgical drapes.

A 510(k) is a process under which a manufacturer notifies FDA of its intent to market a device that is identical to, or similar to, a marketed device.

Most Class II devices require 510(k) clearance. A 510(k) is a process under which the manufacturer notifies FDA of its intent to market a device that is identical to or similar to a marketed device (see below). The manufacturer must submit data demonstrating the equivalence, and FDA clears for marketing devices that meet the criteria. Under FDAMA, however, FDA exempted some Class II devices from 510(k) requirements. FDA may continue to add additional Class II devices to the exemption list on its own initiative or in response to a petition from an interested person. It is important to note that there are certain limitations to the 510(k) exempt status of otherwise exempt Class I and Class II devices. These limitations are spelled out in the *Code of Federal Regulations* and summarized in Table 1.[2]

Generally, Class III devices are those that must receive premarket approval by FDA to ensure their safety and effectiveness. They are life-sustaining, life-supporting, and implantable devices, or new devices that have been found not to be substantially equivalent to legally marketed devices. In general, Class III devices require FDA approval of a premarket approval application (PMA). Examples of Class III devices that require a PMA are heart valves, silicone gel-filled breast implants, drug-eluting

Table 1: General Exemption From 510(k) Requirements

Exemption	Exemption Limitations
Premarket notification (510(k)) not required: 1. To the extent the device has existing or reasonably foreseeable characteristics of commercially distributed devices within its generic type.	A premarket notification (510(k)) must be submitted when: 1. The device is intended for a use different from the intended use of the legally marketed device in that product classification (e.g., the device is intended for a different medical purpose), or the device is intended for lay use where the former intended use was by healthcare professionals only; 2. The modified device operates using a different fundamental scientific technology than the legally marketed device in that generic type of device (e.g., a surgical instrument cuts tissue with a laser beam rather than with a sharpened metal blade, or an in vitro diagnostic device detects or identifies infectious agents by using deoxyribonucleic acid (DNA) probe or nucleic acid hybridization technology rather than culture or immunoassay technology)

stents, and certain bone growth stimulators. Class III devices that were on the market prior to May 28, 1976, may be marketed via the 510(k) notification route until FDA calls for PMAs for these devices by publishing a notice in the *Federal Register*.

Custom devices are exempt from registration and from otherwise applicable performance standards or premarket approval and clearance requirements.

Certain devices ordered by members of the health professions to conform to their special needs or to those of their patients are considered "custom devices." This term is distinguished from "customized" devices which, by their nature, are required to be customized to meet each individual's specific anatomical needs. Under section 520(g) of the FDCA, custom devices are exempt from registration and from otherwise applicable performance standards or premarket approval and clearance requirements. This exemption applies only to devices that are 1) ordered by physicians or dentists for their own use or for a specific patient identified in the order, 2) not generally available in finished form, and 3) not labeled or advertised for commercial distribution. In addition, custom devices must not be generally available to other licensed practitioners. Custom devices, although exempt from the 510(k) notification requirement, still must comply with all other general control requirements including the QSR regulations; investigational use of devices; banned devices; and restrictions on sale, adulteration, and misbranding. Traditionally, FDA has interpreted the term "custom device" very strictly so that many devices claimed to be "custom" by manufacturers have been determined not to be custom devices by FDA.

Congress provided a mechanism for changing the classification of a device if new information emerges regarding its safety and effectiveness. FDA has reclassified hundreds of devices from either Class III to Class II or from Class II to Class I. As noted above, in most cases, FDA has exempted Class I devices from its 510(k) requirements and has also exempted some Class II devices. When FDA reclassifies a device, it reclassifies the "generic type" of device, not the specific device for which a reclassification petition was submitted. Thus, a manufacturer may expend significant resources preparing a reclassification petition and indirectly benefit competitors that manufacture devices within the same generic type.

FDA can also use its enforcement discretion in determining if certain devices require 510(k) clearance (e.g., convenience kits comprising legally marketed devices that are simply being assembled in kit form strictly for the "convenience" of the purchaser or user). Historically, convenience kits were the subject of 510(k) review. FDA determined, however, that under certain circumstances, premarket clearance for convenience kits is not necessary. Therefore, FDA published a list of generic types of convenience kits that are exempt from FDA's 510(k) requirements, but not exempt from the registration, listing, prohibition against misbranding, and QSR regulations. To be subject to the policy, all components of the kit must be legally marketed (e.g., subject to a cleared 510(k) notification, exempt from FDA's premarket notification requirements, or have pre-amendments status), and further processing of the kit cannot significantly affect the safety or effectiveness of the kit or its components.

The intended use of a device is also a significant factor in determining its classification.

The intended use of a device also is a significant factor in determining its classification. For example, lasers that are used for most dermatological and urological procedures are regulated as Class II devices. If the same laser (with certain modifications), however, is capable of performing ophthalmic procedures such as LASIK, the device would be a Class III device and require PMA approval for that indication.

How does one determine under what classification a device falls? Part 800 of the *Code of Federal Regulations* (C.F.R.) identifies, describes, and classifies hundreds of products by device type (e.g., ophthalmic devices are covered in 21 C.F.R. Part 886). If a device has the same intended use and meets the general description of the device described in the classification regulation, the "new" device will likely fall under that regulation.

If a "new" device is not classified, the sponsor should determine the regulatory pathway used by competitors with similar products. Certain information about cleared 510(k) notifications and approved PMAs is publicly available after FDA has taken final action on the submission. This information is helpful in determining how a device will be regulated by FDA.

Another means for determining the likely classification of a device is to have a pre-submission meeting with FDA to discuss the device's description, technological characteristics, and intended uses. A person may submit a written request under section 513(g) of the FDCA that requires FDA to identify the classification of a device and applicable premarket requirements. Alternatively, under section 513(c) of the FDCA, any interested party may submit a citizen's petition requesting that FDA downclassify a Class III device to Class I or Class II, or upclassify a Class I device to Class II or III or a Class II device to Class III. FDA's Guidance for Submitting Reclassification Petitions explains the procedures and requirements for a reclassification petition. A person also may submit a 510(k) notification for a device and see if FDA clears the submission or finds the device not substantially equivalent, which means that a PMA will be necessary for the device.

Where an unclassified device is determined to not be substantially equivalent, and thus Class III, a company can request reclassification based upon the low level of risk of the device.

A company that submits a 510(k) notice for an unclassified device, which is determined to be not substantially equivalent and thus Class III because of the lack of a clear predicate device, can request immediate reclassification into Class I or II based upon the low level of risk of the device. This process is known as the "de novo review" process. The manufacturer's request for a de novo classification must be made within thirty days of receiving a not substantially equivalent determination. The request for de novo classification must describe the device and provide a detailed recommendation for classification. If FDA classifies the device into Class I or Class II, the product is then considered cleared and may be marketed. That newly classified device may also serve as a predicate device for substantial equivalence determinations for future devices. On the other hand, if the agency does keep the device in Class III, PMA approval for the device will be required before marketing.

Medical Device User Fees

Under the Medical Device User Fee and Modernization Act of 2002 (MDUFMA), FDA established user fees for the review of certain premarket submissions. The revenue generated by those user fees is intended to provide financial stability for FDA's medical device review program in return for improved and predictable performance by the agency in the review of new marketing submissions. Under MDUFMA, user fees were required for the review of: 510(k) submissions; PMA applications; biologic license applications (BLAs), premarket reports (PMRs); product development protocols (PDPs); panel-track PMA supplements; BLA efficacy supplements; real-time PMA supplements; and premarket notifications (510(k)).

The Food and Drug Administration Amendments Act of 2007 (FDAAA), among other things, extended FDA's authority to collect user fees until

2012. FDAAA restructured the fee schedule to provide manufacturers with more predictability and stability in the payment of medical device user fees. FDAAA also added the user fee provisions to additional types of submissions. For example, FDA may collect user fees for: thirty-day notices (for PMAs); PMA annual reports; and 513(g) requests for designation. Fees also are required for initial and annual establishment registrations for each facility engaged in covered activities, such as manufacturing, importation, specification development, and contract sterilization.

Revenues generated from FDA's user fee program are to be used to expedite the medical device review process in accordance with FDA performance goals. In consultation with industry, after FDAAA was enacted, the agency restructured its performance goal framework to emphasize deadlines for "final decisions" rather than the agency's previous incremental, or "cycle goals" scheme. The performance goal framework also encouraged a more informal, interactive process between FDA and the medical device industry. To this end, FDA published a guidance document on February 28, 2008, entitled Interactive Review for Medical Device Submissions: 510(k)s, Original PMAs, PMA Supplements, Original BLAs, and BLA Supplements. The purpose of the guidance document was to recommend an interactive premarket review process for submissions, designed to expedite FDA's review of device applications while continuing to assure device safety and effectiveness.

Investigational Device Exemptions

Purpose of an Investigational Device Exemption

An investigational device exemption allows an unapproved device to be shipped in interstate commerce for purposes of conducting supportive clinical research.

Devices used on human subjects to conduct investigations of the device's safety and effectiveness are considered "investigational devices" under section 520(g) of the FDCA. These devices have not been approved for commercial distribution by FDA for their investigational use. An investigational device exemption (IDE) allows an unapproved device to be shipped in interstate commerce for purposes of conducting clinical research that can be submitted in support of a 510(k) or PMA submission. Without this exemption, shipment of an unapproved device in interstate commerce would violate the FDCA. Notably, although an approved IDE application exempts a device from certain provisions of the FDCA, it does not exempt it from other federal, state, or local regulations. For example, an investigational device that emits radiation may be subject to radiological health regulations, including product performance standards for equipment such as lasers and diagnostic x-rays. Investigational devices must also comply with FDA's advertising and labeling requirements regarding such devices.

Significant Risk and Nonsignificant Risk Devices

The IDE regulation describes two types of device studies: 1) significant risk and 2) nonsignificant risk. The IDE regulation defines a significant risk device as an investigational device that: 1) is intended as an implant and presents a potential for serious risk to the health, safety, or welfare of a subject; 2) is purported or represented to be for use in supporting or sustaining human life and presents a potential for serious risk to the health, safety, or welfare of a subject; 3) is for a use of substantial importance in diagnosing, curing, mitigating, or treating disease, or otherwise preventing impairment of human health and presents a potential for serious risk to the health, safety, or welfare of a subject; or 4) otherwise presents a potential for serious risk to the health, safety, or welfare of a subject. Some examples of significant risk studies include clinical trials on cardiac pacemaker/pulse generators; balloon dilation catheters for benign prostatic hyperplasia; implantable prostheses (ligament, tendon, hip, knee, and finger); and intraocular lenses.

A significant risk device:

1) *is intended as an implant and presents a potential for serious risk to the health, safety, or welfare of a subject;*
2) *is purported or represented to be for use in supporting or sustaining human life and presents a potential for serious risk to the health, safety, or welfare of a subject;*
3) *is for a use of substantial importance in diagnosing, curing, mitigating, or treating disease, or otherwise preventing impairment of human health and presents a potential for serious risk to the health, safety, or welfare of a subject; or*
4) *otherwise presents a potential for serious risk to the health, safety, or welfare of a subject.*

A nonsignificant risk device study is one that does not pose a significant risk to patients. Some examples of nonsignificant risk studies include clinical trials on daily wear contact lenses, denture repair kits, general urological catheters, and externally worn monitors for insulin reactions.

Significant risk studies must meet all of the regulatory requirements set forth in 21 C.F.R. Part 812, including the requirements that the sponsor obtain approval from FDA of the IDE, and approval of the investigational plan and informed consent from each participating Institutional Review Board (IRB) before commencing the study. If the investigation does not present a significant risk to the health of the patients, the sponsor may begin without obtaining FDA approval of the study (nonsignificant risk studies are "deemed" to have IDE approval by FDA), provided that each reviewing IRB approves the study. An IRB must make two separate decisions: 1) whether the proposed investigation is a significant or nonsignificant risk study; and 2) whether the investigation should be approved. Informed consent must be obtained from each subject regardless of whether it is a significant or nonsignificant risk study.

An assessment of whether a device study presents a nonsignificant risk is made initially by the sponsor. If the sponsor believes a study poses a nonsignificant risk, the sponsor provides the IRB with the study proposal, an explanation of why the study is a nonsignificant risk, and other supporting information (e.g., any reports of prior investigations). The sponsor or investigator must also advise the IRB whether the study subjects must undergo a procedure as part of the investigational study (e.g., a surgical procedure), so it can evaluate the potential harm that could be caused by the procedure in addition to the potential harm that could be caused by the device.

Institutional Review Boards (IRBs)

An IRB must be assured that:
1) risks to subjects are minimized and are reasonable in relation to anticipated benefits and knowledge to be gained,
2) subject selection is equitable,
3) informed consent materials and procedures are adequate, and
4) provisions for monitoring the study and protecting the privacy of subjects are acceptable.

IRBs are committees (independent or affiliated with medical institutions) that are composed of qualified experts who are tasked with reviewing and approving biomedical research, as well as continuing review of ongoing research, to assure the protection of the rights and welfare of human subjects. In deciding whether a study (whether nonsignificant risk or significant risk) is approvable, an IRB must be assured that: 1) risks to subjects are minimized and are reasonable in relation to anticipated benefits and knowledge to be gained, 2) subject selection is equitable, 3) informed consent materials and procedures are adequate, and 4) provisions for monitoring the study and protecting the privacy of subjects are acceptable. To ensure that the risks to the subjects are reasonable in relation to the anticipated benefits, the risks and benefits of the investigation are compared to the risks and benefits of alternative devices or procedures. If all reviewing IRBs agree that the study presents a nonsignificant risk and is approvable, the investigation may proceed without FDA approval. If any reviewing IRB determines that the study poses a significant risk, the sponsor must notify FDA that a significant risk determination has been made and an IDE application must be submitted and approved before beginning the study. Moreover, at any time, FDA may overrule a nonsignificant risk determination by an IRB and require the sponsor to submit an IDE application to FDA.

IDE Exempt Investigations

In general, clinical investigations of devices to support a market application are subject to the IDE requirements. There are, however, limited exemptions from the IDE regulations. For example, per 21 C.F.R. § 812.2(c), a diagnostic device that complies with the labeling requirements in 21 C.F.R. § 809.10(c) is exempt from the IDE regulations if the testing: 1) is noninvasive, 2) does not require an invasive sampling procedure that presents significant risk, 3) does not by design or intention introduce energy into a subject, and 4) is not used as a diagnostic procedure without confirmation by another medically established diagnostic product or procedure. These studies also still must comply with FDA's IRB and informed consent requirements. Certain other studies also are exempt from FDA's IDE regulations, including a device undergoing consumer product testing, a device that is legally marketed provided it is used in accordance with its cleared labeling (or labeling in effect prior to May 28, 1976, for pre-amendments devices), and a custom device unless the device is being studied to determine its safety or effectiveness for commercial distribution.

Content of an IDE

Per 21 C.F.R. § 812.20, the sponsor of the proposed human clinical investigation that is not exempt per 21 C.F.R. § 812.2(c) must include the following information in an IDE application:

(1) name and address of sponsor;
(2) report of prior investigations, including biocompatibility, in vitro, and in vivo testing, as well as published and unpublished adverse information;
(3) investigational plan, including a description of the intended use of the device, objectives and duration of the study, analysis of risk, justification, patient population, monitoring procedures, and the protocol;
(4) device description and description of manufacturing;
(5) example of investigator agreement;
(6) certification that all investigators who will participate in the study have signed the investigator agreement;
(7) names, addresses and chairpersons of IRBs;
(8) participating institutions;
(9) statement of noncommercialization;
(10) claim of categorical exclusion from environmental assessment;
(11) labeling; and
(12) informed consent materials.

An IDE application that does not contain all required information will be returned to the sponsor for revision before FDA begins a substantive review.

FDA's guidance document entitled Center for Devices and Radiological Health's Investigational Device Exemption (IDE) Refuse to Accept Policy includes an IDE "refuse to accept" checklist, which provides a listing of all the elements required in the IDE. If an IDE does not contain all of these elements, it will be returned to the sponsor for revision before FDA begins a substantive review.

IDE Review Process

FDA has thirty days to review the IDE application. Technically, an IDE application is considered approved thirty days after it has been received by FDA, unless FDA notifies the sponsor that the IDE is approved with conditions or disapproved prior to the thirty days. In practice, however, sponsors await an approval notification from FDA so as not to begin studies that might have to be stopped or modified a short time later. If FDA disapproves an IDE, the sponsor may respond to the deficiencies and/or request a regulatory hearing under 21 C.F.R. Part 16. Should FDA approve the IDE with conditions, the sponsor has forty-five days in which to address the conditions of approval.

Notably, sponsors of clinical studies of any Class III or any implantable device may submit an investigational plan (including the clinical protocol) to FDA for review, in order to reach agreement on the proposed plan. In practice, FDA also typically agrees to review investigational plans for Class I and II nonimplantable devices, and neither Blue Book Memorandum #D95-1 (Goals and Initiatives for the IDE Program) nor IDE Guidance #99-1 (Pre-IDE Program: Issues and Answers) make distinctions with respect to class or type of device. The plan can be submitted prior to the actual official submission of the IDE application or prior to seeking approval from an IRB to conduct a study. This IDE provision states that any agreement reached by the sponsor and FDA must be made part of the administrative record and may be changed only: 1) with the written agreement of the sponsor, or 2) pursuant to a decision made by the director of the office in which the device is reviewed that a substantial scientific issue essential to determining the safety or effectiveness of the device has been identified. Such a determination must be documented after providing the study sponsor with an opportunity for a meeting with the director during which the scientific issues involved are documented.

Informal, nonbinding guidance is also available via the pre-IDE process to allow the reviewing division to provide guidance and feedback on development of supporting preclinical data or the investigational plan for incorporation into the IDE application. These meetings can take many forms, including conference calls, video conference calls, or face-to-face meetings.

IDE Supplements

Sponsors of significant risk studies are required to obtain approval of an IDE supplement before making a change in the investigational plan that may affect scientific soundness of the rights, safety, or welfare of subjects.

Pursuant to FDA's IDE regulations, sponsors of significant risk studies are required to obtain approval of an IDE supplement before making a change in the investigational plan that may affect its scientific soundness or the rights, safety, or welfare of subjects. Under section 201 of FDAMA, FDA was required to promulgate new regulations that allow study sponsors to make modifications to investigational devices and study protocols without submitting IDE supplements to FDA. The regulations set forth several specific changes that no longer require IDE supplements: 1) developmental changes in the device (including manufacturing changes) that do not constitute a significant change in design or basic principles of operation and that are made in response to information gathered during the course of investigation; and 2) changes or modifications to clinical protocols that do not affect: a) the validity of data or information resulting from the completion of an approved protocol, or the relationship of likely patient risk to benefit relied upon to approve a protocol; b) the scientific soundness of an investigational plan submitted in the IDE; or c) the rights, safety, or welfare of the human subjects involved in the investigation.

Moreover, the IDE regulations state that these types of changes can be made if the sponsor of the study 1) determines, on the basis of credible information, that the change or modification meets the specified criteria; and 2) submits to FDA, not later than five days after making the change or modification, a notice of the change or modification. The intent of this provision is to place the burden on the study sponsor to determine whether proposed changes necessitate the filing of an IDE supplement. Of course, FDA has the option to disagree with the sponsor's determination and can later require an IDE supplement at its discretion.

Investigational Device Labeling Requirements

Per 21 C.F.R. § 812.5, investigational devices are subject to specific labeling requirements. The labeling of investigational devices must include:

There are specific labeling requirements for investigational devices.

(1) name and place of business of the manufacturer, packer, or distributor;
(2) the quantity of contents;
(3) the statement, "CAUTION—Investigational device. Limited by federal (or United States) law to investigational use";
(4) all relevant contraindications, hazards, adverse effects, interfering substances or devices, warnings and precautions;
(5) no false or misleading statements; and
(6) no representation that the device is safe or effective for the purposes for which it is being investigated.

Note that a manufacturer also may include a statement that the product has an approved IDE.

Sponsor and Investigator Responsibilities

Per the IDE regulations, sponsors of IDE investigations and the investigators participating in the IDE investigation have various responsibilities. Investigators are responsible for the following: 1) ensuring that the study is conducted according to investigational plan and applicable FDA regulations; 2) obtaining informed consent from study subjects; 3) supervising the use of the device; and 4) returning unused investigational devices to the sponsor or disposing of them as the sponsor directs. Sponsors are responsible for: 1) selecting qualified investigators and providing them with the information they need to conduct the study properly; 2) obtaining IRB review and approval as necessary; 3) ensuring proper monitoring of the study; 4) investigating any unanticipated adverse events that occur during the study and taking appropriate action; and 5) informing FDA and IRBs about significant new information. (21 C.F.R. § 812.40.)

Sponsors and investigators have recordkeeping and reporting responsibilities.

In addition to the above responsibilities, both sponsors and investigators are subject to recordkeeping responsibilities. Per 21 C.F.R. § 812.140(a), investigators must keep records of: 1) correspondence with the sponsor, FDA, IRB, other investigators, and monitors; 2) receipt and disposition of investigational devices; 3) study subjects' case history and exposure to the device; 4) documentation of informed consent; and 5) the protocol and any deviations. Sponsors are responsible for maintaining records of the following per 21 C.F.R. § 812.140(b): 1) correspondence with investigators, FDA, IRB, other sponsors, and monitors; 2) shipment and disposition of investigational devices; 3) signed investigator statements; 4) name and address of each investigator; and 5) name and address of each IRB that has reviewed the study.

Finally, both sponsors and investigators are subject to reporting responsibilities. For investigators, per 21 C.F.R. § 812.150(a), the following must be reported: 1) unanticipated adverse effects reports (should be submitted to the sponsor and IRB of any unanticipated adverse device effect occurring during the study within ten working days after the investigator first learns of the event); 2) progress reports (should be submitted to the sponsor and IRB, and the investigator should monitor progress reports on the study at regular intervals (at least yearly)); and 3) final reports (should be submitted to the sponsor and IRB within three months of the end of the study).

Sponsors' reporting requirements include: 1) evaluating the reports of unanticipated adverse effects from the investigator and reporting results to FDA, all reviewing IRBs, and participating investigators within ten working days after sponsor first receives notice of the effect; 2) submitting a current investigator list to FDA every six months; 3) submitting progress reports at regular intervals (at least yearly) to all IRBs and, for a significant risk study, to FDA; and 4) for significant risk studies, notifying FDA of termination of the study within thirty days and submitting final reports to FDA, all reviewing IRBs, and participating investigators within thirty days of the end of the study. For nonsignificant risk studies, a final report must be submitted to all reviewing IRBs within six months after study termination. (21 C.F.R. § 812.150(b).)

Disqualification of Investigators

Per 21 C.F.R. § 812.119, an investigator can be disqualified by FDA from performing clinical research for failure to comply with regulatory requirements, or for repeated or deliberate submission of false information to a sponsor. Should a study investigator be disqualified, FDA typically will examine the study data to determine whether it is reliable. If found unreliable, this can be a basis for withdrawing approval of the IDE or marketing application that included the unreliable data.

Registration Requirements for Clinical Trials

FDAAA established registration requirements for "applicable clinical trials." An applicable device clinical trial is defined as:

1) "a prospective clinical study of health outcomes comparing an intervention with a device subject to [510(k), PMA and Humanitarian Device Exemptions premarket requirements] against a control in human subjects (other than a small clinical trial to determine the feasibility of a device, or a clinical trial to test prototype devices where the primary outcome measure relates to feasibility and not to health outcomes)"; and

"Applicable clinical trials" must meet registration requirements established by the Food and Drug Administration Amendments Act of 2007.

2) "a pediatric postmarket surveillance [requirement]"

Thus, per FDAAA, it may be the case that a study being conducted under an approved IDE must be registered with the ClinicalTrials.gov data bank.

Information required to be provided upon registration includes, but is not limited to: the study title; a brief summary of the study written for the lay public; the study design; the primary purpose of the study; the study phase; the study type; the disease or condition being studied; the intervention name and type; the start date; the expected completion date; the sample size; and the primary and secondary endpoints. The sponsor also must provide recruitment information including: eligibility criteria; gender; age limits; policies on accepting healthy volunteers; recruitment status; and individual site status. In addition, contact information for the sponsor's facility, as well as certain administrative information (e.g., the unique protocol identification number, the name and contact information for the individual responsible for the study, etc.), must be provided.

FDAAA also requires that product submissions, including 510(k)s, PMAs, and humanitarian device exemption applications, be accompanied by a certification that the applicant has complied with the clinical trial registration requirements. FDAAA requires that the certifications be submitted to FDA. FDA also has created a certification form, Form FDA 3674, which is available on FDA's website.

As of publication of this book in mid-2008, the agency is reviewing the legislation and developing guidance on which clinical trials meet the above definition and are required to report to ClinicalTrials.gov. Until FDA issues such guidance, the sponsor remains responsible for determining whether its study meets the definition of an applicable trial and, therefore, is subject to the reporting requirements.

Humanitarian Device Exemptions

The humanitarian device exemption applies to devices that:

- *are designated to treat or diagnose a disease or condition that affects fewer than 4,000 persons per year,*
- *are not available otherwise and there is no comparable device available,*
- *do not expose patients to unreasonable or significant risk, and*
- *the benefits to health outweigh the risks.*

To encourage the discovery of devices that benefit a small number of patients in the United States, FDA may grant a humanitarian device exemption (HDE) from the effectiveness requirements of the FDCA after finding that: 1) the device is designated to treat or diagnose a disease or condition that affects fewer than 4,000 individuals per year; 2) the device is not available otherwise, and there is no comparable device available to treat or diagnose the disease or condition; 3) the device will not expose patients to unreasonable or significant risk; and 4) the benefits to health from its use outweigh the risks.

Two distinct steps are necessary to obtain approval to market a humanitarian device. First, the sponsor must submit a request to FDA's Office of Orphan Products Development (OOPD) seeking a determination that the disease or condition that the device is intended to treat or diagnose affects or is manifested in fewer than 4,000 individuals in the United States per year. The request for humanitarian use designation (HUD) should provide the following: 1) the precisely defined proposed indication(s) for use based upon current medical and scientific knowledge; 2) a brief description of the device, including illustrations and a discussion of its principle of operation; and 3) documentation, with authoritative references appended, of the target population demonstrating that the rare disease or condition affects or is manifested in fewer than 4,000 people in the United States per year. FDA must approve, disapprove, or return the HUD request for additional information within forty-five days of the request.

Second, if OOPD determines that the device is eligible for a humanitarian designation, an HDE application must be submitted to FDA's Office of Device Evaluation (ODE). It is similar in both form and content to a PMA; however, it is not required to contain the results of scientifically valid clinical investigations demonstrating that the device is effective for its intended purpose.

The application also must contain a report by an independent certified public accountant verifying that the amount charged does not exceed the costs of the device's research, development, fabrication, and distribution. Manufacturers of pediatric devices receiving an HDE, however, are permitted to sell their devices for a profit, provided that the devices meet all other HDE requirements. Despite this, the number of pediatric devices distributed during a year may not exceed the annual distribution number specified by FDA when the HDE was granted.

The HDE application must also estimate the number of patients that would be required to generate data to support a full PMA, and an explanation of why such a study is not feasible or why the cost of conducting such a study could not reasonably be expected to be recovered. Such application must also include a description of all pediatric subpopulations that suffer from the disease or condition that the device seeks to address and the approximate number of affected pediatric patients. Finally, as previously stated, all HDE applications must include certification that the applicant has complied with the clinical trial registration requirements. FDA is required send the applicant an approval order, approvable letter, or order denying approval within seventy-five days of receipt of an HUD request accepted for filing and for which there were no major amendments.

A device that is subject to an HDE can be used prior to IRB approval if a physician determines that such approval cannot be obtained in time to prevent serious harm or death to a patient.

The use of an HUD must initially and continually be reviewed by an IRB. The IRB does not, however, have to approve each use of the HUD, but rather the use of the HUD at the facility. A device that is subject to an HDE can be used prior to IRB approval providing that a physician determines that such approval cannot be obtained in time to prevent serious harm or death to a patient. Where a physician does use an HDE device without approval from an IRB, the physician afterward must notify the chairperson of the IRB and identify the patient involved, the date the device was used, and the reason for the use.

HDEs will be granted for an unlimited timeframe. Nevertheless, FDA may require the sponsor of the HDE device to demonstrate continued compliance with the HDE regulations if FDA believes that such a demonstration is necessary to protect the public health, or if FDA has reason to believe that the criteria for the HDE are no longer met. FDA can suspend or withdraw the HDE only after providing the holder of the HDE an opportunity for an informal hearing.

510(k) Premarket Notification Process

Overview

The 510(k) process involves a comparison of a company's new device to one or more legally marketed devices (i.e., predicate device(s)). A predicate device is a legally marketed Class I or Class II device, or a Class III device for which PMAs are not yet required. According to FDA's regulations, a manufacturer is required to file an FDCA section 510(k) premarket notification prior to: 1) initial marketing of a device; 2) making a change or modification to a cleared device that could significantly affect the safety or effectiveness of the device; or 3) making a major change or modification to the intended use of its previously cleared device. The regulations require manufacturers to submit to FDA a 510(k) notification at least ninety days prior to the applicant's intended introduction into the market of a device that requires premarket clearance. A device that requires 510(k) clearance may not be marketed until the applicant receives an "order" from FDA, which states that the new device is substantially equivalent to a legally marketed predicate device (21 U.S.C. § 360(k)).

To be "substantially equivalent," a new device must have:

- *the same intended use as a predicate; and*
- *either the same technological characteristics as the predicate device or*
- *different technological characteristics, but the information submitted must not raise new questions of safety and effectiveness and must demonstrate substantial equivalence.*

For a new device to be found "substantially equivalent" to one or more legally marketed predicate devices, it must have 1) the same intended use as a predicate; and 2) either a) the same technological characteristics as the predicate device or b) different technological characteristics, but the information submitted must not raise new questions of safety and effectiveness and must demonstrate substantial equivalence. A device that is the subject of a 510(k) notification may have multiple predicate devices, as certain features of the device may be substantially equivalent to certain predicate devices, while other features may be substantially equivalent to other predicates (21 U.S.C. § 360c(1)(l)(a)). FDA has developed a decision tree that facilitates making the substantial equivalence determination. With regard to 510(k) submissions, FDA is directed to limit its determination as to whether the product is substantially equivalent based on the device's proposed labeling included in the 510(k) filing.

Initially, the agency required proof of equivalence to an actual pre-amendments device (i.e., one that was on the market prior to May 28, 1976). The Safe Medical Devices Act of 1990 (SMDA) made it clear, however, that a postamendments Class I or Class II device may be found substantially equivalent to any legally marketed Class I or Class II device or Class III device for which FDA has not yet called for PMAs. The predicate device, therefore, need not be a pre-amendments device, but it cannot be a device that was removed from the market by FDA or determined to be misbranded or adulterated by judicial order. (21 U.S.C. § 360c(l)(2).)

Contents of a 510(k) Premarket Notification

The format and information required in a 510(k) premarket notification, outlined below, are specified in 21 C.F.R. §§ 807.87, 807.90, 807.92, and 807.93. The contents of a premarket notification include the following:

- **Device Name.** The device name, including both the trade or proprietary name and the classification name, must be included in a 510(k) premarket notification.
- **Identification.** The applicant's name and street address must be included in a 510(k) premarket notification.
- **Registration Number.** If applicable, the FDA establishment registration number of the owner or operator submitting the premarket notification should be included.
- **Classification.** The applicant should include the class of the device (i.e., Class I, II, or III). If known, include the appropriate classification panel.
- **Description.** The 510(k) notification should include a physical description of the new device, together with an explanation of its intended use, principles of operation, power source, composition, and other information necessary to understand the device.
- **Substantial Equivalence Comparison.** Applicants should attempt to make a comparison of the new device to its predicate as easy as possible for the FDA reviewer. The 510(k) notification should, therefore, include a discussion of the similarities and differences between the device and its predicate device(s), and should make use of comparative tables whenever possible.

Applicants should attempt to make a comparison of the new device to its predicate as easy as possible for the FDA reviewer.

- **Software.** Applications for computerized devices must follow the appropriate CDRH guidance.[3]
- **Standards.** The applicant should identify any mandatory or voluntary standards met by the device.
- **Performance.** Performance data are often needed to help demonstrate that the proposed device is as safe and effective as the predicate device.
- **Biocompatibility.** Submissions for devices that directly contact the body must include a description of the characteristics of their materials. This description should compare the device to its predicate in sufficient detail to determine biocompatibility, as well as the kind of tests needed to determine biocompatibility. Any material differences

between the new device and the claimed predicate device must be stated explicitly, but it is just as important to state whether the materials comprising the two devices are identical. Manufacturers need to provide biocompatibility test data for any materials found in the new device that are not present in the predicate device.

- **Sterility.** Submissions for devices that are labeled sterile must cite their sterilization method as well as the method used to validate the sterilization cycle and the sterility assurance level that the validated method ensures.
- **Labeling.** Although applicants may submit drafts of their device labeling, the submission should be representative of the final version.
- **Class III Certification and Summary.** All 510(k) submissions for Class III devices must have a special added certification statement by which the applicant must certify in its 510(k) premarket notification that it has searched for all available information relative to that device's safety and effectiveness, and the 510(k) notification must include citations to any adverse safety and effectiveness data.
- **510(k) Summary or Statement.** A premarket notification must include either a summary of the 510(k) safety and effectiveness information upon which the substantial equivalence determination is based or a statement that this information will be made available by the 510(k) applicant to any person within thirty days of a written request.
- **Truthful and Accuracy Statement.** All 510(k) applicants must include a statement certifying that all information in the application is truthful and accurate and that no material fact has been omitted.

In addition, ODE has issued many device-specific guidance documents that contain requirements for data and information to be submitted with the 510(k). The data and information may include engineering testing data, information regarding applicable national and international standards, and/or human clinical data. These documents are posted on FDA's website, which should be consulted frequently as documents are added and removed from the site as necessary.

Hybrid 510(k) Premarket Notifications

"Hybrid 510(k)s" are premarket notifications that include clinical data to demonstrate substantial equivalence to a predicate device.

Some premarket notifications contain clinical data. Those 510(k)s that include clinical information in order to demonstrate substantial equivalence are often referred to as "hybrid 510(k)s."[4] For these hybrid submissions, FDA requires that the 510(k) notification be supported by clinical data demonstrating equivalence of the new device to its predicate device(s). The data collected is intended to validate that any technological differences between the device under consideration and the predicate device(s) do not raise any new questions of safety and efficacy.

In most cases in which a PMA or 510(k) includes clinical data, FDA requires study sponsors to either disclose certain financial interests of the clinical investigators or certify that the clinical investigators do not hold any disclosable financial interests. Under FDAAA, any 510(k) that contains clinical data must be accompanied by a certification that the applicant has complied with the clinical trial registration requirements.

Device Modifications

One of the most difficult decisions for 510(k) holders is when to submit a new premarket notification for changes that the holder intends to make to one of its legally marketed devices. As stated above, FDA's regulations require that a new 510(k) notification be cleared by FDA before the holder makes a change or modification to the device that "could significantly affect the safety or effectiveness of the device, e.g., a significant change or modification in design, material, chemical composition, energy source, or manufacturing process"; or makes a major change or modification in the intended use of the device.[5] FDA has disseminated a guidance document to assist manufacturers in determining which modifications require the submission of new 510(k) notices.[6]

Although the 510(k) holder is responsible for making the initial determination as to whether a change or modification could significantly affect safety or effectiveness, FDA may second-guess the company's decisions. If FDA disagrees with the company's decision not to file a new 510(k) notification for a device modification or change, the agency may make the company file a 510(k) notification and discontinue marketing the device while the 510(k) is pending. The agency may also take enforcement action against the company. As a practical matter, however, if the company has made a good faith effort to document the reasons that it did not submit a new 510(k) for the device change, if the reasons appear genuine, and there are no demonstrated safety problems with the modified device, FDA may use its enforcement discretion to allow the company to continue marketing the device while the new 510(k) notification is pending.

"The New 510(k) Paradigm"

The New 510(k) Paradigm
- *Traditional 510(k)*
- *Special 510(k): Device Modification Option*
- *Abbreviated 510(k)*

To streamline the evaluation of 510(k)s, FDA developed "The New 510(k) Paradigm" (March 20, 1998), which offered manufacturers three alternative approaches for seeking 510(k) clearance.[7] The new paradigm retained the traditional methods of demonstrating substantial equivalence (through adequate device descriptions, appropriate preclinical testing and, occasionally, clinical trials). In addition, under the 510(k) Paradigm, the device manufacturer has the option of submitting a "Special

510(k)" for certain types of device modifications or an "Abbreviated 510(k)."

Under the Special 510(k): Device Modification option, a manufacturer that intends to modify its own legally marketed cleared device may conduct the necessary verification and validation activities to demonstrate that the design outputs of the modified device meet the design input requirements. Special 510(k)s are usually processed by the ODE within thirty days of receipt. Modifications that affect the intended use or alter the basic fundamental scientific technology of the device are not eligible for this alternate type of submission, but may be eligible for the proposed new Abbreviated 510(k) route as described below.

Device manufacturers may submit an Abbreviated 510(k) when 1) a device-specific guidance document exists; 2) a special control has been established; or 3) FDA has recognized a relevant consensus standard. Abbreviated 510(k)s include summary information that describes how special controls have been used to address the risks associated with the device type and a declaration of conformity with any relevant recognized standards, if applicable.

Review Process

In responding to a 510(k) notification, FDA can
1) decide that a device is substantially equivalent to a legally marketed device that does not require premarket approval;
2) decide that it is not substantially equivalent (NSE); or
3) notify the applicant that additional information is required to determine whether the device is, in fact, substantially equivalent.

FDA responds to a 510(k) notification in one of three ways. FDA can 1) decide that a device is substantially equivalent to a legally marketed device that does not require premarket approval; 2) decide that it is not substantially equivalent (NSE); or 3) notify the applicant that additional information is required to determine whether the device is, in fact, substantially equivalent. A decision by FDA that a device is substantially equivalent to a predicate device gives the 510(k) holder the right to commercially market it in the United States. A finding that a device is not substantially equivalent to the predicate device means that it is a "new" Class III device, thus requiring approval of a PMA before being marketed (unless FDA downclassifies the entire device category from Class III to either Class I or Class II or clears the device through the de novo classification process described above). It generally takes four to twelve months from the time of submission to obtain 510(k) premarket clearance, but the process can take longer if FDA requires additional information. There are no assurances that FDA will ultimately clear the 510(k).

In making a request for information, FDA is directed to consider the "least burdensome means of demonstrating substantial equivalence." In a guidance document, FDA defined the least burdensome concept as "a successful means of addressing a premarket issue that involves the most appropriate investment of time, effort, and resources on the part of industry and FDA."[8] FDA has also developed a number of principles for applying the least burdensome concept, which may serve as useful starting points in discussions with reviewers. First, information unrelated to the regulatory decision should not be part of the decision-making process. Second, alternative approaches to all regulatory issues should be considered to optimize time, effort, and resources. Third, all reasonable mechanisms to lessen review times should be used. While it is often advisable to at least raise with FDA least burdensome arguments, the agency ultimately determines what amount and type of data and information are necessary to support marketing applications.

Although FDA's response to applications under section 510(k) establishes, for all practical purposes, whether a particular device can be marketed without a PMA, FDA does not "approve" a premarket notification in the same way that it approves a PMA. FDA's response to section 510(k) notifications makes clear that its findings under this provision extend only to whether a device is substantially equivalent to a predicate device and not whether if it is safe and effective for its intended use(s).

If FDA determines that a device is not substantially equivalent, the applicant may:

- resubmit another 510(k) with new data,
- request a Class I or II designation through the de novo process,
- file a reclassification petition, or
- submit a premarket approval application (PMA).

Third-Party Review

FDA-accredited third parties can conduct initial review of 510(k)s for low-to-moderate risk devices.

On August 1, 1996, FDA began a voluntary Third-party Review Pilot Program for selected medical device 510(k)s to 1) provide manufacturers of eligible devices with an alternative 510(k) review process that could yield more rapid marketing clearance decisions; and 2) enable FDA to use its scientific review resources for higher-risk devices, while maintaining confidence in the review by third parties of low-to-moderate risk devices.

In 1997, with the passage of FDAMA, Congress codified and expanded the pilot program. FDAMA directed FDA to accredit third parties (Accredited Persons) in the private sector to conduct the initial review of 510(k)s for low-to-moderate risk devices; specified that an Accredited Person may not review any Class III device, "Class II devices that are permanently implantable, life-supporting, or life-sustaining," or Class II devices for which clinical data are required; and set limits on the number of Class II devices that may be ineligible for Accredited Person review because clinical data are required. In early 2001, FDA clarified that all

Class I devices and all Class II devices that are not permanently implantable, life sustaining, or require clinical data are eligible for third-party review.

Within thirty days of receiving the written classification and substantial equivalence recommendation from the accredited party, FDA must make its decision as to whether the device is substantially equivalent. If the agency does not adopt the recommendation of the accredited party, FDA must provide the 510(k) applicant and the reviewer a statement explaining in detail its reasons.

PMA Approval Process

An approved PMA is, in effect, a license granted to the applicant to market a particular medical device. Under section 515 of the FDCA, a PMA must be filed if a proposed device is not substantially equivalent to a legally marketed Class I or Class II device, or if it is a pre-amendments Class III device for which FDA has called for PMAs.

A PMA differs significantly from a 510(k) premarket notification in the amount of information that must be submitted to FDA.

A PMA differs significantly from a 510(k) premarket notification in the amount of information (particularly clinical data) that must be submitted to FDA. In contrast to 510(k) notices, which must demonstrate that the new device is "substantially equivalent" to a predicate device, a PMA must be supported by valid scientific evidence to demonstrate the "safety and effectiveness" of the device. PMAs typically include the results of extensive clinical trials, bench tests, laboratory studies, animal studies, and references to any standards relevant to a device's safety or effectiveness. The PMA also must contain a complete description of the device and its components; a detailed description of the methods, facilities, and controls used to manufacture the device; the proposed labeling and advertising literature; and any training materials. In addition, all published and unpublished literature concerning the prior use of the product must be included, as well as a bibliography of all published reports that were not submitted and were known to the applicant concerning the device's safety and effectiveness. The review time for a PMA is significantly longer than for 510(k) notifications.

The following table summarizes the major distinctions between 510(k) notices and PMAs.

	510(k) Premarket Notification	**Premarket Approval (PMA)**
Devices Subject to Requirement	Few Class I, most Class II, and some Class III pre-amendments devices	All Class III postamendments devices and some Class III pre-amendments devices
Clinical Data Requirements	Most are not supported by clinical data; Hybrid 510(k) notifications include clinical data	Clinical studies usually required to support submission
Evidence of Safety and Efficacy Required	Information and data to support the "substantial equivalence" of the device to a legally marketed predicate device	Clinical data and/or scientific evidence supporting "safety and efficacy" claims
Marketing Rights	No exclusivity	Like a Product License
Average FDA Review Time[9]	54 FDA days (06 – 07 FY) 95 total days (06 – 07 FY)	283 FDA days (06 FY) 335 total days (06 FY)
Regulations on Device Changes	Must file new 510(k) if the change "could significantly affect" the safety or efficacy of the device	Must file a new PMA, some form of PMA supplement, or annual report depending on the nature and effect of change on the safety and effectiveness of the device
Advisory Panel Review	No Advisory Panel Review for almost all 510(k) devices	Advisory Panel Review for some but not all PMAs. Generally, no Advisory Panel Review for PMA Supplements

FDA's Least Burdensome Approach policies also apply to PMAs. FDA has directed its reviewers to consider whether preclinical data (including well-designed bench and/or animal testing) are adequate to meet the

FDA ultimately determines what amount and type of data and information are necessary to support marketing applications.

statutory standard and, when clinical data are needed, and to consider alternatives to randomized, controlled trials as well as the use of surrogate endpoints. For example, the sponsor may be allowed to rely on valid non-U.S. data, published data, or studies using nonconcurrent controls such as historical data, objective performance criteria, or patients as their own control. As with the least burdensome requirements for 510(k)s, while it is often advisable to at least raise with FDA least burdensome arguments, the agency ultimately determines what amount and type of data and information are necessary to support marketing applications.

Contents of a PMA

The format and information required in a PMA are outlined in 21 C.F.R. § 814.20:

- The name and address of the applicant.
- A table of contents that specifies the volume and page number for each item referred to in the table. A PMA shall include separate sections on nonclinical laboratory studies and on clinical investigations involving human subjects.
- A summary in sufficient detail that the reader may gain a general understanding of the data and information in the application. The summary shall contain the following information:
    - *Indications for use.* A general description of the disease or condition the device will diagnose, treat, prevent, cure, or mitigate, including a description of the patient population for which the device is intended.
    - *Device description.* An explanation of how the device functions, the basic scientific concepts that form the basis for the device, and the significant physical and performance characteristics of the device. A brief description of the manufacturing process should be included if it will significantly enhance the reader's understanding of the device. The generic name of the device as well as any proprietary name or trade name should be included.
    - *Alternative practices and procedures.* A description of existing alternative practices or procedures for diagnosing, treating, preventing, curing, or mitigating the disease or condition for which the device is intended.
    - *Marketing history.* A brief description of the foreign and U.S. marketing history, if any, of the device, including a list of all countries in which the device has been marketed and a list of all countries in which the device has been withdrawn from marketing for any reason related to the safety or effectiveness of the device. The description shall include the history of the marketing of the device by the applicant and, if known, the history of the marketing of the device by any other person.

- *Summary of studies.* An abstract of any information or report described in the PMA under paragraph (b)(8)(ii) of this section and a summary of the results of technical data submitted under paragraph (b)(6) of this section. Such summary shall include a description of the objective of the study; a description of the experimental design of the study; a brief description of how the data were collected and analyzed; and a brief description of the results, whether positive, negative, or inconclusive. This section shall include the following:
    - A summary of the nonclinical laboratory studies submitted in the application;
    - A summary of the clinical investigations involving human subjects submitted in the application including a discussion of subject selection and exclusion criteria, study population, study period, safety and effectiveness data, adverse reactions and complications, patient discontinuation, patient complaints, device failures and replacements, results of statistical analyses of the clinical investigations, contraindications and precautions for use of the device, and other information from the clinical investigations as appropriate (any investigation conducted under an IDE shall be identified as such).
- *Conclusions drawn from the studies.* A discussion demonstrating that the data and information in the application constitute valid scientific evidence within the meaning of 21 C.F.R. § 860.7 and provide reasonable assurance that the device is safe and effective for its intended use. A concluding discussion shall present benefit and risk considerations related to the device including a discussion of any adverse effects of the device on health and any proposed additional studies or surveillance the applicant intends to conduct following approval of the PMA.

- A complete description of:
    - The device, including pictorial representations;
    - Each of the functional components or ingredients of the device if the device consists of more than one physical component or ingredient;
    - The properties of the device relevant to the diagnosis, treatment, prevention, cure, or mitigation of a disease or condition;
    - The principles of operation of the device; and
    - The methods used in, and the facilities and controls used for, the manufacture, processing, packing, storage, and, where appropriate, installation of the device, in sufficient detail so that a person generally familiar with current good manufacturing practice can make a knowledgeable judgment about the quality control used in the manufacture of the device.

- Reference to any performance standard under section 514 of the act or the Radiation Control for Health and Safety Act of 1968 (42 U.S.C. 263b et seq.) in effect or proposed at the time of the submission and to any voluntary standard that is relevant to any aspect of the safety or effectiveness of the device and that is known to or that should reasonably be known to the applicant. The applicant shall—

- Provide adequate information to demonstrate how the device meets, or justify any deviation from, any performance standard established under section 514 of the act or under the Radiation Control for Health and Safety Act, and
- Explain any deviation from a voluntary standard.

- The following technical sections which shall contain data and information in sufficient detail to permit FDA to determine whether to approve or deny approval of the application:
  - A section containing results of the nonclinical laboratory studies with the device including microbiological, toxicological, immunological, biocompatibility, stress, wear, shelf life, and other laboratory or animal tests as appropriate.
  - A section containing results of the clinical investigations involving human subjects with the device including clinical protocols, number of investigators and subjects per investigator, subject selection and exclusion criteria, study population, study period, safety and effectiveness data, adverse reactions and complications, patient discontinuation, patient complaints, device failures and replacements, tabulations of data from all individual subject report forms and copies of such forms for each subject who died during a clinical investigation or who did not complete the investigation, results of statistical analyses of the clinical investigations, device failures and replacements, contraindications and precautions for use of the device, and any other appropriate information from the clinical investigations. Any investigation conducted under an IDE shall be identified as such. Information on clinical investigations involving human subjects shall include the following:
    - A statement with respect to each study that it either was conducted in compliance with the institutional review board regulations in 21 C.F.R. Part 56, or was not subject to the regulations under 21 C.F.R. §§ 56.104 or 56.105, and that it was conducted in compliance with the informed consent regulations in 21 C.F.R. Part 50; or if the study was not conducted in compliance with those regulations, a brief statement of the reason for the noncompliance.
    - A statement that each study was conducted in compliance with 21 C.F.R. Part 812 or 21 C.F.R. Part 813 concerning sponsors of clinical investigations and clinical investigators, or if the study was not conducted in compliance with those regulations, a brief statement of the reason for the noncompliance.

- For a PMA supported solely by data from one investigation, a justification showing that data and other information from a single investigator are sufficient to demonstrate the safety and effectiveness of the device and to ensure reproducibility of test results.

- The following:
  - A bibliography of all published reports not submitted under this section, whether adverse or supportive, known to or that should reasonably be known to the applicant and that concern the safety or effectiveness of the device.
  - An identification, discussion, and analysis of any other data, information, or report relevant to an evaluation of the safety and effectiveness of the device known to or that should reasonably be known to the applicant from any source, foreign or domestic, including information derived from investigations other than those proposed in the application and from commercial marketing experience.
  - Copies of such published reports or unpublished information in the possession of or reasonably obtainable by the applicant if an FDA advisory committee or FDA requests.
- One or more samples of the device and its components, if requested by FDA. If it is impractical to submit a requested sample of the device, the applicant shall name the location at which FDA may examine and test one or more devices.
- Copies of all proposed labeling for the device. Such labeling may include, e.g., instructions for installation and any information, literature, or advertising that constitutes labeling under section 201(m) of the act.
- An environmental assessment. If the applicant believes that the action qualifies for exclusion, the PMA shall provide information that establishes to FDA's satisfaction that the action requested is included within the excluded category and meets the criteria for the applicable exclusion.
- A financial certification or disclosure statement or both as required by 21 C.F.R. Part 54.
- Such other information as FDA may request. If necessary, FDA will obtain the concurrence of the appropriate FDA advisory committee before requesting additional information.

Review Process

Upon receipt of a PMA, FDA makes a threshold determination as to whether it is sufficiently complete to permit a substantive review. If so, FDA will accept the application for filing. Once accepted, FDA begins an in-depth review of the submission. FDA often asks for more information or clarification of information already provided in the application, which extends the review period. Additionally, if FDA determines that additional clinical trials are necessary, the PMA review may be delayed for the additional period of time required to conduct the studies and to submit the results in an amendment to the pending PMA.

FDA often asks for more information or clarification of information already provided in the application, which extends the review period.

In 1998, the Center for Devices and Radiological Health (CDRH) implemented a "modular approach" for PMA submissions to expedite the PMA review process. Instead of waiting for all sections to be complete, the modular approach allows sponsors to submit parts of their application as soon as they are ready for filing. CDRH and the sponsor must come to a mutual agreement as to which elements will be included in each module. This approach opens communications between the sponsor and CDRH at every step in the application process.

At some point during the review period, FDA usually convenes an advisory committee (typically a panel of clinicians) to evaluate the application and to recommend whether FDA should approve the device. FDA is not bound by the recommendation of the advisory panel. Toward the end of the PMA review process, FDA usually inspects the manufacturer's facilities to ensure compliance with applicable QSR requirements.

If FDA's evaluations of both the PMA and the manufacturing facilities are favorable, FDA may issue either an approval letter or an "approvable" letter, which contains a number of conditions that must be met in order to secure final PMA approval. When and if the manufacturer satisfies those conditions, FDA will issue an approval letter authorizing commercial marketing of the device for specific indications. If FDA's evaluation of the PMA or the manufacturing facilities is not favorable, FDA will deny approval of the application or issue a "non-approvable" letter, which identifies the major deficiencies with the PMA which must be resolved before the application is approved.

Types of changes that require a PMA supplement submission:

1) new indications for use of the device;
2) labeling changes;
3) the use of a different facility or establishment to manufacture, process, or package the device;
4) changes in manufacturing facilities, methods, or quality control procedures;
5) changes in sterilization procedures;
6) changes in packaging;
7) changes in the performance or design specifications, circuits, components, ingredients, principle of operation, or physical layout of the device; and
8) extension of the expiration date of the device based on data obtained under a new or revised stability or sterility testing protocol that has not been approved by FDA.

Device Modifications

Approval of a PMA supplement is required before making a change that affects the safety or effectiveness of the device. Supplements to a PMA often require the submission of the same type of information required for an initial PMA, except that the supplement generally is limited to the information needed to support the safety and effectiveness of the proposed modification, or clarify safety and effectiveness of an existing device (i.e., new adverse event information, higher than predicted failure rates, etc.). The regulations identify types of changes that require the submission of a PMA supplement if the change affects safety or effectiveness. These include 1) new indications for use of the device; 2) labeling changes; 3) the use of a different facility or establishment to manufacture, process, or package the device; 4) changes in manufacturing facilities, methods, or quality control procedures; 5) changes in sterilization procedures; 6) changes in packaging; 7) changes in the performance or design specifications, circuits, components, ingredients, principle of operation, or physical layout of the device; and 8) extension of the expiration date of the device based on data obtained under a new or revised stability or sterility testing protocol that has not been approved by FDA. Many of these changes, such as a change in the manufacturing site, are presumed to affect safety and efficacy and require a PMA supplement.

Additionally, when a PMA supplement is required for an incremental change to the design of a device that affects safety and effectiveness, the PMA supplement must be approved by FDA if 1) nonclinical data demonstrate that the design modification creates the intended additional capacity, function, or performance of the device; and 2) clinical data from the approved PMA application and any supplement provide a reasonable assurance of safety and effectiveness of the modified device. FDA is allowed to require, when necessary, additional clinical data to evaluate the design modification of the device to provide a reasonable assurance of safety and effectiveness.

When a PMA supplement is required for an incremental change to the design of a device that affects safety and effectiveness, the PMA supplement must be approved by FDA if:
1) nonclinical data demonstrate that the design modification creates the intended additional capacity, function, or performance of the device; and
2) clinical data from the approved PMA application and any supplement provide a reasonable assurance of safety and effectiveness of the modified device.

There are several types of submissions that may be used to obtain FDA approval for a modification to a PMA device. These include: a new PMA; a traditional PMA Supplement; a thirty-day notice; a thirty-day supplement; a Special PMA Supplement for Changes Being Effected; PMA Manufacturing Site Change Supplement; or a PMA Annual Report. FDA has disseminated a draft guidance document to assist manufacturers in determining which type of PMA Supplement is required for various types of device modifications.[10]

PMA Annual Reports

FDA requires that the PMA holder report a change for which a PMA supplement is not required in a periodic (annual) report. This change may be made before it is reported to FDA. FDA guidance on PMA changes also allows manufacturers to make certain very minor changes to their approved devices by simply documenting the change information in the firm's files. As a practical matter, most companies include in their annual reports at least general information about all changes that have been made to this device that have not been the subject of an approved supplement, in order to put FDA on notice of the changes.

Annual reports must also contain a bibliography and a summary of unpublished reports of data from any clinical investigations or nonclinical laboratory studies involving the device or related devices and any reports in the scientific literature concerning the device. The annual report should summarize information pertaining to the original PMA, as well as any subsequent PMA supplements and should include all postapproval reports for PMA supplements. The annual report should also describe any adverse device effects.

THE PDP IS AN ALTERNATIVE TO THE PMA PROCESS

An alternative to the PMA process is the Product Development Protocol (PDP) (FDCA § 515(f)). While the PDP option lay dormant for nearly twenty years, FDA issued a proposal in April 1997 and a revised draft guidance on July 27, 1998 (Contents of a Product Development Protocol) to revamp and revive it. Though it is still rarely used, the proposed PDP process includes the following steps: 1) an applicant submits a summary outline of the proposed PDP; 2) FDA determines whether the PDP outline submission is sufficient; 3) FDA and the applicant meet to discuss PDP eligibility issues, concerns, approach, available guidance, and potential panel consultation; 4) PDP is formally filed and FDA conducts a "filing review"; 5) proposed PDP is referred to advisory panel for recommendation, if necessary; 6) advisory panel submits its recommendation to FDA; 7) FDA reaches its decision and issues either an approval letter or feedback concerning the disapproval of the PDP, with suggested modifications; 8) upon approval, the applicant develops preclinical data as required by the PDP; 9) applicant and IRB meet to discuss preclinical results and determine whether clinical studies may begin; 10) the applicant gathers clinical data and notifies FDA of its intent to submit a Notice of Completion; and 11) FDA reviews the Notice of Completion. The agency has 120 days in which to review a PDP protocol, which is not deemed approved if FDA does not decide within the 120-day time frame, and ninety days in which to declare a protocol complete or not completed, once it has received the notice of completion. If all requirements are met, FDA declares the PDP complete, permitting the device to legally go to market.

The PDP procedure is optional; FDA cannot require a sponsor to use the PDP process for determining market approval.

Under 21 C.F.R. § 814.19, a device with a completed PDP will be considered to have an approved PMA. The PDP procedure is optional; FDA cannot require a sponsor to use the PDP process for determining market approval. The major distinguishing feature of a PDP from a PMA approach is FDA's early involvement at the design or preclinical testing phase. Thus, the PDP approach involves a close relationship between FDA and the sponsor in designing appropriate preclinical tests and clinical investigations to establish the safety and effectiveness of the device. The requirements for proof of safety and effectiveness are no less stringent under a PDP than they are under a PMA; thus, the PDP process offers little advantage if the device already has undergone considerable design investigation and evaluation. Historically, the PDP rarely has proven to be feasible for a manufacturer and to be overly demanding of FDA's resources.

Radiological Health

The Electronic Product Radiation Control provisions of the FDCA, which are set forth in sections 531 through 542 (originally enacted as the Radiation Control for Health and Safety Act of 1968 and incorporated into the FDCA by the SMDA) give FDA responsibility for all *medical* and *nonmedical* electronic products that emit any ionizing or nonionizing electromagnetic or particulate radiation or any sonic, infrasonic, or ultrasonic wave. FDA's implementing regulations are codified in 21 C.F.R. Parts 1000 through 1299. These regulations set forth the following three types of requirements: 1) performance standards, 2) reporting requirements, and 3) labeling. Such products must comply with all of the applicable requirements unless they are exempted from certain requirements by regulation.

All medical and nonmedical electronic products that emit any ionizing or nonionizing electromagnetic or particulate radiation or any sonic, infrasonic, or ultrasonic wave must comply with applicable performance, reporting, and labeling requirements.

FDA has issued radiation performance standards intended to control unnecessary human exposure to potential hazardous ionizing and nonionizing radiation and to ensure the safe and effective use of such radiation. Performance studies apply to products such as television receivers and diagnostic x-ray systems.

Manufacturers must submit product reports (including supplements and abbreviated reports), annual reports, and notices of defect or noncompliance. Manufacturers must document any actual or possible unexpected exposure during manufacturing, testing, or use of any electronic product in the appropriate report or notice.

Electronic products subject to a standard must bear label(s) identifying the name and address of the manufacturer, the date of manufacture, and the manufacturer's statement that the product complies with the Department of Health and Human Service's radiation standards or similar language.

FDA has made available product-specific guidance documents and information packages to assist manufacturers in meeting the reporting requirements for radiation-emitting products.

If the product is a medical device, these requirements are in addition to any premarketing or postmarketing requirements that apply to the device.

Conclusion

FDA's regulations on devices are quite extensive and often complex. This chapter summarizes FDA's premarket requirements for devices. It does not address postmarketing requirements, including QSR compliance, medical device reporting, tracking, or product recalls. It is also certainly not an exhaustive account of what is necessary to comply with all of the premarket device requirements. Nonetheless, it highlights the basic requirements for marketing devices in the United States.

Endnotes

1. Special thanks are extended to Laurie Clarke for her significant contributions to the prior version of this chapter. The authors also would like to thank Jennifer Henderson, Kelliann Payne, Lina Kontos, Robert Berlin, Danielle Woodlee, and David Blazina of Hogan & Hartson for their valuable contributions to this chapter.
2. In vitro diagnostic devices have specific exemption limitations not listed here.
3. Office of Device Evaluation, Center for Devices and Radiological Health, Food and Drug Administration. Guidance for the Content of Premarket Submissions for Software Contained in Medical Devices (May 11, 2005).
4. If information concerning similarity to a predicate device must be obtained through a clinical trial, the trial is subject to the requirement of the IDE regulation, 21 C.F.R. § 812.22.
5. 21 C.F.R. § 807.81(a)(3)(i).
6. Office of Device Evaluation, Center for Devices and Radiological Health, Food and Drug Administration. 510(k) Memorandum: Deciding When to Submit a 510(k) for a Change to an Existing Device (January 10, 1997).
7. Office of Device Evaluation, Center for Devices and Radiological Health, Food and Drug Administration. The New 510(k) Paradigm—Alternate Approaches to Demonstrating Substantial Equivalence in Premarket Notifications—Final Guidance (March 20, 1998).
8. *See* Office of Device Evaluation, Center for Devices and Radiological Health, Food and Drug Administration. The Least Burdensome Provisions of the FDA Modernization Act of 1997: Concept and Principles; Draft Guidance for FDA and Industry (May 3, 2001).
9. U.S. Food and Drug Administration, Office of Device Evaluation, Annual Report, Fiscal Year 2006-2007 at 44-50.
10. Office of Device Evaluation, Center for Devices and Radiological Health, Food and Drug Administration. Draft Guidance for Industry and FDA Staff—Modifications to Devices Subject to Premarket Approval (PMA)—The PMA Supplement Decision-Making Process (March 9, 2007).

Chapter 8

Combination Products

Suzanne O'Shea, Baker & Daniels, LLP, Indianapolis, IN

Key Points

- **A combination product comprises two or more different types of regulated components. It can be a drug/device, a biologic/device, a drug/biologic, or a drug/device/biologic.**
- **The Safe Medical Devices Act of 1990 directs FDA to assign review of a combination product to an agency center based on the product's primary mode of action (PMOA).**
- **The PMOA is the single mode of action that provides the most important therapeutic effect of the combination product. Drug-coated vascular stents, for example, are regulated as devices because the mechanical scaffolding of the stent provides the most important therapeutic action.**
- **A sponsor of a combination product can submit a request for designation where the jurisdiction of the reviewing center is unclear or in dispute.**
- **FDA has issued a guidance describing the assessment of user fees for combination products.**

What the Statute and Regulations Say

A combination product is one that has multiple characteristics. It could be a drug/device, a biologic/device, a drug/biologic, or a drug/device/biologic. Increasingly in the past decade there have been more and more products that have been designated by the Food and Drug Administration (FDA) as combination products. An example might be a device whose purpose is to deliver a drug to a patient, or a product used during surgery.

Products that combine two products of the same type are not regarded as combination products. For example, a fixed combination drug product comprising two or more drug ingredients in a single dosage unit is not a combination product. Similarly, products comprising two or more devices, or two or more biological products, are not combination products. Products comprising a drug and a cosmetic, or a drug and a dietary supplement, are also not considered combination products, although they raise some of the same issues as combination products.

The Safe Medical Devices Act of 1990 addresses the threshold combination product issue: when a product comprises more than one type of product, which FDA center will review and regulate it?

The first statutory reference to combination products occurred in the Safe Medical Devices Act of 1990. The statute addresses the threshold combination product issue: when a product comprises more than one type of product, which FDA center will review and regulate it? The statute directs the agency to assign combination products to an agency center for review based on the product's primary mode of action (PMOA), but significantly contains no definition of "combination products" or PMOA:

> The Secretary shall designate a component of the Food and Drug Administration to regulate products that constitute a combination of a drug, device, or biological product. The Secretary shall determine the primary mode of action of the combination product. If the Secretary determines that the primary mode of action is that of—
>
> (A) a drug (other than a biological product), the persons charged with premarket review of drugs shall have primary jurisdiction,
>
> (B) a device, the persons charged with premarket review of devices shall have primary jurisdiction, or
>
> (C) a biological product, the persons charged with premarket review of biological products shall have primary jurisdiction.
>
> FDCA § 503(g); 21 U.S.C. § 353(g)

Regulations issued shortly thereafter included the following definition(s) of combination products:

- A product comprising two or more regulated components—i.e., drug/device, biologic/device, drug/biologic, or drug/device/biologic—that are physically, chemically, or otherwise combined or mixed and produced as a single entity (21 C.F.R. § 3.2(e)(1)). Examples include drug-coated stents, an implantable replacement joint coated with a growth factor, and a monoclonal antibody with a therapeutic drug attached.
- Two or more separate products packaged together in a single package or as a unit and comprising drug and device products, device and biological products, or biological and drug products (21 C.F.R. § 3.2(e)(2)). An example would be a kit containing a drug and a device applicator.
- A drug, device, or biological product packaged separately that according to its investigational plan or proposed labeling is intended for use only with an approved individually specified drug, device, or biological product where both are required to achieve the intended use, indication, or effect and where upon approval of the proposed product the labeling of the approved product would need to be changed

(e.g., to reflect a change in intended use, dosage form, strength, route of administration, or significant change in dose) (21 C.F.R. § 3.2(e)(3)). An investigational device intended to deliver an already approved drug product in a new way for a new use would fit this definition.

- Any investigational drug, device, or biological product packaged separately that according to its proposed labeling is for use only with another individually specified investigational drug, device, or biological product where both are required to achieve the intended use, indication, or effect (21 C.F.R. § 3.2(e)(4)). An investigational device intended to deliver an investigational new drug would be deemed a "combination product" under this definition.

The statute does not address the statutory provisions under which a combination product is to be regulated. In practice, combination products are almost always regulated under the type of application ordinarily submitted to the center with jurisdiction over the product. In other words, combination products assigned to the Center for Drug Evaluation and Research (CDER) are ordinarily reviewed under the new drug provisions of the Federal Food, Drug, and Cosmetic Act (FDCA); combination products assigned to the Center for Devices and Radiological Health are ordinarily reviewed under the device provisions; while combination products assigned to the Center for Biologics Evaluation and Research (CBER) are ordinarily reviewed under the licensing provisions of the Public Health Service Act or the device provisions of the FDCA.

Combination products are almost always regulated under the type of application ordinarily submitted to the center with jurisdiction over the product.

An exception to the above is FDA's final rule "Regulations Restricting the Sale and Distribution of Cigarettes and Smokeless Tobacco to Protect Children and Adolescents." FDA asserted that it had the discretion to choose the premarket approval authority for combination products that provides the best public health protection (61 Fed. Reg. 44395, 44402 (Aug. 28, 1996)). In practice, combination products are almost always reviewed under the premarket approval authority ordinarily used by the lead reviewing center.

Primary Mode of Action and Assignment of a Lead Agency Center

Intercenter Agreements

In 1991, CBER, CDER, and CDRH entered into three Intercenter Agreements (ICAs): a CBER–CDER Intercenter Agreement, a CBER–CDRH Intercenter Agreement, and a CDER–CDRH Intercenter Agreement. Although they differ in content, format, and scope, the ICAs share the common purpose of explaining how various categories of both combination and single-entity medical products were classified and assigned at the time the agreements were written in 1991. The ICAs constitute guidance that is not binding on the public or the agency.

The usefulness of Intercenter Agreements (ICAs) is becoming increasingly limited as new products are developed that were not envisioned when the ICAs were established.

At the time the ICAs were written, they were the major jurisdictional statements issued by the agency, but their usefulness is becoming increasingly limited as new products are developed that were not envisioned when the ICAs were established. Since 1991, FDA has continued to classify and assign many new products not specifically covered by the ICAs. The body of jurisdictional decisions has therefore grown significantly, and over time, the ICAs have become incomplete statements.

In 2006, the agency published a *Federal Register* notice in which it concluded that while the CDER–CDRH and CBER–CDRH ICAs continue to provide useful nonbinding guidance about the assignment and classification of products, the CBER–CDER ICA was rendered almost completely out of date by the transfer of many therapeutic biological products from CBER to CDER in 2003. For these reasons, the agency proposed to continue the CDER–CDRH and the CBER–CDRH ICAs in effect, and to rescind the CBER–CDER ICA. As of the writing of this chapter, this proposal had not been finalized.[1]

Primary Mode of Action

As noted above, the FDCA requires that combination products be assigned to an agency center on the basis of the product's PMOA, but does not include a definition of PMOA. In 2005, FDA amended the combination product regulations to include a definition of PMOA.

The amended regulations begin by defining mode of action as "the means by which a product achieves an intended therapeutic effect or action. For purposes of this definition, 'therapeutic' action or effect includes any effect or action of the combination product intended to diagnose, cure, mitigate, treat, or prevent disease, or affect the structure or any function of the body" (21 C.F.R. § 3.2(k)).

PMOA is defined as "the single mode of action of a combination product that provides the most important therapeutic action of the combination product. The most important therapeutic action is the mode of action expected to make the greatest contribution to the overall intended therapeutic effects of the combination product" (21 C.F.R. § 3.2(m)).

In many cases, this definition suffices to determine a combination product's PMOA. The preamble to the final rule provides several examples, including a drug-coated vascular stent. A vascular stent provides a mechanical scaffold to keep a blood vessel open while the drug is slowly released from the stent to prevent the buildup of new tissue that would re-occlude the artery. This product has two modes of action—the device mode of action contributed by the stent and the drug mode of action contributed by the drug coating. The stent itself provides the most important therapeutic effect of the product, while the drug augments the effectiveness of the stent. Accordingly, drug-coated stents are generally assigned to CDRH for review and regulation under the device provisions of the act.

In contrast, a drug-eluting disc, which is surgically implanted and contains a drug that is slowly released for prolonged, local delivery of chemotherapeutic agents to a tumor site, also has device and drug modes of action. In this case, however, the chemotherapeutic drug makes the most important contribution to the therapeutic effect of the product. Products like this are assigned to CDER for review and regulation under the new drug provisions of the FDCA.

In some cases, FDA has not been able to determine which component makes the major therapeutic contribution to the product. For example, consider a contact lens that corrects vision and also contains a drug that will be delivered from the lens to treat glaucoma. This hypothetical product has both drug and device modes of action, but the two modes of action are independent of one another, and neither appears to be subordinate to the other. In cases like this, where it is impossible to say that one component provides the most important therapeutic action of the product, the agency follows an assignment algorithm set out in the regulations.

Where it is impossible to say that one component provides the most important therapeutic action of the product, FDA follows an assignment algorithm set out in the regulations.

The first step of the algorithm is to determine whether one agency center regulates other combination products presenting similar questions of safety and effectiveness with regard to the combination product as a whole. In this case, CDER regulates glaucoma drugs presenting questions of safety and effectiveness similar to those presented by the drug in the combination product, and CDRH regulates devices presenting questions of safety and effectiveness similar to those presented by the contact lens in the combination product but neither agency center regulates combination products that present questions similar to those presented by both the contact lens and the glaucoma drug.

When no agency center regulates combination products presenting questions of safety and effectiveness with regard to the combination product as a whole, the agency proceeds to the second step of the algorithm; the agency considers which center has the most expertise related to the most significant safety and effectiveness questions presented by the combination product. In this case, the most significant safety and effectiveness questions are related to the characterization, manufacturing, and clinical performance of the drug component, while the safety and effectiveness questions raised by the vision-correcting contact lens are considered more routine. As a result, the corrective contact lens with a glaucoma drug product would be assigned to CDER for review. If a second manufacturer were to submit a marketing application for a similar product, the similar product would be subsequently assigned to CDER under the first step of the algorithm. (21 C.F.R. § 3.4(b).)

Requests for Designation

A request for designation is a formal process by which the sponsor of a combination product requests that FDA assign the product to a center for review when it is unclear or disputed as to which center has jurisdiction over the product.

A request for designation (RFD) is the formal process by which a sponsor of a combination product requests that the agency assign a combination product to a center for review when it is unclear or in dispute as to which center has jurisdiction over the product. An RFD is limited to fifteen pages, and contains summary information about the product and its intended use. FDA recommends that an RFD be submitted as soon as sponsors have enough information about the product to enable FDA to make a decision.

An RFD is also to contain the sponsor's assessment of the modes of action of the components of the combination product, as well as the sponsor's description of the product's PMOA. Sponsors may include data on these points if it is useful to the determination of the product's modes of action and PMOA. The sponsor is also given the opportunity to recommend which center should have jurisdiction over the product.

By statute, the agency is allowed sixty days to respond to RFDs. The agency's decision is in the form of a designation letter. Decisions made in an RFD letter are unique in two respects. First, the agency may change these decisions without the consent of the sponsor only to protect the public health or for other compelling reasons. Second, if the agency does not issue a designation letter in response to an RFD within the sixty-day time period, the sponsor's recommendation as to assignment of the product takes effect. The agency rarely, if ever, fails to issue an RFD letter within the sixty-day time frame.[2]

Consults and Collaboration

Even though one agency center is designated as the lead, the other center will likely be involved in the review. In general, participation by the other relevant agency center is either a consultative review or a collaborative review. The RFD designation letter will state the role of the other center.

A consult occurs when one center requests advice from another center on a specific question or issue. A collaboration occurs when two or more centers have primary review responsibilities, generally for a defined portion of a submission. Regulatory and scientific decisions will be made by the management of each center for that portion of the review assigned to it, including the decision to approve or refuse to approve the product.

FDA has issued a Standard Operating Procedure (SOP) for the Intercenter Consultative/Collaborative Review Process.[3] The objective of this SOP is to improve intercenter communication on combination products, as well as the timeliness and consistency of intercenter consultative and collaborative reviews.

A frequent concern about consults and collaborations is that they will slow down the review process. To allay such concerns, the SOP states that "all consulted and collaborating reviewers should be held accountable and receive credit for thorough and timely expert reviews and advice. Every effort should be made to meet the due date identified by the request originator." The SOP also stresses the importance of frequent, ongoing communication between the primary reviewer and the consulting or collaborative reviewer.

Combination Product Issues

Adverse Event Reporting

FDA has not issued a regulation covering the reporting of adverse events for combination products. The agency has, however, issued for comment purposes only, a concept paper on postmarket safety reporting for combination products.[4]

FDA has not issued a regulation covering the reporting of adverse events for combination products.

The postmarket safety reporting requirements for drugs, biologics, and devices share many similarities. For example, each requires the reporting of deaths and serious adverse events, as well as the submission of periodic or follow-up reports. In general, appropriate postmarket safety reporting is achieved by following the requirements for the type of marketing application used for approval or clearance of the combination product. For example, a drug/device combination product approved under a new drug application would be subject to the postmarket reporting requirements for drugs.

There are some differences in the adverse event reporting requirements of drugs, devices, and biological products, however, and if combination products were subject only to the postmarket reporting requirements associated with the marketing application, some reporting requirements would not apply. For example:

- Both drug and device regulations require that deaths or serious injuries be reported. In addition, device postmarket safety regulations require reporting of device malfunctions where no death or serious injury occurred, but the device would be likely to cause or contribute to a death or serious injury if the malfunction were to recur (21 C.F.R. § 803.20(3)(ii)). Reporting for drugs and biological products does not include an analogous requirement to report a product failure. For some combination products containing a device constituent part that is regulated under the drug or biological product provisions of the act, it may be necessary to also comply with the device requirements should an adverse event occur that is attributable to the device constituent part.

For some combination products containing a device constituent part that is regulated under the drug or biological product provisions of the act, it may be necessary to also comply with the device requirements should an adverse event occur that is attributable to the device constituent part.

- The device regulations also require reporting within five days of a reportable event that requires remedial action to prevent an unreasonable risk of substantial harm to the public health, as well as reportable events for which FDA makes a written request. (21 C.F.R. § 803.10(c)(2)(i).) For some combination products containing a device constituent part that are regulated under the drug or biological product provisions of the act, it may be necessary to also comply with the device requirements if the adverse event is attributable to the device constituent part.
- For drugs and biological products, regulations require reporting of adverse events that are both serious and unexpected within fifteen days of the sponsor's receipt of information about the event. (21 C.F.R. § 314.80(c).) Device postmarket safety regulations require reporting of any serious injury within thirty days. For some combination products containing a device and a drug or biological product, that are regulated under the device provisions of the act, it may be necessary to also comply with the drug and biological product requirements when the adverse event is attributable to the drug or biological product constituent part.
- The biological product regulations require a written report within seven days of any blood-related death (21 C.F.R. § 606.170). For some blood-containing combination products regulated under the drug or device provisions of the act, it may be necessary to also comply with this requirement.

Current Good Manufacturing Practices

While FDA has issued a draft guidance on current Good Manufacturing Practices (cGMPs) for combination products, as of this writing FDA had not issued a proposed or final regulation covering the application of cGMPs (including 21 C.F.R. Parts 210 and 211 for drugs and biological products and Quality System Regulations (QSRs) for devices, 21 C.F.R. Part 820.)[5]

Current Good Manufacturing Practices and QSRs are intended to ensure that drugs; biological products; human cells, tissues, and cellular and tissue based-products; and devices are made properly. Each set of regulations, however, is somewhat different because each is tailored to the characteristics of the types of products for which they were designed. Each set of regulations contains certain express or specific requirements that may be only generally expressed in the other set of regulations. For example, the cGMP regulations for drugs and biological products specifically require calculation of yield and stability while QSRs contain more general design validation provisions. Similarly, QSRs have detailed Corrective and Preventive Action (CAPA) provisions, while cGMPs contain more general production record requirements.

Under the draft current Good Manufacturing Practices (cGMP) guidance, each drug, biological product, or device constituent part of a combination product, taken individually, is subject only to its governing cGMP regulations until it is actually combined with another type of constituent part to form a combination product.

Under the draft guidance, each drug, biological product, or device constituent part of a combination product, taken individually, is subject only to its governing cGMP regulations until it is actually combined with another type of constituent part to form a combination product. For example, when the constituent parts of a combination product are separately marketed, such as a new device intended for use with an individually specified, already approved drug product marketed by a different manufacturer, the device constituent part would be subject only to the QSRs, while the drug constituent part would be subject only to the cGMP regulations.

On the other hand, for combination products in which the constituent parts are physically, chemically, or otherwise combined or co-packaged, it generally should not be necessary for manufacturers to maintain two separate manufacturing systems to ensure compliance with both sets of regulations during and after joining the constituent parts together. Compliance with both sets of regulations during and after joining the constituent parts of a combination product can generally be achieved by using either the cGMP or QSRs because it should be possible to develop and implement a practice that complies with a more specific requirement in one set of regulations even while using the more general requirement framework included in the other set of regulations.

The following chart, from the draft guidance, identifies key provisions of the cGMP and QSRs that differ in their specificity. FDA recommends that manufacturers of constituent parts that are co-packaged or physically, chemically, or otherwise combined carefully consider these provisions during and after joining the constituent parts to ensure compliance with both cGMP and QSRs.

Key Current Good Manufacturing Practice Provisions to Consider During and After Joining Together Co-Packaged and Single-Entity Combination Products

If The Operating Manufacturing Control System Is Part 820 (QS Regulation)		If the Operating Manufacturing Control System Is Part 210/211 (cGMP Regulation)	
Carefully Consider These Specific cGMP Requirements	Title	Carefully Consider These Specific QS Requirements	Title
§ 211.84	Testing and approval or rejection of components, drug product containers, and closures	§ 820.30	Design controls
§ 211.103	Calculation of yield	§ 820.50	Purchasing controls
§ 211.137	Expiration dating	§ 820.100	Corrective and preventative actions
§ 211.165	Testing and release for distribution		
§ 211.166	Stability testing		
§ 211.167	Special testing requirements		
§ 211.170	Reserve samples		

According to the draft guidance, it may be important to consider other specific requirements to ensure compliance with both cGMP and QSRs depending upon the particular combination product. An example is aseptic control assurance for drug and biological product constituent parts unable to withstand terminal sterilization.

In the draft guidance, FDA recommends that manufacturers present information to the agency during the development phase about how they intend to achieve compliance with both sets of regulations during and after joining the constituent parts together of proposed combination products that will have constituent parts that are physically, chemically, or otherwise combined, or that will be co-packaged. For example, FDA recommends that a pre-investigational new drug (pre-IND) or pre-investigational device exemption (pre-IDE) meeting include a discussion of the sponsor's implementation of cGMPs, including consideration of risks of the combination product, its technology, and any anticipated postmarket development and postapproval changes. FDA recommends that the sponsor include all critical manufacturers in these discussions and include information on critical steps that may be conducted at source/contract firms and any special testing. FDA's Office of Combination Products is available as a resource to sponsors in the resolution of cGMP concerns.

Number of Applications

According to FDA regulations, "the designation of one agency component as having primary jurisdiction for the premarket review and regulation of a combination product does not preclude . . . in appropriate cases, the requirement by FDA of separate applications." (21 C.F.R. § 3.4(c).) This regulation suggests that most of the time combination products will be reviewed and regulated under one application.

FDA has also issued a concept paper intended to clarify the number of marketing applications necessary for approval or clearance of a combination product.[6] According to the concept paper, while a combination product is assigned to an agency center based on the product's PMOA, the PMOA does not automatically determine the type of marketing application that will be used. Depending on the type of product, approval or clearance could be obtained either through a single marketing application, or through separate marketing applications for the individual constituent parts of the combination product.

Depending on the type of product, approval or clearance could be obtained either through a single marketing application, or through separate marketing applications for the individual constituent parts of the combination product.

For most combination products, a single marketing application should be sufficient to ensure product safety and effectiveness. FDA review of a combination product under a single application addresses the combination product as a whole and its constituent parts.

Although two applications for a combination product have rarely been required, the concept paper notes that there are some circumstances in which two applications could be necessary to ensure safety or effectiveness of the combination product. According to the concept paper, two applications might be required in the following circumstances:

- when the constituent parts are separate and complex products;
- when one constituent part has uses beyond the combination product;

- when a Biologics License Application for further manufacture is appropriate to ensure the identity, safety, purity, and potency of certain biological products when the product as a whole is being regulated under the drug or device provisions;
- to effect labeling revisions for a constituent part that is already approved for uses that do not include the proposed combination product indication;
- to maintain regulatory consistency.

Additionally FDA, under some circumstances, may accept two applications from the manufacturer when one would suffice to ensure the safety and effectiveness of the product. FDA recognizes that certain regulatory mechanisms (such as new drug exclusivity or orphan drug benefits) are associated only with certain types of marketing applications and that sponsors may wish to derive specific benefits that accrue under a particular application. In addition, when two manufacturers are involved in the development and manufacture of a combination product, each manufacturer may prefer its own application. The concept paper requests stakeholder perspectives on appropriate FDA responses when sponsors desire to have multiple applications.

User Fees

Congress first authorized FDA to collect fees from companies that manufacture drugs and biological products under the Prescription Drug User Fee Act of 1992 (PDUFA), and from companies that manufacture devices under the Medical Device User Fee and Modernization Act of 2002 (MDUFMA). FDA has issued a guidance describing the assessment of user fees for combination products.[7]

In general, combination products reviewed under one application will be subject to the user fees associated with that type of application.

In general, combination products reviewed under one application will be subject to the user fees associated with that type of application. For example, a biologic/device or a drug/device combination product for which a device premarket approval (PMA) application is required would be subject to the PMA fee under MDUFMA.

In instances where one application would suffice but the sponsor(s) elect to submit two applications covering the constituent parts of a combination product, FDA believes that the user fees associated with both applications should be payable. Although sponsors may still be eligible for fee waivers or reductions, FDA assesses the two fees because review of two applications when one would suffice places an extra burden on FDA resources.

On the other hand, when FDA requires two applications for a combination product, sponsors are encouraged to consider submitting a request for user fee waiver or reduction. In particular, according to the guidance, FDA will look closely at whether a PDUFA "barrier to innovation" waiver may be applicable to reduce the additional fee burden associated with FDA's requirement for two marketing applications.

Both PDUFA and MDUFMA provide waivers or reductions of fees associated with the submission of applications by small businesses, although the eligibility standards and amount of the fee waiver or reduction differ. Sponsors of combination products requiring two applications should consider applying for the small business waiver or reduction under PDUFA and/or MDUFMA if they meet the qualification criteria.

Both PDUFA and MDUFMA provide waivers or reductions of fees associated with the submission of applications by small businesses, although the eligibility standards and amount of the fee waiver or reduction differ.

Other than certain specific situations, such as marketing applications submitted by small businesses, standard MDFUMA fees are required for nearly all device marketing applications. In contrast, PDUFA provides for waivers or reduction of fees where:

- Such waiver is necessary to protect the public health.
- The assessment of the fee would present a significant barrier to innovation because of limited resources or other circumstances.
- The fees to be paid by such person will exceed the anticipated present and future costs incurred by the Secretary in conducting the process for the review of human drug applications for such person.

Combination products that incorporate cutting-edge, innovative technologies that hold promise for advancing patient care may also be eligible for waiver or a reduction of fees as FDA believes that assessment of two marketing application fees could represent a significant barrier to its development. To be eligible for the "innovative combination product" waiver under PDUFA's "barrier to innovation because of . . . other circumstances" provision, FDA considers the following factors:

- the combination product as a whole is innovative;
- FDA is requiring two fee-bearing marketing applications for the product;
- the applications request approval only of the two components of the combination product for use together (i.e., neither application includes an independent use for that constituent part of the combination product); and
- the applicant does not qualify for a small business waiver or have limited resources.

FDA considers the following factors in determining whether a combination product is innovative for purposes of the waiver application:

- the product addresses an unmet medical need in the treatment, diagnosis, or prevention of disease and therefore provides significant, meaningful advantage over alternatives;

- factors such as whether one of the two applications includes a new molecular entity, has been designated as a priority drug, is eligible for expedited device review, or has been granted fast track status; and
- the existence of treatment alternatives (which would weigh against deciding that a product is innovative).

For innovative combination products requiring two applications, FDA would expect to reduce PDUFA fees as follows in appropriate situations:

- For products requiring a MDUFMA application and a PDUFA application, FDA would expect to reduce the PDUFA fee by the amount of the MDUFMA fee. Thus a sponsor would pay the full MDUFMA fee associated with the MDUFMA application, and a PDUFA fee reduced by the amount of the MDUFMA fee. The total amount paid would be the equivalent of one PDUFA fee.
- For products requiring two PDUFA applications (for combination products comprising a drug constituent part and a biological product constituent part), FDA would expect to reduce each PDUFA fee by half. In such a case, the total amount paid would be equivalent to one PDUFA fee.

The ''innovative combination product'' waiver provides for a possible waiver only of application fees; the waiver is not applicable to annual product and establishment fees.

According to the guidance, the ''innovative combination product'' waiver provides for a possible waiver only of application fees; the waiver is not applicable to annual product and establishment fees. FDA reviews requests for waivers of product and establishment fees, as well as requests for waivers or reductions of application fees not qualifying for the ''innovative combination product'' waiver, under criteria applicable to both combination and noncombination products.

FDA's Office of Combination Products

Immediately following formal creation of the combination products category in 1990, the task of designating a lead agency center for review and regulation of combination products was assigned to the Office of the Chief Mediator and Ombudsman in the Office of the Commissioner. Over the years, a number of concerns have been raised about combination products, including concerns about the consistency, predictability, and transparency of the assignment process; issues related to the management of the review process when two or more FDA centers had review responsibilities for a combination product; and lack of clarity about the postmarket regulatory controls applicable to combination products.

FDA's Office of Combination Products (OCP) was established on December 24, 2002, as required by MDUFMA, to address such concerns. The law gives OCP broad responsibilities covering the regulatory life cycle of combination products. As outlined in MDUFMA, the responsibilities of OCP include:

The Medical Device User Fee and Modernization Act of 2002 gives FDA's Office of Combination Products broad responsibilities covering the regulatory life cycle of drug-device, drug-biologic, and device-biologic combination products.

- assigning an FDA center to have primary jurisdiction for review of a combination product;
- ensuring timely and effective premarket review of combination products by overseeing reviews involving more than one agency center;
- ensuring consistency and appropriateness of postmarket regulation of combination products;
- resolving disputes regarding the timeliness of premarket review of combination products;
- updating agreements, guidance documents, or practices specific to the assignment of combination products; and
- submitting annual reports to Congress on the office's activities and impact.

By most accounts, OCP has been successful in meeting these objectives.[8] In particular, the annual report to Congress provides a great deal of detail about the activities of the OCP.

ENDNOTES

1. The most recent information relative to these ICAs is available at www.fda.gov/oc/combination/intercenter.html.
2. Additional details about RFDs can be found in 21 C.F.R. §§ 3.7 – 3.9, and in a guidance document issued by the Office of Combination Products, "How to Write a Request for Designation (RFD)" available at www.fda.gov/oc/combination/Guidance-How%20to%20Write%20an%20RFD.pdf.
3. Available at www.fda.gov/oc/ombudsman/intercentersop.pdf.
4. See www.fda.gov/oc/combination/adveventconcept.html.
5. For the most up-to-date information, see www.fda.gov/oc/combination/OCLove1dft.html.
6. See www.fda.gov/oc/combination/singlesepconpaper.html.
7. See www.fda.gov/oc/combination/userfees.html.
8. For further information, please see the OCP website at www.fda.gov/oc/combination.

Chapter 9

The Cosmetics Regulatory Process

Elizabeth H. Anderson and Frances K. Wu, The Personal Care Products Council, Washington, D.C.

Key Points

- The Federal Food, Drug, and Cosmetic Act (FDCA) defines cosmetics as articles applied to the human body to cleanse, beautify, alter the appearance, etc.
- FDA prohibits "adulterated" cosmetics, which includes not only contaminated ingredients or packaging, but also use of unapproved color additives or banned ingredients.
- FDA prohibits "misbranding," which includes false or misleading labeling by claims about the product, inaccurate labeling such as net content declaration, having a misleading container size or amount, and other violations.
- Cosmetics are not subject to premarket approval by FDA, but the product and ingredients must be tested for safety. If the manufacturer cannot substantiate safety, a warning is required.
- Color additives are the only cosmetic ingredients that must be pre-approved or "listed" by FDA. Color additives are subject to the Delaney Clause, which bars using any color shown to cause cancer "in man or animal."
- Coal tar hair dyes are subject to special regulatory requirements.
- FDA monitors compliance through random inspections of cosmetic facilities.
- The cosmetic industry has several self-regulatory programs to work with FDA in assuring ingredient and product safety.
- The "intended use" doctrine states that cosmetic or drug status is determined by labeling claims about the intended use of the product.
- Cosmetic product labeling is governed by the FDCA and the Fair Packaging and Labeling Act (FPLA). Cosmetic labels must state the statement of identity, net contents, ingredients, any required warning, and other information.

What the Law and Regulations Say

Under the Federal Food, Drug, and Cosmetic Act (FDCA), the standards governing cosmetics differ significantly from those governing foods, medical devices, or drugs, largely because of the relatively few risks associated with their use.

Section 201(i) of the FDCA defines a "cosmetic" as:

> 1) an article intended to be rubbed, poured, sprinkled, or sprayed on, introduced into or otherwise applied to the human body or any part thereof for cleansing, beautifying, promoting attractiveness, or altering the appearance; and
>
> 2) an article intended for use as a component of any such article; except that such term shall not include soap.[1]

The FDCA prohibits the introduction into interstate commerce of any cosmetic that is "adulterated." Section 601 of the FDCA is very specific about what makes a cosmetic adulterated:

- if it bears or contains any poisonous or deleterious substance that may render it injurious to users under conditions of use prescribed in the labeling thereof, or under such conditions of use as are customary or usual;
- if it consists in whole or in part of any filthy, putrid, or decomposed substance;
- if it has been prepared, packed, or held under unsanitary conditions whereby it may have become contaminated with filth, or whereby it may have been rendered injurious to health;
- if its container is composed, in whole or part, of any poisonous or deleterious substance that may render the contents injurious to health; or
- if it is not a hair dye and it is, or it bears or contains, a color additive that is unsafe within the meaning of section 721(a).

FDA regulations provide that the mere presence of certain ingredients in the formulation may render a cosmetic product adulterated.

Further, Food and Drug Administration (FDA) regulations provide that the mere presence of certain ingredients in the formulation may render a cosmetic product adulterated. Examples of such ingredients include the antibacterial agent bithionol; mercury as an eye makeup preservative (except at strict limits); vinyl chloride included as a propellant in cosmetic aerosol products such as hairsprays; certain halogenated salicylanilides; zirconium in aerosol cosmetics; and specified cattle materials.

The FDCA also prohibits the sale of any cosmetic that is "misbranded." Under section 602 of the FDCA, a cosmetic is misbranded:

- if its labeling is false or misleading in any particular;
- if in package form unless it bears a label containing 1) the name and place of business of the manufacturer, packer, or distributor; and 2) an accurate statement of the quantity of the contents in terms of

weight, measure, or numerical count: *Provided* That under the clause (2) of this paragraph reasonable variations shall be permitted, and exemptions as to small packages shall be established, by regulations prescribed by the Secretary.

- if any word, statement or other information required by the act to appear on the label or labeling is not prominently placed thereon with such conspicuousness (as compared to other words, statements, designs, or devices in the labeling) and in such terms as to render it likely to be read and understood by the ordinary individual under customary conditions of purchase and use;
- if its containers are so made, formed, or filled as to be misleading;
- if it is a color additive and its packaging and labeling are not in conformity with regulations issued under section 721 (this requirement does not apply to color additives marketed and intended for use only in or on hair dyes as defined in section 601(a)); or
- if its packaging or labeling is in violation of an applicable regulation issued pursuant to sections 3 or 4 of the Poison Prevention Packaging Act of 1970.

FDA regulations require that a manufacturer substantiate the safety of a finished cosmetic product and each of its ingredients. Because cosmetics are not required to be approved by FDA before marketing, FDA enacted a labeling requirement for products where safety has not been substantiated before marketing. A product is considered misbranded if substantiation is not available, unless the following warning appears on the principal display panel: "*Warning* — The safety of this product has not been determined." (21 C.F.R. § 740.10(a)). FDA has made it clear that the safety substantiation requirement does not require that new testing be conducted in every case "where reasonable scientific opinion would regard the available data as adequate."

FDA regulations require that a manufacturer substantiate the safety of a finished cosmetic product and each of its ingredients. A product is considered misbranded if substantiation is not available, unless the following warning appears on the principal display panel: "Warning—The safety of this product has not been determined."

Color Additives

The only cosmetic ingredients that must be pre-approved or "listed" by FDA to be used in a finished cosmetic product are color additives. Certain color additives also must be "certified," meaning each production batch must be approved by FDA.

FDA approves color additives specifically for use in a cosmetic, a drug, or a food, or any combination of those products (e.g., D&C Green No. 5, FD&C Yellow No. 5). FDA also may put limitations on the cosmetic use of a color additive, such as where it may be used ("externally except eye area"), and may establish maximum allowable use levels (e.g., "Lip products (5% maximum)"). Use of an unapproved color in a cosmetic makes the product adulterated under the FDCA and subject to FDA seizure and other legal action. The requirement for pre-approval of color additives stems from the Color Additive Amendments of 1960.

These amendments prohibited use of a color additive unless a regulation permitted the additive's use. The FDCA defines "color additive" as a "dye, pigment, or other substance [which] when added or applied to a food, drug or cosmetic, or to the human body or any part thereof, is capable (alone or through reaction with any other substance) of imparting color thereto . . . ."

The Delaney Clause imposes an absolute ban on any color "if, after tests which are appropriate for the evaluation of the safety of additives for such use, or after other relevant exposure of man or animal to such additive, it is found by the Secretary to induce cancer in man or animal."

The Color Additive Amendments also contain "The Delaney Clause," a provision named for its author, Congressman James Delaney (D-NY). This provision was intended to guard against cancer-causing ingredients and imposes an absolute ban on any color "if, after tests which are appropriate for the evaluation of the safety of additives for such use, or after other relevant exposure of man or animal to such additive, it is found by the Secretary to induce cancer in man or animal." (21 U.S.C. § 379e(b)(5)(B)). A court case concluded that Congress intended for FDA to deny approval of a color additive if it posed a risk, even a *de minimis* or trivial one, of inducing cancer in animals.

There is an exemption for colors used in hair dyes. Hair dye products are cosmetics that generally must use FDA-approved color additives; however, in 1938, when cosmetics were regulated by the FDCA for the first time, Congress included an exemption from the nonadulteration provision for coal tar hair dyes.

Section 601(a) of the FDCA states that a cosmetic is adulterated if it contains any deleterious substance that could harm the user even if the product is used according to the labeling or customary use. This prohibition, however, does not apply to coal tar hair dyes if their labels bear the following statement:

> Caution This product contains ingredients, which may cause skin irritation on certain individuals, and a preliminary test according to accompanying directions should first be made. This product must not be used for dyeing the eyelashes or eyebrows; to do so may cause blindness.

In addition, the label should have adequate directions for preliminary testing such as patch test directions. If the label lacks the caution statement and patch test directions, FDA can take regulatory action. This exemption applies only to coal tar hair dyes and not to other coloring ingredients in hair dyes, or eyebrow and eyelash dye products.

FDA Enforcement Authority

The primary means for FDA to monitor the cosmetics industry is through random inspections of cosmetic facilities. FDA also checks imports at ports of entry and investigates consumer or competitor complaints about specific products. If FDA perceives a violation through information obtained during a facility inspection or an import inspection, it may send the company a "warning letter." The warning letter typically issues from FDA's district office, which oversees the facility or the place of import in the United States, but may occasionally come from the Center for Food Safety and Applied Nutrition at FDA headquarters.

FDA monitors the cosmetics industry through random inspections of cosmetic facilities, checks imports at ports of entry, and investigates complaints about specific products.

Inspection of cosmetic manufacturing establishments is one of FDA's primary means of cosmetic product oversight. FDA is not required to notify the facility in advance of inspection. The inspection usually is routine, but could be triggered by FDA's belief that a company's product(s) is being manufactured or marketed in violation of the law.

A Cosmetic Facility

FDA's authority during a cosmetic inspection is less comprehensive than for biologics or drugs, for example. A manufacturer is not legally required to provide FDA inspectors with master formula records, batch production records, products or ingredient analyses, safety testing data of any type, and consumer complaint files or adverse experience data. Moreover, companies are not required to produce any financial data or other business records; however, if requested by an FDA inspector, companies are required to provide access to and copies of shipping records showing movement of cosmetics in interstate commerce.

The right of FDA inspectors to take photographs during an inspection is an area of continuing controversy among FDA, industry, and the courts. In its Inspections Operations Manual (IOM), FDA takes the position that it has the authority to take photographs. The FDA IOM instructs inspectors not to request permission to take photographs but to take the camera into the firm and use it as necessary, as with any other inspectional equipment. Industry has taken the posture that it may deny inspectors the ability to take photographs, particularly when necessary to protect trade secrets regarding manufacturing equipment, formulations, or processes.

In the course of cosmetic inspections, FDA inspectors frequently take samples of finished and unfinished materials and labeling. FDA frequently samples products to ensure that the cosmetic is using FD&C approved color additives.

FDA and Inspection of Cosmetic-Drugs Under FDAMA

FDAMA allows facilities that manufacture drugs or products regulated both as cosmetics and drugs (such as skincare products containing sunscreen and antiperspirant/deodorant products) to be inspected to the same extent as prescription drug manufacturers.

The Food and Drug Administration Modernization Act of 1997 (FDAMA) changed FDA's inspection authority for drugs but *not for cosmetics.* Section 704 of the FDCA, however, as amended by FDAMA, allows facilities that manufacture drugs or products regulated both as cosmetics and drugs (such as skincare products containing sunscreen and antiperspirant/deodorant products) to be inspected to the same extent as prescription drug manufacturers. Under such circumstances, FDA has authority to request all records that could determine whether a cosmetic drug is adulterated or misbranded. The following records may be available under the OTC Drug Inspection Authority:

- Quantitative Formulas, specifications for all active and inactive ingredients and all testing done to assure that ingredients met those specifications; all records relating to the manufacture of the drug, including batch records, validation records, stability testing data, and all other types of records either required to be maintained under drug Good Manufacturing Practice (GMP) regulations or that bear upon compliance with drug GMP regulations;
- all testing of ingredients and finished products relating to microbial content; all release specifications for finished product, all testing of finished products to determine compliance with release specifications, and all records relating to investigations of batches that in any way failed release specifications; all testing and other safety substantiation for inactive and active ingredients, and for finished products;
- all data relating to product packaging; all consumer complaints of any type relating to safety and effectiveness;
- all testing to support product claims of any type;
- all consumer complaints about product performance or other product attributes.
- formula records, manufacturing batch records, adverse reaction reports, and evidence of GMP compliance for cosmetic drugs.

This expanded inspection authority does not apply to cosmetic products that are not drugs.

Labeling Deficiencies

FDA has issued warning letters to cosmetic companies in recent years alleging labeling deficiencies. These deficiencies fall into several basic categories. The largest category by far consists of labeling claims that, under the "intended use" doctrine, convert a cosmetic into a drug. In determining the intended use of a product, FDA scrutinizes not only the claims and representations made about a product but also whether the mandatory labeling information is present (such as listing ingredients). The resulting warning letter for labeling violations would allege that the product is "misbranded" under section 602 of the FDCA.

As with other FDA-regulated products, if FDA believes a cosmetic is adulterated or misbranded under the statute, the agency may opt to take several actions including seizure, refuse entry into the United States if it is a foreign product, go to federal district court to obtain a restraining order to prevent further shipments, or initiate a criminal enforcement action. Examples of products seized as "adulterated" in the past include various eyebrow and eyelash dye products, and nail preparations containing methyl methacrylate.

Industry Self-Regulation

CIR was designed to help companies substantiate the safety of ingredients used in cosmetics and the final formulation without duplicating safety testing already done by others.

♦ Cosmetic Ingredient Review

In the past, the cosmetic industry sought an FDA program to publicly substantiate the safety of cosmetic ingredients. Due to other resource commitments, FDA declined and suggested that the cosmetics industry establish its own program to evaluate cosmetic ingredient safety.

In response, the cosmetic industry developed and adopted a number of self-regulatory programs, with the Cosmetic Ingredient Review (CIR) becoming the cornerstone of the cosmetic industry's self-regulatory effort. This industry-funded body was established in 1976 by the Cosmetic, Toiletry, and Fragrance Association (CTFA) (now known as the Personal Care Products Council). The CIR was designed to help companies substantiate the safety of ingredients used in cosmetics and the final formulation without duplicating safety testing already done by others.

As part of the ingredient safety assessment, the available scientific data on an ingredient is reviewed by a seven-member expert panel. Panel conclusions are publicly announced by CIR without private review or comment by the industry. The panel's scientists are nominated by consumer, scientific, and clinical groups; government agencies; and industry. They are chosen from several scientific disciplines such as dermatology and toxicology. The expert panel also has three nonvoting members representing a consumer group, industry, and FDA.

The scientific review of each ingredient goes through several stages. The technical staff of CIR prepares a Scientific Literature Review summarizing known data gleaned from databases and industry studies. The Literature Review is made available for public comment with a request for any data, published or unpublished, that the review has not included. After sixty days, the comments received (including data submissions), are incorporated into the document for panel consideration. After a series of public meetings, the panel issues a Tentative Report.

The Tentative Report may reach any one of four tentative conclusions: safe as used, safe with certain qualifications, unsafe, or insufficient data available to CIR to support safety. The Tentative Report is available for comment for sixty days. All comments are analyzed and a response developed. The Final Report incorporates any changes based on public comment and is published in the peer-reviewed *Journal of the American College of Toxicology*. Final Reports on ingredient safety also appear in the *CIR Compendium*, published annually.

A primary goal of CIR is to minimize duplication of ingredient safety testing; consequently CIR has deferred or excluded review of ingredients that are subject to other safety assessments. Examples include over-the-counter (OTC) drug active ingredients, fragrance ingredients (reviewed by the Research Institute for Fragrance Materials), ingredients in new drug applications, color additives reviewed by FDA under section 721 of the FDCA, and those subject to any final FDA regulation. The chemicals taken from CTFA's *International Cosmetic Ingredient Dictionary and Handbook* were ranked according to potential biological activity, frequency of use, concentration of use, route of exposure (e.g., inhalation), area of exposure (e.g., the eyes), and any special group of users (e.g., infants).

♦ Voluntary Registration and Reporting Programs

Since the mid-1970s the industry has participated in two voluntary programs administered by FDA: registration of cosmetic facilities (including foreign facilities) and registration of cosmetic product ingredients statements.

Since the mid-1970s, the industry has participated in two voluntary programs administered by FDA. One involves the voluntary registration of cosmetic facilities, including foreign facilities. Upon registering, a facility is assigned a registration number by FDA. The other program involves the voluntary registration of cosmetic product ingredient statements. FDA has developed an electronic database with industry input into which such information should be reported (and updated where necessary). The facility and formula information is entered into an FDA database that enables the agency to notify and investigate the appropriate entities in the event of an adverse incident involving a cosmetic product. The programs apply only to products sold at retail and excludes products sold for professional use.

♦ Voluntary Industry Code of Practice

In 2006, the Personal Care Products Council adopted a Consumer Commitment Code designed to reinforce industry practices already in place and to initiate additional actions intended to enhance cosmetic safety. The code incorporates existing practices such as the current reporting of manufacturing establishments and includes a new Safety Information Summary Program that provides FDA with relevant cosmetic product information and makes ingredient safety readily available upon request. The code went into effect on January 1, 2007, and is open to all members of the industry.

The Cosmetic/Drug Distinction

In determining whether a product is a "cosmetic" or a "drug," it is important to examine the definitions for "cosmetic" and "drug" in the FDCA. As noted earlier, the term "cosmetic" means:

> 1) articles *intended* to be rubbed, poured, sprinkled, or sprayed on, introduced into or otherwise applied to the human body or any part thereof for cleansing, beautifying, promoting attractiveness, or altering the appearance, and
>
> 2) articles *intended* for use as a component of any such articles; except that such term shall not include soap. (emphasis added) (FDCA § 201(i); 21 U.S.C. § 321(i))

"Drug" means:

> articles *intended* for use in the diagnosis, cure, mitigation, treatment, or prevention of disease in man or other animal; and . . . articles (other than food) intended to affect the structure or any function of the body of man or other animals . . . ." (emphasis added) (FDCA § 201 (g)(1); 21 U.S.C. § 321(g)(1))

The key words in the cosmetic and drug definitions are "intended for use" and "intended to be." The manufacturer's intent to market a "cosmetic" versus a "drug" is determined from the claims or representations made for the product in advertising or labeling. If the claims refer only to beautifying or promoting attractiveness, the product is a "cosmetic" and must be labeled in compliance with FDA regulations governing cosmetics.

The key words in the definitions of cosmetic and drug are, respectively, "intended to be" and "intended for use."

The marketer can intend that products be both cosmetics *and* drugs if they contain both cosmetic and drug claims, such as an antiperspirant

Cases providing preeminent judicial guidance on the cosmetic/drug distinction:
- *"Sudden Change"*
- *"Line Away"*
- *"Magic Secret"*

(drug)/deodorant (cosmetic) product. Cosmetic-drugs must comply with both the cosmetic and drug regulatory requirements for that product.

As cosmetic products become more sophisticated and offer greater benefits to consumers, FDA periodically has questioned whether the claims for some products cause them to become drugs, a category subject to more stringent regulation. The cosmetic/drug issue has been an occasional battleground between FDA and manufacturers. Three cases from the late 1960s remain the preeminent judicial guidance on when a "cosmetic" becomes a "drug." In one, the court held that claims associated with a product called "Sudden Change" (represented as giving a "face lift without surgery"; promising to "lift out puffs") were sufficient to make the product a "drug." In another case, the court held that claims for the product "Line Away" (such as "made in a pharmaceutical laboratory"; packaged under "biologically aseptic conditions"; creates a "tingling sensation" while "at work"; "tightening" facial skin; and "discouraging new wrinkles from forming") made this product a "drug." In a third case, involving a product called "Magic Secret," the court held that claims that the product was "pure protein" and that it caused an "astringent sensation" were *not* sufficient to cause consumers to conclude that the product would do anything more than alter their appearance, which was a cosmetic benefit.

These cases still provide guidance when determining whether a claim is a cosmetic or drug claim. Additionally, FDA issued regulatory letters to dozens of cosmetic manufacturers in 1987 challenging manufacturers' claims for skincare products as "drug" claims. While most of those matters were resolved privately, FDA's response to a citizen petition arising out of one of those matters made it clear that the agency relies heavily on the decisions in *Sudden Change*, *Line Away,* and *Magic Secret* when determining the "drug" or "cosmetic" status of a product. Additionally, it showed that the agency still applied the standards of the "ignorant, unthinking and credulous" consumer when deciding the meaning of those claims. At the same time, FDA declined to establish guidelines for cosmetic treatment claims, stating that each claim or group of claims had to be viewed in context to determine whether it was a cosmetic or drug claim.

The agency has taken the position, however, that the mere presence of an ingredient at levels that will "affect the structure or function of the body" is sufficient to make the product a drug, regardless of the claims in advertising and labeling, a position that represents a divergence from its past practice. An example involves the presence of hormone ingredients in a topical preparation. FDA concluded that the mere inclusion of hormones, even in the absence of drug claims, made the products "cosmetic-drugs" subject to a monograph.[2]

Labeling Requirements

Labeling:
- *The FDCA requires that label information be placed on the immediate container of a cosmetic.*
- *The FPLA only requires label information to appear on the outer container of a cosmetic.*

FDA regulates cosmetics labeling under two federal laws—the FDCA and the Fair Packaging and Labeling Act (FPLA). FDA has issued labeling regulations under these laws in 21 C.F.R. Part 701. Labeling cannot be false or misleading, and label information must be prominent and conspicuous.

The FDCA requires that label information be placed on the immediate container of a cosmetic. If the retail package consists of an immediate container enclosed in an outside container (e.g., cologne bottle in a box), both the inner and outer containers must display the mandatory information. There are exceptions; for example, a product contained in a transparent package or shrink-wrap would not have to be labeled if it surrounds a container otherwise properly labeled. If the information is easily legible through the outer container (see-through package or shrink-wrap) then the individual products inside the container can bear all the required labeling information.

A final concept affecting label placement under the FDCA is the distinction between "label" and "labeling." The FDCA defines "labeling" more broadly than "label":

> The term "labeling" means all labels and other written, printed, or graphic matter
> (1) upon any article or any of its containers or wrappers, or
> (2) accompanying such article.

Thus, the term "labeling" includes pamphlets, leaflets, and other written material accompanying a cosmetic product, but not necessarily affixed to it.

Unlike the FDCA, the FPLA requires label information to appear only on the outer container of a cosmetic. Thus, if a retail package consists of an immediate container enclosed in an outside container (e.g., a jar of face cream in a box), the FPLA does not apply to the immediate (or inner) container label. It is sufficient to place the required information on the outer container only. If a cosmetic product is displayed for sale in its immediate container only (e.g., a deodorant in an aerosol can), however, the immediate container must comply with the FPLA.

These interpretations are consistent with the purpose of the FPLA, which is to provide purchasers with certain information at the point of retail sale so that they can compare ingredients in products and make value comparisons prior to purchase.

Only products intended to be displayed to retail purchasers are subject to the requirements of the FPLA. (A "consumer commodity is defined to include any food, drug, device or cosmetic sold at retail for use by the consumer in the home.") Therefore, shipping containers used to transport bulk quantities of a product need not comply with the act. Similarly, cosmetics intended as free gifts or samples and not for sale, and products sold to salons for application to customers by professional cosmetologists, are not subject to these requirements.

The FPLA requires that certain information appear on the principal display panel (PDP). The PDP is defined as "that part of a label that is most likely to be displayed, presented, shown, or examined under normal and customary conditions of display for retail sale."

The label of a cosmetic must state the identity or name of the product. It is also permissible to include a common or usual name, an appropriately descriptive name, a fanciful name understood by the public, or an appropriate illustration or vignette representing the intended cosmetic use. The statement of identity is required only to appear on the outer container. Most marketers, however, put it on both the inner and outer containers.

The purpose of the quantity statement is to allow consumers to make a value judgment about the products they are purchasing. The net quantity of contents tells the consumer how much of the cosmetic is in the container. The quantity statement must appear on both the inner and outer container under both the FDCA and the FPLA.

Under the 1992 amendments to the FPLA, the net quantity of contents in cosmetic labeling must be expressed in *both* the English and metric systems. The quantity declaration for "English" units is stated in avoirdupois pounds and ounces for weight or mass; and fluid ounces for fluid measure statements. The metric declaration of net contents must be stated in kilograms, grams, or milligrams for solid, semisolid, or viscous cosmetics, and liters or milliliters for liquid cosmetics.

Both the FDCA and FPLA require that the name and the place of business of the manufacturer, distributor, or packer must appear on both the inner and outer cosmetic containers. The place of business must include the city, state, and zip code. A street address is required only if it does not appear in a local telephone directory.

For products not sold at retail and for free samples, ingredient statements are not mandatory.

For products intended for retail sale, FDA requires ingredient labeling under the authority of the FPLA. Consequently, the ingredient declaration must appear on the outer container only. Cosmetic ingredients must be listed "in descending order of predominance" on "an appropriate information panel." For products not sold at retail and for free samples, ingredient statements are not mandatory.

There are two exceptions to the listing of all ingredient names. First, flavors and fragrances may be listed generically rather than by "name." As a result, the term "fragrance" or "flavor" may appear in the ingredient declaration in descending order of predominance. The second exception is when FDA has granted a manufacturer's petition for a trade secret exemption. If trade secret status is granted for the ingredient, the words "and other ingredient(s)" must appear at the end of the ingredient statement.

Ingredients must be listed by established name. FDA regulations identify a priority list of sources to determine the appropriate name for an individual cosmetic ingredient. Unless FDA has established a name by regulation, CTFA's *International Cosmetic Ingredient Dictionary and Handbook* is the primary source for an "adopted name." If an ingredient does not appear in the CTFA dictionary, alternative sources are listed in order of priority such as the U.S. Pharmacopoeia and others. Only if the ingredient does not appear in the recognized sources can the manufacturer choose to use a name generally recognized by consumers or, in the absence of that, a chemical or other technical name.

Warning statements on cosmetic labels are required under the authority of the FDCA "whenever necessary or appropriate to prevent a health hazard that may be associated with the products." Warnings must appear on both the inner and outer containers, be prominent and conspicuous, and meet minimum type size requirements. FDA regulations require warnings with specific language for cosmetics in self-pressurized containers (e.g., aerosols), feminine deodorant sprays, certain bubble baths, and cosmetics that have not been substantiated adequately for safety. In addition, the FDCA requires a specific warning for coal tar hair dyes. FDA does not require specific flammability warnings for cosmetics, including aerosol or alcohol-based cosmetics, but many companies include such warnings voluntarily.

Warning statements on cosmetic labels are required under the authority of the FDCA "whenever necessary or appropriate to prevent a health hazard that may be associated with the products."

Conclusion

In sum, safety substantiation by cosmetic manufacturers of their ingredients and products and proper labeling remain the cornerstones of the regulatory scheme governing cosmetic products. These longstanding requirements, together with the voluntary industry reporting and registration programs, have rendered cosmetics one of the safest of all of the FDA-regulated product categories.

Endnotes

1. "Soaps" are not considered a cosmetic and, therefore, are exempt from all provisions of the FDCA. Soap products must, however, comply with the Federal Trade Commission's regulations issued under the Fair Packaging and Labeling Act (FPLA).
2. See 21 C.F.R. § 310.530 ("use of the word 'hormone' in the . . . ingredient statement is an implied drug claim").

Chapter 10

The Regulation of Foods and Food Additives

Daniel A. Kracov & Joshua M. Glasser, Arnold & Porter LLP, Washington, D.C.

Key Points

- Although FDA has primary authority over the regulation of most foods, USDA regulates meat and poultry products, BATF regulates alcoholic beverages, and the FTC has jurisdiction over food advertising.
- Adulteration is the central concept underlying FDA's regulation of the safety of food products. There are a number of statutory bases for a food to be adulterated, including the presence of poisonous or deleterious substances, insanitary practices in food processing, or the use of unapproved food additives.
- Under the Food Quality Protection Act, a special regulatory framework applies to pesticides in food. EPA registers pesticide products and sets tolerances for the presence of pesticide residues in food products. These tolerances are then enforced by FDA.
- FDA applies its general regulatory authorities to products of food biotechnology. FDA asks developers of bioengineered foods to notify the agency of their intent to market a food from a bioengineered plant at least 120 days before marketing. Special labeling is required only when the use of biotechnology so alters a food's characteristics or composition that the information about the change is material and should be revealed to consumers.
- The concept of economic adulteration permits FDA to prevent consumer fraud. For example, the agency may ensure that damage to a food product is not concealed from the consumer, or that a food is not made to appear to be of greater value than it is, such as by the addition of unnecessary water to add weight.
- Misbranding is the statutory term for violations relating to the labels and labeling of food products, as opposed to actual composition and safety. The central standard in the FDCA permits FDA to deem a product misbranded if its "labeling is false or misleading in any particular."
- FDA and USDA administer extensive regulations governing the labeling of food products, including the basic components of the label, mandatory nutrition labeling, and complex rules governing the nutrient content and health claims.
- Dietary supplement products are regulated under the FDCA as amended by the Dietary Supplement Health and Education Act of 1994. Those amendments provide a separate definition for dietary supplements, as well as special rules governing the safety and labeling claims for such products.

Introduction

Foods represent the most basic of the Food and Drug Administration's (FDA's) public health responsibilities: ensuring that what is eaten on a daily basis is both wholesome and fairly represented to the public. This responsibility requires an understanding and careful balance of many factors, including chemical and biological safety risks, evolving information on nutrition and health, food marketing concerns, and, more recently, food supply security—all within an increasingly complex statutory framework.

Agency Jurisdiction

An article is a "food" if it is used for human or animal food or drink, if it is a chewing gum, or if it is used as a component of any food.

The Federal Food, Drug, and Cosmetic Act (FDCA) gives FDA jurisdiction to regulate most foods in interstate commerce. Under FDCA § 201(f), an article is a "food" if it is used for human or animal food or drink, if it is a chewing gum, or if it is used as a component of any food. This is not necessarily a commonsense definition. For FDCA purposes, a food can include items that are not intended for consumption, such as seeds and rejected eggs. Raw, unprocessed food substances may or may not be foods. For example, although inedible green coffee beans were found to be a food within the statutory definition, *U.S. v. Green Coffee Beans*, 188 F.2d. 555 (2d Cir. 1951), the agency does not consider raw sugar to be a food because it contains certain impurities that can be removed only by the refining process. The agency also construes the term "food" to encompass substances migrating to food from food-contact articles such as containers and cutting surfaces.

In addition to the FDCA, there are other important food regulatory authorities at the federal level. The production and labeling of most meat and poultry products are regulated by the U.S. Department of Agriculture (USDA) under the Federal Meat Inspection Act and the Poultry Products Inspection Act. USDA exercises exclusive jurisdiction over the inspection of meat products until they leave a plant, but FDA and USDA have concurrent jurisdiction over misbranding and adulteration of meat products after inspection. Under an agreement between the agencies, FDA generally informs the USDA's Food Safety and Inspection Service when an apparent violation is encountered involving meat or poultry products, and usually will not initiate action against such products. USDA also regulates the production of eggs and egg products under the Egg Products Inspection Act. FDA has jurisdiction over game meats, such as deer and rabbit, as well as seafood products. FDA also regulates food products containing a relatively small proportion of meat—such as a dressing with bacon bits—interpreted as less than or equal to 3 percent meat.

FDA shares regulatory authority over alcoholic beverages with the Department of Treasury's Alcohol and Tobacco Tax and Trade Bureau (TTB). Although FDA may regulate ingredients used in alcoholic beverages, TTB generally is responsible for regulation of alcoholic beverage labeling, and has primary responsibility for recalls of alcoholic beverages.

The Federal Trade Commission (FTC) has primary responsibility over food advertising. The FTC frequently takes enforcement action in specific cases of deceptive food advertising, and routinely consults with FDA when such advertising raises issues of safety or nutrition.

Food Safety

Food safety, under the Federal Food, Drug, and Cosmetic Act, focuses on the legal definition of "adulteration."

The regulation of food safety under the FDCA centers around the legal definition of "adulteration." The term is defined by a range of acts specified in the FDCA that cause a food to be adulterated and, therefore, in violation of the statute.

Poisonous or Deleterious Substances

The first adulteration provision under the FDCA is found in section 402(a)(1), which incorporates two standards under which a food may be deemed adulterated:

> If it bears or contains any poisonous or deleterious substance which may render it injurious to health; but in case the substance is not an added substance such food shall not be considered adulterated under this clause if the quantity of such substance in such food does not ordinarily render it injurious to health.

This is the primary provision used by FDA to regulate the safety and purity of whole foods as opposed to the discrete ingredients added to foods.

The first part of the standard is much broader than it appears, for the term "added" can include the artificial introduction of a substance into a food by indirect means. Thus, in *United States v. Anderson Seafoods*, 622 F.2d 157 (5th Cir. 1980), the court determined that if a portion of the total amount of mercury found in swordfish resulted from industrial pollution, then all of the mercury in that product could be treated as an added substance subject to the "may render injurious" standard. Although the mere presence of an added poisonous or deleterious substance in a food does not satisfy the "may render" standard for proof of adulteration, FDA typically is given broad deference in its construction of the standard. *United States v. Lexington Mill & Elevator Co.*, 232 U.S. 399

(1914). Any "added" substance potentially could be subject to this standard, including microbial contamination.

The second part of section 402(a)(1), the "ordinarily render injurious to health" standard, is rather narrow in comparison. This provision applies to substances that are inherent in whole foods, such as toxins naturally present in fruits and vegetables. Such substances must be shown to be harmful before they result in food adulteration. As a result of the broad construction of the "may render" standard for "added" substances, this basis for adulteration is rarely invoked.

Unavoidable Contaminants

A food bearing or containing a poisonous substance is not considered adulterated if the quantity of the added substance is within an established tolerance level.

Under FDCA § 402(a)(2), a food is adulterated if it contains any avoidable added poisonous or deleterious substance that is "unsafe" within the meaning of FDCA § 406. An "unsafe" substance under section 406 is "any poisonous or deleterious substance added to any food, except where such substance is required in the production thereof or cannot be avoided by good manufacturing practice."

Section 406 permits FDA to establish tolerances for such "unavoidable contaminants." Such tolerances may limit the quantity of the substance in or on the food to the extent necessary for the protection of public health. If a tolerance is in effect, a food bearing or containing the poisonous substance is not considered adulterated if the quantity of the added substance is within the tolerance level. This tolerance provision permits the agency to take into account not just the presence of the poisonous or deleterious substance in the particular food in question, but the "other ways in which the consumer may be affected by the same or other deleterious substances."

Section 406 tolerances may be developed only through formal rulemaking, a time-consuming and resource-intensive process. As a result, the agency generally has adopted "action levels," which technically are nonbinding enforcement guidelines that identify levels of contamination above which FDA may bring an enforcement action. Both tolerances and action levels are based on the unavoidability of the added substances, and they do not establish a permissible level of contamination where the added substance is avoidable.

The agency also may establish "regulatory limits" through informal rulemaking, representing the level at which the agency would consider a food adulterated under section 402(a)(1). Such a regulatory limit may be appropriate where a substance cannot be avoided by current Good Manufacturing Practices (cGMPs) or there is insufficient information to establish a tolerance.

Filthy, Putrid, or Decomposed Substances

A food may be considered adulterated under FDCA § 402(a)(3) "if it consists in whole or in part of any filthy, putrid, or decomposed substance." As a practical matter, virtually any natural food product will have some level of filth—whether mold or insect parts—that has little or no impact on its safety or quality. The courts have tried to give these statutory terms their "usual and ordinary meaning," but with little consistency. Thus, in *United States v. Tomato Paste*, 22 F. Supp. 515 (E.D. Pa 1938), the presence of worm fragments rendered tomato paste filthy, while in *United States v. Canned Tomato Paste*, 236 F.2d 208 (7th Cir. 1956), a paste that had a small number of insect fragments, fly eggs, and rodent hairs was not adulterated.

Although FDA does not have authority to set tolerances for decomposition or filth in food, the agency has developed "defect action level" guidances.

The agency does not have authority to set tolerances for decomposition or filth. Nevertheless, to bring some consistency to this area, and based on its enforcement discretion under the FDCA, the agency has developed "defect action levels." Defect action levels are guidances that indicate levels of filth, mold, and other contaminants that are not likely, taken alone, to result in an enforcement action, and can be achieved by applying cGMPs. It is important to note that a defect action level cannot be met by blending highly contaminated food with uncontaminated food, for FDA considers the finished product to be adulterated regardless of the net level of contamination.

Containers

Under FDCA § 402(a)(6), a food may also be adulterated if it is in a container that "is composed, in whole or in part, of any poisonous or deleterious substance which may render the contents injurious to health." This provision has rarely been invoked by FDA, which typically relies upon its other adulteration and indirect additive authorities.

Unfit for Food

A food may also be adulterated "if it is otherwise unfit for food" under FDCA § 402(a)(3). This provision describes a condition in which a food is in an inedible state, and does not necessarily depend upon the presence of filth or decomposition. The "unfit for food" adulteration provision is based on the perception of the average consumer. For example, in *United States v. Herring Roe*, 87 F. Supp. 826 (D. Me. 1949), the court found that in order for a fish roe to be unfit for food, it must be so tough and rubbery that the average consumer under ordinary conditions could not eat it. This statutory basis for adulteration is rarely used, largely because other adulteration provisions are less subjective and easier to prove.

Sanitation/Good Manufacturing Practices

One of the most important adulteration provisions is FDCA § 402(a)(4), which deems a food to be adulterated "if it has been prepared, packed, or held under insanitary conditions whereby it may have been contaminated with filth, or whereby it may have been rendered injurious to health." This provision does not require FDA to prove that a food product has been contaminated or rendered injurious to health. Rather, the mere presence of the insanitary conditions and the possibility that those insanitary conditions may have resulted in the adulteration is enough to bring the charge. Typically, the agency looks for evidence of rodent droppings, insect parts, unscreened windows, or other insanitary practices where food is processed to bring a case under this provision.

FDA determined that one of the most effective ways to ensure sanitary conditions in food production was through controls on food manufacturing operations.

In 1967, FDA determined that one of the most effective ways to implement section 402, and thereby maintain a safe and sanitary food supply, would be through controls on manufacturing operations. That year, the agency published the first set of proposed food current Good Manufacturing Practices (cGMP) rules. After many revisions and several unsuccessful lawsuits challenging FDA's authority to promulgate the regulations, the cGMP rules have become an established condition of doing business in the food industry, and are found at 21 C.F.R. Part 110. Dietary supplements cGMP rules are found at 21 C.F.R. Part 111.

The food cGMP regulations impose affirmative obligations on manufacturers to control the risk of chemical, microbiological, and other contamination of food. The underlying theory is that effective sanitation requires careful planning and vigilance in every phase of production, and that manufacturers must carry the primary responsibility for maintaining a safe and sanitary food supply. FDA recognizes, however, that manufacturing operations can vary widely and still be safe and sanitary, and the umbrella cGMP rules allow for some flexibility in methods of compliance. The rules are couched in terms of a mandatory *result*, together with permissive guidelines for *methods* of compliance.

The umbrella cGMPs touch every aspect of food production, including raw material inspection, employee training, plant design, equipment specifications and cleaning, quality control testing, and distribution of finished products. While recordkeeping requirements exist in other areas, FDA did not impose specific recordkeeping requirements in general food cGMPs. Daily production logs, manuals, and other written records, however, provide proof to an FDA inspector that a company's compliance programs exist. The inspector then can verify that the written program reflects that company's actual, current practices.

The cGMP regulations require plant managers to take precautions to ensure that food products are not contaminated by employees. Four requirements are prescribed with regard to personnel practices: 1) any person with evidence of disease must be excluded from any operation where he or she may come into contact, either directly or indirectly, with food; 2) employees must maintain proper hygiene, including hand washing; 3) employees must be trained in sanitary practices; and 4) employees must be adequately supervised.

Under the food cGMPs, manufacturing facilities must be designed, constructed, and maintained to protect against contamination of food. The regulations provide a partial checklist of points for plant managers to follow, setting forth requirements for the maintenance of grounds, construction of physical plants, adequate lighting and ventilation, pest control, use and storage of chemicals, water supply and plumbing, and waste removal.

"Umbrella" cGMP regulations address:

- *personnel practices*
- *plant design*
- *equipment specifications and cleaning*
- *production controls*
- *quality control testing*
- *product distribution*

The cGMP regulations also govern construction, cleaning, and maintenance of equipment. Manufacturers must use only tools that can be properly cleaned and maintained, and must protect them from corrosion or contamination. Conveyor belts and other manufacturing systems, freezer and cold storage systems, compressed air cleaning systems, and instruments for measuring and regulating manufacturing conditions (e.g., temperature, acidity, and water flow) must be well maintained.

Other cGMP provisions address production controls, including inspection of raw materials, in-process monitoring, and storage and transport. Manufacturers must adhere to adequate sanitation principles in all production procedures, including receiving, inspecting, transporting, preparing, manufacturing, packaging, and storing foods. To meet the prescribed quality control standards, manufacturers must periodically test their products for chemical, microbial, or extraneous material contamination, and either reject or reprocess any products that they determine to be contaminated. Similarly, raw materials must be inspected to ensure that they are clean and suitable for processing, and must be stored properly to avoid contamination and minimize deterioration. Moreover, manufacturers must monitor such factors as time, temperature, humidity, and pH to ensure that mechanical breakdowns, delays, and temperature fluctuations do not contribute to the decomposition or contamination of food. The rule also details specific techniques for preventing and minimizing microbiological contamination of batters and sauces, refrigerated foods, and acidified and dehydrated foods. Finished food must be transported and stored under conditions that will protect it against contamination and deterioration of the food and the container.

The "umbrella" food cGMPs are still in place, and FDA continues to rely on sampling and testing of conditions at the time of inspection of end products to regulate adulteration. In recent years, however, FDA has moved toward expansion of the Hazard Analysis Critical Control Point

(HACCP) concept in the processing of foods. HACCP is a preventive strategy that is based on the development by the food producer of a plan that anticipates food safety hazards and identifies the specific critical points in the production process where a failure would likely result in a hazard being created or allowed to persist. Such critical control points are monitored systematically, and corrective action is taken when control over those points is lost.

To date, FDA has issued rules imposing HACCP requirements on the processing and importation of fish and fishery products, 21 C.F.R. Part 123, and juice products, 21 C.F.R. Part 120. USDA's Food Safety and Inspection Service has imposed HACCP requirements on meat and poultry production. According to FDA, the expansion of HACCP to other segments of the food industry is within FDA's adulteration-related authorities and its general authority to ensure efficient enforcement of the law.

Food Additives

In the decades after the passage of the FDCA, the number of chemicals added to foods for functional purposes increased enormously, yet there was no mechanism for FDA premarket clearance based on a safety evaluation. To take action against an ingredient in the product, FDA could rely only on its evaluation of the product, already on the market, under its general adulteration standards for added substances. In 1954, congressional hearings before Congressman James Delaney (D-NY) focused on the safety of additives in the food supply, revealing that only 200 of the 1,400 chemicals known to be added to foods had been shown to be safe. This uncertainty suited neither FDA nor food companies, for there were no clear additive safety standards.

The need for food additive regulation led to the passage of the Food Additives Amendment of 1958.

The consensus regarding the need for food additive regulation led to the passage of the Food Additives Amendment of 1958, in which Congress provided the agency with a framework for food additive regulation that mandated proof of safety prior to marketing. Under section 201(s) of the FDCA, the term "food additive"

> . . . means any substance the intended use of which results or may reasonably be expected to result, directly or indirectly, in its becoming a component or otherwise affecting the characteristics of any food (including any substance intended for use in producing, manufacturing, packing, processing, preparing, treating, packaging, transporting, or holding food; and including any source of radiation intended for any such use), if such substance is not generally recognized, among experts qualified by scientific training and experience to evaluate its safety, as having been adequately shown through scientific procedures (or, in a case of a substance used in food prior to

> January 1, 1958, through either scientific procedures or experience based on common use in food) to be safe under the conditions of its intended use. . . .

This definition is quite broad, encompassing any substance that may reasonably be expected to directly or indirectly affect or become a part of a food. Such substances are presumed to be unsafe—and therefore adulterate a food—unless the additive has been the subject of a premarket approval by FDA.

There are significant exceptions to the food additive definition, most notably generally recognized as safe (GRAS) substances, pesticide chemical residues, and dietary supplements. One additional, but relatively small, category of excepted uses of such substances are those that are subject to a "prior sanction." Prior sanctioned substances are those that were the subject of FDA or USDA safety opinions prior to 1958 and are "grandfathered" as part of the 1958 legislation. Such substances are still subject to the general adulteration standards and, in large part, have been eclipsed by the premarket approval and GRAS framework over time.

Any food that bears or contains any food additive that is unsafe is considered adulterated.

Any food that bears or contains any food additive that is unsafe within the meaning of FDCA § 409 (i.e., unapproved or used outside the parameters of an approval) is considered adulterated. Section 409 provides a formal petition process for the approval of food additives by the agency, which applies a science-based safety standard to review of food additive petitions. At a minimum, a food additive petition must include the name of the substance; its chemical identity and composition; the proposed conditions of its use; proposed labeling; physical effects data; technical effects (and levels) data; information on the manufacturing process, facilities, and controls; methods of detecting and determining the quantity of the additive in the finished food; the results of safety investigations; and an environmental assessment. 21 C.F.R. Part 171.

The term "safe" for purposes of food additive approval means that there is a reasonable certainty in the minds of competent scientists that a substance is not harmful under its intended conditions of use. The agency considers the probable levels of consumption of the additive, and the cumulative effect of the additive and related substances in the diet in arriving at its determination. The toxicological testing requirements for food additives are the subject of a guidance document, known as the "Red Book." FDA will calculate the exposure to the additive based upon an estimated daily intake that is within an acceptable daily intake (ADI) derived from data on toxicological effects and the determination of a "no observable adverse effect level" to which an appropriate safety factor (typically 1/100) is applied. If FDA finds an additive to be safe, it issues a regulation specifying the conditions under which the additive may safely be used. *See* 21 C.F.R. Parts 172-178.

Although food additives are subject to a general safety standard, there is a significant exception. Section 409(c)(3)(a) of the FDCA contains what is commonly referred to as the "Delaney Clause," which provides that "[n]o additive shall be deemed to be safe if it is found to induce cancer when ingested by man or animal, or if it is found after tests which are appropriate for the evaluation of the safety of food additives, to induce cancer in man or animal."

Due to the absolute nature of the Delaney Clause, FDA has made significant efforts to avoid it by adopting policies of construction and interpretation. One statutory exception is the DES Proviso, which provides that the Delaney Clause does not prohibit the use of a compound if "no residue" of that compound administered to food producing animals can be "found" in meat, milk, or eggs by an approved analytical method. FDCA § 409(c)(3)(A). The agency also may make a scientific determination that a substance does not technically or directly "induce" cancer.

Under the Delaney Clause, no additive is deemed safe if it induces cancer when ingested by humans or animals, or is found after appropriate testing to induce cancer in humans or animals.

FDA interprets the term "additive" in the Delaney Clause to apply only to the additive as a whole and not its unavoidable, nonfunctional constituents. 47 Fed. Reg. 14,464 (Apr. 2, 1982). If carcinogenic constituents of an additive are detected, FDA conducts a risk assessment under the general safety standard for food additives. FDA first applied this "constituents policy" in its 1982 approval of the color additive D&C Green No. 6, which contains the carcinogenic contaminant n-toluene. The policy has been applied on numerous occasions since then, and has been challenged and upheld in court. Other efforts by FDA to avoid the Delaney Clause, however, such as the argument that it is too rigid and should be subject to a *de minimis* exception, have been rejected by the courts.

The Delaney Clause has consistently been criticized as outdated in light of current methods of assessing the risk of carcinogenicity. Nevertheless, although its applicability to pesticide residues was eliminated as part of the 1996 enactment of the Food Quality Protection Act (FQPA), the Delaney Clause remains in force in the food and color additive areas.

Indirect Additives/Food Contact Substances

The food additive definition is extremely broad, extending beyond substances intentionally added for a functional purpose to include even nonedible items—such as adhesives, packaging, and food contact surface materials—that "may reasonably be expected" to become a component or otherwise affect the characteristics of a food. These migrating indirect additives generally are subject to the same food additive and GRAS frameworks applicable to direct food additives.

FDA has established a process for determining when the likelihood or extent of migration to food of a substance used in a food contact article is so trivial as not to require food additive approval. This "threshold of regulation" exempts from food additive regulation those noncarcinogenic substances in food contact articles that result in a dietary concentration of the substance of 0.5 parts per billion (ppb) or less. Also exempted are regulated direct food additives when used in food contact articles at levels that result in a dietary exposure of 1 percent or less of the ADI for the additive as determined by the agency. 21 C.F.R. § 170.39. Such substances may not have a technical effect in the food, and must be the subject of a submission to FDA documenting eligibility for the terms of the threshold regulation, including an environmental assessment.

The 1997 Food and Drug Administration Modernization Act (FDAMA) created a new statutory classification to encompass indirect additives that does not require premarket approval. This class, referred to as "food contact substances," is defined as "any substance intended for use as a component of materials used in manufacturing, packing, packaging, transporting, or holding food if such use is not intended to have any technical effect in such food." Food contact substances typically consist of materials used in food packaging such as plastics, paper, and adhesives, but can also include substances used in the manufacture of food.

FDAMA created a new statutory classification to encompass indirect additives that does not require premarket approval.

Section 409(a)(3) provides that a food additive will not be deemed unsafe if it is a food contact substance and the substance and its use have been approved in a food additive regulation like any other substance, or it is the subject of a notification that has become effective. Under section 409(h), manufacturers may file a notification with FDA regarding a food contact substance 120 days before its introduction into interstate commerce. The notification must identify the food contact substance and its intended use, as well as a description of the manufacturer's determination that the intended use is safe, including the information that forms the basis for that conclusion. All such information will be kept confidential by FDA for 120 days after receipt, at which time it will be available to the public, except for trade secrets or confidential commercial information.

In May 2002, FDA issued regulations governing this provision and a guidance document for industry on submitting food contact notifications (FCNs). 67 Fed. Reg. 35,724 (May 21, 2002) (codified at 21 C.F.R. Part 170, Subpart D); Guidance for Industry: Preparation of Premarket Notifications (May, 2002). A manufacturer of a food contact substance is required to submit a FCN for new uses of food contact substances that are food additives. A notification is effective for the manufacturer that submitted the FCN—or anyone who can demonstrate that the food contact substance being marketed has been manufactured or supplied by the manufacturer—where the food contact substance is being used under the conditions that are the subject of the FCN. A notification becomes effective 120 days after receipt by FDA, at which time the food contact substance may be distributed in interstate commerce, unless FDA makes a determination that, based on the data and information before it, the use of the substance has not been shown to be safe and a food additive petition should be filed requesting that a regulation be issued.

Generally Recognized as Safe Substances

The general recognition of safety is not based on the opinion of the lay population—it is based on the views of experts qualified to evaluate the safety of foods.

In framing the food additive definition, Congress recognized that there was a range of food substances that should not be the subject of the petition requirement. Such substances are not merely safe, they are generally recognized as safe (GRAS). The burden of demonstrating such GRAS status falls upon the proponent of the GRAS use of an ingredient. Moreover, the general recognition of safety is not based on the opinion of the lay population—it is based on the views of experts qualified to evaluate the safety of foods. Although unanimity is not required, GRAS status must at least be a consensus opinion of qualified experts.

The passage of the Food Additives Amendment in 1958 presented a significant transitional problem. Many ingredients, including common foods such as vinegar, vegetable oil, salts, spices, flavors, and gums, did not have a clear regulatory status. FDA clarified the status of those substances by publishing the "GRAS List" to which it subsequently added other categories of substances that the agency deemed to be subject to the GRAS exemption.

In 1970, as a result of banning cyclamate, an artificial sweetener previously considered to be GRAS, due to concern about carcinogenicity, the agency initiated a comprehensive study of substances presumed to be GRAS. In this "GRAS review," FDA evaluated a broad range of substances using contemporary scientific standards. It then issued regulations that affirmed the GRAS status of those ingredients where appropriate. FDA also promulgated a series of regulations setting forth the criteria for determining GRAS status, the category of food substances it considers eligible for GRAS status or GRAS affirmation, and the procedures for petitioning the agency to affirm the GRAS status of other substances. 21 C.F.R. §§ 170.30, 170.35.

Until recent years, a manufacturer could seek, through filing a GRAS affirmation petition, a formal determination from FDA that a given substance is GRAS and therefore appropriate for use in food without being approved as a food additive. *See* 21 C.F.R. Parts 184 and 186. This nonstatutory process generally proved interminable, and was a low priority for FDA's overburdened staff. FDA has long acknowledged, however, that GRAS status may be determined without formal FDA action (referred to as "self-determination of GRAS status"). Thus, the GRAS exception from the food additive definition creates a separate regulatory category for substances which, although intentionally added to food, are not subject to mandatory premarket review.

In making a GRAS self-determination, a company assumes a risk that FDA may not agree with its determination, and may seek withdrawal of the product through informal means or by resort to its seizure or injunctive authorities. This risk usually is minimized by having the product and its planned use(s) reviewed by independent scientific consultants and legal counsel.

The process of determining whether a substance is GRAS involves evaluation of the same safety issues as are raised with respect to food additives, as well as a determination that the terms for GRAS status have been satisfied. For substances used in food prior to January 1, 1958, GRAS status may be established through "experience based upon common use in food." For all other substances, GRAS status must be established through safety data collected by "scientific procedures"; i.e., studies. Experience data may serve, however, to confirm the findings of these studies, including information on use of the substance abroad.

The process of determining whether a substance is GRAS involves evaluation of the same safety issues as are raised with respect to food additives, as well as a determination that the terms for GRAS status have been satisfied.

"Scientific procedures" are defined by FDA to include "those human, animal, analytical, and other scientific studies, whether published or unpublished, appropriate to establish the safety of a substance." 21 C.F.R. § 170.3(h). The GRAS eligibility regulation further states that general recognition of safety through scientific procedures shall "require the same quantity and quality of evidence" as is required to obtain food additive approval and "shall ordinarily be based upon published studies which may be corroborated by unpublished studies and other data and information." 21 C.F.R. § 170.3(b).

It must be remembered, however, that the safety of a substance is evaluated within the context of its intended use. Thus, while a general purpose food ingredient may be deemed or affirmed as GRAS without any limitation on how it may be used, most GRAS determinations are made in the context of one or more specified uses. GRAS substances must comply with applicable specifications, must perform an appropriate function in the food, and must be present in the food at a level no higher than necessary to accomplish that purpose.

For a substance to be GRAS, the pertinent scientific community must be familiar with the substance and believe it to be safe. In other words, GRAS status depends on showing not only that a substance is safe, but also that it is widely viewed as such by experts in the field. FDA evaluates the qualifications of experts whose opinions are offered in support of GRAS status. The GRAS eligibility regulation repeats the statutory requirement that "general recognition of safety may be based only on the views of experts qualified by scientific training and experience to evaluate the safety of substances directly or indirectly added to food." 21 C.F.R. § 170.30(a). Thus, FDA effectively applies the concept of peer review to the scientist as well as to the science, and it relies on documented credentials as one factor in assessing the validity of studies and the integrity of other scientific evidence offered in support of GRAS status.

In April 1997, FDA proposed a new rule which, while not finalized, has largely replaced the prior GRAS petition framework. 62 Fed. Reg. 18,938 (April 17, 1997). Under this notification procedure, companies have the option of notifying FDA of its GRAS self-determination. Rather than publishing a regulation with a finding of safety as it purports to do under the current system, FDA provides a response to the notice within ninety days, in which it either acknowledges the notifier's GRAS determination or identifies problems that it found in the submission.

The stated goal of the GRAS notification proposal is to increase the agency's awareness of private GRAS determinations, make the process by which FDA recognizes GRAS status more efficient, and reduce resources devoted to the nonstatutory GRAS affirmation process. While FDA's response to such notices does not carry the same weight as a GRAS determination by FDA, it enables manufacturers who make their own GRAS determinations to ascertain the agency's position on the matter quickly. Concurrently, the proposal has intensified commercial pressure on those marketing GRAS ingredients to submit notifications to FDA in lieu of private determinations of GRAS status.

Color Additives

Color additives must be shown with reasonable certainty to pose no risk to human health, to accomplish an intended effect, and to not deceive consumers.

Color additives are subject to a separate statutory approval framework under the FDCA. Section 201(t) defines a "color additive" as any material that, when added to food, is capable of imparting color, except those that the Secretary of Health and Human Services, by regulation, determines are used "solely for a purpose or purposes other than coloring." FDCA § 721 provides a framework for the listing and certification of color additives that is similar to the premarket approval process for food additives. Color additives must be shown with reasonable certainty to pose no risk to human health, to accomplish an intended effect, and to not deceive consumers. Section 721 includes a Delaney Clause, although there is no exclusion for GRAS or prior sanctioned colors. Color additives may be subject to precise specifications, and FDA may subject color additives to batch certification to ensure that specifications are met.

Pesticide Residues

Historically, pesticide residues have presented a major regulatory problem. Until the passage of the FQPA in 1996, the Environmental Protection Agency (EPA) was responsible for setting tolerances for pesticide residue on raw agricultural commodities under FDCA § 408, which incorporated a risk-benefit standard. Although a "flow-through" proviso permitted levels of pesticides in processed foods up to the level permitted in raw agricultural commodities under section 408, EPA also set tolerances for pesticide residues that concentrated in processed foods under section 409 (the food additive provision). Those residues, however, were subject to the food additive Delaney Clause. As a result of the judicial rejection of EPA's policy of applying a *de minimis* standard to these residues, *Les v. Reilly*, 968 F.2d 985 (9th Cir. 1993), a number of tolerances for important pesticides were subject to revocation.

The FQPA redefined "pesticide chemical" in FDCA § 201(q)(1) to include any substance that is a pesticide within the meaning of the Federal Insecticide, Fungicide, and Rodenticide Act (FIFRA), including active and inert ingredients in the pesticide. A "pesticide residue" is defined in section 201(q)(2) as a residue in or on a raw agriculture commodity *or* processed food of a pesticide chemical, or any other added substance that is primarily the result of the metabolism or other degradation of a pesticide chemical. These changes took all pesticide residues out of the food additive definition and the food additive Delaney Clause. Instead, all tolerances for pesticide residues in a food must be established on the basis of a single safety standard that requires a reasonable certainty that no harm will result from an aggregate exposure to the pesticide chemical residue, including all anticipated dietary exposures and all other exposures for which there is reasonable information. FDCA § 408(b)(2)(A). Specific consideration also is given to exposures to infants and children, and the consideration of pesticide benefits in tolerance-setting is significantly limited to certain "eligible" residues.

All tolerances for pesticide residues in a food must be established on the basis of a single safety standard that requires a reasonable certainty that no harm will result from an aggregate exposure to the pesticide chemical residue, including all anticipated dietary exposures and all other exposures for which there is reasonable information.

The enforcement of tolerances for pesticide residues is now the responsibility of FDA, although EPA may initiate action if a violation of FIFRA is involved. The FQPA provides for civil penalties as an alternative method of taking enforcement action against the sale of a food that is adulterated by unsafe pesticide residues, although such penalties cannot be applied to farmers.

Food Biotechnology

The use of organisms to make food products, such as yogurt, represents one of the oldest of food technologies. A major scientific development in food science in the last decade, however, has been the application of new biotechnologies, including recombinant DNA techniques and cell fusion, to go beyond traditional methods and make direct genetic modifications to food sources. Food biotechnology, as well as animal cloning for agricultural purposes, has led to a great deal of discussion and inquiries to FDA, and there is a clear consensus that some form of FDA oversight is warranted.

Genetic Modification of Plant Varieties

In 1992, FDA issued a policy under which new plant varieties developed by application of genetic modification are regulated within the existing framework of the FDCA and FDA regulations. 57 Fed. Reg. 22,984 (May 29, 1992).

In general, FDA regulates foods derived from new plant varieties under the general adulteration standard, which requires the producer of a new food to evaluate its safety and ensure that FDA standards are met. FDA applies the food additive and GRAS frameworks to plant products derived from single gene transfers. Food additive petitions under section 409 of the FDCA are required in cases where the food differs in structure, function, or composition so significantly as to raise safety questions that warrant formal premarket review to ensure public health protection.

Food additive petitions are required in cases where the food differs in structure, function, or composition so significantly as to raise safety questions that warrant formal premarket review to ensure public health protection.

FDA has developed a decision tree approach that provides for the assessment of the new plant variety, the characteristics of the host and donor species, the nature of the genetic change, the identity and function of newly introduced substances, and unexpected or unintended effects that accompany genetic changes. Particular concerns that need to be assessed as part of this analysis include:

- toxins known to be characteristic of the host and donor species;
- the potential that food allergens would be transferred from one food source to another;
- the concentration and bioavailability of important nutrients for which a food crop is ordinarily consumed;
- the safety and nutritional value of newly introduced proteins; and
- the identity, composition, and nutritional value of modified carbohydrates, or fats and oils.

Originally, FDA administered a "voluntary" consultation system in which companies would decide whether to consult with the agency pursuant to the decision tree. FDA has since changed this approach, and companies must consult with the agency regarding their intent to market, at least

120 days before marketing. Based upon this notification FDA may determine that additional testing or labeling is necessary, or that a food additive filing may be required.

In 2006, FDA issued a guidance requesting that developers of new proteins in new plant varieties for food submit a safety evaluation to FDA prior to the stage of development where the protein could inadvertently enter the food supply. Guidance for Industry: Recommendations for the Early Food Safety Evaluation of New Non-Pesticidal Proteins Produced by New Plant Varieties Intended for Food Use (June, 2006). A safety evaluation need not be submitted where a protein has been previously reviewed as part of a consultation and no safety concerns were identified, or where a protein has been part of a previous safety evaluation with no identified safety concerns and is later introduced into another plant species.

A safety evaluation should focus on whether the new protein is an allergen or a toxin, and should contain information including a description of its purpose or intended technical effect and a list of any identities and sources of the introduced genetic material. The guidance document states that FDA should respond within 120 days with the results of the safety evaluation.

With respect to labeling of genetically modified foods, FDA applies its general analysis under section 403(i) of the FDCA, which requires that the producer of a food product describe the product by its common or usual name, or, in the absence thereof, an appropriately descriptive term. In addition, under section 201(n), all food product labeling must reveal facts that are material in light of representations made or suggested by labeling or with respect to consequences that may result from use. In other words, a new name or a label disclosure is only required when the application of biotechnology alters a food's characteristics or composition to such a degree as to create an important consumer expectation or safety concern. A good example would be the need to disclose the introduction of a peanut protein into a tomato that could result in an allergic reaction in a susceptible population.

Cloning in Animal Species Used for Food

Animal cloning has raised public concerns, and FDA has conducted an in-depth analysis of animal cloning in the last several years. In 2001, FDA requested that livestock producers and researchers not introduce food from animal clones or their offspring into the food supply until FDA evaluated potential risks to consumers. FDA issued a draft assessment in 2006, and final risk assessment in January 2008, finding that meat and milk from clones of adult cattle, pigs, and goats, and their offspring, are as safe to eat as food from conventionally bred animals.

FDA issued a draft assessment in 2006, and final risk assessment in January 2008, finding that meat and milk from clones of adult cattle, pigs, and goats, and their offspring, are as safe to eat as food from conventionally bred animals.

The result of the FDA risk assessment on animal cloning is that FDA has lifted the voluntary moratorium on products from the offspring of cloned animals. FDA has requested, however, that the voluntary moratorium remain in place temporarily for products from cloned animals. FDA is not requiring labeling or any other additional measures for food from cattle, swine, and goat clones, or their offspring.

Economic Adulteration

The adulteration provisions of the FDCA are not limited to safety issues. "Economic" adulteration under section 402(b) can occur if:

- any valuable constituent has been in whole or in part omitted or abstracted; or
- any substance has been substituted wholly or in part; or
- damage or inferiority has been concealed in any manner; or
- any substance has been added or mixed or packed so as to increase its bulk or weight, or reduce its quality or strength, or make it appear better or greater value than it is.

Early cases in this area dealt with coloring foods in a manner that caused economic adulteration, such as the addition of pumpkin to bakery products to give the appearance of egg content. The addition of water to foods was—and remains—a popular approach to adulteration. Perhaps the most prominent example in recent years was the highly publicized case, *United States v. Beech-Nut Nutrition Corp.*, 871 F.2d 1181 (2d Cir. 1989), involving the economic adulteration of apple juice for babies with a substandard ingredient. In general, the economic adulteration provisions of the FDCA are used only when the agency cannot otherwise regulate nonsafety-related aspects of food formulation.

Misbranding

Misbranding is the statutory term for FDCA violations relating to the labels and the labeling of a food product, as opposed to its actual composition and safety.

Misbranding is the statutory term for FDCA violations relating to the labels and the labeling of a food product, as opposed to its actual composition and safety. The primary basis upon which a food may be deemed misbranded is if "its labeling is false or misleading in any particular" under section 403(a). A failure to reveal material facts under section 201(n) also can constitute misleading labeling under this standard. Other general bases on which FDA may make a misbranding finding include, in part:

- If a food is "offered for sale under the name of another food." FDCA § 403(b).
- "If it is an imitation of another food, unless its label bears, in type of uniform size and prominence, the word 'imitation' and, immediately thereafter, the name of the food imitated." FDCA § 403(c). *See* Standards of Identity, below.
- If "its container is so made, formed, or filled as to be misleading." FDCA § 403(d).

Food Labeling

Two primary statutory authorities—the FDCA and the Fair Packaging and Labeling Act (FPLA)—govern the regulation of food labeling. "Label" is defined under section 201(k) as a display of written, printed, or graphic matter on the immediate container of any article. Under section 201(m), "labeling" is further defined to include all labels and other written, printed, or graphic matter on any article or any of its containers or wrappers, or accompanying such article. Thus, the FDCA requires information appearing on the label to also be included on the outside container or wrapper of the retail package. In contrast, requirements imposed solely by the FPLA apply only to the outside container or wrapper of the retail package.

The FDCA and the Fair Packaging and Labeling Act govern the regulation of food labeling.

Basic Components of the Food Label

Over the years, FDA has developed regulations pertaining to virtually every aspect of food labeling, including specifications for both mandatory and voluntary information. Moreover, a number of exemptions have been recognized to accommodate special packaging and marketing issues, specific product categories, and other attributes that may trigger specific labeling requirements. For example, products with nutrient content claims trigger specific referral and disclosure requirements. Drinks that purport to contain fruit juice must bear information regarding the percentage of juice in the product.

The regulations governing the basic components of the food label are found at 21 C.F.R. Part 101, Subpart A. These regulations specify two areas on a product's label where required information may appear: the Principal Display Panel (PDP) and the Information Panel (IP). The PDP is the part of the label most likely to be displayed, presented, shown, or examined by the consumer under normal and customary conditions of display for retail sale. The IP is that part of the label that is immediately contiguous and to the right of the PDP as observed by the consumer facing the PDP. If there is more than one PDP, each must contain the mandatory label information. Only one IP is necessary, however, even if there is more than one PDP. An IP is not required if all required information is placed on a PDP.

In general, FDA regulations require certain information to appear on the PDP; other information may appear on either the PDP or the IP. For example, the identity and net content statements must appear on the PDP. If an IP is used, all necessary information except the identity and content statements may appear on the IP. If the IP is too small, the information may be split between the IP and the PDP. No one item, however, may be split between the two panels (e.g., part of an ingredient statement on each panel).

Each aspect of the food label is subject to specific requirements. The following are the basic parameters for major components of the food label.

Major components of the food label:
- *identity statement*
- *net quantity of contents statement*
- *responsibility statement*
- *ingredient statement*
- *flavor labeling*
- *nutrition labeling*
- *nutrient content claims*
- *country of origin*

- An "**identity statement**" is the standardized, common, or usual name of the food, or a fanciful name generally used by the public for the particular product. The identity statement should identify accurately or describe either the basic nature of the product or its characterizing properties or ingredients, using simple and direct terms. When the nature of the product is obvious, a fanciful name commonly used by the public may serve as the identity statement.
- The "**net quantity of contents statement**" is the declaration in terms of weight, measure, or numerical count of the unit container and, where carton labeling is necessary, the numerical count and the total package content. The statement should be placed in the bottom 30 percent of the PDP as a distinct item, in the most appropriate units of both the English and metric systems.
- The "**responsibility statement**" states the name, street address, and zip code of the person who manufactures, packs, or distributes the product. In the case of a corporation, the actual corporate name must appear. If the particular business address appears in a current city directory or telephone directory, the street address may be omitted but the zip code must be included. If the principal place of business differs from the place of manufacture, packing, or distribution, only the principal place of business is required.
- The "**ingredient statement**" is a list of the product's ingredients by their common or usual name, in descending order of predominance by weight in the product (except for ingredients under 2 percent of the weight of the product).
- "**Flavor labeling**" details the type of flavoring of the product, including natural, artificial, or a combination of the two. These labeling requirements are quite complex and require careful review. In general, if the label, labeling, or advertisement of a food makes any

direct or indirect representation regarding a primary recognizable flavor, or if the manufacturer or distributor wishes to designate the flavor of the food by any means other than through the statement of ingredients, that flavor becomes the "characterizing flavor" for the purposes of flavor labeling. The choice of which terms and wording to employ in the flavor labeling depend on the type and number of flavors a product contains. If a food contains any artificial flavor that simulates, resembles, or reinforces the characterizing flavor, the name of the food must be accompanied by the name of the characterizing flavor, together with the word(s) "artificial" or "artificially flavored." Such labeling must precede or follow the characterizing flavor in the product, and is expressed as "artificial," "artificially flavored," etc., depending on the type of flavor(s) used, (e.g. artificially orange flavored). The disclosure should appear on the PDP with the identity statement.

- **Nutrition labeling** must appear by way of a prescribed format that provides detailed "Nutrition Facts" on the product. The nutrition labeling requirements are reviewed in detail below.
- If any **nutrient content claims** are made, a disclosure statement referring to nutrition labeling of a specific size relative to the claim must be included along with the claim if there are other food constituents present at certain disclosure levels. Nutrient content claims are subject to specific definitions and are reviewed in detail below.
- Every article of foreign origin must be marked in a conspicuous place to indicate the English name of the **country of origin**.

♦ Ingredient Labeling

A food product is misbranded if the ingredients are not listed in descending order of predominance by weight, as such an ingredient statement is likely to confuse consumers. Ingredients that are present in amounts of 2 percent or less need not be listed in descending order if a qualifying statement such as "Contains ________ percent or less of ________" appears at the end of the ingredient statement, with the second blank filled in with the names of the ingredients present at less than 2 percent.

Each ingredient must be listed specifically by its common or usual name. Collective terms such as "artificial flavors," "natural flavors," "spices," and "artificial flavors," however, may be listed for those ingredients without further elaboration. FDA provides a definition for each of these terms, and lists those items that may be included under them in an ingredient statement. An ingredient statement for flavors is required in addition to any flavor labeling required in conjunction with the identity statement.

Each ingredient must be listed specifically by its common or usual name.

While flavors and spices may be listed generically in ingredient statements, certified colors must be identified individually. Certified colors added to foods are designated in the ingredient statement by a common or usual name (e.g., "FD&C Blue No. 1," "Blue 1," "Blue 1 Lake"). The terms "FD&C" and "No." may be omitted from the name of the color. A collective name, such as "artificial color" or "color added," may still be used to declare noncertified color additives, although many companies choose to list noncertified colors by their common or usual name (e.g., annatto, grape skin extract).

Preservatives must be identified in an ingredient statement, not only by the common or usual name of the preservative, but by a separate description of its function, e.g., "benzoate of soda—a preservative" or "stannous chloride to protect flavor." Incidental additives—those ingredients present in a food at insignificant levels and which do not have any technical or functional effect in the finished food—need not be included in the ingredient statement. There is a specific rule in the case of sulfites. If the sulfites have either a technical or functional effect on the product or are present in an amount greater than 10 parts per 1,000,000, then they are not considered incidental and must be included in the ingredient statement in the same manner as any other ingredient in the product.

The ingredient declaration may appear either on the PDP or the IP, but the entire statement must appear on a single panel.

♦ Allergens

Under the Food Allergen Labeling and Consumer Protection Act (FALCPA) of 2004, all packaged foods labeled on or after January 1, 2006, also must comply with food allergen labeling requirements set forth in FDCA § 403(w). Specifically, a food that is not a raw agricultural commodity and contains a "major food allergen"—defined as milk, egg, fish, crustacean shellfish, tree nuts, wheat, peanuts, and soybeans—is misbranded unless the label identifies, immediately after or adjacent to the list of ingredients, that the food "Contains" the food source from which the allergen is derived. These allergen labeling requirements apply to all foods regulated under the FDCA, including both domestically manufactured and imported products.

♦ Nutrition Labeling

When Congress passed the Nutrition Labeling and Education Act (NLEA), the act reaffirmed the legal basis for FDA's labeling initiative and established an explicit timetable.

In 1990, Congress passed the Nutrition Labeling and Education Act (NLEA), Pub. L. No. 101-535, 104 Stat. 2353 (1990), to require uniform nutrition labeling on most FDA-regulated packaged food products. Extensive regulations are found at 21 C.F.R. § 101.9. USDA has adopted parallel nutrition labeling and nutrient content claims regulations. The statute and regulations provide a number of exemptions from nutrition labeling requirements, which can be lost if claims are made on the label or labeling. The exemptions include:

- food produced by certain small businesses;
- food served in restaurants;
- food served in other establishments for immediate consumption, such as schools, hospitals, and airplanes;
- ready-to-eat foods prepared primarily on-site (for example, at bakeries, delicatessens, and candy stores);
- raw fruits, vegetables, and fish;
- food shipped in bulk, provided that it is not sold in that form to consumers, and is used in the manufacture of foods at another site;
- foods that contain insignificant amounts of all nutrients and food components required to be declared on the nutrition label (for example, coffee beans and tea leaves);
- foods in small packages that have a total surface area of less than twelve square inches. Such foods are required to bear an address or telephone number that a consumer can use to obtain the required information. A modified label format is also provided for intermediate size packages (forty or less square inches), provided that these foods bear no nutrition claims or other nutrition information;
- medical foods;
- infant formulas; and
- dietary supplements (subject to separate labeling requirements).

The regulations require manufacturers to include information about certain nutrients on product labels (mandatory nutrients). Information about certain other nutrients may be listed at the manufacturer's discretion (voluntary nutrients). If a claim is made about any of the voluntary nutrients, or if a food is fortified or enriched with any of them, information about that nutrient then becomes mandatory. The mandatory and voluntary nutrients enumerated in the regulations are the only ones permitted to appear on the nutrition panel. A revision to the mandatory nutrients information, implemented in 2006, requires that food labels list trans fatty acids ("trans fat") on a separate line immediately under the line for saturated fatty acids.

A revision to the mandatory nutrients information that was implemented in 2006 requires that food labels list trans fatty acids ("trans fat") on a separate line immediately under the line for saturated fatty acids.

Those mandatory nutrients (italicized) and the voluntary nutrients are listed below in the order in which they must appear on the label:

Mandatory Nutrients and Voluntary Nutrients	
Listed in the order in which they must appear on the label. Mandatory nutrients are italicized.	***total calories***
	calories from fat
	calories from saturated fat
	total fat
	saturated fat
	trans fat
	cholesterol
	sodium
	potassium
	total carbohydrate
	dietary fiber
	soluble fiber
	insoluble fiber
	sugars
	sugar alcohols
	other carbohydrate (the difference between total carbohydrate and the sum of dietary fiber, sugars, and sugar alcohol if declared)
	protein
	vitamin A
	vitamin C
	calcium
	iron
	other vitamins and minerals (see 21 C.F.R. § 101.9(c))

The regulations go into great detail on the methodology to be used in calculating nutrient content, and discuss specific analytical methods to be used to determine the amount of each dietary component present in foods. In most cases, a food manufacturer is free to use other methods. Where FDA contests the results found by the food manufacturer, however, the agency uses the analytical methods identified in the regulations.

When listing these nutrients, not only their absolute quantitative measure must be identified; the NLEA also requires that reference values for nutrients—the "Daily Value"—be included. The daily value is the average amount of a particular nutrient that an individual should consume in a day. A nutrition label must declare the daily value and, in some cases, the quantity by weight of all nutrients.

FDA has established a detailed format for the presentation of nutrition information on food products. The nutrient declarations are based upon serving size listed in "common household units" such as cups, tablespoons, or teaspoons, except for beverages, which must be listed in fluid ounces. To determine the appropriate serving size for food product, a manufacturer must look to the reference amount in FDA's regulations for the relevant product category. 21 C.F.R. § 101.12. The reference amount customarily consumed (RACC) represents the amount of food from the product category that is customarily consumed per eating occasion. RACCs are not intended as dietary recommendations, but rather as guides to help manufacturers establish appropriate serving sizes. Manufacturers determine the serving size for a product by calculating what fraction of a sales unit equals the RACC. This is rarely an exact fit, so the regulations contain standards to convert RACCs to appropriate serving sizes. For example, if the sale unit of a product weighs at least 67% but less than 200% of the reference amount, the serving size of the product is one unit. Underneath the serving size is the "Number of Servings Per Container."

The nutrient declarations are based upon serving size listed in "common household units" such as cups, tablespoons, or teaspoons, except for beverages, which must be listed in fluid ounces.

FDA has recognized that the levels of nutrients in food products generally will not calculate out as even, uniform numbers. The presentation of a wide array of numerical values, including fractions or decimal places, will render the nutrition label unnecessarily confusing to consumers, and make comparison of values among different products more difficult. Therefore, the regulations provide specific rules for rounding nutrient values on nutrition labels up or down, generally to increments of five or ten. The regulations establish different rounding parameters for different nutrients, and the level of adjustment made will vary for different ranges within individual nutrients (e.g., the different rules discussed above for rounding caloric values above or below fifty).

If standard-size packages (those that have a total surface area available for labeling of more than forty square inches) cannot fit the nutrition panel onto the information panel in the general tabular format, a modified, tabular format, which presents the information in a horizontal, side-by-side display, may be used. If the package lacks sufficient continuous vertical space to utilize even this modified vertical display, the regulations provide for a horizontal format.

Small and intermediate-size packages (those which have a total surface area available for labeling of forty square inches or less) are subject to looser requirements for the presentation of nutrition labeling. The Nutrition Facts label may appear on any label panel, not only the information panel. Moreover, if necessary for reasons of package space, the footnotes to the nutrition label may be omitted and replaced with an asterisked statement at the bottom of the label that percent daily values are based on a 2,000-calorie diet.

Small packages (those with a total surface area of twelve square inches or less available for labeling) are eligible for an even greater exception to the labeling format requirements. If necessary for reasons of space, small packages may omit the full nutrition labeling and instead merely list an address or telephone number through which to obtain nutrition information. If a manufacturer uses the "telephone number exemption," it may not make any claims in the label as to the nutrient content of the product.

If a food contains insignificant amounts of seven or more of the mandatory nutrients and total calories, the manufacturer may use a simplified Nutrition Facts format that omits much of the information that appears in the standard display. "Insignificant amount" is defined as an amount that may be declared as zero under the nutrition labeling regulations, or for total carbohydrates, dietary fiber, and protein, a declaration of "less than 1 g" (see the above discussion of rounding rules). Trans fat does not have to be included if the *total* fat in a food is less than 0.5 gram per serving and the label makes no claims about fat, fatty acids, or cholesterol content. This simplified format contains information on total calories, total fat, total carbohydrate, protein, and sodium only. These five nutrients must be declared, even if they are present in insignificant amounts. If the food product contains calories from fat and/or mandatory nutrients in greater than insignificant amounts, they must be declared on the label. Any nutrients added to the food must be declared as well.

The Nutrition Facts panel must appear on the principal display panel or the information panel. There are, however, exceptions to this requirement. For example, FDA gives packages that have a total surface area available for labeling greater than forty square inches greater flexibility in displaying nutrition information. If the principal display panel and the information panel do not provide sufficient space to accommodate all of the required information, the manufacturer may use any alternate panel that can be seen readily by consumers for the nutrition label.

♦ Nutrient Content Claims (Descriptors)

Manufacturers are permitted to place claims on a label regarding the level of a nutrient in a food, provided that they use only the descriptive terms that FDA has defined by regulation.

Nutrient content claims on food labels also are governed by NLEA. Manufacturers are permitted to place claims on a label regarding the level of a nutrient in a food, provided that they use only the descriptive terms that FDA has defined by regulation. This enables manufacturers to highlight particular nutritional attributes of their products through a uniform frame of reference.

FDA allows two types of nutrient content claims: absolute claims, which describe the level of a nutrient in a serving of a product, and relative claims, which compare the level of nutrient per serving in a product to that of a reference product. Absolute claims may utilize only the particular descriptive terms approved by FDA, which are listed and defined below. Relative claims only can compare products to appropriate classes of reference foods established by FDA for use as the basis for relative claims. All nutrient content claims, whether absolute or relative, must be based on RACCs. Special rules apply to claims for foods with small RACCs.

FDA allows two types of nutrient content claims: absolute claims, which describe the level of a nutrient in a serving of a product, and relative claims, which compare the level of nutrient per serving in a product to that of a reference product.

Labels containing a relative claim must state, in immediate proximity to the claim, the identity of the reference product and the amount by which the reduced product differs from it, expressed as a percentage or a fraction, e.g. "30 percent fewer calories than regular ________." The label also must bear quantitative information comparing calories per serving to the reference product. This can be accomplished by a statement such as "calorie content of regular is 120 calories per 12 oz. serving; calorie content of diet is 2 calories per 12 oz. serving," or by a chart or graph display of the nutrient levels of the reference product, and the corresponding lower levels in the reduced product. This quantitative information must appear either next to the most prominent reduced calorie claim, or on the nutrition information panel.

If a product qualifies for a nutrient content claim, but contains a high level of certain other nutrients, a referral/disclosure statement is required. Specifically, if a food making a nutrient content claim contains more than 13 grams of fat, 4 grams of saturated fat, 60 milligrams of cholesterol, or 480 milligrams of sodium per RACC, then the referral statement must read "See [appropriate panel] for information about [nutrient requiring disclosure] and other nutrients."

A table of FDA-approved nutrient content claims is found at the end of this chapter. The NLEA allows for the submission of petitions requesting that FDA promulgate definitions for new nutrient content claims or accept synonyms for defined terms, or allow the use of implied nutrient content claims in brand names.

♦ Structure-Function Claims

Conventional foods may also bear "structure-function" claims—claims relating a food or food ingredient to an effect on the structure or function of the body. Such claims have been used on foods for many years, and include statements such as "calcium builds strong bones." One of the important distinctions between conventional foods and dietary supplements lies in this area: FDA takes the position that conventional food claims must be derived from the "nutritive value" of the food, an ambiguous concept that FDA regulations define as "a value in sustaining human existence by such processes as promoting growth, replacing loss of essential nutrients, or providing energy." 21 C.F.R. § 101.14(a)(3).

♦ Health Claims

In addition to nutrient content claims, NLEA authorizes the use of health claims—defined as a statement that expressly or by implication characterizes the relationship of certain nutrients to a disease or health-related condition—on food labels. Health claims differ from nutrient content claims in that they focus not on the amount of a particular nutrient supplied by the food product in question, but rather on the potential health benefits of consumption of that nutrient, with the food product in question being but one source of that nutrient.

An "authorized health claim" is permitted only if FDA has promulgated a regulation approving the claim and setting forth the conditions under which it may be used.

An "authorized health claim" is permitted only if FDA has promulgated a regulation approving the claim and setting forth the conditions under which it may be used. A food is misbranded, and may be considered an unapproved drug, if it bears any health claim other than those authorized by FDA, or if it fails to meet the requirements of the regulation authorizing its use. Food products are permitted to bear authorized health claims for certain relationships between a nutrient or a food and the risk of a disease or health-related condition.

FDA may issue an authorized health claim regulation on its own, or in response to a petition from manufacturers. Such a claim may be authorized if the agency determines, based on the totality of publicly available scientific evidence (including evidence from well-designed studies conducted in a manner consistent with generally recognized scientific procedures and principles), that the claim is supported by such evidence.

In addition, a "qualified health claim" is permitted where a claim is based on credible evidence, but the strength of the scientific evidence falls below the threshold for FDA to issue an authorized health claim regulation based on significant scientific agreement (the SSA standard). FDA established a review process for qualified health claims in response to several court decisions, including *Pearson v. Shalala*, 164 F.3d 650 (D.C. Cir. 1999), which ruled on First Amendment grounds that FDA may not reject a health claim found to be potentially misleading unless the agency also reasonably determines that no disclaimer would eliminate the potential deception.

In 2003, FDA established interim procedures for reviewing petitions for qualified health claims. Guidance for Industry and FDA: Interim Procedures for Qualified Health Claims in the Labeling of Conventional Human Food and Human Dietary Supplements (July 2003). Under this interim process, FDA reviews qualified health claim petitions on a case-by-case basis. FDA also has established an evidence-based ranking system to evaluate the scientific evidence supporting qualified health claims.

Guidance for Industry and FDA: Interim Evidence-based Ranking System for Scientific Data (July, 2003).

FDA classifies the strength of scientific validity for a qualified health claim into one of several categories: moderate/good level of comfort (Category B); low level of comfort (Category C); and extremely low level of comfort (Category D). By contrast, a Category A claim (high level of comfort) would meet the requirements for an authorized health claim petition under the SSA standard.

FDA classifies the strength of scientific validity for a qualified health claim into one of several categories: high level of comfort, moderate/good level of comfort, low level of comfort, and extremely low level of comfort.

Under the interim procedures for review of qualified health claims, FDA must respond by letter within 270 days notifying the petitioner whether FDA intends to exercise enforcement discretion with respect to a qualified health claim or to deny the petition. In a letter of enforcement discretion, FDA specifies the nature of the qualified health claim for which FDA has no objections. FDA has developed standardized qualifying language for qualified health claims subject to a letter of enforcement discretion, based on the three levels of support used in the evidence-based ranking system.

FDA posts on its website all petitions requesting a qualified health claim for a sixty-day public comment period. FDA also posts on its website all letters of enforcement discretion and denial letters for qualified health claim petitions. The posted letters of enforcement discretion give notice to manufacturers regarding how FDA intends to exercise its enforcement discretion on the use of the qualified health claim.

In July 2007, FDA released a draft guidance addressing its current thinking on the petition process used to evaluate scientific evidence for both authorized health claims and qualified health claims. The draft guidance makes several recommendations to health claim petitioners regarding the development of proposed claims related to the identification of studies to evaluate the substance/disease relationship and the identification of surrogate endpoints for disease risk.

The FDCA, through the passage of FDAMA, also allows a class of health claims and nutrient content claims which are not required, prior to use, to be codified into a regulation as an authorized health claim or be the subject of letter of enforcement discretion as a qualified health claim. These claims, referred to as "authoritative statement" claims, are permitted if:

- a scientific body of the U.S. government with official responsibility for public health protection or research directly relating to human nutrition (e.g., the National Institutes of Health or the Centers for Disease Control and Prevention) or the National Academy of Sciences or any of its subdivisions, has published an authoritative statement, currently in effect, about the relationship between a nutrient and a disease or health-related condition to which the health claim refers, or which identifies the nutrient level to which the claim refers, as appropriate;

- the person intending to make the claim submits to FDA, 120 days before introducing the food into interstate commerce with such a claim, a notice of the claim, including: 1) the exact words to be used and a concise description of the basis for concluding that the authoritative statement relied upon has been made; 2) a copy of the authoritative statement relied upon; and 3) a balanced representation of the scientific literature relating to the relationship that is the subject of the health claim or nutrient content claim;
- the claim and the food for which it is made are in compliance with FDA regulations prohibiting claims on foods that contain nutrients in amounts that increase the risk of diet-related diseases or health conditions, and the general provisions on misbranding; and
- the claim is stated so that it accurately represents the authoritative statement on which it is based, and it enables the public to understand both the information provided and its relative significance in the context of the total daily diet.

A health claim or nutrient content claim based on an authoritative statement may be made without FDA approval.

During the 120-day period between notification to FDA and the introduction of the food bearing the claim into interstate commerce, FDA may inform the notifier that it has not submitted all of the information required by the act. As noted, a health claim or nutrient content claim based on an authoritative statement may be made without FDA approval. Such a claim may be continued until either: 1) FDA issues a regulation (and the regulation has become effective) prohibiting or modifying the claim, or finding that the requirements of the act for such a claim have not been met, including a finding that the notification did not include all of the information required; or 2) a federal court determines, in the context of an enforcement proceeding, that the statutory requirements have not been met.

Standards of Identity

Section 401 of the FDCA permits FDA to set a certain definition or standard for a food to "promote honesty and fair dealing in the interest of consumers." Such regulations may include establishing a common or usual name for a food, providing a reasonable definition and standard of identity, setting a reasonable standard of quality, or reasonable standards of fill of container. *See* 21 C.F.R. Parts 102 (common or usual names for nonstandardized foods), 103 (quality standards for foods with no identity standards), 104 (nutritional quality guidelines for foods), and 130-169 (general conditions for standards of identity, and specific standards). The development of standards for most products—to the extent developed at all—are subject to informal, notice-and-comment rulemaking procedures rather than formal rulemaking.

To a large extent a standard of identity can be characterized as a recipe for a food that provides consumers with a consistent expectation as to composition and quality. A food may be considered misbranded if it is represented on its label as a food for which a definition and standard of identity has been established, yet fails to conform to that definition and standard even if it is wholesome and its label is otherwise truthful. See FDCA § 403.

A standard of identity can be characterized as a recipe for a food that provides consumers with a consistent expectation as to composition and quality.

Standards also may pertain to the quality of a food product. Products failing to meet a "standard of quality" must disclose the fact of substandard quality in a label statement. "Standards of fill" also commonly are used to protect against "slack fill" or products with excess water levels.

According to section 403(c) of the FDCA, a food is misbranded "[i]f it is an imitation of another food, unless its label bears, in type of uniform size and prominence, the word 'imitation' and, immediately thereafter, the name of the food imitated." FDA regulations further provide that "imitation labeling" is required if a food is a substitute for and resembles another food but is nutritionally inferior to that food. "Nutritional inferiority" is defined as any reduction in the content of the essential nutrient that is present at a measurable amount, not including caloric or fat content with a measurable amount considered to be 2 percent or more of the daily reference value for protein and potassium, and the referenced daily intake for specified vitamins and minerals. Rather than bearing the term "imitation"—which virtually ensures a food product's demise in the marketplace—products that resemble a standardized food but are not nutritionally inferior may bear an appropriate common or usual name, an appropriately descriptive term, or a fanciful name that is not false and misleading.

Under 21 C.F.R § 130.10, a food may bear the name of a standardized food that does not meet the standard if the deviation from the standard is described by a nutrient content claim on the label. This regulation permits the development of healthful versions of standardized foods without requiring labeling that would prevent consumers from buying the product. Among a number of specific limitations, in order for a food product to comply with this "generic" standard of identity:

- nutrients may be added so that the product is not nutritionally inferior to the standardized food;
- the substitute food must possess the same or similar performance characteristics as the standardized food;
- deviations from the non-ingredient provisions of the standard are permitted if intended to produce the performance characteristics;

- deviations must be the minimum necessary to qualify for the nutrient content claim; and
- any significant deviations from the range of performance characteristics for the standardized food must be noted on the label, such as "not recommended for frying."

In May 2005, FDA and the USDA's Food Safety and Inspection Service, which regulates meat and poultry products standards of identity, issued a joint proposed rule to revise their respective food standards processes they employ. 70 Fed. Reg. 29,214 (May 20, 2005). The proposed rule establishes a set of criteria that both agencies would use to evaluate petitions to revise, eliminate, or create a new standard of identity. The proposed rule also would give each agency the ability to propose, on its own initiative, to revise, eliminate, or create a new standard of identity.

Food Security/Safety

FDA has increasingly focused on issues of food security in the last several years.

FDA has increasingly focused on issues of food security in the last several years, in particular following the passage of the Public Health Security and Bioterrorism Preparedness and Response Act (Bioterrorism Act) of 2002 (Pub. L. 107-88). In response to Title III of the Bioterrorism Act, "Protecting Safety and Security of Food and Drug Supply," FDA has proposed and issued regulations governing facility registration, new food import requirements, administrative detention authority, and recordkeeping and access requirements.

FDA is also involved in several other food security/safety initiatives, including coordination with other federal and state agencies to further develop response plans for food emergencies, the recent issuance of the FDA Food Protection Plan, an increased focus on food facility inspections, and the development of an adulterated food registry.

Bioterrorism Act

FDA has issued several food regulations in response to passage of the following Bioterrorism Act sections: food facility registration (section 305): prior notice of imported food (section 307); administrative detention of foods (section 303); and recordkeeping and access requirements for food firms (section 306).

♦ Food Facility Registration

In October 2003, FDA issued an interim final rule requiring domestic and foreign facilities that manufacture, process, pack, or hold food for consumption by humans and animals in the United States to register with FDA by December 2003. 68 Fed. Reg. 58,894 (Oct. 10, 2003). In October 2005, FDA issued a final rule adopting the interim final rule requirements, set forth in 21 C.F.R. Part 1, Subpart H.

The food facility regulations require that a food manufacturer separately register each facility. The registration for foreign facilities also must include the name of the U.S. agent for the facility. FDA is required to compile and maintain an up-to-date list of registered facilities, which is available on its website.

Foreign facilities are not required to register with FDA where the manufactured food undergoes further processing or packaging at another facility outside the United States. In addition, manufacturers of food contact substances are not required to register with FDA. Other establishments excluded from the registration requirements include farms, restaurants and other retail food establishments, and nonprofit food establishments.

♦ Prior Notice of Imported Food

In October 2003, FDA issued an interim final rule establishing prior notice regulations set forth in 21 C.F.R. Part 1, Subpart I. The regulations require that prior notice is given to FDA for all food for humans and animals imported or offered for import into the United States for use, storage, or distribution in the United States. 68 Fed. Reg. 58,975 (Oct. 10, 2003). The prior notice rules apply to food for transshipment through the United States to another country and food for future export, but are not applicable for foods that are imported and then exported without leaving the port of arrival until export.

Prior notice must be given to FDA for all food for humans and animals imported or offered for import into the United States for use, storage, or distribution in the United States.

A prior notice may be submitted by any person with knowledge of the required information, and may be transmitted to FDA by a third party, such as a customer, on behalf of the submitter. Prior notices are submitted electronically to FDA through either 1) the U.S. Customs and Border Patrol (CBP) Automated Broker Interface of the Automated Commercial System (ABI/ACS) or 2) the FDA Prior Notice System Interface. Prior notice submissions must contain detailed production, transportation, and recipient information.

The time requirements for submission of prior notice, and confirmation by FDA for review, are as follows: 1) if the article of food is arriving by road, no less than two hours before arriving at the port of arrival; 2) if the article of food is arriving by rail, no less than four hours before arriving at the port of arrival; 3) if the article of food is arriving by air, no less than four hours before arriving at the port of arrival; or 4) if the article of food is arriving by water, no less than eight hours before arriving at the port of arrival. Except where a food is offered for import by international mail, a prior notice may not be submitted more than five calendar days before the anticipated date of arrival of the food at the anticipated port of arrival.

A food may be refused admission into the United States if the prior notice is inadequate—either due to no prior notice, inaccurate prior notice, or untimely prior notice. A refused food must be exported (unless seized or administratively detained by CBP or FDA under other authority), or it must be held within the port of entry unless otherwise directed by CBP or FDA. A request may be made within five days for FDA to review whether a food refused admission is in fact subject to prior notice requirements or whether the information submitted in the prior notice is accurate. If FDA determines that the food is not subject to prior notice requirements or the prior notice submission is accurate, it will notify the requester that the food is no longer subject to refusal of admission.

♦ Administrative Detention

In June 2004, FDA issued a final rule establishing regulations, set forth in 21 C.F.R. Part 1, Subpart K, authorizing the detention of any food found during an inspection, examination, or investigation conducted under the FDCA, when based on credible evidence or information indicating such food presents a threat of serious adverse health consequences or death to humans or animals. 69 Fed. Reg. 31,659 (June 4, 2004). An officer or qualified employee of FDA may order an administrative detention, which must be approved by the Secretary or a designated official. The detention period must be reasonable and not exceed thirty calendar days. Any person entitled to claim the food if it were seized may appeal the detention order to the Secretary.

♦ Records

Persons who manufacture, process, pack, transport, distribute, receive, hold, or import food in the United States must maintain records and allow FDA access to those records.

In December 2004, FDA issued a final rule establishing regulations, set forth in 21 C.F.R. Part 1, Subpart J, requiring persons who manufacture, process, pack, transport, distribute, receive, hold, or import food in the United States to maintain and allow FDA access to records. 69 Fed. Reg. 71,561 (Dec. 9, 2004). Records to be maintained by food firms relate to the identity of the immediate previous source of all food received and the immediate subsequent recipient of all food released, and records must be retained at or reasonably close to the establishment where the activities covered in the records occurred. The record retention period for human foods ranges from six months to two years depending on the food's shelf life, and the retention period for animal food is one year.

The following persons or facilities are not subject to the recordkeeping and access requirements: farms; restaurants; persons performing covered activities when the food is meat, poultry, or egg products subject to exclusive USDA jurisdiction; and foreign persons, except those who transport food in the United States. The records requirements also do not extend to the following information: recipes for food; financial and pricing data, personnel data, research data, or sales data (other than shipment data regarding sales). In addition, certain persons or facilities—including small retail food establishments and certain nonprofit food establishments—are not subject to the record establishment requirements, but are subject to the availability requirements for existing records.

Other Food Safety/Security Initiatives

FDA is involved with several initiatives in furtherance of its responsibilities in ensuring the safety and security of the nation's food supply.

One area of focus has been the collaboration among FDA, other federal agencies, state governments, and private industry in developing food safety response plans. In September 2004, FDA, USDA, the U.S. Department of Homeland Security (DHS), and the National Association of State Departments of Agriculture signed a cooperative agreement to further develop an integrated national food safety response system, and FDA, DHS, and the Federal Bureau of Investigation have announced a new collaboration with states and private industry to protect the food supply from terrorist threats. In July 2007, FDA announced a national program, the Manufactured Food Regulatory Program Standards, to adopt more uniform standards for state food regulatory programs.

In November 2007, FDA issued the FDA Food Protection Plan: An Integrated Strategy for Protecting the Nation's Food Supply, in response to a directive from the Secretary of Health and Human Services to develop a comprehensive plan to protect the nation's domestic and imported food supply from unintentional and deliberate contamination. The plan uses a science and risk-based approach with three core elements: prevention, intervention, and response. The risk-based approach focuses on key points in the food supply where risks can be reduced or eliminated through timely intervention.

In November 2007, FDA issued the Food Protection Plan to protect the nation's domestic and imported food supply from unintentional and deliberate contamination.

The Food Protection Plan recommends that FDA request additional regulatory authorities to more successfully execute its recommendations, including authority to: 1) issue additional preventive controls for high-risk foods; 2) require food facilities to renew their FDA registrations every two years and allow FDA to modify the registration categories; and 3) and accredit highly qualified third parties for voluntary food inspections.

FDA also has strengthened its inspection program of foreign food facilities. Food contamination traced to foreign food facilities, including a massive recall in 2007 stemming from contaminated vegetable proteins imported from China and used as ingredients in pet food, have led to considerable publicity regarding the need to conduct inspection of foreign facilities manufacturing FDA-regulated products.

Under section 417 of the Food and Drug Administration Amendments Act of 2007 (Pub. L. 110-85), FDA is required within one year of passage, which occurred in September 2007, to create a Reportable Food Registry for "reportable foods," defined as foods (other than infant formula) for which there is a reasonable probability that the use of, or exposure to, the food will cause serious adverse health consequences or death to humans or animals. Responsible parties, defined as persons who submit a food facility registration to FDA for a facility where food is manufactured, processed, packed, or held will be required to notify FDA within twenty-four hours after the party determines that a food is a reportable food.

Medical Foods

"Medical foods" are administered by physicians for dietary management of a specific disease or disorder.

Medical foods have always been a subject of confusion. Although the category was conceived as a special category of foods administered by physicians for dietary management of a specific disease or disorder, it was not until 1988, with the passage of the Orphan Drug Amendments, that a statutory definition was provided for medical foods:

> A food which is formulated to be consumed or administered internally under the supervision of a physician and which is intended for the specific dietary management of a disease or condition for which distinctive nutritional requirements based upon recognized scientific principles are established by medical evaluation.

Pub. L. No. 100-290, 102 Stat. 90 (1988) (codified at 21 U.S.C. § 301 note, 360; 42 U.S.C. § 236 note (1994)). This definition was later incorporated into the NLEA.

For many years, FDA discussed the establishment of regulations for medical foods. In 1996, FDA finally published an advance notice of proposed rulemaking (ANPR) to request comments on its approach to the "broad group of heterogeneous products that are marketed as medical foods." 61 Fed. Reg. 6066 (Nov. 29, 1996). Concerns were expressed about the "medical foods paradox"—while these products are intended for the specific dietary management of a disease or condition for which distinctive nutritional requirements had been established, they could be sold without any nutrition information on their label or labeling and could bear claims that were not evaluated by FDA. Additionally, no mechanism existed to ensure that the formulation of a medical food has been evaluated prior to sale to ensure that it is suitable for the intended patient population. The agency expressed specific concern that such a lack of scrutiny could have adverse public health consequences, especially if claims were not scientifically valid or if product labeling did not disclose information necessary for safe and effective use.

In the medical foods ANPR, FDA expressed the view that Congress did establish a strict standard for medical foods—"distinctive nutritional requirements based upon recognized scientific principles"—thus implicitly providing an expectation that the standard would be met. Accordingly, the agency will look to medical food marketers to provide substantiation of the nutritional efficacy of their medical foods.

Infant Formulas

Under FDCA § 201(z), the term "infant formula" means "a food which purports to be or is represented for special dietary use solely as a food for infants for reason of its simulation of human milk or its suitability as a complete or partial substitute for human milk." Special requirements for infant formula are provided under FDCA § 412, which deems an infant formula adulterated if it does not provide specific nutrients, does not meet quality requirements prescribed by the Secretary, or is not produced in compliance with applicable cGMPs and quality control procedures. Records development and retention requirements also apply to infant formula products, and FDA has the authority to review and copy all records containing microbiological testing results of raw materials used in infant formula powder and unfinished infant formula. FDA also maintains requirements for the labeling of infant formulas, including nutrient content, directions for preparation and use, and a "use by" date. Finally, special requirements also apply to procedures for processing consumer complaints relating to infant formulas.

An infant formula is deemed adulterated if it does not provide specific nutrients, does not meet quality requirements prescribed by the Secretary, or is not produced in compliance with applicable cGMPs and quality control procedures.

Under FDCA § 412(c), persons introducing any new infant formula into interstate commerce must submit a registration with FDA, at least ninety days before the marketing of a new infant formula, that includes the quantitative formulation of the new infant formula or description of any reformulation or change in processing of the formula. A "new infant formula" includes "an infant formula manufactured by a person which has not previously manufactured an infant formula, and . . . . an infant formula manufactured by a person who has previously manufactured infant formula and in which there is a major change, in processing or formulation, from a current or any previous formulation produced by such manufacturer." FDCA § 412(c)(2). Preparations for special uses, such as for infants with inborn errors of metabolism, low birth rate, or other unusual medical or dietary problems, are exempt from the quality factors, quality control procedures, and recordkeeping requirements, subject to terms and conditions established by FDA. Such deviations are based upon an appropriate rationale submitted to the agency which supports the deviation from the general requirements.

CONCLUSION

Food regulation continues to evolve as new challenges arise. As a consequence, the food law framework may undergo further revision in the coming years. Concurrently, the line between so-called "functional foods" and disease will continue to change historical notions as to the relative role of foods in the promotion and maintenance of health. The food regulatory construct will increasingly be subject to scrutiny and challenge due to the potential for food bioterrorism and as part of international harmonization efforts. Even in this era of increasing complexity, however, the traditional concerns that food must be wholesome and truthfully represented remain the central tenets of federal regulation of the food supply.

Approved Health Claims

Approved Claims	Food Requirements	Claim Requirements	Model Claim Statements
Calcium and Osteoporosis § 101.72	High in calcium, Assimilable (Bioavailable), Supplements must disintegrate and dissolve, and Phosphorus content cannot exceed calcium content	The claim states that adequate calcium intake throughout life is linked to reduced risk of osteoporosis, but does not attribute any degree of reduction in risk Indicates that disease depends on many factors by listing risk factors for the disease Sex—Female Race—Caucasian and Asian Age—Bone-forming years (approximately 11 to 35 years) and menopausal women with a family history of the disease Primary target population Females Caucasian and Asian races Teens and young adults in their bone-forming years Additional factors necessary to reduce risk Eating healthful meals Regular exercise Mechanism relating calcium to osteoporosis Optimizes peak bone mass Foods or supplement containing more than 400 mg calcium must state that total intakes of greater than 2,000 mg calcium provide no added benefit to bone health	Regular exercise and a healthy diet with enough calcium helps teens and young adult Caucasian and Asian women maintain good bone health and may reduce their high risk of osteoporosis later in life.

Approved Claims	Food Requirements	Claim Requirements	Model Claim Statements
Sodium and Hypertension § 101.74	Low Sodium	The claim states that diets low in sodium "may" or "might" reduce the risk of high blood pressure Required terms: "Sodium" "High blood pressure" Indicates that high blood pressure depends on many factors Includes physician statement (Individuals with high blood pressure should consult their physicians) if claim defines high or normal blood pressure	Diets low in sodium may reduce the risk of high blood pressure, a disease associated with many factors.
Dietary Fat and Cancer § 101.73	Low fat Fish & game meats: "Extra Lean"	The claim states that diets low in fat "may" or "might" reduce the risk of some cancer, without attributing any degree of reduction of risk Required terms: "Total Fat" or "Fat" "Some types of cancers" or "Some cancers" Indicates that the development of cancer depends on many factors Does not specify types of fats or fatty acids that may be related	Development of cancer depends on many factors. A diet low in total fat may reduce the risk of some cancers.
Dietary Saturated Fat and Cholesterol and Risk of Coronary Heart Disease § 101.75	Low saturated fat Low cholesterol Low fat Fish & game meats: "Extra Lean"	The claim states that diets low in saturated fat and cholesterol "may" or "might" reduce the risk of heart disease, without attributing any degree of reduction of risk Required terms: "Saturated fat and cholesterol"	While many factors affect heart disease, diets low in saturated fat and cholesterol may reduce the risk of this disease.

Approved Claims	Food Requirements	Claim Requirements	Model Claim Statements
		"Coronary heart disease" or "Heart disease" Indicates that the development of heart disease depends on many factors Includes physician statement (Individuals with elevated blood total—or LDL—cholesterol should consult their physicians) if claim defines high or normal blood total and LDL-cholesterol	
Fiber-Containing Grain Products, Fruits, and Vegetables and Cancer § 101.76	A grain product, fruit, or vegetable that contains dietary fiber, or a food that contains the above. Low fat, and good source of dietary fiber under § 101.54 (without fortification)	The claim states that diets low in fat and high in fiber-containing grain products, fruits and vegetables "may" or "might" reduce the risk of some cancers, without attributing any degree or reduction of risk Required terms: "Fiber," "Dietary fiber," or "Total dietary fiber" "Some types of cancer" or "Some cancers" Indicates that development of cancer depends on many factors Does not specify types of dietary fiber that may be related to risk of cancer	Low fat diets rich in fiber-containing grain products, fruits, and vegetables may reduce the risk of some types of cancer, a disease associated with many factors.
Fruits, Vegetables, and Grain Products That Contain Fiber, Particularly Soluble Fiber, and Risk of Coronary Heart Disease § 101.77	A fruit, vegetable, or grain product that contains fiber, low saturated fat, low cholesterol, low fat, and at least 0.6 grams of soluble fiber per RACC (without fortification), and soluble fiber content provided on label	States that diets low in saturated fat and cholesterol and high in fruits, vegetables and grain products that contain fiber "may" or "might" reduce the risk of heart disease, without attributing any degree of reduction of risk.	Diets low in saturated fat and cholesterol and rich in fruits, vegetables, and grain products that contain some types of dietary fiber, particularly soluble fiber, may reduce the risk of heart disease, a disease associated with many factors.

Approved Claims	Food Requirements	Claim Requirements	Model Claim Statements
		Required terms: "Fiber," "Dietary fiber," "Some types of dietary fiber," "Some dietary fibers," or "Some fibers" "Saturated fat" and "Cholesterol" "Heart disease" or "Coronary heart disease" Indicates that development of heart disease depends on many factors. Includes physician statement (Individuals with elevated blood total or LDL-cholesterol should consult their physicians) if claim defines high or normal blood total and LDL-cholesterol	
Fruits and Vegetables and Cancer § 101.78	A fruit or vegetable, low fat, and good source (without fortification) of at least one of the following: Vitamin A, Vitamin C, or dietary fiber	States that diets low in fat and high in fruits and vegetables "may" or "might" reduce the risk of some cancers, without attributing any degree of reduction of risk. Required terms: "Fiber," "Dietary fiber," or "Total dietary fiber" "Total fat" or "Fat" "Some types of cancer" or "Some cancers" Characterizes fruits and vegetables as "Foods that are low in fat and may contain Vitamin A, Vitamin C, and dietary fiber" Characterizes specific food as a "Good source" of one or more of the following: Dietary fiber, Vitamin A, or Vitamin C Does not specify types of fats or fatty acids or	Low fat diets rich in fruits and vegetables (foods that are low in fat and may contain dietary fiber, Vitamin A, or Vitamin C) may reduce the risk of some types of cancer, a disease associated with many factors. OR Broccoli is high in vitamins A and C, and is a good source of dietary fiber.

Approved Claims	Food Requirements	Claim Requirements	Model Claim Statements
		types of dietary fiber that may be related to risk of cancer. Indicates that development of cancer depends on many factors.	
Folate and Neural Tube Defects § 101.79	"Good source" of folate (at least 40 mcg folate per serving) Dietary supplements, or foods in conventional food form that are naturally good sources of folate (i.e., only non-fortified food in conventional food form) The claim shall not be made on products that contain more than 100 percent of the RDI for Vitamin A as retinol or preformed vitamin A or vitamin D Dietary supplements shall meet USP standards for disintegration and dissolution or otherwise bioavailable Amount of folate required in Nutrition Label	States that daily consumption of adequate amounts of folate by a woman during childbearing years may reduce risk of spinal bifida or other neural tube defects, without attributing any degree of reduction of risk Required terms: Terms that specify the relationship (e.g., women who are capable of becoming pregnant and who consume adequate amounts of folate) "Folate," "Folic Acid," "Folacin," "Folate a B Vitamin," "Folic Acid, a B Vitamin," or "Folacin, a B Vitamin" "Neural tube defect," "birth defects, spinal bifida, or anencephaly," "birth defects of the brain or spinal cord anencephaly or spinal bifida," "spinal bifida or anencephaly, birth defects of the brain or spinal cord" Does not imply that folate intake is the only recognized risk factor for neural tube defects. Must also include information on the multifactorial nature and prevalence of neural tube defects, dietary sources of folate, and the	Healthful diets with adequate folate may reduce a woman's risk of having a child with a brain or spinal cord defect.

Approved Claims	Food Requirements	Claim Requirements	Model Claim Statements
		safe upper limit of daily intake.	
Dietary Noncariogenic Carbohydrate Sweeteners and Dental Caries § 101.80	Sugar free, and when a fermentable carbohydrate is present, the food must not lower plaque pH below 5.7. The following are eligible substances: 1) sugar alcohol (xylitol, sorbitol, mannitol, maltitol, isomalt, lactitol, hydrogenated starch hydrolysates, hydrogenated glucose syrups, erythritol, or a combination of these); 2) sugar (D-tagatose); and 3) non-nutritive sweetener (sucralose)	States that noncariogenic carbohydrate sweeteners do not promote dental caries, compared to other carbohydrates, without attributing any degree of reduction of risk. Required terms: "does not promote," "may reduce the risk of," "useful [or is useful] in not promoting," or "expressly [or is expressly] for not promoting" dental caries. "Sugar alcohol," "sugar alcohols," or the name of the sugar alcohols, or D-tagatose, or sucralose (note: D-tagatose may be identified as "tagatose") "Dental caries" or "tooth decay" When the substance that is the subject of the claim is a noncariogenic sugar (i.e., D-tagatose), the claim shall identify the substance as a sugar that, unlike other sugars, does not promote the development of dental caries. Includes statement that frequent between meal consumption of foods high in sugars and starches can promote tooth decay. Packages with less than 15 square inches of surface area available for labeling may use a shortened claim.	Frequent between-meal consumption of foods high in sugars and starches promotes tooth decay. The sugar alcohols in [name of food] do not promote tooth decay. (Full claim) OR Does not promote tooth decay. (Short claim—on small packages only)

Approved Claims	Food Requirements	Claim Requirements	Model Claim Statements
Soluble Fiber from Certain Food and Risk of Coronary Heart Disease § 101.81	Meet requirements for low fat, low saturated fat, and low cholesterol The food product must include one or more of the following whole oat or barley foods: 1) oat bran, 2) rolled oats, 3) whole oat flour, 4) whole grain barley or dry milled barley. The whole oat or barley foods must contain: 1) at least 0.75 g of soluble fiber per RACC of the food product; 2) Oatrim that contains at least 0.75 g of beta-glucan soluble per RACC of the food product; or 3) psyllium husk that contains at least 1.7 g of soluble fiber per RACC of food product. Beta-glucan soluble fiber from the following are eligible sources of soluble fiber: 1) oat bran; 2) rolled oats; 3) whole oat flour; 4) Oatrim; 5) whole grain barley and dry milled barley; and 6) soluble fiber from psyllium husk with purity of no less than 95%. The amount of soluble fiber per RACC must be declared in nutrition label	States that diets low in saturated fat and cholesterol that include soluble fiber from [source] "may" or "might" reduce the risk of heart disease, without attributing any degree of reduction of risk Does not imply that low saturated fat and cholesterol diets that include soluble fiber are the sole means of achieving a reduced risk of CHD Required terms: "Saturated fat" and "cholesterol" "Heart disease" or "coronary heart disease" In specifying the substance the claim uses the term "soluble fiber" qualified by the name of the eligible source of the soluble fiber, which is either whole oat or barley or psyllium seed husk. Claim specifies the daily dietary intake of the soluble fiber source necessary to reduce the risk of CHD Claim specifies the amount of soluble fiber in one serving of the product. For psyllium products — see potential warning/notice statement under 21 C.F.R. § 101.17(f)	Soluble fiber from foods such as [name of source] as part of a diet low in saturated fat and cholesterol may reduce the risk of heart disease. Diets low in saturated fat and cholesterol that include [_____ grams] soluble fiber per day from [source (can include name of food product)] may reduce the risk of heart disease. One serving of [*name of food*] provides_____grams of this soluble fiber.
Soy Proteins and Risk of Coronary Heart Disease § 101.82	Meet requirements for low saturated fat, low cholesterol, and low fat (except that foods made from whole soybeans that contain no fat in	States diets that are low in saturated fat and cholesterol and that include soy protein "may" or "might" reduce risk of heart	25 grams of soy protein a day, as part of a diet low in saturated fat and cholesterol, may reduce the risk of heart disease. A serving of [*name of*

Approved Claims	Food Requirements	Claim Requirements	Model Claim Statements
	addition to that inherent in the whole soybean are exempt from the "low fat" requirement) Shall contain at least 6.25 g of soy protein.	disease, without attributing any degree of reduction of risk. Required terms: "Heart disease" or "coronary heart disease" "Soy protein" "Saturated fat" and "cholesterol" Does not imply that consumption of soy is the only way to reduce risk of coronary heart disease. Claim specifies daily dietary intake levels of soy protein associated with reduced risk. Claim specifies amount of soy protein in a serving of food.	*food*] supplies_____grams of soy protein. Diets low in saturated fat and cholesterol that include 25 grams of soy protein a day may reduce the risk of heart disease. One serving of [*name of food*] provides_____grams of soy protein.
Plant Sterol/Stanol Esters and Risk of Coronary Heart Disease § 101.83	Must meet requirements for low saturated fat and low cholesterol. Must contain at least 0.65 g of plant sterol esters per RACC of spreads or salad dressings, or at least 1.7 g of plant stanol esters per RACC of spreads, salad dressings, snack bars, and dietary supplements. Spreads and salad dressings that exceed 13 g fat per 50 g must bear the statement "*see nutrition information for fat content*" Salad dressings are exempted from the minimum 10% DV nutrient requirement	States diets low in saturated fat and cholesterol that include plant sterol/stanol esters may reduce the risk of coronary heart disease, without attributing any degree of reduction of risk. Required terms: "Heart disease" or "coronary heart disease" "Plant sterol esters" or "plant stanol esters;" except "vegetable oil" may replace the term "plant" if vegetable oil is the sole source of the sterol/stanol ester Claim specifies the daily dietary intake of plant sterol or stanol esters necessary to reduce CHD risk, and the amount provided per serving. Claim specifies that plant sterol or stanol esters should be consumed with two different meals each a day.	Foods containing at least 0.65 gram per of vegetable oil sterol esters, eaten twice a day with meals for a daily total intake of least 1.3 grams, as part of a diet low in saturated fat and cholesterol, may reduce the risk of heart disease. A serving of [*name of food*] supplies_____grams of vegetable oil sterol esters. Diets low in saturated fat and cholesterol that include two servings of foods that provide a daily total of at least 3.4 grams of plant stanol esters in two meals may reduce the risk of heart disease. A serving of [*name of food*] supplies_____grams of plant stanol esters.

General criteria all health claims must meet:

Only information on the value that intake or reduce intake, as part of a total dietary pattern, may have on a disease or health-related condition

Enables public to understand information provided and significance of information in the context of a total daily diet

Complete, truthful, and not misleading

Food contains, without fortification, 10 percent or more of the Daily Value of one of six nutrients (Dietary supplements excepted):

Nutrient	10%DV	Nutrient	10%DV
Vitamin A	500 IU	Calcium	100 mg
Vitamin C	6 mg	Protein	5 g
Iron	1.8 mg	Fiber	2.5 g

All information in one place without intervening material (Reference statement permitted)

Uses "may" or "might" to express relationship between substance and disease

Does not quantify any degree of risk reduction

Indicates disease depends on many factors

Disqualifying nutrients in foods contained at less than the levels specified:

Disqualifying Nutrient	Food	Main Dishes	Meal Products
Fat	13.0 g	19.5 g	26.0 g
Saturated Fat	4.0 g	6.0 g	8.0 g
Cholesterol	60 mg	90 mg	120 mg
Sodium	480 mg	720 mg	960 mg

Low Fat
Food: ≤ 3 g per RACC (and per 50 g if RACC is small)
Meals and main dishes: ≤ 3 g per 100 g and not more than 30% of calories from fat

Low Saturated Fat
Food: ≤ 1 g per RACC and ≤ 15% of calories from saturated fat
Meals and main dishes: ≤ 1 g per 100 g and < 10% of calories from saturated fat

Low Cholesterol
Food: < 20 mg per RACC (and per 50 g of food if RACC is small)
Meals and main dishes: < 20 mg per 100g

Low Sodium
Food: ≤ 140 mg per RACC (and per 50 g if RACC is small)
Meals and main dishes: ≤ 140 mg per 100 g

"Extra Lean"
Seafood or game meat:
< 5 g total fat and 2 g saturated fat and
< 95 mg cholesterol per RACC and per 100 g
Meals and main dishes: < 5 g total fat and < 2 g saturated fat and < 95 mg cholesterol per 100 g and per LS

High in Calcium
Food: ≥ 200 mg per RACC
Meals and main dishes: Contains food that is high in calcium and identifies the food

Good Source of Vitamin A
Food: ≥ 500 IU per RACC
Meals and main dishes: Contains food that is a good source of Vitamin A and identifies food

Good Source of Vitamin C
Food: ≥ 6 mg per RACC
Meals and main dishes: Contains food that is a good source of Vitamin C and identifies food

Good Source of Dietary Fiber
Food: ≥ 2.5 g per RACC
Meals and main dishes: Contains food that is a good source of dietary fiber and identifies food

ABBREVIATION: DV = Daily Value; RACC = Reference Amount Customarily Consumed per Eating Occasion; LS = Labeled Serving; IU = International Units; RACC small = ≤ 30 g or 2 tablespoons or less

To be labeled as "Healthy," a food must meet the definition of "Low" for fat and saturated fat, and neither cholesterol nor sodium may be present at a level exceeding the disclosure levels in 21 C.F.R. 101.13(h). In addition, the food must comply with definitions and declaration requirements for any specific nutrient content claims.

21 C.F.R. 101.65(d)(2)

Conditions for the Use of "Healthy"

Individual Food	Seafood or Game Meat[5/]	Meal or Main Dish
TOTAL FAT low fat	TOTAL FAT < 5 g fat /RACC & /100 g	TOTAL FAT low fat
SATURATED (sat) FAT low sat fat	SATURATED (sat) FAT < 2 g sat fat /RACC & /100g	SATURATED (sat) FAT low sat fat
SODIUM ≤ 480 mg /RACC and LS; or ≤ 480 mg /50 g, if RACC is small	SODIUM ≤ 480 mg /RACC and LS; or ≤ 480 mg /50 g, if RACC is small	SODIUM ≤ 600 mg /LS
CHOLESTEROL ≤ disclosure level	CHOLESTEROL < 95 mg /RACC & /100 g	CHOLESTEROL ≤ 90 mg /LS
BENEFICIAL NUTRIENTS Contains at least 10% of DV / RACC for vitamins A, C, calcium, iron, protein, or fiber The following are excepted: 1) raw fruits and vegetables; 2) frozen or canned single ingredient fruits and vegetables (may include ingredients whose addition does not change the nutrient profile of the fruit or vegetable); 3) enriched cereal-grain products that conform to a standard of identity in 21 C.F.R. 136, 137, 139.	BENEFICIAL NUTRIENTS Contains at least 10% of DV / RACC for vitamins A, C, calcium, iron, protein, or fiber	BENEFICIAL NUTRIENTS Contains at least 10% of the DV /LS of two nutrients (for a main dish product) or of three nutrients (for a meal product) of vitamin A, vitamin C, calcium, iron, protein, or fiber.
FORTIFICATION Per 21 C.F.R. § 104.20	FORTIFICATION Per 21 C.F.R. § 104.20	FORTIFICATION Per 21 C.F.R. § 104.20

OTHER CLAIMS

Food complies with established definition and declaration requirements for any specific nutrient content claim

NOTE: RACC = Reference Amount Customarily Consumed per Eating Occasion, LS = Labeled Serving, DV = Daily Value

RACC small = 30g or less or 2 tablespoons or less

5/ Raw, single ingredient seafood or game meat once processed becomes an individual food, meal or main dish.

Rounding Rules for Declaring Nutrients

Nutrient Serving	(M) or (V)*	Core Nutrient	Units	Increment Rounding**	Insignificant Amount	Other Relevant Information***
Calories	M	X	cal	< 5 cal express as zero < 50 cal express to nearest 5 cal increment > 50 cal express to nearest 10 cal increment	< 5 cal	§ 101.9(c)(1)
Calories from fat	M		cal	< 5 cal express as zero < 50 cal express to nearest 5 cal increment > 50 cal express to nearest 10 cal increment	< 5 cal	If < 0.5 g fat: "*cal from fat*" not required § 101.9(c)(1)(ii)
Calories from saturated fat	V		cal	< 5 cal express as zero < 50 cal express to nearest 5 cal increment > 50 cal express to nearest 10 cal increment	< 5 cal	§ 101.9(c)(1)(iii)
Total fat	M	X	g	< 0.5 g express as zero < 5 g express to nearest 0.5 g increment > 5 g express to nearest 1 g increment	< 0.5 g	§ 101.9(c)(2)
Saturated fat	M		g	< 0.5 g express as zero < 5 g express to nearest 0.5 g increment > 5 g express to nearest 1 g increment	< 0.5 g	§ 101.9(c)(2)(i)
Trans fat	M		g	< 0.5 g express as zero < 5 g express to nearest 0.5 g increment > 5 g express to nearest 1 g increment	< 0.5 g	§ 101.9(c)(2)(ii)
Polyunsaturated & Monosaturated fat	V		g	< 0.5 g express as zero < 5 g express to nearest 0.5 g increment > 5 g express to nearest 1 g increment	< 0.5 g	§ 101.9(c)(2)(iii) & (iv)
Cholesterol	M		mg	< 2 mg express as zero 2–5 mg express as "less than 5 mg" > 5 mg express to nearest 5 mg increment	< 2 mg	§ 101.9(c)(3)
Sodium	M	X	mg	< 5 mg express as zero 5–140 mg express to nearest 5 mg increment > 140 mg express to nearest 10 mg increment	< 5 mg	§ 101.9(c)(4)
Potassium	V		mg	< 5 mg express as zero 5–140 mg express to nearest 5 mg increment > 140 mg express to nearest 10 mg increment	< 5 mg	§ 101.9(c)(5)
Total carbohydrate	M	X	g	< 0.5 g express as zero < 1 g express as "Contains less than 1 g" OR "less than 1 g" > 1 g express to nearest 1 g increment	< 1 g	§ 101.9(c)(6)

Nutrient Serving	(M) or (V)*	Core Nutrient	Units	Increment Rounding**	Insignificant Amount	Other Relevant Information***
Dietary fiber	M		g	< 0.5 g express as zero < 1 g express as "Contains less than 1 g" OR "less than 1 g" > 1 g express to nearest 1 g increment	< 1 g	§ 101.9(c)(6)(i)
Soluble & Insoluble fiber	V		g	< 0.5 g express as zero < 1 g express as "Contains less than 1 g" OR "less than 1 g" > 1 g express to nearest 1 g increment	< 0.5 g	§ 101.9(c)(6)(i)(A) & (B)
Sugars	M		g	< 0.5 g express as zero < 1 g express as "Contains less than 1 g" OR "less than 1 g" > 1 g express to nearest 1 g increment	< 0.5 g	§ 101.9(c)(6)(ii)
Sugar alcohol	V		g	< 0.5 g express as zero < 1 g express as "Contains less than 1 g" OR "less than 1 g" > 1 g express to nearest 1 g increment	< 0.5 g	§ 101.9(c)(6)(iii)
Other carbohydrate	V		g	< 0.5 g express as zero < 1 g express as "Contains less than 1 g" OR "less than 1 g" > 1 g express to nearest 1 g increment	< 0.5 g	§ 101.9(c)(6)(iv)
Protein	M	X	g	< 0.5 g express as zero < 1 g express as "Contains less than 1 g" OR "less than 1 g" > 1 g express to nearest 1 g increment	< 1 g	§ 101.9(c)(7)
When declaring nutrients other than vitamins and minerals that have RDIs as a % DV	**M**		**% DV**	express to nearest 1% DV increment	< 1% DV	
Vitamins & minerals (express as % DV)	M		% DV	< 2% of RDI may be expressed as: (1) 2% if actual amount is 1.0% or more (2) zero (3) an asterisk that refers to statement "Contains less than 2% of the Daily Value of this (these nutrients) (nutrients)".... (4) for Vit A, C, calcium, iron: statement "Not a significant source of________ (listing the vitamins or minerals omitted)" < 10% of RDI express to nearest 2% increment > 10%–< 50% of RDI express to nearest 5% increment > 50% of RDI express to nearest 10% increment	< 2% RDI	Vitamins and minerals other than Vit. A, C, calcium and iron, listed in (8)(iv), are mandatory if added as nutrient supplement in food or if claim is made § 101.9(c)(8)(iii) & (iv)

Nutrient Serving	(M) or (V)*	Core Nutrient	Units	Increment Rounding**	Insignificant Amount	Other Relevant Information***
Beta-carotene (express as % DV)	V		% DV	≤10% of RDI for vitamin A express to nearest 2% DV increment > 10%–< 50% of RDI for vitamin A express to nearest 5% DV increment > 50% of RDI for vitamin A express to nearest 10% DV increment		§ 101.9(c)(8)(vi)

* (M) = Mandatory and (V) = Voluntary

** To express to the nearest 1 g increment, amounts exactly halfway between two whole numbers or higher (e.g., 2.50 to 2.99 g) round up (e.g., 3 g), and amounts less than halfway between two whole numbers (e.g., 2.01 to 2.49 g) round down (e.g., 2 g).

*** *NOTES FOR ROUNDING % Daily Value (DV) for Total Fat, Saturated Fat, Cholesterol, Sodium, Total Carbohydrate, Fiber, and Protein:*

(1) To calculate % DV, divide either the actual (unrounded) quantitative amount or the declared (rounded) amount by the appropriate RDI or DRV. Use whichever amount will provide the greatest consistency on the food label and prevent unnecessary consumer confusion (§ 101.9(d)(7)(ii)).

(2) When % DV values fall between two whole numbers, rounding shall be as follows:

—for values exactly halfway between two whole numbers or higher (e.g., 2.50 to 2.99) the value shall round up (e.g,, 3%)

—for values less than halfway between two whole numbers (e.g., 2.01 to 2.49) the values shall round down (e.g., 2%).

Definitions of Nutrient Content Claims

NUTRIENTS*	FREE	LOW	REDUCED/LESS	COMMENTS[1]
	Synonyms for "Free": "Zero," "No," "Without," "Trivial Source of," "Negligible Source of," "Dietarily Insignificant Source of" Definitions for "Free" for meals and main dishes are the stated values per labeled serving	Synonyms for "Low": "Little," ("Few" for Calories), "Contains a Small Amount of," "Low Source of"	Synonyms for "Reduced/Less": "Lower" ("Fewer" for Calories) "Modified" may be used in statement of identity Definitions for meals and main dishes are same as for individual foods on a per 100 g basis	For "Free," "Very Low," or "Low," must indicate if food meets a definition without benefit of special processing, alteration, formulation or reformulation; e.g., "broccoli, a fat-free food" or "celery, a low calorie food"
Calories § 101.60(b)	Less than 5 calories per reference amount and per labeled serving Not defined for meals or main dishes	40 calories or less per reference amount consumed if reference amount is greater than 30 grams (and per 50 g if reference amount is smaller) Meals and main dishes: 120 cal or less per 100 g	At least 25% fewer calories per reference amount than an appropriate reference food (or for meals and main dishes, at least 25% fewer calories per 100 g) Reference food may not be "Low Calorie" Uses term "Fewer" rather than "Less". . . .	"Light" or "Lite": If 50% or more of the calories are from fat, fat must be reduced by at least 50% per reference amount. If less than 50% of calories are from fat, fat must be reduced at least 50% or calories reduced at least 1/3 per reference amount § 101.56 "Light" or "Lite" meal or main dish product meets definition for "Low Calorie" or "Low Fat" meal and is labeled to indicate which definition is met For dietary supplements: Calorie claims can only be made when the reference product is greater than 40

NUTRIENTS*	FREE	LOW	REDUCED/LESS	COMMENTS[1]
				calories per serving
Total Fat § 101.62(b)	Less than 0.5 g per reference amount and per labeled serving (or for meals and main dishes, less than 0.5 g per labeled serving) No ingredient that is fat or understood to contain fat except as in note 2	3 g or less per reference amount (and per 50 g if reference amount is small) Meals and main dishes: 3 g or less per 100 g and not more than 30% of calories from fat	At least 25% less fat per reference amount than an appropriate reference food (or for meals and main dishes, at least 25% less fat per 100 g) Reference food may not be "Low Fat"	"_____% Fat Free": OK if food meets the requirements for "Low Fat" 100% Fat Free: Food must be "Fat Free" "Light": See above For dietary supplements: Fat claims cannot be made for products that are 40 calories or less per serving
Saturated Fat § 101.62	Less than 0.5 g saturated fat and less than 0.5 g trans fatty acids per reference amount and per labeled serving (or for meals and main dishes, less than 0.5 g saturated fat and less than 0.5 g trans fatty acid per labeled serving) No ingredient that is understood to contain saturated fat except as in note 2	1 g or less per reference amount and 15% or fewer calories from saturated fat Meals and main dishes: 1 g or less per 100 g and less than 10% of calories from saturated fat	At least 25% less saturated fat per reference amount than an appropriate reference food (or for meals and main dishes, at least 25% less saturated fat per 100 g) Reference food may not be "Low Saturated Fat"	Next to all saturated fat claims, must declare the amount of cholesterol if 2 mg or more per reference amount, and the amount of total fat if more than 3 g per reference amount (or 0.5 g or more of total fat for "Saturated Fat Free") (or for meals and main dishes, per labeled serving) For dietary supplements: Saturated fat claims cannot be made for products that are 40 calories or less per serving

NUTRIENTS*	FREE	LOW	REDUCED/LESS	COMMENTS[1]
Cholesterol § 101.62(d)	Less than 2 mg per reference amount and per labeled serving (or for meals and main dishes, less than 2 mg per labeled serving) No ingredient that contains cholesterol except as in note 2	20 mg or less per reference amount (and per 50 g of food if reference amount is small) Meals and main dishes: 20 mg or less per 100 g	At least 25% less cholesterol per reference amount than an appropriate reference food (or for meals and main dishes, at least 25% less cholesterol per 100 g) Reference food may not be "Low Cholesterol"	CHOLESTEROL CLAIMS ONLY ALLOWED WHEN FOOD CONTAINS 2 g OR LESS SATURATED FAT PER REFERENCE AMOUNT, OR FOR MEALS AND MAIN DISHES PRODUCTS, PER LABELED SERVING SIZE FOR "FREE" CLAIMS OR PER 100 g FOR "LOW" AND "REDUCED/ LESS" CLAIMS Must declare the amount of total fat next to cholesterol claim when fat exceeds 13 g per reference amount or labeled serving (or per 50 g of food if reference amount is small), or when the fat exceeds 19.5 g per labeled serving for main dishes or 26 g for meal products For dietary supplements: cholesterol claims cannot be made for products that are 40 calories or less per serving

NUTRIENTS*	FREE	LOW	REDUCED/LESS	COMMENTS[1]
Sodium § 101.61	Less than 5 mg per reference amount and per labeled serving (or for meals and main dishes, less than 5 mg per labeled serving) No ingredient that is sodium chloride or generally understood to contain sodium except as in note 2 "Salt Free" must meet criterion for "Sodium Free"	140 mg or less per reference amount (and per 50 g if reference amount is small) Meals and main dishes: 140 mg or less per 100 g "Very Low Sodium": 35 mg or less per reference amount (and per 50 g if reference amount is small). For meals and main dishes: 35 mg or less per 100 g	At least 25% less sodium per reference amount than an appropriate reference food Reference food may not be "Low Sodium"	"Light" (for sodium reduced products): If food is "Low Calorie" and "Low Fat" and sodium is reduced by at least 50% "Light in Sodium" If sodium is reduced by at least 50% per reference amount. For meals and main dishes, "Light in Sodium" meets definition for "Low in Sodium" "No Salt Added" and "Unsalted" must meet conditions of use and must declare "This is Not A Sodium Free Food" on information panel if food is not "Sodium Free" "Lightly Salted": 50% less sodium than normally added to reference food and if not "Low Sodium" so labeled on information panel
Sugars § 101.60(c)	"Sugar Free": Less than 0.5 g sugars per reference amount and per labeled serving (or for meals and main	Not defined. No basis for a recommended intake	At least 25% less sugars per reference amount than an appropriate reference food (or for meals and	"No Added Sugars" and "Without Added Sugars" are allowed if no sugar or sugar containing

NUTRIENTS*	FREE	LOW	REDUCED/LESS	COMMENTS[1]
	dishes, less than 0.5 g per labeled serving) No ingredient that is a sugar or generally understood to contain sugars except as in note 2 Disclose calorie profile (e.g., "Low Calorie")		main dishes, at least 25% less sugar per 100 g) May not use this claim on dietary supplements of vitamins and minerals	ingredient is added during processing. State if food is not "Low"or "Reduced Calorie" The terms "Unsweetened" and "No Added Sweeteners" remain as factual statements Claims about reducing dental care are implied health claims "Sugars" do not include sugar alcohols

NOTES:

[1]Restaurant Foods that bear claims are exempt from certain accompanying information that must be provided by foods from other sources. See specific provisions for more information.

[2]Except if the ingredient listed in the ingredient statement has an asterisk that refers to the footnote (e.g., "adds a trivial amount of fat").

*"Small Reference Amount" = reference amount of 30 g or less or 2 tablespoons or less (for dehydrated foods that are typically consumed when rehydrated with water or a diluent containing an insignificant amount, as defined in § 101.9(f)(1) of all nutrients per reference amount, the per 50 g criterion refers to the prepared form of the food).

Statement "See _____ panel for nutrition information" must accompany all content claims when levels exceed: 13 g Fat, 4 g Saturated Fat, 60 mg Cholesterol, or 480 mg Sodium per reference amount, per labeled serving or, for foods with small reference amounts, per 50 g, disclosure statement is required as part of claim (e.g., "See side panel for information on fat and other nutrients").

Other Nutrient Content Claims

"Lean"	On seafood or game meat that contains < 10 g total fat, 4.5 g or less saturated fat and < 95 mg cholesterol per reference amount and per 100 g (for meals & main dishes, meets criteria per 100 g and per label serving). On mixed dishes not measurable with a cup (as defined in 21 C.F.R. 101.12(b) in table 2) that contain less than 8 g total fat, 3.5 g or less saturated fat and less than 80 mg cholesterol per reference amount.
"Extra Lean"	On seafood or game meat that contains < 5 g total fat, 2 g or less saturated fat and < 95 mg cholesterol per reference amount and per 100 g (for meals and main dishes, meets criteria per 100 g and per label serving)
"Good Source," "Contains," or "Provides"	Contains 10% or more of Daily Value (DV) to describe protein, vitamins, minerals, dietary fiber or potassium per reference amount May be used on meals or main dishes to indicate that product contains a food that meets definition but may not be used to describe meal or main dish itself May not be used for total carbohydrates
"High," "Rich in," or "Excellent Source of"[4]	Contains 20% or more of Daily Value (DV) to describe protein, vitamins, minerals, dietary fiber, for potassium per reference amount May be used on meals or main dishes to indicate that product contains a food that meets definition but may not be used to describe meal or main dish itself May not be used for total carbohydrates
"More," "fortified," "enriched," "added, "extra," or "plus"	10% or more of the DV per reference amount May only be used for vitamins, minerals, protein, dietary fiber and potassium
"High Potency"	May be used on foods to describe individual vitamins or minerals that are present at 100% or more of the RDI per RACC or on a multi-ingredient food product that contains 100% or more of the RDI for at least 2/3 of the vitamins and minerals with RDIs and that are present in the product at 2% or more of the RDI (e.g., "High potency multivitamin, multimineral dietary supplement tablets").
"Modified"	May be used in statement of identity that bears a relative claim, e.g., "Modified Fat Cheese Cake, Contains 35% Less Fat Than Other Regular Cheese Cake"
Any Fiber Claim	If claim is made and food is not low in total fat, must state level total fat per labeled serving.
Antioxidant Claims	Each nutrient for which a claim is made has recognized antioxidant activity (scientific evidence that after absorption from GI tract, the substance participates in physiological, biochemical or cellular processes that inactivate free radicals or prevent free radical-initiated chemical reactions) An RDI has been established for each antioxidant nutrient present

	Each antioxidant nutrient is present in amounts sufficient to qualify for a claim of "high," "good" or "more" Beta-carotene may be the subject of an antioxidant claim when the level of vitamin A present as beta-carotene in the food is sufficient to qualify for the claim. Claim must identify the particular nutrients for which it is made, and may not use terms such as "complete" or "antioxidant complex"

4 Dietary supplement of vitamins and minerals can not use these claims to describe any nutrient or ingredient (e.g., fiber protein, psyllium, bran) other than vitamins or minerals

Relative Claims

To bear a relative claim about the level of a nutrient, the amount of that nutrient in the food must be compared to an amount of nutrient in an appropriate reference food as specified below.

"Light"/"Lite"	(1) A food representative of the type of food bearing the claim, e.g., average value of top three brands for representative value from valid data base; and (2) A similar food (e.g., potato chips for potato chips)
"Reduced" and "Added" (or "Fortified" and "Enriched")	(1) An established regular product or average representative product and (2) A similar food
"More" and "Less" (or "Fewer")	(1) An established regular product or average representative product and (2) A dissimilar food in the same product category which may be generally substituted for labeled food (e.g., potato chips for pretzels) or a similar food

Accompanying Information for Relative (or Comparative) Claims

- For all relative claims, percent (or fraction) of change and identity of reference food must be declared in immediate proximity to the most prominent claim. Quantitative comparison of the amount of the nutrient in the product per labeled serving with that in the reference food must be declared on the information panel. A relative claim for decreased levels of a nutrient may not be made if the nutrient content of the reference food meets the requirement for a "low" claim for that nutrient (e.g., 3 g fat or less).

Implied Claims

- Claims about a food or ingredient that suggest that the nutrient or ingredient is absent or present in a certain amount or claims about a food that suggest a food may be useful in maintaining healthy dietary practices and which are made with an explicit claim (e.g., "healthy, contains 3 grams of fat") are implied claims and are prohibited unless provided for in a regulation by FDA. In addition, the agency has devised a petition system whereby specific additional claims may be considered.
- Claims that a food contains or is made with an ingredient that is known to contain a particular nutrient may be made if the product is "Low" in or a "Good Source" of the Nutrient associated with the claim (e.g., "good source of oat bran").
- Equivalence claims: "Contains as much [*nutrients*] as a [*food*]" may be made if both reference food and labeled food are a "Good Source" of the nutrient on a per serving basis (e.g., "Contains as much vitamin C as an 8 ounce glass of orange juice").
- The following label statements are generally not considered implied claims unless they are made in a nutrition context: 1) avoidance claims for religious, food intolerance, or other non-nutrition related reasons (e.g., "100% milk free"); 2) statements about non-nutritive substances (e.g., "no artificial colors"); 3) added value statements (e.g., "made with real butter"); 4) statements of identity (e.g., "corn oil" or "corn oil margarine"); and 5) special dietary statements made in compliance with a specific Part 105 provision.

The term "healthy" and related terms ("health," "healthful," "healthfully," "healthfulness," "healthier," "healthiest," "healthily" and "healthiness") may be used if the food meets the requirements in 21 C.F.R. § 101.65(d)(2).

Claims on Food for Infants and Children Less Than 2 Years of Age

Nutrient content claims are not permitted on foods intended specifically for infants and children less than 2 years of age except:
1) Claims describing the percentage of vitamins and minerals in a food in relation to a Daily Value.
2) Claims on infant formulas provided for in Part 107.
3) The terms "Unsweetened" and "Unsalted" as taste claims.
4) "Sugar Free" and "No Added Sugar" claims on dietary supplements only.

Terms Covered That Are Not Nutrient Content Claims

"Fresh"	A raw food that has not been frozen, heat processed, or otherwise preserved
"Fresh Frozen"	Food that was quickly frozen while still fresh

Chapter 11

The Regulation of Dietary Supplements

Daniel R. Dwyer and Anthony L. Young, Kleinfeld, Kaplan and Becker, LLP, Washington, D.C.

Key Points

- With the enactment of the Dietary Supplement Health and Education Act (DSHEA) in 1994, dietary supplements were given their own set of safety standards and labeling laws. Previously, they were regulated as either foods or drugs.
- The definition of "dietary supplement" is very broad. Any "dietary ingredient" intended to supplement the diet could, in theory, be a dietary supplement, so long as it meets the other criteria in the definition.
- Regardless of the form of a dietary supplement, it may not be represented as a conventional food or for use as the sole item of a meal or of the diet.
- The first use of an ingredient determines its eligibility for use as a dietary supplement. If a product is first marketed as a dietary supplement and is later approved as a drug or biologic, it can continue to be marketed as a dietary supplement. If the ingredient is first marketed, however, as a drug or biologic, it is not normally eligible to be regulated as a dietary supplement.
- As a practical matter, safety substantiation for dietary supplements should be similar to that for foods. Careful written documentation by one or more qualified experts supporting the safety of the ingredient for its recommended use will help a manufacturer not only meet its regulatory obligations under the FDCA, but also minimize the risk of products liability in the event that something goes wrong.
- "New dietary ingredients" are those that have not been marketed in the United States before October 15, 1994. If a new dietary ingredient has not been present in the food supply as an article used for food in a form in which the food has not been chemically altered, then the marketer must submit a notification to FDA at least seventy-five days before marketing the product with information demonstrating that the product will reasonably be expected to be safe.
- Comprehensive GMP regulations for dietary supplements become effective in 2008, 2009, or 2010, depending on company size. They establish process controls to assure dietary supplement quality.
- A dietary supplement label must include: a) a statement of identity; b) an ingredient statement; c) nutrition information in the form of a Supplement Facts box; d) the name and place of business of the manufacturer, packer, or distributor; and e) an accurate statement of the quantity of contents.

Key Points (Continued)

- **Within thirty days of making a structure-function claim, the marketer must notify FDA that it has included such claim on the label or labeling of its dietary supplement.**
- **The Federal Trade Commission (FTC) regulates dietary supplement advertising. The FTC has published a guide to assist in understanding its rules, entitled "Dietary Supplements: An Advertising Guide for Industry."**

INTRODUCTION

For many years, Food and Drug Administration (FDA)-related laws provided only two regulatory options for dietary supplements: they could be regulated as either "foods" or "drugs." Under most circumstances, vitamin and mineral supplements were regulated as foods. As a result, FDA took the position that ingredients in dietary supplements had to meet the same safety standards as ingredients added to foods—that is, they had to be "generally recognized as safe" (GRAS) or covered by a food additive regulation.

FDA also normally took the position that labeling claims for dietary supplements were governed by the same standards as those for foods. As a result, many health-related claims—even claims that, by today's standards, would be considered relatively benign claims about a dietary supplement's effect on the healthy structure or function of the body—could cause a supplement to be regulated as a drug. From shortly after the enactment of the Federal Food, Drug, and Cosmetic Act (FDCA), FDA brought actions against marketers of "dietary supplements" that made very frank drug claims as well as those making claims that would now be considered to be structure-function claims. These reported cases helped shape the rich history of our food and drug law.

In 1994, however, much of this rich history was reversed with the enactment of the Dietary Supplement Health and Education Act (DSHEA), an amendment to the FDCA. DSHEA adopted, for the first time, a legal definition for "dietary supplement" and included provisions specifically applicable to dietary supplements (related primarily to the safety, labeling, and ingredients to be used in such products). As a result, dietary supplements now possess a unique niche in the framework of food law. Dietary supplements are still "foods" under the law, and many of the laws and regulations applicable to foods continue to apply. Dietary ingredients in dietary supplements, however, no longer need to be GRAS or covered by a food additive regulation to be legally marketed. In addition, there are some unique health-related claims that are permitted only for dietary supplements and not for conventional foods.

What Is a "Dietary Supplement"?

Statutory Definition

DSHEA codified a new definition for dietary supplements. A product is a "dietary supplement" only if it conforms to section 201(ff) of the FDCA, which establishes various criteria governing 1) ingredients, 2) formulation, 3) intended use, and 4) relationship to drugs and biologics. These criteria are as follows:

Ingredients. A dietary supplement must contain one or more of the following: 1) a vitamin, 2) a mineral, 3) an herb or other botanical, 4) an amino acid, 5) a dietary substance for use by man to supplement the diet by increasing the total dietary intake, or 6) a concentrate, metabolite, constituent, extract, or combination of any of the ingredients listed above. In addition, a dietary supplement may not be a tobacco product.

A product is a "dietary supplement" only if it meets various criteria governing
- *ingredients*
- *formulation*
- *intended use*
- *relationship to drugs and biologics*

If this list of eligible ingredients seems almost all-encompassing, it is because of the phrase in the fifth part of the definition. The phrase "dietary substance for use by man to supplement the diet by increasing the total dietary intake" might lead one to conclude that any new substance added to the diet would be defined by this phrase because it will increase the dietary intake of that substance to above zero. FDA, however, has interpreted "dietary substance" to mean a substance that is or has been in the diet and used for food, and not a substance that is for the first time intended for use to supplement the diet. The rationale for this position is straightforward; "dietary" means of, or pertaining to, the diet and one cannot increase the total dietary intake of a substance that is not presently in the diet.

Formulation. Dietary supplement ingredients may be formulated either into products that are *intended for ingestion* in capsule, tablet, liquid, powder, softgel, or gelcap form, or into products that are in conventional food form (such as beverages or nutrition bars). Regardless of how they are formulated, however, a dietary supplement may not be *represented as* a conventional food or for use as a sole item of a meal or of the diet.

If a product looks, smells, and tastes like a conventional food, can it be marketed as a dietary supplement? The answer would appear to be "yes," but only so long as the product is not "represented as" a conventional food. And there's the rub: at this time, from FDA's perspective, it does not take much to "represent" a product as a conventional food. For example, describing a product as a "shake in chocolate and vanilla flavors" or as a "good tasting and satisfying treat," may be enough to "represent" it as a conventional food and exclude it from dietary supplement status. It might even be possible to "represent" a product as a conventional food by marketing it in retail stores next to conventional foods, but FDA has never formally taken this position. As a general rule, if a product can be consumed primarily for its taste or aroma, or if it can be substituted for a conventional food in the diet, then there is a risk that FDA could regulate it as a conventional food and not a dietary supplement. While there have been no court decisions on this issue, FDA has publicly objected to the characterization of soup, yogurt snack products, and candy bar-like products as dietary supplements. In addition, it should be noted that—as the statutory language provides—FDA takes the position that products represented as "meal replacements" are ineligible for dietary supplement status.

What does "intended for ingestion" mean? A court opinion states "The ordinary and plain meaning of the term 'ingestion' means to take into the stomach and gastrointestinal tract by means of enteral administration." *United States v. Ten Cartons Ener-B Nasal Gel*, 888 F. Supp. 381, 393-94 (E.D.N.Y.), *aff'd*, 72 F.3d 285 (2d Cir. 1995). As a result, FDA has taken the position that nasal products, topical skin products, sublingual tablets, sprayed products that are absorbed from the mouth, aromatherapy products, gargles, and throat lozenges are ineligible for dietary supplement status because they are not "intended for ingestion."

A dietary supplement may not be intended for use as a conventional food.

Intended Use. A dietary supplement must be labeled as a dietary supplement and be intended to supplement the diet. As discussed above, it may not be intended for use as a conventional food. Also, it may not be intended for use as a drug; that is, it may not be intended for use in the diagnosis, cure, mitigation, treatment, or prevention of disease. (A dietary supplement, however, is not a "drug" if it is labeled with an authorized health claim, even though that claim may refer to a disease. Health claims are described later in this chapter.)

Relationship to Drugs and Biologics. A dietary supplement may, under some circumstances, include substances that are approved or investigational drugs—if the substances were used first as foods or dietary supplements.

Approved Drugs. Under the statute, a product is eligible for regulation as a dietary supplement if it is or includes an article that was approved as a new drug or licensed as a biologic, so long as the article was marketed as a dietary supplement or as a food *prior* to the date it was approved as a drug or biologic (unless FDA has issued a regulation stating otherwise). If the article was not marketed as a dietary supplement or food prior to the approval date, then it is ineligible for dietary supplement status (unless, again, FDA has issued a regulation stating otherwise).

Investigational Drugs. If an article is authorized for use in substantial clinical investigations that have been instituted and the existence of which have been made public, and if the article was not marketed as a dietary supplement or food prior to the date when it was authorized for investigational use, then it is ineligible for dietary supplement status (unless FDA has issued a regulation stating otherwise).

The Definition of "Article." The rules summarized in the two paragraphs above refer to "articles"; that is, if an "article" was marketed as a dietary supplement before being approved as a new drug, it is then eligible for dietary supplement status. But what exactly is an "article"? A court decision suggests that it is any substance that is intended to be in a dietary supplement. For example, if the dietary supplement is formulated to contain an ingredient that has been approved as a new drug, and if it is sold or promoted based on the presence of that ingredient, then that ingredient may be considered the relevant "article" for purposes of determining whether the product is eligible for dietary supplement status. This may be true even if the ingredient is a relatively minor constituent in the overall dietary supplement product.

An article marketed as a dietary supplement before being approved as a new drug is eligible for dietary supplement status.

The court decision dealt with a product containing red yeast rice, called "Cholestin," which was marketed as a dietary supplement for cholesterol reduction. FDA argued that the red yeast rice was manufactured purposely to contain high levels of lovastatin, an approved cholesterol-lowering drug that was not marketed as a food or dietary supplement prior to approval. FDA also argued that Cholestin was promoted for its lovastatin content. Therefore, FDA considered lovastatin to be the relevant "article" for purposes of determining whether Cholestin was eligible for dietary supplement status. The manufacturer argued that Cholestin simply contained red yeast rice, a traditional Asian product that happens to include some lovastatin as a minor constituent. It considered red yeast rice to be the relevant "article." The court found for FDA, concluding that, in this case, the relevant "article" was lovastatin.

The manufacturer in that case also argued that, even if lovastatin were the relevant "article," it was eligible for dietary supplement status because it had been marketed as a constituent of many traditional foods prior to its having been approved as a drug. The court rejected this argument, however, agreeing with FDA that, for lovastatin to have been marketed in foods prior to approval as a drug, the marketed foods must have been promoted for their lovastatin content, or the lovastatin must have been increased or optimized as a constituent. As a result, Cholestin was determined to be a drug, not a dietary supplement, because it contained lovastatin, an article that was not marketed as a dietary supplement or food before it was approved as a drug. *Pharmanex Inc. v. Shalala*, 35 F. Supp. 2d 1341 (D. Utah 1999), *rev'd and remanded,* 221 F.3d 1151 (10th Cir. 2000).

Dietary Supplement Safety

Under the law, all dietary supplements must be safe (i.e., not "adulterated").

- A dietary supplement is considered adulterated if either it, or any dietary ingredient contained in it, presents a "significant or unreasonable risk of illness or injury" under conditions of use recommended or suggested in labeling (or if no conditions of use are suggested or recommended in the labeling, under "ordinary" conditions of use).
- A dietary supplement also is considered adulterated if either it, or any dietary ingredient contained in it, bears or contains any poisonous or deleterious substance that may render it injurious to health.

There is a parallel between dietary supplements and GRAS food substances: the law leaves the initial determination of safety up to the manufacturer and FDA has no authority to review the safety of a product prior to marketing. Unlike GRAS food substances, however, there is no requirement that dietary supplements be "generally recognized" in the scientific community "as safe," or that safety be based on data and information that is published or otherwise generally available to the scientific community.

The exact scope of data needed to support safety has not been as clearly elucidated for dietary supplements as it has been for foods.

A comparison of the safety standards for dietary supplements and GRAS food substances is interesting. Whereas dietary supplements may not present a "significant or unreasonable risk of illness or injury," FDA has concluded that GRAS status must be based on "reasonable certainty that the substance is not harmful under the intended conditions of use." (62 Fed. Reg. 18,937 (Apr. 17, 1997).) It is possible that, to have some confidence that one's dietary supplement does not present a "significant or unreasonable risk of illness or injury," one would have to have a "reasonable certainty that the substance is not harmful"—but that is entering into the realm of speculation. Suffice it to say that the exact scope of the data needed to support safety has not been as clearly elucidated for dietary supplements as it has been for foods.

Accordingly, a manufacturer would be well advised to substantiate the safety of dietary supplements in a manner that would be recognized as adequate by the scientific community. As a practical matter, such substantiation would be not unlike that used for foods. For well-known dietary ingredients, it might be appropriate to rely on a conclusion based on a general recognition of safety supported by a long period of common use at the levels intended for the target population, or supported by adequate studies reported in the scientific literature. Where there is any question, however, about the safety of a particular ingredient or product, or about the interpretation of the scientific literature, it would be prudent to obtain the supporting opinion of qualified experts. Regardless of how a safety conclusion is reached, the company should document its conclusion in sufficient detail to substantiate that it has addressed the relevant safety issues. Careful documentation of the safety of a dietary supplement will help a manufacturer not only to meet its regulatory obligations under the FDCA but also to minimize products liability in the event that something goes wrong.

It is particularly important that a dietary supplement manufacturer prepare labeling with clear conditions for use and warnings consistent with the safety profile of its dietary supplement. Under the statute, if labeling does not limit the conditions for use, then a dietary supplement may be considered adulterated if it presents a significant or unreasonable risk of illness or injury under all "ordinary" conditions of use—which can be a very broad category of uses. In most cases, then, it is prudent to limit the conditions of use recommended or suggested in labeling through the use of clear directions and warnings. For example, in March 2002, FDA issued a Consumer Advisory with respect to dietary supplements containing the botanical ingredient kava.[1] Following this advisory, many manufacturers and distributors of such products included cautionary information from the advisory on product labels.

FDA bears the burden of proof on each element to show that a dietary supplement is adulterated.

DSHEA offers dietary supplement manufacturers two protections in the event of a legal action by FDA against the safety of a product. First, it specifies that FDA shall bear the burden of proof on each element to show that a dietary supplement is adulterated. Second, the manufacturer has the opportunity to present its views to FDA (i.e., to try to persuade FDA not to refer the case to a U.S. Attorney). The burden of proof on FDA to show that a dietary supplement is not safe was firmly established in 2006 when the Tenth Circuit Court of Appeals held that "Congress expressly placed the burden of proof on the government to determine whether a dietary supplement is adulterated" and further stated that: "The burden remains on the agency to show that the risks associated with a dietary supplement outweigh benefits and are, therefore, unreasonable." (*Nutraceutical Corporation v. von Eschenbach* (459 F.3d 1033).)

In reaching its decision, the court relied upon the standard of review for such FDA decisions that has evolved over the past twenty years: "The review of scientific literature is properly the province of the FDA, to which this Court grants deference based on its expertise" (459 F.3d at 1043). Using this standard, and its own review of the record, the court found that FDA had made its case by the "preponderance of the evidence" standard set out in DSHEA.

As a practical matter, the burden of proof provision of DSHEA, as applied by the court in *Nutraceutical Corporation*, means that FDA may, through rulemaking, deem a dietary supplement (or dietary ingredient) to be adulterated. In so doing, FDA has the burden to show by a preponderance of the evidence that the risks are either significant or outweigh the benefits and are, therefore, unreasonable. In such a rulemaking, FDA's review of scientific information would normally be given deference because of the agency's expertise.

New Dietary Ingredients

If a dietary supplement contains a "new dietary ingredient," then: 1) it is subject to an additional safety requirement, and 2) information on the ingredient may need to be reported to FDA prior to marketing the product.

Manufacturers are responsible for determining whether their ingredients meet the "new dietary ingredient" definition.

- ***What is a "new dietary ingredient"?*** It is any dietary ingredient that was not marketed in the United States in a dietary supplement before October 15, 1994. Manufacturers are responsible for determining whether their ingredients meet this definition of "new."
- ***What additional safety requirements apply?*** There is an additional standard for a "new dietary ingredient": If a dietary supplement is, or contains, a "new dietary ingredient" for which there is inadequate information to provide reasonable assurance that such ingredient does not present a significant or unreasonable risk of illness or injury, then the product is considered adulterated. Therefore, manufacturers must ensure that their "new" ingredients are adequately substantiated as being safe. (Of course, as discussed above, *all* dietary ingredients should be substantiated as being safe.)
- ***When does information need to be reported to FDA?*** If a dietary supplement contains a new dietary ingredient, but the ingredient has been present in the food supply as an article used for food in a form in which the food has not been chemically altered, then it need not be reported to FDA. A report, however, must be submitted if this is not the case; that is, if the ingredient has not been present in the food supply, or if its form has been chemically altered for use in a dietary supplement as compared with its form in the food supply (known as a "reportable new dietary ingredient" or "reportable NDI").
- For a reportable NDI, two requirements must be met. First, there must be a history of use or other evidence establishing that the dietary ingredient, when used under the conditions recommended or suggested in the labeling of the dietary supplement, will reasonably be expected to be safe. Second, at least seventy-five days before being introduced or delivered for introduction into interstate commerce, the manufacturer or distributor of the dietary ingredient or dietary supplement must submit information to FDA, including any citation to and copies of published articles or unpublished reports of

safety studies, that is the basis on which the manufacturer or distributor has concluded that a dietary supplement containing such dietary ingredient will reasonably be expected to be safe. (Note that FDA will keep the seventy-five-day notification confidential for ninety days after its receipt; after that time it becomes public, except for trade secrets or confidential commercial information.)

If these two conditions for a reportable NDI are not met, then the dietary supplement is deemed adulterated, and may be subject to FDA enforcement action if and when it is marketed.

FDA has established a docket in which NDI notifications are filed.[2] From this docket, it is possible to determine how FDA has addressed each NDI notification that it has received.

A petition process also is available for reportable NDIs: the FDCA permits a petition to be filed proposing the issuance of an order prescribing the conditions under which an NDI reasonably will be expected to be safe. FDA must make a decision on such a petition within 180 days of its filing.

Facilities that manufacture, process, pack, or hold food, including dietary supplements, for consumption in the United States must be registered with FDA.

Facility Registration

Under the Public Health Security and Bioterrorism Preparedness and Response Act of 2002, owners, operators, or agents in charge of domestic or foreign facilities that manufacture, process, pack, or hold food, including dietary supplements, for consumption in the United States are required to register the facility with FDA. Retail establishments are exempt from registration.

Foreign facilities that manufacture, process, pack, or hold food also are required to register unless food from that facility undergoes further processing (including packaging) by another foreign facility before the food is exported to the United States. If the subsequent foreign facility performs only a minimal activity, however, such as putting on a label, both facilities are required to register.

All facilities are also subject to the recordkeeping requirements of the Bioterrorism Act.

cGMPs

A dietary supplement is adulterated if it has been prepared, packed, or held under conditions that do not meet current Good Manufacturing Practice (cGMP) regulations, including regulations requiring, when necessary, expiration date labeling. FDA promulgated cGMP regulations for dietary supplements on June 25, 2007 (72 Fed. Reg. 34,751; 21 C.F.R. Part 111). FDA established three compliance dates for the regulations—June 25, 2008, for businesses employing 500 or more employees; June 25, 2009, for businesses employing fewer than 500 (but twenty or more full-time equivalent employees); and June 25, 2010, for businesses that employ fewer than twenty full-time equivalent employees.

The focus of the regulations is the requirement for each manufacturer to implement a system of production and process controls that covers all stages of manufacturing, packaging, labeling, and holding of the dietary supplement to *ensure the quality* of dietary supplements and that dietary supplements are packaged and labeled as specified in the master manufacturing record required for each product.

FDA does not require expiration dating for dietary supplements but it is, for the most part, a market necessity.

FDA did not propose to require expiration dating for dietary supplements because, while "there are current and generally available methods to determine the expiration date of some dietary ingredients, for example vitamin C, we are uncertain whether there are current and generally available methods to determine the expiration dating of other dietary ingredients, especially botanical dietary ingredients." (68 Fed. Reg. 12,157, 12,203-4 (Mar. 13, 2003).) In the final cGMP rule, FDA confirmed this decision. Nonetheless, as a practical matter, expiration dating, or shelf-life dating as it is sometimes called, is for the most part a market necessity. And FDA has made clear that "any expiration date that you place on a product label (including a 'best if used by' date) should be supported by data." (72 Fed. Reg. 34,855-6.)

Third-Party Substantiation of Identity, Purity, and Safety

Prior to the promulgation of cGMPs for dietary supplements, a number of organizations made efforts to establish voluntary criteria for the identity, purity, and safety of dietary supplements. Industry trade associations established voluntary cGMP systems whereby manufacturers could submit to inspections in order to assure customers of the integrity of their facilities and processes. These voluntary programs form the basis for educating the dietary supplement industry with respect to compliance with the FDA cGMP. The U.S. Pharmacopoeia now publishes monographs for dietary supplement ingredients. In addition the National Institutes of Health (NIH), through the Office of Dietary Supplements, provides information on dietary supplements and the safety of ingredients.[3]

Products That Combine an OTC Drug with a Dietary Supplement

A number of companies have considered marketing a combination over-the-counter (OTC) drug and dietary supplement product. For example, a combination of low-dose aspirin and vitamin E, or an OTC cough suppressant and vitamin C, have been considered. In theory, such combination products should be "legal," provided: a) the "drug side" of the product falls under an OTC monograph and is labeled properly; b) the "dietary supplement side" of the product does not make drug claims; and c) and the dietary supplement ingredients can be deemed safe and suitable inactive ingredients that do not cause the product to become a "new drug," requiring submission of a new drug application.

FDA advises against the marketing of combination over-the-counter drug and dietary supplement products.

FDA, however, has strongly advised against the marketing of such products in a series of letters to companies, noting "serious concerns about the marketing of any such combination product," and stating that it would take "appropriate measures" against such products. From FDA's perspective, these combination products raise several public health issues. For example:

- **Safety and Efficacy:** The addition of a new ingredient to a legally marketed drug product could affect/interact with the safety and efficacy of the drug component.
- **Potentially Misleading:** Consumers may potentially believe that both components have been subjected to the more stringent drug regulatory requirements, when, in fact, only the drug component may have been reviewed by the agency for safety and effectiveness.
- **Consumer Confusion:** It is uncertain under what circumstances the disclaimer required by DSHEA for certain dietary supplement claims (as discussed further below) could appear on a combination product without causing consumer confusion.

These policies remain in effect as FDA firmly seeks to maintain the boundaries between drugs and dietary supplements.

Postmarketing Surveillance and the Dietary Supplement and Nonprescription Drug Consumer Protection Act

In 1993, FDA initiated adverse event monitoring for special nutritional products, including dietary supplements. This database consisted of reports from FDA's MedWatch program; FDA's field offices; other federal, state, and local public health agencies; and letters and phone calls from consumers and health professionals. In 2002, FDA announced that this system was limited and that the information in it was provided in a manner that made it difficult for users to appropriately interpret adverse events. Accordingly, FDA removed this information from its website and the Center for Food Safety and Applied Nutrition (CFSAN) then developed a new system for tracking and analyzing adverse event reports involving foods, cosmetics, and dietary supplements.

As the dietary supplement industry matured, it came to understand that a mandatory system for adverse event reporting would benefit all its various "stakeholders"—industry, consumers, healthcare professionals, and regulators. On December 22, 2006, the Dietary Supplement and Nonprescription Drug Consumer Protection Act was signed into law. This law requires adverse event reporting and recordkeeping for dietary supplements and nonprescription drugs marketed without an approved new drug application and requires dietary supplement manufacturers, packers, or distributors to report serious adverse events that may be associated with the use of their dietary supplements to FDA.

Manufacturers, packers, or distributors of dietary supplements are required to report serious adverse events that may be associated with use of their products to FDA.

The basic requirement of the law is that serious adverse events (those events that report death, a life-threatening experience, inpatient hospitalization, a persistent or significant disability or incapacity, or a congenital anomaly or birth defect; or require, based on reasonable medical judgment, a medical or surgical intervention to prevent a serious outcome) must be reported to FDA within fifteen business days of receipt. These reports and records associated with these reports must be kept, along with all other reports of adverse events (i.e., nonserious adverse events), for six years, and made available to FDA inspectors upon request. As with all reports of adverse events to FDA, submission of the report is not regarded as an admission that the dietary supplement involved caused or contributed to the adverse event being reported.

To facilitate reporting of adverse events, the law also requires that manufacturers and distributors include a domestic telephone number or domestic address on the label of their products through which they may receive a report of an adverse event.

Dietary Supplement Labeling

Required Components of the Dietary Supplement Label

The basic required labeling components for conventional foods that are described in FDA regulations at 21 C.F.R. § 101, Subpart A are also applicable to dietary supplements. A dietary supplement label must include:

- a statement of identity (e.g., "dietary supplement" or "_______ supplement" (with the name of the dietary ingredient in the blank));
- an ingredient statement;
- nutrition information;
- the name and place of business of the manufacturer, packer, or distributor; and
- an accurate statement of the quantity of contents, in terms of weight, measure, or numerical count.

The basic required labeling components for conventional foods are also applicable to dietary supplements.

If any of the above information does not appear in the correct format on a dietary supplement label, then the product will be considered misbranded and subject to FDA enforcement action (unless an exemption applies). Additionally, as with conventional food claims, any claims on dietary supplement labels or labeling must be truthful and not misleading in any aspect. False or misleading claims on dietary supplement labels will render the product misbranded.

In April 2005, FDA published a dietary supplement labeling guide which provides plain language information regarding the labeling of dietary supplements.[4]

Nutrition Labeling

Following enactment of the Nutrition Labeling and Education Act (NLEA) some confusion existed as to the type of nutrition information to be included on dietary supplement labels. The NLEA Nutrition Facts box (required for foods) was not easily translated to dietary supplements. DSHEA subsequently clarified this point, requiring that dietary supplements bear nutrition labeling "in a manner appropriate" for these products.

To this end, FDA promulgated regulations set forth in 21 C.F.R. § 101.36 that specify the detailed nutritional labeling requirements for dietary supplements. The regulations require a Supplement Facts box that is similar in format and appearance to the Nutrition Facts box required for conventional foods. The Supplement Facts box and its contents must appear on the label in the precise format and type size set forth in the regulations. The box must state "Supplement Facts" across the top and must include information such as the serving size, servings per container (unless it appears as part of the net contents declaration), a listing of any dietary ingredients that have a reference daily intake (RDI) or a daily reference value (DRV) and their subcomponents (e.g., total calories, calories from fat, total fat, saturated fat, cholesterol, sodium, total carbohydrate, dietary fiber, sugars, protein, vitamin A, vitamin C, calcium, and iron), and the amount per serving and percent daily value (if applicable) of such ingredients. These ingredients are referred to in the regulations as "(b)(2)-dietary ingredients" (based on the section of the regulations in which they are defined, section 101.36(b)(2)). Certain other listed nutrients *may* be declared with these ingredients, but they *must* be declared if a claim is made about them.

The regulations also discuss dietary ingredients for which RDIs and DRVs have not been established. In contrast to the (b)(2)-dietary ingredients, these ingredients are referred to as "other dietary ingredients," and if present in the dietary supplement, must be declared with their amounts in a separate section of the Supplement Facts box, just below the (b)(2)-dietary ingredients.

The Supplement Facts box required for dietary supplements is similar in format and appearance to the Nutrition Facts box required for conventional foods.

Proprietary blends and sources of dietary ingredients also must be declared consistent with the regulations. The regulations also specify how to declare ingredients for multivitamin and botanical products.

The following is an example of a Supplement Facts box for a dietary supplement containing dietary ingredients with and without RDIs and DRVs. Other examples are provided in the regulations at 21 C.F.R. § 101.36.

Supplement Facts

Serving Size 1 Tablet

	Amount Per Serving	% Daily Value
Vitamin A (as retinyl acetate and 50% as beta-carotene)	5000 IU	100%
Vitamin C (as ascorbic acid)	60 mg	100%
Vitamin D (as cholecalciferol)	400 IU	100%
Vitamin E (as dl-alpha tocopheryl acetate)	30 IU	100%
Thiamin (as thiamin mononitrate)	1.5 mg	100%
Riboflavin	1.7 mg	100%
Niacin (as niacinamide)	20 mg	100%
Vitamin B_6 (as pyridoxine hydrochloride)	2.0 mg	100%
Folate (as folic acid)	400 mcg	100%
Vitamin B_{12} (as cyanocobalamin)	6 mcg	100%
Biotin	30 mcg	10%
Pantothenic Acid (as calcium pantothenate)	10 mg	100%

Other ingredients: Gelatin, lactose, magnesium stearate, microcrystalline cellulose, FD&C Yellow No. 6, propylene glycol, propylparaben, and sodium benzoate.

Ingredient Labeling

The declaration of ingredients on a dietary supplement label is required. Under some circumstances, ingredients may be declared in the Supplement Facts box as source ingredients (e.g., in the declaration "calcium (as calcium carbonate)" the source ingredient is calcium carbonate). Ingredients that are not declared in the Supplement Facts box should appear immediately below the Supplement Facts box or, if there is insufficient space, immediately contiguous and to the right of the box. The detailed requirements for the declaration of ingredients on dietary supplement products can be found at 21 C.F.R. §§ 101.4(g), (h), and 101.36(d).

Optional Labeling Claims for Dietary Supplements

There are three categories of optional claims that can be made on dietary supplement labels and labeling: 1) structure-function claims, 2) health claims, and 3) nutrient content claims.

Three categories of optional claims can be made on dietary supplement labels and labeling:
- *structure-function claims*
- *health claims*
- *nutrient content claims*

♦ **Structure-Function Claims**

DSHEA added section 403(r)(6) to the FDCA, which sets forth four types of optional claims for dietary supplements. These claims are commonly referred to as "structure-function claims" and may be made on a dietary supplement if they:

- ♦ claim a benefit related to a classical nutrient deficiency disease (e.g., scurvy) and disclose the prevalence of such disease in the United States; or
- ♦ describe the role of a nutrient or dietary ingredient intended to affect the structure or function in humans (e.g., "calcium builds strong bones"); or
- ♦ characterize the documented mechanism by which a nutrient or dietary ingredient acts to maintain such structure or function (e.g., "antioxidants maintain cell integrity"); or
- ♦ describe general well-being from consumption of a nutrient or dietary ingredient.

These claims are permitted on dietary supplement labels and labeling so long as certain conditions are met:

- ♦ ***Substantiation.*** The manufacturer making the claim must have substantiation that the claim is truthful and not misleading. This means that prior to making a claim, the manufacturer must have substantiation that provides a reasonable basis for the express or implied claim being conveyed. FDA has published a guidance document entitled "Substantiation for Dietary Supplement Claims Made Under Section 403(r)(6) of the Federal Food, Drug, and Cosmetic Act" which provides guidelines for proper claim substantiation.[5]

- ***Notification.*** Within thirty days of making a structure-function claim, the manufacturer, packer, or distributor must notify FDA's Office of Nutritional Products, Labeling and Dietary Supplements that it has included such a statement on the label or labeling of its product. Details on the information to be included in this notification are set forth in FDA regulations at 21 C.F.R. § 101.93. If FDA objects to the claim, it will send a "Courtesy Letter" to the notifier, normally within thirty days, explaining why the claim is considered by FDA to be unlawful. This Courtesy Letter provides guidance so that the manufacturer or retailer will have fair warning of FDA's position with regard to the claim. If the notifier fails to remove the claim from its labeling following a Courtesy Letter, it may be considered by FDA to be operating in violation of the law; there is a risk that FDA will initiate official enforcement action against the notifier and/or the product in the future.
- ***Disclaimer.*** The following disclaimer in boldface type must accompany a structure-function claim: **"This statement has not been evaluated by the Food and Drug Administration. This product is not intended to diagnose, treat, cure, or prevent any disease."** FDA regulations at 21 C.F.R. § 101.93 require that the disclaimer either appear immediately adjacent to the statement or appear elsewhere on the same page as the statement and linked to it by a symbol (e.g., asterisk). If the statement is linked by a symbol, it must be set off in a box.

What is an appropriate structure-function claim?

A structure-function claim cannot state or imply that the dietary supplement treats, cures, mitigates, or prevents disease.

In January 2000, FDA published a final regulation (21 C.F.R. § 101.93(f), (g)) in an attempt to define structure-function claims and to clarify how such claims can be distinguished from unapproved health claims or "disease" claims. Notably, a structure-function claim may not state or imply that the dietary supplement treats, cures, mitigates, or prevents disease. If it does, then the product may be subject to enforcement action as a drug, and/or as a dietary supplement that is labeled with an unauthorized health claim. Prohibited disease claims include those that assert that the product:

- has an effect on a specific disease or class of diseases,
- has an effect on the characteristic signs or symptoms of a disease,
- has an effect on an abnormal condition associated with a natural state, if the condition is uncommon or can cause significant harm,

- has an effect on a disease as described by one or more of the following:
  - the name of the product,
  - a statement about an ingredient in the product that has been regulated by FDA as a drug,
  - citation of a publication on the immediate product label so as to imply disease prevention or treatment,
  - use of the term "disease" except in general statements that do not refer to a specific disease or product, or
  - pictures, symbols or vignettes,
- belongs to a class of products that is intended to diagnose, mitigate, treat, cure, or prevent disease,
- is a substitute for a product that is a therapy for disease,
- augments a therapy or drug action intended to diagnose, mitigate, treat, cure, or prevent disease,
- has a role in the body's response to a disease,
- treats, prevents, or mitigates adverse events associated with a disease therapy, or
- otherwise suggests an effect on a disease or diseases.

Distinguishing between structure-function claims and "disease" claims is one of the most troublesome issues confronting label-writers for dietary supplements. The difficulty in distinguishing such claims is evidenced by a few examples: "helps promote digestion" is a permissible structure-function claim whereas "relieves acid indigestion" is a disease claim, and "helps support cartilage and joint function" is a structure-function claim, whereas "maintains normal bone density in post-menopausal women" is an implied disease claim (implying treatment for osteoporosis). The preamble to FDA's January 2000 final rule (65 Fed. Reg. 1,000 (Jan. 6, 2000)) provides a good discussion of these issues. In addition, FDA has published a guidance document entitled "Structure/Function Claims Small Entity Compliance Guide" that provides simple, straightforward guidance for making these claims.[6]

♦ Health Claims

Health claims either expressly or by implication characterize the relationship of a conventional food or dietary supplement to a disease or health-related condition. Described in more detail in FDA regulations at 21 C.F.R. § 101.14, a health claim generally is not permitted unless FDA has promulgated a regulation setting forth the conditions for use of such claim, including the specific permissible language for the claim. An example of an approved health claim published in FDA regulations is as follows: "25 grams of soy protein a day, as part of a diet low in saturated fat and cholesterol, may reduce the risk of heart disease. 1 capsule provides X grams of soy protein."

A health claim generally is not permitted unless FDA has issued a regulation stating the conditions for use of such claim, including the specific permissible language of the claim.

FDA may issue a health claim regulation on its own or in response to a petition from a manufacturer. When FDA receives a petition requesting approval of a new health claim, the claim may be authorized only if FDA determines that there is significant scientific agreement among experts qualified by scientific training and experience to evaluate such claims (based on the totality of scientific evidence), and that the claim is supported by such evidence.

FDA has grappled with the standard for substantiation of health claims (i.e., what represents "significant scientific agreement"). In July 2007 FDA published a draft guidance entitled "Evidence-Based Review System for the Scientific Evaluation of Health Claims."[7]

FDA has accepted certain "qualified" health claims for use in dietary supplement labeling although these qualified health claims do not appear in FDA regulations and the process for the formal regulatory approval of such claims is still evolving.

"Qualified" health claims may be made for dietary supplements as well as conventional foods.

An example of a qualified claim negotiated by FDA and the industry is as follows: "As part of a well-balanced diet that is low in saturated fat and cholesterol, folic acid, vitamin B6 and vitamin B12 may reduce the risk of vascular disease." A disclaimer immediately adjacent to the claim in the same font size must appear: "FDA evaluated the above claim and found that, while it is known that diets low in saturated fat and cholesterol reduce the risk of heart disease and other vascular diseases, the evidence in support of the above claim is inconclusive." Qualified health claims may also be made for conventional foods.

FDA has also provided a guidance to the industry with respect to submissions in support of qualified health claims entitled FDA's Implementation of "Qualified Health Claims."[8] The number of qualified health claims reviewed by FDA continues to grow.[9]

♦ Nutrient Content Claims

Nutrient content claims are used by manufacturers to highlight specific nutritional attributes of their products through a uniform frame of reference. Examples of such claims are "good source of Vitamin C" or "low in fat." The regulations pertaining to nutrient content claims are set forth beginning at 21 C.F.R. § 101.13 and apply both to conventional foods and to dietary supplements. These regulations specify the types of nutrient content claims that are permissible and their requirements. Generally, to make such claims, the specific language used must be defined in the regulations. If not already defined, a manufacturer may submit a petition to FDA for approval and publication in the regulations.

Specific nutrient content claims also are permitted, provided the manufacturer provides notice to FDA at least 120 days prior to making the claim that an authoritative statement is supported by a scientific body of the U.S. government. FDA must then issue a regulation or seek a court order to prohibit the claim. This method was utilized with respect to nutrient claims for DHA, EPA, and ALA from fish oils. Several years after three petitions were filed with respect to these ingredients, FDA published a proposed regulation in early 2008 that would disallow all but one of the claims.

The primary difference between the regulation of nutrient content claims for conventional foods and dietary supplements is that, for claims about an ingredient that is not defined in the regulations or for which FDA has not established an RDI or DRV, dietary supplements may make nutrient content claims that characterize the percentage level of a dietary ingredient (e.g., "contains 200% of the lycopene in a tomato"). For conventional foods, any such claims cannot be made without approval by FDA through publication in a regulation or acceptance of an authoritative statement of a scientific government body.

Information About Dietary Supplements That Is Not Regulated as "Labeling" (Third-Party Literature)

The definition of labeling for all FDA-regulated products is found in section 201(m) of the FDCA. It includes "all labels and other written, printed, or graphic matter (1) upon any article or any of its containers or wrappers, or (2) accompanying such article." This definition is important because it means that "labeling" encompasses more than just the label, which is the written material appearing on the immediate product container. "Labeling" has been interpreted broadly by the Supreme Court and may include promotional materials, such as brochures, letters, and videos, even if they don't physically accompany the product at the time of the sale. (Websites, according to FDA, may be considered labeling, at least under some circumstances—although the Federal Trade Commission (FTC) also considers them to be advertising.) Therefore, claims found in these promotional vehicles are subject to FDA's jurisdiction.

"Labeling" has been broadly interpreted by the Supreme Court and may include promotional materials.

If a dietary supplement is promoted through its labeling to treat, diagnose, cure, mitigate, or prevent disease, then FDA may consider the product to be a drug that cannot be marketed without prior approval of a new drug application. Prior to DSHEA, it was FDA's position that books and other publications disseminated by a dietary supplement manufacturer were labeling, even if they were written by third parties, if that literature discussed a dietary supplement product. DSHEA, however, exempts this type of literature from being regulated as labeling. This exemption often is referred to as the "third-party literature" exemption. It permits manufacturers, distributors, and retailers to disseminate scientific literature, books, and other publications so long as the criteria set forth in section 403B of the FDCA are met. Such a publication may be used in connection with the sale of a dietary supplement when it meets *all* of the following criteria:

- it is not false or misleading;
- it does not promote a particular manufacturer or brand of a dietary supplement;
- it presents a balanced view of the information;
- it is physically separate from the dietary supplements, if displayed in a store; and
- it does not have any information appended to it (e.g., a sticker with a company's name or logo).

As a result, marketers of dietary supplements are permitted to legally disseminate publications that refer to disease treatment and prevention, so long as the above criteria are met. Note that DSHEA's legislative history suggests that this exemption does not apply to a summary of a publication other than an official abstract of a peer-reviewed scientific publication. Significantly, the language of the law does not include this limitation. To date, the effect of the more restrictive language included in the legislative history, however, has not been established.

The FTC regulates claims in dietary supplement advertising.

Dietary Supplement Advertising

The FTC is the federal agency generally responsible for regulating product advertising. With respect to FDA-regulated products, the FTC and FDA have worked together under a longstanding agreement governing the division of responsibilities between the two agencies. FDA has primary responsibility for regulating claims in labeling and the FTC has primary responsibility for regulating claims in advertising. This means that dietary supplement claims found in traditional advertising media such as television, radio, and print will be regulated and enforced primarily by the FTC, whereas claims found on dietary supplement labels and brochures will be regulated and enforced primarily by FDA. Claims found on the Internet and in promotional videos have been considered either advertising or labeling, and therefore both the FTC and FDA have taken enforcement action against false claims appearing in these promotional vehicles.

In 1998, the FTC published a guide, Dietary Supplements: An Advertising Guide for Industry. Throughout the guide, the FTC reiterates its basic common-sense principles used to regulate advertising for any product: 1) all advertising must be truthful and not misleading; and 2) *before* disseminating an advertisement, advertisers must have adequate substantiation for all claims (the Prior Substantiation Doctrine). The guide further explains that, just as with other product claims, claims for dietary supplements generally will require substantiation with "competent and reliable scientific evidence." This is defined as: "tests, analyses, research, studies, or other evidence based on the expertise of professionals in the relevant area that have been conducted and evaluated in an objective manner by persons qualified to do so, using procedures generally accepted in the profession to yield accurate and reliable results."

If the weight of the evidence does not support a claim, the claim should not be made, even if qualified.

While there is no fixed formula for the type and number of studies a manufacturer must have to substantiate its claims, in most cases if the weight of the evidence does not support the claim, it should not be made, even if qualified. Manufacturers and retailers must consider all relevant research relating to the claimed benefit of their dietary supplement and should not focus only on research that supports the effect, while discounting research that does not.

To ensure compliance with the FTC guidelines, manufacturers and retailers should: 1) carefully draft advertising claims with particular attention as to how claims are qualified and what express or implied messages are actually conveyed; and 2) carefully review the support for a claim to make sure it is scientifically sound, adequate in the context of the surrounding body of evidence, and relevant to the specific product and claim advertised.

In recent years, the FTC has been quite active in taking enforcement action against dietary supplement manufacturers and retailers making false, misleading, or unsubstantiated claims about their products. As a result, some dietary supplement marketers have been required to pay consumer redress of up to $20 million, or more, due to false or misleading advertising claims made in advertising materials challenged by the FTC. In seeking redress, it is the FTC's position in the cases that it brings that sellers must return all "ill-gotten gains" to consumers. This means the value of the sales to consumers, not the net profits. In the usual case, the FTC requires the production of detailed financial information to track "ill-gotten gains" to assure that they are accounted for. In more than one recent case, the FTC has required the sale of company owners' homes, cars, and boats as part of the resolution of the case.

In addition to the FTC, state attorneys general are also active from time to time in enforcing against false or misleading dietary supplement claims, and such actions often result in the payment of extensive monetary damages.

The Future of Dietary Supplement Regulation

Over the almost fourteen years since DSHEA was passed, the regulatory scheme for dietary supplements has matured with regulations covering labeling, cGMP, and a law that mandates the reporting of serious adverse events and the retention in company files of all adverse events. At the same time, FDA enforcement resources have been stretched and strained as more and more products regulated by the agency come from sources outside the United States. Against this background, the future of the dietary supplement industry may, in the main, be under the control of the industry itself. Over the next decade, the industry will come into compliance with cGMP through a learning process as FDA inspectors and manufacturers interact over the nuances of these regulations. At the same time, there will be a body of adverse event information that will be developed that will provide signals to both the industry and to regulators regarding dietary supplement safety.

The future of the dietary supplement industry is in its own hands.

The dietary supplement industry is still perceived by healthcare professionals, the media, and legislators as "unregulated." This is probably because the products come mainly in pill form, which gives them the appearance of drugs, and the products are not approved by FDA prior to marketing. While ephedrine alkaloid-containing dietary supplements remained on the market, the industry was barraged with bad publicity, usually associated with serious adverse events alleged to be associated with the use of products containing this ingredient. That publicity adversely affected the entire product category while often spiking ephedra sales upward. If the industry were to market another product alleged to cause serious adverse events at a level approaching what was reported with ephedra, legislative action to change the present regulatory structure would be a likely consequence. Accordingly, the future of the dietary supplement industry is in its own hands.

Conclusion

FDA's promulgation of cGMPs for dietary supplement manufacture and distribution, and legislation mandating adverse events reporting, have taken the dietary supplement category to a higher level of regulation.

The Dietary Supplement Health and Education Act of 1994 created a new regulatory scheme for dietary supplements. Since enactment, FDA has promulgated regulations implementing the law. Two recent events, the promulgation by FDA of cGMPs for dietary supplement manufacture and distribution, and the enactment of legislation mandating the reporting of serious adverse events associated with the use of dietary supplements, have taken this relatively newly created product category to another, higher, level of regulation.

Endnotes

1. See www.cfsan.fda.gov/~dms/addskava.html.
2. See www.fda.gov/ohrms/dockets/dockets/95s0316/95s0316.htm.
3. See http://ods.od.nih.gov/.
4. See www.cfsan.fda.gov/~dms/dslg-toc.html.
5. See www.cfsan.fda.gov/~dms/dsclmgui.html.
6. See www.cfsan.fda.gov/~dms/sclmguid.html.
7. See www.cfsan.fda.gov/~dms/hclmgui5.html.
8. See Questions and Answers at www.cfsan.fda.gov/~dms/qhcqagui.html.
9. FDA's determinations may be found at www.cfsan.fda.gov/~dms/lab-qhc.html.

Chapter 12

Regulation of Promotion and Distribution

Wayne L. Pines, APCO Worldwide Inc., Washington, D.C.

Key Points

- **The promotion of medical products is central to their proper use. FDA's jurisdiction over promotional materials for medical products includes virtually everything issued by a company or an agent of that company that is product-specific.**
- **A few basic principles apply to FDA's regulation of advertising and promotion: materials must be truthful and not misleading, must contain a fair balance of benefits and risks, and must provide for full disclosure of prescribing (drugs) or usage (devices) information.**
- **FDA is especially concerned about the promotion of off-label uses for approved drugs and devices, the pre-approval promotion of new medical products, the lack of fair balance, and comparative claims of superiority.**
- **FDA does not prohibit any communication techniques from being used to promote medical products, but there are nuances of policy that apply to each technique.**
- **FDA generally enforces the law by issuing letters to companies in violation. The letters cite the alleged violation and seek remedy. Consent decrees have been used for more serious violations. Most enforcement actions stem from FDA's review of materials submitted by companies or from competitors' complaints.**
- **Other statutes also apply to marketing medical products.**
- **Settlements under the False Claims Act and anti-kickback statute have changed the way that pharmaceutical and medical device companies market their products.**

Overview

The promotion of medical products is central to their success and optimum use. Promotion encompasses a variety of objectives: informing consumers about new and existing products that may be of value in improving their health; educating healthcare providers about new and existing products and how to use them; providing information needed by those who finance or pay directly for medical products, such as managed care organizations or hospitals; and positioning products to differentiate them from those of competitors.

There also is the need to keep other audiences informed about research and new products. The public demands such information; everyone wants to know about medical progress. Investment capital for new companies is dependent on understanding the research progress, as well as the potential market value of new products. Maintaining investment community interest in a company hinges upon focused communications. Healthcare providers need to know, on a continuing basis, what kinds of advances are being made in their specialty areas.

These forms of communication, when initiated by a medical products company or by one of its agents (e.g., an advertising or public relations agency), are regulated by the Food and Drug Administration (FDA). Promotional materials issued by medical products companies or their agents are among the most regulated of all forms of communication in the United States. FDA's concerns about product communications that are controlled (directly as well as indirectly) by drug or device companies centers primarily upon the communications that promote the products "off-label," make claims that are false and/or misleading, make unsupported comparisons with other products, and/or overstate efficacy or minimize risk.

"Off-label," in particular, has come to be a controversial term. Basically it means that the claims made in the promotional materials or statements are not included in or are not consistent with the officially approved labeling for the product. FDA's underlying concern with "off-label" promotional efforts is that they may result in patients being prescribed unproven therapies or ones that may be less effective or more risky than therapies approved for that use by FDA. The agency also is concerned that "off-label" promotion can undermine companies' incentive to conduct additional studies that will establish safety and efficacy for the new use.

FDA concern about off-label promotion raises First Amendment issues.

There is inherent controversy in this area. Some have concerns that FDA's declaration of regulatory control over communications has elements that conflict with the First Amendment (free speech) protection afforded by the U.S. Constitution. This is especially true when FDA seeks to regulate information that is generally accepted as being medically truthful, but that is not included in the official labeling or that does not meet FDA's definition of "substantial evidence." Denying the right of companies to communicate truthful and nonmisleading information, many contend, is in fact contrary to the interests of patients and the public health in general.

Others argue that advertising and promotion should be regulated more aggressively. Some contend that physicians should receive medical information from traditional scientific sources, not from drug or device companies with an interest in selling a product. Abuses of promotion and marketing efforts by companies over the years have reinforced this view.

Concerns also have been raised about the extent of FDA's jurisdiction. FDA has assumed regulation of all product-specific communications by a medical products company, even before the product is approved and available. FDA also assumes jurisdiction over conversations that take place between a company's sales representative and a physician, and the sales information provided to an accountant at a managed care organization. FDA also regulates what is said by a physician who receives compensation from a drug or device company to promote a product.

One ambiguous facet of the issue is that FDA does recognize the need for and value of communicating legitimate and accurate product information in the period before a product or new use is approved and there is no labeling to provide parameters. FDA's own regulations establish the legitimacy of "scientific exchange"—the well-recognized need for scientists to communicate with each other about research findings, and for companies to communicate research information. It is when such "exchange" crosses over into "commercialization"—and the line has never been defined with precision—that FDA regulators become concerned.

"Scientific exchange" has never been defined with precision.

In its enforcement actions, FDA also seems to draw a distinction based on who within the company is involved in the communication of "nonpromotional," scientific information. The basis for FDA enforcement actions is generally the content of what is said, not who says it. FDA has indicated, however, that it is less suspicious when medical personnel deal with "off-label" information. At the same time, it must be recognized that medical personnel who use the opportunity to promote a product "off-label" or before approval are subject to the same restrictions as all other company employees.

Because of these issues, the regulation of promotional materials is one of the most challenging areas of FDA regulation. The agency's approach is continually evolving to meet new communications technologies and creative programming by marketing staffs. At the same time, medical products companies generally have learned to work within the agency's regulatory framework. Larger companies have full-time regulatory staffs dedicated to assuring compliance with FDA requirements. Smaller companies often rely on consultants to keep them up to date on FDA promotional policies.

Drawing a line between violative and permitted activities usually requires experienced judgment. Within companies, FDA promotional policies often are a source of conflict between the marketing and communications staffs on the one hand, and regulatory and legal staffs on the other. The marketing and public relations teams want their companies to be appropriately aggressive based on their understanding of the rules; regulatory and legal staffs want to make sure the company is in compliance, even when the rules are vague and evolving. Each company's management must decide its own policies and internal processes in designing and implementing marketing and communications programs, and whether to seek FDA review in advance for certain materials.

What the Law Requires

The legal basis for FDA's authority to regulate medical product communications dates from the 1962 Drug Amendments. Before 1962, promotional activities for prescription drugs were regulated by the Federal Trade Commission (FTC). The 1962 amendments gave FDA authority over prescription drug advertising after Congress heard testimony of alleged abuses by pharmaceutical companies in seeking to market their products to physicians. The concern about marketing abuses by medical products companies has been a recurring theme and frequently has been the subject of hearings before Congress or media stories.

The pharmaceutical advertising section of the Federal Food, Drug, and Cosmetic Act (FDCA), as enacted in 1962, consists of a single paragraph in the section of the law that defines a "misbranded" product (FDCA § 502(n); 21 U.S.C. § 352(n)). It requires that the generic name of the drug appear "prominently" in promotional materials, that the drug's formula appear, and that a "brief summary" relating to side effects, contraindications, and effectiveness appear in all advertising. It also prohibits FDA from requiring that advertising materials be approved in advance, except in "extraordinary circumstances." FDA issued detailed regulations in the 1960s and 1970s to establish specific requirements for paid advertising for prescription drugs.

FDA regulation has adapted to the changing environment.

Since 1962, there have been dramatic changes in how medical products are marketed, in the audiences that need and want to know about them, and in communications technology generally. No longer are medical products promoted just to healthcare providers. No longer is the printed medical journal or the visit by the company's sales representative the primary vehicle of communicating product information. FDA has adapted to this continuously evolving environment.

Further, similar requirements for medical devices (FDCA § 502(r); 21 U.S.C. § 352(r)) have evolved from the requirements of the 1962 Drug Amendments, as well as guidances and enforcement actions that affect the marketing of all FDA-regulated medical products—human drugs and biologicals, veterinary drugs, and medical devices.

FDA regulations that apply to the promotion of medical products are contained in several sections of the *Code of Federal Regulations* (Title 21). Among the applicable sections are Part 200 and, most particularly, Part 202 for pharmaceutical promotion, Part 510 for veterinary drugs, Part 601 for biological products, and Part 801 for medical devices. The sections that deal with human prescription drugs generally set the policies for prescription veterinary drugs.

The formal regulations, however, provide only a small measure of the information needed to comply with FDA requirements. The regulations are most helpful when it comes to understanding the requirements for traditional paid advertising directed at physicians—the oldest form of marketing now being practiced and the regulatory objective of the 1962 amendments. Much of FDA policy in this area is set forth in other FDA documents, most prominently in guidances and enforcement action letters issued by the agency. To keep up with evolving policies, careful attention must be paid to the warning letters and other correspondence that involve specific companies or products. Further, policies have been elucidated in the meetings and symposia where FDA regulators speak.

It's Basic!
A few basic principles underlie all of FDA's regulation of promotion and advertising.

UNDERLYING PRINCIPLES

A few basic principles underlie FDA's regulations, guidances, and regulatory actions regarding promotion and advertising. Essentially, any medical product that fails to adhere to these principles in its promotional practices could be viewed as "misbranded" by FDA and subject to an enforcement action.

The basic principles that underlie FDA's advertising and promotion policies, and that apply to all medical products categories, are:

- **Product-specific promotional information issued by medical products companies is regulated.** While the 1962 amendments envisioned that FDA primarily would regulate advertising directed at physicians, because that was the principal means of promoting prescription drugs at the time, over the years FDA has expanded the horizons of its jurisdiction to include all promotional information. While some attorneys dispute FDA's expanded view of its jurisdiction, as a practical matter FDA does regulate, to varying degrees, not just prescription drug advertising but also sales materials, information directed at consumers, press materials, information provided to the investment community, sales materials for managed care organizations and hospitals, and oral statements made by any company employee or representative that discuss a specific product.
- **FDA regards promotional materials issued by drug companies as either "advertising" or "labeling."** "Advertising" consists of traditional paid advertising (e.g., when a company pays to place an advertisement). "Labeling," or more precisely "promotional labeling," to distinguish the term from being confused with the package insert, includes everything else (e.g., brochures, booklets, direct mail pieces,

press releases, letters to formulary committees, slide kits, and audio-visual materials). "Advertising" and "promotional labeling" must meet the same general standards for truthfulness, accuracy, and balance.

There is one disclosure requirement that differentiates "advertising" and "promotional labeling." When paid advertising appears, the risk disclosure requirements can be met with the inclusion of a "brief summary" of risk information, whereas materials classified as "promotional labeling" generally must be accompanied by the full package insert.

Sometimes materials issued by or on behalf of a medical products company that do not mention a specific product, such as information about a disease, may be regarded as "labeling" or "promotional labeling" if the materials are intended to be used in conjunction with the promotion of a product or if a reasonable person would be able to identify the product based on the implicit claim.

All information in promotional materials issued by or on behalf of a drug or device company must be truthful and not false and/or misleading.

- **Under FDA's regulations, all information in promotional materials issued by or on behalf of a drug or device company must be truthful and not false and/or misleading.** FDA, however, imposes requirements above and beyond simple accuracy and truthfulness. For example, a press release may accurately and truthfully describe new research on an unapproved use of an approved product, but if it also does not include a "fair balance" of risk factors and provide for "full disclosure" of risk information, then it could be regarded by FDA as violative. Further, if the issuance contains information inconsistent with FDA-approved labeling, even if that information is medically accurate, truthful, and well accepted by experts in the medical field, that information may be regarded by FDA as violative.
- **All information must be fairly balanced with risk information.** FDA defines "fair balance" as a "balanced presentation of benefits and risks." This means that, in an advertisement, to the extent that a particular benefit is described, the medical risks associated with that benefit also must be described. In a press release, when benefits are described, FDA expects that the major adverse experiences and side effects also will be described. "Fair balance" also may mean that a product's limitations must be delineated. "Fair balance" is hard to define with any better precision because it differs for each individual product.

Television advertising that is product-specific must also meet the "fair balance" requirement by including risk information within the advertising itself. Further, television advertising must also meet the "brief summary" requirement. It does so by making "adequate provision" for the recipient of the information to obtain prescribing information.

"Adequate provision" for television advertising directed to a consumer audience can be met through mechanisms set forth by FDA (initially in an August 1997 draft guidance, and then again two years later in a final guidance). It was this guidance that basically opened the door to product-specific direct-to-consumer (DTC) television advertising. FDA stated that the "adequate provision" requirement could be met for television by including in the commercial an 800 number that the consumer can call to ask for further information to be mailed, faxed or read; a referral to an Internet site; a referral to information in an advertisement in a current issue of a print publication that included the brief summary; or provision of information that healthcare professionals can provide to patients.

- **Companies may make therapeutic claims for products in advertising and promotional labeling only when that claim is consistent with the FDA-approved labeling or, in some cases when the labeling is not up to date, based on "substantial evidence" or "substantial clinical experience."** (As a practical enforcement matter, FDA generally does not permit claims to be made solely on the basis of "substantial clinical experience," but this language remains in the FDA regulations.) This requirement has been very controversial. Even if information is well accepted in the medical community, it may not, in FDA's view, be used in company promotional material if it is not included in FDA-approved labeling or based on what FDA regards as "substantial evidence."

  FDA's rationale in restricting the use of "off-label" information in company promotional materials is that it could mislead healthcare providers and consumers into believing a product is effective for a use when it has not been shown effective to FDA's satisfaction. Further, FDA believes that if companies are permitted to disseminate off-label information, it will remove any incentive they have to conduct needed research on that use. Congress addressed this issue in 1997 legislation, the Food and Drug Administration Modernization Act (FDAMA). This matter also has been addressed in litigation (the Washington Legal Foundation case) and is central to ongoing debates about FDA's policies and its exercise of its enforcement discretion.

- **Material facts about the product must be disclosed in company promotional materials.** If an advertisement or promotional piece fails to mention a material fact that would influence the prescribing, use, or purchase of a product, then the piece could be regarded by FDA as being violative.

- **The rules governing advertising and "promotional labeling" apply to any product-specific information issued or caused to be issued by a company, *either directly or through any agent.*** There was a time when FDA would hesitate to initiate regulatory action when a medical products company hired a third party, such as a physician, to

The rules governing advertising and promotional labeling apply to any product-specific information issued or caused to be issued by a company, either directly or through any agent.

speak on behalf of the company's product and make off-label statements. FDA has made clear that any third parties hired by a company to speak publicly about a product in a promotional context must keep the remarks within approved labeling and otherwise comply with the same rules that apply to the company itself.

The same principle applies to an advertising or public relations agency hired by a medical products company to promote a product, and it further applies when a company provides money to a third-party organization to issue information on behalf of one of its products. The indictment in the spring of 2006 by the U.S. Attorney in the Eastern District of New York of a physician for alleging promoting "off-label" uses on behalf of a pharmaceutical company underscores the government's concern with off-label promotion.

Off-label promotion
FDA believes that promoting a marketed product for an unapproved use poses a significant potential threat to the public health.

Specific FDA Concerns

In the view of FDA, promoting a marketed product for an unapproved use poses a significant potential threat to the public health. FDA is concerned that if healthcare providers and consumers are led to believe that a marketed product is safe and effective for a use for which it is not approved, then adverse health consequences may result. FDA further argues that permitting manufacturers to promote their products for unapproved uses would reduce their incentive to perform the studies and research necessary to obtain FDA approval of such indications.

FDA regulations provide that the standard for whether a claim can be made is "substantial evidence" or "substantial clinical experience." As a practical enforcement matter, however, FDA usually relies on the approved labeling as the basis for judging whether a claim is acceptable for promotional purposes. Thus, FDA might take enforcement action even when medical scientists uniformly believe that a particular use is safe and effective.

FDA rules and enforcement policy seek to discourage drug and device companies from disseminating information about "off-label" uses. This policy is controversial, as the argument has been made that the standard for dissemination of "off-label" information in a nonpromotional context should be whether the claim itself is medically justified and supported, even if it has not been incorporated into the official FDA labeling. The argument is premised on the fact that FDA labeling lags behind science, and drug and medical device companies should be entitled to provide truthful and nonmisleading information.

Some of the specific kinds of "off-label" promotional activities that FDA objects to are: implying in an advertisement that a drug is useful for a particular use when it has not been shown to be (for example, FDA objected to a photograph in an advertisement for a drug that depicted a young woman, when the drug was indicated for older people); posting information on the Internet that indicates that a medical device is useful for a broad range of procedures when it was approved under a 510(k) application only for a limited type of procedure; or suggesting that a drug is useful as first-line therapy when it was approved only as second-line therapy.

FDAMA established circumstances under which peer-reviewed studies that describe or mention "off-label" uses for approved drugs could be disseminated to health professionals. Under the law and its implementing regulation, the company must have studied or be studying the "off-label" use, and must intend to seek FDA approval for that use. Many other criteria also had to be met, including submitting the peer-reviewed article to FDA at least sixty days in advance of dissemination. There also had to be disclosure of the "off-label" nature of the study and the package insert had to accompany the distribution of the article. The law established a procedure for companies to seek FDA approval of disseminating peer-reviewed studies.

Relatively few companies used the process and, as a result, this provision of FDAMA sunsetted in 2006 and was not reauthorized by Congress. In February 2008, FDA issued a draft guidance that set forth its criteria for when companies could distribute peer-reviewed medical journal articles.

FDA also objects to the commercialization of a product before approval. The agency's view was set forth in 1994 correspondence which expressed its interpretation of section 312.7 ("scientific exchange") of the regulations:

> Prior to approval, promotional materials provided by the sponsor are often inaccurate with respect to the indications and risk information that ultimately appear in the approved product labeling. This inaccuracy occurs because the sponsor does not know what indications and other information the final product labeling will contain. Additionally, the sponsor's assessment of the drug may be overly optimistic, exaggerating efficacy while minimizing risk. Thus, the sponsor's biases may be incorporated into the promotional materials it provides prior to approval of final product labeling. Such promotional materials do not fulfill the needs of healthcare providers or benefits managers to obtain balanced, accurate information about new drugs, but instead disseminate misinformation and create potential risk and misuse.

Investigational products may not be commercialized, but can be discussed as "scientific exchange."

FDA has a somewhat different policy for medical devices in the pre-approval stage, recognizing that purchasers need to commit large sums of money to buy certain devices. Medical device companies may notify potential customers about a new product whose 510(k) application is still being reviewed by FDA, but may make no conclusory claims with regard to effectiveness or safety, and may not take orders for the product.

Another principal concern of FDA is comparative claims made by companies for their products. In an environment in which competition in the medical products industries is intense, all companies seek to differentiate their products, and all want to claim that their product is superior. Examples of comparative claims are "drug of choice," "unsurpassed," or "more effective."

Comparative claims
FDA requires that any claim of superiority for a prescription drug be supported by "substantial evidence" and not be based solely on a comparison of labeling information.

FDA requires that any claim of superiority for a prescription drug be supported by "substantial evidence," usually two adequate and well-controlled studies or in some cases a single large multicenter trial. The studies must be "head-to-head" (i.e., they must be designed prospectively to directly compare the products). Generally, the agency wants two such studies, but it will permit a limited claim (e.g., our product is better absorbed, or works faster, or is more easily swallowed by patients) to be made on the basis of a single study. FDA prohibits a claim of superiority based solely on a comparison of data in the two products' labeling.

FDA also requires that any comparative claim be clinically relevant to patients. In addition, if a comparative claim is made, it cannot be false or misleading and cannot leave out other measurements by which the company's product is inferior to its competitor.

Two kinds of comparative claims that companies have increasingly been making involve cost-effectiveness (our product is more cost-effective than our competitor's) or quality-of-life claims (our product helps patients obtain a high quality of life, either in absolute terms or in comparison with our competitor's product). FDA generally requires that any such claims be proven by studies. Quality-of-life claims must report not just positive findings but also negative ones.

With regard to cost-effectiveness claims, in the 1997 FDAMA, Congress recognized the need of companies to provide such information to medical products purchasers (as contrasted with prescribers). The law said that cost-effectiveness information could be supplied to managed care organizations, but only to such organizations, if the information is "competent and reliable." This language is stated in the statute but is subject to FDA interpretation. The legal history of FDAMA made clear that the same information that is provided to product purchasers based on "competent and reliable" data may not also be provided to consumers or even to healthcare providers in their capacity as prescribers.

Communications Techniques

In the modern world, there are many ways for information to be communicated. FDA does not object to the use of any specific mode of communication for medical products information. Medical information can be provided to healthcare providers, consumers, managed care purchasers, or anyone else with whatever communication mechanisms exist: electronic or print, television commercials or journal advertising, Internet or CD/DVD. What FDA is concerned about, however, is the content of these materials and whether it is false or misleading in any way.

Requirements that apply to specific methods of communication are as follows:

Reminder ads are exempt from risk summaries.

- **Reminder ads**: FDA regulations permit companies to sponsor advertising that does not mention the indications or uses for a product, but that is intended to "remind" readers or viewers of the name. Such advertising may state the name (including the generic name); the ingredients; the dosage form; and the name and address of the manufacturer, packager, or distributor. The advertisement, however, may not mention what the product is used for, and may not make a safety or efficacy claim or any other representation, including a graphic representation, about the use of the product. Such advertising is exempt from the requirement for a "brief summary." "Reminder ads" may not appear for drugs for which there is a "boxed" warning in the FDA-approved labeling, or, in the case of older drugs, whose efficacy has not been reaffirmed by FDA. As a practical matter, the pens and pads that companies have provided are technically "reminder" advertising in that they mention only the product name (including generic name) without indicating its uses.
- **Press releases**: FDA does not have a specific regulation or guidance applying to press releases, but does regulate them as "promotional labeling," and while some attorneys dispute whether FDA has the authority to regulate press releases, as a practical matter both the drug and devices industry generally accede to FDA's position. Based on FDA expectations (as derived from various enforcement actions and statements by FDA), the agency expects promotional press releases to contain "fair balance" within the release itself. Because they are regarded by FDA as "labeling" rather than advertising, FDA expects that press releases be accompanied by the full package insert, not just a "brief summary" of risks.

  It is safer from a regulatory standpoint if press releases contain disclaimers that help put the product into regulatory context (e.g., in a research announcement for a product not yet approved, it is best to make clear that the product is not approved or that an application is pending before FDA, if that is the case). Press releases issued before product approval must avoid saying that the product has been shown to be safe and effective, and should avoid any statements that might be construed as promotional, such as using words like "promising" or "breakthrough."

- **Video news releases:** These ninety-second electronic versions of press releases are regarded by FDA as promotional labeling, and therefore under FDA policy must contain balanced information if they are product-specific. It is best to provide easy access to a package insert as well, or to scroll risk information at the end.
- **Materials for investors**: Investor-directed press releases and other materials, such as annual reports, are subject to the same regulatory requirements, according to FDA policy. FDA, however, recognizes that these materials are not intended to be used in a product promotion context and its enforcement policies are geared accordingly. For example, an annual report handed out at a medical meeting might be regarded as promotional, but FDA has never required annual reports issued to investors that mention ongoing research or newly approved products in this context to include the labeling as an attachment. FDA coordinates closely with the Securities and Exchange Commission in regulating investor materials.
- **Scientific meetings**: The sponsorship by companies of medical and other meetings has been controversial. The concern by FDA and other government agencies is that companies will use the meetings to promote off-label uses of their products, or that companies will exert control over meetings that are depicted as independent.

  Any scientific meeting that is under the content control of a company and that is product-specific must meet all criteria for fair balance and full disclosure. FDA, however, does not regulate the content of legitimate continuing medical education (CME) funded by medical products companies, as long as the CME grant is provided to a third party and the CME is conducted independently of the company.

  Companies that fund CME generally have standard contracts with providers that set forth a specific relationship that is intended to ensure independence of the program, the presenters, and the derivative material, such as monographs or publications. In evaluating whether a CME program is truly independent, FDA looks at about a dozen factors, most particularly who controls the program agenda and speaker selection. The Accreditation Council for Continuing Medical Education accredits CME programs; its rules were tightened in 2006 in an effort to assure a high level of independence from commercial interests.

CME is not regulated by FDA if it is independently conducted.

- **Internet**: FDA does not have a formal Internet policy, but does actively regulate information on the Internet sponsored by medical product companies. For the most part, corporate information that is not product-specific may be put on the Internet at will. So, too, can information about approved products, as long as the information is consistent with labeling and provides ready and easy access to product labeling.

The regulatory challenges arise with links to other Internet sites that contain off-label information, or with chat rooms where off-label information may be discussed. Generally companies do not sponsor such links or chat rooms. Another issue is how to regulate information that emanates from overseas affiliates, especially if it relates to products also sold in the United States. In such cases, companies generally indicate clearly which part of the website is intended for U.S. audiences as contrasted with audiences in countries where the product may be approved for uses not approved in the United States.

- **Homemade materials**: Company personnel in the field sometimes seek to create their own promotional materials to provide to healthcare professionals. Homemade materials usually contain misleading claims and/or lack risk information. FDA discourages this practice, because all promotional materials distributed by a prescription drug or biologics company are required to be submitted to the agency at the time of first use.

  FDA would expect sales representatives who want to distribute their own materials to submit them to appropriate supervisory officials in advance so they can go through the company's approval process. Most, if not all, companies prohibit the creation by field personnel of their own materials.

Companies prohibit "homemade" materials as a matter of policy.

- **Requests for information**: Companies may respond to requests for information from any external source. FDA differentiates, however, between requests that are solicited by the company—that is, that the company has encouraged in any way—and those that are totally unsolicited. If a request for information is solicited, then the company's response must stay within labeling.

  If a request is unsolicited, then information about "off-label" uses that is directly responsive to the inquiry can be provided. Responses to unsolicited requests for information generally are handled by a company's Medical Affairs Department. Companies usually keep records of such requests, and these records are subject to FDA inspection. When "off-label" information is sent to the requester, the customary practice is for the cover letter to make clear that the materials discuss an indication that is not presently approved by FDA.

- **Direct-to-consumer promotion**: Most countries, including those in the European Union, do not permit companies to advertise prescription drug promotional information directly to consumers. The United States is the only country other than New Zealand that permits DTC advertising of prescription products. Companies in the United States also target other promotional materials directly to the consumer, such as materials that may be distributed in a physician's waiting room.

FDA requires that all consumer-directed information must meet the same criteria for accuracy, truthfulness, fair balance, and full disclosure as materials intended for healthcare professionals. Print advertising must fairly present the risks as well as benefits, and also must include the "brief summary" or a consumer version of it.

Advertising of prescription drugs on commercial television is permitted, but it must make "adequate provision" for consumers to obtain further information.

As described above, under a policy announced by FDA in August 1997, and reiterated in August 1999, advertising of prescription drugs on commercial television also is permitted, but it must make "adequate provision" for the consumer to obtain further information via the Internet, a toll-free number, or some other means. FDA encourages disease-oriented or "help-seeking" advertising to consumers that does not mention any product name, but that identifies a disease condition and urges consumers to see their doctors.

Washington Legal Foundation Case

The most celebrated legal case involving the promotion of medical products was brought by the Washington Legal Foundation (WLF). In 1993, WLF filed a citizen's petition with FDA objecting to the agency's policies restricting the ability of pharmaceutical companies to provide scientific information to healthcare professionals that is truthful and nonmisleading but not consistent with FDA-approved labeling for the product. This case evolved into protracted litigation that lasted until 2000.

The case focused on the right of pharmaceutical companies to provide healthcare professionals with truthful and nonmisleading scientific information, including reprints of peer-reviewed materials and sponsorship of CME programs. WLF took the view that the criteria for such communication should be whether the information itself was truthful, not whether the information was consistent with the FDA-approved labeling.

On July 30, 1998, the court enjoined FDA from seeking to limit any pharmaceutical manufacturer's ability to disseminate to healthcare professionals any off-label information published in a peer-reviewed journal, to disseminate bona fide textbooks, or suggest content or speakers for an independent CME program, even when off-label uses are to be discussed. This decision was later vacated.

In 2000, during oral argument on appeal, FDA stated that it viewed its CME guidance as establishing a "safe harbor" for pharmaceutical company sponsorship of medical education, and would take enforcement action against companies that provided peer-reviewed articles to healthcare professionals only if the information itself was false and/or misleading or contrary to the public health. In March 2000, FDA published a notice in the *Federal Register* that reiterated its "safe harbor" position.

FDA's articulation of its policy did not resolve the uncertainty. WLF returned to court to seek clarity, but on November 30, 2000, the district court denied the request. The court criticized FDA for failing to resolve the issue: "After six years' worth of briefs, motions, opinions, congressional acts and more opinions, the issue remains 100% unresolved, and the country's drug manufacturers are still without clear guidance as to the permissibility of this conduct." *Washington Legal Foundation v. Henney,* 128 F. Supp. 2d 11, 15 (D.D.C. 2000).

Enforcement

FDA cannot mandate, but does expect, companies to have in place written policies and procedures for reviewing promotional materials and programs, including an internal review process. The agency also cannot mandate, but does expect, regular training for staff, including the sales force, on regulatory requirements. Training has become a major focus for many companies that want to be sure that everyone in the company, from top management to the sales force, is aware of the company's philosophy toward FDA's rules, especially with regard to how the sales force conducts its activities on a day-to-day basis. Training also is required under corporate integrity agreements (CIAs) signed by companies that settle cases under the False Claims Act or anti-kickback statute (see below).

Submission to FDA
Promotional materials for drugs and biological products, but not devices, must be submitted to FDA at time of first use.

For pharmaceuticals and biological products, FDA regulations require that all product-specific promotional materials must be submitted to FDA at the time of their first use. Promotional pieces for pharmaceuticals are submitted to the Division of Drug Marketing, Advertising and Communications in the Center for Drug Evaluation and Research, and for biologics to the Advertising and Promotional Labeling Staff in the Center for Biologics Evaluation and Research. Medical device and veterinary medicine manufacturers have no requirements for routine submission of promotional materials.

FDA enforcement actions generally are premised on its review of materials submitted at the time of their first use by companies and on its own surveillance of the marketplace. Many actions, however, also are based on competitor complaints (i.e., complaints filed by one company against another, or by healthcare professionals). Such complaints often are submitted formally, in writing, to the FDA division responsible for regulating the advertising and promotion of the product. Many companies encourage their employees to gather intelligence about their competitors' promotional activities to assure that regulation is even-handed.

Typically, when FDA detects a violation, it sends the offending company either an "untitled" letter or a warning letter. Both identify FDA's concern and seek remedial action, such as discontinuation of the promotional piece at issue. The letters indicate that the agency has concluded that a legal violation has occurred and remedial action is required, such as withdrawal of the violative materials. FDA also may request that a "Dear Health Professional" letter be disseminated. It also can seek other corrective measures, such as employee training or preclearance of any new promotional materials for a period of time.

Enforcement letters usually provide ten to fifteen days for the company to respond and present a plan of action. Companies often seek a meeting or teleconference with FDA to discuss the appropriateness of the remedial action. Enforcement letters are made public upon issuance by FDA, and thus become a potential source of negative publicity, as well as a potent enforcement tool. FDA posts warning and untitled letters on its Internet site (www.fda.gov), along with the violative materials.

FDA has other enforcement options. In the 1990s, but not recently, FDA negotiated consent decrees with companies. FDA also has the option to seek a seizure, injunction, or criminal action (misdemeanor or felony) against violative companies or activities. FDA usually includes in its "untitled" letters, and always in its warning letters, the possibility of more stringent action but as a practical matter a seizure, injunction, or criminal prosecution is unlikely.

Over-the-Counter Products

The FTC has authority over the advertising and promotion of nonprescription drugs and nonrestricted devices, as well as foods and cosmetics. The FTC's authority, which predates FDA's, stems from section 5 of the Federal Trade Commission Act, which gives the commission authority to prevent companies from "using unfair methods of competition . . . and unfair or deceptive acts or practices in or affecting commerce." (The FTC technically retains some legal jurisdiction over prescription drug advertising, but as a practical matter defers to FDA.)

The FTC regulates the advertising and promotion of nonprescription drugs, nonrestricted devices, foods, and cosmetics.

FDA and the FTC work together in cases involving medical products because the FTC does not have a medical staff and any FTC action must be based on FDA-approved labeling of over-the-counter (OTC) drugs or nonrestricted devices. FDA and the FTC operate under a 1971 Memorandum of Understanding that sets forth how the relationship between the two agencies will work.

FTC procedures permit companies to engage in formal discussions with staff before any matter is resolved. The usual resolution of an FTC investigation is the signing of a consent decree in which the company admits no wrongdoing but agrees never to repeat the activity to which the FTC has objected. The FTC also has the authority to seek a temporary restraining order or an injunction.

Prescription Drug Marketing Act

The use of drug samples—small quantities of a product that are provided free of charge to a physician so that he or she may provide them free to a patient as a "starter"—has been controversial. There has been concern that control over samples was not sufficient to preclude their diversion into commercial channels or, more important, that samples of drugs subject to potential abuse might be readily diverted.

The Prescription Drug Marketing Act—a section of the FDCA—prohibits the diversion of prescription drugs or biological products into illegitimate commercial channels. It also prohibits the sale of drug samples. The law provides that companies must obtain the signature of a physician for all drug samples. The law also requires record-keeping and careful storage of samples. Whenever a manufacturer discovers any diversion, it must report this to FDA.

FDCA prohibits sale and diversion of drug samples.

False Claims Act

The federal False Claims Act was originally passed during the Civil War to prevent vendors from defrauding the government. The law was amended in 1986, and a dozen years later the government started using the law to bring actions against the pharmaceutical and medical devices industries.

The basic allegation in the cases was that if a drug or device company promoted a product "off-label," and if, as a consequence, the product cost was reimbursed by the government, then that constitutes fraud against the government. The law provides that whistle-blowers can initiate such cases, and the vast majority of cases brought against the drug and device industries have been brought by whistle-blowers, often current or former company employees, who under the law can collect 15 to 30 percent of the fine.

A few dozen such cases have been brought against pharmaceutical and medical device companies, resulting in fines that often are in the hundreds of millions of dollars. The cases also resulted in companies signing CIAs with the government. The cases are brought by the Department of Justice in conjunction with the Office of the Inspector General of the Department of Health and Human Services (OIG DHHS), which usually is intimately involved in negotiating the settlements.

DHHS's interest and authority in this area comes from the fact that it administers the Medicaid and Medicare programs, and the OIG DHHS is responsible for preventing fraud and abuse in these programs. (Medicaid is a joint state/federal healthcare reimbursement program for people who cannot afford treatment, while Medicare is a federal program that reimburses for healthcare for the elderly and disabled.)

Many states also have their own false claims statutes and state attorneys general also have brought cases and have shared in the settlements.

In one settlement, three corporate officials pleaded guilty to misdemeanors and paid substantial fines for their roles in promotional activities. This reflected the government's interest in pursuing individual liability.

The OIG sets standards for internal compliance programs.

In 2003, OIG DHHS issued a guidance explaining what it expects from pharmaceutical companies to avoid making false claims under the False Claims Act. The guidelines, published in the *Federal Register* on May 5, 2003, set forth standards for internal compliance programs for pharmaceutical manufacturers. The guidance contained both broad principles for compliance, such as encouraging a corporate culture of compliance, as well as specific policies that companies are expected to adopt and follow.

The guidance set forth seven elements "that have been widely recognized as fundamental to an effective compliance program." The seven elements constitute the basis for much of the contents of CIAs. The seven elements are:

- **Implementing written policies and procedures:** The written policies should "verbalize" the company's commitment to compliance and address specific areas of fraud and abuse, such as the reporting of pricing and rebate information, and sales and marketing practices.
- **Designating a compliance officer and committee:** The compliance officer and committee are responsible for developing and monitoring the compliance program and should report directly to the board of directors or president/chief executive officer of the company.

- **Conducting effective training and education:** All affected employees should be trained substantively at regular intervals.
- **Developing effective lines of communication:** There should be effective communication between the compliance officer and all employees. Companies should establish a telephone hotline for reporting internal complaints. This safeguards the anonymity of complainants and protects whistle-blowers from retaliation.
- **Conducting internal monitoring and auditing:** There regularly should be audits or other risk evaluation techniques to monitor compliance or identify problem areas.
- **Enforcing standards through well-publicized disciplinary guidelines:** Companies should develop policies and procedures to preclude the employment of individuals or companies excluded from participating in federal healthcare programs and to enforce disciplinary action against employees or contractors who have violated the rules.
- **Responding promptly to detected problems and undertaking corrective action:** Firms should implement policies and procedures for identifying and investigating any instances of noncompliance or misconduct.

Anti-Kickback

Another federal law that applies to marketing medical products is the "anti-kickback" law (42 U.S.C. § 1320a-7b). This law, which dates from 1972, is not part of either the FDCA or the False Claims Act; instead, it relates to the Medicaid and Medicare statutes.

The anti-kickback law relates to the Medicaid and Medicare statutes.

The anti-kickback statutes are intended to prevent overuse of and overcharging for medical products that are subject to government reimbursement under either Medicaid or Medicare (or other government-reimbursed healthcare programs). They prohibit any activity in which a medical products company may try to persuade, other than with sound therapeutic arguments, a physician or another healthcare provider or facility to use a particular product.

Specifically, the law, which is also enforced by the OIG DHHS, prohibits a company from offering "any remuneration (including any kickback, bribe, or rebate) directly or indirectly, overtly or covertly, in cash or in kind" to anyone to induce them to purchase a product or service for which reimbursement may be sought under Medicaid or Medicare. The regulations do provide certain exceptions, also known as "safe harbors," which do permit some marketing activities.

A number of settlements with pharmaceutical and medical device companies have been signed under the anti-kickback law. The cases have entailed significant fines and the signing of CIAs.

PhRMA and AdvaMed Codes

The PhRMA's Code on Interactions with Healthcare Professionals redefines the relationship between healthcare professionals and the pharmaceutical industry.

In 2002, the Pharmaceutical Research and Manufacturers of America (PhRMA)—the trade association of research-oriented drug companies—adopted a Code on Interactions with Healthcare Professionals. It attempted to redefine the relationship between healthcare professionals and the pharmaceutical industry. It was adopted by the PhRMA Board of Directors and became effective in 2002. The code is voluntary but has been adopted by most companies and become the standard of conduct for drug companies. In July 2008, PhRMA updated its code, with the new provisions taking effect in January 2009.

In January 2004, AdvaMed, the trade association representing large medical device companies, issued its own code. It was similar to the PhRMA code except in those areas in which pharmaceutical marketing differs from medical device marketing, such as the ability of device companies to promote their products before approval (but not make any claims or take orders).

Specific provisions of the codes include:

- **Informational presentations:** Presentations by industry representatives and others speaking on behalf of a company are encouraged. Occasional meals (but no entertainment or recreational events) may be offered as long as the meals: 1) are modest as judged by local standards; 2) occur in a venue and manner conducive to informational communication; and 3) take place in conjunction with activities that provide scientific or educational value.
- **Medical education:** Financial support from companies for scientific and educational conferences or professional meetings is permissible provided no strings are attached. Such financial support should be given to the conference's sponsor through a grant.
- **Consultants:** Consultants who provide legitimate services to companies may be offered compensation at fair market value as well as reimbursement for travel, lodging, and meal expenses. Token consulting should not be used. It is not appropriate to pay honoraria, travel, or lodging expenses to nonfaculty and nonconsultant attendees at company-sponsored meetings.
- **Grants:** No grants, scholarships, subsidies, support, consulting contracts, or educational or practice-related items or other remuneration should be provided or offered to a healthcare professional in

exchange for prescribing products. Nothing should be offered or provided in a manner or under conditions that would influence or interfere with the independence of a doctor's prescribing practices.

- **Gifts:** Gifts to physicians are not permitted under the PhRMA code unless they are of an educational nature. This provision, adopted in July 2008, eliminated pens, pads, and other items provided by drug companies, as well as items for display in medical offices.

In January 2006, another PhRMA code, setting forth principles for DTC advertising, took effect. This is a voluntary code with which most major pharmaceutical companies have agreed to comply. It states that "all DTC information should be accurate and not misleading, should make claims only when supported by substantial evidence, should reflect balance between risks and benefits, and should be consistent with FDA approved labeling."

Further, these principles also state that "DTC television and print advertising for prescription drugs should clearly indicate that the medicine is a prescription drug, to distinguish such advertising from other advertising for non-prescription products." Companies should "spend an appropriate amount of time to educate health professionals about a new medicine or a new therapeutic indication before commencing the first DTC advertising campaign" and "should submit all new DTC television advertisements to the FDA before releasing these advertisements for broadcast. . . . DTC television and print advertising should include information about the availability of other options such as diet and lifestyle changes where appropriate for the advertised condition" and "DTC television and print advertisements should be targeted to avoid audiences that are not age appropriate for the messages involved."

The adoption of the PhRMA principles has led to a significant increase in the number of DTC advertising campaigns for prescription drugs submitted to the agency for an advisory opinion. The 2007 Food and Drug Administration Amendments Act contained a provision for a system whereby companies would pay a fee to FDA for a timely review of their DTC television advertisements. The program was not implemented because of congressional objections to industry payments for such reviews.

There has been a significant increase in the number of DTC advertising campaigns for prescription drugs submitted to the agency for an advisory opinion.

Conclusion

FDA's regulation of marketing practices by medical products companies—specifically their promotional programs—has become a highly specialized and especially dynamic field within food and drug law. The rules are set forth in a variety of ways—in FDA regulations, in guidances, and in enforcement actions—but are constantly refined in public discussions by regulators. The policies and their nuances continue to evolve as new products are introduced and new means of communications become available.

In essence, however, the key principles underlying FDA regulation have been constant. Programs and materials must be truthful, they must prominently disclose risk information, "scientific exchange" but no commercialization may take place before a product is approved, and there may be no efforts by medical products manufacturers to persuade or induce healthcare providers to use products for uses not approved by FDA.

Chapter 13

Review of FDA Inspections and Related Regulations

Ronald F. Tetzlaff, Ph.D. & David L. Chesney, PAREXEL Consulting, Duluth, Georgia and Lowell, Massachusetts

Key Points

- **FDA inspections are administrative investigations to determine whether the inspected company is in compliance with the Federal Food, Drug, and Cosmetic Act or other laws enforced by FDA.**
- **Inspectors' actions must comply with general statutory standards of reasonableness (time, limits, manner) and specific procedures as provided by law.**
- **Inspections may be initiated for routine purposes, for cause, or as a follow-up to prior adverse findings. This chapter explains the more common reasons for inspections, with a focus on GMP inspections.**
- **FDA employees who conduct inspections have a wide variety of backgrounds. Inspections are conducted by FDA investigators, chemists, microbiologists, engineers, and various scientists having specialized education and training.**
- **Effective preparation and management of FDA inspections may significantly influence the outcome.**
- **FDA has put in place a variety of policies, procedures, and forms with a bearing on inspections. These are public documents and companies are well advised to be familiar with their content and purpose.**
- **Companies may facilitate FDA inspections by following general guidelines for effective communication and interaction with inspectors and other agency officials.**
- **A trained person should act as escort for FDA during the course of the inspection.**
- **A conference room or office should be set aside for FDA's use during the inspection. A separate conference room should serve as the company's command post for the inspection.**

Introduction

One of the principal functions of the Food and Drug Administration (FDA) is to conduct inspections of facilities that manufacture, process, pack, or hold foods, drugs, medical devices, biologicals, cosmetics, and other products that are subject to FDA regulation. The purpose of FDA inspections is to determine whether regulated products have been processed, packed, or held under conditions that may result in such products being adulterated or misbranded within the meaning of the Federal Food, Drug, and Cosmetic Act (FDCA), or whether products lacking FDA approval (where approval is required) are being sold and shipped. FDA inspections are usually unannounced, and may include examination of manufacturing sites, contract laboratories, warehouses, and quality control laboratories for evidence of violations, including reviews of production and laboratory control records to determine if conditions and practices are in compliance with applicable laws and regulations

FDA inspections are usually unannounced, and may include examination of manufacturing sites, contract laboratories, warehouses, and quality control laboratories for evidence of violations.

Inspections are also conducted under what FDA terms its "bioresearch monitoring" inspections. These inspections are done at sites where clinical investigations are conducted to determine compliance with applicable regulations, commitments made in relevant submissions (e.g., investigational new drug (IND) applications and investigational device exemption (IDE) applications), and to assess data integrity. Under FDA-approved INDs or IDEs, sponsors are permitted to use investigational drugs and devices to obtain safety and effectiveness data needed to support new drug applications (NDAs) and premarket approval (PMA) applications. In addition, under the bioresearch monitoring programs, FDA inspects Institutional Review Boards (IRBs) for compliance with 21 C.F.R. Parts 50 and 56, nonclinical (animal safety testing) laboratories for compliance with the Good Laboratory Practice (GLP) regulations (21 C.F.R. Part 58), and bioanalytical laboratories that support bioequivalence and bioavailability testing of generic drugs, for compliance with 21 C.F.R. Part 320.

Specially trained investigators and laboratory personnel conduct FDA inspections. FDA inspection approaches vary for each of the different types of products regulated. For example, most inspections of food manufacturing facilities and warehouses are intended to determine if products have been processed, packed, or held under insanitary conditions whereby they may have been contaminated with filth, rendered injurious to health, or are otherwise unfit for consumption. For drugs, medical devices, and biologicals, FDA inspections evaluate the adequacy of controls used to ensure the identity, strength, quality, or purity of such products, and to verify that they are in conformance with applicable compendia.

When FDA detects violative conditions or practices during its inspections, evidence is collected to support recommendations for regulatory sanctions against individuals, companies, and/or products, when deemed necessary. Evidence may be in the form of direct observations by investigators, copies of production and control records, and reports to prove violations of laws and regulations, as well as shipping records to prove the connection with interstate commerce necessary to establish federal jurisdiction. Sometimes, samples of products or extraneous material are collected for analysis to support inspection findings.

Inspections that detect significant violations, such as insanitary conditions or noncompliance with current Good Manufacturing Practice (cGMP) regulations, may lead FDA to initiate legal proceedings to effect corrective actions, or to punish responsible persons. Before proceeding to litigation, however, FDA frequently will (but not necessarily) issue a warning letter to advise management of the nature of the violations and the applicable sections of the law that the agency is prepared to invoke against the company or individual. When such warnings are ineffective, or if conditions are egregious or pose imminent health hazards, FDA may initiate formal administrative or judicial actions such as seizures, criminal prosecutions or civil monetary penalties, temporary restraining orders, or permanent injunctions to prevent continued distribution of violative products in interstate commerce.

FDA authority to conduct inspections is derived from section 704 of the FDCA (21 U.S.C. § 374), which defines the conditions under which FDA may conduct its inspections. Inspections may extend to a factory, warehouse, laboratory, or other establishment that manufactures, processes, packs, or holds foods, drugs, devices, and cosmetics. Inspections may encompass facilities, records, finished or unfinished products, files, papers, records, and other documents. Regulations that are relevant to FDA inspections or cGMPs include the following:

FDA authority to conduct inspections is derived from the FDCA, which defines the conditions under which FDA may conduct its inspections.

- food-related regulations, including infant formulas (21 C.F.R. Part 106);
- low-acid canned food (21 C.F.R. Part 113) and food (GMPs) (21 C.F.R. Part 110);
- human and veterinary finished pharmaceuticals, including GMP regulations (21 C.F.R. Parts 210 and 211);
- medical devices (21 C.F.R. Part 820) and quality system regulations;
- and biologicals, such as biological products (21 CFR Part 600) and blood and blood components (21 C.F.R. Part 606).

GMP regulations for drugs, biologics, and devices are binding, and have the force and effect of law. The general food GMPs found at 21 C.F.R.

Part 110 are interpretive and serve as guidance to the food industry. FDA has not promulgated GMPs for the cosmetics industry.

FDA Inspection Authority

Federal Food, Drug, and Cosmetic Act

FDAMA amended the provisions of the FDCA and the biological provisions of the Public Health Service Act, including a number of sections that deal with FDA inspection authority.

The FDCA is the principal law that provides FDA authority to conduct factory inspections. It provides FDA with the authority to inspect any factory, warehouse, or establishment in which foods, drugs, devices, or cosmetics are manufactured, processed, packed, or held for introduction into interstate commerce (or after such introduction). The FDCA also defines prohibited acts and provides for regulatory and administrative sanctions that enable FDA to bring noncomplying companies or persons into compliance with the law. The Food and Drug Administration Modernization Act of 1997 (FDAMA) amended the provisions of the FDCA and the biological provisions of the Public Health Service Act, including a number of sections that deal with FDA inspection authority (such as new provisions that extend FDA's authority to have access to records for over-the-counter (OTC) drugs).

The following chapters of the FDCA are relevant to the FDA inspection process:

Chapter	Topic
III	Defines what acts are prohibited and provides for certain administrative and criminal sanctions (penalties)
IV	Provides the basic definition of what constitutes adulteration and misbranding for foods
V	Defines adulteration and misbranding for drugs
VI	Defines adulteration and misbranding for cosmetics
VII	Establishes FDA authority to conduct inspections
VIII	Provides requirements for imports and exports

FDA's General Inspection Authority

Chapter VII of the FDCA confers general inspection authority on FDA. It authorizes duly accredited FDA personnel to enter and inspect certain types of regulated facilities at "...reasonable times, and within reasonable limits and in a reasonable manner. ..." The specifics of what constitutes a "reasonable time" are not defined in the statute, but precedents exist that establish that a "reasonable time" is any time regulated activities are being conducted. Other specifics of the "reasonableness standard" have been the subject of debate for many years, such as whether the agency has statutory authority to take photographs during inspections.

In 1952, the Supreme Court ruled that the factory inspection provisions of the 1938 FDCA were too vague to be enforced as criminal law (*United States v. Cardiff*). As a result, Congress passed the Factory Inspection Amendments in 1953 to provide clarification to the 1938 act. These amendments provided for FDA to present manufacturers with a written notice of inspection at the beginning of an inspection, and written reports of observations at the conclusion of the inspection. The amendments also required FDA to provide written receipts for samples, as well as reports of analysis for certain types of samples (FDCA § 704). The provision for a written report of observations at the conclusion of an inspection forms the basis for today's Form FDA-483.

Upon initiating an inspection, FDA personnel must display appropriate credentials and give the owner, operator or agent in charge a written notice of inspection.

Upon initiating an inspection, FDA personnel must display appropriate credentials and give to ". . .the owner, operator or agent in charge. . ." a written *notice of inspection*. For this purpose, the agency uses the Notice of Inspection, Form FDA-482.

Section 704 of the FDCA confers to FDA specific authority to conduct inspections of any factory, warehouse, or establishment where food, drugs, devices, or cosmetics are manufactured, processed, packed, or held for introduction into interstate commerce (or after such introduction). For prescription and OTC drugs and restricted medical devices, the inspection authority generally extends to all things having a bearing on whether the products have been manufactured, processed, packed, or held under conditions whereby they may become adulterated or misbranded within the meaning of the law, or which may not be manufactured, introduced into interstate commerce, or sold. For this special category of products, the law grants access to all records, files, papers, processes, controls, and facilities that have a bearing on adulteration or misbranding. The act specifically exempts from FDA inspection certain types of information including financial, sales, and pricing (other than shipment data), research data, and certain personnel data unless such information directly has a bearing on whether a product may be adulterated, misbranded, or otherwise in violation of applicable laws or regulations. Notably, this exception does not apply to research data relating to new drugs that are subject to reporting and inspection under regulations issued pursuant to the new drug provisions of the FDCA, such as under sections 505(i) or (k), 507(d), and others.

For new drugs and medical devices and for licensed biological products, FDA must act on requests for regulatory approvals (including but not limited to NDAs, abbreviated new drug applications (ANDAs), PMAs for devices, biologic license applications (BLAs), and other similar submissions). FDA decisions are based upon information and data contained in applications submitted by sponsors. To verify the accuracy and completeness (integrity) of such information and data relative to pending or approved applications, FDA has authority to access both facilities (on-site inspections) and records. Failure to allow access to records to which FDA is entitled is a prohibited act under section 301 of the FDCA and a refusal may cause the agency to obtain an administrative inspection warrant to compel such access.

With the FDA pre-approval inspection (PAI) program, FDA investigators routinely request access to new drug and biologic development records. The same is true for medical device design history files, which are mandated by the Quality System Regulation (QSR). FDA investigators expect access to records that are retained by personnel with "research" functions or responsibilities if the data support product applications. FDA generally will not be persuaded that access is not permitted because testing performed represents "discovery" rather than "developmental" research.

There are exemptions from inspection that are provided by statute. Section 704(a)(2) of the FDCA states that FDA authority does not include access to records and facilities that manufacture prescription drugs and restricted devices in four specific instances: 1) pharmacies that are in conformance with local laws (provided their activities are limited to dispensing and selling drugs or devices at retail); 2) practitioners who are licensed by law to prescribe or administer drugs (or use devices) if the manufacture or processing is for use in the course of their professional practice; 3) persons who manufacture such products solely for use in teaching, research, or chemical analysis where such products are not for sale; and 4) any other class of person as designated by FDA by regulation.

Upon completion of an inspection, FDA personnel must leave a written report with the owner, operator, or agent in charge.

Section 704(b) requires that FDA, upon completion of an inspection, leave with the owner, operator, or agent in charge a written report that identifies "any conditions or practices or practices observed by him which, in his judgment, indicate any food, drug, device or cosmetic in such establishment" is in violation of the adulteration provisions of FDCA. As previously noted, FDA generally records its observations on a form known as an FDA-483 (List of Inspectional Observations). While the statute itself only mandates that a report be issued for adulteration-related observations, FDA has for many years included other inspection-related observations on the form as a matter of policy. Certain exceptions are described in Chapter 5 of FDA's *Investigations Operations Manual*, which is available at http://www.fda.gov.

When FDA collects a physical sample during the course of an inspection, a written receipt for samples must be provided to the owner, operator, or agent in charge. Such receipt (FDA Form FDA-484) must be issued upon completion of the inspection before leaving the premises. In the case of food samples collected during an inspection, FDA is required by section 704(d) to provide a written report on any sample analyzed for evidence of being filthy, putrid, or decomposed. This provision applies only to foods and does not extend to samples of drugs, devices, or cosmetics that are collected during FDA inspections, nor does it apply to results of analysis for factors other than filth or decomposition.

FDA employees authorized to conduct inspections, while acting in the course of their official duties, are authorized to possess controlled substances as per 21 C.F.R. § 1301.24(a)(1) and other sections; e.g., 21 C.F.R. § 1309.26(a)(1). This permits FDA investigators to collect samples of controlled substances during inspections and other special assignments. The Form FDA-484 prepared by the FDA investigator, however, must contain FDA's Drug Enforcement Administration (DEA) Registration Number and that of the establishment from which the products are obtained. All other inventory controls required by DEA regulations apply to FDA and to anyone providing samples of controlled substances to an FDA investigator.

For many years, controversies have persisted about the legal requirements for process validation in the GMPs, and their application to research and development activities. While there may be some "gray areas" between "pure research" and new drug development activities, firms should expect FDA to routinely request access to the records supporting process validity. While some firms have been reluctant to provide FDA access to drug development records based on the erroneous assumption that FDA is not entitled to "research" data, the FDCA provides FDA with authority to access and copy records and reports required under the new drug provisions. Drug development involves a continuum from "pure" research activities (i.e., discovery related) through transition phases where the activities clearly have a bearing on GMP or validation issues. Therefore, the statutory exemption from access to research data should be considered applicable only until the point when the data is intended to be used in support of an application for FDA approval to permit use of the new drug or medical device in clinical trials (and beyond). At that stage in the development process, the research data that forms the basis of claims made in the relevant submission may be subject to review during FDA inspections. Correspondingly, research data that is not relevant to any current submission to the agency would be considered exempt from inspection, because it has no bearing on the status of any marketed product nor on the validity of any submission to FDA.

While there may be some "gray areas" between "pure research" and new drug development activities, firms should expect FDA to routinely request access to the records supporting process validity.

For drug manufacturers located outside the United States, there is no specific statutory authority for FDA to conduct factory inspections. FDA has an active international inspection program, and inspections are conducted routinely in various parts of the world. While strictly speaking, foreign inspections are voluntary; firms that refuse to allow FDA inspection may find that FDA will invoke administrative sanctions, such as preventing the importation of the company's products into the United States under provisions of section 801. Another potential sanction is the withholding of NDA or ANDA approvals, as well as approval of other regulatory submissions that are made by that firm or by a sponsor who lists the firm in their application(s). When FDA inspections of drug or device manufacturers reveal insanitary conditions or practices that do not conform to current GMP or QSR regulations, FDA may invoke administrative sanctions that result in refusal to permit entry into the United States.

Current Good Manufacturing Practices Concepts

The 1962 Drug Amendments granted FDA authority to promulgate regulations and added a provision that required companies to comply with "current good manufacturing practices."

The 1962 Drug Amendments added two important sections that are relevant to FDA inspections. FDA was granted authority to promulgate regulations and a provision was added that required companies to comply with "current good manufacturing practices" (FDCA § 501(a)(2)(B)). Although the law did not define what constituted "current good manufacturing practices," the act was amended to allow FDA to publish regulations to define its requirements and expectations. FDA published its interpretation of cGMPs in 1963 (currently 21 C.F.R. Parts 210, 211 for human and veterinary drug products, and 21 C.F.R. Parts 225, 226 for medicated premixes and medicated feeds for animals).

The following are examples of the key regulations that had been promulgated to define cGMPs for specific commodities.

- *Foods*—The low-acid canned food regulations (21 C.F.R. Part 113) and the companion rules for acidified food (21 C.F.R. Part 114) were issued as a consequence of a number of botulism outbreaks that occurred during the 1960s and 1970s involving food products packaged in hermetically sealed containers. These regulations define the minimum requirements and controls necessary to ensure such products are processed in a manner that ensures they are safe.
- *Devices*—The Quality System Regulation (QSR) (21 C.F.R. Part 820) defines cGMP for medical device facilities. The QSR applies to the methods, facilities, and controls that are used during the design and manufacture (including packaging, labeling, storage, installation, and servicing).
- *cGMPs for Finished Pharmaceuticals*—These were promulgated in 1963 and have been updated a number of times over the years (usually in reaction to incidents or problems) (21 C.F.R. Part 211). In 2007, FDA issued a Direct Final Rule to amend the drug GMPs in an effort

to modernize the requirements and to better harmonize with regulatory authorities in foreign countries; as of this writing, the date for comments had passed but the effective date had not been reached. The cGMPs describe the minimum FDA requirements for conforming to the cGMP requirements of the FDCA.

FDA published the cGMP regulations as being legally binding requirements; i.e., they define the minimum cGMP that must be followed for the production and control of finished pharmaceuticals. The cGMPs describe the minimum FDA requirements for conforming to the current good manufacturing practices that are cited in the FDCA. Although the cGMPs are substantive, they do not spell out in detail how firms are expected to satisfy the requirements.

The cGMPs are considered broad "umbrella" regulations in that they apply to all finished pharmaceuticals for humans and animals. The language of the regulation is broad enough to describe the requirements for all dosage forms (tablets, capsules, oral liquids, topicals, transdermals, parenterals, etc.), and the requirements apply to both prescription and OTC drugs. Because they apply across the board to all finished drug products, the regulation contains ample use of subjective terms (such as adequate, appropriate, sufficient, and others).

The cGMPs are considered broad "umbrella" regulations in that they apply to all finished pharmaceuticals for humans and animals.

- *Drug Regulations* (21 C.F.R. Parts 300-499)—FDA has promulgated extensive regulations covering many of the administrative details concerning procedures that must be followed when submitting NDAs to FDA. These sections contain detailed requirements for filing NDAs, as well as the requirements for various drug products. The requirements for submissions for postapproval change have been effected directly by FDAMA, which added section 506A to the FDCA. The major effects of this section on FDA inspections are the statutory requirement to validate postapproval changes, and the subdivision of supplements into four principal types: Pre-approval supplement; Changes Being Effected (thirty days); Changes Being Effected (immediate), and Annual Report submissions. This is quite similar to the previous scheme except for the addition of the Changes Being Effected (thirty days) provision. Manufacturers filing this type of submission must wait thirty days before implementing the change, to allow FDA an opportunity to review the change and comment (or object).

New drugs that are intended to be administered to humans or animals must be manufactured in accordance with the cGMP regulations, and the NDAs must certify conformance. If production is done in laboratory research facilities or pilot plant production facilities, the procedures may be different from those used in full-scale production facilities. NDAs must include detailed descriptions of manufacturing and control procedures. If changes are made from NDA commitments, it may be necessary to obtain prior approval from FDA or to notify FDA following the change.

- *Applications for FDA Approval to Market a New Drug or Antibiotic* (21 C.F.R. Part 314)—This section describes requirements for NDAs and various administrative actions followed by the agency for reviewing and approving applications.

- *Other Postmarketing Reports* (21 C.F.R. § 314.81)—FDA inspections frequently are triggered as a result of firms filing an NDA Field Alert as provided for by this section. Applicants are required to submit, within three working days of receipt, information about products that: 1) involve any incident that causes a drug product or its labeling to be mistaken for another (e.g., label mix-up), 2) failure of a distributed product to meet specifications listed in applications, or 3) significant change or deterioration of the drug product (such as physicochemical deterioration or microbiological contamination).

During postapproval inspections, FDA inspection teams review the content of NDAs and the annual reports to compare actual conditions at the facility against commitments.

- *Annual Report* (21 C.F.R. § 314.81)—Sponsors holding approved NDAs must file annual reports. During postapproval inspections, FDA inspection teams review the content of NDAs and the annual reports to compare actual conditions at the facility against commitments. FDA investigators will verify that annual reports have been filed, and that information contained in them is accurate and complete for significant new information. Such information includes summaries about any matter that may affect the safety, efficacy, or labeling including summaries of actions taken in response to new information or intentions to take actions such as supplements, new warnings, or initiate new studies. FDA may verify that annual reports contain distribution data showing the quantity of the drug product distributed and summary of labeling changes made, as well as copies of representative package labels, inserts, etc. FDA will be alert for the presence or absence of reports of new information about experiences, investigations, studies, or tests that involve physical, chemical, or microbiological properties that may affect FDA conclusions about the safety or effectiveness of the drug. Finally, FDA will review documentation about any changes to manufacturing and controls that do not require submissions of supplements under Part 314.70 and the various other summaries that are related to nonclinical and clinical studies.

- *Drug Master Files* (21 C.F.R. § 314.420)—A Drug Master File (DMF) is a submission to FDA that may be used to provide confidential detailed information about facilities, processes, or articles used in the manufacturing, processing, packaging, and storing of one or more human drugs. The submission of a DMF is not required by law or FDA regulation, and a DMF is not a substitute for an IND application, NDA, ANDA, or export application. There is no process whereby a DMF is "approved" or disapproved by FDA. During the conduct of preapproval inspections (PAIs) FDA inspection teams frequently review copies of applicable DMFs that relate to containers, closures, and facilities. FDA will carefully compare commitments made in DMFs (such as specifications, test methods, release limits, and the like) against the corresponding specifications, methods, or release limits that are in place at the user firm. If discrepancies are noted, this may result in an FDA citation.

Five DMFs and the rules for submitting them are listed in 21 C.F.R. § 314.420:

- Type I (now rescinded), see below
- Type II covers drug substances, drug substance intermediates, and material used in their preparation.
- Type III covers packaging material, including toxicological data on these materials, if such data is not otherwise available.
- Type IV covers excipients, colorants, flavors, essences, or materials used in their preparation, including toxicological data.
- Type V covers "accepted reference information," which does not fit any of the above categories. FDA actively discourages this type of DMF. If a firm desires to submit one, prior consultation with FDA is required.

In January 2000, FDA announced a revision of the regulation governing DMFs. FDA removed the provision for submitting Type I DMFs (which formerly covered facilities, operating procedures, and personnel) and the agency no longer permits information submitted in a Type I DMF to be incorporated by reference in IND applications, NDAs, ANDAs, or amendments or supplements to any of these. FDA's stated intention is to eliminate submissions of information that is not needed for FDA to conduct its inspections of manufacturing facilities or is not needed for its review on the chemistry, manufacturing, and controls sections of applications (such as INDs, NDAs, and ANDAs). The effective date of this change was July 10, 2000.

- *Bioavailability and Bioequivalence* (21 C.F.R. Part 320)—This section describes FDA expectations and procedures for determining the bioavailability or bioequivalence of drug products. Companies submitting full or abbreviated NDAs are required to submit evidence demonstrating bioavailability of the drug product or to request a waiver from the bioavailability requirement. The regulation describes changes reported in supplements for which bioavailability studies may be required, such as changes in manufacturing process that alter product formulation or strength beyond variations permitted in the approved application, or labeling changes, or the establishment of a new dosage regimen. This section also describes FDA requirements for requesting a waiver from bioavailability or bioequivalence testing requirements.

- *Biological Product Regulations* (21 C.F.R. Parts 600-680)—Used by FDA for the enforcement of section 351 of the Public Health Service Act, these regulations are similar in content to the drug GMP regulations. Licensing provisions and procedures for Establishment License Applications (ELAs) and Product License Applications (PLAs) are described as

Biological Product Regulations are similar in content to the drug GMP regulations.

are the establishment standards for manufacturing whole blood for transfusions, blood components, and blood derivatives.

Preparing for an Inspection

Inspections are conducted generally by FDA investigators, most of who are assigned to one of FDA's district offices.

Inspections are conducted generally by FDA investigators, most of who are assigned to one of FDA's district offices. Investigators may be assisted by laboratory analysts, engineers, microbiologists, FDA headquarters technical experts, and other specialists. Each district office bears responsibility for inspecting the regulated companies located within its geographic boundaries. FDA also performs inspections abroad for products that are intended to be shipped into the United States.

Each district office maintains files of previous inspection reports, communications with industry, and the results of sample testing. Before performing an inspection, the FDA team usually will review these records to determine whether previous inspections have encountered significant discrepancies or violations. If previous inspections have found problems, the follow-up inspection will assess the adequacy of corrective actions. For pharmaceutical, biologic, and medical device inspections, preparation also may include the review of product approval applications to determine compliance with commitments made to the agency. Previously issued FDA-483s are usually reviewed prior to each inspection, as are the associated narrative Establishment Inspection Reports (EIRs). The inspection team will be alert for patterns and trends that reflect evidence of continuing noncompliance, and/or issues that may suggest potential problems in areas not covered previously.

FDA inspection team members also will review appropriate regulatory standards for the facility to be inspected. For example, the team may utilize applicable compendia, such as the U.S. Pharmacopoeia or National Formulary; relevant trade association guidelines; documents that may constitute industry standards; the *Investigations Operations Manual,* which guides the investigators in procedural matters; and the *Compliance Program Guidance Manual*, which contains several hundred documents that describe inspection procedures for particular industries. While FDA investigators may use industry guidelines and standards as references, they cannot impose them as legal requirements.

When preparing for an FDA inspection of a company that has multiple sites, FDA offices often will coordinate their activities to determine whether violations suggest a larger systemic problem. When FDA finds repeated violations at multiple sites for a single company, the agency may consider taking stronger, corporate-wide measures, including the issuance of injunctions.

FDA Inspection Techniques

During a typical FDA inspection, one or more FDA investigators arrive unannounced at a facility. FDA inspections may be as short as a few hours or last several weeks or months depending on the purpose. A typical inspection of a food processing facility may last for a few days and a complex inspection of a pharmaceutical manufacturer may require more than two weeks. If FDA detects significant objectionable conditions, the inspection may be extended as necessary.

FDA inspection approaches vary considerably depending on the type of product manufactured at the facility. Typically inspections of food manufacturers concentrate on basic sanitation and employee practices. For example, FDA will examine warehouse areas for evidence of rodents, insects, or other vermin, and will observe manufacturing equipment and employee practices for evidence of inadequate cleaning or insanitary employee practices. FDA also is alert for conditions that may lead to food safety issues, such as conditions that may promote microbiological growth in food products, or unsafe handling of insecticides, cleaning agents, and other hazardous materials.

The scope of the inspection will depend upon the purpose of the inspection, the type of product (which determines the applicable regulations), any special concerns such as current complaints, and other factors. For example, FDA inspections of pharmaceutical manufacturers usually include examinations of the facilities and personnel for basic sanitation. In addition, FDA will examine manufacturing and control records to verify conformance with applicable GMPs. Drug products must be manufactured according to manufacturing instructions that have been reviewed and double-checked by at least two persons. The weighing and addition of ingredients must be verified by at least two persons, and personnel must record each significant step in the manufacturing and control operations. Appropriate "in-process" inspections and tests are required to ensure products meet specifications, and before any batch can be released, it must be tested against predetermined specifications. The GMP regulations specify the types of records that must be maintained and the document retention requirements. FDA investigators will examine laboratory facilities and laboratory control records to ensure that appropriate records are being maintained and that test methods are suitable for the intended use. Before any batch can be released it must be tested according to an approved method and if a product is covered by an official compendial monograph (such as the U.S. Pharmacopoeia), it must be tested against this standard.

The scope of the inspection will depend upon the purpose of the inspection, the type of product, any special concerns such as current complaints, and other factors.

A major focus of recent FDA drug and device inspections has been the review of product process validation, as well as the activities surrounding the development of drug formulations and the design of medical devices. FDA expects firms to provide adequate assurances that drugs have the identity, strength, quality, and purity characteristics that they purport or are represented to possess. When pre-approval inspections detect application integrity problems or noncompliance with GMPs, FDA may withhold approval of pending product applications.

During FDA inspections, the team will review records covering the manufacturing and testing of all batches made to date, and the documents that establish the firm is capable of consistently producing a product that meets predetermined specifications (i.e., verify that processes are validated). If early development activities are found by FDA to be deficient or not well documented, firms may not be in a position to justify the validity of their conclusions about the safety and effectiveness of their drug product.

Recent Inspection Trends

For many years, FDA inspectors have adopted a "quality system" approach, as opposed to the more traditional facility- or product-oriented approach. FDA has an established methodology for use of this approach in medical device inspections, known as the Quality System Inspection Technique (QSIT). The QSIT approach is now standard for medical device inspections that focus on compliance with the Quality System Regulation, 21 C.F.R. Part 820.

FDA applies a quality system approach—as opposed to the more traditional facility- or product-oriented approach—to medical device, pharmaceutical, and biologic inspections.

Since 2002, FDA has also applied a quality system approach to pharmaceutical and biologic inspections. FDA has adopted a six-system definition for purposes of inspection as follows:

1. The *Quality System* includes a wide variety of areas that involve how the company manages its quality operations. Included here are nonconformance investigations, the responsibilities and authority of the Quality Unit, the requirement for annual review of product quality performance, and other overall quality management functions.
2. The *Facilities and Equipment System*, which, as the name implies, involves evaluation of the adequacy of the environment and equipment used to produce drugs and biologics.
3. The *Materials System*, which includes evaluation of components, containers and closures, packaging and finishing materials, etc.
4. The *Production System*, which includes review of the controls used to keep manufacturing operations running in compliance with GMP.
5. The *Packaging and Labeling System*, which again as the name implies, involves evaluation of controls to assure that products are properly packaged and carry the correct labels and associated labeling.

6. The *Laboratory Controls System*, which involves evaluation of the procedures, controls, and methods used in the laboratory for the analysis of materials, in process and finished products.

Associated training, change control, and records pertinent to each of the systems are reviewed within the context of the systems themselves.

The quality system approach currently used by FDA differs slightly depending on whether the product is a drug (generally regulated by the Center for Drug Evaluation and Research (CDER)) or a biologic (generally regulated by the Center for Biologics Evaluation and Research (CBER)). Both CDER and CBER have issued compliance programs to FDA Field Offices describing how the quality system approach is to be used for the products they regulate. Both compliance programs (7356.002, "Drug Manufacturing Inspections" and 7345.848, "Inspection of Biological Drug Products") provide for either an abbreviated or comprehensive approach, depending on the history of the company, current concerns, and findings of the inspection. The reader is referred to the cited compliance programs, available at http://www.fda.gov, for further details.

Two Controversial Inspection Issues: Photography and Affidavits

Photography During Inspections

FDA has for many years taken the position that photography is sometimes necessary to a reasonable inspection, and therefore is "just another evidence gathering tool" authorized under the general "reasonableness" standard of section 704 of the FDCA. Industry, however, often takes the position that because the law does not specifically authorize photography, FDA has no right to take photographs, and company policies often state that FDA personnel will not be allowed to take photographs.

FDA has for many years taken the position that photography is sometimes necessary to a reasonable inspection.

FDA's *Investigations Operations Manual* provides the following instructions to investigators in the event they need to take photographs:

> Do not request permission from management to take photographs during an inspection. Take your camera into the firm and use it as necessary just as you use other inspectional equipment. If management objects to taking photographs, explain that photos are an integral part of an inspection and present an accurate picture of plant

> conditions. Advise management the U. S. Courts have held that photographs may lawfully be taken as part of an inspection.

The reference goes on to cite two court cases in support of the agency's position. Whether these cases truly support FDA's position, however, remains contested and this debate continues, remaining unsettled at this writing.

In practice, FDA rarely takes photographs except during food inspections, most commonly to show gross insanitary conditions. It is possible, however, during any inspection that the agency may proceed to take photographs. If companies refuse to permit photography, there is a risk that FDA may go to court (ex parte) to seek an administrative inspection warrant to compel the inspected company to allow photography. FDA has been successful in obtaining such warrants, and has also included provisions mandating photography during inspections in consent decree settlements.

An approach used by some companies is to allow limited photography, provided the agency personnel is willing to wait for the company to obtain a camera so that identical photos can be taken by company personnel. Circumstances under which the authors believe companies may be well justified to refuse photography include the presence of volatile vapors that might explode in the presence of electrostatic discharge, or where camera flashes might create a hazard to operators of dangerous equipment or pose a risk of malfunction of sensors. The final decision as to whether to allow photography during an inspection should be made in concert with legal counsel.

Affidavits

FDA investigators are trained to prepare affidavits to link evidence collected to documents that establish the connection with interstate commerce which is necessary for FDA to establish jurisdiction. Such affidavits may be written and provided to company personnel with a request that personnel sign them. There is no statutory mandate requiring company personnel to sign these affidavits. Here again, the decision whether to sign is one best made by counsel after consideration of all the facts. In the experience of the authors, however, the majority of companies have policies that require company personnel not to read, agree to, nor sign affidavits prepared by FDA personnel during inspections. FDA personnel are familiar with policies and are not likely to be upset by company personnel refusals to sign.

The majority of companies have policies that require company personnel not to read, agree to, nor sign affidavits prepared by FDA personnel during inspections.

FDA-483s

The stated purpose of the List of Inspectional Observations (Form FDA-483) is to cite observations concerning filth, insanitary conditions, or danger to health. In practice, however, FDA reports a wide variety of inspectional observations on the FDA-483, including deviations from approved protocols in clinical trials, recordkeeping problems, deviations from GMPs, and many other general observations related to inspection findings.

The reverse side of the FDA-483 states a dual purpose: 1) for the purposes required by statute and 2) to assist firms to comply with the provisions of the act. The latter category accounts for the majority of FDA-483 observations. Following each inspection, the FDA team prepares an Establishment Inspection Report (EIR) that describes observations made during the inspection and includes exhibits to support findings (including photographs, production and control documents, records of interstate commerce, etc.). The EIR is reviewed and endorsed by district personnel. Reports that are endorsed as violative are referred to district management for a decision about appropriate compliance action(s). When necessary the case is forwarded to the appropriate FDA headquarters center for final review and disposition.

Hosting FDA Inspections

This section describes some of the important points that companies should consider when hosting inspections conducted by FDA employees. It includes information about the types of FDA employees who usually conduct inspections and the logistical issues associated with hosting an inspection. Also described are some commonsense etiquette issues (i.e., "do's and don'ts"), as well as methods to deal with requests that are outside the scope of FDA's inspection authority.

Types of Employees Who Conduct FDA Inspections

Inspections are conducted by FDA investigators, chemists, microbiologists, engineers, and various scientists having specialized education and training.

FDA employees who conduct inspections have a wide variety of backgrounds. Inspections are conducted by FDA investigators, chemists, microbiologists, engineers, and various scientists having specialized education and training. Every employee who participates in an inspection must possess official FDA credentials and must properly display them to an appropriate official of the company at the beginning of each inspection. Each FDA employee is required by law to present a written notice to the owner, operator, or agent in charge before beginning an inspection. FDA uses the "Notice of Inspection" (Form FDA-482) to provide this notice.

The titles of FDA employees who conduct inspections may vary. Each of the more common titles, with a brief description of the duties, follows:

The titles of FDA employees who conduct inspections may vary and include:

- *Consumer Safety Officer*
- *Commissioned Corps Officer*
- *Consumer Safety Inspector*
- *Analyst*
- *Special Agent, Office of Criminal Investigations*

- *Consumer Safety Officer (CSO)*—This is an official job title for personnel management purposes within FDA, and some employees may identify themselves using the CSO job title. The employees who identify themselves as "investigators" are usually CSOs, although several other specialized positions exist in the CSO job series. For example, also included are the following "functional" titles: Investigator, Compliance Officer, Reviewer, Program Analyst, Small Business Representative, Interstate Travel Sanitation Specialist, Sanitarian, Shellfish Specialist, Food Service Specialist, and others. Various FDA headquarters-based personnel who sometimes participate in inspections are also included in the CSO job series.
- *Commissioned Corps Officers*—Commissioned officers of the U.S. Public Health Service are on assignment to the agency in a variety of positions, including as investigators. These employees may provide one of the titles given above for CSO positions, or may use their military title as a member of the commissioned corps, such as Commander, Captain, etc. Commissioned corps officers hold the same status and authority as civil service FDA employees.
- *Consumer Safety Inspector (CSI)*—The CSI is a para-professional level position. CSIs carry out such activities as collecting samples and inspecting warehouses. Many CSIs operate exclusively in import-related activities, mainly collecting samples of products offered for importation at the point of entry into U.S. commerce. CSIs usually identify themselves by that title, but may use the title of "Inspector."
- *Analyst*—An analyst normally works in FDA laboratories, but occasionally may participate in on-site inspections. Functional job titles include chemist, microbiologist, biologist, or entomologist. Infrequently, certain para-professional laboratory personnel, such as physical science technicians, may assist on inspections. Laboratory personnel occasionally conduct inspections alone, but normally they are present to assist the investigators with laboratory portions of more complex inspections.
- *Special Agent, Office of Criminal Investigations (OCI)*—Special Agents rarely take part in regulatory inspections. If a special agent from OCI is participating in an FDA inspection, his or her presence would provide a signal that the inspection has a special or unusual purpose. Companies that are visited by special agents should consider this to

be highly unusual, and should consider seeking the advice and assistance of legal counsel. Special agents have full police powers, including the right to carry firearms and make arrests. A special agent, however, may be assigned to accompany an investigator on an inspection as part of his or her on-the-job training or orientation to agency operations. Companies should ask for and expect to be provided with a full and complete explanation about the purpose of a special agent's presence during a regulatory inspection.

Logistics While an Inspection Is in Progress

A trained person should act as escort for FDA personnel during the course of the inspection. For complex industries, it is advisable to have multiple persons who can fill this role. There may be multiple FDA staff present for the inspection, and an escort should be available for each FDA employee. One or more persons should be designated to act as scribe to maintain an accurate transcript of questions, answers, and any significant discussions about issues, concerns, or corrective actions reported to FDA.

There may be multiple FDA staff present for the inspection, and an escort should be available for each FDA employee.

The person(s) serving as scribe should not be the designated escort. The escort should not be burdened by trying to take notes while meeting the needs of FDA personnel (such as monitoring FDA activities and responding to requests from the investigators). Written policies or procedures should be prepared in advance, describing how inspections are to be handled by the firm. The policy or procedure should include, but not be limited to, the company's position on such matters as access to areas of the company, photography, affidavits, collection of samples, providing copies of documents, and granting FDA requests for interviews with company employees.

A conference room or office should be set aside for FDA's use during the inspection, as needed. This facilitates review of the large number of documents that may be requested by FDA. The location of the conference room may be near document storage areas, photocopying resources, or production areas depending on the inspection objectives. For lengthy inspections (several weeks or longer) companies may wish to consider dedicated clerical support for the FDA team during the inspection.

A separate conference room should be available to serve as the company's command post for the inspection. This room should be near, but not too near, the room dedicated to FDA's use. It should be located in an area of the company not subject to inspection by FDA, such as administrative office space, to enable frank discussions to take place without risk of them being overheard by the investigators.

Companies are encouraged to have daily debriefing of all company personnel who were involved with FDA during the course of an inspection. Debriefings should include key issues covered by FDA, topics discussed, information provided, any allegations of violations made by the Investigators, corrective actions taken or promised, and any other significant issues.

After the inspection, the company should prepare its own final report, providing a permanent record of the inspection. The record furnishes the company's perspectives and is supported by original notes taken by company personnel during the inspection. Each company should establish a policy as to whether to keep permanent copies of the notes taken during an inspection. If notes are maintained, procedures should define how they are to be identified (signed and dated), how they will be preserved, and by whom. The benefits of having the notes available in the event of litigation must be weighed against any possible adverse consequences of maintaining potentially problematic information. The final decision on retention of original notes should be determined with advice of legal counsel.

Managing the Exit Discussion

At the conclusion of an inspection and prior to leaving the premises, FDA will issue a Form FDA-483, List of Inspectional Observations. By FDA policy, the inspection team will afford the inspected company an opportunity to present their views and ask questions during the exit discussion.

Some companies elect not to comment during the exit discussion, preferring to comment only in writing and after the fact.

While most companies will discuss the List of Observations with the FDA inspection team to better understand the basis for each observation, some companies elect not to comment during the exit discussion, preferring to comment only in writing and after the fact. Each company must decide the best strategy in this regard. Ultimately the decision whether or not to hold an exit discussion may depend on the advice of counsel. Opting not to have the exit discussion precludes an important opportunity to ensure FDA understands the company's position, and to ensure that the company understands the basis for FDA's findings. Even if the company does not agree, understanding FDA's position is critical for preparation of an appropriate response.

If a decision is made to participate in an exit discussion, among the objectives of the discussion should be the following, at a minimum:

- ensure a correct understanding of FDA's reason for citing items on the 483 (even if the company disagrees, a clear understanding will be essential to a good response);
- ensure that the facts stated on the 483 are accurate;

- ensure that the wording of the 483 is complete and not misleading (for instance, inadvertent omission of a word like "not" from a sentence may change the entire meaning); and
- request that FDA delete items from the 483 if the inspection team agrees they are inaccurate or erroneous. (FDA policy is to delete items that can be shown to be in error or not factually correct.)

Ensure that the right people are present for the discussion. Generally, this means senior management and subject matter experts for topics that were covered during the inspection. It is best to avoid having large numbers of people present who will not be contributing substantively to the discussion and those who have little or no authority to make commitments for the company.

It is important to decide in advance who will control the discussion from the company's perspective, and who will speak for the company regarding actions in response to the 483 and who may offer time lines for corrections. Care should be taken to avoid characterizing FDA's observations as "violations" or "deviations," instead simply refer to them as FDA-483 "items" or "citations."

The decision of whether or not to have counsel present for the exit discussion is best determined on a case-by-case basis. In the experience of the authors, most companies elect not to have counsel present unless there appears to be an imminent risk of enforcement action, or a significant dispute has arisen over FDA authority. The ultimate decision is best left to senior management in collaboration with counsel.

Etiquette Points for Dealing with FDA Investigators

The etiquette for dealing with FDA staff is fairly straightforward and is based on an understanding of FDA inspection authority, FDA policy for the conduct of inspections, the company's policy, and an understanding of FDA's ethical restrictions. FDA staff work under a very restrictive standard of ethical conduct, which is repeatedly and strongly reinforced over the course of their employment with the agency. The standard is one of avoidance of even an *appearance* of a conflict of interest. Therefore, it is inadvisable to offer anything of more than nominal value. Refreshments such as coffee, tea, or soft drinks are generally acceptable and will not be seen as inappropriate. The utmost care should be taken to avoid any offer that could be construed as a bribe or gratuity.

Utmost care should be taken by the company to avoid any offer to FDA inspectors that could be construed as a bribe or gratuity.

Requests Outside the Scope of FDA Authority

Historically, FDA has taken the position that during an inspection it may ask for any type of information, but will insist upon access only to statutorily mandated areas and information.

Historically, FDA has taken the position that during an inspection it may ask for any type of information, but will insist upon access only to statutorily mandated areas and information. In practice, FDA investigators will routinely request whatever information they believe they need, and will not, as a rule, take the initiative to explain to the company being inspected just which types of information must be provided versus information requested on a purely consensual basis. Historically, FDA has taken the position that it is the company's responsibility to know the difference.

For these reasons, FDA investigators may sometimes request access to areas or information that are outside the scope of the general inspection authority under section 704. The investigators usually will answer questions from the company if asked whether release of the information or access to the area is within the scope of section 704. Since it may be assumed, however, that the investigator's interests are served by obtaining the information on a consensual basis, caution and careful consideration are required before a company accedes to such a request.

There are cases where a company may decide to agree to such a request. For example, if an investigator asks about a company's annual volume of business (a common question), and such information is already a matter of public record, a company may decide that answering will serve to promote goodwill and honest communication while not disclosing information of a proprietary or damaging nature. The factors to be considered in deciding whether to supply information to FDA when the company is not legally required to do so include, among others:

- understanding the reason for FDA's request;
- an assessment of the potential adverse consequences of disclosure;
- an assessment of the benefits of cooperating with the inspector's request versus not cooperating; and
- an assessment of the ease with which the agency may be able to obtain the information from alternative sources, and whether the procedure of obtaining the information in that way might expose the company to questions at suppliers, customers, or others.

Note: *There is no statutory requirement or precedent that requires FDA to inform a company (or individual persons) of their rights during the context of an FDA inspection.* While companies have argued that FDA investigators should provide Miranda warnings or similar warnings to company officials (especially when the agency develops an awareness that the matter under investigation may be referred for criminal prosecution), courts have consistently found that Miranda warnings are not required in the context of an FDA inspection. The FDA *Investigations Operations Manual* instructs investigators to provide Miranda warnings only when the person being interviewed is in custody or under detention, and therefore is not free to leave.

Forms Commonly Used During FDA Inspections

FDA uses several forms for a wide variety of purposes during regulatory inspections. The forms are commonly referred to by either their name or their number. For example, the Notice of Inspection may be referred to as the "Notice of Inspection," the "Notice," the "FDA-482," or simply the "482." FDA employees and industry representatives use the terms interchangeably. The forms FDA-482, FDA-483, and FDA-484 are designed to comply with statutory requirements imposed on FDA by section 704 of the FDCA (see details below). The majority of the current content of section 704 of the FDCA was established through the Factory Inspection Amendments to the FDCA in 1953, with some subsequent modification by the 1997 FDAMA.

FDA-482, Notice of Inspection

This form is issued to the "owner, operator or agent in charge" of a facility at the beginning of an inspection. Its purpose is to comply with the provisions of section 704(a) of the FDCA that require that written notice be given before an inspection is undertaken. The form lists the name and address of the facility being inspected, and bears the signature(s) and typed or printed name(s) of the FDA employee(s) conducting the inspection. The form cites the sections of the law that grant inspection authority. In addition to the FDCA, the form cites authorities granted by other laws enforced by FDA, and therefore it is used for all inspections, regardless of which law is being enforced. This is convenient for the agency, because in many cases the inspection is in fact being conducted under authority granted by more than one statute. For example, an inspection of a licensed blood bank may be conducted under both the FDCA and section 351 of the Public Health Service Act.

Form FDA-482 cites authorities granted by other laws enforced by FDA, and therefore it is used for all inspections, regardless of which law is being enforced.

FDA-483, Inspectional Observations

This form is issued at the conclusion of the inspection in accordance with section 704(b) of the act. By law, the investigators must list those observations which, in their judgment, may indicate that a food, drug, medical device, or cosmetic processed, packed, or held on the inspected premises consists in whole or in part of a filthy, putrid, or decomposed substance, or has been prepared, packed, or held under insanitary conditions whereby it may have become contaminated. As previously described, the agency uses this form to cite a wide variety of observations, far beyond the scope of what is required by statute. Generally speaking, the form is used to list all potential violations that can be directly observed by the investigators. Certain exceptions exist for issues that generally involve suspected violations that cannot be easily established through inspection observations, such as the adequacy of label claims, status of a drug as a new drug, and other issues. The *Investigations Operations Manual,* Chapter 5, lists these exceptions.

This form is also used to list recordkeeping violations, GMP deviations, discrepancies noted in the review of clinical trial records, and a host of other conditions and practices that range far from its statutorily mandated use. If the FDA employee(s) believe it is necessary to re-initiate any part of the inspection after the FDA-483 has been issued, they will issue a new FDA-482 and another inspection will officially commence.

FDA-484, Receipt for Samples

This form is used to account for any physical evidence removed from the premises being inspected. Product samples (raw materials, in-process goods, and finished products) are listed on the FDA-484, as are samples of extraneous material that may be taken to document conditions observed during the inspection. Extraneous material may include live or dead insects, rodent filth, foreign material, spillage, residues, bacterial swabs, and so forth. Documentary evidence such as labels, copies of production records, invoices, and shipping records are not listed on the FDA-484.

Firms undergoing inspection should request that Form FDA-484 be issued daily when samples are collected, to keep management fully apprised of any materials leaving the premises.

Practices may vary as to the timing of issuance of the FDA-484. Some investigators will issue the form each day when samples are collected. Others will wait until the conclusion of the inspection and issue the form then, to cover all samples collected during the inspection. Firms undergoing inspection should request that the form be issued daily when samples are collected, to keep management fully apprised of any materials leaving the premises. The inspected firm also may elect to charge FDA for the materials taken, as they sometimes amount to a considerable value.

Controlled substances present a special case. FDA investigators and special agents are authorized to collect samples of controlled substances under DEA regulations. In these cases immediate completion of all required paperwork, including the FDA-484, is essential.

FDA-463, Affidavit

This form is often prepared by the inspecting FDA employee at the conclusion of an inspection. This form historically has been used primarily to document the connection with interstate commerce necessary to establish jurisdiction, but in recent years its use has expanded to serve as a vehicle to also document individual responsibility. The FDA employee may represent that the statements related to the individual employee job responsibility are intended to qualify the individual to make the statements that follow on the affidavit. Many FDA employees will refer to such statements to bolster other evidence of individual responsibility that has been gathered during the inspection.

Affidavits come in several forms, with individual form numbers. All have basically the same purpose. There are several fill-in-the-blank affidavits intended to serve common purposes, such as a "Dealer's Statement," "Warehouseman's Statement," affidavits for use with United Parcel Service shipments, and so forth. The FDA-463 is the most common one, however, and is simply a blank page with the necessary introductory wording preprinted on it with a space for the affiant's name and the name of the FDA employee taking the statement.

In regulatory inspections, FDA uses affidavits principally to establish linkage between evidence that is collected by investigators and the element of interstate commerce. Should the inspection lead to legal action and a trial, the agency's lawyers will subpoena the original records and call the affiant to testify, using the affidavit as a record of his or her prior statements.

In regulatory inspections, FDA uses affidavits principally to establish linkage between evidence that is collected by investigators and the element of interstate commerce.

Because company attorneys often advise their clients not to sign FDA affidavits, investigators are trained to read the affidavit out loud and ask if the statements are true. When a verbal affirmation is received, the investigator will so annotate the affidavit, and will secure a witnesses' signature if possible. The investigator will ask the proposed affiant why he or she is not willing to sign, and also will annotate the reason given. For this reason, many attorneys advise clients not to read or listen to the content of FDA affidavits. The decision of whether to read, sign, or verbally affirm an affidavit should be made based on advice of legal counsel. Experienced FDA investigators are accustomed to this response and will generally not press the matter further when they encounter refusals to sign or listen to the content of affidavits.

Other Forms

Other forms for special purposes may come into play during a regulatory inspection. Examples include facsimile forms used to make manual "true copies" of invoices or shipping documents; consumer complaint forms used by the agency to record complaints; the FDA-472, a special form of the FDA-484 issued to truck drivers or operators of other interstate conveyances; and various other special purpose forms such as checklists used to record inspectional observations.

FDA Policies and Administrative Procedures

The actions of FDA employees are directed by a variety of internal policies, procedures, guidelines, and guidance documents that are issued by FDA headquarters units.

The *Investigations Operations Manual* contains a wide range of information, from administrative matters to detailed instructions for preparing and routing of inspection reports. Instructions found in its chapters include instructions for filling out FDA forms and expense reports, and policies and guidance for how to effectively interact with company managers. This manual contains basic reference information that is used on a day-to-day basis by investigators.

The manual is of primary importance during litigation involving FDA inspections, because it defines the standard of conduct and procedures that FDA personnel are expected to follow during their day-to-day activities. The manual provides the basis of the presumption of official regularity in the performance of duty. Investigators are expected to justify and obtain approval for any deviation from established procedures outlined in the manual.

Most compliance programs are now available from FDA's Internet website and are valuable references for use in preparing for particular types of FDA inspections.

The *Compliance Program Guidance Manual* is a compilation of specific instructions for directed inspections of segments of the industries regulated by FDA. The manual is divided into chapters by industry. It serves as the primary document that guides the conduct of most inspections. Most compliance programs are now available from FDA's Internet website and are valuable references for use in preparing for particular types of FDA inspections.

FDA *Compliance Policy Guides* (CPGs) are internal policy documents. FDA describes issues and responses in simple policy statements, which field personnel use during their inspections to support their findings. Many CPGs establish informal internal action levels for analytical findings on regulatory samples. Others establish "direct reference" procedures, where the local FDA office can expedite the processing of regulatory actions by eliminating the need for technical or policy reviews by headquarters staff. If "direct reference" criteria are met, the district may initiate legal proceedings without the need for concurrence and prior approval by some of the usual reviewing offices in FDA headquarters. CPGs are not enforceable documents, because they have not been subjected to notice-and-comment rulemaking.

The *Regulatory Procedures Manual* is maintained by the Office of Enforcement within the Office of Regulatory Affairs (ORA). It addresses policies and procedures for processing regulatory actions by the field force. It also establishes standard format and provides certain standardized templates with language for pleadings in criminal and civil cases. In addition, the manual provides regulatory guidance in certain other nonlitigation matters, such as product recalls.

The *Investigations Training Manual* consists of a series of outlines used during the initial orientation/basic training program for new investigators. This manual provides training in the basic provisions of the FDCA and other laws enforced by FDA, and orientation to the major reference documents, programs, and procedures used by field personnel. The manual is used heavily by new investigators during their initial months on the job, but usually is not often referred to following completion of basic training.

FDA *Field Management Directives* (FMDs) are documents that address administrative and compliance matters dealt with by the field force. Most of the topics in these documents are of limited significance for inspections. Exceptions include FMDs on recall management, consumer complaints, and the classification of Establishment Inspection Reports.

FDA *Staff Manual Guides* are issued at the highest level of the agency, and are mainly human resources and financial management documents. They also contain formal delegations of authority, establish position names, describe procedures for the issuance of official credentials, and state policies involving ethical conduct and other matters which have bearing on regulatory inspections.

Inspection Technical Guides and their earlier versions known as *Inspection Bulletins* are produced and distributed by ORA. These documents are short, focused technical references on topics relevant to inspections.

Inspection Technical Guides *are short, focused technical references on topics relevant to inspections.*

All of the aforementioned manuals and publications are accessible from FDA's Internet website, http://www.fda.gov.

Product Recalls and Market Withdrawals

Recall is an effective method of removing or correcting consumer products that are in violation of laws administered by FDA.

With few exceptions, a product *recall* is a voluntary action to remove a product from channels of distribution. Manufacturers and distributors initiate recalls to protect the public from products that represent a risk of injury or gross deception, or are otherwise defective. A market *withdrawal* is removal of a product from the market where the violation is not severe enough to result in regulatory action by FDA if the product is not withdrawn. Product recalls and market withdrawals may frequently trigger inspections, or, if discovered for the first time during an inspection for another purpose, companies can expect FDA to direct significant attention to these activities. Therefore, an understanding of FDA's view of recall activities is a necessary predicate to good inspection management.

The FDCA authorizes FDA to order recalls of medical devices, under certain circumstances and subject to certain controls, but there is no similar authority for foods, drugs, or cosmetics. According to the document "FDA Recall Policies" found on FDA's website, "The Federal Food, Drug, and Cosmetic Act. . . does not generally authorize FDA to 'order' a manufacturer to recall a food, cosmetic or supplement. The agency may request a product recall if the firm is not willing to remove dangerous products from the market without FDA's written request. Only when a medical device, human tissue products, and infant formula pose a risk to human health. . . the law specifically authorizes FDA to prescribe a recall and to rule on the scope and extent of the same." In situations involving serious hazards to health, however, FDA often does *request* firms to take a recall action. Typically, in these instances, the request will be made under the signature of the Associate Commissioner for Regulatory Affairs and often will be hand delivered to a responsible official of the company, to underscore the agency's concern. If a company fails to respond to FDA's request for a recall, the agency must then rely on other measures, such as multiple seizure actions or injunctions, to remove the product from the market.

FDA's general policy about recalls is in 21 C.F.R. §§ 7.3 and 7.40-7.59. Removal of a product from channels of distribution is deemed to be a "recall" when 1) the product is not under the control of the recalling firm and 2) it is in violation of law to the extent that FDA would take action to remove it from distribution channels if it was not recalled. In most cases, firms will recall products voluntarily when these conditions are met. FDA classifies recalls as Class I, Class II, or Class III. The criteria for these classifications reflect the agency's assessment of the relative degree of health hazard represented by the reason for recall. The definitions of the three classification levels are as follows:

- *Class I* is a situation in which there is a reasonable probability that the use of, or exposure to, a violative product will cause serious adverse health consequences or death.
- *Class II* is a situation in which use of, or exposure to, a violative product may cause temporary or medically reversible adverse health consequences or where the probability of serious adverse health consequences is remote.
- *Class III* is a situation in which use of, or exposure to, a violative product is not likely to cause adverse health consequences.

The agency monitors to ensure that recalls are carried out effectively. The degree of monitoring activities and their nature (i.e., telephone calls, visits by investigators, and so forth) is dictated by the classification assigned to each recall, the product involved, and the steps necessary to ensure effectiveness of the recall. For example, a Class III recall of a food product might receive little or no monitoring, while a Class I recall of a contaminated drug product might require a visit by an investigator to 100% of the locations that should have been notified of the recall, to make certain that the notification was received and instructions were properly followed.

FDA sometimes requests the court to direct the company to recall products by seeking a court order called an "injunction." When such products are foods, drugs, or cosmetics, where FDA has no explicit statutory authority to order a recall, courts must decide that the agency's general injunctive powers, granted under section 302, are sufficiently broad to allow the court to issue an injunction. In some cases, the court has in fact ordered the company to recall. In other cases, the court has found that the lack of explicit authority to order a company to carry out a recall prevents the court from ordering a recall in connection with an injunction action.

FDA sometimes requests the court to direct a company to recall products by seeking a court order called an "injunction."

Chapter 14

FDA Enforcement: How It Works

Arthur N. Levine, Arnold & Porter LLP, Washington, D.C.

Key Points

- **Some enforcement actions may be brought directly by FDA against products, individuals, or companies. Other enforcement actions must be brought by the DOJ on behalf of FDA. In either setting, the evidence for these actions almost always arises from FDA inspections and/or investigations by FDA's OCI.**
- **The enforcement action that FDA uses most frequently is the issuance of a 483 list at the conclusion of an FDA inspection. This tool has been effective in promoting compliance through corrective action. Companies may facilitate FDA inspections by following procedures for effective communication and interaction with inspectors and other agency officials. Where FDA believes that a company's response to a 483 has been inadequate, it may issue a warning letter.**
- **An FDA enforcement tool that can have a dramatic and immediate effect on a company or a product is the issuance of adverse publicity.**
- **Seizure actions are brought to remove a violative product from commerce. Such products may be seized without any notice to the company or prior judicial hearing.**
- **FDA may recommend, and DOJ may bring, injunction cases to prevent a company from continuing to manufacture and market products in a way that does not comply with FDA regulations.**
- **DOJ may file criminal charges against individuals and companies for violations of either the FDCA or other federal criminal laws, or both. An individual may be prosecuted for violating the FDCA even if he or she did not know of or participate in the events that led directly to the violation. It is enough if the individual had the power and authority to prevent or correct the violation but failed to do so. The existence of this doctrine of "strict liability" has been an important underpinning of FDA enforcement for more than sixty years.**

Introduction

The Food and Drug Administration (FDA) is a law enforcement organization. It enforces the law through a variety of administrative actions and, with the approval and assistance of the Department of Justice

(DOJ), through judicial actions. The agency can take action against products, companies, and individuals. FDA has broad discretion to decide which violations it will take enforcement action against; what kind of action to take; and which products, companies, or individuals to bring the action against. FDA takes enforcement actions to remove violative products from the market or prevent their distribution in the first place, to obtain compliance with FDA requirements, to punish persons responsible for causing violations, and to deter others from violating FDA requirements in the same or similar ways.

The Source of FDA's Enforcement Powers

FDA's enforcement power comes primarily from the Federal Food, Drug, and Cosmetic Act.

FDA's enforcement power comes primarily from the Federal Food, Drug, and Cosmetic Act (FDCA). FDA is empowered to take enforcement action against products that are either "adulterated" or "misbranded" as defined in the FDCA, and against companies and individuals who cause products to become adulterated or misbranded. FDA also can prevent the marketing of products that are required to be approved by the agency but that do not have approval.

The FDCA is not static; it has been amended by Congress repeatedly over the years. Many of the amendments expand FDA's enforcement powers by defining conduct that constitutes a crime or authorizing FDA to take action through a civil money penalty.

In addition to the violations defined in the FDCA, FDA can define and establish requirements that are "binding" and have "the full force and effect of law." FDA does this by promulgating regulations—all of which are codified in Title 21 of the U.S. *Code of Federal Regulations* (C.F.R.). For this reason, when FDA promulgates a regulation, interpreting some requirement in the FDCA, it is establishing a new, more specific, legal requirement. Then FDA can take an enforcement action against a noncompliance with that requirement.

FDA also promotes compliance by issuing informal guidance documents that announce its interpretation of the FDCA and FDA regulations. These guidance documents are not legally binding on either FDA or on the industries regulated by it. They influence how companies act, however, because FDA usually will not take enforcement action if a company is operating consistent with its advice.

FDA's Enforcement Philosophy

A primary guiding principle in FDA's enforcement policy is to use all appropriate legal means to secure compliance with FDA laws and regulations.

- FDA encourages and expects compliance with the laws and regulations it enforces.
- FDA conducts inspections and investigations over the industries it regulates to continuously assess compliance and discover noncompliance.
- FDA protects the public health by using its enforcement tools, both administrative and judicial, according to the seriousness of the violation.

Historically, FDA has made decisions regarding enforcement action by weighing six factors:

- the seriousness of the violation,
- the number of people affected by the violative conduct or product,
- the extent to which people would be affected,
- the strength of the evidence of violation,
- the likelihood of success of the enforcement action, and
- the need for FDA to resolve the problem.

How FDA Brings Enforcement Actions

Enforcement actions are built on evidence of noncompliance with FDA requirements.

For the most part, enforcement actions are built on evidence of noncompliance with FDA requirements that is gathered by FDA investigators from the district offices during FDA inspections or by agents in FDA's Office of Criminal Investigations (OCI), supplemented by information obtained from other sources. The agency also may rely on information that a company submits to meet FDA requirements (such as adverse reaction reports) or that a company submits voluntarily (such as information about product recalls).

For most administrative and civil judicial actions, compliance officers in the district office evaluate the evidence. The district office makes an initial decision about whether a violation exists, its significance, the need for enforcement action, and the kind of action that seems appropriate. In some situations, the power to initiate an enforcement action rests with the district office and no further review within FDA is required. In other situations, a summary of the evidence and a recommendation for enforcement action is sent to the Office of Compliance in the FDA center that has jurisdiction over the product. That office may either authorize the action or, if required by FDA internal procedures, obtain further review and concurrence of the proposed action from either FDA's Office of Regulatory Affairs or its Office of the Chief Counsel (OCC), or both. For criminal enforcement, the evidence is most often reviewed and assessed by OCI.

As a general matter, either the center compliance office or OCC must review and approve administrative and civil enforcement actions that could have a significant impact upon a company or FDA policy. Regardless of the review process, there is usually a district compliance officer who has primary responsibility for handling every enforcement action.

Types of Enforcement

FDA may bring enforcement actions through either administrative or judicial procedures. Administrative enforcement may be brought by the agency itself; it does not need either approval from DOJ to initiate the action or an order from a federal court to impose a sanction. As a result, administrative enforcement can be resource efficient for FDA. Individuals and companies that are the subject of FDA administrative enforcement actions may challenge those actions in court but, in most instances, a court will not intervene in FDA's administrative initiative until the agency has taken final action. For some administrative actions, FDA regulations or established practice require the agency to provide an opportunity for a hearing, or an informal meeting, before FDA makes its decision.

Judicial enforcement actions involve DOJ and the federal courts. FDA does not have the power to go to court itself to obtain an order against a product, company, or individuals. Rather, the agency may recommend to DOJ that an action be filed on its behalf. The department may either accept FDA's recommendation, modify it (by revising the alleged violations, naming different products or persons as defendants, or changing the type of action to be sought), or decline the recommendation altogether. Enforcement of the FDCA is brought in federal court in the state in which the products are located, the facility in which the products were manufactured is located, or where the company or individuals who may have been responsible for the violation do business.

The two types of enforcement actions—administrative and judicial—are not mutually exclusive.

These two types of enforcement action—administrative and judicial—are not mutually exclusive. First, FDA repeatedly has announced that it is free to use either or both to accomplish its enforcement objectives. Second, FDA's inability to resolve a problem administratively often will be used to justify a subsequent request to DOJ for judicial enforcement. Finally, the mere threat of judicial enforcement, particularly prosecution, provides FDA with significant leverage in discussions with potential defendants relative to lesser administrative sanctions. Both types of enforcement actions have two predictable consequences. They lead to greater FDA scrutiny of the responsible companies in the future and they decrease FDA's confidence in the companies and individuals against whom enforcement actions have been brought.

Enforcement Trends

Over the past decade, FDA has altered significantly its approach to enforcement actions. Congress has given the agency additional enforcement authorities. The agency has developed compliance policies and procedures that are more varied, more resource-efficient, and more swift than many of the traditional enforcement actions. As a result, FDA's current enforcement approach relies more heavily on administrative (rather than judicial) enforcement actions; greater coordination between district offices and with the relevant FDA offices of compliance and of product evaluation; greater coordination with state enforcement authorities, and with professional and trade associations; greater use of adverse publicity; greater reliance on rulemaking to promote compliance; and the use of informal policy guidance documents to leverage companies to meet FDA's compliance expectations even if those expectations are not legally binding. In the area of judicial enforcement, FDA has focused on cases involving fraud, intentional or knowing violations of the FDCA, and on cases involving product defects with significant consequences for users.

While there have been fewer FDA seizure and injunction cases in the past decade, the number of criminal convictions has increased.

Recent enforcement trends reflect FDA's efforts to maintain a robust and credible enforcement program in an era of limited resources. While there have been fewer FDA seizure and injunction cases in the past decade, the number of criminal convictions has increased.

Congressional expansion of FDA's regulatory authority is not always matched by a commensurate increase in the agency's budget. Thus, FDA continuously re-evaluates its enforcement programs to identify ways to maintain deterrence and promote compliance with the resources it has. One agency strategy is to focus on enforcement actions that will have a substantial impact, and to pursue those actions vigorously. It has been persistent in obtaining full compliance in those circumstances where it has taken action.

Administrative Enforcement

FDA has a wide variety of administrative enforcement powers. Many are informal; they can be imposed without significant review within the agency. Others are brought only after extensive review. Many of FDA's administrative enforcement powers apply to all FDA-regulated products; some apply only to certain products.

List of Inspectional Observations

Over the past five years, FDA has conducted, on average, about 18,000 inspections per year of manufacturing and related facilities in the United States.

The core of FDA's enforcement programs has been, and remains, the inspections conducted by FDA investigators. These inspections gather the evidence of noncompliance that supports the agency's enforcement actions. Over the past five years (2003-2007), FDA has conducted, on average, about 18,000 inspections per year of manufacturing and related facilities in the United States. During this same period, FDA has increased its inspections of facilities outside this country that make products for sale here (from about 700 in 2003 to just over 1,000 in 2007).

At the conclusion of an FDA inspection, the FDA investigators may issue a List of Inspectional Observations (FDA Form 483). This form—provided to a company following a facility inspection—identifies those observations that, in the opinion of the investigator, are deviations from FDA requirements. FDA investigators issue 483 Lists of Observations in about 60 percent of all inspections. The 483 should be viewed not only as part of an FDA inspection but also as an FDA enforcement action because, almost without exception, it results in corrective action by a company to achieve compliance with FDA requirements. FDA expects that the company's corrective actions not only address the investigator's specific observations but also will address the systems, procedures, or organizational structure that may, unless changed, permit a recurrence of the noncompliances or similar deficiencies to those listed in the 483.

In most circumstances, a company's response to the 483 will resolve the noncompliance and no further enforcement action will be sought. A company can, however, expect a follow-up inspection during which FDA will look to verify implementation of the corrective measures described in the 483 response.

Warning Letters

An FDA warning letter is just that: a written warning from FDA that a company is, in the agency's view, not operating in compliance with FDA requirements. The primary purpose of the letter is to achieve compliance by threatening judicial enforcement if the company's noncompliance is not remedied.

In the late 1980s and early 1990s, warning letters became the most prominent type of FDA enforcement action. Even after that peak, during the period from 1993 to 2002, FDA issued, on average, about 1,200 warning letters per year. From 2003 to 2007, that number had fallen to about 550 per year.

Whether a warning letter is initiated by the district or the center, a warning letter represents a formal declaration by the agency that the operations and conditions at a facility do not comply with FDA requirements and that products manufactured in that facility will continue to be either adulterated or misbranded unless the company changes its systems, policies, procedures, or performance.

In most cases, a warning letter is based on the results of an FDA inspection that the agency believes has demonstrated reasonably significant deviations from FDA requirements. Therefore, the noncompliant circumstances described in the warning letter closely parallel the items in the 483. In most cases, but not all, if a company has made an adequate and sufficiently comprehensive response to the 483, FDA will not issue a warning letter. An adequate response to the 483, however, does not mean that a warning letter will not be issued anyway.

The basic elements of a warning letter are fairly straightforward. The letter summarizes the facts or circumstances found during an FDA inspection, a labeling review, an adverse reaction report, a recall, or some other underlying event. The letter asserts that those facts or circumstances cause the recipient's products to be adulterated or misbranded, and describes the fact giving rise to a finding of noncompliance. The letter provides the recipient with fifteen working days to notify the agency of the corrective actions that the company intends to take. Finally, the letter notifies the recipient that a failure to make an adequate response may lead to a product seizure, an injunction, or some other enforcement action.

A warning letter may, in some circumstances, be more than a warning. In many settings, the issuance of a warning letter results in the facility that is the subject of the letter being put on "compliance hold." As a result, FDA may not approve a pending product application or reissue an export certificate for a product manufactured at that facility until the issues raised in the letter are resolved to FDA's satisfaction.

A warning letter may, in some circumstances, be more than a warning.

Typically, warning letters will advise the recipient that the instance(s) of noncompliance described in the letter should not be read as a comprehensive list, and that the recipient has an obligation to consider the issues raised by the warning letter as they may apply to other of the company's products or activities. This standard language reflects FDA's effort to maximize the degree of corrective action obtained from issuing the warning letter. It also underscores the need to review the significance of the letter beyond the particular instances of noncompliance described in it.

The legal authority for a warning letter is found in that section of the FDCA that allows FDA to issue "a suitable written notice or warning" when it believes that a violation exists but has chosen not to pursue a judicial sanction, at least initially. While the issuance of a warning is authorized, it is not required. In addition, FDA is under no obligation to issue a warning letter before recommending a judicial enforcement action. FDA has found warning letters to be effective in obtaining compliance and has chosen to use them in numerous situations where, in earlier years, it may have recommended a seizure action or an injunction.

Warning letters are public information.

Like 483s, warning letters are public information. Many warning letters are automatically made available by FDA to the public and press, without the need for a formal Freedom of Information request. Therefore, once issued, they stand as a public accusation by FDA that a company's operation does not meet FDA standards and that the company's product(s) violate the law. Moreover, FDA routinely sends a copy of warning letters to federal procurement agencies, such as the Department of Defense and the Veterans Administration. These referrals can lead to a decision to terminate federal government contracts to purchase products implicated in the warning letter. These are a few of the many reasons why, as a practical matter, a company almost always will make a comprehensive written response to a warning letter.

The primary objective when responding to a warning letter is to demonstrate a serious and significant effort by the company to address the allegations of noncompliance. FDA expects, and most companies provide, a response that goes beyond any particular examples or circumstances of noncompliance referenced in the letter to include a comprehensive, "systemic" solution designed to preclude a recurrence of the problems. While some deficiencies may be amenable to specific corrections, many can be addressed only through new or revised company policies and procedures, organizational restructuring, employee training, and/or other broad-based activities. Nevertheless, companies generally do not promise more than they can or are willing to deliver. Therefore, most companies try to describe their corrective actions as precisely as possible, often including particular dates or implementation schedules.

If FDA discovers that commitments made in a response to a warning letter have not been met and there is no compelling explanation, the recipient can anticipate a significant escalation of FDA enforcement action. Accordingly, commitments that are made in response to a warning letter cannot be made lightly; well-counseled companies assess realistically what changes they are prepared to make, in what amount of time, and how broadly the changes will be applied throughout the company.

If a company disagrees with the alleged instances of noncompliance discussed in the warning letter, it may decide to explain why a change is unnecessary or would create even greater problems. In some circumstances, a company that disagrees with the agency may choose to make a change anyway because the company believes that it is unlikely that it will be able to convince FDA that its present processes and procedures are adequate. Often, a company will express its disagreement with FDA and explain its position, but implement changes anyway.

As is apparent, a warning letter can result in a significant amount of corrective action by a company. While these corrections are the principal objective in issuing the letter, it serves another important FDA enforcement purpose: a warning letter documents that the company, and the particular person to whom it is addressed, has received formal notice that the company's operations are not satisfactory. If the same or similar noncompliances continue, the existence of this "prior notice" or "prior warning" may be a significant element in FDA persuading DOJ to bring either an injunction action or a criminal prosecution.

Because a warning letter can result in nearly as much corrective action as can be obtained through a judicial injunction action, and because injunctions are resource intensive for FDA and require approval by DOJ, FDA is much more likely to issue a warning letter than it is to seek an injunction where it believes that a company's policies, processes, and procedures need to be changed in order to prevent continued noncompliance.

Adverse Publicity

The FDCA authorizes FDA to issue publicity to warn the public about possible adverse consequences associated with the use of the products it regulates. This statutory authority provides FDA with a broad platform to not only issue public advisories but also to publicize significant enforcement actions.

Generally, FDA does not routinely issue press announcements of its enforcement actions. There is no assurance, however, that FDA will refrain from seeking publicity about these actions.

As a matter of general practice, FDA does not routinely issue press announcements of its enforcement actions, such as the issuance of a warning letter, the institution of a seizure, the signing of a consent decree of injunction, or even a criminal conviction. There can be no assurance, however, that FDA will refrain from seeking publicity about any of these events. Because the effects of FDA-initiated adverse publicity can be devastating to a product or company, the agency's ability to issue such publicity cannot be taken lightly. Indeed, an FDA press release about a public health problem with a product can be the most immediate and effective form of enforcement action—it can end the product's marketability. FDA has significant media and public credibility, particularly when it comes to product-specific safety concerns.

While FDA may be willing to provide notice to a company that publicity about it or one of its products is about to issue, it generally does not negotiate with the company about the text of the FDA announcement. Nor will FDA share the text of a press communication with a company in advance. Thus, a company can try to contain the potential adverse effects of FDA publicity by issuing its own, preemptive statement. Ultimately, however, there is relatively little a company can do in most circumstances to significantly diminish the effect of an agency adverse press release.

Although FDA does not routinely issue press releases for enforcement actions, it is more likely to issue a press release to announce a criminal prosecution, an enforcement action against a large corporation, or an enforcement action that involves a well-recognized product or brand. Where FDA has initiated judicial enforcement, a press release may be issued by the U.S. Attorney's Office that is responsible for handling the case. Many U.S. Attorneys' Offices routinely issue press releases on criminal cases.

Adverse publicity issued by either FDA or DOJ may be reported in the local media and, in many circumstances, may become a national story. Any adverse publicity sought by FDA will be reported by the food, drug, and device trade press, and often by the investment community press.

FDA may publicize the results of its enforcement action by means other than a standard "press release."

FDA may publicize the results of its enforcement action by means other than a standard "press release." These include interviews with the press; appearances on television and radio talk shows; speeches at consumer programs, medical and professional association meetings, and professional conferences; descriptions of the enforcement action in congressional testimony; or providing information to be released during a congressional hearing.

While FDA seeks publicity only when it deems it necessary, it publishes lists of violative products that have been recalled or have been the subject of other enforcement action in its enforcement report. Some of these reports often are repeated or summarized in the trade press, including trade publications that report on specific types of FDA enforcement actions, such as warning letters and inspectional observations.

Of course, adverse publicity based on an FDA enforcement action can result merely because the action is public. Indictments in criminal cases, complaints in injunction and seizure cases, warning letters, 483s, and other FDA enforcement initiatives are all public documents. Copies of these documents can be obtained from a court, from FDA, and, in many cases, through the Internet. Copies of these documents also can be obtained from FDA under the Freedom of Information Act, either in the name of the requestor or anonymously by obtaining copies through a requesting service.

Recalls

With very few exceptions, product recalls by companies are voluntary. As a result, FDA is often unaware of the recall until it has begun. When a company recalls a product because it is adulterated or misbranded, FDA counts that as an enforcement action even though it is undertaken voluntarily. For certain products, however, FDA has the authority to order a recall.

Although companies are not required by law to report recalls to FDA, recalls of FDA-regulated products are reported to the agency every year by companies in deference to FDA's request that it be advised. Because a recall involves the removal from the market of a product that is adulterated or misbranded within the meaning of the FDCA, companies report their recalls so that FDA knows that the products are already being removed from commerce and, therefore, an enforcement action is unnecessary. Companies also report their recalls to FDA to maintain a good relationship with the agency, and to demonstrate that they have the capacity to identify their own noncompliances and the willingness to take action without being forced to do so.

From 1998 to 2007, companies increased the number of recalls from approximately 3,500 per year to more than 5,500 in 2007. Each recall may affect one particular manufactured lot of a product or all of a product made during a substantial period of time. Some recalls involve many products.

There are, of course, many reasons for a company to recall a product quite apart from FDA; these include a desire that customers not receive an inferior product, a desire to limit exposure to liability litigation if a user were injured as a result of use of a product (a use that could have been avoided by a recall), a desire to avoid adverse publicity associated with the distribution of a defective or inferior product, and a desire to maintain the reputation of the company or of the product/brand.

A recall strategy addresses:

- *the depth of a recall,*
- *the need for a public warning,*
- *a communication plan, and*
- *a process for checking the effectiveness of the recall.*

Most companies that decide to recall a product adhere to FDA's recall guidelines. These guidelines advise companies to follow a recall strategy that addresses the depth of the recall (to the wholesale or retail level); the need for a public warning; a communication plan to notify wholesalers, retailers, hospitals, and others being asked to return the product; and a process for checking the effectiveness of the recall.

The agency can and often does request that a company conduct a recall. When FDA learns about the distribution of a product that it believes presents a significant public health risk or a gross fraud, and where a company has not taken action to remove the product from the market, FDA may contact the company directly and request that the company conduct a recall.

If a company does not respond to such a request, FDA in effect can initiate the recall on its own by contacting the company's accounts—distributors, warehousers, hospitals, or individuals—and advising them directly of FDA's conclusion that the product is adulterated or misbranded and should not be used. During these FDA-initiated recalls, the agency may request that the product be returned to the manufacturer. FDA has initiated a recall in this way very rarely, and there is no direct statutory authority for such a recall. The basis for an FDA-initiated recall would appear to be FDA's authority to notify the public of any dangers associated with the use of FDA-regulated products together with its authority to seek adverse publicity. While companies may complain about FDA initiating a recall, the agency will do so when it concludes that a significant public health problem exists, that other enforcement actions may be inefficient or burdensome, and that the company has not itself taken adequate action.

Although FDA lacks general authority to order a product recall, Congress specifically has provided FDA with that authority in three product areas:

- Medical Devices: FDA may order a company to conduct a recall if it finds "a reasonable probability that a device intended for human use could cause serious adverse health consequences or death." Before ordering a recall of a dangerous medical device, FDA must provide the company with an opportunity for an informal hearing to discuss whether a recall is necessary. FDA can exercise this authority even if the company already has voluntarily recalled some of the product.
- Biologics: FDA can order the recall of a licensed biological product if it presents "an imminent or substantial hazard to the public health."
- Infant Formula Products: FDA can order the recall of infant formula products that lack the required nutrients or are otherwise adulterated or misbranded.

Enforcement Concerning Product Approvals

Many FDA-regulated products can be sold only if FDA approves an application for marketing. By the same token, the FDCA provides that FDA may withdraw its approval in a number of circumstances, including noncompliance with good manufacturing practice (GMP) requirements, false or misleading labeling, new evidence that the product is no longer safe or effective, or the submission of false statements to FDA.

The FDCA provides that FDA may withdraw its product approval.

To withdraw a product approval, FDA must publish a notice in the *Federal Register* of its intention to withdraw and invite comments from the company holding the approval as well as others. Next, the agency must publish a notice of an administrative hearing to decide whether the approval should be withdrawn. In most circumstances, however, no hearing is held. Rather, FDA and the company marketing the product settle the dispute, usually by providing for an orderly withdrawal of the product from the market or by agreeing on a labeling change.

When a public health hazard exists, FDA may temporarily suspend its approval of certain product applications without any prior notice or opportunity for an administrative hearing. FDA approvals of new drug and new animal drug applications may be suspended summarily if FDA finds that the product creates an "imminent hazard" to the public health. An approved biologics license can be summarily suspended if continued distribution would create a danger to health. FDA may revoke a permit to make thermally processed foods in hermetically sealed containers if the manufacturer is not in compliance with FDA's low-acid canned foods regulations.

FDA may temporarily suspend the approval of the premarket application for a medical device, but only after providing an opportunity for an informal hearing. If there is reasonable probability that the continued distribution of the device would cause serious adverse health consequences or death, the agency may order the temporary suspension of the distribution of drugs covered by an approved abbreviated new drug application (ANDA) but only after it has provided an opportunity for a hearing on any disputed facts. The suspension of distribution of an ANDA drug is authorized if FDA finds that the applicant has engaged in bribery or submitted false statements, or has engaged in flagrant and repeated material violations of the drug GMP requirements so that such violations undermine the safety of the drugs and have not been corrected within a reasonable period of time.

In addition to withdrawing or temporarily suspending product approvals, FDA may refuse to review one or more of a company's product applications, even if they contain the required evidence of safety and effectiveness, if FDA concludes that data in the pending application is unreliable and possibly fraudulent. This deferral of review is one element of FDA's "Applications Integrity Policy." When FDA questions the reliability of data in a pending product application and invokes this policy, the company that submitted the application must do four things for FDA to proceed with its review:

FDA may refuse to review a product application if the agency concludes that the data in the pending application is unreliable and possibly fraudulent.

- cooperate with FDA in looking for the cause of any wrongdoing that has resulted in the submission of false or unreliable data;
- identify to FDA those individuals who were or may have been associated with any wrongdoing, and remove them from positions of authority on FDA matters;
- conduct a comprehensive internal review to assess the integrity of its product development and application processes; and
- provide a written commitment to FDA to develop a corrective action plan.

In addition, FDA may conduct its own "validity assessment" to ensure that any potential causes of unreliable or false data have been identified and remedied. These activities can take a long time, depending on the apparent source and scope of the data integrity problem. Some companies have had FDA review of their product applications deferred for one to three years while they undertook the prescribed corrective program.

Enforcement Against Imported Products

FDA, working with the U.S. Customs Service, has authority to prevent products from entering U.S. commerce if those products appear to be adulterated or misbranded, or otherwise violate the FDCA.

When a product is identified by an importer as an FDA-regulated product, that declaration is communicated to FDA by an electronic link between the Customs Service and the agency. If FDA requests, the Customs Service will hold the product for FDA examination or sampling. In fact, FDA examines only a very small portion of the FDA-regulated products that are offered for importation each year—about 2 percent. This reflects the enormous volume of import entries of FDA-regulated products each year and the lack of FDA resources available. If FDA decides to take an enforcement action against an import, however, its powers are significant.

FDA examines only a small portion of the FDA-regulated products that are offered for importation each year.

First, the standard for taking enforcement action is relatively low. FDA may refuse entry into U.S. commerce if the product merely "appears" to be violative. Second, FDA's interference with an import can have a significant economic impact, particularly for perishable products or products with short shelf lives. Thus, even the temporary detention of an import for examination pending a final decision on entry often leads to "voluntary" corrective action by the importer without FDA having to ask the Customs Service to issue a formal refusal of entry. Finally, FDA may block importations of products by placing an automatic detention on all products that meet the detention criteria. For example, if FDA has evidence demonstrating that a certain product made in a particular country has regularly been shown to be contaminated, FDA can issue, on the basis of that historical data, an automatic detention to preclude the importation of all entries of that product from that country.

Because products can be refused entry on the basis of examination, sampling, or "otherwise," and because importation of products from outside the United States traditionally has been considered a privilege, not a right, FDA's authority to control the importation of violative products has been generally sustained. A few courts, however, have questioned whether such FDA detention criteria are individual enforcement actions that the agency may pursue at its discretion, or whether they are "rules" that FDA can impose only after rulemaking. Notwithstanding this unresolved legal issue, FDA and the Customs Service have established an effective, even if very selective, enforcement process for imports.

As a result of congressional action to prevent acts of bioterrorism by the use of poisonous food, FDA is authorized to detain any food offered for import into the U.S. if the agency has "credible evidence" that the food presents a threat of "serious adverse health consequences or death" to humans or animals. The importer or owner of the food may appeal

FDA's decision. In addition, food establishments must register with FDA and FDA is authorized to hold any imported food if the foreign manufacturing facility is not registered. To allow FDA to exercise its regulatory powers over imported food, companies must give FDA notice of their intent to import foods into the United States prior to its arrival at an American port.

Civil Money Penalties

For certain products, Congress has authorized the agency to obtain a civil money penalty. A civil money penalty is a fine that is assessed against a company, an individual, or both. FDA has civil money penalty authority in nine program areas.

Civil Money Penalty Authority

1. *Medical devices*
2. *Prescription drug marketing*
3. *Radiation-emitting products*
4. *Biological products*
5. *Generic drugs*
6. *Mammography quality*
7. *Childhood vaccinations*
8. *Foods containing unsafe pesticides*
9. *Drug clinical studies, labeling, and advertising*

In most of them, FDA has been authorized to impose the penalty itself, administratively. In a few areas, only federal courts have the authority to impose the penalty.

Under the Safe Medical Devices Act of 1990 (SMDA), FDA was given the authority to impose a civil money penalty for most violations of FDA requirements applicable to medical devices. FDA can impose these fines administratively; it does not need the approval of DOJ or an order from a court. For many violations, FDA can assess a penalty only if the violation is "significant" or "knowing," or a company can avoid a fine by showing that, notwithstanding the violation, it has operated in "substantial compliance" or that there have been no product defects or significant adverse consequences as a result of the violation. FDA may impose a civil money penalty of up to $15,000 for each violation or up to $1,000,000 for all violations involved in a single civil money penalty proceeding. A company or an individual that has been fined by FDA may appeal the fine to a federal court of appeals.

FDA also may seek a civil money penalty against companies or individuals for violating provisions of the FDCA covering radiation-emitting products. Violations that could lead to a fine include the manufacture or distribution of an electronic product that does not meet applicable federal standards, issuing false certificates of compliance with standards, or the failure to permit an FDA inspection or make an FDA-required report. For radiation-emitting products, FDA cannot impose a civil money penalty administratively. Therefore, FDA must request that DOJ file a complaint for a penalty in a federal court. Civil money penalties for radiation-emitting products are limited to $1,000 for each violation or up to $300,000 for a related series of violations.

Under the PDMA FDA is authorized to seek civil money penalties only against companies, not individuals.

Under the Prescription Drug Marketing Act (PDMA), FDA is authorized to seek civil money penalties but only against companies, not individuals. A company can be assessed a fine if a representative of the company has been convicted of selling drug samples or if the company fails to report to FDA the fact that any of its representatives have been convicted of such violation. Under certain circumstances, a company can avoid a civil money penalty by demonstrating that it could not reasonably have been expected to have detected the violation, notwithstanding its having an internal audit system to detect possible wrongdoing by its employees. The fines that may be imposed range from $50,000 to $1,000,000, depending on the number of violations, the similarity of violations if more than one company representative is involved, and the number of violations that have occurred within a certain time period. FDA has asserted its authority to impose penalties in this area administratively, although the PDMA refers only to the assessment of a civil money penalty by a federal court.

FDA also may impose a civil money penalty against a company that has failed to comply with an FDA order to recall a defective biological product. The penalty is not imposed for the distribution of the product but for failing to comply with FDA's recall order. Thus, this penalty resembles a fine for contempt and, accordingly, is based on each day of continued noncompliance with the FDA recall order, up to $100,000 per day.

The Generic Drug Enforcement Act of 1992 gave FDA authority to impose civil money penalties administratively for a number of prescribed violations involving ANDAs. Civil penalties may be assessed against companies or individuals for making false statements, failing to disclose a material fact, destroying evidence, obstructing an FDA investigation, or bribing or attempting to bribe an FDA employee. In addition, a company may be assessed a civil money penalty if it uses the services of an individual who has been debarred by FDA from work on drug products. The maximum fine is $250,000 for an individual and $1,000,000 for a company, for each violation.

FDA also may impose a penalty under the National Childhood Vaccine Injury Act of 1986 (for destroying, altering, or falsifying documents submitted by a vaccine manufacturer under the childhood compensation program) and under the Mammography Quality Standards Act of 1992 (for a testing facility's failure to obtain the required certificate for operation or for failing to comply with applicable standards). In addition, the Food Quality Protection Act of 1996 authorized civil money penalties for introducing into interstate commerce a food that contains an unsafe pesticide.

In 2007, the Food and Drug Administration Amendments Act (FDAAA) was enacted. This legislation authorized FDA to seek civil money penalties for additional violations of the FDCA. Under the FDAAA, the agency may impose a civil money penalty if a company fails to comply with FDA requirements to register clinical trials and their results in the National Institutes of Health registry or submits registration or study data information that is false or misleading. A penalty of $10,000 may be imposed; violations that are not corrected within thirty days are subject to a civil penalty of up to $10,000 per day until the violation is corrected.

The FDAAA also requires drug companies to develop risk evaluation and mitigation strategies and established new postapproval safety labeling requirements. Failure to comply with these requirements can result in civil money penalties of up to $250,000 per violation and up to $1,000,000 for all violations adjudicated together. If the violations continue, a company can face additional penalties of up to $10,000,000 depending on how long the violation persists. The new amendments also authorized civil money penalties against companies that issue false or misleading direct-to-consumer advertisements, up to $500,000 if violations recur.

Except where explicitly required by the statute, FDA can impose a civil money penalty without a showing of knowing, willful, or intentional conduct by the person who is fined.

Civil money penalty procedures:
- *filing a complaint;*
- *if defendant does not challenge complaint, penalty is addressed without any further proceedings;*
- *if defendant challenges complaint, the case may be settled or go forward.*

FDA has established procedures for imposing civil money penalties. Under these procedures, the penalty process is initiated by filing a "complaint" alleging the violations on which the proposed penalty is based. If a defendant does not want to challenge the allegations in a complaint, a penalty can be assessed without any further proceedings. If the company or an individual challenges the complaint, FDA and the defendant may settle the case and agree upon a fine, or, if they are unable to reach agreement, the case will go forward. Either there will be a hearing or the hearing officer may decide that there are no genuine issues of material fact justifying a hearing, and he or she may issue a decision on the basis of stipulated facts and other documentation presented by both sides. In a civil money penalty proceeding, subpoenas can be issued by FDA and by the defendant. There is no right to issue subpoenas, however; the hearing officer may accept or reject a request for the issuance of a subpoena by either party.

FDA has used its civil money penalty authorities infrequently. Part of the reason is that some of these authorities are relatively new. Another reason is that developing a penalty case is resource intensive and may not be as attractive as other enforcement actions because the penalty itself does not correct the problem and FDA does not gain control over the operation of the company as it does by an injunction.

Referral to State Authorities

Nearly all states have adopted food, drug, and device laws nearly identical to the FDCA. Most of those states amend their laws to incorporate significant new amendments to the FDCA. More than twenty states have provisions in their laws by which amendments to the FDCA are automatically adopted into and become part of the state law. Given the common definitions of adulteration and misbranding between federal and state laws, and a significant degree of similarity in enforcement authorities, FDA has the option of asking the state authorities to take an enforcement action. The state authorities may take enforcement action against any product manufactured or distributed within their state that violates state law.

To foster cooperation and coordination between FDA and the states, the agency has established a task force with the National Association of Attorneys General. In recent years, the states, Attorneys General have had a particular interest in bringing enforcement actions against consumer fraud. Once one state has initiated an action, the Attorneys General in other states often will file or threaten to initiate enforcement actions in their states. This strategy has often resulted in an "agreement" between the company and the Attorneys General for many states in which a company stops making certain promotional claims, issues "corrective advertising," and establishes employee retraining programs.

In addition to enforcement tools similar to those of FDA, state health officials have two additional tools. First, state officials usually can suspend the license of a manufacturer, distributor, or retailer to practice within the state. (Almost all businesses must obtain a state license to operate.) Second, in all states but one, health officials have the authority to embargo violative products on the spot. They do not need to go to court to have the products seized.

In addition to referring certain noncompliant conduct for state enforcement action, FDA may commission state health officials to gather evidence for the agency to use in its federal enforcement action under the FDCA.

FDA has the power to debar either a company or an individual. FDCA § 306, 21 U.S.C. § 335a.

Debarment

In limited settings, FDA has the power to debar either a company or an individual. FDA's debarment authority applies to ANDAs, may implicate other drugs and, under the bioterrorism laws, applies to food importation.

An individual who has been debarred may not provide any services to a company that has any approved or pending drug product applications.

Thus, when a company submits a drug product application, it must certify to FDA that it has not used the services of any debarred individual in developing or submitting the application.

An individual may be debarred if he or she has been convicted of a felony under federal law for illegal conduct relating to the development or approval of any drug product. An individual also may be debarred if that individual has been convicted of a felony relating to the regulation of any drug, not just activity concerning approval. Debarment may be based on the fact that the individual has been convicted of any one of a number of other federal or state crimes, or "materially participated" in any conduct that was the basis of a conviction, even though that individual was not convicted. Finally, FDA may debar an officer or director of a company or some other "high managerial agent" if that person knew that others at the company were engaging in criminal conduct but did not report that conduct to FDA or the appropriate compliance official within the company.

When a drug company has been debarred, FDA will not accept or review any ANDA submitted by that company. In other words, during the period a company is debarred, FDA will not approve any new ANDAs for that company, although the company may continue to submit and FDA may continue to approve other product applications, and the company may continue to manufacture and distribute any drugs for which it already obtained FDA marketing approval. A company may be debarred if it has been convicted of a felony relating to the development or approval of any ANDA or if that company has been convicted of certain specified federal crimes or state law. FDA may not debar either an individual or a company until it has provided an opportunity for a hearing on any disputed issues of material fact.

The names of individuals and companies that have been debarred are published in the *Federal Register*. While FDA has debarred many individuals, FDA has not debarred any active drug companies. Because companies can be debarred only if they have been convicted of a crime, FDA is somewhat limited in its ability to exercise this power because it must await action by DOJ or by a State Attorney General to file criminal charges against a company and obtain a conviction.

While FDA has debarred many individuals, FDA has not debarred any active drug companies.

Congress has authorized FDA to debar persons who are convicted of a felony relating to food importation or who have engaged in a pattern of offering for import adulterated food that presents a threat of serious adverse health consequences or death to humans or animals.

The SMDA provides for additional enforcement authorities against noncompliant medical devices.

Additional Enforcement Powers for Medical Devices

In addition to all of its enforcement tools for FDA-regulated products generally, the agency has additional specific enforcement powers regarding medical devices. These authorities were provided by Congress primarily in the SMDA.

For medical devices, an FDA investigator has the power, during an inspection, to order that a device be detained if the investigator has reason to believe that it is adulterated or misbranded. The detention may last only twenty days and is designed to provide FDA with an opportunity to decide whether to bring a seizure action against the product or to obtain an injunction against the company. If FDA decides that it needs more time to consider its next step, however, the period of detention may be extended an additional ten days.

FDA also may order that a device manufacturer issue a notification to distributors, retailers, doctors, or users of a device if the agency has concluded that the device presents an unreasonable risk of substantial harm to the public and that notification is necessary to eliminate that risk. The only prerequisite to FDA invoking this authority is to "consult with the persons who are to give the notice." In effect, this provision authorizes FDA to mandate that a manufacturer distribute adverse information about its product, which is likely to result in modification of the conditions under which the device is used, cessation of the use of the device due to anxiety associated with the notification, or the return of the device by those who believe that it is no longer safe.

FDA may order a device manufacturer to "immediately cease distribution" of a device and to "immediately notify health professionals and device user facilities. . . to cease use" of it. FDA may invoke this authority if it finds that there is a reasonable probability that the device would cause serious adverse health consequences or death. FDA may make that finding on its own and issue a cease distribution order without giving the company an opportunity for any hearing. FDA must provide an opportunity for such a hearing, however, within ten days after issuing its order. At that time, the agency may withdraw or modify the order, or it may amend the order to require the company to recall the device. In other words, this statutory provision gives FDA the authority to issue both an injunction and a mandatory recall administratively.

Finally, FDA may declare a device to be restricted in its sale, distribution, or use. In invoking these restrictions, FDA may require either that the device be made available only on prescription or may impose "such other conditions" as it believes are necessary to provide a reasonable assurance that the product can be used safely and effectively. If FDA declares a device to be restricted—which it may do only by regulation—

it also gains control over certain aspects of the advertising of that device. A restricted device is the only kind of device over which FDA has any authority over advertising.

Three types of judicial enforcement:
- *seizure*
- *injunction*
- *prosecution*

JUDICIAL ENFORCEMENT

The FDCA authorizes three types of judicial enforcement: product seizure, injunction, and prosecution. The first two are civil sanctions; the last is criminal.

Seizure

Under section 304 of the FDCA, a product that is adulterated or misbranded is subject to seizure. Products may be seized in a manufacturing facility, a warehouse, or distribution facility; from a truck or other carrier of the product; from a retail store; from a hospital or doctor's office; or from a consumer. In most cases, seizures are made at the facility where the products were made, or from the warehouse or distribution center where they are held.

At one time, FDA pursued over 200 seizures each year. During the past five years, FDA has used seizure actions very infrequently (twenty-five seizure actions in 2003 and only six in 2007).

FDA can recommend a seizure to the U.S. Attorney in the state where the products are located. If the U.S. Attorney agrees to initiate the seizure action, he or she will file a "complaint" in the federal court. The complaint identifies the products and describes the ways in which they are adulterated or misbranded, or both. After the complaint is filed, the clerk of the court issues a warrant for the "arrest" (the seizure) of the products. Usually, a Deputy U.S. Marshal will make the seizure. In nearly all situations, products are seized where they are found ("in place"), and cannot be moved or handled without the court's permission.

There is no judicial hearing before the products are seized, so once the seizure is accomplished, FDA has—temporarily—won the case. After that, the court will either condemn the products or the court can find that the allegations in the complaint have not been proven and release the products from seizure.

Recently, FDA has used seizures in three settings: seizures designed to remove from the market products that FDA believes present a serious public health risk, seizures of products that violate the law in a way that FDA wants to publicly highlight, and "mass seizures." FDA may recommend a "mass seizure" of all products that have been manufactured or are being warehoused under violative conditions. Typically, a mass seizure will be brought where the products are alleged to be adulterated because they have not been manufactured in compliance with GMP regulations, or they have been manufactured or held under insanitary conditions. Where such manufacturing or storage conditions exist, all of the products are adulterated. A mass seizure can significantly disrupt normal business operations. As a result, there is often a prompt resolution.

In the vast majority of seizure cases, the products are condemned either by default or consent.

In the vast majority of seizure cases, the products are condemned either by default or consent. One reason for this success rate is that FDA usually does not recommend a seizure action unless it has reasonably strong evidence that the products are adulterated or misbranded. Another is the absence of a judicial hearing before the seizure is accomplished—the owner of the seized products is at a substantial disadvantage because the products remain under seizure during the lengthy judicial process. Thus, it is often in the owner's best business interest to resolve the seizure promptly.

In many seizures, the owner or manufacturer allows the products to be condemned by "default." When this occurs, the court usually will order that they be destroyed. In other situations, the manufacturer will file a claim to the seized products and enter a consent decree agreeing that the court may condemn them. Where products are condemned as part of a consent decree, the decree usually gives the owner or manufacturer an opportunity to recondition them—by relabeling, sorting, cleaning, or similar procedures—in order to salvage as many of them as possible for distribution. Under typical FDA consent decrees, FDA decides whether the products have been reconditioned successfully. Once they have been reconditioned and FDA has released them, the products may be distributed just like any other product because they are no longer in violation of the FDCA. Condemned products that cannot be reconditioned to FDA's satisfaction will be destroyed.

In recent years, the settlement of a seizure action has been by agreement to enter into a consent decree that not only resolves the seizure but also includes injunctive language designed to address the underlying causes of the violations. In this way, FDA uses the seizure as leverage to obtain manufacturer agreement to an even broader decree—one that is frequently more rigorous than FDA would have otherwise secured. On a few occasions, the owner or manufacturer not only believes that the seized products are not adulterated or misbranded but also that FDA-supervised reconditioning is not acceptable. In those cases, the owner or manufacturer will contest the seizure with the hope of demonstrating to the court that the products are not violative and should be released for distribution as is. At trial, the government has the burden of showing, by a preponderance of evidence, that the seized products are violative.

Injunction

Through an injunction FDA hopes to force a company to make significant changes in its operations. An injunction is a court order that the company cease manufacture and distribution of products unless and until the company complies with FDA requirements. A court will issue an injunction if it believes that, without an injunction, violations are likely to recur. The injunction is designed to prevent such recurrence. Usually FDA will seek injunctive relief only after other enforcement actions have been unsuccessful in bringing about corrective action. Most often, FDA will seek injunctive relief for persistent violations of its GMP regulations, or for repeated noncompliance with FDA requirements for labeling and promotion.

FDA recommends injunction actions to the Office of Consumer Litigation, the part of DOJ assigned to review FDA cases. Typically, the complaint for injunction proposed by FDA will identify, in substantial detail, those practices that FDA believes do not comply with its regulations. It is FDA's hope that after reading the lengthy complaint a judge would be inclined to enter an order of injunction against the defendants.

It is FDA's policy that an injunction case should be brought not only against the company but also against company officials who have the most direct responsibility for the alleged violations. Thus, for example, an injunction might include as defendants the company president, the vice president for operations, the director of quality assurance, and, possibly, the plant manager. It has been FDA's experience that by naming corporate individuals as defendants it obtains the maximum amount of cooperation in achieving compliance, as well as the maximum amount of deterrence against other corporate officials who have similar responsibilities in their companies.

There are three types or phases of an injunction. If the alleged violations create a significant and immediate public health risk, FDA will request that DOJ seek a temporary restraining order (TRO). If a court enters a TRO, it will prevent the company from shipping violative products for up to twenty days until there can be a further judicial hearing. A TRO can be entered without a formal hearing before the court. In most cases, however, a court will not enter a TRO without some informal opportunity for a company to appear and offer either an explanation or some assurance about the operations of the company. A court can enter a TRO, however, without any representative from the company being present.

Most FDA injunctions include a request for preliminary relief.

Whether or not a TRO is sought, most FDA injunctions include a request for "preliminary" relief. A preliminary injunction usually prevents the defendants from making or distributing products until the noncompliant procedures and practices are corrected, and until there can be a full judicial hearing on a permanent injunction. In many cases, however, a preliminary injunction may be in effect for several weeks. During that time, a company may negotiate with DOJ to settle the case. A preliminary injunction may be entered only after a judicial hearing.

If neither a TRO nor a preliminary injunction has been entered, the company may continue to operate until a full hearing on a permanent injunction is held and the court has ruled. Usually, FDA seeks both a preliminary and a permanent injunction. In some cases, however, where violations have persisted over a long time but the consequences are not particularly significant, FDA may seek only a permanent injunction.

FDA has pursued injunctive relief somewhat selectively over the past few years. In the five years from 2003 to 2007, FDA recommended approximately eighty injunction actions to DOJ—on average, about fifteen per year. Most of these injunction cases are based on alleged violations of FDA's GMP regulations for drugs and devices.

FDA has pursued injunctive relief somewhat selectively over the past few years.

Most injunction actions filed on behalf of FDA are resolved through the entry of a consent decree of permanent injunction that has been negotiated between DOJ and the defendants. This often occurs because the defendants decide that FDA has sufficient evidence to win an injunction after judicial hearing or they want to resolve the dispute with FDA as quickly as possible. Most consent decrees of injunction contain four standard provisions:

- First, the defendants must cease manufacture and distribution "unless and until" they make a number of corrections in their policies and procedures, which are specified in the consent decree itself.
- Second, the defendants must submit a written report to FDA describing the corrections they have implemented to achieve compliance.
- Third, the defendants must retain an independent expert consultant to review their operation and to report to the defendants, and certify to FDA, that the company is in compliance. Based on the consultant's report, the defendants also must certify to FDA that they are in compliance.
- Finally, FDA will make an inspection, at the defendants' expense, to verify that the company is operating in compliance with the FDCA, and that the corrections are adequate and have been fully implemented.

If these four conditions are met, FDA will notify the court that the company can resume manufacture and distribution, although the company is still operating under the consent decree. In addition, the defendants usually must agree to hold all the products in their possession or under their control on the date the consent decree is entered until FDA determines that the products are suitable for release or until the products are reconditioned to FDA's satisfaction. Some injunctions against large corporations require that many facilities be brought into compliance. This is time consuming and expensive.

Some injunctions against large corporations require that many facilities be brought into compliance. This is time consuming and expensive.

The terms of the consent decree will generally reflect the specific underlying nature of noncompliance with FDA requirements alleged in the complaint, as well as the significance of the noncompliance, the type of product, the consequences for users if the product is not in compliance, and the regulatory history of the company and the individual defendants. It will also reflect DOJ's assessment of the defendants' ability to demonstrate that effective corrective actions have already been implemented, and that the likelihood that the violations will recur is significantly reduced. Finally, the terms of the consent decree will reflect the "give and take" of the negotiation processes.

As a result, a consent decree may impose requirements or give FDA additional powers not conferred by the FDCA itself. For example, companies often are required to have their operations audited routinely by an independent expert and to submit the audit reports to FDA even after they are allowed to resume operations under the consent decree. Some consent decrees require the defendants to conduct ongoing employee training programs. Under some decrees, FDA is authorized to order recalls of the defendants' products. In a consent decree based on allegations of unsubstantiated advertising, the defendants may be required to recall and destroy all material that promotes a product for an unapproved use, submit new promotional material to FDA for advance approval, and conduct a corrective advertising program including issuance of "Dear Doctor" letters and corrective advertisements to appear in journals named by FDA. In some recent consent decrees, the defendants have agreed to pay FDA's costs in investigating and bringing the injunction action, or they have been required to set aside an amount of money to ensure adequate funds for process improvements even after the resumption of operations under the consent decree.

Consent decrees may permit the enjoined company to continue to make and distribute medically necessary products. In some cases, a consent decree may allow the company to continue to manufacture and ship its products—or most of them—while it is implementing corrective action and undergoing verification of such action by external audit. Such "going forward" decrees are less disruptive for companies although the required remedial programs are usually comprehensive, very burdensome, and can take years to be fully implemented.

Two recent appellate court discussions have upheld FDA's position that the government can obtain equitable monetary relief—restitution or disgorgement—as part of an injunction under the FDCA. The theory of this relief is that companies should not be allowed to retain the profits they have made from the sale of violative products before the injunction was entered. So far, FDA has sought this additional relief selectively and important legal issues about its imposition remain.

Complaints for injunction and consent decrees are public documents. Injunction actions are widely reported by FDA trade press and, depending upon the nature of the problem and the size of the defendants, often are reported in the lay press.

If a company maintains continuous compliance for two years, FDA generally does not object to a request by the defendants that the court vacate the injunction.

Even though a consent decree is agreed to by both FDA and the defendants, it is a court order just as if it had been entered by the court after the defendants had challenged the injunction and lost. Because a consent decree is a court order, any knowing violation of it constitutes a contempt of court. The power of the court to hold individuals in contempt undoubtedly is designed to encourage compliance with the court's order.

Developing injunction cases is time consuming for FDA. In addition, there is no guarantee that DOJ will agree to file an injunction that FDA recommends, although in most cases the department accepts FDA's recommendation. While the primary burdens of a consent decree fall upon the defendants, FDA has certain obligations to monitor and supervise the defendants' compliance activities. Thus, an injunction is not completely a one-way street. For these reasons, FDA does not recommend injunction cases lightly. It usually reserves this type of enforcement for companies that have failed repeatedly, after notice from the agency, to adequately correct significant noncompliance with FDA requirements.

Criminal Prosecution

While the FDCA identifies numerous "prohibited acts," most criminal cases are based on either the shipment of adulterated or misbranded products in interstate commerce or the manufacture of a product under conditions that cause it to be adulterated or misbranded. Any individual or company that engages in those prohibited acts or causes any such violation may be punished, criminally. FDA's policy is to recommend criminal charges against individuals as well as companies. FDA believes that criminal charges against the company alone, without individual defendants, does not provide adequate deterrent or adequate punishment.

Under FDA criminal law an individual can be prosecuted even without knowing about the violative conduct or without intent to violate the law.

The most fundamental feature of FDA criminal law is that an individual can be prosecuted even without knowing about the violative conduct or without intent to violate the law. Rather, the prosecution is based on the individual's responsibility for the conduct that results in the violation, as reflected in the individual's power and authority in the company. This "strict liability" basis for criminal prosecution is based upon two Supreme Court decisions. The first, *United States v. Dotterweich*, was decided in 1943. In that case, the Supreme Court said that a violation of the FDCA is committed by all company officials who are "responsible" for the violative conduct.

The strict liability basis for criminal prosecution is based upon two Supreme Court decisions.

More than thirty years later, the Supreme Court reaffirmed and amplified the standard of criminal strict liability under the FDCA in its decision in *United States v. Park*. The Court described the standard for criminal liability under the FDCA this way:

> The Act imposes not only a positive duty to seek out and remedy violations when they occur but also, and primarily, a duty to implement measures that will ensure that violations will not occur. The requirements of foresight and vigilance imposed on responsible corporate agents are beyond question demanding and even onerous but they are no more stringent than the public has the right to expect of those who voluntarily assume positions of authority in business enterprises whose services and products affect the health and well being of the public that supports them. . . . [It is enough if the] defendant had, by reason of his position in the corporation, responsibility and authority either to prevent in the first instance or promptly to correct the violation complained of, and that he failed to do so. . . . We are satisfied that the Act imposes the highest standard of care and permits conviction of responsible corporate officials, who in light of this standard of care, have the power to prevent or correct violations.

The Court also observed that

> . . . those corporate agents vested with the responsibility, and power commensurate with that responsibility, to devise whatever measures are necessary to ensure compliance with the Act bear a "responsible relationship" to, or have a "responsible share" in, violations.

Under the strict liability standard of the "*Park* doctrine," a person who has a responsible relationship to the violations may be prosecuted for a failure to detect, prevent, or correct the violations. The only legal defense under the *Park* doctrine is a showing that the violation occurred notwithstanding "extraordinary" efforts to prevent it. In such a circumstance, the courts have held that compliance is, in effect, impossible. Of course, any individual defendant may show that he or she did not stand in a responsible relationship to the violative conduct because the defendant lacked the necessary power or authority. For that reason, the individual would try to demonstrate that he or she was powerless to prevent the violation and cannot be convicted for what was impossible.

The ability to recommend a criminal prosecution based on the *Park* doctrine provides FDA with a substantial amount of discretion in choosing targets for criminal action. In recent years, however, DOJ has hesitated to file criminal charges against individuals based only on the *Park* doctrine. Rather, it has preferred to bring criminal charges against individuals who have intentionally violated the law or who have been grossly negligent or have recklessly disregarded the FDCA. Nonetheless, the *Park* doctrine has had a significant deterrent effect on individuals who must consider the possibility that unless they exercise the necessary control over their companies they can be held personally criminally liable if the company does not comply with the law.

Traditional FDA recommendations for prosecution under the *Park* doctrine have become few and far between. In fact, virtually all FDA criminal cases in recent years have been handled by FDA's OCI. This office was created to investigate the kinds of intentional criminal cases that DOJ would prefer to prosecute. Working directly with Assistant U.S. Attorneys around the country, FDA's OCI has developed cases that have resulted in many, many more criminal cases than the previous FDA referral process. In the five years between 2003-2007, OCI accounted for approximately 1,500 criminal convictions. In 2007, OCI reported nearly 350 convictions.

The Park *doctrine has been a valuable part of FDA's criminal enforcement but most criminal cases brought in recent years involve intentional violations.*

OCI investigates cases concerning willful misconduct involving FDA-regulated products, obstruction of justice, submitting false information to FDA, mail fraud, wire fraud, racketeering, criminal conspiracy, and product tampering. In addition to these offenses, in recent years FDA's OCI has increased its investigations into persons who make or distribute counterfeit drugs. While OCI opened six counterfeit drug cases in the year 2000, it opened more than fifty such cases in 2006.

Most of the violations investigated by OCI are criminal offenses defined by the federal criminal laws, not the FDCA. In some of these cases, while the investigation has focused on federal, non-FDCA felonies, the defendants may resolve the investigation by agreeing to plead guilty to FDCA *Park* violation. Even where a plea bargain may involve a conviction for an FDCA violation, the penalties associated with these cases often include fines of several million dollars and periods of incarceration for some defendants.

OCI investigations often use evidence-gathering tools that are not available to FDA. These include the use of a grand jury to issue subpoenas for evidence, a grant of immunity to individuals in exchange for their cooperation against targets of the investigation, and electronic surveillance (wiretapping). OCI investigators often work with agents from the Federal Bureau of Investigation (FBI), the Customs Service, and other federal law enforcement investigative agencies to develop these cases.

Some OCI investigations result not only in criminal convictions but also fines and other sanctions for violating federal healthcare fraud and abuse laws. Recently, investigations involving the Department of Health and Human Services' (DHHS's) Inspector General, FDA's OCI, and the FBI have resulted in not only criminal convictions, but large settlements—involving hundreds of millions of dollars—for violations of the federal false claims and anti-kickback laws.

The vast majority of criminal cases involving FDA are resolved by conviction of the defendants as part of a plea bargain. For a corporate defendant, the plea bargain may involve not only the payment of a fine but also an agreement to establish a corporate compliance program that contains many elements of an FDA injunction. For individuals, a plea bargain may involve not only a recommendation regarding a fine or against imprisonment but also may involve an agreement by the defendant not to participate in certain FDA-regulated activities.

Violations of the FDCA under the Park *doctrine are misdemeanors.*

Violations of the FDCA under the *Park* doctrine are misdemeanors. Violations of the FDCA with intent to defraud or mislead and most violations of the federal criminal laws are felonies. The distinction between misdemeanors and felonies, however, has been significantly affected as a result of the U.S. Sentencing Guidelines under which fines against corporations and periods of incarcerations are calculated through a complex scheme. In addition, a company can be placed on corporate probation, a sentence that has some of the characteristics of an FDA injunction. Under the Guidelines, a company can reduce the level of its fine if it can demonstrate that, notwithstanding the violations, it had an effective corporate compliance program designed to detect and prevent violations of law, a program that resembles the standard of liability in the *Park* case.

Conclusion

FDA has a variety of effective enforcement tools available to it and broad discretion in deciding which tools to use to remedy violations of the FDCA. FDA will do whatever it believes is necessary to achieve compliance with the FDCA and FDA regulations and usually pursues enforcement without concern for business consequences. FDA enforcement has been an effective deterrent in promoting compliance among FDA-regulated companies.

Chapter 15

Being Prepared

William Vodra, Arnold & Porter, Washington, D.C.

Key Points

- **A crisis for a company regulated by FDA may take many forms, but usually it involves public allegations of legal violations that endanger consumers, resulting in multiple legal proceedings and negative publicity that can threaten the company's reputation and even its survival.**
- **The crisis generally will be based on either an apparent risk to the public health or a plausible charge of fraud.**
- **Although every crisis has acute phases that must be properly managed, the company facing the crisis will have to make a prolonged and steady commitment of resources. Endurance and patience are essential.**
- **Five principles of crisis management are:**
  - **Recognize a possible crisis early and act accordingly.**
  - **Get ahead of the potential crisis by anticipating its possible scope.**
  - **Staff the crisis adequately.**
  - **Ensure truth and consistency in public statements.**
  - **Deal effectively with FDA and other constituencies.**
- **Not all crises can be prevented, but good crisis management programs contribute to limiting and resolving the unavoidable crisis.**

Characteristics of a Crisis for a FDA-Regulated Firm

Anyone working in the food and drug field will meet the greatest challenges during a "regulatory crisis." Every business tries hard to prevent a disaster, but despite the best of these efforts, one still may be encountered. For firms that are regulated by FDA, the nature of the product means that crises inevitably will occur. It is essential to keep in mind the motto of the Boy Scouts: "Be Prepared."

Crises pose unusual and unique demands on a company. Important steps should be taken early during a crisis to manage it as well as possible. Crisis prevention activities may assist in containing the unavoidable crisis.

The characteristics of a regulatory crisis include:

- allegations of violations of FDA law endangering consumers;
- public awareness of these allegations;
- multiple legal proceedings involving parties other than the company and FDA that influence and complicate the interactions between the regulators and the regulated; and
- significant threats to the company's reputation or products, and perhaps to the organization and key employees as well.

A "regulatory crisis" is not a normal confrontation with FDA. Any business regulated by FDA has numerous and diverse opportunities to run afoul of regulations. Indeed, given an intensive audit by the agency, any company on any particular day could be found in violation of some legal requirement. These "routine" violations generally do not trigger any formal FDA action. The agency looks at whether a business is substantially in compliance with legal requirements, determined in part by whether the firm has control of its operating processes and systems. If FDA believes the systems generally are under control, the agency usually will bring the "routine" violations to the company's attention and recommend voluntary remedial action.

In a regulatory crisis, the alleged violations plausibly create an immediate and significant danger to consumers.

In a regulatory crisis, the alleged violations plausibly create an immediate and significant danger to consumers. The injury would result from one or more of three common elements:

- a product is unsafe as made, labeled, used, or promoted;
- consumers are being defrauded; or
- the government is failing to protect the public because it was misled by the company.

If no risk of serious harm to users of the product is perceived, a confrontation between FDA and a company over the alleged violations will rarely develop into a "crisis."

A regulatory crisis inevitably involves public awareness. Normally, "routine" violations result in a relatively private dialogue between the regulatory agency and the regulated firm. When news media make the public aware of the alleged misconduct, however, a regulatory crisis can explode. Perceptions about the business and its products are always at the core of the situation. Firms supplying foods, drugs, medical devices, cosmetics, and other FDA-regulated items must maintain a high degree of consumer and healthcare professional confidence. In 2003, manufacturers of certain antidepressants warned of potential increased risk of suicide in children and adolescents, amidst charges that these risks had been concealed previously. Shortly thereafter, prescription rates for these drugs fell by 18 percent. In a regulatory crisis, therefore, a firm is challenged to maintain the trust of the consuming public in its products and in its corporate image.

During a regulatory crisis, parties other than the company and FDA inevitably become active players. Furthermore, important events and pressures emerge in many arenas at the same time. For example, a company may be faced simultaneously with different lawsuits asserting claims for product liability, securities law violations, wrongful discharge of employees, unfair trade practices, or denial of insurance coverage. Inquiries can be initiated by congressional committees, corporate directors, and federal agencies in addition to FDA. Investigative news reporters can start a search for scandal. Similar regulatory activities, litigation, and investigations may erupt in other countries where the product is marketed or the firm does business.

A regulatory crisis could result in:

- *plummeting sales,*
- *share values falling,*
- *cumulative sanctions, or*
- *civil and criminal liability.*

A regulatory crisis is marked also by enormous stresses within a company. Sales of individual products may plummet. The sales force, operating on a commission basis, immediately loses personal income. Workers in production and distribution areas may be laid off if sales soon do not recover. Even employees not directly responsible for the involved products may worry about the company's ability to respond to the emergency. In short, morale is put in jeopardy throughout the organization.

Second, if the company's securities are publicly traded, values of shares of stock may fall. In May 2007, after the *New England Journal of Medicine* published a study purporting to show that Avandia (rosiglitazone) increased the risk of heart attacks in diabetic patients, the manufacturer's stock price dropped more than 10 percent in days, wiping out $15 billion in market value. Such precipitous declines expose firms to litigation for alleged failure to disclose risks (thus overvaluing the stock), as well as hostile takeover bids. Even without these dire consequences, management remains answerable to existing shareholders for loss in market value. In the short term, a crisis will require senior executives to devote significant energy to responding to Wall Street analysts.

Third, the potential exposure of the company to cumulative sanctions—criminal prosecution, civil fines and penalties, disgorgement of profits or restitution to consumers, debarment from government procurement programs, and punitive damages in private litigation—can be staggering. Bankruptcy is not unheard of; it was the fate of Able Laboratories following a crisis involving the reliability of generic drug products. Managing these risks can demand resources for years after the immediate crisis has passed.

Finally, individuals within the company may be exposed to civil and criminal liability, as well as debarment from further employment in the industry. The ability of law-respecting "white collar" employees faced with allegations of criminal wrongdoing to bear up under investigations, hearings, depositions, and media coverage is highly variable. This personal element frequently is overlooked in the heat of activities, but can be critical to the firm's ability to survive the crisis intact.

These stresses give a regulatory crisis another dimension that often is not appreciated until it is experienced. Within the company during a crisis, profound interpersonal tensions can emerge. Resources previously committed to future projects are diverted to addressing the problems at hand. Root cause assessments may turn individuals and operating units against each other. Employees begin to consider new career opportunities. The more serious and prolonged the crisis, the more intense becomes the pressure on the company to find a quick and decisive resolution. Management's ability to keep the organization functioning can be severely challenged.

Although a regulatory confrontation may originate between a company and FDA at any time, it becomes a regulatory crisis when it spreads into the public domain and invites other parties to become involved. Preparedness may not prevent a crisis, but it is critical to weathering it successfully.

Evolution of a Crisis

Major crises tend to fall into two patterns: the public health crisis and the fraud crisis.

Major crises tend to fall into two patterns: the "public health" crisis and the "fraud" crisis.

The preponderance of the most serious FDA regulatory crises have begun with a real or perceived danger to the public health associated with a marketed product. In some circumstances, the questions relate to product quality and alleged contamination of a product, whether by diethylene glycol in toothpaste, melamine in pet food, oversulfated chrondroitin sulfate in heparin, or *E. coli* on spinach. Other situations emerge from new discoveries questioning the safety of an established product. Newspapers routinely break stories about possible links between products and terrifying hazards, even when the underlying studies are preliminary and inconclusive. In recent years, American society has been buffeted by scares such as whether antidepressants cause patients to commit suicide, whether preservatives in childhood vaccines produce autism, whether a widely used class of anti-arthritis drug triggers heart attacks, and whether drug-coated coronary stents are more dangerous than earlier "bare-metal" stents. In response to intense criticism for failing to disclose data on potential product safety issues, FDA now regularly publicizes early notices about unconfirmed reports of possible risks. These situations seem to explode with little prior warning.

When a food, drug, device, or cosmetic in active use is discovered—or merely alleged—to present a significant risk of illness, injury, or death, both the company and FDA must deal with urgent health questions:

- Should the product be temporarily or permanently removed from the market?
- Should new warnings or risk minimization controls restrict use of the product?
- Should consumers be advised to get medical care?

These issues must be addressed promptly and with a public conclusion—even if that conclusion is no more than a conscious choice to defer any action until more information is available.

A public health crisis need not present any actual dangers to the public.

A public health crisis need not present any actual dangers to the public. Consumer advocacy groups, scientific researchers, investigative journalists, members of Congress, and even organizations with political agendas unrelated to FDA regulation can make widely publicized accusations that specific products or classes of products are endangering the public health. In every case, Congress and the public expect FDA to review the data dispassionately and to reach a reasoned conclusion about the merits of the allegations. Even though the allegations ultimately prove baseless, the mere fact that they were made can have long-term adverse consequences for the product. For example, public attacks linking Bendectin, a drug for morning sickness during pregnancy, with birth defects were unequivocally rejected by FDA as unsupported by any scientific evidence; nevertheless, continued product liability litigation and hostile publicity led the manufacturer to remove the product from the market.

After any immediate remedial actions are taken to address a public health crisis, FDA almost always will investigate whether the firm either could have prevented the problem or actively concealed it. The search is always looking to answer the critical pair of questions: what did the company know and when did the company know it?

Allegations that company officials knew a product was dangerous but hid that information from the public and regulators make great headlines and can profoundly influence future events. To illustrate, each of the most prominent criminal prosecutions of pharmaceutical manufacturers in the 1980s (Eli Lilly & Co. for Oraflex, Smith Kline & French for Selacryn, and Hoescht AG for Merital) followed public claims that the drug firm had evidence that its product could cause a fatal side effect prior to marketing, failed to disclose that evidence adequately to FDA during premarket review, and as a result was able to sell the product with insufficient warnings.

A "fraud crisis" also may emerge independent of any prior public health crisis. In this situation, it is alleged that the firm committed fraud on someone—FDA, other government bodies, or the public—in connection with obtaining approval of or marketing a product. The assertions may relate to misrepresentations in or omissions from applications submitted to FDA, to misleading promotional claims, or to inconsistent statements made to other bodies or to investors. The public accountability of FDA and the agency's concern for the integrity of its processes require these allegations to be pursued diligently. For example, FDA recently brought a successful prosecution against a company and its chief executive officer, based on charges that it knowingly and deceptively marketed an approved product for sterilizing reusable surgical devices.

Many of the examples just discussed first appeared to be "public health" crises, with widespread stories of illness or deaths linked to the products. But in each case, as well as the other examples, the crisis evolved into a "fraud" crisis where the company was under a lengthy investigation for misconduct.

Duration of a Crisis

A fraud crisis attracts episodic attention:

- *when allegations are first exposed*
- *whenever there are important subsequent revelations*
- *if litigation results, when cases are tried*

To most outsiders, a crisis seems like a bomb explosion: noisy and brief. The public perceives crisis activities as short-lived or episodic. The situations flare, attract considerable attention, and soon become forgotten. The public health problem, for example, is addressed promptly: the product is removed, relabeled, or given a "clean bill of health." A fraud crisis attracts attention episodically: when the allegations are first exposed; whenever there are important subsequent revelations; and, if litigation results, when cases are brought or tried.

This image is deceptive for those actually involved in a FDA regulatory crisis. For a business, management of the problems can require resources for many months or years. The company still must respond to the potential litigations and investigations that are spun off by the initial controversy. Probably it will engage in its own internal investigation and analysis of "what went wrong" and "how could we do better." And it may need to implement changes in personnel and procedures as a result of the crisis.

The litigation surrounding the diet drugs fenfluramine and dexfenfluramine (aka "Phen/Fen Litigation") illustrate the amount of time resolution of these problems can take. In 1997, medical reports linked these drugs with cardiac disease; they were withdrawn from the market almost immediately. The products became the target of product liability lawsuits, which resulted in a class action settlement and an adjudication procedure for processing claims. Claimants could nevertheless litigate if certain conditions were met. Over a decade later, individual cases were still in the courts.

Understanding how long a crisis might last is important for a company. The problems will divert resources for extended periods and require recurring management attention. As patience wears thin, the desire for a "quick fix" will intensify.

Preparing for a Crisis in Today's Business World

In today's downsized corporation, different crisis management strategies are needed.

The common recommendation for crisis management involves having designated teams available, written procedures, training exercises, and mock rehearsals. There is great merit in this approach, but in the downsized corporation of today, other strategies are needed. Many firms no longer have the capacity for training and rehearsing. Moreover, given regular personnel turnover, the potential benefits from developing and maintaining a state of readiness may not appear to managers and directors to be worth the investment.

Thus, additional ways must be found to prepare for managing the future regulatory crisis.

Contemporary crisis management requires at least five elements:	
1	Recognize a possible crisis early and act accordingly.
2	Get ahead of the potential crisis by anticipating its possible scope.
3	Staff the crisis adequately.
4	Ensure truth and consistency in public statements.
5	Deal effectively with FDA and other constituencies.

The first challenge is to recognize a potential crisis early so that appropriate steps can be taken. This step is perhaps the most difficult to take. Most firms and individuals in a potential—or actual—crisis situation cannot accept easily the possibility that something terrible might happen. Not only does the potential for a crisis suggest that the lives of many people will be disrupted; it implies some failure or error on the part of someone in the organization. By the same token, being the bearer of bad news is neither welcomed nor honored. Consequently, the natural human incentives always work against thinking the unthinkable. This tendency toward complacency frequently can lead a company into giving insufficient attention to an emerging issue until too late.

Firms must attempt to get ahead of any potential crisis. To anticipate the possible scope of problems that may have to be addressed, the company must assume a "worst case" scenario. As with warnings about possible crises, this unpleasant exercise is not welcomed and may be greeted with criticisms of "doom-saying." While it might be hoped that such prognostications at least would soften the shocks when things go from bad to worse, it should not be a surprise that—when predicted scenarios come to pass—people will complain they were not really warned about this or that possibility.

Firms must attempt to get ahead of any potential crisis. To anticipate the possible scope of problems that may have to be addressed, the company must assume a 'worst case' scenario.

Legal advisers need to assess the company's potential vulnerabilities so that immediate actions can take them into account. These vulnerabilities include potential exposure to enforcement action by FDA or other governmental agencies; claims for damages from consumers, customers and vendors, third-party insurers, employees, and stockholders; and investigations from legislative bodies. Nonlawyers must be involved also, for many of the most pressing demands for rapid response from the company will arise from media and business considerations, not simply legal obligations. Interested and indirectly affected constituencies may include shareholders (particularly major investors and securities analysts); suppliers and distributors; employees and their unions; insurance carriers; and federal, local, and foreign government agencies. These constituencies cannot be overlooked when focusing on the ultimate consumers of the product, lay media, or regulators such as FDA.

Once the potential or emerging crisis is identified and its dimensions are sketched out, the company must promptly allocate adequate and qualified resources. Two groups of inside employees are essential to handling the situation: those who will be responsible for corporate management of the crisis and those who uniquely possess the factual background essential to support the crisis management effort. These indispensable people must be made available, even if it means that other assignments do not get accomplished. To help them focus on the crisis, these individuals should have job priorities adjusted promptly.

Beyond these essential persons, the company should ensure that adequate numbers of people with knowledge, skills, or experience appropriate to the demands of the crisis are located and assigned. Transferring people will not be easy, as it necessitates a painful process of choosing priorities among competing needs of the business. Here lies the importance of understanding the potential extended duration of a crisis: projects potentially could be postponed not merely for a few weeks, but indefinitely unless other resources are found.

A further staffing consideration is the ability of each individual to function under prolonged stress. Most scientists, regulatory affairs, marketing, and business management people are not trained to—nor do they wish to—work in the adversarial circumstances of, for example, a criminal investigation by FDA or extended civil litigation. Thus, the composition of a crisis management team should take into account the long-term demands on its members.

For a variety of reasons, bringing in outside resources is almost always prudent and necessary. They probably have more experience in crises, particularly if the company and its current management have been fortunate enough to have avoided any FDA crisis in recent memory.

For a variety of reasons, bringing in outside resources is almost always prudent and necessary. They probably have more experience in crises, particularly if the company and its current management have been fortunate enough to have avoided any FDA crisis in recent memory. They also are not being pulled from other corporate commitments. Finally, they usually are more accustomed to a stressful and adversarial environment. Companies should avoid a natural tendency to attempt to manage the situation using only internal resources; a delay in bringing in the appropriate resources can be costly.

During a crisis, it is imperative to ensure the truth and consistency of public statements. A regulatory crisis generally involves allegations that a product appears to endanger the public health. These allegations will become public through news reports. Consequently, the business is pressured to respond to public inquiries and attacks. Carefully managing the media is critical, particularly in the early stages of a crisis. In addition, if there are parallel proceedings—such as lawsuits, congressional hearings, or inquiries from other government agencies and/or governments—the company will be making statements in those arenas.

These pressures can be the most difficult for lawyers or regulatory affairs officials. These individuals often prefer to have matters resolved quietly, out of the spotlight, as much as possible. In a regulatory crisis, however, this approach does not serve the company's interests well. The business must maintain consumer and public trust. It may be compelled to undertake remedial actions and self-correction activities to reassure the public. If company officials are so worried about future liabilities that these immediate priorities are ignored, the business will hurt itself for both the short- and the long-term.

All public statements must be accurate and truthful, and be capable of being proven so, for they likely will be closely scrutinized in the future in many different circumstances.

All public statements must be accurate and truthful, and be capable of being proven so, for they likely will be closely scrutinized in the future in many different circumstances. The company must avoid injuring itself through its public statements. In an era of "spin doctors" the tendency to rebut an allegation with a plausible tale or statement of principle may make the company briefly look good. But if the assertion cannot be substantiated—or worse, later can be proven wrong—the statement will haunt the company for a long time. In dealing with press communications, despite the best public relations effort, no company is going to be able to control media coverage. At most, the story can be influenced toward accuracy and balance. Thus, the value of an unsubstantiated assertion is limited, while the risks are not.

Another common tendency of companies is to make sweeping promises of corrective or remedial actions, in an effort to forestall FDA regulatory activity. It is critical to ensure that any promises to government regulators both can be kept and will be kept. FDA has seen firms pledge to undertake changes in manufacturing processes, for example, that were technologically impossible. Such promises undermine credibility and certainly do not deter an FDA enforcement action. Similarly, failure to fulfill a commitment made in the urgency of the hour must be explained later. The explanation that the cost of the commitment proved unacceptable to corporate management will not be favorably received by FDA. The company also should be careful to avoid any inference that the failure to have previously implemented a particular step or activity represents an admission of past legal violations. FDA has been known to interpret an unqualified pledge to take corrective steps as an admission of prior noncompliance.

Companies should avoid the following when making public statements:
- *unsubstantiated assertions*
- *sweeping promises of corrective or remedial actions*
- *inconsistent statements*

A third dimension of public statements involves assuring consistency among statements. Given the potential breadth and duration of a regulatory crisis, the company must ensure adequate coordination and communication among those who are making statements on behalf of the firm. A few years ago, one firm was embarrassed (and worse) when a spokesperson in a European country defended the safety of its product on the basis of a particular study; it turned out that the company had previously advised FDA that it could not establish the integrity of that study. The challenge of assuring consistency is especially important with respect to assertions made under oath or under legal rules proscribing false statements. Once a firm makes a sworn statement of fact to one government body, it cannot readily deny the truth of the statement before another agency or in court. To be sure, as information changes, prior statements no longer may be fully accurate, but the burden will be on the firm to demonstrate that its information evolved.

The last principle in contemporary management of a FDA crisis is to deal with FDA effectively. As with attempts to control the media during a crisis, efforts to control the actions and responses of FDA generally are doomed to failure. The agency has been mandated by Congress to protect the public and to ensure the integrity of its own processes, by independent investigation and evaluation of the underlying facts. FDA automatically fails in this duty if it accepts a company's story uncritically and without scrutiny. The more serious the alleged threat to the public, the more egregious the alleged fraud on the agency or the consumer, or the more public the allegations become, the greater will be the likelihood that FDA will conduct its own investigation, notwithstanding the statements and promises from the regulated firm.

Complicating the situation is the fact that FDA has two distinct roles, one seeking to protect the public health, the other charged with enforcing the law. In the first capacity, there is no inherent conflict between the agency and the company, which has no interest in injuring its customers. In a metaphorical sense, the marketer sits side-by-side with FDA confronting the public health issue with the best science and medicine both can bring to bear. Cooperation and candor assist both in resolving the safety issues.

But when the question is "What did the company know and when did it know it?", FDA and the firm are in an adversarial mode. In this situation, cooperation and candor may result in facilitating a criminal prosecution. Because the Federal Food, Drug, and Cosmetic Act (FDCA) contains strict criminal liability penalties, the intent or good faith of the firm and its officers is irrelevant to conviction. This fact infuses interactions between the company and FDA with inherent tensions and problems for lawyers, regulatory affairs personnel, and business managers.

The regulated business must communicate with FDA throughout the regulatory crisis.

To complicate the situation further, FDA has no voluntary disclosure program analogous to those of the Department of Defense or Environmental Protection Agency. These programs provide incentives to companies to reveal instances of violations in exchange for a commitment by the government not to impose the most severe sanctions legally available. Because of the strict liability provisions of the FDCA, voluntary disclosure of any violation is tantamount to an admission of criminal wrongdoing.

Despite these special burdens, the regulated business must communicate with FDA throughout a regulatory crisis. In doing so, it should avoid unnecessary confrontations, recognizing the high levels of stress already present. These interactions are not occasions for company employees to vent their past frustrations with regulatory processes at FDA. Nor should irrelevant agendas be incorporated into the situation.

The most sensitive and difficult communication between a company and FDA during a crisis involves "bad news." For the reasons just outlined, the natural tendency is to say nothing. If FDA is likely to learn the bad news eventually, however, the firm should be the first to tell the agency. This process permits the company to put the information into context and offer appropriate explanations. Disclosure also may enhance the credibility of the company with the agency.

The problems that can occur when others convey the bad news first are illustrated by the history of silicone breast implant regulation in the early 1990s. FDA had completed an interim review and concluded that the implants could continue to be marketed. During the same time, plaintiffs' counsel in product liability litigation identified internal corporate documents suggesting unanswered safety issues with the implants. These documents were supplied to FDA and apparently surprised officials, leading the agency to reverse its policy and suspend product marketing immediately. A subsequent investigation, however, led both FDA and the Department of Justice to conclude that the documents did not contain any material safety information not previously known to the agency. But by then the damage was done.

Dealing with FDA during a crisis involves complex and difficult choices. Handling the interactions effectively will never guarantee an outcome that the company might consider optimal. Unnecessary confrontations and a loss of credibility, however, will increase the probability of an undesirable outcome from the firm's perspective.

Crisis Prevention

Some crises cannot be prevented, so preparation to deal with the inevitable crisis is important. Crisis prevention, however, remains a useful exercise. To the extent that prevention succeeds, it is all to the good. But even if a crisis occurs, strong crisis prevention programs can limit the scope and duration of any public health crisis and reduce the potential for a subsequent fraud crisis.

Strong crisis prevention programs can
- *limit the scope of a crisis*
- *reduce the duration of a crisis*
- *lessen the potential for a subsequent fraud crisis*

FDA is interested in knowing whether a firm has control of its operating systems and processes. FDA looks at two key factors: the "closed-loop" design of each system and the documentation of the critical decisions.

From the perspective of FDA, every regulated activity is or should be governed by a system. Each system should contain five fundamental elements:	
1	Written specifications or performance goals that the activity is to attain,
2	Written operating procedures by which the activity is to be conducted in order to meet the specifications or goals,
3	Training employees in the procedures,
4	Monitoring activity to detect failures to meet the specifications or goals, and
5	A self-correcting mechanism to identify the cause of each failure and institute appropriate remedial action.

The fifth element gives the system its "closed-loop" nature. Once the system has identified a failure, in theory it can identify what corrective action is needed. In somewhat oversimplified terms, the problem arose because:

- the specifications did not include all of the necessary targets for the system to attain; or

- the specifications were adequate but the operating procedures were deficient in assuring the correct conduct of the activity; or
- the specifications and procedures were both adequate, but employees were insufficiently trained to follow the procedures; or
- the specifications, procedures, and training were adequate, but adherence to the training and procedures was insufficiently ensured.

The effort to identify the source of the failure, sometimes termed a "root cause analysis," not only permits the system to restore itself to compliance; it is also an essential prerequisite to meaningful corrective action.

FDA believes that these five elements should exist for all aspects of FDA-regulated activities, from the manufacture of individual products, to the development of labeling and promotional material, to the research and development process for new products, to the identification and reporting of adverse events. Good crisis prevention programs will ensure that each regulated operating system or activity has all five elements in place and functioning.

The primary contribution of these crisis prevention programs to crisis management lies in providing the company an opportunity to identify the situation early and to initiate steps to limit the scope and duration of any public health crisis. Secondarily, the existence of strong internal closed-loop systems may lead FDA to conclude that enforcement actions are not needed to bring about compliance from the company. Many of the elaborate and intrusive consent decrees obtained by the agency against individual firms reflect a sense that FDA had lost confidence in each firm's ability to get its own house in order and under control.

The existence of strong internal closed-loop systems may lead FDA to conclude that enforcement actions are not needed to bring about compliance from the company.

Documentation of internal decisions represents the second major crisis prevention activity of importance to FDA. The agency recognizes that its investigations have 20/20 hindsight accuracy. What is ultimately pivotal to initiating enforcement action against the firm is the agency's assessment of how the company performed when making the decisions that are now under FDA review. Successful prosecutions are less likely if the firm's actions were not unreasonable; the fact that a decision proved wrong does not make it unreasonable, even in hindsight.

Nevertheless, an action that looks reasonable in *post hoc* argument may not prevent enforcement actions. What the agency is looking for is a conscious decision, not inadvertent actions. Hence, FDA will look for documentation that shows the company made a decision that was:

- reasonable,
- reasoned,

- timely, in that it occurred within the applicable time limits (e.g., by FDA reporting regulations or prior to product release in accordance with good manufacturing practices), and
- documented contemporaneously.

The last three items avoid *post hoc* arguments to defend actions that might have been reasonable.

The benefit of such documentation to crisis management is that it can defuse and resolve questions about the company's conduct. If a firm can demonstrate through memoranda or other papers generated at the time decisions were being made that it promptly reached a reasoned decision, taking into account what was known and what the law required, all that FDA—or any private litigant—can argue in a court is that a different decision would have been more reasonable. Because the law generally recognizes that reasonable persons can disagree, these documents provide an important defense.

Documentation leading to a company's reasoned decision can defuse and resolve questions about the company's conduct.

Conclusion

An FDA regulatory crisis may not be avoidable. If and when it strikes, a firm that is prepared to respond early and effectively will have an enormous advantage. The company that is not faces serious threats to its reputation, financial health, and potentially, its viability.

Chapter 16

Research and the FDA

Gary L. Yingling, J.D., B.S.Pharm., M.S., & Ann M. Begley, J.D., B.S.N., K&L Gates LLP, Washington, D.C.

Key Points

- **Each of FDA's five substantive centers has its own requirements for research.**
- **Experimental animal research is regulated closely by both the PHS and the USDA to ensure the humane treatment of laboratory animals.**
- **In clinical research, the essential purpose of an institutional review board is to review research to assure it meets the ethical obligations of a clinical study, whereas the principal investigator controls the integrity of the research and manages the other professionals conducting the research and the sponsor must monitor the study and the principal investigator's research to assure compliance.**
- **To assure that persons involved as subjects in a clinical study are properly informed, FDA requires that investigators obtain written informed consent from study subjects.**
- **When submitting data to FDA for review, a major consideration will be the integrity of the data.**

INTRODUCTION

Research is central to the mission of the Food and Drug Administration (FDA)—not just research that FDA itself does, but more particularly the research that companies must submit to gain approval to market their products in the United States. This chapter provides an overview of the regulatory framework for research required by the centers for the various products regulated by FDA.

Each of FDA's five substantive centers has its own requirements for research. The centers require research studies to gain approval or marketing authorization for at least some of the products subject to their jurisdiction. The Center for Drug Evaluation and Research (CDER), the Center for Biologics Evaluation and Research (CBER), and the Center for Devices and Radiological Health (CDRH) each have statutory, regulatory, and guidance documents creating standards and expectations of how the research is to be conducted. The Center for Veterinary Medicine (CVM) has a similar expectation but not as detailed, and the Center for Food

Safety and Applied Nutrition (CFSAN) has a much less formalized expectation but an expectation nonetheless.

FDA's research requirements and expectations have significant impact on how research is conducted in the United States and, to some degree, in other countries. These regulatory standards continue to evolve as new methodologies and technologies emerge.

Animal Research

A number of years ago, animal research was not the subject of government regulation and there was little dialogue relative to the ethical treatment of animals. Not so today. While not the subject of significant regulation by FDA, experimental animal research is regulated closely by both the U.S. Public Health Service (PHS) and the U.S. Department of Agriculture (USDA). Both PHS and USDA have established rules and standards governing the humane treatment of laboratory animals. Of particular relevance to those conducting preclinical research are USDA's Animal Welfare Regulations, which include provisions covering the licensing and registration of research facilities, as well as attending veterinarians; standards for adequate veterinary care; recordkeeping requirements; compliance quality standards; and various other research practices (see 9 C.F.R. Chapter 1, Subchapter A, Parts 1-3). These regulations require all animal research laboratory facilities to register and submit to federal inspection. Also, researchers are required to adhere to Good Laboratory Practices (GLPs) when conducting animal experiments (21 C.F.R. Part 58) if the collected research data is going to be submitted to FDA in support of a product application.

Each facility is required to establish and maintain an Institutional Animal Care and Use Committee to review and approve study protocols for proposed research involving the use of animals and to monitor ongoing animal studies.

Additionally, each facility is required to establish and maintain an Institutional Animal Care and Use Committee (IACUC) to review and approve study protocols for proposed research involving the use of animals and to monitor ongoing animal studies. Under this system, there are instances when an IACUC will not allow an experiment because it is basically torture to the animal. For example, twenty years ago one could remove both of a rat's kidneys making the animal uremic as part of an experimental design (bilateral nephrectomy). Today, it would be unethical to approve such a study design and an IACUC would most likely approve no greater than 5/6 removal. While such limitations on experimental design do create challenges, most can be overcome without compromising the objectives of the proposed study.

Clinical Research

Institutional Review Board

Regulatory controls on clinical research start with the Institutional Review Board (IRB). Research involving human subjects that raises questions of safety cannot be undertaken without having the proposed experiment, protocol, and informed consent reviewed by an IRB. An IRB is responsible for ensuring that the health and rights of human test subjects are adequately protected in a clinical research setting.

The origin of the IRB dates back to 1964, when the Declaration of Helsinki was adopted by the World Medical Assembly and one of the recommendations was that research be reviewed by an independent committee. The Department of Health, Education and Welfare issued a policy in 1971 governing federally funded studies that required that research be reviewed by "an appropriate institutional committee" charged with determining whether the rights and welfare of subjects are protected. The Belmont Report, a 1979 document issued by the National Commission for the Protection of Human Subjects of Biomedical and Behavioral Research, stated that an ethical review of research was necessary to protect human subjects. Thus, the federal policy resulted in two different set of regulations, the Department of Health and Human Services (DHHS) regulation that covers research done at federally funded facilities (45 C.F.R. Part 46), and FDA's regulation that requires IRB review of all research submitted to FDA (21 C.F.R. Part 56). Normally, a food taste-testing panel falls outside "research" but depending on the product and questions asked, it may not.

FDA and the Office for Human Research Protections (OHRP) (within the DHHS) have specific regulations governing the various types of IRBs that may be established, their responsibilities and membership, and the need for minutes reflecting their decision making. The essential purpose of an IRB is to review research to assure it meets the ethical obligations of a clinical study. The IRB can be an academic IRB, organized within an academic institution such as a university; an IRB organized by a clinical site that is conducting studies; or an independent IRB that acts as an IRB for clinical investigators or others who do not wish to undertake the obligation of creating an IRB organization. Additional information regarding FDA's regulation of the IRB and the board's composition and responsibilities can be found in Chapter 5 of this book.

The essential purpose of an IRB is to review research to assure it meets the ethical obligations of a clinical study.

In the drug and device area, both FDA and OHRP exercise inspectional jurisdiction. FDA's inspection is normally done as part of an on-site inspection by an FDA bioresearch monitoring professional, while most of OHRP's are done by correspondence and conference call. While the styles may be different, the objectives are the same. Each agency wants to assure that the IRB is fulfilling its ethical obligations to protect the human subject in clinical research.

Informed Consent

Because of the concern about assuring that persons involved as subjects in a clinical study are properly informed, FDA requires that investigators obtain informed consent from study subjects for "all clinical investigations regulated by the FDA" that support product applications (21 C.F.R. Part 50). The informed consent statement/form, simply stated, must explain to the person who is considering whether to become a clinical subject, the following: the purpose of the study; its potential benefits, if any; and especially the risks that are potentially associated with participation in the study. The objective is to provide sufficient information so the person can make an informed decision on whether to participate in the study.

FDA has created regulations that specifically address the information that must be included in the informed consent document.

FDA has created regulations that specifically address the information that must be included in the informed consent document. Some of the required elements of informed consent include: descriptions of any reasonably foreseeable risks and of any benefits that may be reasonably expected; the informed consent must be written using language understandable to the subject (fifth-grade level; translated, etc.); it must include an explanation of who to contact with questions about the research or a subject's rights during the study; the written informed consent must be reviewed and approved by the IRB; it must provide the subject with sufficient opportunity to consider whether or not to participate in the study; and the informed consent must be signed by the subject or the subject's legal representative to confirm the patient was informed (see 21 C.F.R. § 50.25).

It really does not matter whether the study concerns a food ingredient, a drug, cosmetic, or device; the expectation is that a person being asked to participate in a research study should be provided with complete and understandable disclosure of the benefits and risks of study participation and provide his or her informed consent on a form examined and approved by an IRB. During its inspection of a clinical study, one of the main focus points of an FDA bioresearch monitoring inspection or an OHRP audit will be whether the written informed consent that was signed by the study subject or representative fulfills the FDA or DHHS regulation of fully and properly informing the subject. Failure to inform has often been the basis for FDA to disallow data or OHRP to question a research institution's compliance.

The Sponsor/Sponsor-Investigator

The sponsor is the person or organization who takes responsibility for and initiates a clinical investigation. The sponsor is responsible for monitoring the conduct of the study being conducted by the principal investigator (PI) to assure compliance and collection and analysis of the study data. The sponsor may be a pharmaceutical company, a private or academic organization, or an individual. The sponsor-investigator, however, is an individual who both initiates and conducts a clinical investigation and under whose immediate direction the investigative drug is being administered and dispensed. It is the sponsor or sponsor-investigator who generally seeks FDA approval before beginning a clinical study. A new requirement for clinical study sponsors is the need to list the study on The National Institutes of Health's website (www.clinicaltrials.gov) before the enrollment of the first subject.

Principal Investigator

The principal investigator has primary responsibility for the FDA clinical research process.

When one considers clinical research performed for the purpose of making a scientific data submission to FDA, careful attention should be paid to the PI because that person has primary responsibility for the FDA clinical research process. It is the PI who controls the integrity of the research and manages the other professionals conducting the research. FDA, by requiring the drug/biologic investigator to sign a Form 1572, places the ultimate responsibility for the clinical investigation on the PI. A Form 1572 is a "Statement of Investigator" Form. No investigator may participate in an investigation until he/she provides the sponsor with a completed and signed Form 1572 (21 C.F.R. § 312.53(c)). By signing the form, the investigator agrees, among other things, to conduct the investigation according to the approved protocol, to personally conduct or supervise the described investigation, to inform patients that drugs are being used for investigational purposes, to ensure that requirements related to informed consent and IRBs are met, to report any adverse events that occur in the course of the investigation to the sponsor, to report unanticipated problems involving risks to the subjects and others to the IRB, and to ensure compliance with all other applicable FDA regulations.

In the device process, the PI will sign an agreement with the sponsor which will include language that commits the PI to following the FDA regulations governing device studies.

Whether the investigational product is a drug or a device, the PI is responsible to several different parties in the research process. For example, when the study protocol is not followed, FDA holds the PI absolutely responsible. The IRB looks to the PI to advise it of unanticipated problems and to properly perform the informed consent process. When a Contract Research Organization (CRO) is employed, the CRO will expect the PI to follow the protocol in coordinating the research and enrolling patients. Finally, the sponsor will expect the PI to enroll patients, provide accurate and complete case report forms, submit adverse event reports, and follow the protocol. The data collected by the PI are a critical part of the drug/device application process. As can be seen from these expectations, the PI is the foundation on which all studies are based.

Clinical research is first and foremost data collection, and the clinical site is only as good as its data collection process.

The most significant challenge for sponsors and FDA is that few physicians doing their first clinical study as a PI understand that clinical research is not clinical medical practice. Clinical research is first and foremost data collection, and the clinical site is only as good as its data collection process. The average medical professional who agrees to perform a clinical study and signs a 1572 or device letter agreement may have little understanding of the time and effort that will be required of the staff or the investigator personally. The PIs remain ultimately responsible if there are problems at the study site. The obligation is significant because the investigator can face criminal and civil sanctions should the staff fail to fill out the case report forms correctly. Unfortunately, many PIs do not fully appreciate the level of responsibility they have assumed and fail to properly educate themselves or their staff. (See FDA Guidance for Industry—Protecting the Rights, Safety, and Welfare of Study Subjects—Supervisory Responsibilities of Investigators, available at www.fda.gov/cder/guidance/index.htm.)

Center for Food Safety and Applied Nutrition

Food additives, color additives, and Food Contact Notifications require the submission of scientific studies and data to support marketing. Almost all of the studies are focused on safety and involve the use of various animal models and some tissue testing. Parties are expected to submit both supportive and other data when making submissions to FDA (i.e., provide FDA with information supporting approval of their submission, as well as information of which they are aware that does not necessarily support approval of their submission).

When submitting data to FDA for review, a major consideration will be whether the collected data is statistically significant. For example, were enough animals placed in the study to provide a statistically significant result? Most submissions also require a statement certifying that the study was conducted in accordance with GLPs. GLPs for nonclinical laboratory studies are discussed at 21 C.F.R. Part 58. These regulations include requirements pertaining to organization and personnel, facilities, testing, test and control articles, study protocols and recordkeeping among other things. While one might think that all laboratories practice GLPs, in fact this is not the case; many laboratories have not adopted the procedures necessary to satisfy GLP standards. Data from a laboratory that does not practice GLPs will, in all likelihood, be rejected by FDA.

Center for Veterinary Medicine

The CVM is concerned with both pharmaceutical and food testing in that the center is charged with approval of animal feeds, animal drugs, and the level of drug that may be present in the animal tissue to be eaten by humans. This creates a unique situation not found in any of the other centers; CVM has oversight responsibility relative not only to animal feeds, but also with respect to the pharmaceuticals given to animals and the level of the pharmaceutical given the animal that can be present in the animal tissue at the time of slaughter.

CVM has oversight responsibility relative not only to animal feeds, but also with respect to the pharmaceuticals given to animals and the level of the pharmaceutical given the animal that can be present in the animal tissue at the time of slaughter.

For the most part, testing in animals is similar to safety testing for human foods in that it requires no pretesting submission to FDA. CVM, however, is increasingly focused upon the potential implications associated with the presence of residual levels of drugs that remain in animal tissue of food products ingested by humans. Where the drug is being tested in a food-producing animal and the intent is to use the tissue from that animal for human food, CVM will require research testing that evaluates not only the effect of the drug on the animal, but also the level of residue of the drug in the animal tissue to be eaten by human consumers.

Where questions of animal and consumer safety are involved, an investigational new animal drug (INAD) application (referred to in the regulations as a "Notice of Claimed Investigational Exemption for a New Animal Drug") must be filed with FDA before shipping the test article in interstate commerce. Studies evaluating the impact of such drug residues on human health will likely be required (21 U.S.C. § 512(j)). The legal requirements for conducting studies, tests, and investigations under an INAD exemption are located at 21 C.F.R. Part 511). Among other things, these include labeling the product as investigational, ensuring that the test product is used for tests only in animals and not humans, maintaining adequate shipment records, and actually filing the INAD application. Usually this responsibility lies with the sponsor. Trials using the investigational drug may commence at any time following the submission of the INAD to FDA so long as the regulatory requirements mentioned above are satisfied. Additionally, animals treated with the investigational product may not be used for food until expressly authorized by FDA. Before conducting a study, drug sponsors are encouraged to consult with the agency on study design.

New animal drugs used for tests in vitro and in laboratory research animals are less strictly regulated and covered by the provisions of 21 C.F.R. § 511.1(a). Generally, if the animal tissue is not going to be used as a human food, then submission of an application prior to testing is not required.

Center for Drug Evaluation and Research and Center for Biologics Evaluation and Research

Unlike preclinical research, clinical drug research with human subjects requires FDA notification and involves more active FDA oversight. This is meant to protect the safety and general well-being of the human test subjects participating in the study and to ensure the integrity of the collected test data.

Before a clinical trial can begin, FDA must be notified to ensure that the research will be useful and not result in a study that would expose subjects to the risk of research without providing data that would be useful in a drug approval.

Before a clinical trial can begin, FDA must be notified to be sure the proposed test/experiment/research will be useful and not result in a study that would expose subjects to the risk of research without providing data that would be useful in a drug approval. To be sure the research will be of value, a well-designed and IRB-approved protocol should be used that includes appropriate controls such as informed consent and study monitoring. FDA requires that an investigational new drug (IND) application be submitted to the agency at least thirty days before the drug or biologic is shipped and administered to a test subject. Among other things, the IND should be accompanied by a copy of the IRB-approved protocol and any preclinical laboratory data supporting the proposed investigation. An FDA Form 1571 should be submitted, which identifies the phase of the study and specifies the sponsor's commitment to follow regulatory requirements.

An FDA Form 1572 signed by the PI should also be filed with the IND. By signing the FDA Form 1572, the PI commits to conducting the study in accordance with FDA regulations, including properly obtaining informed consent from each study participant, following the protocol, accurately recording all collected data, and ensuring that all of the investigational product is accounted for. In addition, the PI may work with sub-investigators who also must be listed in the filing with FDA so that the agency knows who is involved with conducting the study. During the thirty-day period before the study is allowed to start, FDA will review the IND to assure that research is appropriate and the subjects will not be subjected to unreasonable risk. If the agency does not place a clinical hold on the IND within thirty days, then the IND becomes effective and the sponsor can begin clinical trial. As a practical matter, the sponsor will generally seek some type of assurance from FDA that the sponsor can proceed with the study before actually starting; there have been times when FDA has delayed beyond thirty days in providing its view that the study has been placed on clinical hold.

Once the IND has been at the agency for thirty days and assuming that a clinical hold has not been placed on the IND, the sponsor/CRO can send the drug to the PI. The PI can then enroll subjects into the study provided they meet the inclusion/exclusion criteria of the protocol and are properly consented into the study. During the study, the PI or the staff collect data from the subject and record it in the patient's clinical records and the case report forms (CRFs) for forwarding to the CRO or sponsor for review and analysis.

During the clinical study, it is likely that the PI will be monitored by the sponsor/CRO to assure that the PI is following the protocol and fully understands the study. If problems are identified at the clinical site, the monitor may try to educate the PI or the site may be closed because the quality of the research is such that it cannot be relied on to support any study conclusions. If the monitoring visit goes well, the PI will continue to enroll patients until the enrollment criteria have been met or the study is stopped. At that point, the PI will submit any data (CRFs) not already submitted and either destroy or return any unused drug. The PI's assignment is then concluded. Now the sponsor takes over the leadership role, analyzing the data from various PIs and conducting a statistical evaluation to see if the data supports a conclusion that the drug is better than a placebo.

Center for Devices and Radiological Health

Clinical research in the medical device area is only a little different from that performed in the area of drugs. As noted earlier, the PI does not sign a 1572, but instead agrees in a letter to the sponsor to follow FDA's medical device regulations. The center also does not require as much clinical research; many devices can be proven to be effective based on nonclinical data, including various physical measurements or animal data.

Many devices can be proven to be effective based on nonclinical data.

CDRH also does not require a pre-submission for almost all clinical studies. The center has concluded that there are two types of clinical studies with medical devices. One is a study in which the clinical risk to the patient is basically not an issue; called a "Non-Significant Risk" study. In those cases, FDA has concluded that there is no real value in having the investigational device exemption (IDE) submitted to FDA. The agency relies on the IRB to make the risk determination. If the IRB says there is no significant risk, the sponsor/CRO does not need to file an IDE and the study may begin immediately (see 21 C.F.R. § 812.150). If, however, the IRB says the device does present a significant risk, then the sponsor/CRO must submit an IDE thirty days before the first patient is enrolled.

The IDE submission for the significant risk device is similar to the IND and is governed by 21 C.F.R. Part 812. As with the IND, once the IDE has been at FDA for thirty days, the sponsor/CRO may send the device to the PI. The PI can then seek to enroll patients who meet the study criteria and complete the informed consent process. Once the study is complete, any devices not used are to be returned to sponsor.

Conclusion

As noted, FDA's centers for drugs, biologics, and medical devices have specific statutory and regulatory requirements governing the practice of preclinical and clinical research. Several of these requirements, such as the establishment and maintenance of an IRB, and obtaining the informed consent of study participants, are required for all studies submitted to FDA. It is important for PIs and sub-investigators to fully appreciate their responsibility to ensure that the patient is properly informed, the recordkeeping is accurate, and there is adherence to GLPs.

Chapter 17

International Regulation

Richard Kingham, Covington & Burling LLP, Washington, D.C.

Key Points

- Nearly every industrialized nation maintains regulatory systems comparable to the Food and Drug Administration's (FDA's), although those systems are not always based on the U.S. model.
- Food and drug law is not a recognized specialty outside of North America because most developed countries have not established agencies like FDA.
- Most advanced regulatory systems are in the European Union, Canada, Australia, and Japan.
- EU legislation governing foods, drugs, and similar products is drafted by the European Commission.
- The first European medicines directive required member states to establish premarket approval systems. Today, requirements for marketing authorization applications are harmonized.
- Medical device directives in Europe rely on a new approach to harmonization, developed by the EU.
- Cosmetics directives in Europe provide for ingredient declarations, use of common European nomenclature, and require manufacturers to maintain product dossiers.
- The EU has issued numerous directives, regulations, and decisions affecting food regulation.
- The Health Products and Food Branch is the primary federal regulator in Canada.
- In Australia, drugs, devices, and similar products are regulated by the Therapeutics Goods Administration; foods are regulated by several agencies.
- The Ministry of Health, Labor, and Welfare conducts food and drug regulation in Japan.
- The United States is unusual in the high degree to which it seeks to regulate exports.
- Efforts to coordinate international food and drug regulation and reduce obstacles to trade take three forms: international cooperation, harmonization of regulations and standards, and mutual recognition. Only the last of these actually eliminates duplicative approval requirements, but it has proved the most difficult to achieve.

Introduction

Nearly every industrialized nation maintains regulatory systems comparable to the Food and Drug Administration's (FDA's), although those systems are not always based on the U.S. model. In recent years, FDA has borrowed ideas from other countries, and there has been great pressure from industry and Congress for the agency to move further in that direction.

It is thus essential to have at least a general understanding of international food and drug regulation. This chapter focuses on three topics: regulatory systems outside the United States, FDA regulation of exports and other matters affecting international trade, and international harmonization initiatives.

Foreign Regulatory Systems

"Food and Drug Law" is not a recognized specialty outside North America for the simple reason that most developed countries in Europe and elsewhere have not established agencies like FDA. Instead, regulation of products under FDA's jurisdiction is commonly entrusted to several agencies, often in different ministries or departments. Within product categories, enforcement is sometimes divorced from policymaking and product-approval functions.

Many countries are now looking to the EU as an alternative to the FDA model.

The most advanced regulatory systems are in the European Union (EU), Canada, Australia, and Japan. Perhaps the most important jurisdiction is the EU, which is now the biggest unified market in the industrialized world. As of 2008, the EU comprised twenty-seven member states with a total population of 497 million, compared to 304 million in the United States and 127 million in Japan. The EU's efforts to harmonize national regulation of consumer products provide a lesson in what can reasonably be expected from such initiatives. Many countries are now looking to the EU as an alternative to the FDA model.

EUROPEAN UNION

The Legal Framework

♦ EU or EC?

Technically, European legislation governing foods, drugs, and similar products is drafted by the European Community (EC). The "European Union" is a vaguely defined political entity that may some day form the basis of a federation comparable to the United States. Its name, however, has captured the public imagination, and it is common to refer to the EU when the EC is meant.

♦ Sources of EU Food and Drug Law

There are two main sources of food and drug regulation in the EU: judicial decisions under provisions of the EC Treaty that correspond roughly to the Interstate Commerce Clause of the U.S. Constitution, and harmonizing legislation issued by the EU.

♦ Free Movement of Goods

Article 28 of the EC Treaty guarantees free movement of goods among the member states, and regulations that create obstacles to free movement may be struck down by the courts if they are not justified on specific grounds identified in the treaty (e.g., protecting the health and safety of consumers), or are not "proportional" to the public interests that justify them. The European courts have developed a substantial body of case law relating to national rules on foods, drugs, cosmetics, and other consumer products. Decisions have rendered unenforceable, for example, a French law defining "cassis de Dijon" and a 16th century German beer-purity law that prohibited use of additives.

♦ Harmonization Measures

Beginning in the 1960s, the EU issued a series of measures aimed at harmonizing national regulations of consumer goods so that products are assured free movement and requirements for duplicative national approvals are minimized. The pace was accelerated greatly in 1985, when the EU set the deadline of December 31, 1992, for the issuance of more than 300 measures required to complete the "internal market." Amendments in 1986 to the EC Treaty furthered this "EC-92" initiative by eliminating provisions that allowed individual member states to veto harmonization measures.

Beginning in the 1960s, the EU issued a series of measures aimed at harmonizing national regulations of consumer goods.

Today, the EU maintains comprehensive systems of measures governing foods, drugs, and similar products. The extent of actual harmonization, however, varies greatly among product categories. The following is a brief summary of the major measures.

Medicines

♦ Medicines

The first medicines directive, issued in 1965, required member states to establish premarket approval systems based on proof of efficacy, safety, and quality. Today, requirements for marketing authorization applications are harmonized, as are provisions for labeling, advertising, regulation of wholesalers, good clinical practice, good laboratory practice (GLP), good manufacturing practice (GMP), and other matters.

Until 1995, marketing authorizations for medicines were granted country-by-country, and divergent decisions were common. Efforts to establish a coordinated "multistate procedure" (an early version of mutual recognition) were largely ineffective, because there was no mechanism to enforce harmonized decisions.

♦ The European Medicines Agency

Since 1995, a London-based independent agency, the European Medicines Agency, has been responsible for coordinating EU drug approval procedures.

Since 1995, a London-based independent agency, the European Medicines Agency (EMEA), has been responsible for coordinating EU drug-approval procedures. Marketing authorization applications for new biotechnology products and many new chemical entities must be submitted to the EMEA, and applications for certain other innovative products may be submitted on an optional basis. An expert body (the Committee for Medicinal Products for Human Use) reviews applications and renders opinions to the European Commission (the executive branch of the EU), which issues approvals that are effective throughout the EU.

For other products, national approvals also are available. Products that are intended to be marketed in more than one member state, however, must be submitted through mandatory mutual recognition or "decentralized" procedures that are backed up by a binding arbitration process administered by the EMEA.

♦ Current Issues

A directive on clinical trials, which took effect in 2004, established requirements similar to those for investigational new drugs in the United States, although separate approvals or notifications are required in each member state where trials are conducted. An orphan drug regulation provides a ten-year period of marketing exclusivity, and there are now incentives for investment in research on medicines for pediatric use.

EU law provides periods of data exclusivity after new drugs are approved, during which "generic" marketing authorization applications (the EU equivalent of abbreviated new drug applications) cannot be submitted. Under legislation that took effect in 2005 (which applies to innovative products for which marketing authorization applications were submitted after the effective date), the EU recognizes a uniform protection period that is often referred to as "8 + 2 + 1." Generic applications cannot be filed until eight years after the reference product is approved, and generic products cannot enter the market until the end of the tenth year, but this period can be extended to eleven years if a medically significant new use is authorized within the first eight years after the reference product is approved. A special system has been established for approval of follow-on biological products (referred to as similar biological medicinal products, or biosimilars).

Medical Devices

Separate directives establish uniform regulatory requirements for marketing active implantable medical devices (e.g., pacemakers), medical devices, and in vitro diagnostics. All of these directives rely on a "new approach" to harmonization developed by the EU to facilitate the EC-92 initiative. The directives establish relatively general "essential requirements." Products that comply with those requirements are labeled with a mark of conformity (the CE mark) and are entitled to move freely throughout the EU, subject to a "safeguard clause" allowing national enforcement actions in extraordinary circumstances. Essential requirements are supplemented by standards issued by the European standard-setting bodies. Conformity to standards is not mandatory, but constitutes presumptive evidence of compliance with essential requirements.

Manufacturers are legally responsible for determining whether their products conform to essential requirements and thus may bear the CE mark. Conformity assessment procedures depend on the risk classification of a device, which is determined by principles in the medical device directives. For the lowest risk devices, conformity assessments may be performed by manufacturers without any intervention by third parties. Manufacturers must notify member state governments when such products are introduced to the EU market.

Manufacturers are legally responsible for determining whether their products conform to essential requirements.

Conformity assessments for higher-risk devices require interaction with "notified bodies" (quasi-governmental entities designated by member state governments). This may consist of product-specific design reviews or certification of quality systems, or both. Quality systems certifications are based on a European version of the International Organization for Standardization (ISO) 9000 series of standards, with modifications specific to medical devices.

Cosmetics

A directive first issued in 1976 establishes a general safety requirement for cosmetics; sets harmonized labeling requirements; prohibits or restricts certain ingredients; and requires affirmative listing of specified categories of ingredients (ultra violet filters, preservatives, and color additives). The European Commission, working with the Scientific Committee on Cosmetology and the member state governments, periodically revises the ingredient lists.

The directive provides for ingredient declarations, using a common European nomenclature, and requires manufacturers to maintain product dossiers. The dossiers must include reports of safety evaluations, which are subject to inspection by member state governments. Manufacturers must submit product notifications to the member states where products are manufactured or first enter the EU. The directive also includes a controversial ban on testing of cosmetic products and new cosmetic ingredients in animals.

The EU has issued numerous directives, regulations, and decisions affecting food regulation.

Foods

♦ Harmonizing Measures

The EU has issued numerous directives, regulations, and decisions affecting food regulation. These include "horizontal" measures on labeling, additives, contaminants, hygiene, and food-contact materials, and "vertical" measures establishing standards for particular foods (e.g., chocolate, fruit juices, mineral waters, and sugars). The European Food Safety Authority, which has replaced the Scientific Committee on Food, advises the European Commission on all matters with a direct or indirect impact on food safety, and other technical issues relating to food legislation.

Two new regulations dealing with nutrition and health claims, and the fortification of foods, applied from last year. They are the first pieces of specific legislation to control such claims and the fortification of foods in the EU. Not all aspects of food regulation are harmonized, however, and there is still scope for national variations. The European Commission has adopted a package of legislative proposals which would introduce harmonized EU legislation on food enzymes for the first time and upgrade current rules for flavorings and additives. A proposed regulation on the provision of information to consumers, which would replace the existing framework directive on food labeling, is also being considered.

♦ Free-Movement Principle

A 1989 EU "communication" seeks to prevent member states from enforcing national requirements that create obstacles to free movement unless there is a clear public health or consumer protection benefit, and requires member states to establish expedited procedures for approving imports from other EU countries that comply with food regulations in the country of origin.

OTHER JURISDICTIONS

Canada

♦ Laws and Agencies

The principal federal statute is the Food and Drugs Act (passed in 1953, but with predecessor legislation dating back to 1860), supplemented by the Food and Drug Regulations and numerous guidance documents.

The principal federal statute is the Food and Drugs Act (passed in 1953, but with predecessor legislation dating back to 1860), supplemented by the Food and Drug Regulations and numerous guidance documents. The Health Products and Food Branch (HPFB) in "Health Canada" (the Department of Health) is the primary federal regulator, although certain aspects of food regulation are entrusted to Agriculture and Agri-Food Canada, other federal departments, and a Canadian Food Inspection Agency established in 1997.

The HPFB maintains a system of premarket approval for new drugs, for which applicants submit new drug submissions and obtain notices of compliance. A procedure for abbreviated new drug submissions provides for an eight-year data exclusivity period to protect innovators, with provision for linkage to patent expiry. A separate system governs medicines containing old active ingredients, for which submissions are required to obtain drug information numbers or GP numbers.

For many years, Canada maintained a relatively simple notification system for most medical devices, with more elaborate requirements for safety substantiation of specified products. The HPFB has established a premarket screening procedure, in which the level of scrutiny depends on relative risk based on classification principles similar to those used in the EU. The ISO 9000 series of standards for quality systems also plays a role.

The Food and Drug Regulations contain requirements for labeling of cosmetics and for notifications of new products, and the HPFB has issued guidelines on permissible claims. Drug/cosmetic products are permitted, but must be registered as proprietary medicines and meet other requirements for drugs (e.g., GMP).

Food additives require prior approval, and the Food and Drug Regulations establish requirements for labeling. The HPFB has issued numerous informal guidelines, including detailed guidance on health-related claims for foods.

Australia

Drugs, devices, and similar products are regulated by the Therapeutic Goods Administration (TGA) in the Commonwealth Department of Health and Ageing. Foods are regulated by several federal and state agencies, with standards set by the Australia-New Zealand Food Authority. Cosmetics that are not classified as drugs are subject only to general regulations for consumer products. The TGA has entered into a mutual recognition agreement with the EU concerning medical device regulation.

Drugs, devices, foods, and cosmetics are regulated at the national level by the Ministry of Health, Labor, and Welfare (MHLW). The Pharmaceutical Affairs Law of 1960 governs drugs, devices, and cosmetics, while the Food Sanitation Law of 1947 governs foods.

Japan

Drugs, devices, foods, and cosmetics are regulated at the national level by the Ministry of Health, Labor, and Welfare (MHLW). The Pharmaceutical Affairs Law governs drugs, devices, and cosmetics, while the Food Sanitation Law governs foods.

Drugs ordinarily require a manufacturing or import license (*kyoka*) and a product license (*shonin*). Data requirements for marketing authorization applications are set out in guidelines issued by the MHLW. New chemical entities are subject to a period of postmarket "re-examination," during which abridged applications for generic copies are not accepted. There are simplified procedures for approval of products containing established active ingredients.

Medical device regulation was revised in 1995, and the current system assigns devices to several classes based on relative risk. Product approvals are no longer required for the lowest risk devices, but quality standards apply.

Cosmetic products require premarket approval. Applications for products containing novel active ingredients require safety data, as do those for "quasi-drugs," a category that includes many products regulated as ordinary cosmetics in Europe and the United States.

Food imports require prior notification. Detailed labeling requirements apply, and there is a system of premarket approval of food additives, with different requirements for "chemical compound additives" and substances of natural origin.

FDA Regulation of Foreign Trade

General Controls on Exports

Every developed country regulates imports of foods, drugs, and similar products, but the United States is unusual in the degree to which it seeks to regulate exports. Section 801 of the Federal Food, Drug, and Cosmetic Act (FDCA) permits exports of foods, drugs, and other articles that are adulterated or misbranded under U.S. law if they conform to the specifications of foreign purchasers, do not conflict with foreign law, and meet certain other requirements. FDA has narrowly interpreted the exemption provisions of the section to restrict exports of banned color additives, aflatoxin-contaminated feedstuffs, and similar products. The agency has asserted that exporters bear the burden of proving compliance with foreign law and has demanded proof of compliance, including letters from foreign government officials.

The United States is unusual in the degree to which it seeks to regulate exports.

Exports of Unapproved Drugs and Devices

♦ Historical Background

Unapproved drugs (and, since 1976, unapproved devices) have presented the most difficult problem. By a quirk of legislative drafting in 1938, the new drug application requirement was not linked to the adulteration and misbranding provisions of the FDCA. As a result, the export exemption in section 801 was ineffective for unapproved new drugs. It is unclear whether Congress intended this result, because it chose seven years later (without discussion) to regulate penicillin, and later other antibiotics, under the adulteration provisions and thus make them eligible for the export exemption.

♦ FDA Enforcement Policy

In the decades following 1938, FDA consistently took the position that exports of unapproved new drugs were prohibited. The agency extended the ban not only to finished products but also to bulk pharmaceuticals, applied the export restriction to foreign trade zones, and prohibited import of unapproved products intended solely for re-export.

The agency permitted exports of "chemical intermediates" used to manufacture drug substances, on the theory that they were not new drugs, but refused to apply a similar policy to precursors of biological products.

♦ The 1968 and 1976 Amendments

By the 1960s, the U.S. ban on exports of unapproved drugs, whatever its historical origins, had become a matter of political significance. Consumer groups drew attention to the "dumping" of unsafe and ineffective medicines in developing countries and urged the United States to provide moral leadership to the industrialized world. When it enacted the Animal Drug Amendments of 1968 and the Medical Device Amendments of 1976, Congress specifically incorporated special procedures for FDA approval of exports of banned or unapproved devices in a conscious effort to drastically deter such exports.

♦ The 1986 Export Amendments

By the 1980s, the political climate had changed. There was increased concern about the competitiveness of U.S. businesses in world markets, and manufacturers argued that U.S. export controls served mainly to encourage companies to locate research and manufacturing facilities abroad.

In 1984, FDA issued regulations permitting exports of unapproved drugs for clinical trials, subject to permits. In 1986, Congress enacted amendments that allowed exports of unapproved drugs to any of twenty-one listed countries, subject to specified conditions, including FDA permits. The legislation included special provisions for unfinished biologics and drugs for tropical diseases.

♦ Current Law

The FDA Export Reform and Enhancement Act of 1996, among other things, lifted the import-re-export ban.

The FDA Export Reform and Enhancement Act of 1996 lifted the import/re-export ban, allowed exports of unapproved drugs and premarket approval devices to any country if they were approved in one of several designated jurisdictions, permitted exports for clinical trials in the listed jurisdictions, and eliminated the requirement for prior approval of most exports (although a simple notification was still required). The legislation also authorized FDA to expand the list of designated countries and to permit, on a case-by-case basis, exports of products not approved in listed countries.

International Initiatives

Efforts to coordinate international food and drug regulation and reduce obstacles to trade take three forms: international cooperation, harmonization of regulations and standards, and mutual recognition. Only the last of these actually eliminates duplicative approval requirements, but it has proved the most difficult to achieve.

Efforts to coordinate international regulation and reduce obstacles take three forms:
- *international cooperation,*
- *harmonization of regulations and standards, and*
- *mutual recognition.*

Cooperative Agreements

♦ General

Information exchanges and other cooperative efforts among government agencies have existed for many years. FDA, for example, began "tripartite" meetings with drug regulators in the United Kingdom and Canada more than twenty-five years ago, and the World Health Organization (WHO) has long maintained an international clearing house for information on adverse drug reactions. FDA officials now meet periodically with their counterparts in the European Commission.

More recently, FDA has entered into formal information sharing agreements with the EU and Japanese authorities relating to drug approvals, inspections, and safety reporting. FDA and the EMEA have also agreed to procedures for providing joint scientific advice to pharmaceutical companies on development of new drug products.

Responding to public concern about imports of contaminated drugs, cosmetics, and other products, FDA is currently in the process of establishing inspection posts in countries that export significant quantities of products to the United States.

♦ Memoranda of Understanding

FDA's more formal cooperative agreements with foreign regulatory agencies are commonly set out in memoranda of understanding (MOUs), exchanges of letters, and similar documents. Typically, these are signed by FDA and its counterparts in foreign countries, but approval by the U.S. Secretary of State may also be required. Agreements cover a wide range of topics, from information exchanges to mutual acceptance of inspections and product standards.

The precise legal status of these agreements has never been entirely clear. They are not treaties within the meaning of the U.S. Constitution, and they cannot supersede FDA's obligations under U.S. statutes or regulations. Some FDA officials have expressed concern that such agreements might impermissibly delegate FDA enforcement functions to foreign governments. Nevertheless, MOUs and similar agreements have great practical importance for the industrial sectors affected.

International efforts to harmonize food and drug regulatory standards have proliferated.

Harmonization

In recent years, international efforts to harmonize food and drug regulatory standards have proliferated. WHO, the Organization for Economic Cooperation and Development (OECD), international standard-setting bodies (especially the ISO), and numerous sectoral and regional organizations have played a role in the process. The Uruguay Round amendments to the General Agreement on Tariffs and Trade (GATT), signed in 1994, enhanced the significance of these initiatives, because signatory countries now may be required to justify failure to implement agreed-upon international standards.

♦ Major Initiatives

Codex Alimentarius

Among the oldest efforts is the Codex Alimentarius Commission, established by the United Nations Food and Agriculture Organization and the WHO in 1962 to develop international standards for foods. The Codex Commission, whose members include representatives of more than 150 countries, aims to protect the health of consumers and ensure fair international trade in food. Major areas of activity include food labeling, food additives and contaminants, food hygiene, pesticide residues, veterinary drug residues, analytical methods, and food inspection. The Codex Commission is advised by expert committees, such as the Joint Expert Committee on Food Additives and the Joint Meeting on Pesticide Residues.

Although the United States has long participated in Codex activities, it has given a relatively low priority to implementing Codex standards.

International Conference on Harmonization

The International Conference on Harmonization of Technical Requirements for Registration of Pharmaceuticals for Human Use (ICH), established in 1989, has been an extraordinarily productive initiative. Sponsors include FDA; the Japanese MHLW; the European Commission; and the national trade associations of the pharmaceutical industries in the United States, the EU, and Japan, with coordination from the International Federation of Pharmaceutical Manufacturers & Associations. Other governments and international entities participate as observers.

From its inception, the ICH decided not to seek mutual recognition, but to focus instead on harmonization of technical requirements for product registration. Activities have been undertaken in the areas of safety (e.g., toxicology testing), efficacy (clinical testing), and quality (manufacturing and chemistry). The result has been a series of consensus documents that participants transpose into guidelines or regulations. The volume of documents has been considerable. In some cases, however, full implementation requires issuance of new regulations or other legislation; this has proved difficult to accomplish, especially in the United States. The ICH has also developed a "common technical document" to help harmonize marketing authorization applications.

Medical Devices

A Global Harmonization Task Force, with participants from the United States, Canada, the EU, Japan, and other countries, is seeking to duplicate the accomplishments of the ICH for medical devices.

A Global Harmonization Task Force, with participants from the United States, Canada, the EU, Japan, and other countries, is seeking to duplicate the accomplishments of the ICH for medical devices. One of the greatest forces for international harmonization of medical device regulation has been the ISO 9000 series of quality systems standards, which can be used as the basis for external certification of companies' systems for controlling the design, testing, production, and distribution of any product or service. The EU's decision to use modified versions of ISO 9001 and 9002, coupled with notified-body certifications, as one means of compliance with its medical device directives greatly enhanced the significance of the standards, as did FDA's decision to incorporate major elements of the standards in its regulations governing GMPs for devices.

♦ Effect of GATT and Other Agreements

International agreements aimed at eliminating nontariff barriers to trade lend increased importance to harmonization initiatives. Much attention has been devoted to the North American Free Trade Agreement (NAFTA), but GATT is potentially more significant, because it includes an effective enforcement mechanism.

Under GATT, measures that might affect international trade must not be stricter than necessary for protection of human, animal, or plant health; must not be maintained without sufficient scientific evidence; and must be based on scientific principles. The World Trade Organization has been established to enforce these requirements.

Mutual Recognition

FDA maintains agreements with many countries on shellfish sanitation inspections.

FDA traditionally has been reluctant to enter into broad mutual recognition agreements with foreign countries, and such agreements have often been confined to narrow sectors or areas of regulation. For example, the existence of OECD guidelines for GLP, based in large measure on the U.S. GLP regulations, made it possible for FDA to enter into MOUs with several countries for mutual acceptance of GLP inspections. FDA maintains agreements with many countries on shellfish sanitation inspections. Mutual recognition, however, has proved much more difficult to accomplish for product sectors that are subject to premarket approvals and similar controls. A 1997 U.S./EU Mutual Recognition Agreement, which covered six product sectors (including drugs and medical devices), proved much less useful than was hoped. In particular, an arrangement for mutual recognition of GMP inspections for pharmaceuticals was never put in operation, largely due to FDA's reluctance to accept the results of inspections by certain national authorities in the EU.

Chapter 18

Fundamental Issues Facing 21st Century Regulation

Michael R. Taylor, School of Public Health and Health Services, George Washington University, Washington, D.C.

Key Points

- There is a longstanding consensus in American society that the government should regulate food and medical products to protect and promote public health and maintain public confidence in products.
- The Food and Drug Administration's (FDA's) job is made difficult by the diversity of the demands placed on the agency—there are many different ideas about what constitutes success for FDA—and the fact that FDA's external environment and what people demand of the agency change over time.
- Technological change is a constant feature of modern society and greatly affects the challenges faced by FDA.
- The marketplace for foods, drugs, and medical devices has been changed dramatically by new demands for and new sources of information about products and by globalization of the market for food and drug products and ingredients.
- Individualism is a persistent feature of American society and affects the demands the public places on FDA and the policies Congress expects FDA to implement, such as in the areas of experimental drugs and dietary supplements.
- At the same time changes in technology and the marketplace and heightened individual demands are making FDA's role more complex and difficult, the domestic elements of the federal government have been in a period of budget and philosophical retrenchment.
- In this changing environment, FDA's longstanding mission remains clear—to protect and promote public health—but how FDA fulfills that mission requires continual refinement to deal with its new challenges.
- FDA's success in fulfilling its mission depends increasingly on how it interacts with other government agencies at federal, state, and local levels and globally.
- The changes in FDA's external environment also require FDA to re-examine the way it works in relation to individuals, industry, and other private institutions.
- Whether and how society is willing to pay for the services FDA provides is a critical issue for the future, and funding success for FDA will depend on building consensus on and broad understanding of what FDA does and how it does it.

The Food and Drug Administration (FDA) traces its origins to the last years of the 19th century. The first comprehensive national legislation governing foods and drugs was passed at the beginning of the 20th century. Now, in the first decade of the 21st century, it is timely to consider some of the fundamental issues that are facing 21st century food and drug regulation.

These include:

- rethinking FDA's mission;
- redefining how FDA works with other government agencies;
- clarifying FDA's role in relation to the individual, the market, and the industry; and
- deciding how society will pay for what it wants FDA to do.

To understand the issues of the future, it is important to review the constants that govern the FDA regulatory enterprise and the changes in the environment surrounding FDA.

The Constant Demand for FDA Regulation

The difficult and controversial issues in food and drug regulation do not have to do with whether government should regulate, but with the manner and success of government regulation.

There is a longstanding public consensus in American society that government has a role to play in protecting public health. Government action to ensure the purity and wholesomeness of food is documented back to biblical times and was a feature of colonial government in America. Serious regulation of pharmaceuticals and medical devices originated more recently in the 20th century, but there is little debate about the legitimacy of some role for government. The difficult and controversial issues in food and drug regulation do not have to do with whether government should regulate, but with the manner and success of government regulation.

To assess how FDA pursues its public health objectives, it is worthwhile to review briefly the rationale for FDA regulation. The products regulated by FDA are not just any consumer products. Food is indispensable to survival, and drugs and medical devices confer life-protecting and life-enhancing therapeutic benefits that are essential to personal well-being and have helped create the high standard of living now taken for granted in industrialized societies.

By their inherent nature, however, foods, drugs, and medical devices not only confer substantial benefits but also carry risks. Food can be rendered poisonous by the presence of naturally occurring or added toxicants, and chronic dietary imbalance in calorie intake or in such nutrients as fat and sodium is associated with an increased risk of heart disease, stroke, and cancer, the leading causes of death in the United States. While medicines and medical devices can provide immense benefits, they pose inherent risks as well and their failure to work as intended or claimed can result in harm, especially when alternative beneficial therapies are available.

Multiple theories are available to justify government intervention in the marketplace for foods, drugs, and medical devices. Economists would say that intervention is justified when market mechanisms fail to provide the safety and effectiveness attributes consumers seek and for which they are willing to pay. Markets work to the extent that consumers have all of the information and expertise they need to assess the risks and benefits of products, and to bargain effectively for the desired level of safety and effectiveness. As most economists and average citizens would agree, the market for foods, drugs, and medical devices is imperfect in this regard, and increasingly so, as products become technologically more complex and citizens are increasingly far removed from the production of their food and an understanding of the science and technology underlying sophisticated pharmaceuticals and medical devices.

Public health experts and officials tend to justify government regulation on less theoretical and more utilitarian grounds. They see the actual public health impact of contaminated food and dangerous or ineffective pharmaceuticals and medical devices. They demand that the best available science be marshaled and that standards be set on the public's behalf to prevent the resulting health problems. This necessarily implies a role for government.

Individual consumers and patients do not think about economic theory or social utility in the broad sense, but rather about their own welfare and the welfare of their families. Most citizens want to know that someone—the proverbial "they"—is looking out for the safety and effectiveness of the foods, drugs, and medical devices used by their families.

Finally, the demand for effective FDA regulation has been led, on many occasions, by the regulated industries—typically when some safety-related crisis or controversy has undermined the public's confidence in industry's products. This phenomenon is typified by the food industry's call in recent years for strengthening FDA oversight of food safety following illness outbreaks associated with fresh produce and public concern about the safety of fish and pet food coming from China. Companies that produce health-related products for consumers have a stake not only in the safety and effectiveness of their products but also in maintaining public confidence.

These several distinct rationales for FDA regulation add up to the overriding constant in FDA's external environment. The public at large and a wide array of interest groups in American society demand the presence of FDA in the marketplace for foods, drugs, and medical devices. This will not change. Moreover, the general public and the many constituencies affected by FDA regulation demand good performance by the agency and often are aggressive in insisting on accountability for good performance through the established governmental and political processes, the media, and other forms of public pressure. What makes FDA's job difficult is the diversity of the demand—there are many different ideas about what constitutes success for FDA—and the fact that FDA's external environment and what people demand of the agency change over time.

What makes FDA's job difficult is the diversity of the demand.

Changes in FDA's External Environment

The changes in FDA's external environment that are important to the future include dramatic advances in the science and technology underlying FDA-regulated products; changes in the nature of the marketplace for foods, drugs, and medical devices; the intensification of demands that the system respond to the needs of individuals; and retrenchment and reform in government.

Science and Technology

Technological change is a constant feature of modern society, and it greatly affects the challenges faced by FDA.

The food supply was transformed by new technologies throughout the 20th century. The chemical revolution transformed pest control in agriculture. Chemical food additives contributed to the revolution in food processing and packaging that has enabled the food industry to meet consumer demand for a wide array of convenient and economical food products. Today, the science of molecular biology and the resulting techniques of genetic modification of food crops promise similar advances in the ability of the American food system to meet consumer needs. As a result, FDA is called upon to make increasingly complex safety judgments, whose correctness and credibility are essential to public health and public acceptance of new technologies.

Technology also has been enlisted to meet consumer demands for nutritionally modified food products, including products that are reduced in fat, calories, and sodium. These products expand the array of choices available to consumers in constructing diets in accordance with the government's dietary guidelines and other public health recommendations, but they raise questions of whether consumers have the information and education they need to use these products effectively.

In the realm of therapeutic products, the impact of science and technology has been even more apparent. The "miracle drugs" of the mid-20th century—the vaccines and antibiotics that contributed so much to reducing the risk of premature death—have been succeeded by new generations of drugs grounded in a much more complete understanding at the molecular level of the causes of human disease. The response of drug researchers and innovators to the acquired immune deficiency syndrome (AIDS) epidemic turned the therapeutic tide on a disease that at first was considered automatically fatal in every case. Now, genomics and nanotechnology provide scientific platforms for further dramatic advances in diagnosis and therapy and increasingly personalized approaches to the practice of medicine. FDA must deal today with a body of science and with therapeutic technologies that barely existed ten or twenty years ago.

FDA must deal today with a body of science and with therapeutic technologies that barely existed ten or twenty years ago.

Changes in the Marketplace

At one level, markets are characterized by the nature of the information available to market participants and the extent to which market participants are able to apply that information to their market transactions. In the markets for foods, drugs, and medical devices, the information demanded by product purchasers, and provided by product sellers and others, has changed dramatically.

In the food arena, the change is most apparent in the area of nutrition information. As public health scientists documented the link between diet and health during the 1980s, consumers began to seek out low-calorie and low-fat foods, including products claimed specifically to be beneficial in reducing the risk of cancer, heart disease, or other adverse health consequences of dietary imbalance. Food marketers responded with an array of products and product claims intended to provide what consumers were looking for. Congress passed the Nutrition Labeling and Education Act of 1990 (NLEA) to bring greater consistency and reliability to the nutrition information and health claims flooding the food marketplace in the hope that reliable information would be a powerful tool for consumers seeking to construct healthy diets. Today, nutritional information and claims are an integral part of food marketing.

The marketplace for food also has been changed in recent decades by the nature of the safety information conveyed to consumers. Concern about food safety has been a persistent issue for the American public

The marketplace for food also has been changed in recent decades by the nature of the safety information conveyed to consumers.

and media, beginning in the 1960s, with the ban of cyclamate; continuing throughout the 1970s and '80s, with controversies over nitrite, saccharin, PCBs, and dioxins; and the present problems with *E. coli* 0157:H7, salmonella and other pathogenic bacteria. These controversies have intensified the pressure on FDA to be the reliable guarantor of food safety—the independent third party whose standards, judgments, and assurances provide the protection and confidence in the food supply that both consumers and the food industry want.

The information environment surrounding therapeutic products also has changed dramatically. The function and value of food is largely self-evident, but a pharmaceutical product is made useful only when accompanied by information concerning how it can be used safely and effectively. The essence of FDA's drug regulatory program is to ensure that reliable information about the safety and effectiveness of drugs is generated before the drugs are marketed. The program also regulates the flow of drug-related information from manufacturers to the marketplace. The effectiveness, as well as the objectives, of this traditional approach to drug regulation is being challenged now by the proliferation of new sources of information about drugs, and by new technologies for transmitting information and making it readily accessible to anyone who is interested in it. FDA's traditional approach also is being challenged by the desire of pharmaceutical companies to market their prescription products directly to consumers through advertising and other means, and by the growing demand of patients to be informed and involved in decisions about drug therapy.

In addition, the information marketplace for drugs is being changed—and made more complicated—by the enhanced role being played by new decision makers, such as health maintenance organizations and other third-party payers, on drug use. Most of these changes in the information environment apply to medical devices as well. The information marketplace for therapeutic products has exploded, and FDA's practical ability to control the flow of information is diminished.

Another critical change in the marketplace for FDA-regulated products is globalization.

Another critical change in the marketplace for FDA-regulated products is globalization. International trade in food is expanding rapidly. The future growth and economic success of American agriculture is heavily dependent on exports. Imports are making an increasingly important contribution to the American diet. For example, about three-quarters of all seafood consumed in the United States is imported, and Americans have come to depend on Mexico and other Latin American countries for fresh produce all year round. This trade creates food safety challenges for FDA and places pressure on regulatory authorities worldwide to maintain both high food safety standards and public confidence in the food supply. The regulatory agencies are responding, trying to establish a level playing field for domestic and imported foods as required by new trade agreements.

Similar pressures exist for drugs and medical devices. A large percentage of the ingredients used to manufacture drugs is imported, placing great strains on FDA's ability to ensure ingredients produced in foreign establishments meet U.S. good manufacturing practices. In addition, scientific research and technology development are now global enterprises. Drug and device companies are innovating for world markets, and they seek maximum consistency from regulatory bodies in data and approval requirements worldwide. Partly as a result of the globalization of science and trade, public health is becoming globalized. In the 21st century, FDA increasingly must work in concert and collaboration with the international community.

Intensification of Individual Demands on the System

Individualism is a persistent feature of American society, and activism among individuals to achieve their individual purposes through (or despite) government became an important feature of the American landscape in the late 20th century and continues as such today. This is reflected in part by the important and growing role that organized, national-level consumer groups play in FDA-related policy debates. It is seen even more graphically, however, in some of the clashes that have occurred between the government and grass-roots groups and individuals.

It is seen even more graphically, however, in some of the clashes that have occurred between the government and grass-roots groups and individuals.

In the early 1990s, dietary supplement users were mobilized to resist efforts by FDA to enforce the food safety laws with respect to nutritional supplements and herbal products. Critics of FDA policy invoked concepts of individual liberty and personal choice, and were successful in gaining enactment of the Dietary Supplement Health and Education Act (DSHEA), which significantly reduced FDA's role in regulating these products. The burden of proof regarding the safety of supplements was shifted from the manufacturer to FDA, and a "safe haven" was created for making nontherapeutic claims about the effect of the supplement on the "structure or function of the body" without prior approval or substantiation to FDA's satisfaction.

Challenges to FDA's role and intervention to protect consumers also have been mounted by patients seeking access to experimental therapies. The statutorily prescribed system of premarket approval for therapeutic products inherently infringes on the understandable desire of desperately ill individuals to have access to any therapy that might be of value, even if still unproven. It does so to achieve the important societal purpose of having the safety and effectiveness of commercially marketed drugs and medical devices proven by their manufacturer. FDA works hard to manage this tension between individual and societal needs through its various programs for providing patients with access to experimental therapies, but the issue will continue to arise, and perhaps in new ways, as, for example, individualized approaches to gene therapy are developed.

Government Retrenchment and Reform

At the same time changes in technology and the marketplace and heightened individual demands on the system are making FDA's role more complex and difficult, the domestic (as opposed to national security) elements of the federal government have been in a period of retrenchment and reform that has affected the resources and tools available to FDA to do its job.

The retrenchment is partly budget driven, with FDA's budget having been constrained by successful efforts in the mid-1990s to balance the federal budget and the current need to address budget deficits resulting from post-9/11 security concerns, the war in Iraq, and tax and spending policies grounded in a "shrink government" political philosophy. FDA's premarket review programs for drugs and medical devices have been amply funded by industry user fees, but resources for FDA's food program and most of its field inspection and compliance activity, which depend on funds appropriated from the U.S. Treasury, have declined in terms of real buying power and continue to lag far behind what is needed to keep up with growing demands on the agency.

There remains, however, an unresolved tension between the persistent public demand for effective regulation to protect public health and the widespread sentiment that government should be less intrusive and heavy handed.

The last twenty-five years have also seen a philosophical shift among many Americans regarding the role of government. Individual citizens and businesses affected by government increasingly have questioned government's role and the means by which government operates. In the public health arena, "regulatory reform" has consisted of reducing the command and control prescriptiveness of regulation, and increasing reliance on performance standards that provide companies greater flexibility in deciding how best to achieve the desired outcome. It also has consisted of efforts to harness market forces to achieve public health objectives, and a call for less confrontation and more cooperation between government and regulated entities. There remains, however, an unresolved tension between the persistent public demand for effective regulation to protect public health and the widespread sentiment that government should be less intrusive and heavy handed.

Fundamental Issues for the 21st Century

The fundamental issues FDA will be grappling with in the 21st century will reflect both the constants and the changes sketched in the preceding sections. The issues can be grouped under four headings: What is FDA's mission? What is FDA's role in relation to other government institutions? What is FDA's role in relation to the individual, the market, the industry, and other private sector entities? How will society pay for what it wants FDA to do?

What Is FDA's Mission?

In the broadest terms, FDA's mission is clear: to protect and promote the public health. This general understanding of FDA's mission gives rise, however, to some difficult issues.

In food regulation, FDA historically has emphasized protection of consumers from foodborne hazards by setting and enforcing standards with respect to chemical and microbiological contaminants, and the nutritional sufficiency of such products as infant formula. This likely will remain FDA's primary role, but, with respect to FDA's core food safety mission of reducing foodborne illness, there are important questions about how FDA can best achieve its public health goals.

FDA's food safety program has historically been based on detecting and reacting to problems after they occur, but, in the view of public health experts and authoritative bodies like the National Academy of Sciences and the Government Accountability Office, today's food safety challenges demand a more forward-looking, preventive approach. What legal tools, expertise, and resources will FDA need to systematically identify and work to prevent significant risks of foodborne illness? What is the proper scope of FDA's food safety leadership role? For example, protection of people from the hazards posed by microbiological contamination of food is closely linked with progress in procedures and technologies for identifying and controlling hazards. As new technologies are developed to detect microbial pathogens with greater speed and reliability and as new control processes and technologies are developed, there will be opportunities to elevate the standard of care for food safety. What role should FDA play both in stimulating the development of the technologies and redefining the technological standard of care for food safety?

The Food and Drug Administration is part of the executive branch of the U.S. government within the Department of Health and Human Services and the Public Health Service. FDA is a scientific regulatory agency that is responsible for the safety of the nation's domestically produced and imported foods, cosmetics, drugs, biologics, veterinary medical products, medical devices, and radiological products. It is one of the oldest federal agencies whose primary function is consumer protection. The agency touches and directly influences the lives of everyone in the United States. FDA is also recognized internationally as the leading food and drug regulatory agency in the world. Many foreign nations seek and receive FDA's help in improving and monitoring the safety of their products.

In the nutrition area, as obesity and obesity-related diseases like diabetes continue to grow as major public health problems, FDA may also be called on to play a more expansive role in promoting public health. The NLEA contemplated not only new labeling requirements but also the nutrition education required to empower consumers to make good use of nutrition information on food labels. Given the public health importance of diet, what should FDA's role be in nutrition education and other efforts to improve the diets of Americans? What role, if any, should FDA play in assessing whether nutritionally modified food products are in fact beneficial to consumers? Should the law be changed to create economic incentives for development of reliable health-related information and claims about food products?

In the therapeutic area, the issue of public health *protection* versus *promotion* often is reduced to whether FDA is reviewing and approving new products rapidly enough. This is, of course, an important issue because the sooner beneficial new products are available to physicians and patients, the sooner the public health benefits of the products will be enjoyed. There are other issues, however, including the relationship between FDA's product approval system and how well both safety and effectiveness are achieved in actual clinical practice. In 2006, the Institute of Medicine issued a scathing report on weaknesses in FDA's oversight of drug safety, and in 2007 Congress gave FDA new authority and resources to strengthen scrutiny of drug safety, especially after products enter the market. The question remains, however, of how FDA can more deeply institutionalize and implement an approach to drug safety that goes beyond the initial approval decision and acts on the basis of the reality that much of what we need to know about drug safety can be learned only after products have been marketed and used in the clinic by physicians and patients.

Questions also remain about FDA's role in assuring the effectiveness of drugs and devices in actual clinical practice. It is well known and widely accepted that much drug and device therapy involves "off-label" uses of approved products. FDA respects the importance of physician discretion within the practice of medicine to prescribe products for off-label uses, but, as the law provides, FDA prohibits drug and device companies from promoting off-label uses. FDA aggressively pursues this policy in the belief that allowing the promotion of off-label uses would undercut the companies' incentives to seek approval for those uses, and could result in false, misleading, or inadequately supported promotional claims regarding safety and effectiveness.

FDA respects the importance of physician discretion within the practice of medicine to prescribe products for off-label uses, but, as the law provides, FDA prohibits drug and device companies from promoting off-label uses.

The evolving legal doctrine of commercial free speech has encumbered FDA's efforts to regulate the flow of industry information about drugs and devices, and FDA and Congress continue to grapple with whether the current approval system for drugs and less so for devices fully meets the public health need for sound therapy. What role should FDA play in stimulating the generation of safety and effectiveness data on off-label uses, especially in such areas as oncology and pediatrics, where off-label uses predominate? Does the current system provide the right incentives for generation of such data? Should FDA play a more affirmative role, perhaps working with other public health agencies, to see that public health is promoted by the optimal generation of high-quality information concerning the safety and effectiveness of all drug and device therapy? How FDA implements the far-reaching provisions of the Food and Drug Administration Amendments Act of 2007 (FDAAA) will provide some of the answers.

How Does FDA Work in Relation to Other Government Agencies?

FDA has undergone a number of internal organizational changes over the years, but its place in the federal government and the basic responsibilities assigned to it have been largely fixed since it was transferred in the 1930s from the Department of Agriculture to what was then the Federal Security Agency (later the Department of Health, Education and Welfare and now the Department of Health and Human Services (DHHS)).

FDA now exists as the agency within DHHS responsible for implementing the Federal Food, Drug, and Cosmetic Act (FDCA) and related statutes. FDA has regulatory responsibilities for foods, drugs, and medical devices under the FDCA, but numerous other DHHS agencies operate in fields closely related to FDA's regulatory responsibility. For example, the Centers for Disease Control and Prevention (CDC) and the National Institutes of Health (NIH) conduct disease surveillance, research, and other activities that contribute essential scientific knowledge to FDA's regulatory activities. CDC has primary responsibility in the federal government for the epidemiological surveillance required to understand the frequency and causes of foodborne illness and other transmissible and chronic diseases.

The National Cancer Institute and the National Heart, Lung and Blood Institute within NIH conduct research and education programs directed at the prevention of illness through dietary change and the treatment of illness through development of effective drug therapies. The Agency for Health Care Policy and Research and the Centers for Medicare & Medicaid Services (both agencies within DHHS) conduct studies about drug and medical device therapies and make decisions about reimbursement for those therapies that have a significant impact on how FDA-regulated therapeutic products are used in practice. They are thus active participants in the information marketplace for therapeutic products, as both generators and consumers of information about the safety and effectiveness of these products.

FDA works with:
- *CDC*
- *NIH*
- *EPA*
- *USDA*
- *FTC*
- *State Agencies*

There are also regulatory agencies outside DHHS that work in areas closely related to FDA's jurisdiction. For example, the Environmental Protection Agency (EPA) is responsible for determining the safety of pesticide residues in food and establishing the legal limits (or tolerances) for such residues. FDA enforces the EPA tolerances. The U.S. Department of Agriculture (USDA) regulates the safety and labeling of most meat and poultry products, as well as certain processed egg products. FDA, on the other hand, regulates fish, game animals used for food, and fresh eggs. FDA regulates most animal drugs, but the Animal and Plant Health Inspection Service within USDA regulates animal biological products. FDA regulates the advertising for prescription drugs, but the Federal Trade Commission regulates advertising for food and over-the-counter drugs.

FDA's role also parallels that played by many state regulatory agencies. Most states have active food safety programs targeted at the retail level (grocery stores and restaurants). In addition, most of the food safety standard setting and inspection with respect to dairy products and shellfish is conducted at the state level, with FDA providing technical expertise and advice. In the pharmaceutical area, state boards of pharmacy regulate the dispensing of prescription drugs and take an active interest in any FDA policy that could affect pharmacy.

Agencies working in fields closely related to, and in some cases overlapping with, FDA's responsibilities illustrate the complexity of the government environment within which FDA works.

These examples of agencies that work in fields closely related to, and in some cases overlapping with, FDA's responsibilities illustrate the complexity of the government environment within which FDA works. This complexity poses serious issues that FDA must continue to grapple with in the future. In the food area, the division of responsibilities for food safety among FDA, USDA, EPA, and CDC creates significant obstacles to the development of a consistent federal food safety program that makes the best use of available resources. Coordination among organizationally separate agencies is inherently difficult, and divergent statutory mandates create gross inconsistencies and inefficiencies in how they assess and manage food safety risks. For example, USDA receives about $1 billion per year to implement outdated inspection programs covering 20 percent of the food supply, while FDA receives a little over half that amount to oversee the remaining 80 percent, including the flood of imported seafood, produce, and food ingredients. Viewed from a risk-based, public health perspective, the current allocation of inspection and other resources between USDA and FDA is not justified.

Organizational fragmentation also makes coordination difficult at a daily operational level. When outbreaks of foodborne illness occur, FDA and USDA must coordinate with CDC and state health departments to investigate the outbreak, determine its cause, and recommend actions to contain and end the outbreak. The agencies work hard to foster cooperation, but communication between multiple agencies can be difficult, and overlapping responsibilities for such matters as communicating with the public can create uncertainty and confusion. This can affect both the quality of the government effort to manage the outbreak and the credibility of the effort in the mind of the public.

How FDA and the other food safety agencies manage their resources, set their priorities, and coordinate their efforts will determine their success in the 21st century. How should resources be allocated among the agencies? Is there a need for statutory change to permit a more efficient, risk-based allocation of resources? How should FDA and the other agencies allocate their resources internally? Is FDA placing sufficient emphasis on efforts to proactively reduce public health risks? How should it balance investment in regulatory initiatives with investments in research and education? What opportunities exist to enhance operational collaboration among the federal food safety agencies and with the states?

With regard to therapeutic products, how should FDA be working with other DHHS agencies and the private sector to improve the information marketplace? Who is responsible for enhancing the quantity and quality of data available to support good decisions about off-label uses of drugs and medical devices? What should be FDA's role in relation to other agencies in assessing cost-effectiveness claims for therapeutic products? Is there a need for policy or statutory change to enhance the incentives for generation of data on safety, effectiveness, and pharmacoeconomics?

These issues may appear to be of interest only to people who work in government or Washington, D.C., but they profoundly affect the government's ability to make decisions and take actions that are critical to the welfare of consumers, patients, and the regulated industry. The organizational complexity that has grown up in the federal government with regard to food, drug, and medical device regulatory matters is an obstacle to the kind of "high-performance government" that the public increasingly expects. There are no snap solutions to this problem, but FDA, as well as Congress, will be challenged to grapple with these issues in the coming years by budget and operational necessity, and by the constant pressures to improve both protection and promotion of public health.

What Is FDA's Role in Relation to the Individual, the Market, Industry, and Other Private Entities?

The changes in FDA's external environment and in the demands placed on FDA to protect and promote public health will require FDA to re-examine the way it works in relation to individuals and private institutions in society.

The changes in FDA's external environment and in the demands placed on FDA to protect and promote public health will require FDA to re-examine the way it works in relation to individuals and private institutions in society.

The demands of individuals for safe food and safe and effective medical products historically have provided much of the political impetus and energy for government regulation of foods, drugs, and medical devices. Moreover, most public health experts today agree that individual responsibility and empowerment of individual consumers and patients to make wise choices are key to achieving society's public health goals. This theme of individual responsibility is ascendant in many areas of contemporary society. One of the on-going challenges for FDA in the 21st century will be to invent ways to facilitate the exercise of individual responsibility and empower consumers.

In the area of diet and health, this means equipping people as fully as possible with the best insights that science can provide concerning what constitutes a healthy and health-promoting diet. The NLEA created a new regulatory framework for making disease-related health claims, but commercial free speech pressures have resulted in FDA adopting policies to allow "qualified claims" in the absence of the scientific evidence required to support an NLEA health claim. Are NLEA and these other FDA policies working effectively to maximize the flow of useful diet and health information to consumers? Are they working optimally to stimulate investment in the research required to support scientifically valid claims? Empowering and educating consumers to choose healthier diets remains one of today's most important public health challenges. Publicly supported health research is likely to remain the primary source of the basic information, but the market will continue to be the conduit for this information. To advance public health in this area, FDA still must forge a *modus vivendi* with the market that works to provide individuals with the information and choices they need to construct healthy diets.

Because FDA lacks the resources to police the dietary supplement marketplace effectively, claims abound for serious health-related conditions that FDA cannot vouch for and that many experts would say have not been proven scientifically.

Implementation of DSHEA has raised some fundamental issues in this arena. In addition to removing FDA from a premarket approval role to ensure the safety of dietary supplements, DSHEA effectively has freed supplement manufacturers from any premarket review of claims about the effectiveness of supplements in addressing important disease and health-related problems. Structure-and-function claims for supplements, which prior to DSHEA were legally considered drug claims requiring premarket approval, are now exempt from premarket approval. Because FDA lacks the resources to police the dietary supplement marketplace effectively, claims abound for serious health-related conditions—such as improving mental function and heart health—that FDA cannot vouch for and that many experts would say have not been proven scientifically.

DSHEA left explicit disease-related claims subject to premarket approval under a "substantial scientific agreement" standard. In 1999, however, the supplement industry won a commercial free speech case that appears to require FDA to approve disease-related claims for supplements without a showing of efficacy for the disease-related purpose, provided the claim is "qualified" so as not to be misleading. This effectively leaves it to consumers to sort out the meaning of disease-related supplement claims for themselves, with the manufacturer's advertising or labeling commonly being the sole source of information on which they rely. For supplements, this takes FDA out of its traditional role of providing the consumer an assurance that supplement products promoted for significant diseases or health-related purposes can be used safely and effectively. Consumer satisfaction and protection are left largely to the private marketplace.

In the therapeutic area, the critical role of physicians and other "learned intermediaries" continues. Individuals will increasingly seek a decision-making role, however, as they become better educated and informed, through the Internet and other means, and as the markets for healthcare in general and therapeutic products in particular more closely resemble the markets for other consumer products.

In the traditional therapeutic area of drugs and medical devices, FDA's premarket approval role and the critical role of physicians and other "learned intermediaries" continue. Yet, individuals will continue seeking a decision-making role in this area as they become better educated and informed. Like FDA, well-informed and empowered consumers are important to public health in the therapeutic area, just as they are in the realm of diet and health. FDA can anticipate continuing pressure to reexamine its policies and requirements toward patient labeling, direct-to-consumer advertising, and the flow of information for off-label uses in light of the changed nature of the marketplace for therapeutic products and the demand for individual empowerment. One innovation that will drive change will be the ability to target drug therapy to individual consumers based on their individual characteristics.

As government's role and FDA's external environment change, so too will FDA's relationship with its constituencies. FDA has a long tradition of collaborating with the scientific and health professional communities, but the changing world also challenges FDA to craft new forms of collaboration with regulated companies and industry groups. The Prescription Drug User Fee Act of 1992 and its subsequent reauthorizations are examples of collaboration based on the common interest of government, industry, and patients in a successful drug review process. The pace, rigor, and credibility of that process are critical to the success of the drug industry, and to the protection and promotion of public health. The FDAAA calls for greater collaboration through the Reagan-Udall Foundation and new ways to control the risks associated with drugs through REMS (risk evaluation and mitigation strategy).

Collaboration of this kind, based on common interests, will be essential to FDA's future success in other areas as well. FDA's 2007 Food Protection Plan calls for greater collaboration with industry on food safety and greater responsibility for industry in implementing preventive control systems, such as the Hazard Analysis and Critical Control Point (HACCP) system FDA has required for seafood and juice products. Congress is considering legislation to mandate this approach, which embodies a new form of collaboration based on the common interest in reducing foodborne illness and maintaining public confidence in the food supply. HACCP-based approaches also raise fundamental questions, however, about the proper balance between collaboration, clear delineation of distinct roles, and institutional credibility. While HACCP places great responsibility on the food industry to design and implement plant-specific food safety procedures, FDA must still be responsible for establishing performance-oriented standards to ensure that a company's HACCP system meets society's food safety expectations. Then the challenge is implementation. What level of inspection oversight and what manner of interaction between FDA inspection and the plant is appropriate to make HACCP successful and give the public confidence that the government is providing rigorous and effective oversight? In general, government and industry should not be adversaries, but the public must know that government will take appropriate action when needed to protect the public's interest.

How Will Society Pay for What It Wants Government to Do?

FDA is a chronically underfunded agency.

This last fundamental question also may be the most critical in a time of expanding challenges and government retrenchment. FDA is a chronically underfunded agency. While user fees have proven effective in supporting product-licensing systems, funding for food safety and to maintain adequate inspection and compliance capabilities remains an important issue. The value to the payer and payee of fees for product licensing reviews is obvious, which makes it feasible to set the fees fairly and pass them politically, but this has not proven to be the case for most other FDA program areas.

If FDA is to receive adequate funding from tax revenues, via the congressional appropriations process, FDA must have a focused, long-term strategy for being successful in that process. That requires, as a start, asking itself and its constituencies fundamental questions of the kind outlined in this chapter. Recognizing the diversity of interests and values that swirl around FDA, it is nevertheless imperative that FDA forges a new societal consensus on what FDA's mission is, how it should go about its work within the government, and how it should engage individuals and institutions outside government.

Today more than ever government agencies need active public and constituency support to be successful. This is as it should be in a democracy. But support comes with understanding and general agreement about the agency's mission and means of pursuing it. Building that understanding and agreement in line with today's realities and in contemporary terms is essential to FDA's success in the 21st century.

Index

D

E

F

G

J

K

L

M

N

O

P

Q

R

S

T

U

V

W